중·고등 영어도 역시 1위 해커스다.

해커스북 중·고등

HackersBook.com

[중고등영어 1위] 한경비즈니스 선정 2020 한국품질만족도 교육(온·오프라인 중·고등영어) 부문 1위 해커스

해커스 수능영어듣기 모의고사 20+4회가 특별한 이유!

최신 경향과 출제 패턴을 반영한 문제로 실전 대비!

1

최신 수능 출제경향을
그대로 반영한
**양질의
영어듣기 모의고사**

2

난이도 높은 문제로
만점 굳히기!
고난도 모의고사

3

대표 기출문제로
수능 기본기를 탄탄히!
**14개 유형별
핵심 전략**

해커스 수능영어듣기 모의고사 20+4회

기본   실전

다양한 버전의 음성으로 편리한 학습!

4

여러 가지 버전으로
실전에 대비할 수 있는
**기본 속도/고속 버전/
고사장 버전 MP3**

5

복습이 간편해지는
**딕테이션 MP3/
문항별 MP3**

6

모든 음성 버전을
한 손에 쏙!
**문제 음성 듣기
QR코드**

해커스 수능영어듣기 모의고사 시리즈를 검토해주신 선생님들

경기
김보경   성일고등학교
김성철   코코스영어학원
연원기   신갈고등학교
이지혜   리케이온 어학원
전상호   평촌 이지어학원

대전
신주희   파써블영어학원

부산
이승의   에이치큐(HQ)영수학원

서울
김종오   입시형인간학원
양세희   양세희 수능영어학원

해커스 어학연구소 자문위원단 2기

강원
안서아   숲어학원 남산캠퍼스
최현주   최샘영어

경기
강민정   김진성의 열정어학원
강상훈   평촌RTS학원
강유빈   일링영어수학학원
권계미   A&T+ 영어
김남균   SDH어학원 세교캠퍼스
김보경   성일고등학교
김세희   이화킴스영어전문학원
김은영   신갈고등학교
나한샘   해법영어교실 프라임수학학원
두형호   잉글리쉬피티 어학원
박은성   GSE 어학원
박지승   신갈고등학교
배동영   이바인어학원탄현캠퍼스
서현주   웰어학원
연원기   신갈고등학교
윤혜영   이루다학원
이미연   김상희수학영어학원
이선미   정현영어학원
이슬기   연세센크레영어
이승주   EL영어학원
이주의   뉴욕학원
이충기   영어나무
이한이   엘케이영어학원
장명희   이루다영어수학전문학원
장소연   우리학원
장한상   티엔디플러스학원
전상호   평촌 이지어학원
전성훈   훈선생영어학원
정선영   코어플러스영어학원
정세창   팍스어학원
정재식   마스터제이학원
정필두   정상어학원
조원웅   클라비스영어전문학원
조은혜   이든영수학원
천은지   프링크어학원
최지영   다른영어학원
최한나   석사영수전문

경남
김선우   이해성 김해 의대관
라승희   아이작잉글리셔
박정주   타임영어 전문학원
이지선   PMS영재센터학원

경북
김대원   포항영신중학교
김주훈   아너스영어
문재원   포항영신고등학교
성룡   미르어학원
엄경식   포항영신고등학교
정창용   엑소더스어학원

광주
강창일   MAX(맥스) 에듀학원
김태호   금호고등학교
임희숙   설월여자고등학교
정영철   정영철 영어전문학원
조유승   링즈영어학원

대구
구수진   석샘수학&제임스영어 학원
권익재   제이슨영어교습소
김광영   e끌리네영어학원
김보곤   베스트영어
김연정   달서고등학교
김원휘   글로벌리더스어학원
위영선   위영선영어학원
이가영   어썸코칭영어학원
이승현   학문당입시학원
이정아   능인고등학교
조승희   켈리외국어학원
주현아   강고영어학원
최윤정   최강영어
황은진   상인황샘영어학원

대전
김미경   이보영의토킹클럽유성분원
성태미   한울영수학원
신주희   파써블영어학원
이재근   이재근영어수학학원
이혜숙   대동천재학원
최애림   ECC송촌제우스학원

부산
고영하   해리포터영어도서관
김미혜   더멘토영어
김서진   케이트예일학원
김소희   윤선생IGSE 센텀어학원
박경일   제니스영어
성현석   닉쌤영어교습소
신연주   도담학원
이경희   더에듀기장학원

서울
이아린   명진학원
이종혁   대동학원
이지현   7번방의 기적 영어학원
전재석   영어를담다
채지영   리드앤톡영어도서관학원

갈성은   씨앤씨(목동) 특목관
공현미   이은재어학원
김시아   시아영어교습소
김은주   열정과신념영어학원
박병배   강북세일학원
신이준   정영어학원
신진희   신진희영어
양세희   양세희수능영어학원
윤승완   윤승완영어학원
이계윤   씨앤씨(목동) 학원
이상영   와이즈(WHY's) 학원
이정욱   이은재어학원
이지연   중계케이트영어학원
정미라   미라정영어학원
정용문   맥코칭학원
정윤정   대치명인학원 마포캠퍼스
조용현   바른스터디학원
채가희   대성세그루영수학원

세종
김주년   드림하이영어학원
하원태   백년대계입시학원
홍수정   수정영어입시전문학원

울산
김한중   스마트영어전문학원
오충섭   인트로영어전문학원
윤창호   로제타스톤학원
임예린   와엘영어학원
최주하   더 셀럽학원
최호선   마시멜로영어전문학원

인천
권효진   Genie's English
송숙진   예스영어학원
임민선   SNU에듀
정진수   원리영어
함선임   리본에듀학원
황혜림   SNU에듀

전남
류성준   타임영어학원

전북
강동현   커넥트영수전문학원
김길자   군산맨투맨학원
김두환   해남맨체스터영수학원
김유경   이엘 어학원
노빈나   노빈나영어학원
라성남   하포드어학원
박지연   박지연영어학원
변진호   쉐마영어학원
송윤경   줄리안나영어국어전문학원
이수정   씨에이엔영어학원
장윤정   혁신뉴욕어학원

제주
김랑   KLS어학원
박자은   KLS어학원

충남
문정효   좋은습관 에토스학원
박서현   EiE고려대학교 어학원 논산
박정은   탑씨크리트학원
성승민   SDH어학원 불당캠퍼스
손세윤   최상위학원 (탕정)
이지선   힐베르트학원

충북
강은구   강쌤영어학원
남장길   에이탑정철어학원
이혜인   위즈영어학원

해커스

수능영어듣기 모의고사 20+4회

고난도

기본

해커스 어학연구소

CONTENTS

교재 구성과 특징 ········· 4

기출 유형 분석

기출 유형 01 **목적 파악** 8

기출 유형 02 **의견 파악** 9

기출 유형 03 **관계 파악** 10

기출 유형 04 **그림 내용 불일치 파악** 11

기출 유형 05 **할 일/부탁한 일 파악** 12

기출 유형 06 **금액 정보 파악** 13

기출 유형 07 **이유 파악** 14

기출 유형 08 **언급 유무 파악** 15

기출 유형 09 **내용 불일치 파악** 16

기출 유형 10 **도표 정보 파악** 17

기출 유형 11 **짧은 대화의 응답 파악** 18

기출 유형 12 **긴 대화의 응답 파악** 19

기출 유형 13 **상황에 적절한 말 파악** 20

기출 유형 14 **세트 문항** [주제/세부 내용 파악] 21

영어듣기 모의고사

01회 영어듣기 모의고사 ········· 24

02회 영어듣기 모의고사 ········· 30

03회 영어듣기 모의고사 ········· 36

04회 영어듣기 모의고사 ········· 42

05회 영어듣기 모의고사 ········· 48

06회 영어듣기 모의고사 ········· 54

07회 영어듣기 모의고사 ········· 60

08회 영어듣기 모의고사 ········· 66

09회 영어듣기 모의고사 ········· 72

10회 영어듣기 모의고사 ········· 78

11회 영어듣기 모의고사 · · · · · · · · · · · · · · · 84

12회 영어듣기 모의고사 · · · · · · · · · · · · · · · 90

13회 영어듣기 모의고사 · · · · · · · · · · · · · · · 96

14회 영어듣기 모의고사 · · · · · · · · · · · · · · · 102

15회 영어듣기 모의고사 · · · · · · · · · · · · · · · 108

16회 영어듣기 모의고사 · · · · · · · · · · · · · · · 114

17회 영어듣기 모의고사 · · · · · · · · · · · · · · · 120

18회 영어듣기 모의고사 · · · · · · · · · · · · · · · 126

19회 영어듣기 모의고사 · · · · · · · · · · · · · · · 132

20회 영어듣기 모의고사 · · · · · · · · · · · · · · · 138

21회 **고난도** 영어듣기 모의고사 · · · · · · · · · · 144

22회 **고난도** 영어듣기 모의고사 · · · · · · · · · · 150

23회 **고난도** 영어듣기 모의고사 · · · · · · · · · · 156

24회 **고난도** 영어듣기 모의고사 · · · · · · · · · · 162

정답 및 해설 [책 속의 책]

교재 구성과 특징

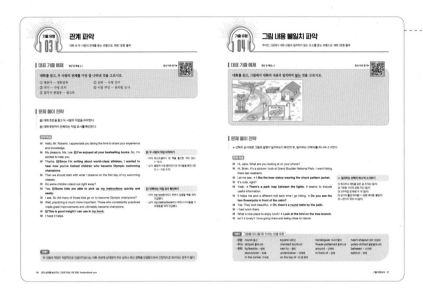

🔎 기출 유형 분석

수능에 반드시 출제되는 14개 대표 문제 유형을 철저히 분석했습니다. 유형별 기출 문제에 문제 풀이 전략을 단계별로 적용해 보고, 빈출 어휘 및 표현을 익히며 수능 기본기를 다질 수 있습니다.

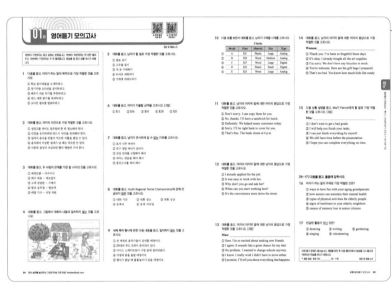

🔎 영어듣기 모의고사 20회

최신 고 1-2 학력평가와 수능의 출제 경향을 완벽히 반영한 모의고사를 풀면서 점진적으로 듣기 실력을 키워나갈 수 있습니다.

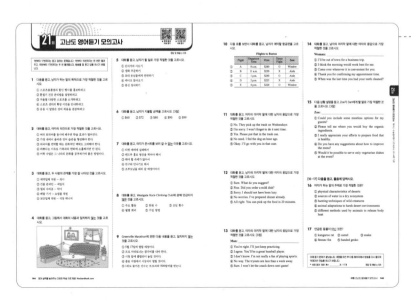

🔎 고난도 영어듣기 모의고사 4회

실제 수능과 비슷한 난이도의 문제로 구성된 고난도 모의고사를 통해 수능 실전 감각을 끌어올릴 수 있습니다.

Dictation

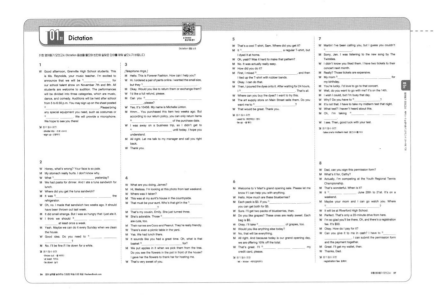

매회 문제 풀이 후 Dictation을 하며 문제 풀이 시 놓쳤던 정답 단서를 확인하고 내용을 정확하게 듣는 연습을 할 수 있습니다.

듣기 필수 표현에 따로 정리되어 있는 시험에 자주 출제되는 표현들을 편리하게 복습할 수 있습니다.

정답 및 해설

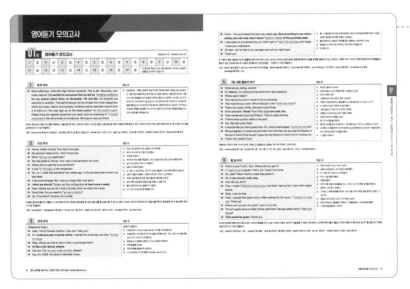

스크립트와 해석을 나란히 확인하며 지문 내용을 한눈에 빠르게 파악할 수 있습니다.

스스로 정답의 근거를 확인하고 상세한 해설을 읽어보면서 다시 틀리는 일이 없도록 오답을 점검할 수 있습니다.

다양한 버전의 MP3

- 실전과 동일한 속도의 **기본 속도 MP3**
- 실전보다 빠른 **고속 버전 MP3**
- 실제 수능 시험장에서 듣는 것 같은 **고사장 버전 MP3**
- 틀린 문제만 골라 다시 들으며 복습하는 **문항별 MP3**
- 영어 지문만 들으며 Dictation하는 **딕테이션 MP3**

MP3 스트리밍 QR코드

매회 모의고사와 Dictation에 있는 QR코드로 간편하게 음성을 이용할 수 있습니다.
HackersBook.com에서 MP3 파일 다운로드도 가능합니다.

해커스북 중·고등

www.HackersBook.com

기출 유형 분석

기출 유형 01   **목적 파악**

기출 유형 02   **의견 파악**

기출 유형 03   **관계 파악**

기출 유형 04   **그림 내용 불일치 파악**

기출 유형 05   **할 일/부탁한 일 파악**

기출 유형 06   **금액 정보 파악**

기출 유형 07   **이유 파악**

기출 유형 08   **언급 유무 파악**

기출 유형 09   **내용 불일치 파악**

기출 유형 10   **도표 정보 파악**

기출 유형 11   **짧은 대화의 응답 파악**

기출 유형 12   **긴 대화의 응답 파악**

기출 유형 13   **상황에 적절한 말 파악**

기출 유형 14   **세트 문항** [주제/세부 내용 파악]

목적 파악

담화의 목적을 묻는 유형으로, 매회 1문항 출제

대표 기출 예제   정답 및 해설 p.2

음성 바로 듣기▶

다음을 듣고, 남자가 하는 말의 목적으로 가장 적절한 것을 고르시오.

① 도서관의 변경된 운영 시간을 안내하려고
② 독후감 쓰기 대회의 일정을 공지하려고
③ 책갈피 디자인 대회 참가를 독려하려고
④ 기한 내 도서 반납을 촉구하려고
⑤ 전자책 이용 방법을 설명하려고

문제 풀이 전략

1 담화 초반에 나오는 소개말을 듣고 화자와 청자가 누구인지 파악한다.

2 목적을 여러 번 반복해서 말해주므로, 담화에서 반복되는 내용을 파악한다.

전략 적용

M **1** Hello, Lockwood High School students. This is your school librarian, **Mr. Wilkins.** I'm sure you're aware that our school library is hosting a bookmark design competition. **2** I encourage students of all grades to participate in the competition. The winning designs will be made into bookmarks, which will be distributed to library visitors. We're also giving out a variety of other prizes. **2** So don't let this great opportunity slip away. Since the registration period for the bookmark design competition ends this Friday, make sure you visit our school library to submit your application. **2** Come and participate to display your creativity and talents.

1 화자와 청자 파악하기

화자는 학교 사서 선생님이고, 청자는 고등학교 학생들이다.

2 반복되는 내용을 통해 목적 파악하기

encourage라는 직접적인 표현을 써서 대회 참가를 독려한다는 목적을 밝힌 뒤, 반복해서 기회를 놓치지 말고 참가하기를 독려하는 발언을 했다.

TIP! 목적을 말할 때 쓰이는 빈출 표현

· 공지/안내:	announce 공지하다	inform 알리다	remind 상기시키다	notify 알리다
· 독려/권장:	encourage 독려하다	recommend 추천하다	suggest 제안하다	
· 요청/당부:	request 요청하다	ask 요구하다	urge 간청하다	hope 희망하다

의견 파악

대화 속에 드러난 화자의 의견을 묻는 유형으로, 매회 1문항 출제

▌대표 기출 예제 정답 및 해설 p.2

음성 바로 듣기▶

대화를 듣고, 여자의 의견으로 가장 적절한 것을 고르시오.

① 사과를 먹으면 장운동이 원활해진다.
② 사과 껍질은 피부 상태 개선에 도움이 된다.
③ 충분한 수면은 건강한 피부 유지에 필수적이다.
④ 사과를 먹기 전에 껍질을 깨끗이 씻어야 한다.
⑤ 주기적인 수분 섭취는 피부 노화를 늦춘다.

▌문제 풀이 전략

1 대화 초반을 듣고 중심 소재를 파악한다.

2 대화 중반에 직접적으로 언급되는 화자의 의견을 파악하여 정답을 고른다.

3 대화 후반에 화자의 의견이 한번 더 진술되는 경우가 많으므로, 끝까지 들으며 맞게 풀었는지 확인한다.

전략 적용

M Honey, do you want some apples with breakfast?
W Sounds great. **1 Can you save the apple peels for me?**
M Why? What do you want them for?
W I'm going to use them to make a face pack. **2 Apple peels are effective for improving skin condition.**
M Where did you hear about that?
W I recently read an article about their benefits for our skin.
M Interesting. What's in them?
W It said apple peels are rich in vitamins and minerals, so they moisturize our skin and enhance skin glow.
M That's good to know.
W Also, they remove oil from our skin and have a cooling effect.
M Wow! Then I shouldn't throw them away.
W Right. **3 Apple peels can help improve our skin condition.**
M I see. I'll save them for you.

1 중심 소재 파악하기

사과 껍질에 관한 대화가 시작되었다.

2 화자의 의견 파악하기

여자가 사과 껍질이 피부 상태를 개선하는 데 효과적이라는 의견을 밝혔다.

3 반복 진술된 의견 확인하기

여자가 사과 껍질의 피부 개선 효과를 한번 더 언급했다.

TIP! 의견을 말할 때 쓰이는 빈출 표현

• I think/believe/guess (that) ~. 저는 ~하다고 생각합니다.
• I don't think/believe (that) ~. 저는 ~하지 않다고 생각합니다.
• You need to ~. 당신은 ~해야 합니다.
• You should not ~. 당신은 ~하면 안 됩니다.
• Why don't you ~? ~하는 건 어떻겠습니까?

기출 유형 03 관계 파악

대화 속 두 사람의 관계를 묻는 유형으로, 매회 1문항 출제

대표 기출 예제

정답 및 해설 p.2

음성 바로 듣기▶

대화를 듣고, 두 사람의 관계를 가장 잘 나타낸 것을 고르시오.

① 평론가 ― 영화감독   ② 심판 ― 수영 선수
③ 작가 ― 수영 코치   ④ 서점 주인 ― 유치원 교사
⑤ 잡지사 편집장 ― 광고주

문제 풀이 전략

■ 대화 초반을 듣고 두 사람의 직업을 파악한다.

■ 대화 후반까지 반복되는 직업 묘사를 확인한다.

전략 적용

W   Hello, Mr. Roberts. I appreciate you taking the time to share your experience and knowledge.

M   My pleasure, Ms. Lee. ■ **I've enjoyed all your bestselling books.** So, I'm excited to help you.

W   Thanks. ■ **Since I'm writing about world-class athletes, I wanted to hear how you've trained children who became Olympic swimming champions.**

M   Then we should start with what I observe on the first day of my swimming classes.

W   Do some children stand out right away?

M   Yes. ■ **Some kids are able to pick up** my instructions **quickly and easily.**

W   I see. So did many of those kids go on to become Olympic champions?

M   Well, practicing is much more important. Those who consistently practiced made great improvements and ultimately became champions.

W   ■ **This is good insight I can use in** my book**.**

M   I hope it helps.

■ 두 사람의 직업 파악하기

• 여자: 베스트셀러가 된 책을 출간한 적이 있다. (→ 작가)
• 남자: 올림픽 수영 챔피언이 된 아이들을 훈련시켰다. (→ 수영 코치)

■ 반복되는 직업 묘사 확인하기

• 여자: **my book**이라고 하면서 집필할 책을 재차 언급했다.
• 남자: **my instructions**라고 하면서 아이들을 가르쳤음을 재차 언급했다.

TIP!
두 사람의 직업이 직접적으로 언급되기보다는, 대화 초반에 상대방의 주요 성과나 최근 경력을 언급함으로써 간접적으로 묘사되는 경우가 많다.

기출 유형 04 그림 내용 불일치 파악

주어진 그림에서 대화 내용과 일치하지 않는 요소를 묻는 유형으로, 매회 1문항 출제

대표 기출 예제   _{정답 및 해설 p.3}

음성 바로 듣기▶

대화를 듣고, 그림에서 대화의 내용과 일치하지 <u>않는</u> 것을 고르시오.

문제 풀이 전략

● 선택지 순서대로 그림과 설명이 일치하는지 확인한 후, 일치하는 선택지를 하나씩 소거한다.

전략 적용

M   Hi, Jane. What are you looking at on your phone?

W   Hi, Brian. It's a picture I took at Grand Boulder National Park. I went hiking there last weekend.

M   Let me see. ● **I like the bear statue wearing the check pattern jacket.**

W   It's cute, right?

M   Yeah. ● **There's a park map between the lights.** It seems to include useful information.

W   It helps me pick a different trail each time I go hiking. ● **Do you see the two flowerpots in front of the cabin?**

M   Yes. They look beautiful. ● **Oh, there's a <u>round</u> table by the path.**

W   I had lunch there.

M   What a nice place to enjoy lunch! ● **Look at the bird on the tree branch.**

W   Isn't it lovely? I love going there and being close to nature.

● 일치하는 선택지 하나씩 소거하기

① 체크무늬 재킷을 입은 곰 조각상 (일치)
② 가로등 사이의 공원 지도 (일치)
③ 오두막집 앞 화분 두 개 (일치)
④ 길가의 **둥근** 테이블 (→ **사각** 테이블: 불일치)
⑤ 나뭇가지 위의 새 (일치)

TIP! 그림을 묘사할 때 쓰이는 빈출 표현

· 모양:	round 둥근	square 네모난	rectangular 직사각형의	heart-shaped 하트 모양의
· 무늬:	striped 줄무늬의	checked 체크무늬의	flower-patterned 꽃무늬의	polka-dotted 물방울무늬의
· 위치:	by/beside ~ 옆에	next to ~ 옆에	around ~ 근처에	between ~ 사이에
	above/over ~ 위에	under/below ~ 아래에	in front of ~ 앞에	behind ~ 뒤에
	in the corner 구석에	on the top of ~의 맨 위에		

할 일/부탁한 일 파악

대화 속 화자가 앞으로 할 일 또는 상대방에게 부탁한 일을 묻는 유형으로, 둘 중 한 유형으로 매회 1문항 출제

▌대표 기출 예제　정답 및 해설 p.3

음성 바로 듣기▶

대화를 듣고, 남자가 할 일로 가장 적절한 것을 고르시오.

① 음식 재료 주문하기　　　　　② 와인 잔 포장하기

③ 추가 메뉴 선정하기　　　　　④ 초대 문자 메시지 보내기

⑤ 노래 목록 확인하기

▌문제 풀이 전략

1 대화 초반부터 나오는 이미 한 일이나 상대방이 할 일은 함정이므로 선택지에서 소거한다.

2 대화 후반에 문제에서 물어보는 화자가 할 일이 언급되므로, 대화 후반의 내용을 잘 확인한다.

전략 적용

W　Honey, I'm so excited for our restaurant's reopening event tomorrow.

M　So am I. Let's see. **1 We've ordered enough ingredients, right?**

W　I think so. We need to remind our loyal customers of the event.

M　**1 I already sent text messages.**

W　Good. **1 I hope people like the new menu items that we added.**

M　Don't worry. We have a great chef. So I'm sure the new dishes will be a hit.

W　What about the live music? **1 Did you confirm the song list with the band?**

M　Not yet. And we also need to wrap wine glasses to give as gifts for the customers.

W　Okay. **2 Could you wrap them?**

M　**2 Sure. I'll do it now.**

W　Great! **1 Then I'll contact the band.**

1 이미 한 일/상대방이 할 일 소거하기

• 이미 한 일
: 음식 재료 주문하기, 초대 문자 메시지 보내기, 추가 메뉴 선정하기는 이미 끝냈다고 했다.

• 상대방이 할 일
: 노래 목록 확인하기는 상대방이 하겠다고 했다.

2 화자가 할 일 확인하기

여자가 와인 잔을 포장해 줄 수 있는지 묻자, 남자가 지금 하겠다고 했다.

TIP!

할 일/부탁한 일의 정답 단서는 대화 후반에 조동사 can/could 또는 will을 쓴 문장으로 나오는 경우가 많다.

금액 정보 파악 고난도 유형

대화 속 화자가 지불할 금액을 묻는 유형으로, 주로 3점짜리로 매회 1문항 출제

▌대표 기출 예제   정답 및 해설 p4

음성 바로 듣기 ▶

대화를 듣고, 여자가 지불할 금액을 고르시오. [3점]

① $36   ② $45   ③ $50   ④ $54   ⑤ $60

▌문제 풀이 전략

1 대화에서 언급되는 가격 정보와 구매하려는 품목의 개수를 간단히 메모하며 듣는다.

2 할인을 받을 수 있거나 배달비가 별도로 발생하는지 등의 추가 정보를 확인한다.

전략 적용

M Welcome to Daisy Valley Restaurant.

W Hi. I'd like to order some food to go. How much is the shrimp pasta and the chicken salad?

M **1 The shrimp pasta is $20, and the chicken salad is $10.**

W **1 I'll take two shrimp pastas and one chicken salad, please.**

M Sure. Would you like some dessert, too?

W Yes. What do you recommend?

M **1 The mini cheese cake is one of the best sellers in our restaurant. It's $5 each.**

W Great! **1 I'll order two of them.**

M Okay. Let me confirm your order. Two shrimp pastas, one chicken salad, and two mini cheese cakes. Is that correct?

W Yes. And I have a birthday coupon here. Can I use it?

M Let me see. *[Pause]* Yes. **2 You can get a 10% discount off the total.**

W Terrific. I'll use this coupon. Here's my credit card.

1 가격 정보와 구매 개수 메모하기

- 새우 파스타: 20달러 × 2접시   = 40달러
- 치킨 샐러드: 10달러 × 1접시   = 10달러
- 미니 치즈 케이크: 5달러 × 2조각   = 10달러

∴ 총 60달러

2 추가 정보 확인하기

생일 쿠폰으로 10% 할인을 받을 수 있다고 했으므로, 지불할 금액은 54달러이다.

TIP! 가격을 설명할 때 쓰이는 빈출 표현

- **가격:** It's $10 each. 개당 10달러입니다.
  It's $10 per person. 1인당 10달러입니다.
  It costs $10. 10달러입니다.
- **할인:** I'll give you a $10 discount on it. 10달러만큼 할인해드리겠습니다.
  You can get a 10% discount off the total. 총액에서 10% 할인받으실 수 있습니다.
  You'll get 10% off the total price. 총액에서 10% 할인받으시겠습니다.
  The discount coupon doesn't apply to ~. 할인 쿠폰이 ~에는 적용되지 않습니다.
  I can give you a dozen shuttlecocks worth $10 for free. 10달러 상당의 셔틀콕 12개를 무료로 드리겠습니다.

이유 파악

대화 속 화자의 행동에 대한 이유를 묻는 유형으로, 매회 1문항 출제

대표 기출 예제   정답 및 해설 p.4

음성 바로 듣기 ▶

대화를 듣고, 남자가 K-Trend Festival에 갈 수 <u>없는</u> 이유를 고르시오.

① 영화관에서 일해야 해서
② 유학 설명회에 참석해야 해서
③ 경제학 시험공부를 해야 해서
④ 태권도 시합에 출전해야 해서
⑤ 동생을 공항에 데려다줘야 해서

문제 풀이 전략

1 대화 중반에 상대방이 이유를 추측해서 물어보는 것은 함정이므로 이어지는 대답까지 잘 듣고 선택지에서 소거한다.

2 대화 후반에 진짜 이유가 언급되므로, 대화 후반의 내용을 잘 확인한다.

전략 적용

W   Sam, do you want to go to the K-Trend Festival with me this Saturday?

M   Hi, Olivia. Is that the festival held at Central Square?

W   Yeah, that's it. There'll be many attractions including Taekwondo performances that incorporate K-pop dance moves.

M   Really? Sounds cool! What time does it start?

W   It starts at 5 p.m. **1 Will you be working at the movie theater at that time?**

M   **1 No, I'm not working this Saturday.** But I can't come to the festival.

W   Too bad. **1 Do you have to study for your economics exam?**

M   **1 Actually, I already took the exam yesterday.**

W   Then, what's the matter?

M   **2 I have to take my younger sister to the airport on Saturday evening.**

W   Where's she going?

M   She's going to Canada to study abroad.

W   That's awesome. I hope she has a good experience there.

1 상대방이 추측한 이유 소거하기

여자가 추측한 이유 두 가지, 영화관에서 일해야 해서와 경제학 시험공부를 해야 해서는 모두 축제에 갈 수 없는 이유가 아니라고 했다.

2 진짜 이유 확인하기

남자가 진짜 이유는 그날 저녁 여동생을 공항에 데려다줘야 해서라고 말했다.

TIP! 이유를 물을 때 쓰이는 빈출 표현

· **What's the matter?** 무슨 일이야?
· **What made you ~?** 뭐 때문에 ~한 거야?
· **Why can't you ~?** 왜 ~할 수 없는 거야?
· **Why not?** 왜 안 돼?
· **I don't get why you ~.** 네가 왜 ~하는지 이유를 모르겠어.

언급 유무 파악

대화에서 언급되지 않은 것을 묻는 유형으로, 매회 1문항 출제

대표 기출 예제

정답 및 해설 p.4

음성 바로 듣기▶

대화를 듣고, 졸업 사진 촬영에 관해 언급되지 <u>않은</u> 것을 고르시오.

① 날짜　　　　② 장소　　　　③ 복장
④ 참여 학생 수　　⑤ 소요 시간

문제 풀이 전략

● 선택지 순서대로 내용이 언급되므로, 언급된 선택지를 하나씩 소거한다.

전략 적용

[Telephone rings.]

W　Hello, Jennifer Porter speaking.

M　Hi, Ms. Porter. This is Steve Jackson from Lifetime Photo Studio.

W　Oh, how are you?

M　Good. I'm scheduled to shoot your school's graduation photos on Wednesday, ● **November 23rd**. So, I'm calling to confirm the details.

W　Sure. As we previously discussed, the place will be ● **Lily Pond Park**.

M　Okay. Could you tell me the exact number of students taking part in the photo session?

W　Let me check. *[Pause]* Well, it'll be ● **180 students**.

M　I see. The same as you said before.

W　That's right. How long will it take to shoot the photos?

M　It'll take ● **almost three hours**. We should finish by noon.

W　Great. Is there any other information you need?

M　No, I'm all set. Bye.

● 언급된 선택지 하나씩 소거하기

① 날짜: 11월 23일 (언급)
② 장소: 릴리 호수 공원 (언급)
③ 복장 (→ 미언급)
④ 참여 학생 수: 180명 (언급)
⑤ 소요 시간: 약 3시간 (언급)

내용 불일치 파악

담화 속 설명과 일치하지 않는 것을 묻는 유형으로, 매회 1문항 출제

대표 기출 예제
정답 및 해설 p.5

음성 바로 듣기 ▶

> Greenville Houseplant Expo에 관한 다음 내용을 듣고, 일치하지 <u>않는</u> 것을 고르시오.
>
> ① 3일 동안 진행될 것이다.
> ② 식물 관리 방법에 관한 강의가 매일 있을 것이다.
> ③ 희귀종을 포함한 다양한 식물을 구입할 수 있다.
> ④ 티켓 구입은 온라인으로만 가능하다.
> ⑤ 에메랄드 컨벤션 센터에서 열릴 것이다.

문제 풀이 전략

● 선택지 순서대로 내용이 언급되므로, 일치하는 선택지를 하나씩 소거한다.

전략 적용

W   Hello, listeners. I'm Melinda Jones from the organizing committee of the Greenville Houseplant Expo. I'm here to announce that the expo will ● **run for three days** starting on March 17th, 2023. ● **Just on the opening day, there'll be a lecture on plant care methods.** This lecture will be given by Dr. Evans, host of the TV show *Plants Love You*. Most importantly, you can ● **buy a variety of plants, including rare species**, exhibited in the expo. Due to its popularity, you'd better get your tickets early. Tickets are ● **available through online purchase only.** If you're a plant lover, come to the expo, which will ● **take place at the Emerald Convention Center**, and refresh your houseplant collection.

● **일치하는 선택지 하나씩 소거하기**

① 3일 동안 진행 (일치)
② 식물 관리 방법에 관한 강의는 **개막일에만** 있음
  (→ **매일** 있음: 불일치)
③ 희귀종을 포함해 다양한 식물 구입 가능 (일치)
④ 티켓 구입은 온라인으로만 가능 (일치)
⑤ 에메랄드 컨벤션 센터에서 열림 (일치)

TIP!

일치하는 않는 선택지는 주로 담화 속 설명의 일부 내용을 반대로 바꿔서 출제되므로, 선택지의 세부 내용에 주목하며 들어야 한다. 특히 대회, 강연, 축제 등의 행사에 관해 설명하는 담화가 자주 출제되므로, 진행 시기, 개최 장소, 시행 횟수, 참가 비용, 참가 대상, 신청 방법과 같은 세부 내용을 놓치지 않고 잘 들어야 한다.

도표 정보 파악

주어진 도표에서 대화 속 화자가 선택할 것을 묻는 유형으로, 매회 1문항 출제

대표 기출 예제 정답 및 해설 p.5

음성 바로 듣기▶

다음 표를 보면서 대화를 듣고, 여자가 구매할 첼로 케이스를 고르시오.

Hard Cello Cases

	Model	Price	Interior Material	Length (inches)	Wheels
①	A	$140	Nylon	51	X
②	B	$160	Cotton	49	O
③	C	$175	Velvet	53	X
④	D	$190	Cotton	52	O
⑤	E	$215	Cotton	55	X

문제 풀이 전략

● 도표에서 조건으로 제시된 항목 네 가지가 순서대로 언급되므로, 조건에 맞지 않는 선택지를 하나씩 소거한다.

전략 적용

M Welcome to Uptown Music Shop. How can I help you?

W Hi, I'm looking for a hard cello case.

M All right. Here's our catalog. These are the ones we have in stock. How much are you willing to spend?

W ● **I can spend up to $200.**

M Okay. How about the interior material? Do you have a preference?

W Well, ● **I don't want the velvet one.** It seems difficult to take care of.

M Right. Then how about the length?

W I have a full-size cello, so ● **I want a case that's at least 50 inches long.**

M Now you have two options left. Do you need wheels on your case?

W ● **No, I don't need them.** I won't carry it around a lot.

M Then this is the one for you.

W Thank you. I'll take it.

● 조건에 맞지 않는 선택지 하나씩 소거하기

· 가격: 200달러까지 (→ E 소거)
· 안감: 벨벳 원하지 않음 (→ C 소거)
· 길이: 최소 50인치 (→ B 소거)
· 바퀴: 필요 없음 (→ D 소거)

TIP! 가격 조건을 말할 때 쓰이는 빈출 표현

도표에는 항상 Price(가격)가 제시되므로, 가격 조건을 말할 때 쓰이는 표현을 익혀두는 것이 좋다.

· I can spend up to $100. 100달러까지 쓸 수 있어요.
· I don't want to spend more than $100. 100달러 넘게 쓰고 싶지 않아요.
· No more than $100. 100달러가 넘지 않게요.
· I'd like to keep it under $100. 100달러 미만으로 하고 싶어요.
· My maximum budget is $100. 최대 예산은 100달러예요.

짧은 대화의 응답 파악

'남-여-남' 또는 '여-남-여'로 이어지는 짧은 대화의 마지막 말에 대한 가장 적절한 응답을 묻는 유형으로, 매회 2문항 출제

대표 기출 예제 정답 및 해설 p.5

음성 바로 듣기▶

대화를 듣고, 남자의 마지막 말에 대한 여자의 응답으로 가장 적절한 것을 고르시오.

① Never mind. I'm selling my old helmet.
② All right. I'll buy a bigger one that fits you.
③ No way. You should not ride a bicycle at night.
④ Great. I think it matches your bicycle perfectly.
⑤ No. We don't have to worry about the tight schedule.

문제 풀이 전략

1 대화의 첫 문장을 듣고, 대화 상황을 파악한다.

2 대화 속 마지막 말의 의도를 파악하여, 이에 대한 응답을 추론한다.

전략 적용

M **1** **Mom, I'd like to get a new bicycle helmet.** Can you buy me one?
W I'll buy you a new helmet if you need it. But what's the problem with the one you have now?
M **2** **My helmet feels too tight. It hurts my head.**

1 대화 상황 파악하기

아들이 엄마에게 새 자전거 헬멧을 갖고 싶다고 했다.

2 마지막 말의 의도 파악하기

헬멧이 너무 꽉 끼어서 머리가 아프다고 했다. 즉, 새 것이 꼭 필요하다고 말하려는 의도이므로, 새것을 사 주겠다는 응답이 나와야 한다.

TIP!

남자의 응답을 고를 때는 '여자-남자-여자'의 순서로, 여자의 응답을 고를 때는 '남자-여자-남자'의 순서로 대화가 짧게 이루어진다. 따라서 마지막 말을 놓치지 않도록 집중하며 듣는다.

긴 대화의 응답 파악 [고난도 유형]

긴 대화의 마지막 말에 대한 가장 적절한 응답을 묻는 유형으로, 주로 3점짜리로 2문항 출제

대표 기출 예제   정답 및 해설 p.6   음성 바로 듣기▶

대화를 듣고, 남자의 마지막 말에 대한 여자의 응답으로 가장 적절한 것을 고르시오. [3점]

Woman: _____

① Not really. It's better to speak in simple sentences.

② Yes. Try to memorize words by learning the root words.

③ That's right. I'm glad you've studied the proper examples.

④ Exactly. That way you can use the proper words in context.

⑤ I don't think so. Always use an Italian-to-Italian dictionary.

문제 풀이 전략

1 처음부터 끝까지 전체적인 대화의 흐름을 파악하며 듣는다.

2 대화 속 마지막 말의 의도를 파악하여, 이에 대한 이어질 응답을 추론한다.

전략 적용

M **1** Can I come in, Professor Rossini?

W Of course. Come on in, Ben. What brings you here?

M **1** I came to ask for advice on studying Italian.

W Is there anything specific you're having trouble with?

M Yes. **1** I'm experiencing difficulty using words properly. Could I get some tips?

W Sure. First, let me ask how you use your dictionary.

M Well, I use it to look up words that I don't know the meanings of.

W **1** Dictionaries provide example sentences for most words. Do you read them, too?

M No, I don't pay attention to the example sentences.

W Knowing the meaning of words is important, but **1** you should also understand the context in which the words are properly used.

M **2** I see. So you're suggesting that I study the example sentences as well, right?

1 대화의 흐름 파악하기

남자가 교수를 방문함
→ 이탈리아어 공부에 대한 조언을 구함
→ 단어를 적절히 사용하기 어렵다고 토로함
→ 교수가 사전 속 예문을 읽는지 물어봄
→ 예문으로 단어가 사용되는 맥락을 이해할 수 있다고 설명함

2 마지막 말의 의도 파악하기

남자가 교수에게 예문도 공부해야 된다고 제안한 것인지 되물었다. 즉, 교수의 조언을 재확인하려는 의도이므로, 앞서 설명했던 예문 공부의 효과를 재설명해 주는 응답이 나와야 한다.

TIP!

대화 초반에는 중심 소재가 언급되고, 이후 대화가 진행되며 점차 대화 주제가 구체화된다. 또한 마지막 말만 듣고 정답을 고르기 어려운 경우가 많으므로, 대화의 전체 흐름을 이해하고 있어야 한다.

기출 유형 13

상황에 적절한 말 파악 고난도 유형

담화 속 인물이 주어진 상황에서 하기에 가장 적절한 말을 묻는 유형으로, 매회 3점짜리로 1문항 출제

대표 기출 예제 정답 및 해설 p.6

음성 바로 듣기▶

다음 상황 설명을 듣고, Katie가 Jacob에게 할 말로 가장 적절한 것을 고르시오. [3점]

Katie: _____

① You should check how many nursing homes there are.
② Why don't you reuse the activity you prepared last time?
③ How about preparing multiple activities for your next visit?
④ You need to gain more practical knowledge about nursing.
⑤ You'd better speak to the residents of the neighborhood.

문제 풀이 전략

1 담화 초반을 듣고 등장인물이 처한 상황을 파악한다.

2 담화 후반 wants to tell/suggest가 나오면 그 뒤에 이어지는 말을 확인한다.

전략 적용

M **1** Jacob just started volunteering at a nursing home and is planning his next visit. He recalls that not every resident in the nursing home enjoyed the activity he had prepared last time. To avoid this situation, he tries to find an activity that all residents in the nursing home can enjoy. But he can't come up with one that everyone would like. He asks his friend Katie for advice because she has lots of experience volunteering at a nursing home. Katie thinks there's no single activity that can interest all the residents. **2** So Katie wants to suggest to Jacob that next time he should plan more than one activity. In this situation, what would Katie most likely say to Jacob?

1 등장인물이 처한 상황 파악하기

Jacob은 요양원에서 자원봉사를 시작했다. 다음 방문을 앞두고, 지난번에 자신이 준비했던 활동을 모두가 즐겼던 것은 아니었다는 사실을 떠올렸다.

2 wants to suggest 뒤의 말 확인하기

Katie는 Jacob에게 다음번에 한 가지 이상의 활동을 계획하라고 제안하고 싶다고 했다.

TIP! 상황별 빈출 정답 표현

• 제안하는 상황: Why don't you ~? ~하지 않을래?　　　　How about ~? ~하는 게 어때?
• 조언하는 상황: You'd better ~. ~하는 편이 좋겠어.　　　　You have/need to ~. ~해야 해.
• 당부하는 상황: Don't forget to ~. ~하는 것을 잊지 마.　　　Make sure ~. 반드시 ~해.

세트 문항 (주제/세부 내용 파악)

긴 담화 하나에 대해 담화의 주제를 묻는 문제와 담화에서 언급되지 않은 세부 내용을 묻는 문제, 총 두 문제가 세트로 구성된 유형으로, 매회 한 세트씩 출제 (유일하게 두 번 반복해서 들려줌)

대표 기출 예제 정답 및 해설 p.7

음성 바로 듣기 ▶

[01~02] 다음을 듣고, 물음에 답하시오.

01. 여자가 하는 말의 주제로 가장 적절한 것은?

① how metals advanced human civilization
② how techniques applied to metals improved
③ where most precious metals originated from
④ why metals were used in the fashion industry
⑤ why ancient civilizations competed for metals

02. 언급된 금속이 아닌 것은?

① gold　　② silver　　③ iron
④ aluminum　　⑤ nickel

문제 풀이 전략

1 담화 초반 Today 뒤에 이어지는 말을 듣고 주제를 파악한다.

2 세부 내용은 서수나 순서 표현을 써서 선택지 순서대로 언급되므로, 언급된 선택지를 하나씩 소거하며 듣는다.

3 두 번째로 들려주는 음성을 들으며 문제를 맞게 풀었는지 확인한다.

전략 적용

W　Hello, students. Perhaps no material on earth has been more important in human history than metal. **1Today, we're going to discuss the contribution of metals to the development of civilization. 2First, gold** was considered the most valuable metal due to its beauty and scarcity. Because of its visual appeal and ability to be easily shaped, it's been used to decorate religious places and objects. **2Second, silver** was mainly prized for being the shiniest of all metals. It's been one of the main forms of currency since it was the chief metal used for making coins. **2Next, iron** became widely used once humans discovered techniques to strengthen it. This metal was fashioned into tools that revolutionized farming, and later, machines that industrialized the world. **2Finally, aluminum** is the most abundant metal in the world and is also lightweight. That's why it's been essential to countless industries in modern society from automotive to aerospace to household products. Now, let's watch a short related video.

1 Today 뒤의 말 확인하기

금속이 문명의 발전에 기여한 바를 논의할 것이라고 했다.

2 세부 내용 선택지 하나씩 소거하기

First, Second 등의 서수 표현과 **Next, Finally** 등의 순서 표현을 써서 금, 은, 철, 알루미늄을 차례대로 언급했다.

3 두 번째 음성 들으며 확인하기

TIP!

담화를 처음 들려줄 때는 첫 번째 문제(주제 파악) 풀이에 집중하고, 두 번째 들려줄 때 두 번째 문제(세부 내용 파악) 풀이에 집중하는 방식도 가능하다. 두 가지 방식으로 모두 풀어본 뒤 자신에게 더 맞는 것을 고르면 된다.

해커스북 중·고등

www.HackersBook.com

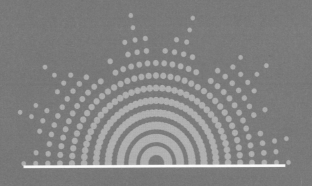

영어듣기
모의고사

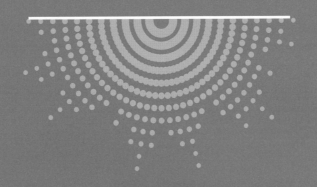

01회~20회   영어듣기 모의고사

21회~24회   **고난도 영어듣기 모의고사**

01회 영어듣기 모의고사

정답 및 해설 p.8

1번부터 17번까지는 듣고 답하는 문제입니다. 1번부터 15번까지는 한 번만 들려주고, 16번부터 17번까지는 두 번 들려줍니다. 방송을 잘 듣고 답을 하시기 바랍니다.

1 다음을 듣고, 여자가 하는 말의 목적으로 가장 적절한 것을 고르시오.

① 학교 동아리들을 소개하려고
② 장기자랑 오디션을 공지하려고
③ 배우기 쉬운 악기를 추천하려고
④ 댄스 대회 참가를 독려하려고
⑤ 오디션 결과를 발표하려고

2 대화를 듣고, 여자의 의견으로 가장 적절한 것을 고르시오.

① 냉장고를 적어도 일주일에 한 번 청소해야 한다.
② 건강을 유지하려면 반드시 식단을 관리해야 한다.
③ 집에서 음식을 만들어 먹으면 지출을 줄일 수 있다.
④ 음식에서 이상한 냄새가 날 때는 먹으면 안 된다.
⑤ 식중독 증상이 의심되면 빨리 병원에 가야 한다.

3 대화를 듣고, 두 사람의 관계를 가장 잘 나타낸 것을 고르시오.

① 패션모델 — 디자이너
② 회사 대표 — 제조업자
③ 고객 상담원 — 구매자
④ 항공 승무원 — 탑승객
⑤ 배달 기사 — 식당 직원

4 대화를 듣고, 그림에서 대화의 내용과 일치하지 않는 것을 고르시오.

5 대화를 듣고, 남자가 할 일로 가장 적절한 것을 고르시오.

① 염료 섞기
② 고무줄 묶기
③ 새 옷 구매하기
④ 티셔츠 세탁하기
⑤ 가게에 데려다주기

6 대화를 듣고, 여자가 지불할 금액을 고르시오. [3점]

① $11   ② $16   ③ $18   ④ $20   ⑤ $21

7 대화를 듣고, 남자가 콘서트에 갈 수 없는 이유를 고르시오.

① 표가 너무 비싸서
② 친구 생일 파티가 있어서
③ 코딩 강의를 신청해야 해서
④ 피아노 연습을 해야 해서
⑤ 중간고사를 쳐야 해서

8 대화를 듣고, Youth Regional Tennis Championship에 관해 언급되지 않은 것을 고르시오.

① 대회 기간   ② 대회 장소   ③ 대회 상금
④ 등록비   ⑤ 등록 마감일

9 새해 축하 행사에 관한 다음 내용을 듣고, 일치하지 않는 것을 고르시오.

① 전 세계의 음악가들이 공연할 예정이다.
② 20대의 푸드 트럭이 준비되어 있다.
③ 아이스 스케이트장이 시청 앞에 설치되었다.
④ 자정에 종을 울릴 예정이다.
⑤ 행사가 끝날 때 불꽃놀이가 있을 예정이다.

10 다음 표를 보면서 대화를 듣고, 남자가 구매할 시계를 고르시오.

Clocks

	Model	Price	Material	Size	Type
①	A	$31	Plastic	Large	Analog
②	B	$29	Wood	Medium	Analog
③	C	$27	Wood	Large	Digital
④	D	$25	Plastic	Small	Digital
⑤	E	$23	Wood	Large	Analog

11 대화를 듣고, 남자의 마지막 말에 대한 여자의 응답으로 가장 적절한 것을 고르시오.

① Don't worry. I can copy them for you.
② No, thanks. I'll have a sandwich for lunch.
③ Definitely. We helped many customers today.
④ Sorry. I'll be right back to cover for you.
⑤ That's fine. The bank closes at 6 p.m.

12 대화를 듣고, 여자의 마지막 말에 대한 남자의 응답으로 가장 적절한 것을 고르시오.

① I already applied for the job.
② It was easy to work with her.
③ Why don't you go and ask her?
④ When can you start working here?
⑤ It's the convenience store down the street.

13 대화를 듣고, 여자의 마지막 말에 대한 남자의 응답으로 가장 적절한 것을 고르시오. [3점]

Man: _____

① Sure. I'm so excited about making new friends.
② I agree. It sounds like a great chance for my dad.
③ No problem. I wanted to change schools anyway.
④ I know. I really wish I didn't have to move either.
⑤ I promise. I'll tell you about everything that happens.

14 대화를 듣고, 남자의 마지막 말에 대한 여자의 응답으로 가장 적절한 것을 고르시오.

Woman: _____

① Thank you. I've been so forgetful these days.
② It's okay. I already bought all the art supplies.
③ I'm sorry. We don't have any bicycles in stock.
④ You're welcome. Here are the gift bags I prepared.
⑤ That's too bad. You know how much kids like candy.

15 다음 상황 설명을 듣고, Mia가 Patrick에게 할 말로 가장 적절한 것을 고르시오. [3점]

Mia: _____

① I don't want to get a bad grade.
② I will help you finish your tasks.
③ I can just finish everything by myself.
④ We still have time before the presentation.
⑤ I hope you can complete everything on time.

[16~17] 다음을 듣고, 물음에 답하시오.

16 여자가 하는 말의 주제로 가장 적절한 것은?

① ways to have fun with your aging grandparents
② how seniors can maintain their mental health
③ types of physical activities for elderly people
④ signs of loneliness in your elderly neighbors
⑤ causes of memory loss in senior citizens

17 언급된 활동이 <u>아닌</u> 것은?

① drawing ② writing ③ gardening
④ singing ⑤ volunteering

이제 듣기 문제가 끝났습니다. 채점을 마친 후 다음 페이지에서 방송을 다시 들으며 딕테이션 연습을 하시기 바랍니다.

* 채점 결과: 맞은 개수 _____개 / 17개   정답 및 해설 p.8

01회 Dictation

Dictation 정답 p.8

01회 영어듣기 모의고사 Dictation 음성을 들으며 빈칸에 알맞은 단어를 채워 넣으시기 바랍니다.

1

W Good afternoon, Grenville High School students. This is Ms. Reynolds, your music teacher. I'm excited to announce that we will be 1)_____ _____ for our school talent show on November 7th and 8th. All students are welcome to audition. The performances will be divided into three categories, which are music, dance, and comedy. Auditions will be held after school from 5 to 6:30 p.m. You may sign up on the sheet posted 2)_____ _____ _____ _____. Please bring any special equipment you need, such as costumes or 3)_____ _____. We will provide a microphone. We hope to see you there!

↘ 듣기 필수 표현
· divide into ~으로 나누다
· sign up 신청하다

2

W Honey, what's wrong? Your face is so pale.
M My stomach really hurts. I don't know why.
W What 1)_____ _____ _____ yesterday?
M We had pasta for dinner. And I ate a tuna sandwich for lunch.
W Where did you get the tuna sandwich?
M It was 2)_____ _____ _____ _____ the refrigerator.
W Oh, no. I made that sandwich two weeks ago. It should have been thrown out last week.
M It did smell strange. But I was so hungry that I just ate it.
W I think we should 3)_____ _____ _____ at least once a week.
M Yeah. Maybe we can do it every Sunday when we clean the house.
W Good idea. Do you need to 4)_____ _____ _____?
M No. I'll be fine if I lie down for a while.

↘ 듣기 필수 표현
· throw out ~을 버리다
· at least 적어도
· lie down 눕다

3

[Telephone rings.]

M Hello. This is Forever Fashion. How can I help you?
W Hi. I ordered a pair of pants online. I wanted the small size, but they 1)_____ _____ _____ _____.
M Okay. Would you like to return them or exchange them?
W I'd like a full refund, please.
M Can you 2)_____ _____ _____ _____ _____, please?
W Yes. It's 10456. My name is Michelle Linton.
M Hmm... You purchased this item two weeks ago. But according to our return policy, you can only return items 3)_____ _____ _____ of the purchase date.
W I was away on a business trip, so I didn't get to 4)_____ _____ _____ until today. I hope you understand.
M All right. Let me talk to my manager and call you right back.
W Thank you.

4

W What are you doing, James?
M Hi, Melissa. I'm looking at this photo from last weekend.
W Where was it taken?
M This was at my aunt's house in the countryside.
W That must be your aunt. Who's that girl in the 1)_____ _____ _____?
M That's my cousin, Emily. She just turned three.
W She's adorable. Those 2)_____ _____ _____ are cute, too.
M Their names are Coco and Peanut. They're really friendly.
W There's even a picnic table in the yard.
M Yes. We had lunch there.
W It sounds like you had a great time. Oh, what is that basket 3)_____ _____ _____ for?
M We put apples in it when we pick them from the tree. Do you see the flowers in the pot in front of the house? I gave her the flowers to thank her for hosting me.
W That's very sweet of you.

5

W That's a cool T-shirt, Sam. Where did you get it?

M It 1)_____ _____ _____ a regular T-shirt, but I dyed it at home.

W Oh, yeah? Was it hard to make that pattern?

M No. It was actually really easy.

W How did you do it?

M First, I mixed 2)_____ _____ _____, and then I tied up the T-shirt with rubber bands.

W Okay. I can do that.

M Then, I poured the dyes onto it. After waiting for 24 hours, I 3)_____ _____ _____ _____. That's all.

W Where can you buy the dyes? I want to try this.

M The art supply store on Main Street sells them. Do you want me to 4)_____ _____ _____?

W That would be great. Thank you.

↘ 듣기 필수 표현
· used to (예전에는) ~였다
· tie up ~을 묶다

6

M Welcome to V Mart's grand opening sale. Please let me know if I can help you with anything.

W Hello. How much are these blueberries?

M Each pack is $3. If you 1)_____ _____ _____, you can get both for $5.

W Sure. I'll get two packs of blueberries, then.

M Do you like grapes? These ones are really sweet. Each bag is $5.

W Okay. I'll take 2)_____ _____ of grapes, too.

M Would you like anything else today?

W No, that will be everything.

M All right. And because today is our grand opening day, we are offering 10% off the total.

W That's great. I'll 3)_____ _____ _____ my credit card, please.

↘ 듣기 필수 표현
· let ~ know ~에게 알려주다

7

W Martin! I've been calling you, but I guess you couldn't 1)_____ _____.

M Sorry, Jen. I was listening to the new song by The Twinkles.

W I didn't know you liked them. I have two tickets to their concert next month.

M Really? Those tickets are expensive.

W My mom 2)_____ _____ _____ _____ for my birthday.

M You're lucky. I'd love to go to that concert.

W Well, do you want to go with me? It's on the 14th.

M I wish I could, but I'm busy that day.

W Why? Do you have to 3)_____ _____?

M It's not that. I have to take my midterm test that night.

W What test? I haven't heard about this.

M Oh, I'm taking 4)_____ _____ _____ _____.

W I see. Then, good luck with your test.

↘ 듣기 필수 표현
· take one's midterm test 중간고사를 치다

8

W Dad, can you sign this permission form?

M What's it for, Cathy?

W Actually, I'm competing at the Youth Regional Tennis Championship.

M That's wonderful. When is it?

W It 1)_____ _____ June 20th to 21st. It's on a weekend.

M Maybe your mom and I can go watch you. Where 2)_____ _____ _____ _____?

W It will be at Riverford High School.

M Perfect. That's only a 20-minute drive from here.

W I'm so glad you'll be there. Oh, and there's a registration fee. It's $50.

M Okay. How do I pay for it?

W Can you give it to me in cash? I have to 3)_____ _____ _____. I can submit the permission form and the payment together.

M Great. I'll get my wallet, then.

W Thanks, Dad.

↘ 듣기 필수 표현
· registration fee 등록비

9

M Welcome to our New Year's celebration. I'm David Allen, the mayor of Rockville, and I'm thrilled to be here with you on the last day of the year. This evening, many of our 1)_____ _____ _____ will be performing live music. Additionally, we have food from all over the world. Please visit one of our 20 food trucks for a delicious meal. An ice-skating rink has also been set up in front of city hall, so please 2)_____ _____ _____ _____ yourselves! We'll be ringing the bell at midnight to celebrate the start of the New Year. We will finish the night with a spectacular fireworks display. You won't want to miss that, so be sure to stick around 3)_____ _____ _____ _____.

↘ 듣기 필수 표현
· all over the world 전 세계에
· stick around 머무르다

10

W Gary, did you buy a clock for your living room?

M No, not yet. I want to order one from this website. Can you help me pick one?

W Of course. How much are you willing to spend?

M I don't want to spend 1)_____ _____ $30.

W All right. Which material do you like, plastic or wood?

M I like these ones 2)_____ _____ _____. What do you think?

W I agree. They look nicer than the plastic ones. What about the size?

M I should get a 3)_____ _____. That way, I can read it from across the room.

W That makes sense. Do you want to get an analog or a digital clock?

M I prefer the look of 4)_____ _____.

W Then, that only leaves this one.

↘ 듣기 필수 표현
· be willing to ~할 의향이 있다
· made of ~으로 만든
· make sense 말이 되다

11

M Sarah, can you help the customer who just 1)_____ _____ _____ _____? I'm going to take my lunch break.

W Sorry, I don't think I can. I have to 2)_____ _____ _____ right now.

M I understand. I can do it.

↘ 듣기 필수 표현
· take one's lunch break 점심을 먹다

12

W Dad, I want to get a part-time job this summer. What do you think?

M That's 1)_____ _____ _____. The owner of the convenience store is looking for someone.

W But I don't have 2)_____ _____ _____. Would she hire a student?

↘ 듣기 필수 표현
· part-time job 아르바이트
· look for ~를 구하다

13

W John, I heard that your family is 1)_____ _____ _____! Is that true?

M That's right, Britney. My dad got a new job in Springton.

W I guess that means you'll have to change schools, right?

M Yes, but I'm going to be here until December.

W Really? How is that possible? Springton is so far away from here.

M I'm going to live with my uncle nearby. My parents want me to 2)_____ _____ _____ _____. It's only a couple of months.

W Oh, I'm so happy to hear that! But I'll miss you when you move.

M I'll miss you, too. We have phones, though. We can talk or send messages any time we want.

W You'd better 3)_____ _____ _____ and keep me posted.

↘ 듣기 필수 표현
· get a job 직장을 구하다
· change schools 전학 가다
· far away from ~에서 먼
· keep ~ posted ~에게 계속 소식을 전하다

14

M Honey, what else do we have to do for our son's birthday party?

W Let's see. We've taken care of the guest list, the food, and the decorations.

M Okay. What about 1)_____ _____ _____ for the kids to take home?

W Oh, right. But what should we put inside them?

M How about some candy?

W I don't think that's a good idea. Sugar is bad for their teeth.

M Then, how about 2)_____ _____? We could get some crayons and small sketchbooks.

W I like that idea. *[Pause]* Oh, no!

M What's the matter?

W I 3)_____ _____ _____ his birthday gift. He wanted a bicycle.

M No worries. We still have some time. Let me go to the store right now and see what's in stock.

↘ **듣기 필수 표현**
- take care of ~을 처리하다
- bad for ~에 나쁜
- No worries. 걱정 마.
- in stock 재고가 있는

15

M Mia and Patrick are working on a science presentation together. They 1)_____ _____ _____ _____ the tasks that needed to be done for the presentation. They then divided up these tasks equally. Mia began 2)_____ _____ _____ _____ right away. She finished everything, and now it is two days before the day of the presentation. But Patrick still has not completed any of his tasks. Mia is worried that he will not 3)_____ _____ on time. So Mia wants to tell Patrick that she can assist him in completing his tasks. In this situation, what would Mia most likely say to Patrick?

↘ **듣기 필수 표현**
- divide up ~을 분배하다
- on time 제시간에

16~17

W Hello, *Morning Show* listeners. Staying healthy is important, and it becomes even more important 1)_____ _____ _____ _____. Today, we'll discuss ways our older listeners can take care of their mental health. First, drawing is a relaxing activity, especially for those of you who can no longer walk that well. It's an enjoyable way to express your feelings and stay creative. Another activity that's good for our elderly listeners is writing. Writing in a journal can 2)_____ _____ _____ your thoughts and improve your memory. Next, gardening is a great way to get fresh air and enjoy the outdoors. It also provides gentle exercise. Lastly, volunteering is a wonderful way to connect with the community. It can also prevent feelings of loneliness. I hope you 3)_____ _____ _____ _____. Please visit our website for more wellness tips!

↘ **듣기 필수 표현**
- no longer 더 이상 ~않다
- connect with ~와 가까워지다

▲ 문제 음성
바로 듣기

▲ 고사장 버전
바로 듣기

정답 및 해설 p.14

1번부터 17번까지는 듣고 답하는 문제입니다. 1번부터 15번까지는 한 번만 들려주고, 16번부터 17번까지는 두 번 들려줍니다. 방송을 잘 듣고 답을 하시기 바랍니다.

1 다음을 듣고, 남자가 하는 말의 목적으로 가장 적절한 것을 고르시오.

① 강당에 접근하지 말 것을 요청하려고
② 상륙 예정인 태풍에 대해 경고하려고
③ 지붕 방수 공사 일정을 안내하려고
④ 학교 안전사고 예방법을 소개하려고
⑤ 수리 과정이 지연되는 이유를 설명하려고

2 대화를 듣고, 남자의 의견으로 가장 적절한 것을 고르시오.

① 자동차로 출퇴근하는 것이 가장 편리하다.
② 대기 오염 문제가 점점 더 심각해지고 있다.
③ 지하철역 안에서는 질서를 잘 지켜야 한다.
④ 환승 할인으로 교통비를 절약해야 한다.
⑤ 환경을 위해 대중교통을 이용해야 한다.

3 대화를 듣고, 두 사람의 관계를 가장 잘 나타낸 것을 고르시오.

① 택배 기사 — 고객
② 담임 선생님 — 학부모
③ 치과 접수원 — 환자
④ 아파트 경비원 — 입주민
⑤ 택시 운전사 — 탑승객

4 대화를 듣고, 그림에서 대화의 내용과 일치하지 않는 것을 고르시오.

5 대화를 듣고, 여자가 할 일로 가장 적절한 것을 고르시오.

① 가구 배치하기
② 광고지 나눠주기
③ 접시 설거지하기
④ 과일 주문하기
⑤ 바닥 걸레질하기

6 대화를 듣고, 여자가 지불할 금액을 고르시오. [3점]

① $30 ② $32 ③ $36 ④ $38 ⑤ $40

7 대화를 듣고, 남자가 이사를 결심한 이유를 고르시오.

① 가족과 가까이에서 살고 싶어서
② 대학원에 입학할 예정이어서
③ 도시 근처에 새 직장을 얻어서
④ 미술관 관람을 자주 하고 싶어서
⑤ 현재 사는 곳에 아는 사람이 없어서

8 대화를 듣고, Midtown Music Festival에 관해 언급되지 않은 것을 고르시오.

① 개최 장소 ② 주차 비용 ③ 개최 날짜
④ 티켓 가격 ⑤ 참여 가수

9 Community Baking Contest에 관한 다음 내용을 듣고, 일치하지 않는 것을 고르시오.

① 7월 5일에 대회가 열린다.
② 주방 도구가 제공될 것이다.
③ 학교 웹사이트에서 접수 신청을 할 수 있다.
④ 외부의 유명 강사를 심사위원으로 초빙했다.
⑤ 부문별 우승자에게 1,000달러가 주어진다.

10 다음 표를 보면서 대화를 듣고, 남자가 구매할 여행 가방을 고르시오.

Suitcases

	Model	Price	Size	Front Pockets	Color
①	A	$85	Large	O	Red
②	B	$65	Large	O	Red
③	C	$60	Large	O	Blue
④	D	$40	Medium	X	Red
⑤	E	$45	Small	X	Blue

11 대화를 듣고, 여자의 마지막 말에 대한 남자의 응답으로 가장 적절한 것을 고르시오.

① When does the car make that noise?
② You should consider buying that car.
③ I'm worried because it doesn't turn on.
④ Be careful not to get in a traffic accident.
⑤ I guess we should get it checked by a mechanic.

12 대화를 듣고, 남자의 마지막 말에 대한 여자의 응답으로 가장 적절한 것을 고르시오.

① Why not? I don't mind at all.
② Of course. Here is the camera.
③ Really? I should buy that smartphone.
④ Good. Is that a photograph of your family?
⑤ I'm sorry. My hand was shaking when I took the picture.

13 대화를 듣고, 여자의 마지막 말에 대한 남자의 응답으로 가장 적절한 것을 고르시오.

Man: _____

① What time will the room be available?
② But I've already made a reservation.
③ That place is very popular with kids.
④ Everyone in my group is an adult.
⑤ Please provide me with a refund.

14 대화를 듣고, 남자의 마지막 말에 대한 여자의 응답으로 가장 적절한 것을 고르시오. [3점]

Woman: _____

① Okay. I'll give you a call on Sunday morning.
② All right. Let's meet together if she wants to.
③ Thanks. I appreciate you showing me around.
④ I'm sorry. But next weekend doesn't work for me.
⑤ Good. She should get here on Saturday afternoon.

15 다음 상황 설명을 듣고, Gordon이 Isabella에게 할 말로 가장 적절한 것을 고르시오. [3점]

Gordon: _____

① These shoes are extremely comfortable.
② Could you tell me which color you prefer?
③ The brand you have selected is very popular.
④ Would you like to try on a white pair instead?
⑤ I'm afraid the ones you want are currently out of stock.

[16~17] 다음을 듣고, 물음에 답하시오.

16 여자가 하는 말의 주제로 가장 적절한 것은?

① languages which are commonly spoken
② a trait shared by several different languages
③ countries that have more than one official language
④ why some languages have begun to disappear
⑤ what made some languages more popular

17 언급된 언어가 <u>아닌</u> 것은?

① English ② Chinese ③ French
④ Hindi   ⑤ Spanish

이제 듣기 문제가 끝났습니다. 채점을 마친 후 다음 페이지에서 방송을 다시 들으며 딕테이션 연습을 하시기 바랍니다.

* 채점 결과: 맞은 개수 _____개 / 17개   정답 및 해설 p.14

02회 영어듣기 모의고사 Dictation 음성을 들으며 빈칸에 알맞은 단어를 채워 넣으시기 바랍니다.

1

M Attention, students. This is Principal Carson. As you know, a 1)_____ _____ _____ through this area last night. After we checked our buildings, we found that the 2)_____ _____ _____. The high winds weakened the building's roof. Obviously, this could be a serious safety threat. So we would like to ask you to keep away from the auditorium. We 3)_____ _____ _____ _____ the auditorium soon. We will inform you when we have a set schedule. Thank you for your cooperation.

↘ 듣기 필수 표현
· keep away from ~에 가까이 가지 않다

2

M Do you usually drive to work, Mia?

W Yeah. What about you?

M I take the subway instead.

W I didn't realize that. Do you find the subway more convenient?

M Not really. I have to 1)_____ _____, and both transfer stations are pretty crowded at rush hour.

W Why don't you just drive, then? You have a car.

M Well, using public transportation is 2)_____ _____ _____.

W What do you mean?

M Cars and trucks release many harmful materials into the air. If everyone used public transportation, 3)_____ _____ _____ would be a lot better.

W Hmm... I never considered that. I might start taking the subway as well.

M I'm glad to hear that.

↘ 듣기 필수 표현
· at rush hour 출퇴근 시간에

3

[Cell phone rings.]

M Hi. Is this Janet Patterson?

W Yes. Who's calling, please?

M I'm with Express Shipping Company. I'm having 1)_____ _____ _____ _____. Is your address 1278 Oak Drive?

W No. It's 1078 Oak Drive.

M Got it. I'll 2)_____ _____ _____ in about 30 minutes.

W I was just on my way out. Could you leave it by my front door?

M Actually, that won't work. I need you to sign for the package.

W In that case, would you be able to come after 4 p.m.? I have to take my daughter to the dentist right now.

M That's fine. I also have some boxes to 3)_____ _____ at an apartment building across town.

W Thanks so much. I really appreciate it.

4

M What are you looking at, honey?

W It's a picture of my childhood home.

M Wow. It's really nice. Why are there 1)_____ _____ in the front yard?

W My parents and I liked to sit there and watch the sunset.

M Is that your bicycle next to the front door?

W Yeah. I used to ride my bike every day.

M Sounds fun. Oh, the flowers in the pot 2)_____ _____ _____ _____ are really pretty.

W I agree. My mom put them there.

M Where was your bedroom?

W You see the three square windows on the second floor? The middle one was my room.

M I see. Oh, the house 3)_____ _____ _____. Does that mean you had a fireplace?

W Yes. In the living room.

M You are lucky to have grown up in such a wonderful home.

↘ 듣기 필수 표현
· used to ~하곤 했다
· grown up 성장하다, 자라다

5

M Amy, are we almost ready for the grand opening of our café tomorrow?

W I think so. I just 1)_____ _____ _____ .

M What about the tables and chairs? Should I finish setting them up?

W I took care of that this morning.

M Thanks. And I've already washed all the dishes, so they are ready to use.

W Great. Hmm... do we need to 2)_____ _____ _____ _____ to make juice?

M No. We received a shipment this morning with everything we need.

W Then, I will hand out 3)_____ _____ · in the area around our café.

M Good plan. The more people know about our café, the busier we will be tomorrow.

↘ 듣기 필수 표현
· wash the dishes 설거지를 하다
· hand out ~을 나눠주다

6

M Welcome to Super Cinema.

W Thanks. Are there still seats available for the 3 p.m. showing of *Jungle Adventure*?

M Yes. How many tickets do you need?

W I need tickets for two adults and one child. How much do the tickets cost?

M It's 1)_____ _____ _____ and $10 for children 12 and under.

W That's good. My kid is 11.

M Okay. Will you be paying with cash or credit card?

W Credit card. Could you check if I get a 20% discount with this credit card?

M Let me see. *[Pause]* Actually, no. You qualify for 2)_____ _____ _____ .

W Oh, okay. Thanks for checking.

M No problem. I'll 3)_____ _____ _____ _____ now.

↘ 듣기 필수 표현
· qualify for ~을 받다, ~자격을 얻다

7

W Hi, Mike. I heard you're planning to move to Chicago next month.

M That's right. I'm moving there on May 1st.

W Why did you make that decision? Does your family live there?

M Actually, I 1)_____ _____ _____ in Chicago right now.

W Then, I guess it must be for work. Did you 2)_____ _____ _____ _____ _____ ?

M No. That's not it. I'm taking some time off from work.

W Then, you will have lots of time to visit all the art galleries there.

M Well, I think I'll be too busy for that.

W Really? Why?

M I'm going to enter graduate school. I plan on 3)_____ _____ _____ _____ . That's why I'm relocating to Chicago.

W Wow, that's very impressive.

↘ 듣기 필수 표현
· make a decision 결정을 내리다
· take time off from work 일을 쉬다, 휴직하다

8

M What are you doing on the computer, honey?

W I'm 1)_____ _____ for the Midtown Music Festival. I'm planning to go with my best friend.

M That sounds like fun. Where will the event be held?

W It will take place at the Warren Performing Arts Center.

M That's convenient. There's a subway station right across the street.

W I think I might drive, though. The center 2)_____ _____ _____ for special events.

M Great. When is the festival?

W It's on Saturday, July 15th. It's an all-day event.

M Are tickets expensive?

W They're only $15 each.

M Wow. That's quite cheap.

W I know. I think the event organizers received funding from the city government. So they aren't 3)_____ _____ _____ _____ _____ .

M That's great to hear.

9

W You're listening to *About Town* on Radio KR100. I'm your host Diane Ramsey with a special announcement. The Pineville Cooking School is holding its fifth annual Community Baking Contest on July 5th. The contest will be held at the school, and all [1]_____ _____ _____ _____. There will be three categories of competition, which are cakes, pies, and bread. Those who wish to participate must sign up on the school's website. There is no entry fee, but all competitors must bring their own ingredients. The five judges are [2]_____ _____ at the school. Also, prizes of $1,000 will be awarded to the winner of [3]_____ _____. The deadline to sign up is this Friday, so visit the website soon!

10

M Excuse me. Could you help me find a new suitcase?

W Of course. Are you planning on [1]_____ _____ _____ soon?

M Yeah. I'll be visiting Spain for a family vacation next month.

W Sounds like fun. Then, how much are you looking to spend?

M [2]_____ _____ _____ $65.

W Got it. We have a number of models in that price range.

M Oh, I should mention that I don't want a small suitcase. A small one won't be [3]_____ _____ _____ _____ all my clothes.

W Okay. And what about a front pocket?

M Oh, I definitely want one with a front pocket.

W Then, these two models [4]_____ _____ _____.

M Both of those look good. But I prefer the blue one.

W That's a great choice.

↘ 듣기 필수 표현
· look to ~할 생각이다, ~할 것을 고려하다
· a number of 많은

11

W Honey, [1]_____ _____ _____ that our car has been making a strange noise?

M No. But I haven't driven it for a few days. What does the noise sound like?

W I hear [2]_____ _____ _____ every time I turn the car on.

↘ 듣기 필수 표현
· make a noise 소리를 내다
· turn on 시동을 걸다, ~을 켜다

12

M Karen, you upgraded your cell phone to [1]_____ _____ _____, right?

W Yes, I did. It takes great photographs and videos. It can prevent camera shake.

M Wow, that sounds cool! I was also thinking of buying one. Can [2]_____ _____ _____ _____ with your phone?

13

[Telephone rings.]

W Thank you for calling Jackson Steakhouse. How can I help you today?

M Hi. I would like to make a dinner reservation for tomorrow night.

W Of course. How many people will be [1]_____ _____ _____?

M There will be eight in total.

W And what time would you like to book a table for?

M Hmm... would it be [2]_____ _____ _____ a private room?

W One of our private dining rooms will be available at 8 p.m. tomorrow. Does that work?

M Could we come at 7 instead?

W Unfortunately, there's no private room available at that time. They're [3]_____ _____.

M In that case, 8 p.m. is fine. And my name is Jason Sutherland.

W Thanks, Mr. Sutherland. Will you [4]_____ _____ _____ _____? We can provide special chairs for them if necessary.

↘ 듣기 필수 표현
· make a reservation 예약하다

14

M Denise, do you ¹)_____ _____ _____ for Saturday? There's a science-fiction movie playing that I really want to watch.

W I'd love to, Jim. But I'm going to be busy all weekend.

M What plans do you have?

W I think I mentioned before that my family will be ²)_____ _____ _____.

M Oh, right. She's from Vietnam, right?

W Yes. She will be arriving on Friday evening. I'm going to spend the weekend showing her around.

M That's nice of you.

W Well, I want to make sure she feels comfortable here.

M Why don't we do some sightseeing with her together?

W Good idea. She would probably enjoy ³)_____ _____ _____ here.

M I'm free all day on Saturday.

↘ 듣기 필수 표현
· show ~ around ~를 구경시켜 주다
· do sightseeing 관광하다

15

M Isabella is shopping at a department store for ¹)_____ _____ _____ _____ _____. She has tried on several pairs, and there is one that she really likes. The sneakers ²)_____ · _____ _____ and are very comfortable. However, they are black, and she would prefer white. She asks Gordon, who works at the store, to bring her the sneakers in white. Unfortunately, that color is very popular, and there are none left. Gordon has to tell Isabella that there are no shoes in ³)_____ _____ _____ available right now. In this situation, what would Gordon most likely say to Isabella?

↘ 듣기 필수 표현
· try on ~을 신어보다

16~17

W Good morning. Last class, we talked about languages that were at risk of disappearing. Today, I want to discuss some languages that are ¹)_____ _____ _____ _____. The first of these is English, and there are over 1.5 billion speakers of this language worldwide. Interestingly, many of these people have learned it ²)_____ _____ _____. Next, I'd like to mention French. It has about 300 million speakers. Most of them live in Europe and Africa. It is also an official language of ³)_____ _____ _____, including the United Nations. Thirdly, there is Hindi, with around 600 million speakers. Most of the people who live in India use this language. Finally, there are about 550 million Spanish speakers. In fact, this is the official language of much of Central and South America. Now, let's watch a video that shows how to say ⁴)_____ _____ _____ in each of these languages.

↘ 듣기 필수 표현
· at risk of ~의 위험에 처한

1번부터 17번까지는 듣고 답하는 문제입니다. 1번부터 15번까지는 한 번만 들려주고, 16번부터 17번까지는 두 번 들려줍니다. 방송을 잘 듣고 답을 하시기 바랍니다.

1 다음을 듣고, 여자가 하는 말의 목적으로 가장 적절한 것을 고르시오.

① 설문 조사 결과를 발표하려고
② 특별 경품 추첨 행사를 홍보하려고
③ 미식축구 경기의 생중계 일정을 공지하려고
④ 개인 연락처 작성 시 주의 사항을 설명하려고
⑤ 방송국 앱을 통한 경기 시청 방법을 안내하려고

2 대화를 듣고, 남자의 의견으로 가장 적절한 것을 고르시오.

① 자기 적성에 맞는 직업을 찾아야 한다.
② 성격 검사로 본인의 장점을 파악할 수 있다.
③ 새로운 것을 계속 배우고 시도하는 것은 중요하다.
④ 자신감이 있어야 기회가 왔을 때 잡을 수 있다.
⑤ 한 직장에서 오래 일하기는 어려운 일이다.

3 대화를 듣고, 두 사람의 관계를 가장 잘 나타낸 것을 고르시오.

① 잡지 기자 — 조종사
② 소설 작가 — 승무원
③ 시험 출제위원 — 대학생
④ 라디오 진행자 — 선장
⑤ 영화감독 — 사회 운동가

4 대화를 듣고, 그림에서 대화의 내용과 일치하지 않는 것을 고르시오.

5 대화를 듣고, 남자가 할 일로 가장 적절한 것을 고르시오.

① 세트장 페인트칠하기
② 인쇄소에서 광고지 찾아오기
③ 큰 사이즈 포스터 출력하기
④ 라디오 방송국에 광고하기
⑤ 지역 신문사에 연락하기

6 대화를 듣고, 여자가 지불할 금액을 고르시오. [3점]

① $90   ② $95   ③ $100   ④ $115   ⑤ $120

7 대화를 듣고, 남자가 여자를 바이올린 수업에 데려다줄 수 없는 이유를 고르시오.

① 늦게까지 일해야 해서
② 귀가 중 사고를 당해서
③ 몸 상태가 좋지 않아서
④ 할머니 댁에 들러야 해서
⑤ 차가 너무 막혀서

8 대화를 듣고, Modern Sculpture Exhibition에 관해 언급되지 않은 것을 고르시오.

① 장소   ② 참여 작가   ③ 입장료
④ 할인 정보   ⑤ 종료 시각

9 Wild Plant Expo에 관한 다음 내용을 듣고, 일치하지 않는 것을 고르시오. [3점]

① 일주일 동안 진행된다.
② Central Convention Center에서 열린다.
③ 다양한 야생화와 희귀 식물을 감상할 수 있다.
④ 여러 전문가의 특별 강연이 매일 있을 것이다.
⑤ 주민일 경우 입장료는 5달러이다.

10 다음 표를 보면서 대화를 듣고, 여자가 구매할 러닝머신을 고르시오.

Treadmills

	Model	Track Width	Maximum Speed	Price	Folding
①	A	44 cm	12 km/h	$350	X
②	B	46 cm	14 km/h	$450	O
③	C	48 cm	16 km/h	$550	X
④	D	50 cm	18 km/h	$650	O
⑤	E	50 cm	20 km/h	$750	X

11 대화를 듣고, 여자의 마지막 말에 대한 남자의 응답으로 가장 적절한 것을 고르시오.

① He called to tell me he has the flu.
② Learning the drums is too difficult.
③ I will meet with my teacher after school.
④ My drum set needs to be repaired.
⑤ The lesson ended at 3 p.m. today.

12 대화를 듣고, 남자의 마지막 말에 대한 여자의 응답으로 가장 적절한 것을 고르시오.

① Yes. We ran out of maple syrup.
② I think so. Check inside the refrigerator.
③ Me too. That was so sweet and delicious.
④ No, thanks. I already had a big breakfast.
⑤ Not at all. Feel free to have these pancakes.

13 대화를 듣고, 여자의 마지막 말에 대한 남자의 응답으로 가장 적절한 것을 고르시오.

Man: _____

① He looks just like my friend's puppy.
② We should put the posters in public places.
③ I think I saw it on the building next to our house.
④ Let's get the puppy something else to eat.
⑤ I'll call my father right now to check.

14 대화를 듣고, 남자의 마지막 말에 대한 여자의 응답으로 가장 적절한 것을 고르시오.

Woman: _____

① I usually like to have milk in my coffee.
② This café helps to protect the environment.
③ We need to recycle as many cups as we can.
④ You should remember to bring your tumbler.
⑤ I use old towels to clean instead of wet tissue.

15 다음 상황 설명을 듣고, Susan이 Alex에게 할 말로 가장 적절한 것을 고르시오. [3점]

Susan: _____

① Let's find another beach to visit, then.
② I think it's too expensive to drive there.
③ Why don't we take a train to the beach?
④ How about getting an X-ray of your back?
⑤ Don't you want to take a road trip with me?

[16~17] 다음을 듣고, 물음에 답하시오.

16 남자가 하는 말의 주제로 가장 적절한 것은?

① foods that can boost your energy
② foods that are good for healing diseases
③ recipes to strengthen the immune system
④ what foods to avoid when you have a cold
⑤ results of studies on cancer treatment

17 언급된 식품이 아닌 것은?

① ginger   ② garlic   ③ honey
④ onions   ⑤ mushrooms

이제 듣기 문제가 끝났습니다. 채점을 마친 후 다음 페이지에서 방송을 다시 들으며 딕테이션 연습을 하시기 바랍니다.

* 채점 결과: 맞은 개수 _____ 개 / 17개   정답 및 해설 p.20

Dictation 정답 p.20

03회 영어듣기 모의고사 Dictation 음성을 들으며 빈칸에 알맞은 단어를 채워 넣으시기 바랍니다.

1

W Attention, football fans. I'm Kerry Platt, host of SBH Sports Network. Would you like to 1)_____ _____ to a football game? If so, enter our special prize-drawing event by following these simple steps. First, download the SBH Sports Network application on your phone. Next, fill out 2)_____ _____ _____, and enter your contact information. Then, watch our Friday night game of the week on SBH. During the live broadcast, one lucky person who filled out a survey will be selected at random. We'll give them two tickets to see 3)_____ _____ _____ _____ _____. This is an amazing opportunity, so don't miss this chance!

↘ **듣기 필수 표현**
· prize-drawing event 경품 추첨 행사
· fill out ~을 기입하다
· contact information 연락처 정보
· at random 무작위로

2

W What are you doing, Justin?

M Hi, Kate. I'm doing a personality test.

W That sounds like a fun way to 1)_____ _____ _____.

M Yeah. The results will also show what jobs fit my personality.

W Oh, are you looking for a new job? I thought you enjoyed working at the bank.

M I do. But I've worked there 2)_____ _____ _____, and I really want to learn some different skills.

W You are taking a big step.

M Maybe so. But I think it's important to 3)_____ _____ _____ new things.

W Yeah. I guess that will help you prepare for unexpected changes.

M Also, it will help me feel confident in myself to succeed in learning something new.

W I see. That makes sense.

↘ **듣기 필수 표현**
· take a big step 크게 도약하다
· make sense 일리가 있다, 말이 되다

3

M Thanks for agreeing to the interview, Captain Simone.

W It's my pleasure, Mr. Roberts. I always enjoy reading your articles in *Harrisburg Magazine*.

M Thanks. Now, I understand that you 1)_____ _____ _____ a flight attendant.

W That's correct. I wanted to fly, but there weren't many opportunities for women.

M Even now, there are few women who fly planes.

W Right. Back then, I couldn't even imagine being in charge of my own plane.

M But you 2)_____ _____ _____ _____ flight school. What inspired you to do that?

W Well, I realized that I could pass the flight tests if I worked hard. And I wanted to follow my dream.

M But was it difficult being the 3)_____ _____ _____ for NW Airlines?

W It was lonely sometimes, but I had to do it.

M Well, I think our readers will be inspired by your story. Thank you.

↘ **듣기 필수 표현**
· agree to ~에 응하다
· be in charge of ~을 담당하다

4

M Mom, are you finished with the preparations for the party to celebrate Dad's promotion?

W Yes. What do you think?

M I like the flowers in the basket. They look fresh.

W Thanks. I 1)_____ _____ _____ _____ _____. What about the picture of your dad on the wall?

M Dad is all smiles in that picture. It looks great.

W I thought so, too.

M And those two gift boxes 2)_____ _____ _____ must be for Dad. What did you get for him?

W One of the boxes has chocolates in it, and the other one has a new watch.

M I also like the star-shaped balloons in the corner.

W Yeah, they are cute. And I moved the side table in front of them. That's where the cake will be.

M Good idea. You did a great job 3)_____ _____.

W Thanks. I hope your dad likes it.

↘ **듣기 필수 표현**
· be all smiles 아주 행복해 보이다

5

W Mr. Evans, how are the preparations for the school musical going?

M They're taking longer than we expected, Ms. Bennett. We still need 1)_____ _____ _____ _____.

W I see. I'll ask the art students to help paint the set. What else needs to be done?

M The posters and flyers have already been printed out. So we need to pick them up from the printing center.

W I'll call and 2)_____ _____ _____ to the school.

M Great. Also, we need to promote the musical. I'd like to put an announcement in the local newspaper.

W Good idea. We should also see if the local radio station can run an advertisement.

M That would be awesome. Should I call the station?

W No. Let me do it. You should 3)_____ _____ _____.

M Okay, I'll do that now.

↘ 듣기 필수 표현
· print out ~을 인쇄하다
· run an advertisement 광고를 내다

6

M Welcome to Bamboo Garden Restaurant.

W Hi. We 1)_____ _____ _____ _____ for six people at 6 p.m.

M Right this way. *[Pause]* Are you here for the buffet?

W Yes. It's $15 per person on weekdays, right?

M I'm sorry, but that's only until 4 p.m. After that, it's $20 per person for the dinner buffet.

W Oh, okay. Is it 2)_____ _____ _____ for kids?

M How old is your child? Kids under five can eat for free.

W That's good. He's just four.

M Okay. So, that will be five adults having the dinner buffet.

W That's correct. And is there a way I can get any additional discounts?

M Yes. If you sign up for a membership card, we will give you 3)_____ _____ _____ _____.

W All right. I'll do that right now.

↘ 듣기 필수 표현
· for free 무료로
· sign up 등록하다, 가입하다

7

[Cell phone rings.]

W Hello, Dad?

M Hi, Elena. I'm really sorry, but I can't 1)_____ _____ _____ _____ your violin lesson today.

W That's okay. I can take the bus. Are you working late tonight?

M No. I actually finished work early today.

W Then, are you meeting Grandmother?

M No. I'm not meeting anyone tonight.

W It must be because you're 2)_____ _____ _____ _____.

M I'm feeling fine. I can't drive you because I'm stuck in traffic right now. I won't be able to get home in time.

W Oh, I see. Don't worry about it, Dad. Just 3)_____ _____ _____.

M Thanks, sweetie.

↘ 듣기 필수 표현
· work late 늦게까지 일하다
· stuck in traffic 차가 막히는

8

M What do you want to do tomorrow, Luna? It's finally the weekend.

W Hi, Jack. Well... the Modern Sculpture Exhibition is going on.

M That sounds interesting. Where is 1)_____ _____ _____?

W It's at the Fantasia Art Gallery. We can take the bus to get there.

M Perfect! Do you know who is participating?

W I don't know, but I'll look it up online now. *[Pause]* Oh, there will be statues by Jamie Adams and Kelly Peterson.

M I've 2)_____ _____ _____. They're quite famous, so we should go.

W Exactly! Also, the entrance fee is very cheap. It costs only $5.

M When 3)_____ _____ _____ _____? I think I can go after 2 p.m.

W That's fine. It is open until 5 p.m. Let's meet at 2:30 in front of the gallery.

M Sure. See you then!

↘ 듣기 필수 표현
· look up ~을 찾아보다
· entrance fee 입장료

9

M Good morning, listeners. This spring, the Wild Plant Expo will be here in Golden City. The expo will ¹⁾ _____ _____ _____ _____ starting May 3rd. It'll be held in the Central Convention Center. Visitors can enjoy a wide variety of wild flowers and ²⁾ _____ . Also, there will be special lectures every day by Dr. Garret, who is a ³⁾ _____ _____ _____ . The tickets are $15 a person, but residents of our city can participate for just $5. If you're interested in plants or gardening, ⁴⁾ _____ _____ _____ _____ . Thank you.

↘ 듣기 필수 표현
· a variety of 다양한

10

M Hello. Can I help you with anything?

W Yes. I want to buy a treadmill.

M Okay. Will you use it for running or walking?

W I want it for running. The weather is too cold for me to ¹⁾ _____ _____ _____ _____ .

M In that case, I'd recommend a track that's wider than 45 centimeters. It'll be more comfortable when you run.

W Got it. Is there anything else I should consider?

M The maximum speed should be at least ²⁾ _____ _____ _____ .

W Hmm... All right.

M How much are you willing to spend?

W I want to keep it under $700.

M Then, you can choose from these two. Do you need one that folds up to save space?

W No, I don't. I have ³⁾ _____ _____ _____ .

M Then, I recommend this one.

W Perfect. I'll take it.

↘ 듣기 필수 표현
· be willing to ~할 의향이 있다
· fold up 접히다

11

W Michael, why are you ¹⁾ _____ _____ ? You're supposed to go to a drum lesson.

M Actually, my teacher canceled today's lesson, Mom.

W Really? ²⁾ _____ _____ _____ to him?

↘ 듣기 필수 표현
· be supposed to ~하기로 되어 있다

12

M Honey, what are you doing?

W I'm going to ¹⁾ _____ _____ _____ for breakfast. Do you want some?

M Sure! But ²⁾ _____ _____ _____ _____ maple syrup?

↘ 듣기 필수 표현
· for breakfast 아침 식사로

13

W Nate, what's that sound?

M I think it's a puppy. Oh, it's over there by the bushes.

W He ¹⁾ _____ _____ _____ _____ .

M Yeah, he must be somebody's pet. Do you have anything to feed him?

W Yes. I have some sausage snacks in my bag. Here you go.

M Wow, he was so hungry! By the way, doesn't the puppy ²⁾ _____ _____ ?

W Yeah. I think you're right! Wasn't there a poster in the neighborhood?

M Right. One of our neighbors was looking for their lost puppy. But I can't remember who.

W We should ³⁾ _____ _____ _____ . Then, we can contact the owner.

↘ 듣기 필수 표현
· by the way 그런데

14

M Oh, it's nice to run into you at this café, Aletha. Are you
¹⁾_____ _____ your coffee?

W Yeah. I ordered a latte. Oh, here it is.

M Why did they serve your latte in a tumbler?

W I always ask them to ²⁾_____ _____ _____
_____ _____.

M Isn't that inconvenient?

W It's a little annoying to always carry a tumbler. But this way, I don't throw away a cup whenever I get coffee.

M Oh, so using your tumbler is a way of protecting the environment, right?

W Yeah. This one simple thing ³⁾_____ _____
_____ _____ _____.

M That's pretty smart. What else do you do to protect the earth?

↘ 듣기 필수 표현
· run into ~를 우연히 만나다
· throw away ~을 버리다

15

W Alex and Susan are close friends who enjoy spending time together. They both like swimming, but there are no beaches nearby. So when Susan recently got her driver's license, they made plans to ¹⁾_____
_____ _____ _____ to the beach during summer vacation. They found a good place to stay and made reservations. However, a week before the trip, Susan started to ²⁾_____ _____ _____
_____ in her back. Now, Susan is worried that she can't drive safely because the pain distracts her while she is driving. So she wants to suggest to Alex that they should ³⁾_____ _____ _____ _____
instead. In this situation, what would Susan most likely say to Alex?

↘ 듣기 필수 표현
· driver's license 운전 면허증
· make a reservation 예약을 하다

16~17

M Hello. This is Dr. Matthew Ashland. Previously, I told you about foods that can give you more energy, like chocolate. Today, I want to talk about some ¹⁾_____
_____ that have the power to help cure illnesses. First, people have been using ginger for hundreds of years to treat stomachaches. You can ease an upset stomach or ²⁾_____ _____ with a cup of ginger tea. Similarly, garlic is good for your immune system. Many people eat it to get better from a cold. Another food that helps when you're sick is honey. This sweet liquid can be ³⁾_____ _____ _____ a sore throat. Finally, mushrooms are full of nutrients. Studies have even found that certain types of mushrooms can help patients with cancer. So try consuming these foods when you're not feeling well to ⁴⁾_____ _____
_____. Now, let's watch a short video about some other healing foods.

↘ 듣기 필수 표현
· upset stomach 배탈
· be good for ~에 좋다
· immune system 면역 체계
· be full of ~으로 가득 차 있다

04회 영어듣기 모의고사

정답 및 해설 p.26

1번부터 17번까지는 듣고 답하는 문제입니다. 1번부터 15번까지는 한 번만 들려주고, 16번부터 17번까지는 두 번 들려줍니다. 방송을 잘 듣고 답을 하시기 바랍니다.

1 다음을 듣고, 여자가 하는 말의 목적으로 가장 적절한 것을 고르시오.

① 채용 박람회를 홍보하려고
② 변경된 면접 일정을 알리려고
③ 참여 기업 추천을 요청하려고
④ 진로 상담의 이점을 설명하려고
⑤ 합격 이력서 예시를 소개하려고

2 대화를 듣고, 남자의 의견으로 가장 적절한 것을 고르시오.

① 인사는 예절의 기본이다.
② 적절한 농담은 대화에 도움이 된다.
③ 아이들은 예절의 중요성을 배워야 한다.
④ 식사 중에 말을 많이 하는 것은 예의가 아니다.
⑤ 지나치게 격식에 얽매이지 않는 것이 중요하다.

3 대화를 듣고, 두 사람의 관계를 가장 잘 나타낸 것을 고르시오.

① 집 주인 — 이사업체 직원
② 주차장 직원 — 운전자
③ 건물 관리인 — 청소업자
④ 고등학교 교사 — 학부모
⑤ 부동산 중개업자 — 고객

4 대화를 듣고, 그림에서 대화의 내용과 일치하지 않는 것을 고르시오.

5 대화를 듣고, 여자가 할 일로 가장 적절한 것을 고르시오.

① 호텔 예약하기
② 배구 경기 관람하기
③ 방탈출 게임 체험하기
④ 가게 전화번호 찾아보기
⑤ 스승의 날 행사 기획하기

6 대화를 듣고, 여자가 지불할 금액을 고르시오. [3점]

① $60   ② $70   ③ $72   ④ $75   ⑤ $80

7 대화를 듣고, 남자가 밴드 연습에 참여할 수 없는 이유를 고르시오.

① 어머니의 가게 일을 도와야 해서
② 다친 손가락이 아직 덜 나아서
③ 영어 숙제를 제출해야 해서
④ 체스 동아리 모임에 가야 해서
⑤ 수학 시험공부를 해야 해서

8 대화를 듣고, Applewood Farm에 관해 언급되지 않은 것을 고르시오.

① 입장료   ② 이동 시간   ③ 주차 가능 여부
④ 운영 시간   ⑤ 체험 활동 종류

9 Global Science Olympiad에 관한 다음 내용을 듣고, 일치하지 않는 것을 고르시오. [3점]

① 로마에서 열릴 예정이다.
② 4년에 한 번씩 개최된다.
③ 4월 22일부터 28일까지 진행된다.
④ 전 세계에서 100명의 학생이 출전한다.
⑤ 학교에서 학생 두 명이 참가한다.

10 다음 표를 보면서 대화를 듣고, 여자가 구매할 플래너를 고르시오.

Planners

	Model	Type	Price	Blank Pages	Cover Color
①	A	Weekly	$16	X	Cream
②	B	Monthly	$14	X	Navy
③	C	Daily	$12	O	Pink
④	D	Monthly	$10	O	Beige
⑤	E	Weekly	$8	O	Black

11 대화를 듣고, 여자의 마지막 말에 대한 남자의 응답으로 가장 적절한 것을 고르시오.

① Why not? We'll have great time together.
② Are you sure? Why don't you check the fridge?
③ That's true. I haven't seen the neighbors lately.
④ That's perfect. I would love to get a new grill.
⑤ No, thanks. I'm still too full from dinner.

12 대화를 듣고, 남자의 마지막 말에 대한 여자의 응답으로 가장 적절한 것을 고르시오.

① Which movie do you want to see this afternoon?
② Would you like to meet next weekend instead?
③ Did you check if the tickets were sold out?
④ What time will you be able to get here?
⑤ How did you know I was still sick?

13 대화를 듣고, 여자의 마지막 말에 대한 남자의 응답으로 가장 적절한 것을 고르시오.

Man: _____

① Exactly. I prefer green tea to coffee.
② I know. I cleaned the kettle last week, too.
③ Let's see. Wash them with soap and water first.
④ Okay. I'll get a towel and dry them completely.
⑤ No, thank you. I don't want any more tea.

14 대화를 듣고, 남자의 마지막 말에 대한 여자의 응답으로 가장 적절한 것을 고르시오.

Woman: _____

① Don't worry. I promise to find it for you.
② Sounds good. I'll wear the silver necklace.
③ Don't bother. It was inside my purse all along.
④ Thank you so much. I'll be there in 20 minutes.
⑤ I'm sorry. I hope you have better luck next time.

15 다음 상황 설명을 듣고, Milo가 Anna에게 할 말로 가장 적절한 것을 고르시오. [3점]

Milo: _____

① No way. You don't know anything about music.
② I agree. I think this song is going to be a big hit.
③ Believe me. My fans will love my new music style.
④ You're right. My voice sounds good on this ballad.
⑤ My mistake. My fans will be disappointed in me.

[16~17] 다음을 듣고, 물음에 답하시오.

16 남자가 하는 말의 주제로 가장 적절한 것은?

① benefits of commonly used fabrics
② hidden problems with popular fabrics
③ types of fabrics that come from animals
④ comparison of natural and man-made fabrics
⑤ how technology changed the fashion industry

17 언급된 직물이 <u>아닌</u> 것은?

① cotton   ② linen   ③ wool
④ silk   ⑤ nylon

이제 듣기 문제가 끝났습니다. 채점을 마친 후 다음 페이지에서 방송을 다시 들으며 딕테이션 연습을 하시기 바랍니다.

* 채점 결과: 맞은 개수 _____개 / 17개   정답 및 해설 p.26

04회 Dictation

04회 영어듣기 모의고사 Dictation 음성을 들으며 빈칸에 알맞은 단어를 채워 넣으시기 바랍니다.

1

W Attention, students and job seekers. Are you unsure about your career path? Would you like the chance to meet professionals 1)_____ _____ _____ _____? Then, come to the career fair at Centerville College! The fair will run from 9 a.m. to 5 p.m. on April 15th. Companies in a variety of industries, including travel, medicine, and technology, 2)_____ _____. Their booths will be set up so visitors can experience job interviews and learn more about possible careers. Please check the school website for the complete list of participants. Attendees should 3)_____ _____ _____ a résumé and questions! We hope to see you there.

↳ 듣기 필수 표현
· career path 진로
· set up ~을 설치하다

2

M Jean, what's the matter? You look upset.

W I'm concerned about my daughter. She's nine, but she still doesn't 1)_____ _____ _____.

M Oh, really? What happened?

W Her uncle visited us yesterday, but she didn't greet him. And she made rude comments during dinner.

M Oh, she can't do that. In my opinion, kids need to learn that 2)_____ _____ is important.

W I told her not to behave rudely. But she kept saying it was just a joke.

M I think you need to explain how her uncle felt. She should know that 3)_____ _____ is different from being playful.

W Okay, I'll do that. I'll let her know the importance of having good manners.

M Good luck. I hope you can 4)_____ _____ _____ her attitude.

↳ 듣기 필수 표현
· be concerned about ~을 걱정하다
· make a comment 말하다
· in one's opinion ~의 생각에
· different from ~과 다른

3

W So now you've seen all of the apartments on our list. Do you have any questions?

M Actually, I have a few about the last apartment we saw. First, how much is the rent?

W It's $1,000 a month. It's much 1)_____ _____ _____ _____ in the area.

M Okay. How many parking spots would I get?

W 2)_____ _____ comes with two underground parking spots.

M That's good. Lastly, isn't Pomona High School nearby? My son goes there.

W Yes. It's just a 10-minute walk from here.

M That's perfect. All the places you've shown me were great, but I can really 3)_____ _____ _____.

W That's wonderful. Do you think you'll take the apartment?

M I think so. I'm excited to move in!

↳ 듣기 필수 표현
· come with ~이 딸려 있다
· move in 입주하다, 이사 오다

4

M Emily, how are the preparations going for your wedding?

W The wedding planner just sent me this picture of the wedding hall.

M Wow. That three-layer wedding cake looks incredible!

W Thanks! But is the 1)_____ _____ _____ _____ at the front of the stage too big?

M Not at all. It will look nice in the photos.

W I'm glad you think so. The curtains will make a pretty background for photos, too.

M I agree. The leaf patterns on the curtains are beautiful. And I see 2)_____ _____ _____ on the left side of the stage. Will that be enough?

W Yes. One is for the wedding host, and the other is for the singer.

M Got it. But is it a good idea to 3)_____ _____ _____ on either side of the aisle?

W Oh... Those could be dangerous.

M Maybe you should mention that to the wedding planner.

W I will.

↳ 듣기 필수 표현
· on either side 양쪽에

5

W Hi, Coach Wilson. How are things going with the school volleyball team?

M Good, Principal Smith. The team 1)_____ _____ _____ in Boston next month.

W Okay. Have you made all the arrangements?

M Almost. I've booked hotel rooms for the athletes and arranged transportation. Now, I just 2)_____ _____ _____ a team-building event.

W Do you have any ideas?

M I can't think of anything yet.

W How about an escape room? There's one near the school that the teachers went to last year.

M Oh, that would be perfect. The players will have to work together to 3)_____ _____ _____ to escape.

W I can look up the phone number of that place if you like.

M Sure. I'd appreciate that.

↘ 듣기 필수 표현
· make an arrangement 준비를 하다
· work together 힘을 합치다
· look up ~을 찾아보다

6

M Welcome to the Pine City Christmas Light Festival.

W Hello. How much is 1)_____ _____ _____?

M It's $10 for adults and $5 for children under the age of 12.

W I need tickets for four adults and four children.

M Sure. Also, we are 2)_____ _____ _____ to take pictures with Santa Claus.

W Oh, great. How much does it cost?

M It's 3)_____ _____ _____.

W Can I get one with all of the kids in it?

M Certainly. That would be fine.

W Okay. I'll take one of those. Also, I'm 4)_____ _____ _____ Pine City. Do I get a discount?

M Yes. Residents get $10 off the total.

W Great. I'm glad I asked.

M So that's four adult tickets, four child tickets, one photo with Santa, with the discount.

W That's right. I'll pay in cash.

↘ 듣기 필수 표현
· under the age of 나이가 ~ 미만의

7

W Hi, Robert. Is your finger feeling better? It 1)_____ _____ when you cut it on that guitar string.

M Hey, Jenny. It's much better now. I've been playing again.

W That's great. Do you think you can 2)_____ _____ _____ _____ on Thursday night?

M I'm sorry, but I can't.

W Why not? Do you have to work on your English homework?

M No. I 3)_____ _____ that.

W I see. Maybe you have to help your mom at her store, then.

M No, my brother will help my mom at that time. Actually, I have to 4)_____ _____ _____ _____ _____.

W Got it. But I will see you at chess club tomorrow, right?

M For sure. See you there.

↘ 듣기 필수 표현
· at that time 그때
· For sure. 물론이지.

8

M What should we do with the kids today, honey?

W The weather is so nice. I thought we could visit a place called Applewood Farm. The entrance fee is only $2 a person.

M That's a great idea. But is it 1)_____ · _____ _____? Traffic might be bad because it's the weekend.

W It's not too far. It only takes 30 minutes to drive there.

M All right. And are you sure they're open today?

W Yes. I just 2)_____ _____ _____. They're open from 9 a.m. to 6 p.m.

M Then, we'll have plenty of time. Do you know what kinds of activities they have?

W We can pick apples there. Also, 3)_____ _____ _____ _____.

M Oh, I bet the kids will love that. Let's go!

W Sure. I'll get the kids ready.

↘ 듣기 필수 표현
· plenty of 충분한, 많은
· I bet ~. 틀림없이 ~하다.

9

W Attention, Palmas High School students. This is your principal, Ms. Garcia. I have a very exciting announcement to make. The Global Science Olympiad is ¹⁾_____ _____ _____ _____, Italy this spring. This event only happens once every four years. This year, it will run from April 22nd to 28th. More than 200 students ²⁾_____ _____ _____ _____ will take part in competitions that will test their knowledge of various scientific fields, such as physics and chemistry. I am extremely proud to say that ³⁾_____ _____ _____ _____ have been selected to attend this important event. Stephanie Kane and Michael Park will compete in the chemistry category. Congratulations to Stephanie and Michael, and good luck in Rome!

↘ 듣기 필수 표현
· take part in ~에 참가하다

10

M Welcome to Office Buddy.

W Hello. I need a planner, but I can't decide which one to buy.

M Do you want separate pages for each day? Or do you prefer to make weekly or even monthly plans?

W I don't like ones with ¹⁾_____ _____.

M Then, you'll want to look at our weekly or monthly planners. How much would you like to spend?

W I'd rather spend less than $15.

M All right. Would you prefer one ²⁾_____ _____ _____ _____ at the back?

W Yes. I like to write out my thoughts. So a planner with many blank pages would be good.

M Okay. What colors do you like ³⁾_____ _____ _____?

W I like dark colors like navy and black.

M Then, I think you should get this planner.

↘ 듣기 필수 표현
· would rather ~하는 게 낫다
· write out ~을 자세히 쓰다

11

W ¹⁾_____ _____ _____ _____ for dinner tonight, honey?

M We have prime beef ²⁾_____ _____ _____. I can cook some steaks on the grill.

W That would be nice. Why don't we invite the neighbors over?

↘ 듣기 필수 표현
· for dinner 저녁 식사로
· invite ~ over ~를 초대하다

12

[Cell phone rings.]

M Hey, Marie. I'm sorry, but I ¹⁾_____ _____ _____ at the theater.

W Really? But I'm almost there. We're supposed to meet in 10 minutes.

M I'm so sorry. I've been ²⁾_____ _____ _____ since I woke up this morning.

↘ 듣기 필수 표현
· be supposed to ~하기로 되어 있다

13

M Hi, Mom. Did you have a good day?

W Yes, I did. What are you doing, Paul?

M I just finished cleaning the electric kettle. You ¹⁾_____ _____ _____ _____ it this morning.

W Oh, I see. Thank you for doing that, sweetie.

M No problem. Now, I just need to plug it in.

W Wait. Your hands are wet, aren't they? You shouldn't ²⁾_____ _____ _____ _____.

M I already shook all the water off my hands.

W That's not enough. It's dangerous to touch cords and plugs while ³⁾_____ _____ _____ _____.

↘ 듣기 필수 표현
· plug ~ in ~에 전원을 연결하다
· shake off ~을 털어내다

14

[Telephone rings.]

M Hello. This is the security desk at River Valley Mall. How can I help you?

W Hi. Do you have a ¹⁾_____ _____ _____ center there?

M We do. Did you lose something at the mall?

W I might have. I think I lost my necklace there yesterday.

M Can you ²⁾_____ _____ in detail?

W Yes. It's silver with a round locket pendant.

M What else can you tell me about it?

W You can open the locket. Inside, there is ³⁾_____ _____ _____ my hamster.

M Okay. I'll call you again if I find it.

W Wait. There's one more thing. The letter J is stamped on the back of the pendant.

M Oh, I think I see your necklace here. You can ⁴⁾_____ _____ _____ _____ now if you like.

↘ 듣기 필수 표현
· in detail 상세하게
· stamp on ~을 각인시키다

15

W Milo is a rock musician, and Anna is his manager. Milo is making his second album. Last night, Anna went to Milo's studio to listen ¹⁾_____ _____ _____ _____. She was surprised to find out that it's a ballad, which is different from his other songs. Anna thinks he ²⁾_____ _____ _____ _____ _____ his new album because his fans might be disappointed. However, Milo wants to show them that he can play more than just rock music. So Milo wants to tell Anna that ³⁾_____ _____ _____ _____ because he thinks his fans will like his new style of music. In this situation, what would Milo most likely say to Anna?

↘ 듣기 필수 표현
· find out ~을 알다

16~17

M Hello, everybody. Previously, we talked about how technology changed the fashion industry. Today, I want to talk about the advantages of ¹⁾_____ _____ _____. First, cotton is one of the most popular fabrics. Clothing made from the cotton plant is soft and comfortable. This material is good at absorbing moisture, so it is often used to make towels. Next, there is wool, which comes from sheep. Because it ²⁾_____ _____ _____, it is used to make winter clothing, such as coats, sweaters, and scarves. Additionally, silk from the silkworm has been used to make clothing for hundreds of years. It is light, smooth, and shiny, but also very strong. Another strong fabric is nylon. This is a fabric that is cheap and easy to wash. Moreover, it does not ³⁾_____ _____ _____, so it is used to make all kinds of clothing. Now, let's look at page 105 in our textbook for more information on these fabrics.

↘ 듣기 필수 표현
· made from ~으로 만든
· come from ~에서 나오다

05회 영어듣기 모의고사

정답 및 해설 p.32

1번부터 17번까지는 듣고 답하는 문제입니다. 1번부터 15번까지는 한 번만 들려주고, 16번부터 17번까지는 두 번 들려줍니다. 방송을 잘 듣고 답을 하시기 바랍니다.

1 다음을 듣고, 여자가 하는 말의 목적으로 가장 적절한 것을 고르시오.

① 마케팅부에서 근무할 직원을 모집하려고
② 50주년 창립 기념식을 홍보하려고
③ 상품 디자인 업무에 대해 설명하려고
④ 새롭게 바뀐 회사 이름을 발표하려고
⑤ 회사 로고 디자인 공모전을 안내하려고

2 대화를 듣고, 여자의 의견으로 가장 적절한 것을 고르시오.

① 돈이 인생의 전부는 아니다.
② 진로를 선택할 때 부모님의 의견을 고려해야 한다.
③ 좋아하는 일을 직업으로 선택해야 한다.
④ 컴퓨터 프로그램으로 생활 환경을 개선할 수 있다.
⑤ 성공한 사업가가 되기 위해서는 부지런해야 한다.

3 대화를 듣고, 두 사람의 관계를 가장 잘 나타낸 것을 고르시오.

① 안경사 — 고객
② 교사 — 학부모
③ 학생 — 환경 운동가
④ 작가 — 독자
⑤ 사서 — 경비원

4 대화를 듣고, 그림에서 대화의 내용과 일치하지 않는 것을 고르시오.

5 대화를 듣고, 여자가 할 일로 가장 적절한 것을 고르시오.

① 펜 빌려주기
② 병원 시설 소개하기
③ 동의서 서명하기
④ 봉사자 조끼 반납하기
⑤ 물품 보관함 비우기

6 대화를 듣고, 여자가 지불할 금액을 고르시오. [3점]

① $25　　② $27　　③ $30　　④ $36　　⑤ $40

7 대화를 듣고, 남자가 보고서 마감일을 맞출 수 없는 이유를 고르시오.

① 어머니 간호를 해야 해서
② 조사 자료를 못 찾아서
③ 학생회 활동으로 바빠서
④ 수술이 예정되어 있어서
⑤ 주제를 정하지 못해서

8 대화를 듣고, Green Planet Special Lecture에 관해 언급되지 않은 것을 고르시오.

① 강연 장소　　② 티켓 가격　　③ 강연 주제
④ 시작 시각　　⑤ 참가 가능 인원

9 현장 학습에 관한 다음 내용을 듣고, 일치하지 않는 것을 고르시오.

① <로미오와 줄리엣> 공연을 관람할 것이다.
② 오전 9시 30분에 극장에 도착하는 일정이다.
③ 연극 공연이 끝나면 함께 점심을 먹을 예정이다.
④ 현장 학습 비용은 15달러이다.
⑤ 허가서는 금요일까지 제출해야 한다.

10 다음 표를 보면서 대화를 듣고, 두 사람이 구매할 포토 달력을 고르시오.

Photo Calendars

	Model	Size	Price	Number of Photos	Processing Time (days)
①	A	Medium	$42	36	5
②	B	Large	$52	36	7
③	C	Medium	$48	24	5
④	D	Large	$44	24	3
⑤	E	Small	$46	12	3

11 대화를 듣고, 여자의 마지막 말에 대한 남자의 응답으로 가장 적절한 것을 고르시오.

① Not really. I don't even have to wear a cast.
② Yes. I can't walk on it for at least six weeks.
③ Of course. The X-ray showed that my ankle is fine.
④ I don't think so. It just happened yesterday morning.
⑤ No problem. The doctor will be with you in a minute.

12 대화를 듣고, 남자의 마지막 말에 대한 여자의 응답으로 가장 적절한 것을 고르시오.

① Does this restaurant serve steak?
② We requested a table near the window.
③ I would like to get the Greek salad, please.
④ Please check if our food is coming out soon.
⑤ This steak has not been cooked long enough.

13 대화를 듣고, 남자의 마지막 말에 대한 여자의 응답으로 가장 적절한 것을 고르시오. [3점]

Woman: _____

① It's okay. I really needed a new camera anyway.
② Maybe. I can't remember what I bought last week.
③ No way. My bank account must have been hacked.
④ Great. That gives me plenty of time to shop online.
⑤ Okay. I'll look up the number and call them right now.

14 대화를 듣고, 여자의 마지막 말에 대한 남자의 응답으로 가장 적절한 것을 고르시오.

Man: _____

① I'm sorry. But I've already been there.
② Sure. I would love to go and check it out.
③ No. They accept cash but not credit cards.
④ Not really. It sounds too expensive for me.
⑤ I know. I don't like vintage shopping either.

15 다음 상황 설명을 듣고, Jonathan이 Stella에게 할 말로 가장 적절한 것을 고르시오. [3점]

Jonathan: _____

① Let's get off the train at the stop after this one.
② We just need to buy tickets on an express train.
③ You should have paid closer attention to where we were.
④ We need to explain to a ticket agent what happened.
⑤ I think our grandmother will be happy to see us.

[16~17] 다음을 듣고, 물음에 답하시오.

16 여자가 하는 말의 주제로 가장 적절한 것은?

① types of dumplings around the world
② recipes for cooking international dishes
③ the history of dumplings in different countries
④ features of world-famous cooking academies
⑤ reviews of the world's top-rated restaurants

17 언급된 나라가 <u>아닌</u> 것은?

① Poland　　② Mexico　　③ Vietnam
④ Korea　　⑤ China

> 이제 듣기 문제가 끝났습니다. 채점을 마친 후 다음 페이지에서 방송을 다시 들으며 딕테이션 연습을 하시기 바랍니다.
>
> * 채점 결과: 맞은 개수 _____ 개 / 17개　　　　정답 및 해설 p.32

Dictation 정답 p.32

05회 영어듣기 모의고사 Dictation 음성을 들으며 빈칸에 알맞은 단어를 채워 넣으시기 바랍니다.

1

W Good morning, Bluetech Company employees. This is Dana Brand from the marketing department. As you know, we 1)_____ _____ _____ the company's 50th anniversary next month. In honor of this, we have decided to design a new company logo, and we need your help! We are 2)_____ _____ _____ _____ _____, and all employees are welcome to enter. The winning logo will be chosen based on the quality and originality of the design. All entries must 3)_____ _____ _____ _____ to match our company's name. Please send me your work by e-mail. I look forward to seeing your designs!

↘ 듣기 필수 표현
· in honor of ~을 기념하여
· based on ~에 근거하여
· look forward to ~을 기대하다

2

W Have you 1)_____ _____ _____ _____, Tony?

M Not yet, Mom. I can't decide what to major in. I'm interested in computer science, but I think I should study business.

W Well, let's talk about it. What do you like about computer science?

M I love computers. My dream is to 2)_____ _____ _____ that improve people's lives.

W That's great. Now, why do you think you should study business?

M I also want to make lots of money. CEOs are usually paid very well.

W I see. I think you should choose to do what you love 3)_____ _____ _____.

M But money is important, too.

W Of course. But if you enjoy what you do, you'll have a greater 4)_____ _____ _____. The money will come later.

M That makes sense. Then, I should study computer science.

↘ 듣기 필수 표현
· major in ~을 전공하다
· be paid well 보수가 좋다
· make sense 말이 되다

3

W It's great to meet you, Mr. Cooper.

M You too, Ms. Harris. I've heard so much about you from my son.

W Derek is a wonderful student. He's doing well in class.

M That's good to hear. I 1)_____ _____ because we had to move right in the middle of the school year.

W He was a bit shy when he first entered my class, but he's making friends and getting used to the new environment.

M Is there anything he 2)_____ _____ _____ _____?

W Well, I think he's having trouble reading the board from the back of the class.

M Oh, really? I should take him to 3)_____ _____ _____ _____.

W Yes. I think that would be a good idea.

M Thank you for letting me know.

↘ 듣기 필수 표현
· make a friend 친구를 사귀다
· get used to ~에 익숙해지다

4

M Hi, Aunt Tina. It looks like you did some remodeling here in the living room.

W Yeah, we changed a few things this summer. What do you think?

M Oh, I love the new L-shaped sofa.

W Thanks! We wanted to get one that 1)_____ _____ _____ _____.

M It's perfect for that. It was a good idea to install a new shelf above the fireplace, too.

W I thought so. I wanted the room to look more modern.

M And you moved that plant 2)_____ _____ _____, right?

W Yeah! Good eye. What do you think about the round coffee table?

M I much prefer it to the old one.

W We're thinking about replacing the polka dot rug, too.

M Really? I think it makes the room more fun.

W The dots are 3)_____ _____.

M Hmm... Maybe you're right.

↘ 듣기 필수 표현
· prefer A to B A를 B보다 더 좋아하다

14

M Hi, Jessica! What are you doing this afternoon?

W I'm going to a vintage furniture store.

M I've never been to one before. Would you recommend it?

W Yeah. The furniture there is ¹⁾_____ _____, so it helps me save money.

M Oh, that's a great reason to shop there.

W Also, I actually don't like modern designs. I think ²⁾_____ _____ _____ _____ _____ _____.

M Oh, I see. So you can find lots of ³⁾_____ _____. But aren't you worried about the quality?

W Not at all. I've bought several pieces, and they are all in great shape.

M What furniture are you going to buy this time?

W I need some new chairs. Why don't you ⁴⁾_____ _____ _____?

↘ **듣기 필수 표현**
· in great shape 상태가 좋은

15

M Jonathan and his little sister Stella are going to visit their grandparents by train. It's their first time traveling by themselves. It's ¹⁾_____ _____ _____ _____, so Jonathan plays games on his phone while Stella sleeps. Suddenly, Jonathan realizes that they have just ²⁾_____ _____ _____. He points this out to Stella, and they get off the train at the next stop. Stella becomes scared and starts crying. However, Jonathan is not worried because he thinks they can get permission to take another train that goes back. So Jonathan wants to tell Stella that they should talk to a ticket agent about ³⁾_____ _____. In this situation, what would Jonathan most likely say to Stella?

↘ **듣기 필수 표현**
· by themselves 그들끼리만
· point A out to B A를 B에게 알려주다
· get off ~에서 내리다

16~17

W Good evening, I'm Sophie Laurent. Welcome to my cooking academy. Today, we'll make dumplings, which are small pockets of dough with different ingredients inside. But first, let me tell you about the ¹⁾_____ _____ _____ _____ around the world. In Poland, dumplings are usually filled with potatoes, onions, and cheese. They are served with sour cream. If you go to Mexico, make sure you try an empanada. This dumpling's name comes from a Spanish word that means "wrapped in bread." In Korea, people eat dumplings with their families during the Lunar New Year. The ²⁾_____ _____ _____ _____ meat, vegetables, and even kimchi. Finally, in China, dumplings come in many different shapes. They are commonly filled with pork and shrimp. Many other countries around the world also have ³⁾_____ _____ _____ of dumplings. Now, let me teach you my own special recipe.

↘ **듣기 필수 표현**
· be filled with ~으로 채워지다
· come from ~에서 유래하다
· come in ~으로 나오다

06회 영어듣기 모의고사

정답 및 해설 p.38

1번부터 17번까지는 듣고 답하는 문제입니다. 1번부터 15번까지는 한 번만 들려주고, 16번부터 17번까지는 두 번 들려줍니다. 방송을 잘 듣고 답을 하시기 바랍니다.

1 다음을 듣고, 여자가 하는 말의 목적으로 가장 적절한 것을 고르시오.

① 온라인 쇼핑몰 이용을 권장하려고
② 최신 주방용품의 신기능을 소개하려고
③ 가전제품 할인 행사를 홍보하려고
④ 블랙 프라이데이 행사의 유래를 설명하려고
⑤ 전자제품 할인 제외 품목을 안내하려고

2 대화를 듣고, 남자의 의견으로 가장 적절한 것을 고르시오.

① 부모는 자녀가 가능한 실패를 겪지 않도록 도와야 한다.
② 틀린 문제를 다시 푸는 것은 성적 향상에 효과적이다.
③ 어려운 숙제일수록 학습 능력 향상에 도움이 된다.
④ 아이들이 실수로부터 배우는 것은 중요하다.
⑤ 부부간에 교육관이 다르면 한쪽으로 통일해야 한다.

3 대화를 듣고, 두 사람의 관계를 가장 잘 나타낸 것을 고르시오.

① 촬영감독 — 각본가
② 배우 — 메이크업 아티스트
③ 가수 — 프로듀서
④ 모델 — 패션 디자이너
⑤ 발레리나 — 사진작가

4 대화를 듣고, 그림에서 대화의 내용과 일치하지 않는 것을 고르시오.

5 대화를 듣고, 여자가 할 일로 가장 적절한 것을 고르시오.

① 선글라스 챙기기
② 일기예보 확인하기
③ 테니스 시합 촬영하기
④ 샌드위치 구매하기
⑤ 응원 팻말 만들기

6 대화를 듣고, 여자가 지불할 금액을 고르시오. [3점]

① $100　② $110　③ $120　④ $130　⑤ $140

7 대화를 듣고, 남자가 선풍기를 반품하려는 이유를 고르시오.

① 저렴한 에어컨을 찾아서
② 소리가 너무 커서
③ 작동이 잘 되지 않아서
④ 색상이 마음에 들지 않아서
⑤ 날씨가 점차 시원해지고 있어서

8 대화를 듣고, Water for Life 콘서트에 관해 언급되지 않은 것을 고르시오.

① 시작 시각　　② 수용 인원　　③ 모금 목적
④ 입장료　　　⑤ 행사 장소

9 Yearbook Picture Day에 관한 다음 내용을 듣고, 일치하지 않는 것을 고르시오. [3점]

① 사진 촬영은 오전 9시 15분에 시작된다.
② 촬영을 위해 한 학급씩 체육관으로 부를 것이다.
③ 개인 촬영이 끝난 후 단체 사진을 찍는다.
④ 학교 웹사이트에서 사진을 확인할 수 있다.
⑤ 10월 12일에 재촬영이 있을 예정이다.

10 다음 표를 보면서 대화를 듣고, 여자가 구매할 이불을 고르시오.

Blankets

	Model	Price	Size	Care	Material
①	A	$105	Twin	Machine washable	Cotton
②	B	$115	Queen	Machine washable	Wool
③	C	$135	Queen	Dry-cleaning only	Wool
④	D	$145	King	Machine washable	Cotton
⑤	E	$165	King	Dry-cleaning only	Down

11 대화를 듣고, 여자의 마지막 말에 대한 남자의 응답으로 가장 적절한 것을 고르시오.

① No problem. I will go do that right now.
② Of course. You can come with me any time.
③ Definitely. The kids will be happy to see us there.
④ Really? I didn't know the library was closed today.
⑤ Okay. Do you need anything from the grocery store?

12 대화를 듣고, 남자의 마지막 말에 대한 여자의 응답으로 가장 적절한 것을 고르시오.

① I know. He's always so busy with work.
② Really? Next week doesn't work for me.
③ That's true. Maybe I should stay home.
④ No, thanks. I don't need to see a doctor.
⑤ That's fine. Please book an appointment for me.

13 대화를 듣고, 여자의 마지막 말에 대한 남자의 응답으로 가장 적절한 것을 고르시오.

Man: _____

① That's right. Most of them are close friends.
② It's too bad. We have the most talented players.
③ I don't know. They'll probably lose the next game.
④ Good idea. The team should have dinner together.
⑤ I agree. I'll arrange some extra practice time.

14 대화를 듣고, 남자의 마지막 말에 대한 여자의 응답으로 가장 적절한 것을 고르시오.

Woman: _____

① Okay. I'll try to do what you've suggested.
② Got it. I will make more eye contact on stage.
③ Don't worry. I know you'll do a wonderful job.
④ Thank you so much. Your advice really worked.
⑤ Maybe. I'll look inside the dressing room again.

15 다음 상황 설명을 듣고, Eddie가 Jessica에게 할 말로 가장 적절한 것을 고르시오. [3점]

Eddie: _____

① I'm sorry that I arrived at the theater so late today.
② Let's plan to see the movie after you finish dinner.
③ Why don't you come with me to meet my friends?
④ I think you need to check your schedule thoroughly.
⑤ You should apologize to your friend for canceling your plans

[16~17] 다음을 듣고, 물음에 답하시오.

16 남자가 하는 말의 주제로 가장 적절한 것은?

① tips for conserving resources
② easy ways to reduce waste at home
③ how resources are obtained from the Earth
④ environmental problems facing our planet
⑤ importance of natural resources

17 언급된 자원이 아닌 것은?

① water　　② trees　　③ coal
④ electricity　　⑤ gasoline

이제 듣기 문제가 끝났습니다. 채점을 마친 후 다음 페이지에서 방송을 다시 들으며 딕테이션 연습을 하시기 바랍니다.

* 채점 결과: 맞은 개수 _____개 / 17개　　　　정답 및 해설 p.38

Dictation 정답 p.38

06회 영어듣기 모의고사 Dictation 음성을 들으며 빈칸에 알맞은 단어를 채워 넣으시기 바랍니다.

1

W   Attention, shoppers. Did you miss out on the Black Friday sales? Do you want some more great deals? Then, log on to TechStop's online store for our Cyber Monday Sale. There, you will 1)_____ _____ on a wide range of products. We'll offer up to 30% 2)_____ _____ _____ _____ for new electronics, including TVs, computers, and smart phones. Or if you need a new air fryer, toaster, or coffee machine, all of our 3)_____ _____ are on sale for up to 40% off. So mark your calendars, and don't miss this one-day event!

↘ 듣기 필수 표현
· miss out on ~을 놓치다
· log on to ~에 접속하다
· a wide range of 다양한
· up to 최대 ~까지

2

M   What were you doing in Henry's room, honey?
W   I was 1)_____ _____ _____ his math homework. It's finally finished.
M   I hope you didn't do it all for him.
W   Well... I wanted him to get the correct answers.
M   You should let him figure them out 2)_____ _____.
W   But he keeps making mistakes. He doesn't seem to understand the assignments.
M   Yes, but I think it's important to let kids make mistakes and 3)_____ _____ _____.
W   That's true. I just don't want him to get a bad grade.
M   I understand. But it won't be helpful for our son in the end.
W   You're right. I won't do it for him anymore.

↘ 듣기 필수 표현
· figure out ~을 해결하다
· make a mistake 실수를 하다
· in the end 결국

3

[Cell phone rings.]
W   Hello, Nate?
M   Hi, Sharon! How are you?
W   I'm doing well, thanks. I'm so glad you called me back. I 1)_____ _____ _____ _____ on February 16th, and I want you to do my makeup.
M   What kind of event is it?
W   It's a press conference for my new soap opera, *Fallen Angel*.
M   Oh, I heard that your acting in it is great. I 2)_____ _____ _____ _____ it.
W   Thank you. There will be a lot of photographers there.
M   Don't worry. I'll make sure you look amazing. Do you want to 3)_____ _____, or would you prefer heavy makeup?
W   I'd like a natural look.
M   No problem. What time can you 4)_____ _____ _____ _____?
W   What about 3 in the afternoon?
M   That works for me. I'll see you then.

4

M   Hey, Kelly. What do you have in the box?
W   Hi, Ralph. It's the cookie house I made for Christmas. I'll show it to you.
M   Wow, that's amazing. What types of cookies did you use?
W   I baked sugar cookies for the walls and roof. Then, I added 1)_____ _____ _____ _____ to make it look like snow.
M   It almost looks real. And you used chocolate squares to make 2)_____ _____ on the house.
W   Yes, and do you see the 3)_____ _____ on the door?
M   Yeah. That's so cute. Oh, and is that 4)_____ _____ _____ by the house?
W   You're right. I used a tree-shaped cookie cutter to make it.
M   The dog in front of the tree is also a nice touch. You did a wonderful job.
W   Thank you. Let's make one together next year.

5

[Cell phone rings.]

M Hi, Jessica. Are you ready to go see Lucy's tennis tournament?

W Yeah. I'm looking forward to it. Lucy really ¹)_____ _____ _____.

M Did you make a cheer sign for her? I didn't have enough time to make one.

W Don't worry. We can share the one I made.

M That's a relief. I did remember to ²)_____ _____ _____ _____, though.

W Good. She'll be happy to watch her games later.

M What about food? We might need some snacks during the tournament.

W I've got that covered. I bought some sandwiches.

M Sounds good. I just ³)_____ _____ _____, and it's supposed to be very sunny today. Don't forget to bring your sunglasses.

W Okay, thank you. I'll ⁴)_____ _____ right now.

M Then, see you at the stadium!

↘ 듣기 필수 표현
· look forward to ~을 기대하다
· That's a relief. 다행이다.
· have got ~ covered ~을 알아서 하다
· be supposed to ~할 예정이다

6

M Welcome to Echo Bay Aquarium. How can I help you?

W Hello. ¹)_____ _____ _____ _____ two adults and two students, please.

M Tickets are $30 each for adults and $25 for students.

W Okay. Can we watch a movie at the Ocean Theater with these tickets?

M No. You have to pay extra. It's $10 for adults and $5 for students.

W I see. What's ²)_____ _____ _____?

M It's a documentary called *Reef Adventure*.

W All right. Can I get tickets for that, too?

M Sure. So that's ³)_____ _____ for two adults and two students.

W That's correct. Can I use this coupon I found online? It's for $10 off the total.

M Yes, you can. How ⁴)_____ _____ _____?

W I'll pay in cash.

↘ 듣기 필수 표현
· pay extra 추가 요금을 내다

7

W Hey, Michael. Why are you loading that fan into your car?

M It's the one I bought yesterday. I'm taking it back ¹)_____ _____ _____.

W Oh, really? Did you finally find an air conditioner for a good price?

M No. Those were still too expensive.

W I remember you wanted a black fan. Was the fan ²)_____ _____ _____ _____?

M That's not it. This one looks fine.

W Is there any problem with it?

M No. It works perfectly.

W I know that the weather is supposed to get cooler soon. Maybe you don't need a fan anymore.

M Summer is almost over, but it's still hot. Actually, I just thought the fan ³)_____ _____ _____.

W Oh, yeah. That can be annoying.

M Seriously. I just want to get my money back.

W Good luck!

↘ 듣기 필수 표현
· take back ~을 반품하다
· get back ~을 돌려받다

8

W Do you want to hang out this weekend, Kyle?

M I'd love to, but I can't. I'll be ¹)_____ _____ _____ _____ _____ called Water for Life.

W That sounds interesting. When is it?

M It's on Saturday at 8 p.m.

W Luckily, I'll be free at that time. Can you tell me more about it?

M We're raising money to ²)_____ _____ _____ in Africa.

W That sounds like a great cause.

M It is! And the tickets are only $10 per person.

W That's ³)_____ _____ _____ _____. I'll definitely be there. Where is it being held?

M It will be at Stanville Park.

W Okay. See you there.

↘ 듣기 필수 표현
· hang out 놀다
· raise money 돈을 모금하다

9

M　Good afternoon, Lakefield High School students. This is your principal, Mr. Morris. I'd like to announce that we will have Yearbook Picture Day on October 12th. The photo shoots will start at 9:15 a.m. We'll call classes into the gym ¹⁾＿＿＿＿ ＿＿＿＿ ＿＿＿＿ starting then. After the photographer finishes with the individual pictures, we'll have group photo shoots. Your photos will be available on the ²⁾＿＿＿＿ ＿＿＿＿. To access them, you just need to log in to the website. For students who will be absent from school on the 12th, there will be ³⁾＿＿＿＿ ＿＿＿＿ ＿＿＿＿ ＿＿＿＿ on October 26th. Thank you.

↘ 듣기 필수 표현
· be absent from　~에 결석하다

10

W　Are you busy, Oliver?

M　No, Susan. Do you need help with something?

W　I want to buy a new blanket, but there are ¹⁾＿＿＿＿ ＿＿＿＿ ＿＿＿＿. Can you help me decide?

M　Sure. What's your budget?

W　I can't spend more than $150.

M　Then, this one is too expensive. How big is your bed?

W　I have a queen-size bed, so ²⁾＿＿＿＿ ＿＿＿＿ ＿＿＿＿ ＿＿＿＿ would fit.

M　That leaves these three options. What about washing it? Is it okay if the blanket can only be dry cleaned?

W　It has to be machine washable. I don't want to spend time taking it to the cleaners.

M　Okay. What ³⁾＿＿＿＿ ＿＿＿＿ would you like?

W　I prefer cotton over wool.

M　Great. Then, you should get this one.

↘ 듣기 필수 표현
· machine washable　세탁기로 세탁할 수 있는
· prefer A over B　B보다 A를 더 좋아하다

11

W　Honey, I'm going to ¹⁾＿＿＿＿ ＿＿＿＿ ＿＿＿＿ now.

M　Okay. Can you stop by the library, too? Our library books are ²⁾＿＿＿＿ ＿＿＿＿.

W　I have to pick up the kids from school, so I won't have time. Can you ³⁾＿＿＿＿ ＿＿＿＿ ＿＿＿＿?

↘ 듣기 필수 표현
· stop by　들르다
· pick up　~를 데리러 가다

12

[Telephone rings.]

M　Hi. This is Dr. Miller's office.

W　Hi. My name is Elsa Peterson. Is Dr. Miller ¹⁾＿＿＿＿ ＿＿＿＿? My back really hurts.

M　I'm afraid he's booked all day. ²⁾＿＿＿＿ ＿＿＿＿ ＿＿＿＿ ＿＿＿＿ ＿＿＿＿ you is tomorrow at 9:30 a.m.

↘ 듣기 필수 표현
· all day　하루 종일

13

W　What's wrong, Coach Stevens? You seem concerned.

M　I am, Principal Klein. I'm worried about how I'll manage this year's soccer team.

W　But you told me we have ¹⁾＿＿＿＿ ＿＿＿＿ ＿＿＿＿.

M　We do, but they don't work together on the field. They have trouble ²⁾＿＿＿＿ ＿＿＿＿ ＿＿＿＿.

W　Oh, no. What do you think the problem is?

M　The players don't seem ³⁾＿＿＿＿ ＿＿＿＿. Some of them don't even celebrate when their teammates score a goal.

W　It sounds like you need to teach them the importance of team spirit.

M　You're right. I have to plan ⁴⁾＿＿＿＿ ＿＿＿＿ ＿＿＿＿ to bring them together and strengthen their bond.

W　What about organizing a team meal so they can become friends off the field?

↘ 듣기 필수 표현
· work together　협력하다
· score a goal　골을 넣다
· bring ~ together　~를 하나로 묶다

14

M Where have you been, Stacy? Our drama club's play is starting in 10 minutes.

W I'm sorry, Mr. James. I 1)_____ _____ _____ _____ right now.

M What's wrong? Do you need some medicine?

W No. I just don't think I can go on stage tonight. My knees 2)_____ _____.

M Ah, it sounds like you're a little nervous. I know what will help you. You need to go to the dressing room and take deep breaths for five minutes.

W Okay. But what if I'm still nervous after that?

M Once you get onto the stage, don't 3)_____ _____ _____ _____.

W Then, where do I keep my eyes?

M You can stare at the back wall. Trust me. If you do these things, you'll 4)_____ _____ _____.

↘ 듣기 필수 표현
· take deep breaths 숨을 깊이 들이쉬다
· What if ~? ~이라면 어떡하지?
· stare at ~을 쳐다보다

15

W Eddie and Jessica are siblings. They have agreed to 1)_____ _____ _____ _____ on Saturday night. Eddie has been looking forward to watching this movie for a long time. But one hour before it is 2)_____ _____ _____, Jessica calls to tell him that she cannot come to the theater. She forgot that she had dinner plans with her friends. This is 3)_____ _____ _____ _____ Jessica has canceled on Eddie at the last minute. So Eddie wants to tell her that she should 4)_____ _____ _____ more carefully. In this situation, what would Eddie most likely say to Jessica?

↘ 듣기 필수 표현
· cancel on ~를 바람맞히다
· at the last minute 마지막 순간에

16~17

M Hello, everybody. Welcome to another episode of the *Planet Rangers* podcast. I'm your host Ken Thompson. Today, I want to tell you about some simple ways to 1)_____ _____ and help the planet. First, saving water is easy to do. Never 2)_____ _____ _____ while you brush your teeth, and take short showers. You can also preserve trees by using less paper. For example, you can use mobile tickets instead of printed ones. Additionally, it's not hard to save electricity. Switch off the lights whenever you leave a room, and 3)_____ _____ _____ as much as possible. Finally, you can cut down on gasoline use by leaving your car at home and taking public transportation instead. Walking and cycling are other great ways to save on fuel while also getting exercise. These small actions can have 4)_____ _____ _____ over time. Thank you for listening, and have a great day!

↘ 듣기 필수 표현
· brush one's teeth 이를 닦다
· take a shower 샤워를 하다
· instead of ~ 대신에
· switch off ~을 끄다
· as ~ as possible 가능한 한 ~하게
· cut down on ~을 줄이다
· over time 시간이 지나면서

정답 및 해설 p.44

1번부터 17번까지는 듣고 답하는 문제입니다. 1번부터 15번까지는 한 번만 들려주고, 16번부터 17번까지는 두 번 들려줍니다. 방송을 잘 듣고 답을 하시기 바랍니다.

1 다음을 듣고, 여자가 하는 말의 목적으로 가장 적절한 것을 고르시오.

① 어린이 병원 개원 소식을 알리려고
② 진료 예약 사유 입력을 요청하려고
③ 병원 웹사이트 개편 일정을 공지하려고
④ 온라인 진료 예약 방법을 설명하려고
⑤ 새로 부임한 의료진을 소개하려고

2 대화를 듣고, 남자의 의견으로 가장 적절한 것을 고르시오.

① 해야 할 일을 마지막 순간까지 미뤄서는 안 된다.
② 과도한 TV 시청은 건강에 해롭다.
③ 지나간 일에 대한 후회를 떨쳐내야 한다.
④ 마감의 압박감 속에서 글을 더 잘 쓸 수 있다.
⑤ 늦게라도 하는 것이 시작도 하지 않는 것보다는 낫다.

3 대화를 듣고, 두 사람의 관계를 가장 잘 나타낸 것을 고르시오.

① 인공지능 전문가 — 기자
② 의사 — 환자 보호자
③ 로봇 공학자 — 라디오 진행자
④ 과학 교사 — 학생
⑤ 교수 — 연구실 조교

4 대화를 듣고, 그림에서 대화의 내용과 일치하지 않는 것을 고르시오.

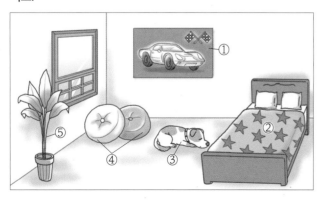

5 대화를 듣고, 여자가 할 일로 가장 적절한 것을 고르시오.

① 빨래 정리하기
② 청소기 돌리기
③ 핫초코 만들기
④ 친구에게 전화하기
⑤ 스키 캠프 등록하기

6 대화를 듣고, 남자가 지불할 금액을 고르시오. [3점]

① $140   ② $150   ③ $180   ④ $190   ⑤ $200

7 대화를 듣고, 남자가 마라톤에 불참하려는 이유를 고르시오.

① 호주로 여행을 가게 돼서
② 장거리 훈련량이 모자라서
③ 시험공부 하느라 바빠서
④ 사진 촬영 일정이 있어서
⑤ 무릎 부상이 덜 회복돼서

8 대화를 듣고, 할아버지의 칠순 잔치에 관해 언급되지 않은 것을 고르시오.

① 장소   ② 참석 인원수   ③ 시작 시각
④ 음식 가짓수   ⑤ 준비한 선물

9 Summer Yoga Program에 관한 다음 내용을 듣고, 일치하지 않는 것을 고르시오.

① 주민센터에서 수업이 진행된다.
② 첫 수업은 다음 주 토요일에 열린다.
③ 초급자와 상급자 모두 참여할 수 있다.
④ 수강생은 개인 요가 매트를 가져와야 한다.
⑤ 회원이 아니면 수강료를 지불해야 한다.

10 다음 표를 보면서 대화를 듣고, 여자가 구매할 물병을 고르시오.

Water bottles

	Model	Size	Price	Material	Straw
①	A	250 ml	$26	Glass	X
②	B	350 ml	$21	Plastic	O
③	C	500 ml	$23	Glass	X
④	D	660 ml	$25	Stainless Steel	O
⑤	E	980 ml	$28	Stainless Steel	O

11 대화를 듣고, 여자의 마지막 말에 대한 남자의 응답으로 가장 적절한 것을 고르시오.

① I'll have my hair cut this weekend.

② I made a reservation for you at the salon.

③ I'm sure he will like the hairdresser there.

④ You should go there to get your hair colored.

⑤ They're losing regular customers these days.

12 대화를 듣고, 남자의 마지막 말에 대한 여자의 응답으로 가장 적절한 것을 고르시오.

① No, thank you. I don't need it.

② I'm sorry. I wish I could help you.

③ Thanks anyway. I'll call back later.

④ No. They're sold out everywhere.

⑤ Yes, please. I'll be right there.

13 대화를 듣고, 여자의 마지막 말에 대한 남자의 응답으로 가장 적절한 것을 고르시오. [3점]

Man: _____

① You're right. I'll start researching rentals now.

② That's too bad. The repairs will be expensive.

③ Let's check. There might be a bus we can take.

④ That's fine. I'll get there early to pick up the car.

⑤ Don't stress. Your parents will understand if you don't go.

14 대화를 듣고, 남자의 마지막 말에 대한 여자의 응답으로 가장 적절한 것을 고르시오.

Woman: _____

① Thanks. But I have all of Hemingway's books.

② Definitely. I love hearing various opinions and ideas.

③ Yes. Discussion is the only way to solve the problem.

④ That's okay. I don't mind reading a new book every week.

⑤ How come? I think it's nice to have friends of different ages.

15 다음 상황 설명을 듣고, Nathan이 Nicole에게 할 말로 가장 적절한 것을 고르시오. [3점]

Nathan: _____

① Let's ask the other group for help.

② We can find more materials at the library.

③ I think we should work on a different topic.

④ I found a lot of information on light pollution.

⑤ Why don't we ask for more time to finish our project?

[16~17] 다음을 듣고, 물음에 답하시오.

16 남자가 하는 말의 주제로 가장 적절한 것은?

① why food is difficult to find in certain regions

② what is needed to survive on a deserted island

③ the best way to escape from an isolated area

④ importance of preparing for emergencies

⑤ how to build a shelter in the mountains

17 언급된 물품이 <u>아닌</u> 것은?

① lighter　　② knife　　③ tent

④ blanket　　⑤ rope

이제 듣기 문제가 끝났습니다. 채점을 마친 후 다음 페이지에서 방송을 다시 들으며 딕테이션 연습을 하시기 바랍니다.

* 채점 결과: 맞은 개수 _____개 / 17개

정답 및 해설 p.44

07회 영어듣기 모의고사 Dictation 음성을 들으며 빈칸에 알맞은 단어를 채워 넣으시기 바랍니다.

1

W Greetings, patients! This is Allison from Princeton Hospital. I'd like to inform you that we have a 1)_____ _____ _____ _____. You can now visit our website to make a doctor's appointment. The system is simple to use. First, 2)_____ _____ _____ and log in. Then, click on "Manage My Appointments." On the next screen, select your doctor to check availability. Choose your preferred date and time. Lastly, type the reason for your appointment, and 3)_____ _____. You can also reschedule or cancel your appointments online. We hope this system will make scheduling appointments more convenient. Thank you.

↘ 듣기 필수 표현
· make a doctor's appointment 진료 예약을 하다

2

M Andrea, don't you have to 1)_____ _____ _____ tomorrow morning?

W Yes, Dad. I'll work on it after I watch this TV program.

M How much more do you have left?

W Honestly... I haven't started writing it yet.

M It's already 5 p.m. You don't have much time.

W It's just a short essay, so it 2)_____ _____ _____.

M That's not a good idea. You should not put off your work 3)_____ _____ _____ _____.

W But I usually do better under pressure.

M Didn't you make the same mistake last time you had an essay assignment?

W You're right. I turned that one in late, and I got a bad grade.

M That's the point. 4)_____ _____ _____ the last minute to do your work. You can relax and watch TV after finishing the essay.

↘ 듣기 필수 표현
· put off ~을 미루다
· under pressure 압박감을 느끼는
· make a mistake 실수를 하다
· turn in ~을 제출하다

3

[Cell phone rings.]

W Hello? This is Lynn Sawyer.

M Hi. It's Donald Porter from *Science for Life*.

W Ah, Mr. Porter. It's nice to hear from you again. I liked 1)_____ _____ _____ _____ the future of robotics.

M Thank you. Now, I'm writing an article on artificial intelligence, and I know you're an expert in that field.

W Sure. I'd be happy to discuss my work on AI with you.

M Great! When 2)_____ _____ _____?

W I'm busy this week, but I have some time the week after that.

M Okay. Are you free next Tuesday at 10 a.m.?

W Yes. That's fine. If you 3)_____ _____ _____ _____, I can show you around and answer any questions you have.

M Thank you. See you then.

↘ 듣기 필수 표현
· hear from ~로부터 연락을 받다
· show ~ around ~를 구경시켜 주다

4

M Hi, Mandy. I rearranged my bedroom. Do you want to see a picture?

W Okay. [Pause] That's 1)_____ _____ _____ _____ on the wall.

M Thanks. I just bought it last week.

W Did you get a new blanket, too? This blanket has a star pattern on it.

M Yeah. My mom got it for me. It's really warm.

W That's awesome. I see your dog sleeping 2)_____ _____ _____ _____.

M Yeah, he likes to sleep in my room sometimes. That's why I put the two heart-shaped cushions 3)_____ _____ _____. They're for him.

W That's so sweet.

M Do you notice anything else that's new?

W Is that 4)_____ _____ _____ _____ the one I gave you? It grew so much!

M That's right. I had to change the pot. Thanks again.

W You're welcome.

5

W Scott, did you hang the laundry?

M Yes, Mom. I 1)_____ _____ _____ _____, too.

W Thanks, dear. You've been a big help while I've been busy with work.

M Well, it's winter vacation, so I have lots of time to help out.

W Okay, but I still want you to enjoy your vacation. Is there anything you'd be interested in doing?

M Yes. I want to go to a sports camp.

W My friend's son is going to a ski camp. Should I 2)_____ _____ and get more information about it?

M Sure! That sounds like fun. Oh, I'm 3)_____ _____ _____ _____. Do you want some?

W Of course. Thank you.

↘ 듣기 필수 표현
· help out 돕다

6

W Welcome to the Lotus Valley Music Festival. Can I help you?

M Hi. How much are the tickets?

W Standard tickets are $55. 1)_____ _____ _____ are $80.

M So... with the standard tickets, I wouldn't have a seat?

W No. And with reserved seats, you can watch the performances in a section closer to the stage.

M Great. I'll take two of those.

W Sure. And for just $20 extra, you can buy a VIP Pass. It will let you get 2)_____ _____ _____ _____ in the VIP Lounge.

M Oh, that would be nice. I'll get 3)_____ _____, please.

W No problem. So that's two reserved seat tickets and two VIP Passes.

M That's right. And can I use this 10% discount coupon?

W Sure. How would you like to pay?

M I'll pay by credit card.

↘ 듣기 필수 표현
· close to ~에 가까운

7

W Hey, Oscar. Do you want to go running after school? The marathon is in a week.

M I'm sorry, but I'm not participating in this year's marathon after all.

W Why not? We've 1)_____ _____ _____. Is it because you have to study for exams?

M No. I'm already prepared for them.

W Are you still hurt? You 2)_____ _____ _____ a while ago.

M No. It's perfectly fine now.

W I don't understand why you'd drop out a week before the race.

M Do you remember 3)_____ _____ _____ _____ I entered last month?

W Yeah. You sent a photograph of a kangaroo.

M Well, I won the grand prize! The reward for winning was a free trip to Australia. I'll leave tomorrow and stay there for nine days.

W No way! Congratulations!

↘ 듣기 필수 표현
· after all 결국
· drop out 빠지다, 손을 떼다
· No way! 말도 안 돼!

8

W Dad, I'm so excited for Grandpa's 70th birthday party.

M Yeah, it will be great to see everyone. I haven't seen your aunt and uncle in a long time.

W I know. We're meeting at the Chinese restaurant downtown, right?

M That's right. I 1)_____ _____ _____ _____ so that there will be enough space for everyone.

W Good. When does the party begin?

M The reservations are for 5 p.m. next Sunday.

W Perfect. I also remember you saying that there will be 2)_____ _____ _____ _____ _____.

M Yes, with barbecue duck as the main dish.

W Wow, I love barbecue duck! And do you think Grandpa will like my gift? I painted a picture of him.

M It's 3)_____ _____ _____ _____ _____. He'll love it.

W I hope so.

↘ 듣기 필수 표현
· in a long time 한동안

9

W Good morning, everyone. I'm Karen Moon, the owner of Moon Yoga Studio. I'm happy to announce that we're offering a Summer Yoga Program. The classes will take place every Saturday here [1)]_____ _____ _____ _____. The first class is scheduled for next Saturday at 7 a.m. We'll accept both beginner and advanced students, so anyone can attend. However, attendees should bring their own yoga mat. There is [2)]_____ _____ to take this class. But I encourage all of you to become members of my studio so you can [3)]_____ _____ _____. If you enjoy the class, you can purchase a membership on my website. I hope to see you all soon!

↘ 듣기 필수 표현
· take place 진행되다, 열리다
· be scheduled for ~로 예정되어 있다

10

M Welcome to Sports Stop. Please let me know if you need anything.

W Hi. Can you help me choose a water bottle?

M Sure. These are our most popular water bottles. They come in many sizes.

W It has to [1)]_____ _____ _____ _____. So anything over 700 milliliters would be too large.

M Okay. How much do you want to spend on it?

W I think $25 and under is reasonable. I don't want to spend more than that.

M And [2)]_____ _____ _____ _____? We have plastic, stainless steel, and glass.

W I don't want a plastic bottle. Either glass or stainless steel would be fine.

M Do you want it to come with [3)]_____ _____?

W Sure. I'd like that. It'll be easier to drink from that way.

M Then, I recommend you get this one.

↘ 듣기 필수 표현
· come in ~으로 나오다, 출시되다
· spend on ~에 (돈, 시간을) 쓰다
· come with ~이 딸려 나오다

11

W Ted, do you know a good place to get a men's haircut in our neighborhood?

M Yes. Amigo Hair [1)]_____ _____ _____ _____ our school. I'm a regular customer there.

W That's good. My brother wants to [2)]_____ _____ _____ _____.

↘ 듣기 필수 표현
· get a haircut 머리를 자르다

12

[Telephone rings.]

M This is King Toys. How can I help you?

W I'm looking for a nutcracker doll. Do you [1)]_____ _____ _____ _____?

M Wait a second. *[Typing sound]* Yes, but there's [2)]_____ _____ _____. Should I set it aside for you?

↘ 듣기 필수 표현
· look for ~을 찾다
· set aside ~을 챙겨두다, 따로 떼어 두다

13

W Honey, are we still going to [1)]_____ _____ _____ for Thanksgiving this weekend?

M I want to, but I'm not sure if we can anymore.

W The car isn't fixed yet?

M No. The repairman says it won't be ready in time. I thought maybe we could [2)]_____ _____ _____ _____, but there are no tickets available.

W Yeah, Thanksgiving is just around the corner.

M I don't know what to do.

W Well, we could [3)]_____ _____ _____.

M Won't that be expensive?

W But we don't have any other choice. Let's pick it up the day before we leave and start driving really early in the morning.

M That's a good idea. Then, we can beat the traffic.

W Exactly. It'll [4)]_____ _____ _____ to enjoy the holiday with family.

↘ 듣기 필수 표현
· around the corner 곧, 임박하여
· pick up ~을 찾아오다, 가져오다
· beat the traffic 교통체증을 피하다

14

M Jenna, what are you doing on your laptop?

W I'm about to 1)_____ _____ _____ _____, Dad. I recently joined an online book club.

M I 2)_____ _____ _____ _____ a book club, too. But we met at the local library.

W Oh, I didn't know that. Well, my book club meets online every Wednesday.

M That sounds convenient. What kind of books 3)_____ _____ _____?

W All of the members are great fans of Ernest Hemingway. So we mostly read and talk about his books.

M Really? Are all the other members students like you?

W No. It's 4)_____ _____ _____ _____. There's even one old woman from India.

M That's great. Are you enjoying the discussions with such a diverse group?

↘ 듣기 필수 표현
· be about to 막 ~하려는 참이다

15

W Nicole and Nathan are classmates in high school. They are working on a group science project together. Nicole 1)_____ _____ _____ as their topic, and they agree to research it. But Nicole catches the flu and ends up missing a week of school. During this time, Nathan searches for some materials, but it isn't easy 2)_____ _____ _____ _____. He also hears that another group is working on the same topic. So when Nicole comes back to school, Nathan wants to tell her that they should 3)_____ _____ _____. In this situation, what would Nathan most likely say to Nicole?

↘ 듣기 필수 표현
· agree to ~하기로 합의하다
· catch the flu 독감에 걸리다
· end up 결국 ~하게 되다

16~17

M Good afternoon. In yesterday's session, we discussed how to build a shelter and find food if you are ever trapped on a mountain. Today, we will look at what equipment you might need to 1)_____ _____ _____ on a deserted island. First, it is important to have a lighter. That way, you can start a fire to keep warm and cook food. Next, a knife is necessary. It can be used to 2)_____ _____ _____ _____, as well as to make a spear to catch fish. A blanket is also very useful. You can wrap yourself in it while you sleep, and it can 3)_____ _____ _____ _____ to sit during the day. Finally, a long piece of rope is another necessity. It can be used to tie up materials, which is useful for collecting items or building a shelter. I hope today's talk has given you some tips that will be helpful if you ever find yourself alone on 4)_____ _____ _____.

↘ 듣기 필수 표현
· start a fire 불을 피우다
· as well as ~뿐만 아니라
· wrap oneself in ~을 몸에 걸치다
· tie up ~을 묶다

08회 영어듣기 모의고사

정답 및 해설 p.50

1번부터 17번까지는 듣고 답하는 문제입니다. 1번부터 15번까지는 한 번만 들려주고, 16번부터 17번까지는 두 번 들려줍니다. 방송을 잘 듣고 답을 하시기 바랍니다.

1 다음을 듣고, 여자가 하는 말의 목적으로 가장 적절한 것을 고르시오.

① 버스 연착을 사과하려고
② 여행 코스를 설명하려고
③ 중간 정차 장소를 안내하려고
④ 탑승객의 불만 사항을 접수하려고
⑤ 버스 음식물 반입 금지를 당부하려고

2 대화를 듣고, 남자의 의견으로 가장 적절한 것을 고르시오.

① 공원에 더 많은 쓰레기통을 설치할 필요가 있다.
② 사회 질서를 위해 엄격한 법이 집행돼야 한다.
③ 콘서트 후 버려지는 쓰레기 문제가 심각하다.
④ 쓰레기 투기에 대한 벌금을 인상해야 한다.
⑤ 봉사활동을 통해 공동체 의식을 기를 수 있다.

3 대화를 듣고, 두 사람의 관계를 가장 잘 나타낸 것을 고르시오.

① 아동문학 작가 — 삽화가
② 동물원 직원 — 방문객
③ 만화가 — 인쇄소 직원
④ 수의사 — 사육사
⑤ 미술관장 — 조각가

4 대화를 듣고, 그림에서 대화의 내용과 일치하지 않는 것을 고르시오.

5 대화를 듣고, 여자가 남자에게 부탁한 일로 가장 적절한 것을 고르시오.

① 공항으로 마중 가기
② 영어 가르쳐주기
③ 항공편 예약하기
④ 저녁 식사 대접하기
⑤ 보고서 제출하기

6 대화를 듣고, 여자가 지불할 금액을 고르시오. [3점]

① $100   ② $125   ③ $135   ④ $145   ⑤ $150

7 대화를 듣고, 남자가 축구 연습에 가지 않는 이유를 고르시오.

① 친구의 발표 준비를 도와야 해서
② 역사 숙제를 끝내야 해서
③ 감기가 다 낫지 않아서
④ 친구와 영화를 보러 가야 해서
⑤ 축구에 흥미를 잃어서

8 대화를 듣고, Dolman Job Fair에 관해 언급되지 않은 것을 고르시오.

① 행사 일자   ② 행사 장소   ③ 주최 기관
④ 참가 기업 수   ⑤ 종료 시각

9 James Harper Exhibit에 관한 다음 내용을 듣고, 일치하지 않는 것을 고르시오. [3점]

① Harper는 생전에 약 240채의 건물을 설계했다.
② Harper의 유명한 건축물의 사진들이 전시된다.
③ 주택 모형들이 가장 주요한 볼거리이다.
④ 안내처 직원에게 해설 관람을 신청할 수 있다.
⑤ 입장료에는 해설 관람 비용이 포함되어 있다.

10 다음 표를 보면서 대화를 듣고, 여자가 구매할 컴퓨터 모니터를 고르시오.

Computer Monitors

	Model	Screen Size (inches)	Cost	Color
①	A	20	$170	White
②	B	22	$200	White
③	C	24	$180	Black
④	D	26	$220	Black
⑤	E	18	$160	Black

11 대화를 듣고, 여자의 마지막 말에 대한 남자의 응답으로 가장 적절한 것을 고르시오.

① Possibly. I'll call there now to check.
② Absolutely. Let's make a reservation.
③ I don't know. I'm not hungry right now.
④ Sorry. You will have to pay for the lunch.
⑤ Thanks. I'm really glad you found my wallet.

12 대화를 듣고, 남자의 마지막 말에 대한 여자의 응답으로 가장 적절한 것을 고르시오.

① It took half an hour to get there.
② But I booked the movie yesterday.
③ Have you seen my ticket anywhere?
④ We had better leave right away, then.
⑤ Do you mind giving me a ride today?

13 대화를 듣고, 남자의 마지막 말에 대한 여자의 응답으로 가장 적절한 것을 고르시오.

Woman: _____

① She has agreed to organize the science festival.
② The presentation about flight was canceled.
③ I'm certain the festival will be a success.
④ Airplanes are a very interesting subject.
⑤ I'll ask her about it in the afternoon.

14 대화를 듣고, 여자의 마지막 말에 대한 남자의 응답으로 가장 적절한 것을 고르시오.

Man: _____

① Congratulations on your daughter's graduation.
② We have nothing else scheduled for that day.
③ We offer a wide variety of Italian dishes.
④ I hope your guests enjoyed our food.
⑤ I'm afraid we don't take credit cards.

15 다음 상황 설명을 듣고, Samantha가 Neal에게 할 말로 가장 적절한 것을 고르시오. [3점]

Samantha: _____

① Should I turn down the TV volume for you?
② Could you play somewhere else while I study?
③ How long are you going to play video games?
④ Can I prepare for the exam in your bedroom?
⑤ Why don't you read books in the living room?

[16~17] 다음을 듣고, 물음에 답하시오.

16 남자가 하는 말의 주제로 가장 적절한 것은?

① how to stay safe during natural disasters
② places where tsunamis are likely to occur
③ why natural disasters have become more common
④ the areas with the greatest risk of hurricanes
⑤ the most serious natural disasters in history

17 언급된 자연재해가 <u>아닌</u> 것은?

① earthquake　② tsunami　③ tornado
④ hurricane　⑤ flood

이제 듣기 문제가 끝났습니다. 채점을 마친 후 다음 페이지에서 방송을 다시 들으며 딕테이션 연습을 하시기 바랍니다.

* 채점 결과: 맞은 개수 _____ 개 / 17개　　　　정답 및 해설 p.50

08회 영어듣기 모의고사 Dictation 음성을 들으며 빈칸에 알맞은 단어를 채워 넣으시기 바랍니다.

1

W Attention, all passengers. Thank you for choosing the Lyon Bus Line for your trip. We want to 1)_____ _____ _____ everyone has a comfortable trip on our buses. That is why we would like to remind everyone of a new rule about food. Recently, we've 2)_____ _____ _____ strong-smelling snacks and spilled beverages. So passengers are no longer 3)_____ _____ _____ food and drinks on the bus. But don't worry! Your driver will make regular stops, so you will have a chance to eat during your trip. Thank you.

↘ 듣기 필수 표현
· no longer 더 이상 ~이 아닌
· make a stop 정차하다, 멈추다

2

M What are you doing this weekend, Mandy?
W I'm going to a concert with my friends.
M Lucky you. That sounds like a lot of fun.
W What about you?
M I'm 1)_____ _____ _____ _____ on Saturday.
W Really? What exactly will you do?
M I belong to a student group that picks up trash in local parks.
W That 2)_____ _____ _____.
M It is, honestly. I am always surprised by how much garbage we see.
W Hasn't our city banned throwing trash on the ground in parks?
M Yeah, but the laws are not strict. The city really needs to 3)_____ _____ _____ for this.
W I agree. But until that happens, it is good that there are people like you to keep our parks clean.

↘ 듣기 필수 표현
· Lucky you. 잘됐네.
· belong to ~에 소속되다, 속하다
· pick up ~을 줍다

3

W Thanks for meeting with me today.
M No problem. I'm really excited to work with you on this project.
W Great. I think your art style will be perfect for 1)_____ _____ _____ _____.
M I hope so. All of the characters you want me to draw are animals, right?
W That's correct. The story is about a group of animals living in the zoo.
M Interesting. 2)_____ _____ _____ will you need in total?
W The book is 20 pages long. I want to include at least 10 pictures in it.
M Okay. 3)_____ _____ _____ _____?
W I'd like you to finish everything by June 10th at the latest. Does that work for you?
M That should be fine.

↘ 듣기 필수 표현
· at least 적어도, 최소한
· at the latest 늦어도

4

M Honey, I just finished setting up the backyard for the summer.
W Wow. It looks great.
M What about the 1)_____ _____ _____ on the fence? Do you think they will provide enough light?
W I do. If not, we can always add more. And the table with the two chairs in the middle of the yard looks really cozy.
M I agree. We can have dinner there on summer nights.
W And the 2)_____ _____ _____ the table is very eye-catching.
M Yeah. It's also practical. It will keep the rain off us.
W Oh, I see you moved the barbecue grill 3)_____ _____ _____ _____.
M Right. I thought that would be a good spot.
W Good idea. The big tree beside it will provide shade while we cook.
M Exactly. We need to stay cool.

↘ 듣기 필수 표현
· keep ~ off (비, 태양 등을) 막다

5

W Chris, what are you doing this afternoon?

M Nothing special. Why are you asking, Miranda?

W Do you 1)_____ _____ _____ _____ in Korea?

M Of course! You stayed with Minyoung and her parents. You told me they were very nice.

W Yes. Well, Minyoung is going to stay with my family for three weeks. I 2)_____ _____ _____ her English.

M Wow, you seem thrilled.

W Yes. But there's an unexpected issue.

M Is it anything I can give you a hand with?

W Actually, I am supposed to 3)_____ _____ _____ at the airport this afternoon. But I haven't finished a report that I need to hand in today.

M And you need someone to meet Minyoung at the airport.

W Could you please do it for me?

M Sure. Why not? But you will have to 4)_____ _____ _____ sometime.

⤵ 듣기 필수 표현
· give ~ a hand ~를 도와주다
· be supposed to ~하기로 하다
· hand in ~을 제출하다

6

M Do you need help with anything today?

W Yes. I want to 1)_____ _____ _____ _____ for Christmas.

M Well, what do you think of this model? It is our best one, and it only costs $50.

W I guess my nephews will like it. I'll take two.

M Great. Do they have helmets already? This helmet is $25.

W I'll take two of those as well.

M Oh, I almost forgot. We are 2)_____ _____ _____ _____ helmets this week.

W That's wonderful. How much of a discount will I get?

M You will 3)_____ _____ _____ the helmets. Is there anything else you need today?

W No. That's everything. Thank you so much for your help.

⤵ 듣기 필수 표현
· as well ~도, 역시

7

W Mark, why are you still at home? I thought you had soccer practice this afternoon.

M I'm not going today, Mom.

W Oh, that's right. You have history homework 1)_____ _____.

M I finished it already.

W Then, are you sick? Should I take you to the doctor's office?

M No. I had a cold last week, but I feel fine now.

W 2)_____ _____ _____ _____ go to a movie or something with your friends?

M I don't have time for anything like that today.

W Then, why are you not going to practice today?

M One of my classmates has to give a speech in front of our class tomorrow.

W What does that have to do with soccer practice?

M I promised that I would 3)_____ _____ _____ _____ _____.

W I see. That is nice of you.

⤵ 듣기 필수 표현
· have a cold 감기에 걸리다
· give a speech 발표하다, 연설하다
· in front of ~의 앞에서
· have to do with ~과 상관이 있다

8

M Denise, have you found a new job yet?

W No. I'm getting 1)_____ _____ _____ about it.

M Well, the Dolman Job Fair is coming up soon. Maybe you should check it out.

W Really? When is it taking place?

M It will be 2)_____ _____ _____.

W Do you know where I should go?

M It'll be at the Star Hotel downtown.

W That's convenient. How many companies will 3)_____ _____?

M Around 50. And many of them are in your field of work.

W Great. Oh, I just remembered that I have a doctor's appointment that day. I won't be free until 5 p.m.

M That's fine. The fair will 4)_____ _____ _____.

W Then, I'll definitely go. Thanks for letting me know about it.

⤵ 듣기 필수 표현
· find a job 직장을 구하다
· come up 열리다, 생기다
· check out ~을 확인하다
· take place 개최되다
· not A until B B는 되어야 A하다

9

W Welcome to the opening of the James Harper Exhibit at the Museum of Modern Architecture. Mr. Harper was one of the [1)]_____ _____ _____ of the 1990s. He designed around 240 buildings during his lifetime. The exhibit includes photographs of his most famous buildings. But the models of the houses that Mr. Harper designed are [2)]_____ _____ _____. These are incredibly detailed. If you would prefer a guided tour of the exhibit, speak to one of the staff members at the information desk. This service is not included in the admission fee, so there will be [3)]_____ _____ _____ _____. I hope all of you enjoy the exhibit.

↘ 듣기 필수 표현
· during one's lifetime 생전에, 일생 동안

10

M What are you doing, Tara?

W I'm looking at computer monitors online. I need to buy a new one.

M Have you [1)]_____ _____ _____ _____ yet?

W No. But I definitely want one with a screen size of at least 22 inches.

M That's a good size. What about cost? How much are you willing to spend?

W I have [2)]_____ _____ _____ _____. I can't go over that amount.

M Well, that seems to leave two models to choose from.

W I know. But I am having a hard time [3)]_____ _____ _____.

M The black one seems best to me.

W You're right. I'll get that one. Thanks for your help.

M No problem.

↘ 듣기 필수 표현
· be willing to ~할 의향이 있다
· have a hard time ~하는 데 어려움을 겪다

11

W What's the matter, Brad? You look really worried.

M I just noticed that [1)]_____ _____ _____ _____ my pocket!

W Did you leave it at the restaurant where we [2)]_____ _____?

12

M Mom, could you [1)]_____ _____ _____ the movie theater?

W Sure. What time do you need to be there?

M Actually, in about 30 minutes. We [2)]_____ _____.

13

M Cindy, are you planning to attend the school's science festival next week?

W Yes, Mr. Parker. It sounds like fun.

M We need some student volunteers for the event. I thought maybe you would be interested in [1)]_____ _____.

W What would I have to do?

M Well, the volunteers will assist the presenters.

W Could I [2)]_____ _____ _____ to help?

M Do you have one in mind?

W Yeah. The school's website says that there will be a presentation about flight.

M Oh, the one about airplane design.

W Right. I'd like to be a pilot someday, so that's a topic I follow closely.

M You should speak to Ms. Clarkson about this. She's in charge of [3)]_____ _____ _____ for the event.

↘ 듣기 필수 표현
· be interested in ~할 의향이 있다
· have ~ in mind ~을 염두에 두다
· be in charge of ~을 담당하다

14

[Telephone rings.]

M You've reached Benson Catering.

W Hi. I'm planning 1)_____ _____ _____ for my daughter. One of my friends recommended your company to provide the food.

M That's wonderful. How many people will be attending?

W I'm expecting 35 guests.

M Okay. What kind of food would you 2)_____ _____ _____?

W My daughter really likes Italian food, so pasta and pizza would be great.

M We can do that. I'll send you a list of dishes you can choose from. Then, you can just pick what you want.

W Perfect. I was planning to hold the event next Saturday.

M Let me check my schedule. [Pause] Oh, no. We are 3)_____ _____ for another event on that day.

W Then, what about next Friday? 4)_____ _____ _____?

15

W Samantha is studying for the final exam in her 1)_____ _____. She finds the subject difficult, and she is having a hard time focusing on her lecture notes. To make things worse, her younger brother, Neal, 2)_____ _____ _____. He is playing video games in the living room, and the volume is very loud. In addition, he keeps shouting and laughing while he plays. Unfortunately, her bedroom is right next to the living room, so she can't ignore him. So Samantha wants to ask Neal to go to another room in the house while she 3)_____ _____ _____ _____. In this situation, what would Samantha most likely say to Neal?

↘ 듣기 필수 표현
· focus on ~에 집중하다
· to make things worse 설상가상으로

16~17

M Good morning. Yesterday, we talked about the 1)_____ _____ _____ _____ _____. Today, I want to discuss what we must do to survive when these disasters happen. First, the key to keeping safe 2)_____ _____ _____ is to protect yourself from falling objects. You should get under something sturdy like a table or a desk. In the case of a tsunami, you must go to high ground as quickly as possible. Move away from the beach, and 3)_____ _____ _____ _____. Next, be sure to stay indoors during a hurricane. The high winds and heavy rains make it unsafe to be outside. Finally, if 4)_____ _____ _____, it is dangerous to be in an underground parking lot or on one of the lower floors of a building. Go to a higher floor or even the roof of the building. I hope this lesson has given you a better understanding of what to do in these situations.

↘ 듣기 필수 표현
· protect A from B A를 B로부터 보호하다
· as ~ as possible 가능한 한 ~하게

09회 영어듣기 모의고사

정답 및 해설 p.56

1번부터 17번까지는 듣고 답하는 문제입니다. 1번부터 15번까지는 한 번만 들려주고, 16번부터 17번까지는 두 번 들려줍니다. 방송을 잘 듣고 답을 하시기 바랍니다.

1 다음을 듣고, 남자가 하는 말의 목적으로 가장 적절한 것을 고르시오.

① 봄 학기 등록 절차에 대해 설명하려고
② 유료 컴퓨터 프로그램을 홍보하려고
③ 코딩 수업 개선 아이디어를 요청하려고
④ 강좌 참가 신청 마감일 변경을 안내하려고
⑤ 과도한 컴퓨터 사용의 유해성을 경고하려고

2 대화를 듣고, 남자의 의견으로 가장 적절한 것을 고르시오.

① 친구끼리는 서로의 약점을 보완해줘야 한다.
② 친구의 의견과 반대되는 견해를 가져도 괜찮다.
③ 갈등 해결을 위해서는 솔직한 대화가 필요하다.
④ 각별한 관계일수록 매너를 지켜야 한다.
⑤ 사람들은 대화하기 쉬운 사람들과 친구가 되려고 한다.

3 대화를 듣고, 두 사람의 관계를 가장 잘 나타낸 것을 고르시오.

① 광고주 — 편집장
② 기자 — 사진사
③ 관람객 — 도슨트
④ 경비원 — 박물관 직원
⑤ 고고학자 — 아나운서

4 대화를 듣고, 그림에서 대화의 내용과 일치하지 않는 것을 고르시오.

5 대화를 듣고, 여자가 할 일로 가장 적절한 것을 고르시오.

① 쿠키 반죽하기
② 지도 그리기
③ 동물 구조하기
④ 부스 설치하기
⑤ 문자 보내기

6 대화를 듣고, 남자가 지불할 금액을 고르시오. [3점]

① $60   ② $64   ③ $80   ④ $88   ⑤ $110

7 대화를 듣고, 여자가 유람선 여행을 갈 수 없는 이유를 고르시오.

① 티켓을 사지 못해서
② 숙제를 해야 해서
③ 배 멀미를 해서
④ 캠핑을 가야 해서
⑤ 저녁 약속이 있어서

8 대화를 듣고, 프랑스어 동아리 겨울 여행에 관해 언급되지 않은 것을 고르시오.

① 목적지   ② 출발일   ③ 활동
④ 경비   ⑤ 인솔자

9 Clean Marine Poster Contest에 관한 다음 내용을 듣고, 일치하지 않는 것을 고르시오. [3점]

① Pinewood High School 학생들이 참가할 수 있다.
② 제출 마감일은 5월 31일이다.
③ 대회 3위는 상금 30달러를 받는다.
④ 수상자는 6월 8일에 발표된다.
⑤ 1위 포스터는 봉사자 증정 티셔츠에 인쇄된다.

10 다음 표를 보면서 대화를 듣고, 두 사람이 구매할 에스프레소 기계를 고르시오.

Espresso Machines

	Model	Price	Brewing Time (seconds)	Cleaning Function	Color
①	A	$200	45	X	Black
②	B	$245	45	O	Silver
③	C	$320	40	O	Blue
④	D	$380	55	X	Green
⑤	E	$415	50	O	White

11 대화를 듣고, 남자의 마지막 말에 대한 여자의 응답으로 가장 적절한 것을 고르시오.

① Can I get the pasta salad, please?

② I think I will order something online.

③ Please wash the vegetables thoroughly.

④ Our reservation is for 6:30 tonight.

⑤ How would you like your steak?

12 대화를 듣고, 여자의 마지막 말에 대한 남자의 응답으로 가장 적절한 것을 고르시오.

① Exactly. Our concert is going to be next Saturday.

② That's great. I enjoyed reading your essay.

③ I'm sorry. But that book isn't available.

④ No. Fair tickets are free for children.

⑤ Sure. I'll be done in five minutes.

13 대화를 듣고, 남자의 마지막 말에 대한 여자의 응답으로 가장 적절한 것을 고르시오. [3점]

Woman: _____

① I agree. It's a really nice magazine.

② Wait. Let me adjust the camera a bit.

③ Really? Maybe I should submit a photo, then.

④ I'm sorry. You don't qualify for the contest.

⑤ No. I'd rather take photos of people.

14 대화를 듣고 여자의 마지막 말에 대한 남자의 응답으로 가장 적절한 것을 고르시오.

Man: _____

① I know. That's why we didn't watch it.

② Yeah. Horror movies give me nightmares.

③ Right. We should have picked the other movie.

④ Not really. I don't always agree with movie critics.

⑤ Great. A science-fiction movie sounds exciting!

15 다음 상황 설명을 듣고, Mr. Penn이 Gina에게 할 말로 가장 적절한 것을 고르시오.

Mr. Penn: _____

① Passing accurately is more important than shooting.

② I can show you some techniques during practice.

③ Rest is required if you want to heal properly.

④ Too much training can cause an injury.

⑤ Scoring a goal requires hard work.

[16~17] 다음을 듣고, 물음에 답하시오.

16 여자가 하는 말의 주제로 가장 적절한 것은?

① how different countries were founded

② nations that have animals on their flags

③ why kings had animals as their symbols

④ national animals of various countries

⑤ changes to flag designs over time

17 언급된 나라가 <u>아닌</u> 것은?

① Mexico ② Sri Lanka ③ Moldova

④ Peru ⑤ Dominica

이제 듣기 문제가 끝났습니다. 채점을 마친 후 다음 페이지에서 방송을 다시 들으며 딕테이션 연습을 하시기 바랍니다.

* 채점 결과: 맞은 개수 _____ 개 / 17개   정답 및 해설 p.56

09회 영어듣기 모의고사 Dictation 음성을 들으며 빈칸에 알맞은 단어를 채워 넣으시기 바랍니다.

1

M Attention, please. I have an update regarding this year's spring computer course. As you may already know, Riverview High School offers a 1)_____ _____ _____ every year. Students have a chance to learn basic coding and create simple computer programs. Originally, the last date that you could apply was March 30th. However, due to the 2)_____ _____ _____ _____, we've decided to close the application period early. Therefore, I need to inform you that the 3)_____ _____ _____ _____ will be March 15th. If you have any questions about the application process, please visit the school's website. Thank you for understanding.

↘ 듣기 필수 표현
· due to ~으로 인해, 때문에

2

M What's the matter, Tory? You're frowning.

W My friend Anna said something rude to me earlier. She really 1)_____ _____ _____.

M Oh, no. I'm sorry to hear that. Did she apologize for it?

W No. She doesn't even know I'm upset.

M Well, maybe you should tell her how you feel. I think you need to have an honest conversation with her so you can 2)_____ _____ _____.

W No. It'll be too uncomfortable. I'll just try to forget about it.

M But if she doesn't know what she did wrong, she will probably do it again. 3)_____ _____ is important for keeping relationships healthy.

W Hmm... I think you're right. Maybe I'll message her about it.

M That's a good idea, but you shouldn't wait too long.

W Okay. I'll send her a text now. Thanks for your advice!

3

M Hi, Dana. My chief editor mentioned that you could help with the article 1)_____ _____.

W Sure. Is this for that story you're reporting on about the Brentwood Museum?

M Right. The museum got a big donation from an anonymous person.

W That's interesting. Do you need pictures 2)_____ _____ _____ _____ for the article?

M Actually, we need new ones.

W I can go over there and take some pictures. What do you need me to do?

M This story is going on the front page of the newspaper. So I'd like a photo of the new sculpture by the main entrance. A few paintings were also donated. Let's get those, too.

W No problem. When do you need my photos?

M The article will be 3)_____ _____ _____ _____.

W Will we make the deadline if I send you the photos in three days?

M Yeah. That would be perfect. Thanks!

4

W Honey, this market is really amazing. I'm glad our tour guide brought us here.

M I think so, too. Let's visit that stall over there.

W You mean the one with the banner that says "Handmade Goods"?

M Right. It caught my eye because of 1)_____ _____. It looks like an interesting place to shop.

W Look at those three jars on the counter. They would be perfect for storing spices.

M I agree. What's that hanging on the wall behind the counter?

W It looks like a large, 2)_____ _____. It seems to be carved out of wood.

M It's beautiful. What do you think of that lantern 3)_____ _____ _____ _____ _____?

W I like it. Maybe we should get it for our garden.

M That's a great idea. It will make our garden more cheerful.

↘ 듣기 필수 표현
· catch one's eye ~의 눈길을 사로잡다

5

W Hey, Shawn. Good job with your fundraising booth yesterday. You sold so many cookies.

M Thanks, Ms. Henderson. I was happy to raise a lot of money for [1]_____ _____ _____.

W You must have been very busy, though.

M I was. I think I'll need some help when I go back to the booth today.

W I would lend a hand, but I have a meeting in an hour.

M I see. Well, is there anyone else who can work at the booth with me?

W I can ask! I'll [2]_____ _____ _____ _____ _____ to the other volunteers right away.

M Thanks for doing that.

W No problem. Oh, could you send me [3]_____ _____ _____ _____ _____?

M Sure. I saved a map that shows where the booth is. You can send the image if you want.

↘ **듣기 필수 표현**
· raise money 돈을 모으다
· go back to ~로 돌아가다
· lend a hand 도와주다

6

W Welcome to Bay Area Amusement Park. How can I help you?

M Hi. How much is a day pass to the park?

W For adults it's $30, and for children it's $20.

M Okay. Then, I'd like tickets for [1]_____ _____ and one child.

W All right. And would you like to buy fast passes with that?

M What is a fast pass?

W It allows you to move to the front of the line of some rides. They're $10 each.

M That's okay. I [2]_____ _____ _____.

W Okay, so you need two adult tickets and one child ticket.

M That's correct. I also have a coupon. Can I use it with this purchase?

W Let me see. *[Pause]* [3]_____, _____ _____. I'll take 20% off of your total.

M Great! Here's my card.

7

M Hey, Kelly. How was your weekend?

W It wasn't very fun. I had to stay home and do homework.

M Oh, no. So you didn't get to enjoy the lovely weather?

W No. It's a shame. The weather was so nice all weekend.

M Well, I have two tickets for a sunset cruise this Saturday. Would you like [1]_____ _____ _____?

W That sounds wonderful, but I can't go.

M Is it [2]_____ _____ _____ _____? Will you still be working on it?

W No. It's finished. I submitted it yesterday.

M Then, it must be because you get sick on boats.

W Actually, I love going on boat rides. But I already have [3]_____ _____ _____ _____ this weekend.

M I see. Well, let's grab dinner sometime this week instead.

W Sure, I'd love to.

↘ **듣기 필수 표현**
· It's a shame. 아쉬워.
· grab dinner 저녁을 먹다

8

W Henry, have you heard about the winter trip the French club is taking?

M No, I haven't. Can you tell me more about it?

W There's some information on their website. It sounds really fun.

M Let's see. *[Pause]* So they're [1]_____ _____ _____ for five days.

W Yeah. They're leaving on November 22nd.

M It says here that they'll be visiting some famous landmarks.

W They're [2]_____ _____, too.

M That's awesome. How much is the trip?

W It says down here that it's $750, and that includes transportation, food, and accommodations.

M Wow, that's really fair. Is it only for [3]_____ _____?

W I think so. But if not enough people sign up, they'll let others join, too.

M Okay. I'll ask my parents about it.

↘ **듣기 필수 표현**
· Have you heard about ~? ~에 대해 들어본 적 있어?
· It says here that ~. 여기에 ~라고 쓰여 있다.

9

W Attention, students. This is Ms. Nelson, the biology teacher. I'd like to remind you all about the Clean Marine Poster Contest. The contest is 1)_____ _____ _____ Pinewood High School students, so I highly encourage everyone to participate. The theme this year is "Save Our Seas." We are now accepting entries, and the submission deadline is 2)_____ _____. Contestants' posters will be hung up in the cafeteria, and students will 3)_____ _____ _____ _____ _____. The first-, second-, and third-place winners will receive cash prizes of $50, $30, and $15, respectively. The winners will be announced on World Oceans Day, which is June 8th. The first-place poster's design will be 4)_____ _____ _____ _____ given to beach-cleaning volunteers.

10

W Honey, don't you think we should change the espresso machine? Ours is too old.

M Actually, I was already looking at some new ones on Webmart.

W Hmm... *[Pause]* These look great, but I 1)_____ _____ _____ _____ more than $400 on an espresso machine.

M Fair enough. How long should the brewing time be?

W I'm happy with anything that makes espresso in 2)_____ _____ _____ _____.

M What about the cleaning function? Is that necessary?

W I do think 3)_____ _____ _____. Espresso machines are pretty hard to clean.

M It looks like we have two colors to choose from, then.

W I really like that shade of blue.

M I like it, but it doesn't go with the color of the kitchen.

W You're right. Let's 4)_____ _____ _____ _____.

M Perfect. I'll order it now.

↘ 듣기 필수 표현
· Fair enough. (생각이나 제안에 대해) 좋아, 타당해.
· go with ~과 어울리다

11

M Ma'am, here is your water. Would you like 1)_____ _____ _____ with the menu?

W No, thanks. I've already decided what I want to order.

M Okay. Then, 2)_____ _____ _____ _____ _____?

12

W Hey, John. I thought you would be at the school fair. What are you doing 1)_____ _____ _____?

M I'm printing out flyers for the jazz band's concert.

W Could I 2)_____ _____ _____ after you? I need to print my English class essay.

↘ 듣기 필수 표현
· print out ~을 출력하다

13

W I love that photo, David. Did you take it for our photography class?

M Yeah, I did. Thanks. Actually, I'm entering it in an amateur photography contest.

W I didn't know there was a contest!

M It's being sponsored by *Art of Our Times*.

W Oh, I love that magazine.

M You should 1)_____ _____ _____, too. Anyone who is not a professional photographer can participate.

W Interesting. So is there 2)_____ _____ _____?

M It's people in nature.

W Oh, so I would need to have a model in the photo?

M Well, there needs to be at least one person.

W Hmm... I usually just take photos of natural settings. I don't think I'll 3)_____ _____ _____.

M Okay, but you should know that the winner will get a free trip to Thailand.

14

M Which movie should we watch at the theater tonight, Elena?

W Here's a list of what's playing right now. Do any of them interest you?

M Hmm... What about this one? It's a [1)]_____ _____.

W You know I'm not a big fan of science fiction.

M That's right. *[Pause]* Maybe we can watch this one. It's a romantic comedy.

W That one got a lot of negative reviews, so I [2)]_____ _____ we should watch it.

M You should choose the movie, then. I'm not as picky as you are.

W All right. Then, let's watch this one! It's a horror movie.

M Are you sure about that? It looks pretty scary.

W Do you think it's a bad idea [3)]_____ _____ _____?

15

M Gina is a member of the school soccer team. She is a talented player, but she has difficulty scoring goals. During games, she frequently misses good chances to score because her shots are inaccurate. As a result, she has been [1)]_____ _____ _____ _____. These days, Gina often continues to practice even when she feels tired or sore. Her coach, Mr. Penn, has [2)]_____ _____ _____ about Gina. He thinks that her training habits are harmful. He believes that Gina should let her body recover more. So Mr. Penn wants to tell Gina that practicing so hard may cause her [3)]_____ _____ _____. In this situation, what would Mr. Penn most likely say to Gina?

↘ 듣기 필수 표현
· score a goal 골을 넣다, 득점하다
· miss a chance 기회를 놓치다
· as a result 결과적으로

16~17

W Hello, students. In class last week, we talked about why countries have certain symbols on their flags. Today, we'll learn about [1)]_____ _____ _____ _____ on them. The first is the flag of Mexico. It shows a golden eagle, which is a character in a famous Aztec legend. The second flag is that of Sri Lanka. It [2)]_____ _____ _____ _____ holding a sword. The lion is the symbol of Sri Lanka because the country's first king had this animal on his flag. Another flag with an animal on it is that of Moldova. This small country, [3)]_____ _____ _____ _____, used to have an unusual animal on its flag. Until the 1800s, it displayed the head of a bull. Finally, the flag of Dominica shows a [4)]_____ _____. This country is the only one with this type of bird on its flag. Now, let's look at some pictures of these flags.

↘ 듣기 필수 표현
· used to (과거에) ~했다

10회 영어듣기 모의고사

정답 및 해설 p.62

1번부터 17번까지는 듣고 답하는 문제입니다. 1번부터 15번까지는 한 번만 들려주고, 16번부터 17번까지는 두 번 들려줍니다. 방송을 잘 듣고 답을 하시기 바랍니다.

1 다음을 듣고, 여자가 하는 말의 목적으로 가장 적절한 것을 고르시오.

① 할 일 목록 작성의 중요성을 강조하려고
② 새로운 스마트폰 앱을 홍보하려고
③ 무료 체험 기간 변경을 예고하려고
④ 알람 설정 방법을 설명하려고
⑤ 정기 구독 취소를 요청하려고

2 대화를 듣고, 남자의 의견으로 가장 적절한 것을 고르시오.

① 아이들에게 컴퓨터 프로그래밍 학습을 시켜야 한다.
② 부모는 아이들이 원하는 것을 모두 사주면 안 된다.
③ 소액이라도 저축하면 미래에 도움이 된다.
④ 가족 구성원 모두가 집안일에 참여해야 한다.
⑤ 아이들은 어릴 때부터 돈의 가치를 배워야 한다.

3 대화를 듣고, 두 사람의 관계를 가장 잘 나타낸 것을 고르시오.

① 정형외과 직원 — 환자
② 간호사 — 방사선사
③ 치위생사 — 의사
④ 목수 — 건축가
⑤ 요리사 — 고객

4 대화를 듣고, 그림에서 대화의 내용과 일치하지 않는 것을 고르시오.

5 대화를 듣고, 남자가 할 일로 가장 적절한 것을 고르시오.

① 재스민차 사기
② 초대장 발송하기
③ 맞춤 팔찌 만들기
④ 식당 예약 전화하기
⑤ 케이크 주문하러 가기

6 대화를 듣고, 여자가 지불할 금액을 고르시오. [3점]

① $100   ② $108   ③ $120   ④ $126   ⑤ $140

7 대화를 듣고, 남자가 야구 경기에 출전할 수 없는 이유를 고르시오.

① 연습 때 부상을 당해서
② 감기가 아직 낫지 않아서
③ 수학 보충 수업이 있어서
④ 학교 연극 오디션을 봐야 해서
⑤ 사촌에게 동네를 구경시켜줘야 해서

8 대화를 듣고, 아이스 스케이팅 프로그램에 관해 언급되지 않은 것을 고르시오.

① 수업 종류   ② 수업 시각   ③ 시작 날짜
④ 준비물   ⑤ 강사 이름

9 Voices of Youth Literary Competition에 관한 다음 내용을 듣고, 일치하지 않는 것을 고르시오. [3점]

① 단편 소설, 시, 수필 중 하나를 제출하면 된다.
② 부문별 1등에게 300달러의 상금이 주어진다.
③ 우승 작품은 신문에 실릴 예정이다.
④ 작품 제출은 3월 31일 자정까지만 받는다.
⑤ 대회 규칙은 웹사이트에서 확인할 수 있다.

10 다음 표를 보면서 대화를 듣고, 두 사람이 예약할 연습실을 고르시오.

Practice Rooms

	Room	Capacity (people)	Minimum Time (hours)	Hourly Rate	Air Conditioning
①	A	1–2	1	$18	O
②	B	2–3	1	$20	X
③	C	2–3	2	$22	O
④	D	3-4	2	$24	X
⑤	E	3-4	2	$26	O

11 대화를 듣고, 여자의 마지막 말에 대한 남자의 응답으로 가장 적절한 것을 고르시오.

① There's plenty of time to eat.
② I'm not hungry at all right now.
③ You told me you had a huge lunch.
④ It will be ready in about 10 minutes.
⑤ I already finished dinner a while ago.

12 대화를 듣고, 남자의 마지막 말에 대한 여자의 응답으로 가장 적절한 것을 고르시오.

① Definitely. That sounds like a lot of fun.
② No way. The park is too crowded today.
③ Of course. I bought two tickets online.
④ Sorry. I already have plans tonight.
⑤ Really? Did you enjoy the concert?

13 대화를 듣고, 여자의 마지막 말에 대한 남자의 응답으로 가장 적절한 것을 고르시오.

Man: _____

① Sorry. We're all sold out of that item.
② Sure. I have some old books I can donate.
③ Okay. I'll put up some signs around school.
④ No, thanks. I don't need anything right now.
⑤ Amazing! You succeeded in raising a lot of money.

14 대화를 듣고, 남자의 마지막 말에 대한 여자의 응답으로 가장 적절한 것을 고르시오.

Woman: _____

① Tours at the Plant Museum start at 10 a.m.
② The job is more interesting than I thought.
③ It takes me an hour to get there by subway.
④ It's difficult to work part-time while studying.
⑤ I'm getting valuable experience at the museum.

15 다음 상황 설명을 듣고, Ava의 아버지가 Ava에게 할 말로 가장 적절한 것을 고르시오. [3점]

Ava's father: _____

① You should review the test paper to learn from your errors.
② I'm impressed that your German skills improved so fast.
③ I must have recommended the wrong subjects for you to study.
④ You'd better sign up for a higher-level German course.
⑤ It's important to double-check your answers to avoid mistakes.

[16~17] 다음을 듣고, 물음에 답하시오.

16 남자가 하는 말의 주제로 가장 적절한 것은?

① characteristics of different art forms
② the importance of clear communication
③ how art has changed throughout history
④ ways art is used to improve mental health
⑤ reasons that painting has become more popular

17 언급된 예술 활동이 <u>아닌</u> 것은?

① painting ② sculpting ③ writing
④ acting ⑤ singing

이제 듣기 문제가 끝났습니다. 채점을 마친 후 다음 페이지에서 방송을 다시 들으며 딕테이션 연습을 하시기 바랍니다.

* 채점 결과: 맞은 개수 _____ 개 / 17개   정답 및 해설 p.62

10회 Dictation

Dictation 정답 p.62

10회 영어듣기 모의고사 Dictation 음성을 들으며 빈칸에 알맞은 단어를 채워 넣으시기 바랍니다.

1

W Attention, listeners! When you're busy, do you have trouble 1)_____ _____ _____ _____? Then, the new smartphone app, List Keeper, can help! With List Keeper, you can keep your task list, shopping list, and reading list in one place. It also helps you finish the most 2)_____ _____ _____. You can set alarms for reminders of what you have to do. You can even share your to-do lists with others, so List Keeper is great for 3)_____ _____ _____. Sign up now for a free 14-day trial, and then 4)_____ _____ only $2 per month.

↘ 듣기 필수 표현
· have trouble ~하는 데 어려움을 겪다
· set an alarm 알람을 맞추다
· sign up 가입하다

2

W How was your weekend, Mark?

M Great. My daughter got a new computer, so I helped her set it up.

W I bet she was happy that you bought her a computer.

M Actually, she 1)_____ _____ _____. She's been saving up for years.

W That's amazing. Did you teach her how to save?

M Yes. I believe kids need to learn 2)_____ _____ _____ _____ from a young age.

W How did you do it? I want to teach my kids, too.

M My wife and I pay her to do chores. For example, she gets $1 every time she cleans her room, and it 3)_____ _____ _____ her piggy bank.

W I see. That sounds like a great way for children to learn about the value of money.

M Yeah, it worked for us.

↘ 듣기 필수 표현
· set up ~을 설치하다
· save up 저축하다

3

W Hello. How can I help you?

M Hi. My name is Terry Lee. I called this morning and made an appointment.

W Okay, just one moment. *[Typing sound]* Yes, you told me 1)_____ _____ _____ _____, right?

M That's right. I fell off a ladder while replacing a ceiling light. I think I sprained my left ankle.

W Do you have any other injuries?

M No, that's it.

W 2)_____ _____ _____ our clinic before?

M No. It's my first time.

W Then, please show me your ID card.

M Here it is.

W Okay. Registration 3)_____ _____. We'll give you an X-ray first. Then, you'll be able to see the doctor.

M All right. Thanks.

↘ 듣기 필수 표현
· make an appointment 예약하다
· fall off ~에서 떨어지다

4

W Hey, Luke. I went to the new café near our school to study last night.

M How was it? I haven't 1)_____ _____ _____.

W I'll show you a picture. *[Pause]* Doesn't it look nice?

M Yes. It looks cozy. Look at the sleeping cat on the counter.

W It's so cute. And the bookshelf on the right made the café feel 2)_____ _____ _____.

M It looks like a great place for studying. I like those striped curtains.

W I thought they were stylish. And isn't that a cool lamp on the table?

M Yeah. That square clock on the wall is beautiful, too.

W Oh, yes. It was useful for keeping track of the time.

M Let me know if you 3)_____ _____ _____ _____. I want to join you.

W Sounds good.

↘ 듣기 필수 표현
· keep track of ~을 관리하다, 기록하다

5

W Hi, Aaron. I can't wait for Irene's surprise birthday party on Sunday.

M Me neither. She's going to be shocked. Did you 1)_____ _____ _____ _____?

W Irene loves seafood, so I booked a room at the Seaside Kitchen.

M Perfect. How many of us will there be?

W There will be 10 people in total.

M Great. Have you found a present for her yet?

W Actually, I 2)_____ _____ _____ _____ during my jewelry-making class. It has her initials on it.

M What a special gift! I got her some of her favorite jasmine tea.

W She'll love that.

M I hope so. Oh, should we order a cake for her? There's a great bakery near my house.

W Okay. Do you mind 3)_____ _____ _____ it?

M Not at all. I'll drop by soon.

↘ 듣기 필수 표현
· Do you mind ~? 괜찮다면 ~해줄래?
· drop by 들르다

6

M Welcome to Wild Water World. Are you here to enjoy our outdoor pools and water slides?

W Yes. How much are tickets?

M It's 1)_____ _____ _____ and $20 for children.

W Okay. We have two adults and two children in our group.

M All right. Also, we have a special promotion going on this weekend. Our lunch buffet tickets are $10 for adults and 2)_____ _____ _____ _____.

W That sounds good. Can I pay for those now, too?

M Certainly. So you want admission and lunch tickets for two adults and two children.

W Right. And I have this coupon. Is it 3)_____ _____ _____?

M You're lucky. Today's the last day you can use it. So you'll get 10% off the total.

W Great. I'll pay with my credit card.

↘ 듣기 필수 표현
· pay with one's credit card 신용 카드로 지불하다

7

W How was baseball practice, Jay? I'm looking forward to watching you play tomorrow.

M Hi, Cindy. Practice was good, but I 1)_____ _____ _____ tomorrow.

W Really? That's too bad.

M I know. But it's out of my control.

W Is it because you're still not 2)_____ _____ _____ your cold?

M No. I'm much better now, except for the occasional cough.

W I remember your cousin is visiting from Calgary. You must be busy showing him around our town, right?

M No. That's not why. I'm 3)_____ _____ the school play tomorrow.

W Oh, that's cool. Good luck with that.

M Thanks. See you later in math class.

W Okay. See you.

↘ 듣기 필수 표현
· out of one's control 제어할 수 없는
· except for ~을 제외하고는
· show A around B A에게 B를 구경시켜 주다

8

M Helen, what are you looking at?

W It's a pamphlet 1)_____ _____ _____ at the community center, Dad.

M Is there anything that looks interesting?

W Yeah. I'm interested in the ice-skating program.

M Let's see here. *[Pause]* They offer beginner and intermediate classes for speed skating. There's also a figure-skating class for advanced skaters.

W Well... I've only skated a few times before, so I should 2)_____ _____ _____ _____.

M It's every Wednesday evening at 7 p.m.

W That works for me. When does it start?

M It starts on January 4th and runs for eight weeks.

W Okay. Is there anything I need to bring?

M You just need a pair of ice skates. They also 3)_____ _____ _____ _____.

W Great. I can't wait to start!

↘ 듣기 필수 표현
· look at ~을 보다
· be interested in ~에 관심이 있다

9

W Good morning, students. This is your principal Ms. Crawley with a special announcement. We are now accepting submissions for the Voices of Youth Literary Competition. All students ¹⁾_____ _____ _____ _____ one of their best short stories, poems, or essays. The first-place winner in each of the three categories will be awarded ²⁾_____ _____ _____ of $500. The winners will also ³⁾_____ _____ _____ _____ in the Glendale County newspaper. Submissions will be accepted online until midnight on March 31st. Please check the Voices of Youth website for full contest rules and ⁴⁾_____ _____ in each category.

↘ 듣기 필수 표현
· be awarded (상을) 받다

10

M Amy, we need to book a practice room for tonight. Our dance performance is tomorrow.

W I know. There aren't many available now. We should have booked it earlier.

M But there are still ¹⁾_____ _____ _____ _____. It just needs to be large enough for the three of us.

W Right. How long do we need to practice for?

M We need it for at least two hours.

W Okay. How much money can we spend?

M ²⁾_____ _____ _____ per hour is fine.

W All right. That leaves us with two options. Oh, it looks like only this one has air conditioning.

M We definitely ³⁾_____ _____ _____. It'll be so hot.

W Then, we should book that one.

M Perfect. Let me call right now.

↘ 듣기 필수 표현
· at least 적어도

11

W Honey, I skipped lunch today. Now, I'm ¹⁾_____ _____.

M I'm making spaghetti and meatballs for dinner. Can you ²⁾_____ _____ _____ _____?

W Of course. Will it take a long time?

↘ 듣기 필수 표현
· skip lunch 점심을 거르다
· take a long time 오래 걸리다

12

M Nancy, do you ¹⁾_____ _____ _____ for Saturday evening?

W No. I was just going to stay home and watch TV. Why?

M There's a free pop concert in Oak Park. We ²⁾_____ _____ _____.

↘ 듣기 필수 표현
· stay home 집에 머물다

13

W Jordan, I'm so glad I found you.

M Hey, Amber. What's up?

W I need help putting up these signs.

M I can help. What are the signs for?

W Our ¹⁾_____ _____ is holding a flea market next Saturday. We are donating the money that we raise to the children's hospital.

M Wow, cool. What time is the flea market?

W It'll start at 10 a.m. and finish at 4 p.m.

M Then, I can participate. Where did you ²⁾_____ _____ _____ you are selling?

W We're collecting them from our teachers and other students. Do you have ³⁾_____ _____ _____? We would really appreciate it.

↘ 듣기 필수 표현
· put up ~을 세우다, 설치하다

14

M Hi, Bailey. I haven't seen you ¹⁾_____ _____ _____!

W Hey, Jake. I know! I've been so busy. I started a part-time job a few weeks ago.

M How is it going?

W It's been pretty good. I'm a tour guide.

M Oh, that sounds like a nice job. Where are you ²⁾_____ _____ _____?

W I work at the Plant Museum.

M Isn't that located next to Lake Park downtown?

W Right. It's ³⁾_____ _____ _____ my house.

M Tell me about it. So what is your commute like?

15

W Ava is taking a German language class this semester at her high school. Ava's father worked in Germany for a long time, so he ¹⁾_____ _____ _____ her. Ava accepted, believing that the lessons would help her get a good grade in the class. Today, however, Ava found out that she ²⁾_____ _____ _____ for the German class. Ava seems very disappointed and says that she is surprised that she failed. In response, Ava's father wants to tell her to ³⁾_____ _____ _____ _____ _____ so she can find out what mistakes she made. In this situation, what would Ava's father most likely say to Ava?

↘ **듣기 필수 표현**
· get a good grade 좋은 성적을 받다
· in response 이에 대해

16~17

M Good evening, everyone. I'm Damien Grey, founder of the Roseberry Art Institute. Art ¹⁾_____ _____ _____ thousands of years. Today in our lecture series, we'll be discussing how doctors can use art activities when they treat mental problems. First, they can use painting to ²⁾_____ _____ _____ who don't speak out about their difficulties. Second, sculpting can be helpful. For example, patients with depression show improvement when they participate in this activity. Third, acting can be ³⁾_____ _____ _____ as well. Acting therapy involves role play and storytelling to help people recognize their problems and solve them. Lastly, singing is used because it lets people express their feelings through lyrics and sound. In these ways, it allows people to communicate their thoughts and emotions when words alone fail, and this can ⁴⁾_____ _____ _____. I hope you found today's talk interesting. Please join us again next week. Thank you.

↘ **듣기 필수 표현**
· speak out 밝히다, 말하다
· participate in ~에 참여하다

▲ 문제 음성 바로 듣기
▲ 고사장 버전 바로 듣기

정답 및 해설 p.68

1번부터 17번까지는 듣고 답하는 문제입니다. 1번부터 15번까지는 한 번만 들려주고, 16번부터 17번까지는 두 번 들려줍니다. 방송을 잘 듣고 답을 하시기 바랍니다.

1 다음을 듣고, 남자가 하는 말의 목적으로 가장 적절한 것을 고르시오.

① 빙판길 안전 운전 방법을 설명하려고
② 자동차 타이어 교체 비용을 안내하려고
③ 보행자 무단횡단 금지를 당부하려고
④ 신호등 교체 공사 일정을 공지하려고
⑤ 눈길 교통사고 소식을 전달하려고

2 대화를 듣고, 여자의 의견으로 가장 적절한 것을 고르시오.

① 정치인들은 지역 주민의 이익을 대변해야 한다.
② 선거 가능 연령을 낮출 필요가 있다.
③ 전자투표를 도입하면 투표율을 높일 수 있다.
④ 유권자는 공약을 확인하고 투표해야 한다.
⑤ 모든 시민은 반드시 투표에 참여해야 한다.

3 대화를 듣고, 두 사람의 관계를 가장 잘 나타낸 것을 고르시오.

① 택시 운전사 — 탑승객
② 호텔 지배인 — 투숙객
③ 부동산 중개인 — 집주인
④ 배관 수리공 — 의뢰인
⑤ 아파트 관리소장 — 방문객

4 대화를 듣고, 그림에서 대화의 내용과 일치하지 않는 것을 고르시오.

5 대화를 듣고, 남자가 할 일로 가장 적절한 것을 고르시오.

① 의자 옮기기
② 책장 설치하기
③ 구연동화 하기
④ 방문객 안내하기
⑤ 반납 도서 정리하기

6 대화를 듣고, 여자가 지불할 금액을 고르시오. [3점]

① $90   ② $100   ③ $110   ④ $120   ⑤ $130

7 대화를 듣고, 남자가 함께 영화를 보러 갈 수 없는 이유를 고르시오.

① 수학 공부를 해야 해서
② 밴드부 연습에 참여해야 해서
③ 가족과 시간을 보내기로 해서
④ 뮤지컬을 보러 가야 해서
⑤ 친구 선물을 사야 해서

8 대화를 듣고, Eastwood Comics Fair에 관해 언급되지 않은 것을 고르시오.

① 개최 장소   ② 개최일   ③ 입장료
④ 참여 만화가   ⑤ 주관사

9 Young Musicians Concert Series에 관한 다음 내용을 듣고, 일치하지 않는 것을 고르시오. [3점]

① 매주 공연이 진행된다.
② 마지막 공연은 10월 2일에 열린다.
③ 공연자 명단은 웹사이트에 올라온다.
④ 입장권은 온라인에서만 구매할 수 있다.
⑤ 지역 주민은 할인을 받을 수 있다.

10 다음 표를 보면서 대화를 듣고, 여자가 등록할 요가 강좌를 고르시오.

Workout World Yoga Classes

	Class	Level	Start Time	Days
①	A	Beginner	7 p.m.	Mondays & Thursdays
②	B	Intermediate	1 p.m.	Tuesdays & Fridays
③	C	Intermediate	10 a.m.	Mondays & Thursdays
④	D	Intermediate	3 p.m.	Mondays & Thursdays
⑤	E	Advanced	11 a.m.	Tuesdays & Fridays

11 대화를 듣고, 여자의 마지막 말에 대한 남자의 응답으로 가장 적절한 것을 고르시오.

① Sure. It's on the corner of Main Street.
② Never mind. I'll visit the store in person.
③ Right. They sell various kinds of rice cakes.
④ No problem. The bookstore opens at 10 a.m.
⑤ Thanks. I'm glad to know about the relocation.

12 대화를 듣고, 남자의 마지막 말에 대한 여자의 응답으로 가장 적절한 것을 고르시오.

① Okay. I should return the swimsuit.
② I'm sorry. I don't feel like swimming today.
③ You're right. You missed the registration date.
④ Perfect. I really enjoyed going to the beach.
⑤ Great plan. We'll have a lot of fun together.

13 대화를 듣고, 여자의 마지막 말에 대한 남자의 응답으로 가장 적절한 것을 고르시오.

Man: _____

① Really? I couldn't find anything to buy.
② Sure. Let me just finish washing the windows.
③ I'm not sure. Where would we park the car, then?
④ Got it. There should be many items for a yard sale.
⑤ I understand. That's a lot of work for you to do alone.

14 대화를 듣고, 남자의 마지막 말에 대한 여자의 응답으로 가장 적절한 것을 고르시오.

Woman: _____

① No. The tickets will cost $15 each.
② Sure. Remind me before you leave.
③ Okay. Be sure to prepare dinner when I return.
④ Of course. I'm so excited to try the rides there.
⑤ Sorry. I should not have spent so much money on snacks.

15 다음 상황 설명을 듣고, Josh가 Emma에게 할 말로 가장 적절한 것을 고르시오. [3점]

Josh: _____

① You should ask your friend to leave.
② Can you hear my TV in your apartment?
③ I'll try my best not to make a lot of noise.
④ Would you mind turning down the volume?
⑤ What is the TV program that you are watching?

[16~17] 다음을 듣고, 물음에 답하시오.

16 여자가 하는 말의 주제로 가장 적절한 것은?

① who is responsible for global warming
② the impact of climate change on animals
③ how the rise in temperatures can be stopped
④ the effects of rising sea levels on plants
⑤ the advantages of protecting wildlife

17 언급된 동물이 <u>아닌</u> 것은?

① polar bear   ② sea turtle
③ Arctic fox   ④ African cheetah
⑤ giant panda

이제 듣기 문제가 끝났습니다. 채점을 마친 후 다음 페이지에서 방송을 다시 들으며 딕테이션 연습을 하시기 바랍니다.

* 채점 결과: 맞은 개수 _____개 / 17개   정답 및 해설 p.68

11회 영어듣기 모의고사 Dictation 음성을 들으며 빈칸에 알맞은 단어를 채워 넣으시기 바랍니다.

1

M Good morning. This is Chief Anthony Walker of the Brownsville Police Department. With winter approaching, I wanted to give everyone some tips for 1)_____ _____ _____ _____. To begin with, make sure that you have proper winter tires on your vehicle. This will greatly reduce your chances of 2)_____ _____ _____ _____. Also, take care when approaching intersections. Follow the traffic lights, and watch for any 3)_____ _____ _____. Finally, do not speed. Drive slowly and carefully because you never know when the road will become slippery. I hope all of you have a safe winter on the road.

↘ 듣기 필수 표현
· to begin with 우선
· take care 주의하다

2

M Hi, Samantha. I haven't seen you in a while. How are you doing?

W I'm fine, Dale. But I don't have much time to chat right now. I'm in a bit of a hurry.

M Where are you going?

W I need to vote for the 1)_____ _____ _____. I have plans tonight, so I want to do this during my lunch break.

M Oh, I forgot that was today. Honestly, voting is too 2)_____ _____ _____ _____.

W Don't tell me you're not planning to vote today. You have to cast your vote.

M It doesn't matter if I do or not. One vote won't 3)_____ _____ _____.

W But it's the responsibility of all citizens to vote.

M I guess you're right. Could I come with you?

W Of course. Let's go now.

↘ 듣기 필수 표현
· in a hurry 급하게, 서둘러
· vote for ~를 뽑다, ~에게 투표하다
· Don't tell me ~. 설마 ~이라는 건 아니겠지.
· cast one's vote 투표하다, 한 표를 행사하다

3

M Good morning. I'm sorry I'm late. The traffic was quite heavy.

W No problem. I'm just glad you came.

M You said you were having a problem with your kitchen sink?

W Actually, it's the one in my bathroom. It 1)_____ _____.

M When did this start?

W Last week. I tried fixing it myself, but it began leaking again yesterday. So I decided to 2)_____ _____ _____.

M I see. It sounds like I will need to replace the pipe under the sink.

W Will that take very long?

M It will depend on the type of pipe. If I have to 3)_____ _____ _____, you will need to wait a couple of days.

W Got it. I'll show you where the bathroom is.

4

M Anna, what do you think of my new home office?

W You 1)_____ _____ _____ really well, Brian. I like the two plants on your desk.

M Thanks. What about the painting of the mountain above the desk?

W It looks great. What is in the 2)_____ _____ _____ the desk?

M That's where I keep all my important work documents.

W How convenient! I'm not sure about the curtains on the window, though. The 3)_____ _____ _____ _____.

M I know. But they were a gift from a friend, so I don't want to take them down.

W That's understandable. Why did you hang 4)_____ _____ _____ _____?

M It's because I like a bright room so I don't strain my eyes.

W Good idea. Well, I think you have an amazing workspace.

M Thanks!

5

W Greg, are you ready to work at the library? It's your first day.

M I am, Ms. Denson.

W Great. Usually, new staff members have to put away 1)_____ _____. But we have already finished that today.

M I see. Maybe I could help visitors find the books they need, then.

W Actually, I have something else for you to do. We are setting up a children's reading room on the second floor.

M What should I do, specifically?

W The tables and chairs were moved there yesterday, but we still need to 2)_____ _____ _____. Could you help with that?

M Of course. I'd be happy to.

W Wonderful. Let's 3)_____ _____ _____ _____ _____ now so I can show you what to do.

↘ 듣기 필수 표현
· put away ~을 치우다, 정리하다

6

M Hello. Are you looking for anything in particular today?

W Yeah. I'm going on a camping trip with some friends next week, so I need to buy a tent.

M This model is one of our most popular tents. It's 1)_____ _____ and very easy to set up.

W How much is it?

M The 2)_____ _____ _____ _____, and the four-person model is $120.

W The one for two people should be fine.

M Okay. Oh, I forgot to mention that we are having a sale, so you'll 3)_____ _____ _____ _____ the tent.

W Great! Also, do you sell camping lanterns?

M We do. These lanterns are $10 each.

W Perfect. I'll take two of them.

M Do you need anything else?

W No. That's it.

↘ 듣기 필수 표현
· in particular 특별히
· That's it. 그게 다예요.

7

W Hi, Paul. How do you think you did on the math test today?

M Pretty good. I studied a lot for it.

W Me too. I was thinking of going to a movie tonight to relax. Do you want to come?

M I'm sorry, but I can't.

W Oh, you have 1)_____ _____ on Friday evenings, right?

M Actually, that's on Thursdays.

W Then, are you 2)_____ _____ _____ your family?

M No. I'm going to see a musical tonight. It's a very popular show, so I'm happy that I managed to get a ticket.

W Great. I hope you 3)_____ _____ _____.

M Thank you. I'll tell you all about it on Monday.

↘ 듣기 필수 표현
· manage to 간신히 ~하다

8

M What are you looking at, Denise?

W It's a brochure for the Eastwood Comics Fair.

M Interesting. Are you planning on going?

W Yeah. It's being held in New York City. I'll be visiting friends there the same day.

M That's great. When will it 1)_____ _____?

W It starts on June 12th. I'll probably only go on the first day.

M Are tickets expensive?

W Not really. 2)_____ _____ _____ is $35.

M That's reasonable. Who is 3)_____ _____ _____?

W A company called New Horizons. It operates a chain of comic-book stores across the country.

M Well, I hope you have a great time at the fair.

W Thanks a lot.

↘ 듣기 필수 표현
· across the country 전국적으로

9

W If you don't have ¹⁾_____ _____ _____ _____ this autumn, why don't you attend the Young Musicians Concert Series? Every week, Milton Hall will be ²⁾_____ _____ _____ with young musicians from the city. The first concert will ³⁾_____ _____ _____ October 2nd. For the last concert, the pianist Matthew Livingston will be performing. A list of performers and their show dates will be posted on our website. Tickets are only sold online. You can get a ticket at a discounted price if you are ⁴⁾_____ _____ _____. Thank you.

10

[Telephone rings.]

M Thank you for calling Workout World. How can I help you today?

W Hi. I'm ¹⁾_____ _____ _____ a yoga class.

M Well, we have a beginner class that is very popular.

W Oh, I've been doing yoga for a while, so I don't want to take a low-level class.

M Okay. We also offer ²⁾_____ _____ _____ classes.

W Great. I'll take an intermediate class. But I can't join a morning class because I'm busy before noon.

M All right. Um, all of our classes meet two days a week. Either on Mondays and Thursdays or Tuesdays and Fridays.

W Tuesdays and Fridays will work for me. I have a ³⁾_____ _____ _____ on Mondays.

M In that case, there is one class that meets your requirements.

W Great. I'd like to sign up for it now.

↘ **듣기 필수 표현**
· either A or B A거나 B인
· in that case 그렇다면, 그런 경우에는

11

W Pardon me. I'm looking for Delight Rice Cakes. Its website says it's ¹⁾_____ _____ _____ the bookstore, but I can't see it.

M Oh, that store has moved to another place.

W Really? Can you give me directions if you ²⁾_____ _____ _____ _____?

↘ **듣기 필수 표현**
· Pardon me. 실례합니다.
· give directions 길을 알려주다

12

M Louise, you're going to ¹⁾_____ _____ _____, right?

W Yes. I'm really looking forward to them. I already bought a swimsuit and goggles.

M That's good. Maybe I should ²⁾_____ _____ _____ _____ lessons as you.

↘ **듣기 필수 표현**
· look forward to ~을 기대하다

13

W Honey, do you have any plans today?

M No. Why?

W I want to do some spring cleaning. It would be great if you could help me.

M Sure. What do you want me to do?

W Well, I was going to begin by washing the windows. Maybe you could ¹⁾_____ _____ _____.

M Of course. We have a lot of stuff stored in there.

W Right. There is ²⁾_____ _____ _____ for the car, now.

M I agree. But I'm not sure where to put everything.

W What do you think about having a yard sale?

M You mean we should sell the items in the garage?

W That's it! You need to figure out ³⁾_____ _____ while cleaning.

↘ **듣기 필수 표현**
· figure out ~을 알아내다

14

M Mom, can I go to Thrill Land with my friends this weekend?

W Is that the 1)_____ _____ _____ that opened last month?

M Right. Michael got three tickets from his parents, so he invited Miles and me.

W How will you get there?

M By bus. It should 2)_____ _____ _____ _____.

W I see. What time will you be home?

M We are planning to leave there at 5 p.m., so I should be back before dinner.

W That's fine, then. Just make sure to call me if you are going to be late.

M Thanks, Mom. Um, could I have some money to 3)_____ _____ _____ that day?

↘ 듣기 필수 표현
· make sure to 꼭 ~하다

15

M Josh and Emma live in the same apartment building. Josh's apartment is 1)_____ _____ Emma's. Emma is watching a TV program with a friend late at night. Unfortunately, the TV is very loud, and Josh hears it easily in his apartment. He has to wake up early in the morning for 2)_____ _____ _____, but he cannot sleep because of the noise. So Josh wants to ask Emma to 3)_____ _____ _____ _____.
In this situation, what would Josh most likely say to Emma?

↘ 듣기 필수 표현
· wake up 일어나다

16~17

W Hello, everyone. In our class last week, I explained why global warming is happening. This afternoon, I want to look at its 1)_____ _____ _____. The most typical example of this is the polar bear. As the Arctic sea ice melts, it becomes hard for polar bears to 2)_____ _____ _____ _____. The sea turtle is another creature facing great hardship. Global warming has caused sea levels to rise, destroying sea turtles' nesting areas on beaches. Next, the African cheetah is particularly vulnerable to climate change. It lives in areas with little water, so the droughts resulting from higher temperatures 3)_____ _____ _____. Finally, the giant panda is another animal that is at risk. The problem is that bamboo, its main source of food, is sensitive to changes in the climate. The plant may die off if 4)_____ _____ _____ _____, and then the panda won't have anything to eat. Now, let's watch a brief video about these animals.

↘ 듣기 필수 표현
· vulnerable to ~에 취약한
· result from ~에서 비롯하다, ~이 원인이다
· at risk 위험에 처한
· sensitive to ~에 민감한
· die off (하나도 남지 않을 때까지) 차례로 죽어가다

12회 영어듣기 모의고사

정답 및 해설 p.74

1번부터 17번까지는 듣고 답하는 문제입니다. 1번부터 15번까지는 한 번만 들려주고, 16번부터 17번까지는 두 번 들려줍니다. 방송을 잘 듣고 답을 하시기 바랍니다.

1 다음을 듣고, 여자가 하는 말의 목적으로 가장 적절한 것을 고르시오.

① 개교기념일 행사 취소를 알리려고
② 글짓기 대회 개최에 대해 공지하려고
③ 이타적인 자세의 중요성을 강조하려고
④ 작문 과제의 마감일 변경을 안내하려고
⑤ 봉사활동 동아리 회원을 모집하려고

2 대화를 듣고, 남자의 의견으로 가장 적절한 것을 고르시오.

① 학생들은 교내 운동부 활동을 해야 한다.
② 잘하는 일을 함으로써 자신감을 얻을 수 있다.
③ 연습은 기량을 쌓기 위한 최선의 방법이다.
④ 학생들의 건강을 위해 학교 체육 시간을 늘려야 한다.
⑤ 힘들다는 이유로 좋아하는 일을 포기해서는 안 된다.

3 대화를 듣고, 두 사람의 관계를 가장 잘 나타낸 것을 고르시오.

① 화가 — 미술관장
② 박물관 직원 — 방문객
③ 여행 가이드 — 관광객
④ 식당 종업원 — 손님
⑤ 주방장 — 수산물 시장 상인

4 대화를 듣고, 그림에서 대화의 내용과 일치하지 않는 것을 고르시오.

5 대화를 듣고, 남자가 할 일로 가장 적절한 것을 고르시오.

① 여행 가방 싸기
② 호텔에 예약 확인하기
③ 셔틀버스 좌석 예약하기
④ 공항 장기주차료 알아보기
⑤ 유로화로 환전하기

6 대화를 듣고, 여자가 지불할 금액을 고르시오. [3점]

① $8   ② $15   ③ $17   ④ $18   ⑤ $20

7 대화를 듣고, 남자가 함께 쇼핑하러 갈 수 없는 이유를 고르시오.

① 농구 경기를 보러 가야 해서
② 겨울옷을 이미 구매해서
③ 아르바이트를 해야 해서
④ 수학 시험공부를 해야 해서
⑤ 친구와 저녁 약속이 있어서

8 대화를 듣고, Landford Garden Show에 관해 언급되지 않은 것을 고르시오.

① 날짜   ② 장소   ③ 입장료
④ 행사 순서   ⑤ 참여업체 수

9 Topics of Interest 강연 시리즈에 관한 다음 내용을 듣고, 일치하지 않는 것을 고르시오. [3점]

① 일주일에 세 번 강연이 열린다.
② 강연이 끝나면 질의응답 시간이 있을 것이다.
③ 참석자들은 다음 달 강연에 관한 소책자를 받았다.
④ 오늘 강연의 주제는 기후 변화이다.
⑤ 오늘의 강연자는 Anne Johnson이다.

10 다음 표를 보면서 대화를 듣고, 남자가 구매할 컴퓨터용 헤드셋을 고르시오.

Computer Headphones

	Model	Price	Material	Microphone	Color
①	A	$52	Plastic	X	Green
②	B	$49	Plastic	X	Green
③	C	$45	Metal	X	Purple
④	D	$41	Metal	O	Purple
⑤	E	$38	Metal	O	Red

11 대화를 듣고, 여자의 마지막 말에 대한 남자의 응답으로 가장 적절한 것을 고르시오.

① Can you help me hang the poster?
② Fill out this application form, then.
③ I'm so happy to have you join the choir.
④ I'll see you at the audition this Saturday.
⑤ We really need someone to play the piano.

12 대화를 듣고, 남자의 마지막 말에 대한 여자의 응답으로 가장 적절한 것을 고르시오.

① Why did you decide to buy that one?
② Could you let me borrow yours for the day?
③ I can give you a 10% discount on the final price.
④ It was much more expensive than I expected.
⑤ I'll send you the store's name and address.

13 대화를 듣고, 여자의 마지막 말에 대한 남자의 응답으로 가장 적절한 것을 고르시오.

Man: _____

① I'd prefer to take the train that departs at 1.
② Could you confirm my seat number, please?
③ Then, I'll take one ticket for the 3 p.m. train.
④ What is the reason for the unexpected delay?
⑤ I believe the schedule may not be accurate.

14 대화를 듣고, 남자의 마지막 말에 대한 여자의 응답으로 가장 적절한 것을 고르시오.

Woman: _____

① No worries. I already turned in my report.
② Okay. I'll go to the teachers' office right now.
③ You're right. I need to rest more to get better.
④ I'm not sure. Why did she miss class yesterday?
⑤ I agree. You should check the attendance record.

15 다음 상황 설명을 듣고, Chloe가 Noah에게 할 말로 가장 적절한 것을 고르시오. [3점]

Chloe: _____

① Why don't we hold rehearsals on weekdays instead of weekends?
② Do you think we have enough time to prepare for the performance?
③ Thank you for creating a schedule of the class's rehearsals.
④ I'd like to put on the play earlier than originally planned.
⑤ We should meet fewer times a week for rehearsals.

[16~17] 다음을 듣고, 물음에 답하시오.

16 남자가 하는 말의 주제로 가장 적절한 것은?

① common sources of cholesterol
② natural treatments for heart disease
③ a condition caused by food allergies
④ foods that prevent heart problems
⑤ healthy methods to cook food

17 언급된 식재료가 아닌 것은?

① broccoli ② brown rice ③ sugar
④ beef ⑤ butter

이제 듣기 문제가 끝났습니다. 채점을 마친 후 다음 페이지에서 방송을 다시 들으며 딕테이션 연습을 하시기 바랍니다.

* 채점 결과: 맞은 개수 _____ 개 / 17개

정답 및 해설 p.74

12회 Dictation

Dictation 정답 p.74

12회 영어듣기 모의고사 Dictation 음성을 들으며 빈칸에 알맞은 단어를 채워 넣으시기 바랍니다.

1

W May I have your attention, please? Kenwood High School is celebrating its 15th anniversary next month. We have a lot of 1)_____ _____, and I'd like to add one more, an essay writing contest. The topic of the essay is helping others, and it should be 500 to 700 words in length. The 2)_____ _____ _____ _____. The judges will be our three English teachers and a special guest. I bet some of you are fans of this guest. We will 3)_____ _____ _____ _____ before the winners are announced. The grand prize is $200. Thank you.

2

M Hi, Sarah. Joel and I are going to a café after school today. Do you want to come with us?

W I'd love to, but I can't.

M Why not?

W I joined the school's 1)_____ _____. I have practice this afternoon.

M That's great. You've always wanted to play on the volleyball team.

W To be honest, I'm 2)_____ _____ _____. The coach is really demanding, and we practice four times a week. It's a lot 3)_____ _____ _____ _____.

M You shouldn't give up on something you enjoy just because it's difficult.

W You really think so?

M Of course. Overcoming difficulties can make you 4)_____ _____ _____.

W I guess you're right. Thanks for the advice.

↘ 듣기 필수 표현
· to be honest 솔직히 말하면
· give up on ~을 포기하다

3

M Do you have a question?

W Yes. Could you tell me 1)_____ _____ _____ this art gallery?

M We'll leave in about 30 minutes. We're going to listen to the artist talk about his paintings first.

W And we'll be going to the National Museum after this?

M That's right. Why? Is there a problem?

W I checked the schedule you handed out on the tour bus this morning. But I couldn't find information 2)_____ _____ _____ _____.

M Oh, we'll get some lunch after I finish showing the group around the museum.

W Where will we be eating?

M I made a reservation at a famous local restaurant. I'm sure everyone will enjoy their seafood.

W Great. Thanks for all your effort. You've really 3)_____ _____ _____ _____.

↘ 듣기 필수 표현
· hand out ~을 나눠주다
· show A around B A에게 B를 구경시켜 주다

4

M Natalie, are you done setting up your booth for our school's science fair?

W I just finished, Mr. Parker. What do you think?

M It looks great. Are those models of volcanoes on the two tables 1)_____ _____ _____ _____ the booth?

W Right. And the poster on the wall to the left shows a volcano erupting.

M That's very interesting. And I see you put a big banner that says "Volcanoes" on the wall behind the table.

W That's correct. I want to make sure everyone knows my topic.

M What is the 2)_____ _____ _____ the banner for?

W Oh, I marked where several famous volcanoes are located.

M Wonderful. What is that 3)_____ _____ in the picture on the right wall?

W It's called a *dol hareubang*. It's a traditional Korean sculpture made from volcanic rock.

5

W Honey, we still have a lot to do before we leave for Paris.

M But we've already 1)_____ _____ _____. I think we're almost ready to go.

W Well, I want to contact our hotel to 2)_____ _____.

M Oh, I didn't think about that. Good idea.

W When I do that, I'll also book us seats on the hotel's airport shuttle bus.

M What can I do to help?

W Could you visit the airport website and find out how 3)_____ _____ _____ _____ ?

M Of course. I'll take care of that now.

W Did you remember to exchange some money? We'll need euros in Paris.

M Don't worry. I did that already.

↘ 듣기 필수 표현
· find out ~을 알아보다
· take care of ~을 처리하다
· exchange money 환전하다

6

M Welcome to Food Express. How can I help you today?

W I'd 1)_____ _____ _____ of French fries, please.

M Of course. Which size would you like? A large is $6, and a small is $5.

W I'll get two large fries and one small.

M Sure. And would you like 2)_____ _____ _____ that?

W Yes. How much is a large cola?

M That'll be $3.

W I'll get one of those, then.

M Would you like to pay with cash or a credit card?

W Cash, please. Oh, I almost forgot. I have 3)_____ _____ _____ 10% off.

M Okay. I'll ring your order up now.

↘ 듣기 필수 표현
· ring ~ up ~을 계산해주다

7

W Billy, Walton's Department Store is 1)_____ _____ _____ _____. All of its winter jackets are 40% off.

M That's good to hear. I need to buy a new coat.

W Do you want to go shopping together on Sunday?

M I'd love to, but I'm going to be busy that day.

W Too bad. Will you be 2)_____ _____ _____ _____ _____ ?

M No. I only work on Saturdays.

W I see. I guess you need to prepare for the big math test on Monday, then.

M Actually, I'm ready for that. My dad got tickets for the 3)_____ _____ _____ on Sunday. We're going together.

W Lucky you. I heard tickets were really hard to get.

M Yeah. There will be a lot of people at the game.

W Okay. Have fun.

↘ 듣기 필수 표현
· Too bad. 안됐다.
· Lucky you. 잘됐네.

8

M Nora, you enjoy gardening, right?

W Yeah. It's been my hobby for several years now. Why?

M The third annual Landford Garden Show is on May 15th. 1)_____ _____ _____ _____ you'd like to go with me.

W That sounds like fun. Where is it being held?

M At the Linden Conference Center. We can get there by subway.

W Great. How much are the tickets?

M They are 2)_____ _____. But I got a couple of free tickets from my company, so you don't have to pay anything.

W Wow. Thank you so much.

M No problem. This year's event should be really amazing. 3)_____ _____ _____ are participating.

W I can't wait. Thanks again for inviting me.

↘ 듣기 필수 표현
· I can't wait. 너무 기대돼.

9

W Welcome to our center's *Topics of Interest* series of lectures. As you know, we will be ¹⁾_____ _____ _____ _____ _____ to attend a lecture. After each lecture, there will be a question-and-answer session. You each have a brochure that ²⁾_____ _____ _____ on the 12 lectures for this month. Our topic for today is climate change. Rising global temperatures pose a significant threat to all life on our planet. We will look at the causes of this problem and ³⁾_____ _____ _____ them. We hope you will enjoy today's lecture. Now, I'd like to present Anne Johnson, our lecturer.

↘ 듣기 필수 표현
· pose a threat to ~에 위협이 되다

10

W Honey, have you decided what Christmas present to get your nephew Craig yet?

M He mentioned that he needs a new pair of headphones for his computer. I was just looking at some models online.

W Let me see... Some of those are quite expensive.

M Yeah, I guess I shouldn't ¹⁾_____ _____ _____ $50. We have a lot of gifts to buy this year.

W Right. And don't get a pair made of plastic. That material breaks very easily.

M That's a good point.

W Do you think he will ²⁾_____ _____ _____?

M Absolutely. He likes to chat with his friends while they play games together.

W Well, that leaves you with a couple of options to choose from.

M I think I'll ³⁾_____ _____ _____ _____ headphones. That's his favorite color.

↘ 듣기 필수 표현
· made of ~으로 만들어진
· Absolutely. 물론이지.

11

W Mr. Baker, I saw on a poster that the City Choir is ¹⁾_____ _____ _____.

M Oh, right. We'll ²⁾_____ _____ _____ this Friday to pick four sopranos. Are you interested?

W Yes. I'd like to participate in it.

↘ 듣기 필수 표현
· participate in ~에 참여하다

12

M Is that a new backpack, Beth?

W Yeah. I got it on sale yesterday. It only ¹⁾_____ _____ _____.

M I need one as well. Could you tell me ²⁾_____ _____ _____ it?

↘ 듣기 필수 표현
· as well ~도, 역시

13

W Next in line, please.

M Hi. Could you tell me what time the train for London departs?

W Well, we have one scheduled for 1 p.m. However, it's ¹⁾_____ _____ _____.

M Are there any more today?

W Yes. There is one train departing at 2 p.m. and another at 3 p.m.

M I see. I need to get to London by 5 p.m., so I guess I'd better take the earlier train.

W Actually, you should consider the train that leaves at 3 p.m.

M Really? Why?

W It's the ²⁾_____ _____, so it takes just under two hours.

M What about the other train?

W The earlier train stops several times between here and London. It won't ³⁾_____ _____ _____ _____ _____.

14

M Hazel, why weren't you at school yesterday?

W I had a really bad cold, so my mother told me to stay home.

M That's unfortunate. Are you 1)_____ _____ today?

W Yeah. I'm just kind of tired. But I'm also a little stressed.

M Why? What's 2)_____ _____?

W I'm supposed to hand in the book report for English class today, but I didn't finish it. I was too sick.

M I'm sure Ms. Kingston will understand if you 3)_____ _____ _____ to her.

W Do you think so? She is pretty strict.

M Of course. Why don't you see her and ask for 4)_____ _____ _____?

↘ **듣기 필수 표현**
· have a bad cold 독감에 걸리다
· That's unfortunate 안 됐네.
· kind of 약간의
· ask for ~을 부탁하다

15

W Noah and Chloe are classmates. Their class will put on a play at the school festival in two months. Last night, Noah made 1)_____ _____ _____. Before making the schedule, Noah asked Chloe for her opinion. She said that she wanted the play to be a success, so rehearsing often was important. However, when Chloe read Noah's schedule this morning, she saw that it included rehearsals five nights a week. Chloe is worried that practicing so much will 2)_____ _____ _____ _____. So Chloe wants to suggest that Noah 3)_____ _____ _____ _____ _____ each week. In this situation, what would Chloe most likely say to Noah?

↘ **듣기 필수 표현**
· put on ~을 공연하다

16~17

M Hello, everyone. As you probably already know, millions of people have heart attacks every year. Today, I'd like to talk about 1)_____ _____ _____ that reduce the risk of heart disease. Most importantly, you need to 2)_____ _____ _____ fruits and vegetables. Broccoli, for example, contains vitamin A, which prevents heart problems. Similarly, whole grains like brown rice are 3)_____ _____ _____ the health of the heart. At the same time, you should avoid eating too much beef and other types of red meat. Most meat is a source of cholesterol, a substance that can lead to heart attacks. Finally, 4)_____ _____ _____ of unhealthy fats you consume, such as those found in butter. Now, let's watch a brief video about how to plan and prepare healthy meals.

↘ **듣기 필수 표현**
· lead to ~을 일으키다, 초래하다

13회 영어듣기 모의고사

정답 및 해설 p.80

1번부터 17번까지는 듣고 답하는 문제입니다. 1번부터 15번까지는 한 번만 들려주고, 16번부터 17번까지는 두 번 들려줍니다. 방송을 잘 듣고 답을 하시기 바랍니다.

1 다음을 듣고, 남자가 하는 말의 목적으로 가장 적절한 것을 고르시오.

① 주택 수리 업체를 홍보하려고
② 백화점 멤버십 가입을 권유하려고
③ 토네이도의 예상 이동 경로를 공지하려고
④ 지역 봉사단체의 연간 계획을 발표하려고
⑤ 재해 복구 기금 모금 행사를 안내하려고

2 대화를 듣고, 남자의 의견으로 가장 적절한 것을 고르시오.

① 건강한 급식을 제공하면 아이들의 식습관이 개선된다.
② 학교는 학생들의 요구를 반영해서 급식을 제공해야 한다.
③ 학생들은 어릴 때부터 영양소에 대해 배워야 한다.
④ 학습 효율을 향상시키려면 식단 개선이 필요하다.
⑤ 부모들은 아이들의 식습관을 관리해야 한다.

3 대화를 듣고, 두 사람의 관계를 가장 잘 나타낸 것을 고르시오.

① 역사 선생님 — 방송 PD
② 작가 — 평론가
③ 학생 — 사서
④ 관람객 — 영화관 직원
⑤ 경비원 — TV 수리 기사

4 대화를 듣고, 그림에서 대화의 내용과 일치하지 않는 것을 고르시오.

5 대화를 듣고, 여자가 남자를 위해 할 일로 가장 적절한 것을 고르시오.

① 매장에 연락하기
② 매니저에게 보고하기
③ 새 카드로 교체해 주기
④ 카드 잔액 환불해 주기
⑤ 카드 기계 수리 신청하기

6 대화를 듣고, 남자가 지불할 금액을 고르시오.

① $50 ② $70 ③ $80 ④ $90 ⑤ $100

7 대화를 듣고, 두 사람이 내일 바다 여행을 갈 수 없는 이유를 고르시오.

① 시험 공부를 해야 해서
② 일기 예보가 좋지 않아서
③ 버스와 기차표가 매진되어서
④ 친구들이 다른 계획이 있어서
⑤ 여행 경비가 비싸서

8 대화를 듣고, 오디션에 관해 언급되지 않은 것을 고르시오.

① 장소   ② 시간   ③ 신청 방법
④ 담당자 이름 ⑤ 이메일 주소

9 Peer Tours에 관한 다음 내용을 듣고, 일치하지 않는 것을 고르시오.

① 가이드 투어를 무료로 제공한다.
② 가이드들은 여행객이 방문할 도시에 거주 중이다.
③ 가이드들이 현지인들만 아는 맛집으로 안내해준다.
④ 가이드에게 통역에 대한 도움을 받을 수 있다.
⑤ 투어 예약은 웹사이트를 통해 신청해야 한다.

10 다음 표를 보면서 대화를 듣고, 두 사람이 이용할 청소 서비스를 고르시오.

Cleaning Services

	Service	Time	Price	Frequency	Laundry
①	A	7 a.m. - 10 a.m.	$120	Biweekly	X
②	B	7 a.m. - 10 p.m.	$125	Biweekly	O
③	C	7 a.m. - 10 a.m.	$145	Monthly	X
④	D	8 a.m. - 11 a.m.	$160	Monthly	O
⑤	E	12 p.m. - 3 p.m.	$165	Weekly	O

11 대화를 듣고, 남자의 마지막 말에 대한 여자의 응답으로 가장 적절한 것을 고르시오.

① The farmer will be back on Sunday.
② I think we can pick them next weekend.
③ I can start planting them in just a second.
④ Let's get a weekend farm next spring.
⑤ I just put the cucumbers in a salad.

12 대화를 듣고, 여자의 마지막 말에 대한 남자의 응답으로 가장 적절한 것을 고르시오.

① Yes. I packed some sweaters, pants, and a coat.
② That's fine. I'll just take a taxi to the airport.
③ Not really. I prefer the one I bought recently.
④ Don't worry. I'm sure you'll find it soon.
⑤ Perfect. I'll give it back to you later.

13 대화를 듣고, 여자의 마지막 말에 대한 남자의 응답으로 가장 적절한 것을 고르시오. [3점]

Man: _____

① I'm sorry. I'll post the photos now.
② It's a deal. You strike a hard bargain.
③ I totally agree. They're a lot of work.
④ That's fine. I'll be at the shelter until 5 p.m.
⑤ You don't have to. You can see the puppies.

14 대화를 듣고, 남자의 마지막 말에 대한 여자의 응답으로 가장 적절한 것을 고르시오. [3점]

Woman: _____

① I really appreciate your help.
② I'll have to go on another weekend.
③ The delivery is scheduled for Saturday.
④ Maybe you can buy her something else.
⑤ I just need to pack, and then I'll be ready.

15 다음 상황 설명을 듣고 Lisa가 Arthur에게 할 말로 가장 적절한 것을 고르시오. [3점]

Lisa: _____

① I'll meet the club president tomorrow.
② Why don't I work on the poster for you?
③ The concert starts at 7 p.m. in the auditorium.
④ I can't help you since I have too many things to do.
⑤ Don't you think the poster needs to be more colorful?

[16~17] 다음을 듣고, 물음에 답하시오.

16 남자가 하는 말의 주제로 가장 적절한 것은?

① reasons animals breed in the same places
② reasons for different parenting styles across species
③ how animals return home after long distance travel
④ ways that sea animals use their sense of smell
⑤ how fish can travel long distances to feed

17 언급된 동물이 <u>아닌</u> 것은?

① salmon　　② sea turtles　　③ seagulls
④ geese　　⑤ whales

이제 듣기 문제가 끝났습니다. 채점을 마친 후 다음 페이지에서 방송을 다시 들으며 딕테이션 연습을 하시기 바랍니다.

* 채점 결과: 맞은 개수 _____ 개 / 17개　　　정답 및 해설 p.80

13회 영어듣기 모의고사 Dictation 음성을 들으며 빈칸에 알맞은 단어를 채워 넣으시기 바랍니다.

1

M Good morning, Martin's Department Store customers. As you know, hundreds of people 1)_____ _____ _____ due to the recent tornado in Pike City. We would like to help them rebuild their lives. So for today only, we will donate one dollar to the victims for each dollar you spend at the store. The funds 2)_____ _____ _____ _____ to the Pike City Volunteer Group. This charity group will use the money to help those most in need. In other words, your donations 3)_____ _____ _____ _____ temporary housing, home repairs, and medical care. Thank you in advance for your help and cooperation.

↘ 듣기 필수 표현
· due to ~으로 인해
· in need 어려움에 처한
· in other words 다시 말해
· in advance 미리

2

M Honey, I heard they're going to provide healthier lunches at the elementary school.

W Why? Aren't they 1)_____ _____ _____?

M Yes, but there will be more fresh fruits and vegetables now.

W I don't think the kids will like that.

M Maybe not at first. But I think serving healthy lunches will improve 2)_____ _____ _____.

W Hmm... Kids 3)_____ _____ _____ _____.

M If they eat fresh fruits and vegetables every day, they'll learn to enjoy the taste.

W I guess that's true.

M And I like that the school is setting a good example.

W What do you mean?

M They will have a positive example of 4)_____ _____.

W That's true. Maybe they'll be more likely to choose healthier foods later in life.

M I hope so!

↘ 듣기 필수 표현
· at first 처음에는
· set a good example 좋은 본보기가 되다

3

M Hi. I'd like to know if the DVD I reserved is available now.

W May I have your student ID? Just a second, please. *[Typing sound]* You reserved *Early American History*, right? It's available.

M Yes. That's the one. What a relief! I need to 1)_____ _____ _____ _____ _____ this week.

W Would you like to take it home or watch it in the library's media room?

M I think I'd 2)_____ _____ _____ _____ because other students will need it, too.

W All right. We have one media room that's free, and the film is about an hour long.

M Sounds good. Oh, could I check out these books first?

W Sure. I can 3)_____ _____ _____ _____.

M Thanks!

↘ 듣기 필수 표현
· What a relief! 정말 다행이네요!
· check out ~을 대출하다

4

M How was your Christmas, Martha?

W It was wonderful. Here's a photo my mother took.

M Oh, did you 1)_____ _____ _____? It's beautiful with that star on top.

W Yes, my family and I did. We do it every year.

M And under the tree, there's a gift 2)_____ _____ _____. Whose gift was that?

W That one was for me. It was a winter coat.

M Ah, that's why the box is so big. Those must be your grandparents 3)_____ _____ _____ _____ by the window.

W Yeah! You can see that they were happy.

M The three socks on the wall look so cute.

W Yeah, they were filled with candy.

M Was this photo taken in the morning? You're 4)_____ _____ _____ with a reindeer on it.

W Right. I was still drinking my coffee.

M It looks like you had the perfect Christmas.

↘ 듣기 필수 표현
· be filled with ~으로 가득 차 있다

5

W Hi. May I help you?

M I bought this gift card here at the outlet mall, but it didn't work at some of the shops.

W I'm sorry about that. Can you tell me where the card didn't work?

M I 1)_____ _____ _____ at Papa's Pizza and Norman's Boutique.

W Hmm... I don't know what the problem is. Can I take a look at it?

M Here you go.

W *[Typing sound]* I've checked it, and it still has $45 on it. I don't see anything wrong with the card.

M Could you 2)_____ _____ _____ _____ _____?

W Sorry, but I can't. Instead, I'll 3)_____ _____ _____ with a new one.

M What if I have the same problem?

W You can come back here, and we'll 4)_____ _____ _____ _____.

↘ **듣기 필수 표현**
· take a look at ~을 보다, 점검하다
· What if ~? ~하면 어떡하죠?

6

W Can I help you find anything, sir?

M Yes, thanks. I'm looking for two pairs of warm gloves.

W Certainly. All our winter accessories are over this way.

M Ah, okay. *[Pause]* How much are these gloves?

W That pair is $25. We also 1)_____ _____ _____ _____ for $35.

M Oh, I need the waterproof ones. They'll keep my hands warm and dry when I'm removing snow from my driveway.

W Do you need anything else?

M I suppose I should get a scarf, too. How about this one?

W 2)_____ _____ _____ _____ $20. But if you buy two, the second will be $10.

M That won't be necessary. Just one wool scarf, please.

W Okay. So that's 3)_____ _____ _____ _____ and a wool scarf.

M That's correct.

W Perfect. The cash register is right over here.

↘ **듣기 필수 표현**
· a pair of 한 켤레의, 한 쌍의
· remove A from B A를 B에서 치우다, 제거하다

7

W Hi, Nathan. I just read your message about the beach trip tomorrow. I was busy studying for my exam last night.

M I understand. You must be disappointed that we 1)_____ _____ _____ _____ _____.

W Yeah. I was really looking forward to it. Is it canceled because of the weather?

M No. It's actually supposed to be sunny and warm.

W Oh, did our friends 2)_____ _____ _____?

M Not at all. Everyone is available.

W Is the trip too expensive?

M No. There's a 3)_____ _____ _____.

W What's wrong?

M Well, all the bus and train tickets for that day are sold out.

W Oh, I see. We should have 4)_____ _____ _____.

M Right. We'll have to make our plans earlier next time.

↘ **듣기 필수 표현**
· look forward to ~을 기대하다
· be supposed to ~하기로 되어 있다
· Not at all. 전혀 아니야.
· sold out 매진된

8

M Megan, you like acting, right?

W Yeah. I'm in the drama club.

M Did you see this flyer? They're 1)_____ _____ _____ a new television show at Grandview Theater.

W Really? Oh, it's next Sunday!

M Yes. The auditions start at 7 a.m. You should go!

W What's the show about?

M It says here that it's a crime show. They need a few young actors and actresses 2)_____ _____ _____.

W That's perfect!

M To sign up for the audition, you just have to email them a photograph and your name. They'll put you on the audition list.

W What's the email address?

M It's grandview@softmail.com. You can see it here on the flyer.

W Thank you 3)_____ _____ _____ _____. I can't wait to audition!

↘ **듣기 필수 표현**
· put ~ on the list ~를 명단에 올리다

9

W Attention, viewers. Do you love traveling? Wouldn't you love to go on a guided tour for free? Well, thanks to Peer Tours, you can. Peer Tours [1)]_____ _____ _____ _____ who can recommend special places you'll like. These expert guides are all people who live in the cities you'll be visiting. Because they are locals, they will bring you to restaurants that [2)]_____ _____ _____ _____ about. Also, if you don't know the local language, our guides can interpret for you. To book your free tour, [3)]_____ _____ _____ 555-1990. Then, we'll connect you with a guide in [4)]_____ _____ _____ _____ _____! If you're interested in leading a tour of your own area, please register on our website.

↘ 듣기 필수 표현
· for free 무료로

10

M Honey, did you check out house cleaning services?

W I'm looking at some now. Do you want to see?

M Sure. [1)]_____ _____ _____ _____ _____ they should come to clean the house?

W I'd like them to be finished before 12 p.m.

M I agree. We're rarely home in the morning anyway, so those times are [2)]_____ _____.

W What about the price?

M I think anything over $150 is too much.

W Okay. So we won't choose this one.

M [3)]_____ _____ do we want them to come?

W I think every two weeks would be good. Since we have a dog and a cat, once a month is not enough.

M That's true. So let's go with [4)]_____ _____ _____. Do we want laundry service, too?

W Of course. That would be a big help.

M Then, let's go with this one!

↘ 듣기 필수 표현
· go with ~을 선택하다

11

M It's good to be back at the weekend farm, Jane. How are the [1)]_____ _____ _____ _____?

W They're doing well, Dad. We should be able to [2)]_____ _____ _____.

M Great. When do you think we should do that?

↘ 듣기 필수 표현
· be back 돌아오다

12

W Paul, are you ready for your flight tomorrow?

M Yes. I've [1)]_____ _____. I'm just feeling a little worried. I can't find the external battery I bought last week.

W Well, I have one that I don't need. You can [2)]_____ _____ _____ _____ if you want.

↘ 듣기 필수 표현
· be ready for ~을 할 준비가 되다

13

[Telephone rings.]

M Hi. Are you Mindy Miller? I'm Brian from the animal shelter.

W Yes. I called earlier [1)]_____ _____ _____.

M Right. So you saw the pictures of the puppies we just rescued.

W They look so cute. I was thinking [2)]_____ _____ one of them.

M That's great, but have you ever owned a dog before?

W Well, my parents had dogs growing up. So I have some experience.

M Having your own dog [3)]_____ _____ _____ _____ _____.

W Oh, I'm aware of that. I know I can do a good job.

M That's good. But keep in mind, these guys love to play.

W I'm a pretty active person, so that's perfect for me.

M Okay. Let's [4)]_____ _____ _____ for you to come and see them.

W What if I come by later today?

↘ 듣기 필수 표현
· be aware of ~을 알다
· keep in mind 명심하다
· come by 들르다

14

M Christine, you seem stressed. What's wrong?

W I'm planning to surprise my grandmother this weekend for her birthday, but it's not going well.

M How so?

W All the train tickets are sold out, and the present I bought online [1)]_____ _____ _____ yet.

M What are you going to do, then?

W Well, I managed to get a bus ticket, and I might send the present by mail later. But I'm still pretty upset about it all.

M I'm sorry you're having so many problems.

W It's okay. I'm just glad I'll [2)]_____ _____ _____ _____.

M Well, is there anything else you need to figure out?

W Actually, I need to find someone to [3)]_____ _____ _____ while I'm gone.

M I can do it. You shouldn't have to [4)]_____ _____ _____ _____.

W Are you sure?

M Yes. Just enjoy your visit with your grandmother.

↘ 듣기 필수 표현
· go well 잘 되어가다
· manage to 간신히 ~하다
· figure out ~을 해결하다
· one's visit with ~와 함께 보내는 시간

15

W Arthur and Lisa are members of a high school music club. The club is holding a concert soon, so they are [1)]_____ _____ _____ it. Arthur and Lisa are in charge of posting flyers throughout the school. The club president also asked them to [2)]_____ _____ _____ _____ to place on the main bulletin board by the school's entrance. Originally, Arthur agreed to make the poster by himself. Lisa was going to make the flyers. However, Arthur has [3)]_____ _____ _____ _____ school work. Now, Lisa thinks she should make the poster instead of Arthur because she has more free time than him. So Lisa wants to suggest to Arthur that she take on his job. In this situation, what would Lisa most likely say to Arthur?

↘ 듣기 필수 표현
· in charge of ~을 맡아서
· take on (일을) 맡다

16~17

M Good afternoon. Yesterday, we talked about animal parenting techniques. Today, I'd like to discuss how animals get home [1)]_____ _____ _____. First, there's salmon. These fish are born in rivers and swim to the ocean when they are young. As adults, the fish return to the same place to lay eggs, guided by their sense of smell. Sea turtles [2)]_____ _____ _____ _____. They hatch on the beach but live in the sea mostly. By sensing the earth's magnetic field, they can find their way home, even from across the ocean. Next, some seagulls from the Arctic go even farther. They can fly from Canada to South Africa. By watching the sun and the stars, they [3)]_____ _____ _____ in the north every year. Whales also go home to breed. They get there thanks to their sense of hearing. They make clicking sounds that [4)]_____ _____ _____ them, so they always know where they are in the sea. Let's take a look at a video.

↘ 듣기 필수 표현
· get home 집에 돌아가다
· lay egg 알을 낳다
· thanks to ~ 덕분에

▲ 문제 음성
바로 듣기

▲ 고사장 버전
바로 듣기

정답 및 해설 p.86

1번부터 17번까지는 듣고 답하는 문제입니다. 1번부터 15번까지는 한 번만 들려주고, 16번부터 17번까지는 두 번 들려줍니다. 방송을 잘 듣고 답을 하시기 바랍니다.

1 다음을 듣고, 남자가 하는 말의 목적으로 가장 적절한 것을 고르시오.

① 상품 품절에 대해 사과하려고
② 쇼핑센터의 신규 지점을 홍보하려고
③ 쇼핑센터의 정기 휴무일을 상기하려고
④ 화재 발생 시 비상 탈출구를 안내하려고
⑤ 쇼핑센터 영업 종료 시각 변경을 공지하려고

2 대화를 듣고, 여자의 의견으로 가장 적절한 것을 고르시오.

① 때로는 아이들에게 스트레스가 이로울 수 있다.
② 걱정거리는 쌓아두지 말고 바로바로 해소해야 한다.
③ 과한 양의 과제는 아이들에게 스트레스를 준다.
④ 부모는 자녀의 교육에 적극적으로 관여해야 한다.
⑤ 발표를 잘하려면 자신감 있는 태도가 중요하다.

3 대화를 듣고, 두 사람의 관계를 가장 잘 나타낸 것을 고르시오.

① 택시 운전사 — 탑승객
② 정형외과 의사 — 환자
③ 제설업체 직원 — 고객
④ 운동선수 — 트레이너
⑤ 기상 예보관 — 아나운서

4 대화를 듣고, 그림에서 대화의 내용과 일치하지 않는 것을 고르시오.

5 대화를 듣고, 남자가 할 일로 가장 적절한 것을 고르시오.

① 방한복 챙기기
② 랜턴 찾아보기
③ 차에 기름 넣기
④ 캠핑용품 차에 싣기
⑤ 슈퍼마켓에서 장 보기

6 대화를 듣고, 여자가 지불할 금액을 고르시오. [3점]

① $8   ② $12   ③ $18   ④ $20   ⑤ $24

7 대화를 듣고, 남자가 친구의 집들이에 갈 수 없는 이유를 고르시오.

① 늦게까지 근무해야 해서
② 독서회 모임에 참석해야 해서
③ 이사 갈 아파트를 보러 가야 해서
④ 다른 친구와 저녁 약속이 있어서
⑤ 해외 출장을 다녀와야 해서

8 대화를 듣고, Greenville Book Fair에 관해 언급되지 않은 것을 고르시오.

① 날짜   ② 장소   ③ 개장 시각
④ 주차 요금   ⑤ 입장료

9 Paper Folding Design Competition에 관한 다음 내용을 듣고, 일치하지 않는 것을 고르시오.

① 청소년 부문의 참가 연령은 12세부터 18세까지이다.
② 디자인은 우편으로 제출해야 한다.
③ 디자인 제출 마감일은 5월 13일이다.
④ 다른 대회에서 사용했던 디자인은 제출할 수 없다.
⑤ 10명의 수상자가 선정될 예정이다.

10 다음 표를 보면서 대화를 듣고, 여자가 구매할 커피 머신을 고르시오.

Coffee Machines

	Model	Capacity	Warranty	Price	Timer
①	A	2 cups	1-year	$30	O
②	B	4 cups	2-year	$45	X
③	C	6 cups	2-year	$40	O
④	D	6 cups	1-year	$55	O
⑤	E	4 cups	2-year	$35	X

11 대화를 듣고, 여자의 마지막 말에 대한 남자의 응답으로 가장 적절한 것을 고르시오.

① Come on! You should enter that contest.
② Awesome! How long have you been drawing?
③ Maybe. I'm not sure if the judges liked it, though.
④ Of course. I wouldn't mind drawing one for you.
⑤ Why not? I'll show it to you tomorrow.

12 대화를 듣고, 남자의 마지막 말에 대한 여자의 응답으로 가장 적절한 것을 고르시오.

① It's no more than two blocks away.
② I'm in a rush, so I'll take a taxi there.
③ Every item in the store is on sale now.
④ The notebooks are popular with students.
⑤ You need to write down your street address.

13 대화를 듣고, 여자의 마지막 말에 대한 남자의 응답으로 가장 적절한 것을 고르시오.

Man: _____

① I'll look at it now and see what I can do.
② Do you plan on buying one immediately?
③ Your water heater will be installed later today.
④ The model you purchased is very reliable.
⑤ I'm just glad I was able to fix it for you.

14 대화를 듣고, 남자의 마지막 말에 대한 여자의 응답으로 가장 적절한 것을 고르시오. [3점]

Woman: _____

① I'm sorry. I'll be out of town all weekend.
② That's fine. I don't have any plans that day.
③ Have fun. I wish I could go this weekend, too.
④ Don't worry. It's just my regular dental checkup.
⑤ Of course! I'll pick you up on Saturday morning.

15 다음 상황 설명을 듣고, Matthew가 Beth에게 할 말로 가장 적절한 것을 고르시오. [3점]

Matthew: _____

① Where are you planning to go on vacation?
② Will you show me how to look after a lizard?
③ Could you take care of my lizard during my trip?
④ Can you recommend an inexpensive pet hotel?
⑤ What do you feed your lizard every day?

[16~17] 다음을 듣고, 물음에 답하시오.

16 남자가 하는 말의 주제로 가장 적절한 것은?

① benefits of driving cars
② ways to encourage subway rides
③ factors that cause environment pollution
④ common problems of living in a city
⑤ alternative methods to go to work

17 언급된 교통수단이 <u>아닌</u> 것은?

① motorcycles ② buses ③ trains
④ subways ⑤ bicycles

이제 듣기 문제가 끝났습니다. 채점을 마친 후 다음 페이지에서 방송을 다시 들으며 딕테이션 연습을 하시기 바랍니다.

* 채점 결과: 맞은 개수 _____ 개 / 17개

정답 및 해설 p.86

14회 Dictation

▲ Dictation
음성 바로 듣기

Dictation 정답 p.86

14회 영어듣기 모의고사 Dictation 음성을 들으며 빈칸에 알맞은 단어를 채워 넣으시기 바랍니다.

1

M Attention, all customers. We hope you are enjoying your time at the Plaza Shopping Center and are finding everything you need in our stores. We would like to notify everyone that our 1)_____ _____ _____ _____ _____ for today. We will close two hours earlier than usual to perform an 2)_____ _____ _____ on this building. This includes making sure that the fire alarm and sprinkler system are working. We 3)_____ _____ _____ _____ this may cause, but it is necessary to ensure the safety of our customers. The shopping center will return to its regular hours of operation tomorrow. Thank you.

2

W What's the matter, honey?

M I'm a little concerned about our son.

W Really? Did something happen?

M You know he is 1)_____ _____ _____ _____ in class next week. He seems really worried about it.

W Well, it will be 2)_____ _____ _____ _____ in front of an audience. He must be nervous.

M I know. But he is really stressed out about it.

W I think it's okay. In fact, stress can sometimes be 3)_____ _____ children.

M What do you mean?

W When children learn to deal with stress on their own, they become better at overcoming difficult situations.

M Interesting. So this could actually be a 4)_____ _____ for him.

W Exactly. Of course, if he asks for our advice, we should give it. But we shouldn't just offer to help because he looks stressed.

↘ 듣기 필수 표현
· deal with ~을 다루다
· on one's own ~ 스스로
· ask for advice 조언을 구하다

3

W How are you doing, Mr. Williams?

M Not very good. I slipped on the ice while 1)_____ _____ from the sidewalk near my house.

W I guess that is why you came to see me today.

M Right. I 2)_____ _____ _____ when I fell. I want you to check it.

W When did this injury occur?

M Two days ago. I thought it would get better, but it seems to have gotten worse.

W I see. Well, you probably pulled a muscle. But we should take an X-ray to be sure.

M Okay. Will it 3)_____ _____ _____? I have to bring my kids to soccer practice.

W No. It won't take more than 20 minutes.

M Great. Thanks so much.

↘ 듣기 필수 표현
· slip on the ice 빙판길에서 미끄러지다
· pull a muscle 근육이 결리다

4

M Is everything ready for Dad's birthday party, Mom?

W I just finished setting up the dining room. What do you think?

M I like the big banner on the wall that says, "Happy Birthday"!

W Thanks. I made it myself.

M Did you also 1)_____ _____ _____ on the table?

W No. I ordered that from the bakery this morning.

M And there are 2)_____ _____ _____ on the table, too. That's a lot of food!

W I wanted to have all of your father's favorites. Oh, do you see the 3)_____ _____ on the cabinet? Those are the ones we got him.

M Great. And I really like the 4)_____ _____ to the right of the presents. They look really cute.

W I think so, too.

↘ 듣기 필수 표현
· set up ~을 꾸미다, 설치하다

5

W Honey, I can't wait for our family camping trip tomorrow.

M I'm really excited, too. We still have a lot of ¹⁾_____ _____ _____, though.

W That's true. I'm going to the supermarket this afternoon to buy the food we need.

M Great. I've ²⁾_____ _____ our tents and sleeping bags into the car.

W Okay. Did you also pack some warm clothes for the kids?

M I took care of that this morning. Um, could you put gas in the car after you go shopping?

W No problem. And while I'm out, why don't you ³⁾_____ _____ the lanterns? I checked in the garage earlier, but I didn't see them.

M Hmm... I think they are somewhere ⁴⁾_____ _____. Don't worry. I'll find them.

W I hope so. We'll need the lanterns at night.

↘ 듣기 필수 표현
- can't wait for ~이 너무 기대되다
- put gas in a car 차에 기름을 넣다

6

M Welcome to Java Café. What can I get for you?

W Hi. Do you sell green tea?

M Of course. A small cup is $2, and a large is $3.

W Great. I'll get two large cups of tea and ¹⁾_____ _____ _____ _____ _____, please.

M Okay. Would you like anything else?

W Oh, how much are these blueberry muffins?

M They are $4 each.

W I'll take ²⁾_____ _____ _____, please.

M So you want two large green teas, one small green tea, and three blueberry muffins to go.

W Right. And I think I can get ³⁾_____ _____ _____ with this coupon.

M That's correct. Would you like to pay with cash or by card?

W Here's my credit card.

↘ 듣기 필수 표현
- to go 테이크아웃하는, 포장해가는

7

W Hi, Greg. Did you hear about Jenna's housewarming party on Thursday evening?

M Yes. But I ¹⁾_____ _____ I can make it.

W Do you have to work late that night?

M No, I don't.

W Then, is it because you have a ²⁾_____ _____ _____? You usually meet with the other members on Thursdays.

M I no longer belong to that club.

W I see. Have you already made dinner plans with other friends, then?

M No. The problem is that I'm scheduled to go on a business trip abroad.

W How long will you be gone?

M I leave tomorrow, and I'll ³⁾_____ _____ on Saturday.

W Then, why don't you visit Jenna next week? She would love to ⁴⁾_____ _____ _____ _____ _____.

M I'll talk to her about it today.

↘ 듣기 필수 표현
- no longer 더 이상 ~이 아닌
- belong to ~의 소속이다
- be scheduled to ~할 예정이다
- go on a business trip 출장 가다

8

M Long time no see, Grace! How are you doing?

W I've been really busy lately. I'm organizing the Greenville Book Fair.

M That sounds interesting. ¹⁾_____ _____ _____ _____?

W On Saturday, June 23rd. It's a one-day event.

M I'll definitely go.

W Great. Then, come to Maple Park on that day.

M Okay. What time does the fair start?

W It ²⁾_____ _____ _____ a.m. But if you're driving, you should come early. Parking is limited.

M Got it. I was planning to take the subway, anyway. And how much is ³⁾_____ _____ _____?

W It's $10, but I'll send you a free ticket.

M Thanks. I really appreciate that.

↘ 듣기 필수 표현
- Long time no see. 오랜만이야.
- Got it. 알겠어.

9

W Hello, everyone. I'm pleased to announce the third annual Paper Folding Design Competition. This competition is open to ¹)_____ _____ _____. For the youth group, we accept participants aged 12 to 18 years. The adult group participants should be 19 or older. You should turn in your design with a ²)_____ _____ _____ _____. The deadline is May 13th. But keep in mind that you should not submit designs that you have used in other contests. We will choose ³)_____ _____ and hold an exhibition with these designs. We hope many of you participate.

↘ 듣기 필수 표현
· turn in ~을 제출하다
· keep in mind ~을 명심하다

10

M Can I help you find anything?

W Yes. My coffee machine ¹)_____ _____, so I want to buy a new one.

M We have a number of models available. Which capacity do you need?

W It has to make ²)_____ _____ _____ _____ of coffee at one time.

M I see. Does the length of the warranty matter to you?

W I'd prefer one with a two-year warranty or longer.

M Okay. What about ³)_____ _____ _____?

W The maximum I want to spend is $40.

M Got it. And are there any special features you are interested in?

W It has to ⁴)_____ _____ _____. I like to set up the coffee machine before I go to sleep and then wake up to the smell of fresh coffee.

M I think we have just what you are looking for.

↘ 듣기 필수 표현
· a number of 많은
· matter to ~에게 중요하다, 문제가 되다

11

W Brett, I heard you won a prize in an ¹)_____ _____. Congratulations!

M Thanks. I was really surprised. I only started drawing last year.

W Wow. You must be really talented. Can I ²)_____ _____ _____?

↘ 듣기 필수 표현
· win a prize 상을 받다

12

M Excuse me. Do you ¹)_____ _____ here?

W Unfortunately, no. But there is a stationery store just down the street.

M I'd like to know ²)_____ _____ _____ _____ from here.

13

[Doorbell rings.]

W Come in. Thank you for coming here on such short notice.

M No problem. You said there's ¹)_____ _____ _____ your hot water heater, right?

W Yes. We have only had cold water in the house since yesterday.

M Is your water heater making any unusual noises?

W Hmm... Now that you mention it, yes. It ²)_____ _____ _____ _____ once in a while.

M Do you know how old the water heater is?

W I think it was ³)_____ _____ _____ _____ ago.

M Most water heaters need to be replaced after 10 years. You probably need a new one.

W I really hope not. A new one would be expensive. It would be great if you ⁴)_____ _____ _____.

↘ 듣기 필수 표현
· on such short notice 이렇게 갑작스러운 요청에도
· Now that you mention it 그 말을 듣고 보니
· once in a while 가끔

14

M Hey, Sandra! What did you do last weekend?

W Hi, James. I just stayed home. How about you?

M I went to an international food festival at the Stanford Cultural Center. It was really fun.

W That sounds great! 1)_____ _____ _____ _____ did you try there?

M I ate some Mexican, Vietnamese, and Russian foods. Everything was delicious.

W I'm so jealous. I wish I had gone to the festival.

M Don't worry. It will be held again this weekend. I'm 2)_____ _____ _____ one more time myself.

W Really? Why don't we check it out together?

M I was just going to suggest that.

W Which day were you thinking of going?

M I have a dentist appointment on Saturday, so Sunday would be best. Does 3)_____ _____ _____ _____?

❯ 듣기 필수 표현
· check out ~을 보러 가다

15

W Matthew has a pet lizard that he loves very much. However, he will be 1)_____ _____ _____ with his parents next month. They will be away from home for two weeks, and he cannot leave his lizard alone for that long. The pet hotels in his city are very expensive, and he does not want his parents to 2)_____ _____ _____. So Matthew wants to ask his friend Beth if she would be willing to look after his lizard while 3)_____ _____ _____. In this situation, what would Matthew most likely say to Beth?

❯ 듣기 필수 표현
· leave ~ alone ~를 혼자 내버려두다
· be willing to ~할 의향이 있다
· look after ~를 돌봐주다

16~17

M Good morning. As I mentioned in the last class, 1)_____ _____ _____ is a major cause of traffic jams. Today, I want to look at some of the other 2)_____ _____ _____ _____ for commuting in cities. First, buses are popular because they go almost everywhere. However, they use roads, so they might not 3)_____ _____ _____. Next, trains are a better option because they run on their own tracks. But there isn't always land available in a city to construct train tracks. That is why subways are often built in major cities. Their tracks go underground in tunnels. But perhaps the best option is bicycles. They take up less room. Plus, they 4)_____ _____ _____ and provide a way to get regular exercise. I hope this lesson has given you some ideas about how we can reduce the amount of traffic on the roads.

❯ 듣기 필수 표현
· traffic jam 교통 체증
· take up ~을 차지하다

15회 영어듣기 모의고사

정답 및 해설 p.92

1번부터 17번까지는 듣고 답하는 문제입니다. 1번부터 15번까지는 한 번만 들려주고, 16번부터 17번까지는 두 번 들려줍니다. 방송을 잘 듣고 답을 하시기 바랍니다.

1 다음을 듣고, 여자가 하는 말의 목적으로 가장 적절한 것을 고르시오.

① 항공권 할인 행사를 홍보하려고
② 출발 게이트 변경을 안내하려고
③ 목적지의 현재 날씨를 알려주려고
④ 비행기 출발 지연에 대해 공지하려고
⑤ 비행 만족도 조사 참여를 요청하려고

2 대화를 듣고, 남자의 의견으로 가장 적절한 것을 고르시오.

① 아이들에게 책을 억지로 읽게 해서는 안 된다.
② 꾸준한 독서 활동은 학습 능력을 향상시킨다.
③ 아이들은 제 나이에 맞는 책을 읽어야 한다.
④ 책을 읽은 후 내용을 정리하는 활동이 필수적이다.
⑤ 독서량을 늘리기 위해서는 적절한 보상이 필요하다.

3 대화를 듣고, 두 사람의 관계를 가장 잘 나타낸 것을 고르시오.

① 공연장 관리인 — 사진작가
② 웨딩 플래너 — 요리사
③ 화원 주인 — 광고주
④ 시상식 주최자 — 수상자
⑤ 플로리스트 — 행사 기획자

4 대화를 듣고, 그림에서 대화의 내용과 일치하지 않는 것을 고르시오.

5 대화를 듣고, 남자가 할 일로 가장 적절한 것을 고르시오.

① 표지 디자인하기
② 인쇄소 주소 보내주기
③ 이메일 발송하기
④ 인쇄물 가져오기
⑤ 사진 촬영하기

6 대화를 듣고, 남자가 지불할 금액을 고르시오. [3점]

① $36   ② $40   ③ $45   ④ $50   ⑤ $55

7 대화를 듣고, 여자가 스웨터를 교환하려는 이유를 고르시오.

① 디자인이 마음에 들지 않아서
② 이미 같은 옷이 있어서
③ 다른 색상을 원해서
④ 사이즈가 맞지 않아서
⑤ 원하던 브랜드가 아니어서

8 대화를 듣고, Lakeshore Movie Night에 관해 언급되지 않은 것을 고르시오.

① 장소   ② 참석자   ③ 영화 제목
④ 제공 간식   ⑤ 시작 시각

9 Los Angeles Santa Claus Parade에 관한 다음 내용을 듣고, 일치하지 않는 것을 고르시오. [3점]

① 작년에는 악천후로 인해 취소되었다.
② 12월 12일에 개최된다.
③ 경찰서에서부터 시작된다.
④ 현지 음악가들이 라이브 공연을 할 것이다.
⑤ 주요 도로는 오후 3시부터 폐쇄될 예정이다.

10 다음 표를 보면서 대화를 듣고, 두 사람이 예약할 투어 프로그램을 고르시오.

City Tours

	Tour	Start Time	Vehicle	Price	Group Size
①	A	9 a.m.	boat	$40	8
②	B	9 a.m.	bus	$25	12
③	C	10 a.m.	bus	$35	30
④	D	10 a.m.	bike	$45	12
⑤	E	2 p.m.	bike	$30	15

11 대화를 듣고, 여자의 마지막 말에 대한 남자의 응답으로 가장 적절한 것을 고르시오.

① Okay. Let's go buy some now.
② No. These clothes don't look clean.
③ Definitely. I need to pack some pants.
④ Perfect. We're ready to go on a trip now.
⑤ Yes. Our train leaves tomorrow morning.

12 대화를 듣고, 남자의 마지막 말에 대한 여자의 응답으로 가장 적절한 것을 고르시오.

① Do you accept credit cards?
② How long do I have to wait?
③ Can I get extra lettuce on it?
④ Where should I park my car?
⑤ What soft drinks do you have?

13 대화를 듣고, 여자의 마지막 말에 대한 남자의 응답으로 가장 적절한 것을 고르시오. [3점]

Man: _____

① Thanks. I'm excited about this new chapter in life.
② Me too. Moving to a new school can be really scary.
③ I see. Maybe you should call your friends to meet soon.
④ Don't worry. Everything will work out for you in the end.
⑤ Perhaps. But I don't know if I have time for sports right now.

14 대화를 듣고, 남자의 마지막 말에 대한 여자의 응답으로 가장 적절한 것을 고르시오.

Woman: _____

① No problem. I'll stop by later, then.
② I see. The sign says to turn right here.
③ Hold on. The presentation will begin shortly.
④ Thanks. I've been looking forward to reading this.
⑤ Certainly. Please follow me to the exam room now.

15 다음 상황 설명을 듣고, Evelyn이 Charlie에게 할 말로 가장 적절한 것을 고르시오.

Evelyn: _____

① You'd better not miss the school festival today.
② None of this would have been possible without you.
③ Let's think of some ways to help you feel better fast.
④ Why didn't you make a doctor's appointment?
⑤ I think you should go home and relax.

[16~17] 다음을 듣고, 물음에 답하시오.

16 여자가 하는 말의 주제로 가장 적절한 것은?

① results of illegally hunting wild birds
② how to reduce plastic pollution in the ocean
③ ways people are negatively affecting animals
④ tips on saving endangered species from extinction
⑤ examples of animals that disappeared from the planet

17 언급된 동물이 아닌 것은?

① elephants   ② crocodiles
③ orangutans   ④ whales
⑤ sparrows

이제 듣기 문제가 끝났습니다. 채점을 마친 후 다음 페이지에서 방송을 다시 들으며 딕테이션 연습을 하시기 바랍니다.

* 채점 결과: 맞은 개수 _____ 개 / 17개   정답 및 해설 p.92

Dictation 정답 p.92

15회 영어듣기 모의고사 Dictation 음성을 들으며 빈칸에 알맞은 단어를 채워 넣으시기 바랍니다.

1

W Attention, passengers traveling on Flight 118 to Seattle. This announcement is an 1)_____ _____ _____ _____ _____. As you know, the flight was originally scheduled to leave at 9:30 a.m. However, the flight has been delayed because of strong winds and ice. Your new departure time will be 1 p.m. Depending on the weather, there could be 2)_____ _____. We apologize for the inconvenience. If you have any questions or concerns about this matter, please talk to our staff at the information desk. Thank you for flying with us, and we hope to 3)_____ _____ _____ _____ _____ soon.

📌 **듣기 필수 표현**
· be scheduled to ~할 예정이다
· depending on ~에 따라

2

W Honey, I think we should make our son, Ben, read more.

M Really? He's only six years old.

W Sure, but he'll start school soon. We need to make sure his reading skills are improving.

M I disagree. I don't think young children should be 1)_____ _____ _____.

W Why is that?

M Well, I've read that it's better for them to do things that they are naturally interested in. If we make him read when he doesn't want to, he might 2)_____ _____ it.

W Hmm... that makes sense.

M This could cause him to avoid books in the future and fall behind in school.

W So we should not 3)_____ _____ _____ _____ he is reading.

M No. But let's encourage him to be creative when he does. He could draw pictures or keep a diary about what he reads.

W Okay. Let's try that.

📌 **듣기 필수 표현**
· start school 입학하다
· fall behind in school 학교에서 뒤처지다
· keep a diary 일기를 쓰다

3

M Ms. Smith, I'm here with your order.

W These are lovely, Mr. Anderson. The tulips are perfect.

M Thanks. I wanted to design something special for the awards ceremony.

W I appreciate that. I can tell that you and your staff 1)_____ _____ _____ these flower arrangements.

M Should we go ahead and set these up in the banquet hall?

W Yes, please. I've got the rest of the decorations ready to go. I'll show you where to put everything.

M Oh, and when would you like us to come back with 2)_____ _____ _____ for the winners?

W Please be here at 5. The caterer is coming with the food at 5:30, so I'll be busy then.

M No problem. This is such a big ceremony. Who are you 3)_____ _____ _____ _____?

W It's for an advertising company. They hold it every year.

M Well, I'm sure it'll be a success.

4

M Angela, is that a picture of your kitchen?

W Yeah. We just renovated it. What do you think?

M I really like it. That's a cool 1)_____ _____ _____ _____.

W Yeah, we drink a lot of tea. And that's our new blender next to the sink. We make fruit smoothies every morning.

M I see. I like that basket you have 2)_____ _____ _____. What's that for?

W Oh, that's where we'll put our fruit. It's empty now, though.

M And what about that jar on the microwave? What's inside?

W I love to bake cookies, and I usually put them in there.

M I hope I get to try some.

W You will. Do you like this cloud-shaped whiteboard on the wall?

M Yes. That'll be useful for 3)_____ _____ _____ you need.

5

M Hi, Grace. How is the magazine going?

W Hey, Phil. Here, take a look at the layout.

M Wow, it looks amazing. Is there anything else we have to do?

W Some of the articles aren't finished yet. So I'll email the writers and tell them to 1)_____ _____ _____ before the end of the week.

M Great. I told the photographers to take more photos for the articles, too. They'll send their photos to you by then.

W Okay. I already 2)_____ _____ _____. And I told the printer that our copies need to be ready by Tuesday morning.

M Who will be 3)_____ _____ _____ _____ from the printer?

W We haven't figured it out yet. But we need someone with a car.

M Well, I can do it.

W Are you sure?

M Of course. You're so busy with other things anyway.

W Thank you. I'll send the address soon.

↘ **듣기 필수 표현**
· figure out ~을 생각해보다

6

W Welcome to Jackie's Art Shop. How may I help you?

M Hi. I'm 1)_____ _____ _____ _____.

W Okay. Here's our paint section. As you can see, we have many paints to choose from. But these two sets are the most popular.

M How much are they?

W This paint set is $30. The other set comes with 2)_____ _____ _____ the paints, so it's $40.

M I'll take the bigger one.

W Okay. Do you need any brushes?

M I have some, but they're very old. So I need some new ones.

W Well, this brush set is highly rated. It's usually $15, but it's 3)_____ _____ _____ _____ right now.

M Then, I'll get that one, too.

W Okay. So you want the large paint set and the brush set.

M Yes, and I have this coupon here for 10% off.

W All right. I'll ring everything up for you.

↘ **듣기 필수 표현**
· come with ~이 딸려 있다
· ring ~ up ~을 계산해주다

7

M Hey, Rose. How was your birthday?

W It was great! My parents took me to a nice place for dinner.

M Did you get any presents?

W I did. They gave me a sweater, but I'm going to 1)_____ _____.

M Is it because you don't like it?

W That's not it. I've wanted to buy a sweater from this brand for a while.

M Is it because of the size? It's difficult to guess someone's size when you're buying them clothes.

W Well, it 2)_____ _____ _____.

M Then, why are you exchanging it?

W This one is black, but I really want the blue one.

M Oh, I see. So are you going to the mall now?

W Yeah. I just hope they 3)_____ _____ _____ _____.

8

W Hey, David. Are you busy this Friday?

M No. I don't 1)_____ _____ _____. Why?

W Our movie club is going to hold the first Lakeshore Movie Night at school, and I'd like you to come.

M That sounds fun. Who is going?

W Jack, Emma, and Nicole will also be there. And we've decided to 2)_____ _____ _____ _____, *Midnight Scream*.

M Oh, I wanted to watch that.

W Do you think you'll come to the event, then?

M I'd love to. What time does it start?

W 3)_____ _____ _____, after all the classes finish.

M Okay. And should I bring anything with me?

W I don't think so, but I'll message you if we need something.

M Sure. I can't wait!

↘ **듣기 필수 표현**
· I can't wait! 정말 기대된다!

9

M Good afternoon, listeners! This is Chris Lee from *Afternoon Tunes*. I want to tell you all about an exciting event [1)]_____ _____ _____. The Los Angeles Santa Claus Parade is finally returning to the city after being canceled last year [2)]_____ _____ _____ _____. The event will be held on December 12th at 1 p.m. The parade will take place along Pine Street beginning at the police station. Some highlights of the parade include Santa and his reindeer, a marching band, and professional dancers. There will also be a concert featuring live music from local musicians. Because many of the main roads in this area will be [3)]_____ _____ _____ p.m., we recommend that you take public transportation to attend this event.

10

M Do you want to book a city tour for tomorrow, Erica?

W Yeah! I was already looking at a few different tour options online.

M Okay, let's pick one together.

W First of all, I don't want to do it [1)]_____ _____ _____ _____.

M Me neither. Let's choose one that starts in the morning, then.

W I also want to avoid the boat tour. I don't think we'd get [2)]_____ _____ _____ _____ _____ on the boat.

M Good point. What's our budget for the tour?

W Well, I'd like to keep it under $40.

M Sounds good. That still leaves us with a couple of options. Another thing to consider is the size of the tour group.

W Oh, don't you think that it's best to go with as small a group as possible?

M [3)]_____ _____ _____ _____. Then, we're all set!

↘ **듣기 필수 표현**
· Good point. 좋은 지적이야.
· as ~ as possible 가능한 ~한
· be all set 다 되다

11

W Honey, I'm going to do some laundry before we [1)]_____ _____ _____ _____.

M Oh, great. I'll help you. I need to wash some clothes, too.

W We'd better run to the store first. It looks like we're out of [2)]_____ _____.

↘ **듣기 필수 표현**
· do laundry 빨래하다
· be out of ~이 다 떨어지다

12

M Welcome to the Burger Hut drive-through. What can I [1)]_____ _____ _____ today?

W Hi. I'd like a cheeseburger combo, but I want to replace the fries with onion rings.

M We can do that. Would you also like to [2)]_____ _____ _____ to your burger?

↘ **듣기 필수 표현**
· replace A with B A를 B로 바꾸다

13

W Richard, I heard that you're moving soon.

M Yes, Elizabeth. My parents both [1)]_____ _____ _____, so we have to move to a different city.

W Oh, I'm sorry to hear it. Everyone at school will miss you.

M I'll miss everyone, too. We've had some great times over the years.

W Definitely. Do you know when you'll start at your new school?

M Yes. I'll start there next week.

W Really? Are you nervous?

M A little bit. But I [2)]_____ _____ _____, so I'm looking forward to getting to know my classmates. Plus, I'll meet people through sports teams.

W That's true. You'll have friends in no time, then.

M I hope so. But I'll always [3)]_____ _____ here, too. I still want to keep in touch with everyone.

W I think that's great. I wish you the best of luck at your new school.

↘ **듣기 필수 표현**
· in no time 곧, 당장에
· keep in touch with ~와 연락하고 지내다
· wish ~ luck 행운을 빌다

14

M Hello, Ms. Garner. What can I help you with?

W Well, I'm having vision problems lately.

M Can you describe them?

W When I drive at night, I can't see the [1)]_____ _____ _____. And in meetings, I haven't been able to read anything on the board since last month.

M Do you have any issues reading books or magazines?

W No. I can see things clearly when they're close.

M It sounds like you need glasses. We'll have to [2)]_____ _____ _____ _____ _____ today.

W Oh, I see. How long will the test take?

M It only takes 10 minutes, but I think you should take some additional tests since this is your first time.

W It sounds like it'll take a long time. I need to go back to work in 20 minutes.

M Why don't you [3)]_____ _____ _____ _____? We're open until 8 p.m.

15

M Evelyn and Charlie are helping to organize their annual school festival. The day before the event, Charlie says that he is not feeling well. The next day, Evelyn notices that Charlie is [1)]_____ _____ _____, and his cheeks are red. But when she asks him how he is feeling, he says he feels fine. Evelyn thinks he is saying that because he would feel bad about [2)]_____ _____ _____ and giving her more work. However, Evelyn is concerned that his health will get worse if he does not take care of himself. So she wants to suggest to Charlie that he [3)]_____ _____ _____ _____ _____. In this situation, what would Evelyn most likely say to Charlie?

↘ 듣기 필수 표현
· feel bad about ~에 대해 죄책감을 느끼다
· take care of ~를 돌보다

16~17

W Good afternoon, class. Last week, we started discussing the many ways that humans are changing the planet. Today, I want to talk about the things humans are doing that harm animals. Animals such as elephants are negatively affected by the first activity, which is [1)]_____ _____. Because people break the law and hunt species they shouldn't, animals like elephants are close to disappearing forever. Next, orangutans and other animals are harmed by deforestation, which is the [2)]_____ _____ _____. This activity has caused countless animals to lose their homes. Animals like whales can be killed by plastic pollution. It's [3)]_____ _____ _____ to the health of animals in general because they often eat it. Lastly, birds that fly in large groups like sparrows die because of tall buildings in cities. They don't perceive windows as barriers and hit them while flying. Now, let's look at some ways that we can help save these animals from [4)]_____ _____.

↘ 듣기 필수 표현
· break the law 법을 어기다
· in general 일반적으로
· save A from B A가 B하는 것을 막다

정답 및 해설 p.98

1번부터 17번까지는 듣고 답하는 문제입니다. 1번부터 15번까지는 한 번만 들려주고, 16번부터 17번까지는 두 번 들려줍니다. 방송을 잘 듣고 답을 하시기 바랍니다.

1 다음을 듣고, 여자가 하는 말의 목적으로 가장 적절한 것을 고르시오.

① 박물관 행사 취소를 공지하려고
② 프로젝터 수리 방법을 설명하려고
③ 티켓 특별 할인 행사를 소개하려고
④ 시설 관리 직원을 모집하려고
⑤ 전시회 위치를 안내하려고

2 대화를 듣고, 여자의 의견으로 가장 적절한 것을 고르시오.

① 관광지의 경관을 유지하기 위한 정책이 필요하다.
② 여행지에서는 자동차를 이용하는 것이 좋다.
③ 건강을 유지하려면 걷기 운동을 꼭 해야 한다.
④ 스페인은 휴가를 보내기에 좋은 장소이다.
⑤ 도보 여행은 최고의 여행 방식이다.

3 대화를 듣고, 두 사람의 관계를 가장 잘 나타낸 것을 고르시오.

① 식당 종업원 — 주방장
② 피부과 의사 — 환자
③ 파티 플래너 — 의뢰인
④ 수강생 — 요리 강사
⑤ 농부 — 양계업자

4 대화를 듣고, 그림에서 대화의 내용과 일치하지 않는 것을 고르시오.

5 대화를 듣고, 남자가 할 일로 가장 적절한 것을 고르시오.

① 나무 옮기기
② 식물 모종 심기
③ 원예 도구 가져오기
④ 가게에서 씨앗 사기
⑤ 정원에 새 흙을 채우기

6 대화를 듣고, 여자가 지불할 금액을 고르시오. [3점]

① $72   ② $90   ③ $100   ④ $106   ⑤ $120

7 대화를 듣고, 여자가 공부를 도와줄 수 없는 이유를 고르시오.

① 시험 준비를 하기 바빠서
② 다른 친구와 약속이 있어서
③ 미술 동아리 모임이 있어서
④ 수업 내용을 이해하지 못해서
⑤ 안과에서 검진을 받아야 해서

8 대화를 듣고, 자선 축구 경기에 관해 언급되지 않은 것을 고르시오.

① 시작 시간   ② 입장료   ③ 상대 팀
④ 수익금 기부처   ⑤ 부대 행사

9 Steel City Film Festival에 관한 다음 내용을 듣고, 일치하지 않는 것을 고르시오.

① 올해로 13번째 개최되는 영화제이다.
② 개막식은 국내에서만 생중계될 것이다.
③ 350편 정도의 영화가 상영될 것이다.
④ 티켓은 다음 주 금요일부터 판매될 것이다.
⑤ 단체 관람객은 티켓 구매 시 할인 혜택을 받을 수 있다.

10 다음 표를 보면서 대화를 듣고, 두 사람이 구매할 겨울 부츠를 고르시오.

Winter Boots

	Model	Available sizes	Price	Color	Waterproof
①	A	3-5	$46	Blue	X
②	B	4-6	$50	Black	O
③	C	4-6	$54	Pink	X
④	D	5-7	$58	Purple	O
⑤	E	5-7	$62	Brown	X

11 대화를 듣고, 여자의 마지막 말에 대한 남자의 응답으로 가장 적절한 것을 고르시오.

① Hold on. Let me see how we can get there.
② I know. It's a vanilla cake with strawberries.
③ That's right. I'd like to make an order, please.
④ Good idea. I'll send you their information.
⑤ I think so. It's open from 9 a.m. to 4 p.m.

12 대화를 듣고, 남자의 마지막 말에 대한 여자의 응답으로 가장 적절한 것을 고르시오.

① Let's go through the park.
② It's supposed to rain soon.
③ I've got their phone number here.
④ It will be ready to pick up next week.
⑤ The laptop's screen is badly damaged.

13 대화를 듣고, 여자의 마지막 말에 대한 남자의 응답으로 가장 적절한 것을 고르시오.

Man: _____

① I'm not sure. Do you have it in lighter color?
② Sure. We also have that skirt in a smaller size.
③ That's correct. You'll need to pay an additional $10.
④ All right. Your refund should go through soon.
⑤ I'm sorry. Our store policy doesn't allow that.

14 대화를 듣고, 남자의 마지막 말에 대한 여자의 응답으로 가장 적절한 것을 고르시오. [3점]

Woman: _____

① Right. We should begin to prepare for the storm.
② I disagree. I really enjoy spending time in nature.
③ Of course. I check the weather forecast every day.
④ That's true. The power station is right by my house.
⑤ Yeah. Storms like that one can do a great deal of damage.

15 다음 상황 설명을 듣고, Liam의 어머니가 Liam에게 할 말로 가장 적절한 것을 고르시오. [3점]

Liam's mother: _____

① Why don't we go hiking on another day?
② The jacket you are wearing seems too heavy.
③ You should check the forecast before we leave.
④ Make sure to wear warm clothes while hiking.
⑤ Do you think I should put on a different coat?

[16~17] 다음을 듣고, 물음에 답하시오.

16 여자가 하는 말의 주제로 가장 적절한 것은?

① the best places to visit to see fireworks
② New Year's Eve celebrations in various cities
③ beliefs about New Year's Eve in different countries
④ popular travel destinations for young people
⑤ economic benefits of hosting festivals

17 언급된 도시가 <u>아닌</u> 것은?

① New York City　　② Sydney
③ Seoul　　④ London
⑤ Rio de Janeiro

이제 듣기 문제가 끝났습니다. 채점을 마친 후 다음 페이지에서 방송을 다시 들으며 딕테이션 연습을 하시기 바랍니다.
* 채점 결과: 맞은 개수 _____ 개 / 17개　　　정답 및 해설 p.98

Dictation 정답 p.98

16회 영어듣기 모의고사 Dictation 음성을 들으며 빈칸에 알맞은 단어를 채워 넣으시기 바랍니다.

1

W Hello, museum visitors. May I have your attention please? Thank you for visiting the Denver Museum of Natural History. Unfortunately, we need to notify you that our *Frozen in Time* event 1)_____ _____ _____ for the rest of the day. This is 2)_____ _____ _____ _____ with a projector system in the conference hall that will require a replacement part. If you purchased tickets to the event, you are welcome to attend a future showing. If you would 3)_____ _____ _____ your event ticket, a full refund will be provided. We apologize for any inconvenience this causes and hope that you enjoy the rest of your visit to the museum.

↘ 듣기 필수 표현
· welcome to 자유롭게 ~할 수 있는

2

W Honey, did you hear that Jackie is 1)_____ _____ _____ _____ _____ across Spain this summer? Doesn't that sound great?

M That sounds a little hard to me.

W I think walking tours are the best way to travel.

M Why not just drive to places? It's much faster.

W Well, when you're walking, you enjoy the scenery more.

M I guess you do notice more things when you're moving slower.

W And it's 2)_____ _____ _____ _____ _____. You get to move around instead of just sitting inside a car.

M Yeah, it would be nice to get some exercise while we're on vacation.

W Exactly. That's why a walking tour is 3)_____ _____ _____ _____.

M I see what you mean. Maybe we should try it.

W Yeah! Let's make a list of places we can go.

↘ 듣기 필수 표현
· get to ~하게 되다
· instead of ~ 대신

3

W The restaurant is busier than usual today! How's everything going in the kitchen?

M So many orders have come in all at once. But we're keeping up!

W Great. Well, the customer at Table 4 ordered a chicken salad, but she has a peanut allergy. Are there any peanuts in the salad?

M No. We don't put peanuts in the salads.

W Okay. I'll go out to her table and let her know.

M By the way, 1)_____ _____ _____ _____ today's special? It's the first time we've made salmon steaks.

W They love it. I think 2)_____ _____ _____ more seafood dishes.

M I'm glad to hear that. And I'll keep that in mind when I update the menu.

W Sounds good. Oh, how much longer will the roast beef take? It's for Table 6.

M I just 3)_____ _____ _____ of the oven. Let me put it on a plate.

W Alright. I'll be right back.

↘ 듣기 필수 표현
· all at once 한꺼번에, 동시에
· keep up 따라잡다
· today's special 오늘의 특선 요리
· keep in mind ~을 참고하다, 명심하다

4

M Check out my living room, Chloe. I just redecorated it recently.

W It's amazing. I love 1)_____ _____ _____. Where did you get it?

M I actually made it myself.

W Wow, I'm impressed. It looks great.

M Thanks. I think it matches the new checked sofa well.

W I see you put a bookcase in the corner of the room.

M Right. That's where I keep all my board games.

W I love board games. And there's a 2)_____ _____
_____ _____. I didn't know you played guitar.

M I just started learning on my own. I'm not very good at it yet.

W I'm sure you'll get better with practice.

M What do you think of 3)_____ _____ _____
on the wall?

W Oh, that's a cool picture. Did you take it yourself?

M Yes. I used a special zoom lens for it.

↘ 듣기 필수 표현
· be good at ~을 잘하다

5

M I'm looking forward to working on the garden, honey!

W Me, too! We have a lot to do today, so I made a plan. First, 1)_____ _____ _____ _____.

M I already bought some flower and vegetable seeds. I got them when I went to buy the small trees.

W Great. Now, we need to fill the garden with new soil.

M 2)_____ _____ _____? The soil we have now seems good enough.

W Oh, really? Well, you have more gardening experience than me, so I trust your judgment.

M Okay. What else do we have to do?

W We have to 3)_____ _____ _____ _____
_____ _____.

M Sounds good. Let's do that now.

W Wait. We need 4)_____ _____ _____ for that. Do you know where they are?

M They're in the garage. I'll go get them.

W All right. I'll start bringing these trees to the garden.

↘ 듣기 필수 표현
· look forward to ~을 기대하다

6

M Hello. How can I help you?

W Hi. Do you still have seats available for the musical *Chicago Nights*?

M 1)_____ _____ do you need?

W Four, please.

M I see. Just a moment. *[Typing sound]* Okay, I found a row where 2)_____ _____ _____ _____
_____.

W Great.

M Are those all adult tickets?

W Actually, we have two adults and 3)_____ _____.

M Got it. It's $30 for adults and $20 for children.

W Oh, I saw an advertisement that said 4)_____
_____ _____ _____ with a theater membership card. Is that right?

M Yes. You can get a 10% discount.

W Here's my membership card and my credit card, then.

M Okay. Let me just ring everything up.

↘ 듣기 필수 표현
· ring ~ up ~을 계산해주다

7

M Hey, Elizabeth. Did you enjoy science class today?

W Yeah. It was interesting. I'm a little nervous about
1)_____ _____ _____ _____, though.

M But you're so good at science. I was actually wondering if you could 2)_____ _____ _____ what we learned because it sounds a bit confusing.

W Oh, I'm sorry, but I can't today.

M Really? Do you have an art club meeting?

W No. I decided to skip it this week.

M I see. I guess you're hanging out with some friends?

W I usually don't see them until the weekend. Today, I have to 3)_____ _____ _____ _____.

M Oh, is everything okay?

W Yes. I just need a regular checkup. I'm feeling fine.

M All right. I'll see you later, then.

↘ 듣기 필수 표현
· hang out 시간을 보내다, 놀다
· not A until B B가 되어서야 A하다

8

M Linda, do you have any plans this weekend?

W No. I'm free. Why?

M I'm participating in a charity soccer game. You should 1)_____ _____ _____ _____!

W Oh, that sounds fun. When is it?

M The game is on Saturday at 11 a.m. It's taking place at the high school's soccer field.

W Good. I can 2)_____ _____ _____ _____ _____.

M You should bring $5 in cash for the ticket.

W Okay. What charity will the money be given to?

M It's an organization that helps the homeless.

W That's a great cause.

M Yes. And you might want to bring some extra money for some of 3)_____ _____ _____.

W Oh, really? Like what?

M For instance, you can pay to have 4)_____ _____ _____ with the school mascot.

W Great. I can't wait!

↘ 듣기 필수 표현
· take place 열리다, 일어나다
· I can't wait! 정말 기대돼!

9

M Good evening, everyone. I'm Graham Bowman, the president of the Pittsburgh Film Federation. This year is 1)_____ _____ _____ of the Steel City Film Festival. This festival attracts a lot of international attention. In fact, the opening ceremony will be broadcast live in cities 2)_____ _____ _____. This year's festival will be the biggest one so far, with about 350 films playing at theaters across the city. Tickets will go on sale starting 3)_____ _____. They can be purchased online through the festival's official website. Special group tickets for eight or more people will also be available at a 15% discount. Don't miss out on the most exciting event of the year! Thank you for your attention.

↘ 듣기 필수 표현
· in fact 실제로, 사실
· so far 역대, 지금까지
· go on sale 판매하다
· miss out on ~을 놓치다

10

W Honey, can you help me choose some winter boots for our daughter?

M Of course. The Northern Shoe Company is having a sale on all winter boots right now. *[Typing sound]* Here are the most popular models for girls.

W Okay. She wears 1)_____ _____ _____.

M All right. What's our budget?

W She needs a new coat and gloves, too. So let's not spend more than $60 on boots.

M We should be able to find a nice pair for less than that. How about the color?

W I think she would like 2)_____ _____ _____.

M Then, we need to decide between these ones.

W Well, it gets pretty wet in the winter. The boots we buy 3)_____ _____ _____.

M Then, we should get this pair.

W Great. I think those are perfect.

↘ 듣기 필수 표현
· have a sale 할인하다
· more than ~보다 많이, ~ 이상의

11

W This cookie is delicious, Henry. 1)_____ _____ _____ _____ _____?

M It's from a new bakery that just opened downtown. They have a wide selection of cakes, too.

W I'd love to 2)_____ _____ about ordering a cake for my son's birthday party.

↘ 듣기 필수 표현
· would love to ~하고 싶다

12

M Honey, I just 1)_____ _____ _____ _____ about your broken laptop screen. It's fixed now, so we can pick it up any time.

W Oh, that's great news. Let's walk over there now.

M Okay, but why are you 2)_____ _____ _____?

13

M Hello. May I help you?

W Yes. I'd like to 1)_____ _____ _____ for this skirt.

M Is there a problem with it?

W It's just too tight for me.

M I see. Unfortunately, our store doesn't offer refunds. We 2)_____ _____ _____.

W Okay. Then, I'd like to try the skirt in a larger size. Do you have any in stock?

M I'll check. Just one moment, please. *[Typing sound]* I'm afraid we're all sold out.

W Hmm... Do you have any designs that 3)_____ _____ _____ this one?

M We do, actually. I recommend this skirt right here. It's one of our best-selling items.

W Oh, I love it! How much is it?

M This one is $30. The skirt you originally purchased was $20.

W So I 4)_____ _____ _____ _____ the difference, right?

↘ 듣기 필수 표현
· have ~ in stock ~의 재고가 있다

14

[Cell phone rings.]

W Hello, Uncle Adam.

M Hi, Sweetie. Are you okay? I 1)_____ _____ _____ _____ earlier.

W Oh, I'm fine. I didn't mean to make you worry. My phone died during the storm.

M I understand. But I 2)_____ _____ _____ _____ about the typhoon last night. It looked bad.

W Yeah, it was a powerful storm. The power went out for several hours, and my Internet wasn't working.

M No wonder I couldn't reach you! Well, that must have been scary.

W It was! And the wind was so strong. I couldn't sleep at all.

M Was there much damage to your neighborhood?

W 3)_____ _____ _____ _____. And some older buildings were damaged.

M That's terrible. Did anyone get hurt?

W I heard that some people were injured, but not too badly.

M That's a relief. You know, events like these show us 4)_____ _____ _____ _____ _____.

↘ 듣기 필수 표현
· go out (불, 전기 등이) 나가다, 꺼지다
· No wonder ~. ~한 것이 당연하다.

15

M Liam and his mother are planning to spend the day 1)_____ _____ _____ _____. After finishing his breakfast, Liam begins to get ready for the hike. As the weather is warm and sunny, he decides to bring 2)_____ _____ _____ _____. He thinks he will get too hot if he wears a heavier one. However, his mother checks the forecast and discovers that the weather is going to be much cooler on the mountain. In fact, there may be some snow near the summit, even though spring is around the corner. She worries that he will 3)_____ _____ _____ and might even get sick. So she wants to tell him to bundle up during the hike. In this situation, what would Liam's mother most likely say to him?

↘ 듣기 필수 표현
· around the corner 곧 다가오는, 임박하여
· bundle up 옷을 따뜻하게 입다

16~17

W Hello, and welcome back to another episode of *What a Wonderful World*. I'm your host, Monica Pierce. Today, I want to talk about New Year's Eve celebrations in different cities around the world. First, there's the famous ball drop in New York City. A gigantic ball is lowered down a pole 1)_____ _____ _____ of a building in Times Square just before midnight. In Sydney, people go to the Sydney Harbour Bridge to 2)_____ _____ _____ _____. The first show takes place early in the evening, while the main show happens at midnight. Next, there is the bell-ringing ceremony at Bosingak Pavilion in Seoul. The bell is rung 33 times 3)_____ _____ _____ of the New Year. Lastly, more than two million people celebrate New Year's Eve in Rio de Janeiro. The city hosts a large beach party that includes a fireworks display and lots of loud music. I hope this talk 4)_____ _____ _____ _____ of where to visit for New Year's Eve. Thanks for tuning in.

↘ 듣기 필수 표현
· tune in 청취하다, 시청하다

▲ 문제 음성
　바로 듣기

▲ 고사장 버전
　바로 듣기

정답 및 해설 p.104

1번부터 17번까지는 듣고 답하는 문제입니다. 1번부터 15번까지는 한 번만 들려주고, 16번부터 17번까지는 두 번 들려줍니다. 방송을 잘 듣고 답을 하시기 바랍니다.

1 다음을 듣고, 여자가 하는 말의 목적으로 가장 적절한 것을 고르시오.

① 과일 배달 서비스를 소개하려고
② 신규 매장의 위치를 설명하려고
③ 생과일주스의 이점을 설명하려고
④ 새로운 메뉴의 출시를 홍보하려고
⑤ 설문조사 제출일 변경을 공지하려고

2 대화를 듣고, 남자의 의견으로 가장 적절한 것을 고르시오.

① 답례를 기대하고 선물을 하면 안 된다.
② 생일 파티는 성대하게 할수록 좋다.
③ 물건보다 경험을 선물하는 것이 더 낫다.
④ 어린이는 보호자와 항상 동행해야 한다.
⑤ 상대의 취향을 고려해서 선물을 골라야 한다.

3 대화를 듣고, 두 사람의 관계를 가장 잘 나타낸 것을 고르시오.

① 리포터 — 선장
② 시장 상인 — 어부
③ 사진작가 — 가이드
④ 여행사 직원 — 고객
⑤ 섬 주민 — 항만 관리자

4 대화를 듣고, 그림에서 대화의 내용과 일치하지 않는 것을 고르시오.

5 대화를 듣고, 남자가 할 일로 가장 적절한 것을 고르시오.

① 시간표 짜기
② 이메일 보내기
③ 간식 구매하기
④ 광고지 붙이기
⑤ 영화감독 만나기

6 대화를 듣고, 여자가 지불할 금액을 고르시오.

① $100　② $105　③ $110　④ $120　⑤ $125

7 대화를 듣고, 남자가 세미나 장소를 변경하려는 이유를 고르시오.

① 학교 회의실이 작아서
② 프로젝터가 고장 나서
③ 주차 공간이 협소해서
④ 선생님들의 요청이 있어서
⑤ 농구 경기와 시간이 겹쳐서

8 대화를 듣고, 글쓰기 워크숍에 관해 언급되지 않은 것을 고르시오.

① 장소　　② 주제　　③ 참가비
④ 강연자　　⑤ 준비물

9 Fall Family Carnival에 관한 다음 내용을 듣고, 일치하지 않는 것을 고르시오. [3점]

① 시청에서 주최한다.
② 포토존이 동쪽 정원에 설치된다.
③ 9월 15일부터 9월 20일까지 열린다.
④ 입장권은 현금으로 지불해야 한다.
⑤ 수익금은 도시 개발 사업에 쓰일 예정이다.

10 다음 표를 보면서 대화를 듣고, 두 사람이 선택할 프랑스어 수업을 고르시오.

French Courses

	Course	Time	Price	Level	Topic
①	A	8 a.m. - 11 a.m.	$230	Beginner	Everyday Conversation
②	B	8 a.m. - 11 a.m.	$270	Intermediate	Literature
③	C	9 a.m. - 12 p.m.	$310	Advanced	Literature
④	D	9 a.m. - 12 p.m.	$250	Intermediate	Everyday Conversation
⑤	E	1 p.m. - 4 p.m.	$320	Intermediate	Everyday Conversation

11 대화를 듣고, 여자의 마지막 말에 대한 남자의 응답으로 가장 적절한 것을 고르시오.

① Sure. I don't need to eat right away.

② Yes. You can have some of my rice cakes.

③ No. I thought you were going to pack some food.

④ You're right. Let's eat lunch before we go hiking.

⑤ I don't think so. We should take photos of this beautiful view.

12 대화를 듣고, 남자의 마지막 말에 대한 여자의 응답으로 가장 적절한 것을 고르시오.

① Here you go. That should help with the stress.

② No problem. It should be fixed by the end of the day.

③ I don't know. It won't charge even when it's plugged in.

④ Thank you! I'll give it back as soon as I'm done.

⑤ That's right. You have a lot of research to do.

13 대화를 듣고, 여자의 마지막 말에 대한 남자의 응답으로 가장 적절한 것을 고르시오. [3점]

Man: _____

① Okay. You can bring him around 4 p.m. tomorrow.

② Good idea. We can have some quality time, then.

③ Don't worry. He should feel better in a few days.

④ Right. We should give him a different dog food.

⑤ Yes. Check if they can see him in the morning.

14 대화를 듣고, 남자의 마지막 말에 대한 여자의 응답으로 가장 적절한 것을 고르시오.

Woman: _____

① That would be great. I will be there as soon as possible.

② Sure. This app shows you the locations of all the national parks.

③ No problem. Just tell me your email address, and I'll send it to you.

④ Thank you. I never know the names of plants I see in the forest.

⑤ You're welcome. I hope your son had a great time today.

15 다음 상황 설명을 듣고, Kylie가 Peter에게 할 말로 가장 적절한 것을 고르시오. [3점]

Kylie: _____

① If you're busy, I can go ahead and do it.

② I would prefer outdoor activities over indoor ones.

③ Don't wait to book our activities because they fill up fast.

④ That one is fully booked, but here are some other options.

⑤ Let's buy our plane tickets now so that we can save some money.

[16~17] 다음을 듣고, 물음에 답하시오.

16 남자가 하는 말의 주제로 가장 적절한 것은?

① effects of artificial food products on the body

② farming methods utilized for fruit cultivation

③ challenges of growing fruit in today's climate

④ why some fruits have become less popular

⑤ examples of fruits changed by humans

17 언급된 과일이 아닌 것은?

① bananas ② watermelons ③ strawberries

④ peaches ⑤ apples

이제 듣기 문제가 끝났습니다. 채점을 마친 후 다음 페이지에서 방송을 다시 들으며 딕테이션 연습을 하시기 바랍니다.

* 채점 결과: 맞은 개수 _____개 / 17개 정답 및 해설 p.104

Dictation 정답 p.104

17회 영어듣기 모의고사 Dictation 음성을 들으며 빈칸에 알맞은 단어를 채워 넣으시기 바랍니다.

1

W   Hello, everyone! At Natural Beverage, our goal is to provide you with the best healthy fruit and vegetable juices. We recently 1)_____ _____ _____ after listening to customer feedback. We're excited to tell you about the new items, including Berry Burst, Mango Explosion, and Harvest Smoothie. They 2)_____ _____ _____ _____ every shop where our juices are sold! These delicious new juices are all-natural and packed with nutrients to 3)_____ _____ _____ throughout the day. So be sure to check out our new flavors soon. Thank you for choosing Natural Beverage!

❯ 듣기 필수 표현
· provide A with B A에게 B를 공급하다
· be packed with ~으로 가득하다
· check out ~을 확인하다

2

M   Honey, what should we give to our daughter Alice for her birthday?
W   Well, why don't we 1)_____ _____ _____ _____ this weekend to look around?
M   Hmm... But we always do that. I'd like to 2)_____ _____ _____ _____ this year.
W   Are you sure? She gets so excited over gifts.
M   Getting a great experience as a gift is better than getting an object that will 3)_____ _____ _____ over time.
W   That's true. I also can't think of any items she wants.
M   An object just takes up space, and if she doesn't like it, we have to return or exchange it.
W   You're right. Doing something 4)_____ _____ _____ would be more special. How about going to the amusement park on her birthday?
M   Great idea. I think such an experience will mean a lot more to her.

❯ 듣기 필수 표현
· look around 둘러보다, 구경하다
· take up space 자리를 차지하다

3

W   Hello. You must be Mr. Jacobs. I'm Olivia Roberts, and I'll be interviewing you today.
M   Welcome aboard. I'm a 1)_____ _____ _____ _____ *Adventures Abroad*.
W   Thank you. I've heard wonderful things about your boat tours.
M   Well, I grew up here, so it's easy 2)_____ _____ _____ _____ .
W   Do you ever get tired of taking people out on your boat?
M   Not at all. The islands here are beautiful, and I enjoy meeting people from all over the world.
W   That's great. So where will we be going today 3)_____ _____ _____ _____ ?
M   We'll sail over to an island which is about 30 minutes away.
W   Do you think 4)_____ _____ _____ _____ ? One of the members of my film crew gets seasick.
M   No. The water should be quite calm today.
W   Okay, then. I think we're ready to go.

❯ 듣기 필수 표현
· get tired of ~에 싫증이 나다
· get seasick 뱃멀미하다

4

M   Hey, Lauren. Have you finished setting up the home office?
W   Yeah, it's 1)_____ _____ . What do you think?
M   It's very cozy. And I love that you put the desk by the window.
W   Right? Then, I can look out at the view while I work.
M   Is that a new lamp on the desk?
W   Yeah. I just bought it.
M   I like how modern it looks.
W   The 2)_____ _____ _____ _____ is also new. I don't have air conditioning, so I thought it would be useful.
M   Definitely. And I like that cushion with a flower on the chair.

W It makes the chair 3)_____ _____ _____ _____.

M That makes sense. But what are in those two boxes next to the desk?

W Oh, those are just full of office supplies.

M I see. Your home office looks great.

↘ **듣기 필수 표현**
· set up ~을 준비하다, 설치하다
· be full of ~으로 가득 차 있다

5

W Tyler, how is the planning going for the Student Film Festival?

M It's going well. I've 1)_____ _____ _____ _____ for all of the movies.

W That's good. Did you put up the flyers around campus?

M I did that this morning, actually.

W Great. I'm thinking about sending an email out to all the students, too.

M Oh, I just sent one. I 2)_____ _____ _____ _____ _____ from the flyer.

W Amazing job. Also, maybe we should sell some popcorn and drinks for attendees. What do you think?

M Yeah. We could set up booths for tickets and snacks.

W Okay. I'll 3)_____ _____ _____ from the store.

M Let me do it. I have time this afternoon. How did the meeting with the directors go?

W It went well. They accepted our invitation to attend the opening ceremony.

↘ **듣기 필수 표현**
· put up ~을 붙이다, 게시하다

6

M Welcome to Wanda's Bakery. May I help you?

W Hello. I'd like to order a wedding cake. What type of cake 1)_____ _____ _____?

M Usually, people order a medium or large vanilla cake.

W How much are they?

M Our medium cake is $100, and the large is $150.

W I'll go with a medium, please.

M I also recommend 2)_____ _____ _____ to the cake. Here are some example photos.

W Oh, wow. These are beautiful.

M It's another $20 for the flowers. Would you like to add some?

W Sure. I'd like to 3)_____ _____ _____ on it.

M So you want one medium wedding cake and some flower decorations.

W That's right. Also, 4)_____ _____ _____?

M Yes. It will be an additional $5.

W Okay. This is the address of the wedding hall. Here's my card.

↘ **듣기 필수 표현**
· go with ~을 선택하다

7

M Hi, Ms. Napa. I need to talk to you about the teacher's seminar.

W Sure, Principal Kim. What's going on?

M We can 1)_____ _____ _____ _____ _____ here at the school. Can you book a conference room at the Skymark Hotel instead?

W Sure, but why is that? Is our meeting room too small?

M No. There will be less than 20 teachers attending.

W Is it because there is a 2)_____ _____ _____ at the same time? It could be noisy.

M That doesn't matter. The gymnasium is far from the meeting room.

W Then, the teachers 3)_____ _____ _____ the change.

M Actually, we can't have it here because 4)_____ _____ _____ _____. It won't be repaired in time.

W Oh, I see! Let me call the hotel right now.

M Thank you.

↘ **듣기 필수 표현**
· at the same time 동시에
· in time 제때

8

W   Hey, Josh. You like to write, don't you?

M   Yeah. I'm working on a few short stories. Why do you ask?

W   There's 1)_____ _____ _____ at the local library next week.

M   Really? That sounds interesting.

W   Yes. I have the brochure here. The theme is crafting a story, and it will focus on short stories and poetry.

M   Oh, that's perfect. I'd love to go.

W   Me too. It says we 2)_____ _____ _____ _____ in advance. They're $5 each.

M   That's fine. And how long is this workshop?

W   It's next Wednesday and Thursday from 6 to 9 p.m.

M   All right. Is there anything else we need to know?

W   It says we should bring 3)_____ _____ _____ _____ we want feedback on. But I think we'd better bring our laptops, too.

M   Then, let's buy our tickets today.

W   Sounds good!

↘ 듣기 필수 표현
· focus on ~에 집중하다
· in advance 사전에, 미리

9

M   Hello, listeners! Are you looking for 1)_____ _____ _____ _____ _____ the beautiful fall season with your family? Then, come to the Fall Family Carnival! This event, hosted by city hall, will feature 2)_____ _____ _____ _____, rides, and refreshments. It will also include a photo zone in the east garden where you can take pictures. The carnival will run from 3)_____ _____ _____ _____ at North Point Park. Entrance to the event will be free for people of all ages, although food and rides require 4)_____ _____ _____. The money that is raised will go towards city development projects. For more information about the carnival, please visit www.fallfamilycarnival.com. We hope to see you there!

↘ 듣기 필수 표현
· of all ages 모든 연령대의
· go towards ~의 비용으로 쓰이다

10

W   Do you want to take a French course with me, Leo?

M   Oh, I'd love to. I really need to 1)_____ _____ _____.

W   I just looked some up on my computer. Check them out.

M   Okay. I don't think I can take this one. I'm too busy 2)_____ _____ _____.

W   Then, we should take one that ends at or before noon. How much do you want to spend?

M   I think 3)_____ _____ _____ _____ of less than $300 is a good idea. What do you think?

W   I agree. And we've taken French classes before, so let's not sign up for a beginner course.

M   Then, we just have to decide on the course topic.

W   We don't need to learn about French literature.

M   No. It'll be more helpful to learn how to use the 4)_____ _____ _____ _____.

W   I guess we've made our selection, then.

M   Great. Let's sign up now.

↘ 듣기 필수 표현
· sign up for ~에 등록하다
· make a selection 선택하다

11

W   Jake, what a beautiful day for hiking!

M   Yeah, the view is amazing. I'm getting a little hungry, though. Should we 1)_____ _____ _____ _____ now?

W   We're almost at the top of the mountain. Let's 2)_____ _____ _____ _____ _____.

↘ 듣기 필수 표현
· get hungry 배가 고파지다

12

M   Are you okay, Jin? You seem really stressed out.

W   My laptop 1)_____ _____. I need it for a science assignment I'm doing right now.

M   Do you 2)_____ _____ _____ _____? I don't need it at the moment.

↘ 듣기 필수 표현
· stressed out 스트레스로 지친
· at the moment 지금

13

W Honey, why didn't you reply to my messages earlier?

M I'm sorry. My phone ran out of battery. Is everything okay?

W I got home earlier and noticed that our dog, Max, was 1) _____ _____ .

M What do you mean?

W He won't eat his food, and he keeps whining. He never does that.

M Maybe it's because he's been alone a lot these days. We've both been 2) _____ _____ _____ , and dogs can get lonely.

W But I'm worried that he could be sick.

M Should we take him to the vet, then?

W I think so. I will feel better 3) _____ _____ _____ _____ that he's okay.

M You're right. We can take him tomorrow.

W Do you want me to make an appointment?

↘ 듣기 필수 표현
· run out of ~을 다 써버리다
· make an appointment 예약을 잡다

14

[Telephone rings.]

W Hello. Murray National Park. This is Gina speaking.

M Hi. I'm calling to ask about 1) _____ _____ _____ _____ for kids.

W Oh, yes. How old is your child?

M My son is five years old.

W Okay. We have many programs for children that age.

M Great. What kinds of activities do they do?

W We encourage them to explore the natural environment. So they 2) _____ _____ _____ in the water, and they learn to identify plants.

M I think my son would really enjoy that.

W Yes, the kids love it. They also make artwork using leaves, rocks, and sticks.

M That's wonderful. Are there any fees to participate?

W No. But you'll need to 3) _____ _____ _____ , such as a plant identification booklet.

M I see. Can you send me a program schedule?

↘ 듣기 필수 표현
· such as ~과 같은

15

W Peter arrives at a resort for his vacation. As he is checking in, he sees a poster that advertises activities at the resort. Although there are many different options, he finds the scuba diving lesson the most interesting. According to the poster, lessons 1) _____ _____ _____ _____ . Peter asks a staff member, Kylie, if he can book a spot during his stay. But when Kylie checks the computer system, she finds out that 2) _____ _____ _____ _____ _____ for the next few weeks. Nevertheless, other fun activities, such as kayaking, still have openings. Therefore, Kylie wants to tell Peter that he can't join the class because it is full, though there are 3) _____ _____ _____ . In this situation, what would Kylie most likely say to Peter?

↘ 듣기 필수 표현
· according to ~에 따르면
· book a spot 자리를 예약하다

16~17

M Good morning, students. Let's continue our discussion of fruit from last class. Today, I'd like to discuss several different fruits that have been 1) _____ _____ _____ . For example, bananas once were hard on the inside and difficult to eat. The modern banana is a hybrid of two wild species. Through selective breeding, people have created bananas that are much tastier than they used to be. Also, watermelons 2) _____ _____ _____ over time. In the past, they had more seeds and paler flesh. The watermelons we eat today look completely different due to human intervention. Strawberries are another fruit that has changed because of humans. Wild strawberries are tasty, but their shelf life is short. So humans bred strawberries that 3) _____ _____ _____ for a longer time. Finally, ancient peaches were tiny fruits with a salty taste. But the peaches we buy at the supermarket today are much larger, sweeter, and juicier. Now, let's watch a short video about some of these fruits.

↘ 듣기 필수 표현
· over time 시간이 지나면서

18회 영어듣기 모의고사

정답 및 해설 p.110

1번부터 17번까지는 듣고 답하는 문제입니다. 1번부터 15번까지는 한 번만 들려주고, 16번부터 17번까지는 두 번 들려줍니다. 방송을 잘 듣고 답을 하시기 바랍니다.

1 다음을 듣고, 남자가 하는 말의 목적으로 가장 적절한 것을 고르시오.

① 식중독 예방 방법을 안내하려고
② 여행 안전 수칙을 설명하려고
③ 야경 투어 참여를 권장하려고
④ 도난 사고 사례를 소개하려고
⑤ 문화 체험 행사 참여를 독려하려고

2 대화를 듣고, 남자의 의견으로 가장 적절한 것을 고르시오.

① 커피 섭취는 집중력 향상에 도움이 된다.
② 충분한 영양 섭취는 두뇌 회전에 필수적이다.
③ 건강을 위해 충분히 수면을 취해야 한다.
④ 커피를 많이 마시면 공부에 방해가 된다.
⑤ 적당한 긴장감은 실수를 하지 않도록 도와준다.

3 대화를 듣고, 두 사람의 관계를 가장 잘 나타낸 것을 고르시오.

① 식품학 교수 — 학생
② 선생님 — 제빵사
③ 잡지사 기자 — 셰프
④ 영양사 — 학부모
⑤ 식당 주인 — 식품 배달원

4 대화를 듣고, 그림에서 대화의 내용과 일치하지 <u>않는</u> 것을 고르시오.

5 대화를 듣고, 남자가 할 일로 가장 적절한 것을 고르시오.

① 식재료 장보기
② 이불 빨래하기
③ 손님방 청소하기
④ 옷장 정리하기
⑤ 공항택시 예약하기

6 대화를 듣고, 여자가 지불할 금액을 고르시오.

① $45   ② $54   ③ $60   ④ $63   ⑤ $70

7 대화를 듣고, 남자가 축구 시합을 취소해야 하는 이유를 고르시오.

① 모든 팀원이 참가할 수 없어서
② 경기장 예약이 다 차서
③ 심판을 섭외할 수 없어서
④ 폭우가 올 예정이어서
⑤ 부상자가 많아서

8 대화를 듣고, Green Haven Pottery Program에 관해 언급되지 <u>않은</u> 것을 고르시오.

① 장소   ② 시간   ③ 비용
④ 신청 방법   ⑤ 수업 정원

9 Riverside High School Debate에 관한 다음 내용을 듣고, 일치하지 <u>않는</u> 것을 고르시오. [3점]

① 오전 9시부터 10시 30분까지 진행된다.
② 모든 학생들은 토론 대회에 참가할 수 있다.
③ 대회 참가를 위해서는 선생님께 알려야 한다.
④ 참가자들은 티셔츠와 참가 증명서를 받는다.
⑤ 우승자들은 전국 토론 대회에 대표로 참가한다.

10 다음 표를 보면서 대화를 듣고, 여자가 구매할 스카프를 고르시오.

Winter Scarves

	Scarf	Material	Price	Machine Washable	Color
①	A	Cotton	$30	O	Black
②	B	Wool	$35	X	White
③	C	Silk	$40	O	Gray
④	D	Cashmere	$45	X	Black
⑤	E	Cashmere	$60	X	White

11 대화를 듣고, 남자의 마지막 말에 대한 여자의 응답으로 가장 적절한 것을 고르시오.

① Usually the letters arrive in one week.
② Unfortunately, she didn't write me back.
③ Maybe we can meet next week for a coffee.
④ Actually, we went to the same summer camp.
⑤ Hopefully I get a chance to go to Amsterdam.

12 대화를 듣고, 여자의 마지막 말에 대한 남자의 응답으로 가장 적절한 것을 고르시오.

① One moment. Let me get my wallet.
② Don't worry. I can just take the bus home.
③ I'm sorry I'm late. I'll be there as soon as I can.
④ I agree. The food at the restaurant was great.
⑤ Thank you. I think I put it on the table.

13 대화를 듣고, 여자의 마지막 말에 대한 남자의 응답으로 가장 적절한 것을 고르시오. [3점]

Man: _____

① Sure. I'll cut up the vegetables now.
② Of course. Come sit over by the fire.
③ Good idea. Let's go for a swim tomorrow.
④ Not yet. I'm still far from the campground.
⑤ No, thanks. I'd like ham and tomatoes on mine.

14 대화를 듣고, 남자의 마지막 말에 대한 여자의 응답으로 가장 적절한 것을 고르시오. [3점]

Woman: _____

① Okay. Your total will be $150.
② Great. Thanks for fixing it so fast.
③ Got it. I'll come by around 5 p.m.
④ Exactly. I'd prefer to rent a smaller model.
⑤ Definitely. Let me write down what parts to get.

15 다음 상황 설명을 듣고, Daniel이 Rose에게 할 말로 가장 적절한 것을 고르시오.

Daniel: _____

① You have to pay closer attention to the math teacher.
② It's important to create a study schedule for yourself.
③ I don't think it's helpful to worry so much about grades.
④ We can go over the math problems again in 10 minutes.
⑤ You need to learn how to concentrate for more than an hour.

[16~17] 다음을 듣고, 물음에 답하시오.

16 여자가 하는 말의 주제로 가장 적절한 것은?

① why some animals cannot be tamed as pets
② ways in which some animals help each other
③ how animals protect themselves from danger
④ different ways in which animals catch prey
⑤ dangerous animals to avoid in the wild

17 언급된 동물이 <u>아닌</u> 것은?

① bees　　② skunks　　③ squid
④ snakes　　⑤ turtles

이제 듣기 문제가 끝났습니다. 채점을 마친 후 다음 페이지에서 방송을 다시 들으며 딕테이션 연습을 하시기 바랍니다.

* 채점 결과: 맞은 개수 _____ 개 / 17개　　　　정답 및 해설 p.110

18회 Dictation

Dictation 정답 p.110

18회 영어듣기 모의고사 Dictation 음성을 들으며 빈칸에 알맞은 단어를 채워 넣으시기 바랍니다.

1

M Hello, everyone! My name is Mateo, and I will be your tour guide for the week. To begin, let me 1)_____ _____ _____ _____ during the trip. First of all, please keep all your belongings in a safe place. Your passport is the most important thing, so I ask that you always have it with you. Secondly, it is very dangerous 2)_____ _____ _____ at night. If you must go out at nighttime, I recommend bringing another tour member. Finally, the tap water here is not safe to drink. You should only drink bottled water. If you 3)_____ _____ _____, you will have an enjoyable trip without any problems. Okay, shall we begin our trip?

2

M How is studying for your test, Jacky?

W It's fine, but I'm a little tired.

M Me too. I think I'll leave the library soon and go have dinner.

W I'll probably 1)_____ _____ _____ _____ and get some coffee to help me stay awake.

M Didn't you already have a few cups today?

W Yeah. I need it to help me focus.

M I understand, but drinking too much coffee will actually 2)_____ _____ _____ for you to study.

W Are you sure?

M Yes! After you drink a lot of coffee, you feel nervous and uncomfortable.

W Oh, I know that feeling.

M And when you stay up late drinking coffee, you are 3)_____ _____ _____ _____. So it's hard to remember what you studied.

W I see what you mean. I'll get some juice instead.

↘ 듣기 필수 표현
· stay awake (자지 않고) 깨어 있다
· stay up late 늦게까지 깨어 있다

3

W Hi, Mr. Hemmings. How are you today?

M I've been pretty busy. I just 1)_____ _____ _____ _____.

W Great. Well... I wanted to ask whether you would be interested in a work-experience program for my class.

M Oh, what is that?

W Students would spend one day 2)_____ _____ _____ in your bakery.

M That sounds good. Are the students interested in becoming bakers?

W Yes. Some of my students want to open their own bakeries. So if you'd like to participate, these students can come here and spend a day with you.

M What do I have to do? I can show them 3)_____ _____ _____ _____ _____.

W Yes. And you can answer any questions they ask. Also, they can help you out.

M Sounds good. I'll sign up for it.

W Thank you so much.

↘ 듣기 필수 표현
· be interested in ~에 관심이 있다
· help out ~를 돕다
· sign up for ~을 신청하다

4

W Is that a photo of the resort you stayed at last weekend, Sean?

M Yeah. That waterslide in the pool was so fun.

W That's your beach towel on the chair, right? I recognize 1)_____ _____ _____.

M You're right. I spent a lot of time relaxing on that chair.

W Did you get some snacks, too?

M No. I just drank a glass of lemonade. You can see it on the table 2)_____ _____ _____.

W It seems so peaceful.

M It wasn't always peaceful. There was a big group of little kids. The resort staff kept warning them not to run.

W That must be why there's a "No Running" sign posted.

M Exactly. Those are ³)_____ _____ _____ in the pool.

W Well, it looks like a really nice resort. Did you have a good time?

M Definitely. You should go there soon.

5

W Honey, your cousins from Germany arrive tomorrow. I can't wait to see them again.

M I know. Is everything ready for their arrival?

W Almost. I have to go to the store to buy some food for them.

M I ¹)_____ _____ _____ for you to take.

W Thanks. Did you wash the blankets?

M I did that earlier today while you cleaned the guest room.

W Great. Did you move our storage boxes ²)_____ _____ _____ _____, too?

M Yeah. They'll need lots of space for their luggage.

W Okay. We need to figure out how they'll get here from the airport.

M I can ³)_____ _____ _____ taxi to pick them up.

W Oh, leave it to me. I'll call right now.

M No. You go to the store. I'll take care of it.

↘ 듣기 필수 표현
· figure out ~을 알아내다
· pick up ~를 데리러 가다
· Leave it to me. 나한테 맡겨.
· take care of ~을 처리하다

6

M Hello. May I help you?

W Yes. I'd like to buy a candle.

M What about this one? It's our ¹)_____ _____ _____, Vanilla Dream.

W Oh, that smells great. How much is it?

M Originally, it was $40. But right now, it's $30.

W I'll take one, please. And do you have any room sprays?

M We do. What kind of scent are you looking for?

W I'm looking for something that ²)_____ _____ _____.

M Try this lemon spray. It has a very clean smell, and it only costs $15.

W Great. I'll take ³)_____ _____ _____ _____.

M All right. So you want the candle and the two bottles of spray, right?

W That's right. Can I ⁴)_____ _____ _____ all of this, please?

M Sure. Here are some free samples, too.

W Thanks. Here's my credit card.

↘ 듣기 필수 표현
· look for ~을 찾다

7

W Hey, William. Our team's first soccer game is this weekend. Are you excited?

M Actually, we have to cancel this Saturday's game.

W Oh, no. I thought everyone on the team could make it.

M Yeah, we ¹)_____ _____ _____ on that day.

W Then, what's the reason? Is there heavy rain in the forecast?

M Not at all. It's going to be very sunny this weekend.

W Hmm... Is it because we couldn't ²)_____ _____ _____ for the game?

M No. I found one who is available. The problem is that there's no field to play on.

W Oh, are they ³)_____ _____ _____?

M Yes. So we'll ⁴)_____ _____ _____ we can schedule a field.

W That's too bad. I was really looking forward to this game.

↘ 듣기 필수 표현
· make it 참석하다

8

M Rebecca, have you seen the posters about the Green Haven Pottery Program?

W Oh, isn't that being held ¹)_____ _____ _____ _____ on Houston Street?

M Yeah, that's right. Would you like to sign up for it?

W Definitely. It would be fun to make our own coffee mugs and plates.

M I agree. The classes will take place ²)_____ _____ _____. They run from 6 to 8 p.m.

W I'm free at that time. Let's sign up for it. But what about the fee for the program?

M It's $150, but there are five classes in total.

W That's fine with me. How do we enroll?

M We have to ³)_____ _____ _____. But we should hurry before the class fills up.

W Let's call today, then.

↘ 듣기 필수 표현
· take place 열리다, 개최하다
· in total 총, 통틀어
· fill up 다 차다, 가득 차다

9

W Hello, students! Do you want to put your debate skills to the test? Then, we ¹)_____ _____ _____ _____ in the Riverside High School Debate this Thursday! The debate will take place from 9 to 10:30 a.m. in the auditorium. All students are welcome to compete. If you want to participate, you must ²)_____ _____ _____ by Tuesday. Competitors will receive a free T-shirt and a certificate for participating. Each of the winners will receive a cash prize of $200. They will also represent the school ³)_____ _____ _____. Please join us, and show off your debate skills! For more information, please visit our school's website.

↘ 듣기 필수 표현
· put ~ to the test ~을 시험해보다
· show off ~을 뽐내다

10

M Welcome to Freeman's Department Store.

W Hi. I'm looking for a new winter scarf.

M Okay. You should ¹)_____ _____ _____ _____ our most popular options over here. We have all kinds of materials to choose from.

W I don't want a wool scarf because ²)_____ _____ _____ _____ _____.

M I understand. So what's your price range?

W I don't want to spend more than $50.

M Got it. And do you prefer one that you can ³)_____ _____ _____ _____?

W Yes. I think that would be convenient.

M Now, you just have to choose ⁴)_____ _____ _____ _____.

W I like the gray one. It'll go with my coat.

M Excellent. Then, we've found the perfect scarf for you.

↘ 듣기 필수 표현
· go with ~과 잘 어울리다

11

M Hey, Chloe. What are you writing?

W I'm ¹)_____ _____ _____ to my friend Alice. She lives in Amsterdam, and we exchange letters often.

M Wow, that's cool. But Amsterdam is so far away. You must have met her ²)_____ _____ _____ _____.

12

[Cell phone rings.]

W Hey, Kyle. Did you get home okay? We're ¹)_____ _____ _____ _____.

M Hi, April. Yeah, but I realized I left my wallet there.

W I can check for you. Do you remember ²)_____ _____ _____ _____?

↘ 듣기 필수 표현
· get home 집에 도착하다

13

W Did we take all of the camping gear out of the car, honey?

M Yes, I moved it all into the campsite.

W Great. I've set up the camping chairs, too.

M Now, we can finally relax. It has been a long day.

W Yes, that [1]_____ _____ _____ was terrible.

M It was. So let's just rest at the campground today. We can start exploring tomorrow.

W That sounds good to me. What should we make for dinner?

M Well, we [2]_____ _____ _____ _____ to make sandwiches.

W Let's cook the meat. We can make sandwiches for lunch tomorrow.

M Okay. Then, we should start a fire.

W I'll go [3]_____ _____ _____. Can you begin preparing the food in the meantime?

↘ 듣기 필수 표현
· set up ~을 설치하다
· start a fire 불을 피우다
· in the meantime 그 사이에, 그동안

14

[Cell phone rings.]

W Hello. This is Linda Allen.

M Hi. I'm calling from Belmont Auto Repair.

W Oh, yes. Did you find out what's [1]_____ _____ _____?

M We did. There's a problem with the engine.

W Okay. How long will it take to fix?

M It could take up to two weeks. We have to [2]_____ _____ _____ _____.

W Two weeks? I can't go without my car for that long.

M We can give you a rental car in the meantime. You'll get a large discount on it because of your situation.

W That's fine, then. Is there anything that [3]_____ _____ _____ _____ _____?

M You just need to bring your license to the shop when you come. You'll have to sign some paperwork, too.

W Great. When can I pick up the car?

M We are open until 7 p.m. today, so [4]_____ _____ _____.

↘ 듣기 필수 표현
· find out ~을 찾아내다
· up tp 최대 ~까지
· go without ~ 없이 지내다

15

M Rose is a high school student. Recently, she took [1]_____ _____ _____ in her math class. Today, she found out that she received a poor grade, so she feels very disappointed. Rose knows that her friend Daniel got an A on the test. So she asks him what she should do [2]_____ _____ _____ _____. He thinks that concentrating is the most important factor when studying. He knows that when Rose studies, she cannot concentrate for more than 10 minutes at a time. In his opinion, this [3]_____ _____ _____. So Daniel wants to tell Rose that she should try to [4]_____ _____ _____ _____ for more than an hour. In this situation, what would Daniel most likely say to Rose?

↘ 듣기 필수 표현
· in one's opinion ~의 생각으로는

16~17

W Hello, students. In the last class, we learned about different ways that animals catch their prey. Today, we'll go over some of the ways that animals [1]_____ _____ _____ _____. First, let's talk about bees. These insects are usually harmless. But if they feel that their hive is threatened, they will use their stinger [2]_____ _____ _____ _____. Second, I should mention skunks, which have a powerful weapon. This gentle creature has a bad-smelling spray that it will use if danger is close by. Third, squid [3]_____ _____ _____ into the water when predators are near. The ink creates a dark cloud that confuses the predator and allows the squid to quickly escape. Lastly, there are turtles. When a turtle [4]_____ _____, it simply hides inside its shell until the threat is gone. Now, let's watch a video that shows these animals and others in action.

↘ 듣기 필수 표현
· go over ~을 살펴보다

19회 영어듣기 모의고사

정답 및 해설 p.116

1번부터 17번까지는 듣고 답하는 문제입니다. 1번부터 15번까지는 한 번만 들려주고, 16번부터 17번까지는 두 번 들려줍니다. 방송을 잘 듣고 답을 하시기 바랍니다.

1 다음을 듣고, 여자가 하는 말의 목적으로 가장 적절한 것을 고르시오.

① 요리 방송 프로그램을 추천하려고
② 식료품점의 신장개업을 알리려고
③ 좋은 그릇 고르는 법을 소개하려고
④ 밀키트 배달 서비스를 홍보하려고
⑤ 주간 식사 계획 방법을 설명하려고

2 대화를 듣고, 남자의 의견으로 가장 적절한 것을 고르시오.

① 쇼핑할 때는 예산을 고려해야 한다.
② 새 옷을 사기 전에 헌 옷을 팔아야 한다.
③ 중고품 가게에서 쇼핑하는 편이 좋다.
④ 재활용을 통해 환경보호를 실천할 수 있다.
⑤ 나만의 스타일을 고수하는 것이 바람직하다.

3 대화를 듣고, 두 사람의 관계를 가장 잘 나타낸 것을 고르시오.

① 약국 직원 — 환자
② 치과 의사 — 식당 주인
③ 동물 훈련사 — 수의사
④ 음식점 손님 — 종업원
⑤ 가구 배달원 — 고객

4 대화를 듣고, 그림에서 대화의 내용과 일치하지 않는 것을 고르시오.

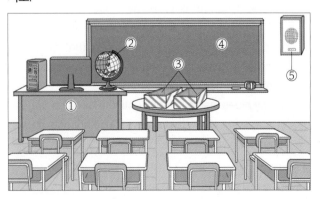

5 대화를 듣고, 여자가 할 일로 가장 적절한 것을 고르시오.

① 선글라스 모아두기
② 티셔츠 주문하기
③ 배경 만들기
④ 카메라 대여하기
⑤ 종이 구매하기

6 대화를 듣고, 여자가 지불할 금액을 고르시오. [3점]

① $90   ② $99   ③ $110   ④ $119   ⑤ $130

7 대화를 듣고, 여자가 여행을 갈 수 <u>없는</u> 이유를 고르시오.

① 돈을 모아야 해서
② 밖으로 나가고 싶지 않아서
③ 가고 싶은 곳의 예약이 다 차서
④ 가족과 시간을 보내고 싶어서
⑤ 국립공원에서 봉사활동을 해서

8 대화를 듣고, Jamestown Whale Festival에 관해 언급되지 <u>않은</u> 것을 고르시오.

① 장소   ② 프로그램   ③ 운영 시간
④ 티켓 가격   ⑤ 추천 교통편

9 The Geography Quiz에 관한 다음 내용을 듣고, 일치하지 <u>않는</u> 것을 고르시오. [3점]

① 지원서는 1월 15일까지 제출할 수 있다.
② 선정된 사람은 31일까지 연락을 받을 것이다.
③ 지원할 때 자기소개 동영상도 제출해야 한다.
④ 지원자들은 쇼에 참가한 적이 있어도 된다.
⑤ 촬영은 2월에 시작될 예정이다.

10 다음 표를 보면서 대화를 듣고, 여자가 구매할 쇼핑 카트를 고르시오.

Grocery Carts

	Model	Material	Price	Wheels	Color
①	A	Fabric	$35	2	Purple
②	B	Aluminum	$60	2	Gray
③	C	Aluminum	$70	4	Black
④	D	Plastic	$90	4	Blue
⑤	E	Plastic	$105	4	White

11 대화를 듣고, 여자의 마지막 말에 대한 남자의 응답으로 가장 적절한 것을 고르시오.

① It should only take about 10 minutes.
② We can either see it at 6 p.m. or 7 p.m.
③ I'd rather go to the park than the theater.
④ We can catch a bus in front of the post office.
⑤ I'm sending some snacks to my friend in Canada.

12 대화를 듣고, 남자의 마지막 말에 대한 여자의 응답으로 가장 적절한 것을 고르시오.

① It'll be worth it if it helps.
② Your new haircut looks amazing.
③ I don't know why my hair gets dry.
④ I should see a doctor to take treatment.
⑤ Can you cut my hair here a little shorter?

13 대화를 듣고, 여자의 마지막 말에 대한 남자의 응답으로 가장 적절한 것을 고르시오.

Man: _____

① We need more information about your submission.
② Let me check my schedule and get back to you.
③ I'm bringing my wife and kids with me.
④ Congratulations on your achievement!
⑤ It would be my honor to do that.

14 대화를 듣고, 남자의 마지막 말에 대한 여자의 응답으로 가장 적절한 것을 고르시오.

Woman: _____

① All right. I'll be back soon.
② Sure. The blanket is in the car.
③ Okay. The pizza should arrive soon.
④ I agree. Let's sit over here in the sun.
⑤ It's great. I'd like to finish the book today.

15 다음 상황 설명을 듣고, David가 Emily에게 할 말로 가장 적절한 것을 고르시오. [3점]

David: _____

① I think the report needs to include charts.
② Can you rewrite this section so it is easier to read?
③ We need to do some research before we write the report.
④ You should add these details to the TV advertisement.
⑤ I think most customers prefer electric cars.

[16~17] 다음을 듣고, 물음에 답하시오.

16 여자가 하는 말의 주제로 가장 적절한 것은?

① effects of technology on students' ability to focus
② challenges of engaging students in the classroom
③ utilization of different technologies to improve education
④ why it is so important to use technology in the classroom
⑤ benefits of limiting student access to technology at school

17 언급된 기술이 아닌 것은?

① computers　　　② tablets
③ smartphones　　④ VR technology
⑤ 3D printing

이제 듣기 문제가 끝났습니다. 채점을 마친 후 다음 페이지에서 방송을 다시 들으며 딕테이션 연습을 하시기 바랍니다.

* 채점 결과: 맞은 개수 _____개 / 17개　　　　정답 및 해설 p.116

19회 Dictation

Dictation 정답 p.116

19회 영어듣기 모의고사 Dictation 음성을 들으며 빈칸에 알맞은 단어를 채워 넣으시기 바랍니다.

1

W Hello, WPR radio station listeners! Are you tired of planning meals every week? Are you too busy to 1)_____ _____ _____? Then, sign up for Green Meal Kits. With this service, you'll get all the 2)_____ _____ _____ to make delicious meals every day. With Green Meal Kits, you don't need any special 3)_____ _____ _____ _____ _____. Our service offers a variety of dishes, and you can make them all in under 40 minutes. Get anywhere from two to seven kits delivered right to your door so you can avoid the 4)_____ _____ _____ _____. Just visit our website at www.greenmeals.com for more information today!

➥ 듣기 필수 표현
· be tired of ~에 싫증이 나다
· sign up for ~을 신청하다
· a variety of 다양한

2

M Hey, Christine. Are you going to Justin's wedding?

W Yes. But I don't have anything to wear. I need to go shopping for a dress.

M Oh, where will you go?

W I'm thinking about going to the mall. I'll definitely find something there.

M Yeah, but I think it would be better to go to 1)_____ _____ _____ instead.

W Why do you think so?

M I read that buying used clothes helps the environment. Making new clothes 2)_____ _____ _____ _____ _____ and creates pollution.

W I had no idea.

M People throw away clothes all the time. Wearing secondhand clothing helps reduce that waste.

W That makes sense. I guess it also saves money.

M Exactly. And you can find a 3)_____ _____.

W You're right. I'll visit a secondhand shop this week.

➥ 듣기 필수 표현
· throw away ~을 버리다

3

W Hi, Mr. Walker. How are you today?

M Not great. I'm experiencing some 1)_____ _____ _____ _____.

W All right. Let's see. *[Pause]* Well, it looks like one of your back teeth is causing the pain.

M What can you do to treat it?

W I'm afraid the tooth needs to be pulled.

M Oh, no... What's that process like?

W Well, I will perform surgery to remove it. And a few months later, I'll put a replacement in.

M I see. Does the surgery take a long time?

W No. The 2)_____ _____ _____ _____, but you'll need a few days to recover afterward.

M This is the busy season for my restaurant, so I can't take time off until next month. Is that okay?

W That should be fine. Let's 3)_____ _____ _____, then. I'll give you some pain medicine for now.

M Okay. Thanks for your help.

➥ 듣기 필수 표현
· perform surgery 수술을 하다
· not A until B B는 되어야 A하다
· take time off 휴가를 내다
· for now 일단은, 당분간은

4

M Hi, Jenny. Are you finished setting up your classroom?

W Yes, I'm all done. Do you want to see a photo of it?

M Of course.

W Here it is. That's my desk at the front of the room.

M Oh, everything looks great. I love that 1)_____ _____ _____ _____.

W Thanks. I thought it would be useful for when we learn about other countries.

M And what are those 2)_____ _____ _____ on the table for?

W The students will put their homework there.

M Your chalkboard behind the table is also nice and big.

W Yes. I wanted a large one for teaching.

M And what is that [3)]_____ _____ _____ the board for?

W Sometimes we watch videos in class, so I thought it would be good to have a speaker for that.

M Yeah, that makes sense.

5

M Ashley, I can't believe the fall festival is this week.

W Me neither. I think our photo booth will be popular, but we should go over our preparations.

M All right. I'm buying some paper tomorrow so we can decorate it. You bought some paint yesterday, right?

W Yes. I also [1)]_____ _____ _____ and sunglasses to put in the booth.

M And we already made the backgrounds for the booth.

W Yeah, they look really good. What about cameras?

M I think I'll rent an extra one. I'm [2)]_____ _____ _____ _____.

W That's a good idea.

M Now, we just need T-shirts for our uniform. Did you like the design I sent you?

W Yeah. Those T-shirts should be perfect.

M Then, let's order them.

W Let me [3)]_____ _____ _____ it. You're so busy these days.

↘ 듣기 필수 표현
· go over ~을 점검하다

6

M Good morning. What can I help you with?

W I need some new running shoes.

M Well, this is our most popular pair right now.

W Oh, those look nice. How much are they?

M They're usually $120, but they're [1)]_____ _____ _____ _____ for $100.

W Great. Do you have a size 8?

M We do have your size. And would you like some new socks as well?

W Yeah. I do need some new ones.

M I recommend these. They're $5, but they are high quality.

W Okay. I'll [2)]_____ _____ _____ of those, then.

M So you would like the shoes and two pairs of socks. Is that right?

W It is. I also [3)]_____ _____ _____ for a 10% discount. Can I use it?

M Yes, you can. And do you need a shopping bag?

W No, thank you. Here's my card.

↘ 듣기 필수 표현
· as well ~도, 또한

7

W Hey, Ron. How are you?

M I just booked a trip for the summer, so I'm happy. It [1)]_____ _____ _____ _____ _____ to decide where to go.

W Where are you going?

M I'm going to Vietnam.

W I've always wanted to go there.

M Are you traveling anywhere this summer?

W No. I can't. I'll stay here.

M Is it because you want to [2)]_____ _____? I know you want to buy a new cell phone.

W I actually bought one already.

M Oh, then is it because you want to spend time with your family at home?

W That's not it, either. I'm [3)]_____ _____ _____ _____ _____.

M Oh, that's really cool. I bet that will be fun.

W I think I'll be busy most of the time, but I'm looking forward to being in the forest.

8

M Honey, are you busy next weekend?

W No. Why do you ask?

M I'd really like to go to the Jamestown Whale Festival.

W What is that?

M It's an event that ¹⁾_____ _____ _____ of gray whales. It will include whale watching, a parade, and musical performances.

W That sounds fun. Does the festival take place all weekend?

M This advertisement says that it will ²⁾_____ _____ _____ _____ to 5 p.m. on both Saturday and Sunday.

W Do we have to buy tickets for it?

M Yes, but they're only $10.

W All right. Let's buy tickets now in that case.

M Sure. It says to purchase them online. And I guess we'll have to rent a car for the festival. The advertisement recommends driving, since there's ³⁾_____ _____ _____ _____.

W That's fine. I can't wait to go!

↘ 듣기 필수 표현
· can't wail to 빨리 ~하고 싶다

9

W Hello, viewers! Have you ever wanted to be a guest on *The Geography Quiz*? Well, this is your ¹⁾_____ _____ _____ on the hit TV show where players answer questions about places around the world. From now until January 15th, we ²⁾_____ _____ _____ on our website for the new season. We will contact everyone who is selected to participate by the 31st. Your application should include your current contact information and a video introducing yourself. ³⁾_____ _____, you must not have appeared on the show before. Filming will begin in February. It will ⁴⁾_____ _____ _____ _____ _____ downtown every Tuesday night at 7 p.m. We hope to see you there!

10

M Tory, what are you shopping for online?

W I'm looking at options for a new grocery cart. Do you want to help me choose one?

M Okay. Let's see. *[Pause]* They all seem nice. But ¹⁾_____ _____ _____ _____ do you want it to be made of?

W I need something durable. I don't think fabric is strong enough. The other materials are okay, though.

M So you have four options left. What about price?

W My budget is $100. I ²⁾_____ _____ _____ _____ that.

M All right. Then, you need to consider how many wheels it has. I think you should get one ³⁾_____ _____ _____. It'll be much easier to move around.

W You're right. That'll be better.

M So the only thing now is color.

W The black one looks really nice.

M I agree.

W Okay. I'll go with this one, then. Thanks!

11

W Honey, do you want to see a movie this afternoon? The new action film you've been ¹⁾_____ _____ _____ _____.

M Sure, but I have to ²⁾_____ _____ _____ _____ first. How about coming along with me to the post office?

W Okay. How are we going to get to the theater?

↘ 듣기 필수 표현
· come along with ~와 같이 가다

12

M What can I do for you today, Daisy? Your hair has ¹⁾_____ _____ _____.

W I'd like to get it cut, but my hair also feels a little dry lately. Is there anything you can do to make it softer?

M Of course. There is a good treatment for that, though ²⁾_____ _____ _____.

13

[Cell phone rings.]

M Hello. This is Trevor Stanton.

W Hi. This is Cecilia Johnson from Seaside Gallery.

M Oh, is this about the art competition?

W Yes. Our judges have 1)_____ _____ _____ as one of the winners.

M Wow, that's amazing! I can't believe it.

W We'd like to invite you to the award ceremony for the competition so we can 2)_____ _____ _____. Would you be able to attend next Friday?

M I think so. What time will it start?

W It will go from 6 p.m. to 9 p.m.

M That's perfect. I'll definitely be there.

W Excellent. Food will be served at the event, and we will display your art, too.

M Great. Is it okay if I bring my family?

W You can bring as many guests as you'd like. And we'd also like you to 3)_____ _____ _____ _____, if you're willing.

14

M Wow, the weather is beautiful today, honey.

W Yes, it is. I'm so glad we came to the river.

M It was a good idea to 1)_____ _____ _____, too.

W Thanks. I thought we would enjoy sitting and reading for a while.

M For sure. I'm starting to get a little hungry, though.

W Yeah, me too. Do you want to go eat somewhere?

M I don't know. I don't really want to 2)_____ _____ _____.

W I could go pick something up. There's a pizza place close by.

M That's a good idea. But I don't really want pizza.

W What about that café over there?

M That would be perfect. I'd love a latte 3)_____ _____ _____.

↘ 듣기 필수 표현
· For sure. 물론이지.

15

M Emily and David work in the marketing department of a company. At the moment, their department is working on a campaign to advertise the company's new electric car. Their task is to 1)_____ _____ _____ that consumers like electric cars. Although they have found a large amount of useful data, David is worried that the report they're writing will be too hard for people to understand. 2)_____ _____ _____ _____ statistics it includes, the report won't be useful unless readers have a clear idea of what the numbers mean. So David wants to tell Emily that they should 3)_____ _____ _____ _____ to the report. In this situation, what would David most likely say to Emily?

↘ 듣기 필수 표현
· at the moment 현재
· have a clear idea of ~을 명확하게 이해하다

16~17

W Hello, teachers. Technology has changed many areas of our lives, including education. Today, let's look at how technology can be used in the classroom to improve learning. First, computers can be used to change the way you 1)_____ _____ _____. You can make presentations or show video clips to the students to engage them. Next, tablets can replace textbooks in the classroom. Tablets are lighter and more convenient to carry around. Plus, tablets make it 2)_____ _____ _____ different books and information online. We can also use VR technology in the classroom. It enables students to take 3)_____ _____ _____ and explore places they might not be able to visit in person. Finally, 3D printing has a lot of potential. For instance, with 3D printing, biology students can easily make models of body parts and cells. This will improve their ability to 4)_____ _____ _____ complex ideas. I hope you've enjoyed hearing about ways to incorporate technology into your teaching. Now, let's look at specific examples of lessons that use these technologies.

↘ 듣기 필수 표현
· in person 직접
· incorporate A into B A를 B에 접목시키다

20회 영어듣기 모의고사

정답 및 해설 p.122

1번부터 17번까지는 듣고 답하는 문제입니다. 1번부터 15번까지는 한 번만 들려주고, 16번부터 17번까지는 두 번 들려줍니다. 방송을 잘 듣고 답을 하시기 바랍니다.

1 다음을 듣고, 남자가 하는 말의 목적으로 가장 적절한 것을 고르시오.

① 스포츠 센터를 홍보하려고
② 테니스 수업 등록을 권유하려고
③ 스포츠 대회 장소를 안내하려고
④ 운동 부족의 위험에 대해 경고하려고
⑤ 농구장 시설 확장 공사를 예고하려고

2 대화를 듣고, 여자의 의견으로 가장 적절한 것을 고르시오.

① 정기적으로 건강 검진을 받아야 한다.
② 증상이 경미하더라도 진료를 받는 것이 좋다.
③ 과잉 진료로 인한 의료 재정 낭비가 심각하다.
④ 물을 충분히 마시면 감기 증상이 완화된다.
⑤ 의사의 처방 없이 약을 복용하는 것은 위험하다.

3 대화를 듣고, 두 사람의 관계를 가장 잘 나타낸 것을 고르시오.

① 각본가 — 평론가
② 패션 디자이너 — 모델
③ 의상 담당자 — 영화감독
④ 역사학자 — 잡지 기자
⑤ 사진작가 — 연예인

4 대화를 듣고, 그림에서 대화의 내용과 일치하지 <u>않는</u> 것을 고르시오.

5 대화를 듣고, 남자가 여자를 위해 할 일로 가장 적절한 것을 고르시오.

① 양궁 가르쳐주기
② 완성작 사진 촬영하기
③ 운동 장비 빌려주기
④ 조각 작품 모델 되기
⑤ 스케치 요령 알려주기

6 대화를 듣고, 여자가 지불할 금액을 고르시오. [3점]

① $108 ② $117 ③ $120 ④ $125 ⑤ $130

7 대화를 듣고, 남자가 바르셀로나를 여행지로 추천한 이유를 고르시오.

① 여행객으로 너무 붐비지 않아서
② 흥미로운 건축물들이 많아서
③ 유서 깊은 유적지가 있어서
④ 맛있는 먹거리로 유명해서
⑤ 바다가 아름다워서

8 대화를 듣고, New Year's Eve Concert에 관해 언급되지 <u>않은</u> 것을 고르시오.

① 장소   ② 시간   ③ 티켓 가격
④ 행사 순서   ⑤ 교통수단

9 Bridge Design Contest에 관한 다음 내용을 듣고, 일치하지 <u>않는</u> 것을 고르시오. [3점]

① 학교에서 매년 열리는 행사이다.
② 대회의 규칙은 작년과 동일하다.
③ 다리 길이는 33cm여야 한다.
④ 학교 물리 선생님이 심사를 맡는다.
⑤ 상위 3개의 튼튼한 다리를 뽑아 시상한다.

10 다음 표를 보면서 대화를 듣고, 두 사람이 구입할 승용차를 고르시오.

Car Models

	Model	Capacity	Model Year	Price (per month)	Electric
①	A	2	2022	$350	X
②	B	4	2022	$375	O
③	C	4	2019	$340	X
④	D	4	2021	$410	X
⑤	E	6	2018	$430	O

11 대화를 듣고, 여자의 마지막 말에 대한 남자의 응답으로 가장 적절한 것을 고르시오.

① I prefer the blue painting.
② It will take about 30 minutes.
③ They're in a box below the sink.
④ I bought them at the supermarket.
⑤ I think you should hang it on the right side.

12 대화를 듣고, 남자의 마지막 말에 대한 여자의 응답으로 가장 적절한 것을 고르시오.

① Okay. Then, we can walk around with them.
② Alright. I'll call them to make a reservation.
③ Sure. I'll grab that table by the entrance.
④ Good idea. It's too cold outside today.
⑤ No, thanks. I'm still feeling full.

13 대화를 듣고, 여자의 마지막 말에 대한 남자의 응답으로 가장 적절한 것을 고르시오. [3점]

Man: _____

① Right. We should send people to the Moon.
② I agree. There's no easy way to solve world hunger.
③ Absolutely. The company has completed the project.
④ Yeah. We need to reduce the amount of money we spend.
⑤ Sure. But it's also important to make scientific progress.

14 대화를 듣고, 남자의 마지막 말에 대한 여자의 응답으로 가장 적절한 것을 고르시오.

Woman: _____

① I might have another ID card.
② I'll give you another copy now.
③ I'll check with the airline right away.
④ You need to print the ticket beforehand.
⑤ The police will be able to help with that.

15 다음 상황 설명을 듣고, Victoria가 James에게 할 말로 가장 적절한 것을 고르시오.

Victoria: _____

① Let's ask the teacher for his opinion.
② I think we should collect seashells on the beach.
③ Why don't we change our topic to more popular one?
④ Our classmates are going to love this topic.
⑤ The seashells are so colorful, aren't they?

[16~17] 다음을 듣고, 물음에 답하시오.

16 남자가 하는 말의 주제로 가장 적절한 것은?

① various causes of personal stress
② effects of vitamins on a person's health
③ the importance of eating healthy snacks
④ ways to cope with stressful situations
⑤ foods that can help to control stress

17 언급된 음식이 아닌 것은?

① chocolate ② almonds ③ strawberries
④ bananas ⑤ milk

이제 듣기 문제가 끝났습니다. 채점을 마친 후 다음 페이지에서 방송을 다시 들으며 딕테이션 연습을 하시기 바랍니다.

* 채점 결과: 맞은 개수 _____ 개 / 17개   정답 및 해설 p.122

Dictation 정답 p.122

20회 영어듣기 모의고사 Dictation 음성을 들으며 빈칸에 알맞은 단어를 채워 넣으시기 바랍니다.

1

M Hello, listeners. Do you want to become stronger and healthier? Would you like to have fun while doing this? Then, 1)_____ _____ _____ _____ Blue Hawaii Sports Center. At Blue Hawaii, we offer a wide range of 2)_____ _____ _____ _____ to choose from. Our facilities include tennis and basketball courts, a swimming pool, and a yoga studio with beautiful views of the ocean. At our gym, you can work out on the latest exercise machines. We have 3)_____ _____ to help you achieve your fitness goals. You can even sign up for a group fitness class. So what are you waiting for? Visit our website for more details.

❯ 듣기 필수 표현
· a wide range of 다양한
· work out 운동하다
· sign up for ~에 등록하다

2

W Hey, David. Are you feeling better today?

M Not really. But I'll just eat soup and drink lots of water for a few days. The illness 1)_____ _____ _____.

W You've been sick for a while. Maybe that's not enough.

M Well, it's just the flu. I'll be fine.

W I understand, but I believe you should go to the doctor even if your symptoms 2)_____ _____ _____.

M I don't really want to spend a lot of time at the doctor's office, though.

W But the doctor will 3)_____ _____ _____ to find out exactly what's wrong with you.

M That's true. I could also get the right medicine, then.

W Definitely. That will help you get better more quickly. It's always a good idea to see a doctor if you're sick.

M You're right. I'll go today.

❯ 듣기 필수 표현
· for a while 한동안
· go to the doctor 병원에 가다
· find out ~을 알아내다
· Definitely. 물론이지.
· get better 회복하다
· see a doctor 진찰을 받다

3

W What's wrong? I think the actors look great.

M I don't know. I'm not happy with the clothes they have on. Their costumes 1)_____ _____ _____.

W That was the clothing style back in the 1940s. I'm sure my research is correct.

M You're right, but they don't have the feel I want for this scene.

W Well, 2)_____ _____ _____ _____ are you looking for?

M This is supposed to be a sad scene. But the colors are too bright and cheerful.

W So you want darker costumes to fit the mood. Are the designs okay?

M The designs are good. It's only the colors that need to be changed.

W Okay, I'll 3)_____ _____ _____ _____ for you to choose from. I need at least a couple of hours.

M Take your time. I want my movie to be perfect.

❯ 듣기 필수 표현
· I'm not happy with ~. ~이 마음에 들지 않아요.
· a couple of 둘의, 두 개의
· Take your time. 천천히 하세요.

4

W I can't believe how quickly you've set up the new children's library, Brian.

M I know. Does it look okay?

W It looks amazing. But what's inside that big wooden box 1)_____ _____ _____ on the wall?

M Oh, that's filled with some cushions and blankets for the kids when they're reading.

W Good idea. I also love 2)_____ _____ _____. It looks soft.

M Yes, I wanted this area to be as comfortable as possible for everyone.

W What's on that poster?

M It's a large tree. Do you like it?

W I do. I think it goes well with the other decorations.

M We also set up a round table in that corner of the room. And we put ³)_____ _____ _____ _____.

W It fits the space nicely. Then, the children can also write or do their homework.

M That's what I was thinking.

↘ 듣기 필수 표현

· set up ~을 준비하다, 설치하다
· be filled with ~으로 가득 차 있다
· go well with ~과 잘 어울리다

5

M Hi, Marisa. How's your project for art class going?

W I haven't started yet, Ben. Actually, I wanted to ask you something related to that.

M Really? What is it?

W This semester I'm taking a sculpture class, so I need to ¹)_____ _____ _____.

M I don't know much about art. I'm not sure how I could help you out.

W Well, you are in the archery club, right?

M Yeah, I've been a member for a long time.

W I'd like you ²)_____ _____ _____ _____ with a bow and arrow.

M Sure. That sounds fun. I can bring my own equipment, too.

W Perfect. I'll ³)_____ _____ _____ of you and do a few sketches.

M What a relief! I thought I'd have to stay in the same position for hours!

↘ 듣기 필수 표현

· related to ~과 관련된
· What a relief! 정말 다행이다!

6

[Phone rings.]

M Green Springs Gourmet Food. How may I help you?

W Hi. This is Rose Whitfield. I'd like to make ¹)_____ _____ _____ _____, please.

M Yes, Ms. Whitfield. What would you like?

W I'd like five orders of seafood pasta. Each order is $20, right?

M Yes, that's correct. Would you like anything else?

W I'd also like a small cheesecake.

M That would be $20. But if you order ²)_____ _____ _____ _____ for $30, you can get a 10% discount on your order.

W Oh, why is that?

M It's our special weekly promotion.

W All right. I'll take the large cheesecake, then.

M Okay. So that's ³)_____ _____ _____ and one large cheesecake. How would you like to pay?

W I'll pay by card.

M Okay. The delivery person will process your payment. It will take about 45 minutes for your order to arrive.

W Thank you.

7

M Have you picked a destination for your summer trip, Penny?

W Not yet. But I've decided I'll choose a city in Europe. Do you have any recommendations?

M I think you should go to Barcelona in Spain.

W Why? Is it because of the beaches there?

M No. They're pretty, but they get too crowded ¹)_____ _____ _____.

W Oh, then I guess it's because of the famous Spanish food. The dishes all look amazing.

M It's very good, but that's not what I meant to say. Actually, I think the top reason to visit Barcelona is ²)_____ _____.

W Really? I didn't know that Barcelona was famous for its architecture.

M It is. There are ³)_____ _____ _____ like palaces and churches.

W That sounds cool. Maybe I'll look into going there after all.

M You should. I think you'd love it.

↘ 듣기 필수 표현

· get crowded 붐비다, 혼잡하다
· be famous for ~으로 유명하다
· look into ~을 자세히 살펴보다
· after all 무엇보다도

8

W Are you doing anything special for New Year's Eve, Daniel?

M I am! I'm going to the city's New Year's Eve Concert.

W I 1)_____ _____ _____ _____. Where is it going to be?

M It will be held at the river park by Williams Bridge. I have the event information here on my phone.

W Okay. So it's from 8 p.m. to 12:30 a.m.

M Yes. They'll have a few 2)_____ _____ _____ in the evening. Then, there's a fireworks show at midnight.

W I really want to go. But parking will probably be a nightmare.

M You're right. I'm going to 3)_____ _____ _____ since there's a Line 2 stop nearby.

W Then, why don't I meet you in the subway station?

M That would be great.

↘ 듣기 필수 표현
· be a nightmare 아주 끔찍하다, 악몽 같다

9

W Hello, students! The Clarkson High School Physics Club is inviting all students to enter our Bridge Design Contest, which takes place 1)_____ _____. Students came up with some very creative designs last year, and we can't wait to see what they do this year. However, we are introducing some 2)_____ _____ _____ this year. The bridge must be made of regular wooden toothpicks and have a length of 33 centimeters. Students will be given four hours to build the bridge. The judge will be our physics teacher, Mr. Weston. He will test how much weight each bridge can hold. Prizes will be awarded to 3)_____ _____ _____ _____ _____. For more details, go to the Physics Club website or check out the notice posted on all bulletin boards.

↘ 듣기 필수 표현
· take place 열리다, 개최되다
· come up with ~을 생각해 내다
· be made of ~으로 만들어지다

10

W What are you looking at, Joe?

M I'm reviewing different cars we can buy. These are our top options.

W Oh, let's see. *[Pause]* Well, I think that this one is too big for us.

M I agree. We don't need 1)_____ _____ _____ _____ since it's just us two.

W That kind of car is also harder to park.

M What about the year it was made? Does that matter?

W I don't want one that is too old. Let's not buy anything 2)_____ _____ _____.

M Okay. And what about the price?

W I'd like to keep it under $400 a month. We're on a limited budget.

M You're right. Now, we should decide if we want an electric car or not.

W I think we should 3)_____ _____ _____ _____. It's better for the environment.

M Okay. Then, let's go with this one.

↘ 듣기 필수 표현
· on a limited budget 예산이 한정된

11

W Honey, I want to 1)_____ _____ _____ on the wall. I think they'll look nice in the living room.

M Sure, I can do it right now. I just need the hammer and some nails.

W Okay, I'll get them. 2)_____ _____ _____ _____ them last?

12

M Let's try this café, Mia. It's crowded, but I heard the coffee is really 1)_____ _____.

W Okay. But all of the tables outside and inside are 2)_____ _____ _____. What should we do?

M We should get our coffees to go.

↘ 듣기 필수 표현
· to go 테이크아웃하는, 포장해가는

13

W Is there any interesting news today?

M Yes. A company called Star Enterprises has announced its first space mission.

W Wow. Tell me more about it.

M Well, the article I read said the research mission will cost about $4 billion.

W $4 billion? That's ¹⁾_____ _____ _____.

M Space exploration is never cheap.

W But what are they going to spend all that money on?

M Well, rockets are expensive, and very few of their parts can be reused after they launch into space.

W That sounds wasteful to me. The money could be used ²⁾_____ _____ _____ _____, like supporting hungry people.

M That's true. But space research leads to the development of new technologies that help everyone. GPS is a good example of this.

W But I still believe it's better to spend money to assist ³⁾_____ _____ _____. Don't you think so?

14

M Welcome to the passport office. May I help you?

W I'm afraid I've ¹⁾_____ _____ _____.

M Are you certain you didn't just misplace it?

W Yes. My backpack was stolen, and my passport was inside it.

M When did this happen?

W It happened earlier today. I hope you can help me. I'm going on vacation, and I ²⁾_____ _____ _____ _____.

M Okay. Did you already report your passport stolen to the police?

W Yes. Here's a copy of the police report.

M I'll get the passport replaced for you. Do you have any other identification?

W I only have this driver's license.

M I see. When is your flight?

W I'm supposed to leave tomorrow morning. Will it be ready by then?

M No. It won't be possible. Can you ³⁾_____ _____ _____?

↘ 듣기 필수 표현
· a copy of 사본 (한 부)
· be ready by ~까지 준비되다

15

W Victoria and James are in the same biology class. Their teacher has asked the students to prepare a presentation about marine life. Victoria and James decided to do a presentation ¹⁾_____ _____. They are interested in this topic, and they have prepared a lot of material for their project. However, James is worried that the students will think ²⁾_____ _____ _____ _____ compared to the other presentations, so he speaks to Victoria about his concern. Victoria disagrees with him. She thinks that they ³⁾_____ _____ _____ _____ their topic. So Victoria wants to tell James that their topic will be ⁴⁾_____ _____ the other students. In this situation, what would Victoria most likely say to James?

↘ 듣기 필수 표현
· ask A to B A에게 B할 것을 요청하다
· compared to ~에 비해
· disagree with ~의 의견에 동의하지 않다

16~17

M Good afternoon. In yesterday's class, we talked about the causes of stress in our life. Today, I want to introduce some foods that can help you ¹⁾_____ _____ _____. First, chocolate is not just a sweet snack. It can also improve your mood. This is because it contains chemicals that cause your body to produce happiness hormones. Second, eating almonds will enable you to respond to stress better. Several studies have shown that people who eat almonds regularly do ²⁾_____ _____ _____ _____ to stressful situations. Next, eating strawberries is another effective way to cope with stress. They are high in vitamin C, which helps to lower the amount of stress-causing chemicals in your body. Finally, warm milk is a great nighttime drink if you are ³⁾_____ _____ _____. It has a calming effect on the mind and can help you get a good night's sleep. I hope today's class has given you some useful tips for managing your stress.

↘ 듣기 필수 표현
· enable A to B A가 B하게 하다
· respond to ~에 반응하다
· cope with ~에 대처하다

21회 고난도 영어듣기 모의고사

정답 및 해설 p.128

1번부터 17번까지는 듣고 답하는 문제입니다. 1번부터 15번까지는 한 번만 들려주고, 16번부터 17번까지는 두 번 들려줍니다. 방송을 잘 듣고 답을 하시기 바랍니다.

1 다음을 듣고, 남자가 하는 말의 목적으로 가장 적절한 것을 고르시오.

① 스포츠용품점의 할인 행사를 홍보하려고
② 환절기 건강 관리법을 설명하려고
③ 겨울철 다양한 스포츠를 소개하려고
④ 스포츠 센터의 확장 이전을 안내하려고
⑤ 운동 시 알맞은 장비 착용을 권장하려고

2 대화를 듣고, 여자의 의견으로 가장 적절한 것을 고르시오.

① 여러 외국어를 동시에 배우면 학습 효과가 떨어진다.
② 가정 내에서 올바른 언어 습관을 형성해야 한다.
③ 외국어를 번역할 때는 문화적인 맥락도 고려해야 한다.
④ 바쁘다는 이유로 가족과의 연락에 소홀해지면 안 된다.
⑤ 어학 수업은 그 나라의 문화를 공부하기에 좋은 방법이다.

3 대화를 듣고, 두 사람의 관계를 가장 잘 나타낸 것을 고르시오.

① 제약업체 직원 ─ 의사
② 건물 관리인 ─ 세입자
③ 열쇠 수리공 ─ 약사
④ 배달 기사 ─ 쇼핑몰 직원
⑤ 보안업체 직원 ─ 식당 매니저

4 대화를 듣고, 그림에서 대화의 내용과 일치하지 <u>않는</u> 것을 고르시오.

5 대화를 듣고, 남자가 할 일로 가장 적절한 것을 고르시오.

① 간식거리 사오기
② 생화 주문하기
③ 초대 손님들에게 연락하기
④ 케이크 찾아오기
⑤ 풍선 장식하기

6 대화를 듣고, 남자가 지불할 금액을 고르시오. [3점]

① $60   ② $72   ③ $80   ④ $90   ⑤ $99

7 대화를 듣고, 여자가 콘서트를 보러 갈 수 <u>없는</u> 이유를 고르시오.

① 티켓 예매에 실패해서
② 밴드부 홍보 영상을 찍어야 해서
③ 해야 할 숙제가 많아서
④ 친구와 만나기로 해서
⑤ 조부모님을 뵈러 갈 예정이어서

8 대화를 듣고, Westgate Rock-Climbing Club에 관해 언급되지 <u>않은</u> 것을 고르시오.

① 주요 활동   ② 회원 수   ③ 모임 횟수
④ 월별 회비   ⑤ 가입 방법

9 Greenville Marathon에 관한 다음 내용을 듣고, 일치하지 <u>않는</u> 것을 고르시오.

① 5월 17일에 열릴 예정이다.
② 프로 마라토너는 참가비를 내야 한다.
③ 시청 앞에 출발선이 놓일 것이다.
④ 종료 지점에서 시상식이 열릴 것이다.
⑤ 1위로 들어온 선수는 트로피와 500달러를 받는다.

10 다음 표를 보면서 대화를 듣고, 남자가 예약할 항공편을 고르시오.

Flights to Boston

	Flight	Departure Time	Price	Direct Flight	Seat
①	A	8 a.m.	$260	O	Window
②	B	11 a.m.	$250	X	Aisle
③	C	1 p.m.	$240	O	Aisle
④	D	2 p.m.	$225	X	Aisle
⑤	E	4 p.m.	$220	O	Window

11 대화를 듣고, 여자의 마지막 말에 대한 남자의 응답으로 가장 적절한 것을 고르시오.

① No. They pick up the trash on Wednesdays.
② I'm sorry. I won't forget to do it next time.
③ Yes. Please put that in the trash can.
④ No need. I fed the dog an hour ago.
⑤ Okay. I'll go with you in that case.

12 대화를 듣고, 남자의 마지막 말에 대한 여자의 응답으로 가장 적절한 것을 고르시오.

① Sure. What do you suggest?
② Fine. Did you order a mild dish?
③ Sorry. I should not have been lazy.
④ No worries. I've prepared dinner already.
⑤ All right. You can pick up the food in 20 minutes.

13 대화를 듣고, 여자의 마지막 말에 대한 남자의 응답으로 가장 적절한 것을 고르시오. [3점]

Man: _____

① You're right. I'll just keep practicing.
② I agree. You'll be a great baseball player.
③ I don't know. I'm not really a fan of playing sports.
④ No way. The tryouts are less than a week away.
⑤ Sure. I won't let the coach down next game!

14 대화를 듣고, 남자의 마지막 말에 대한 여자의 응답으로 가장 적절한 것을 고르시오.

Woman: _____

① I'll be out of town for a business trip.
② I think the morning would work best for me.
③ Come over whenever it is convenient for you.
④ Thank you for confirming my appointment time.
⑤ When was the last time you had your teeth cleaned?

15 다음 상황 설명을 듣고, Zoe가 Dan에게 할 말로 가장 적절한 것을 고르시오. [3점]

Zoe: _____

① Could you include some meatless options for my guests?
② Please tell me where you would buy the organic ingredients.
③ I really appreciate your efforts to prepare food that is healthy.
④ Do you have any suggestions about how to improve the menu?
⑤ Would it be possible to serve only vegetarian dishes at the event?

[16~17] 다음을 듣고, 물음에 답하시오.

16 여자가 하는 말의 주제로 가장 적절한 것은?

① physical characteristics of deserts
② sources of water in a dry ecosystem
③ hunting techniques of wild creatures
④ animal adaptations to harsh desert environments
⑤ different methods used by animals to release body heat

17 언급된 동물이 아닌 것은?

① kangaroo rat   ② camel   ③ snake
④ fennec fox   ⑤ banded gecko

이제 듣기 문제가 끝났습니다. 채점을 마친 후 다음 페이지에서 방송을 다시 들으며 딕테이션 연습을 하시기 바랍니다.

* 채점 결과: 맞은 개수 _____개 / 17개   정답 및 해설 p.128

Dictation 정답 p.128

21회 고난도 영어듣기 모의고사 Dictation 음성을 들으며 빈칸에 알맞은 단어를 채워 넣으시기 바랍니다.

1

M Good morning, shoppers. Autumn is coming to an end, which means that it's almost 1)_____ _____ _____ _____. Whether you are into skating, skiing, sledding, or just playing in the snow, Dolson Sports Equipment has got you covered. We've been providing residents of the Hartford area with high-quality 2)_____ _____ _____ now. And to celebrate our first 10 years in operation, we'll be holding a 3)_____ _____ _____ from November 10th to 25th. Every item will be marked down, and you can expect savings ranging from 20% to 35%. If you are planning to have fun in 4)_____ _____ _____ this winter, make sure to come visit us. We look forward to seeing you!

↘ 듣기 필수 표현
· be into ~에 관심이 있다
· have got ~ covered ~를 책임지다
· mark down ~을 할인하다
· range from A to B A에서 B에 이르다

2

M Hello, Anne. What 1)_____ _____ _____ _____ this afternoon?

W I'm going to my Italian class at the community center.

M I didn't know you were studying Italian.

W I've been taking the class for over a month now.

M Do you find the class interesting?

W Yes. The teacher is amazing. And taking a language class is a great way to 2)_____ _____ _____ _____.

M Can you give me an example?

W Today, we learned a famous Italian expression. It can be translated as, "No matter where you go, you end up at home."

M What does it mean?

W It shows 3)_____ _____ _____ _____ _____ for Italians. Throughout their life, they stay in close contact with their parents and 4)_____ _____.

M Fascinating. You will be an expert on Italy soon.

↘ 듣기 필수 표현
· end up 결국 ~하게 되다
· stay in close contact 긴밀한 관계를 유지하다

3

M Hello. Are you the person who called me?

W Yes. I need some 1)_____ _____ _____ _____.

M Can you describe the problem for me?

W My key broke off in the lock, so I can't get the shutter open.

M I can help. But I need to make sure that you 2)_____ _____ _____. Do you have any documents you can show me?

W Yes, I have one with me. *[Pause]* Here it is.

M Okay, and would you like me to replace your current system? Maybe you would 3)_____ _____ _____ _____ with a keypad.

W Yes, I think it's time for an upgrade. But please hurry. We're supposed to open in an hour.

M Don't worry. I won't keep your customers waiting.

W And there's 4)_____ _____ _____ _____ arriving soon.

M I understand. I'll work as fast as I can.

W Thank you so much!

↘ 듣기 필수 표현
· break off 부러지다, 분리되다

4

M Honey, did you see the picture our daughter sent us?

W Not yet. Can you show me?

M Sure. She wants to know what we think about the living room in her new apartment.

W Oh, I like the rug on the floor. 1)_____ _____ makes it really stand out.

M That's for sure. And the round coffee table on it is beautiful. It 2)_____ _____ _____ _____ _____.

W But I wonder why she decided to put two sofas in her living room.

M Her friends visit her often. She probably wants to make sure there are ³⁾_____ _____ _____.

W Maybe her friends are the people in that picture on the wall.

M That makes sense. What do you think of the curtains?

W The ⁴⁾_____ _____ doesn't really match the rest of the room, in my opinion.

M I agree. She should have chosen something simpler.

↘ 듣기 필수 표현
· stand out 돋보이다

5

M I'm glad we decided to throw a surprise birthday party for Mom tonight. Aren't you?

W To be honest, I'm getting a bit stressed, Matthew. We only have two hours before she ¹⁾_____ _____ _____ _____.

M Well, what else do we still need to do?

W Hmm... Let me think.

M Do you want me to buy some snacks from the store?

W No. It's okay. Dad is doing that now. He'll also get some flowers on his way home.

M Have you called everyone who's invited?

W Of course. I ²⁾_____ _____ _____ _____ earlier this week.

M Then, what should I do?

W Well, I haven't ³⁾_____ _____ _____ _____ from the bakery on 5th Street yet.

M I'll head over there and do that now.

W Great! While you're doing that, I'll ⁴⁾_____ _____ _____ _____. I've got a lot of balloons to blow up.

↘ 듣기 필수 표현
· throw a party 파티를 열다
· to be honest 솔직히 말해서
· head over ~로 가다
· blow up (풍선 등을) 불다

6

W Welcome to West Shore Auto. How can I help you?

M Hi. I flew here ¹⁾_____ _____ _____ _____, and I would like to rent a car.

W Of course. We have a sedan available at $30 per day and an SUV at $45 per day.

M The sedan is fine. I'll need it for two days.

W Okay. Do you have ²⁾_____ _____ _____ for the vehicle?

M Actually, is it possible to have it delivered to my hotel at 4 p.m. today?

W Which hotel are you staying at?

M The Grand Pavilion.

W No problem. But there will be an ³⁾_____ _____ _____ for that service.

M That's fine. I'll pay the fee.

W Okay. And if you download our app, you can get a 10% discount on your total.

M Really? I'll do that right now.

W Sure. [Pause] The coupon ⁴⁾_____ _____. I'll ring you up.

↘ 듣기 필수 표현
· ring up 계산하다

7

M Sarah, you're a big fan of the Golden Stripes, right?

W Yeah. That's one of my favorite bands.

M Well, my cousin gave me ¹⁾_____ _____ _____ _____ _____ on Saturday evening at Domingo Hall. Do you want to go with me?

W Saturday? I'd love to, but I'm afraid I can't.

M Oh, are you meeting your friends?

W Nope. I won't be able to see them at all this weekend.

M You must have a lot of homework, then.

W That's not it. I'm going to be ²⁾_____ _____ _____ visiting my grandparents.

M Too bad. If you'd like, I can ³⁾_____ _____ _____ of the show. Then, you can watch it when you get back.

W Thanks. I really appreciate that.

↘ 듣기 필수 표현
· not ~ at all 전혀 ~ 아닌

8

W Hi, Raymond. I haven't seen you in ages. What 1)_____ _____ _____ _____?

M Well, I joined the Westgate Rock-Climbing Club.

W Really? What types of activities do you do?

M We mostly go to local climbing gyms to climb indoor walls. But once in a while, we go to the mountains 2)_____ _____ _____ _____.

W Interesting. Are there many people in your group?

M Not really. There are 12 members in total. We hope more people will join, though.

W Is there a fee for members?

M Yeah. We each pay $50 per month to 3)_____ _____ _____ _____ _____.

W It sounds like something I would really enjoy. How can I sign up?

M Just stop by our next meeting, and fill out 4)_____ _____ _____. You can come with me, if you want.

W Perfect. Thanks!

↘ **듣기 필수 표현**
· in ages 오랫동안
· once in a while 가끔은
· stop by ~에 들르다
· fill out ~을 작성하다

9

M Welcome back to *Community Update* on LHF Radio. The third annual Greenville Marathon will take place on Saturday, May 17th. There is 1)_____ _____ _____ _____ in this event, and both amateur and professional athletes are welcome. The starting line will be directly in front of city hall, and the race will begin at 10 a.m. The course is 10 kilometers long, and 2)_____ _____ _____ the scenic Elk River. The race will end at Meadow Park, where Mayor Adams will hold a short ceremony to announce the winner. The person 3)_____ _____ _____ _____ _____ this year will receive a trophy and $500. For more information about the event, visit www.greenvillemarathon.com.

10

W Honey, have you booked your flight for your business trip to Boston?

M Actually, I'm looking on a travel website to see what's available. 1)_____ _____ _____ is at 8 a.m.

W But I won't be able to drive you to the airport before 9 a.m.

M In that case, I should look for flights that depart at 11 a.m. or later.

W How much will your company 2)_____ _____ _____ _____ _____ the plane ticket?

M My boss wants me to keep the price under $250.

W Well, that leaves you with these three flights to choose from.

M Now that I think about it, I'd 3)_____ _____ _____ _____.

W Okay. Do you want a window seat or an aisle seat?

M I'd like an aisle seat. That way, it's easier to go to the bathroom.

W Then, you should book this one.

↘ **듣기 필수 표현**
· in that case 그렇다면
· now that ~하니까

11

W Nate, did you take the garbage out? Tomorrow is the pickup day 1)_____ _____ _____.

M I completely forgot, Mom. I'm sorry. I'll take care of that now.

W We 2)_____ _____ _____ _____ if you like. Then, we could go for a walk with the dog afterward.

↘ **듣기 필수 표현**
· take care of ~을 처리하다
· go for a walk 산책하러 가다

12

M Honey, I 1)_____ _____ _____ to cook dinner tonight. Why don't we order in?

W That's a good idea. There's a new Mexican place that I've wanted to 2)_____ _____ _____ _____ now.

M Mexican food? I'm not really in the mood for spicy food tonight. How about getting something else?

↘ **듣기 필수 표현**
· order in 음식을 배달시키다
· be in the mood for ~할 기분이 나다

13

W Why the long face, Greg? Did something happen at school today?

M Yeah, Mom. Do you remember how I wanted to join the school's baseball team?

W Oh, right. The tryouts were today. I guess things 1)_____ _____ _____ for you.

M You can say that again. I made a lot of mistakes, so the coach didn't pick me for the team. It was really embarrassing.

W But your skills improved a lot over the summer. What went wrong?

M I got really nervous 2)_____ _____ _____ _____, and then I couldn't do anything right.

W So there is no chance of you joining the team?

M Not until next year. Maybe I should just give up.

W You shouldn't! You really want to be a baseball player.

M But I will have to 3)_____ _____ _____ before I can try out again.

W Yes, but that will give you more 4)_____ _____ _____.

↘ 듣기 필수 표현
· long face 시무룩한 얼굴
· You can say that again. 정말 그래요.
· give up 포기하다
· try out 도전하다

14

[Telephone rings.]

M Thank you for calling Brighton Dental Clinic. How can I help you?

W Good morning. I'm calling about my appointment with Dr. Nicks this afternoon.

M Could I get your name, please?

W It's Jane Scott.

M You're scheduled for a 1)_____ _____ _____ at 1 p.m., right?

W That's correct. But there's a problem at work, and I have to go to the office to sort it out.

M So you need to 2)_____ _____ _____?

W That's right. I apologize for the short notice.

M That's fine. Are you available later this afternoon?

W I don't think 3)_____ _____ _____ _____ _____ today. And I will be out of town tomorrow. Is there an appointment time available on Monday?

M Let me check. *[Typing sound]* How about 10:30 a.m. or 2 p.m.?

↘ 듣기 필수 표현
· sort out ~을 해결하다

15

M Dan is the owner of a catering company, and Zoe is the manager of an art gallery. Zoe recently hired Dan's company to provide the food for 1)_____ _____ _____ at her gallery. Yesterday, Dan sent her the menu for the event to review. She is happy with the dishes he intends to serve. She also likes that he is planning to use 2)_____ _____ because she wants to provide her guests with healthy food. However, she is concerned because there are no vegetarian dishes on the menu. Therefore, Zoe wants to ask Dan to 3)_____ _____ _____ _____ for her guests as well. In this situation, what would Zoe most likely say to Dan?

↘ 듣기 필수 표현
· intend to ~하려고 생각하다

16~17

W Good morning, students. Yesterday, we began talking about the harsh desert environment. In today's class, we will look at the traits that animals have developed to survive there. Finding and storing water is an issue all animals in the desert must overcome. The kangaroo rat has an advantage in this respect. It can survive 1)_____ _____ _____. Instead, it gets all its moisture from the seeds it eats. The camel is also well-suited to desert life. It can drink more than 75 liters of water at once. This 2)_____ _____ _____ _____ several days' worth of water, allowing it to walk long distances in the desert. Another challenge facing desert animals is the extreme heat. The fennec fox avoids overheating by 3)_____ _____ _____ _____ through its extremely large ears. And the banded gecko avoids the sun entirely. It spends the day hiding under rocks, and then it 4)_____ _____ _____ _____ to hunt. I hope this lesson has helped you develop a better understanding of desert life. Now, let's have a look at a brief video.

↘ 듣기 필수 표현
· in this respect 이러한 점에 있어서

22회 고난도 영어듣기 모의고사

정답 및 해설 p.134

1번부터 17번까지는 듣고 답하는 문제입니다. 1번부터 15번까지는 한 번만 들려주고, 16번부터 17번까지는 두 번 들려줍니다. 방송을 잘 듣고 답을 하시기 바랍니다.

1 다음을 듣고, 남자가 하는 말의 목적으로 가장 적절한 것을 고르시오.

① 기부 행사 참여 방법 변경을 안내하려고
② 신임 아파트 운영위원장을 소개하려고
③ 작년 기부금 사용처 내역을 설명하려고
④ 올해 기부 행사가 취소됐음을 공지하려고
⑤ 통조림 음식 섭취의 유해성을 경고하려고

2 대화를 듣고, 여자의 의견으로 가장 적절한 것을 고르시오.

① 언쟁은 평화적으로 해결되어야 한다.
② 조별 과제를 할 때는 각자의 일을 잘 분담해야 한다.
③ 공동의 목표를 달성하려면 강력한 리더가 필요하다.
④ 역사적 인물을 평가할 때는 다각도에서 고찰해야 한다.
⑤ 조별 과제를 통해 사람들과 협력하는 법을 배울 수 있다.

3 대화를 듣고, 두 사람의 관계를 가장 잘 나타낸 것을 고르시오.

① 응원단장 — 운동선수
② 라디오 진행자 — 축구 감독
③ 스포츠 잡지 기자 — 심판
④ 대회 운영위원 — 후원자
⑤ 재활 전문의 — 환자

4 대화를 듣고, 그림에서 대화의 내용과 일치하지 않는 것을 고르시오.

5 대화를 듣고, 여자가 할 일로 가장 적절한 것을 고르시오.

① 체크리스트 만들기
② 전동 공구 챙기기
③ 배경 음악 고르기
④ 촬영 장비 옮기기
⑤ 동영상 편집하기

6 대화를 듣고, 여자가 지불할 금액을 고르시오. [3점]

① $54 ② $60 ③ $72 ④ $81 ⑤ $90

7 대화를 듣고, 남자가 쇼핑하러 갈 수 없는 이유를 고르시오.

① 치과 검진을 받아야 해서
② 현장학습을 다녀와 피곤해서
③ 가족과 함께 시간을 보내기로 해서
④ 피아노 수업을 들으러 가야 해서
⑤ 역사 공부를 해야 해서

8 대화를 듣고, Emergency First Aid Course에 관해 언급되지 않은 것을 고르시오.

① 시작 시각 ② 참가 인원 ③ 소요 시간
④ 수업 장소 ⑤ 강사 이름

9 Summer Fireworks Festival에 관한 다음 내용을 듣고, 일치하지 않는 것을 고르시오.

① 저녁 9시에 시작해서 11시에 끝난다.
② Harbor Park에서 열릴 예정이다.
③ 4개국 출신의 팀들이 공연을 벌일 것이다.
④ 간식과 음료를 파는 노점상이 설치될 것이다.
⑤ 무료 주차 공간이 제공될 예정이다.

10 다음 표를 보면서 대화를 듣고, 두 사람이 예약할 렌터카를 고르시오.

Rental Cars

	Model	Capacity (persons)	Fuel Efficiency (per liter)	Rental Fee (per day)	Ski Rack
①	A	2	12 km	$40	X
②	B	4	16 km	$55	O
③	C	4	14 km	$45	X
④	D	5	13 km	$40	O
⑤	E	5	10 km	$50	X

11 대화를 듣고, 남자의 마지막 말에 대한 여자의 응답으로 가장 적절한 것을 고르시오.

① It should arrive in about 10 minutes.
② I paid for the taxi with my credit card.
③ Text me as soon as you arrive at the airport.
④ The drive took longer than expected.
⑤ I hope our flight isn't delayed.

12 대화를 듣고, 여자의 마지막 말에 대한 남자의 응답으로 가장 적절한 것을 고르시오.

① No, thanks. The cake was too sweet.
② Yes. The store is on Greenwood Avenue.
③ I'm sorry. The flower delivery will be late.
④ Sure. Is there a particular brand you like?
⑤ No worries. I'll pick you up after work.

13 대화를 듣고, 여자의 마지막 말에 대한 남자의 응답으로 가장 적절한 것을 고르시오.

Man: _____

① My meeting is supposed to begin at 9 a.m.
② I am pretty sure it is the people in Room 302.
③ I'd like a room with a view of the ocean, please.
④ What time will I be able to check in tomorrow?
⑤ Please confirm that my new room is ready.

14 대화를 듣고, 남자의 마지막 말에 대한 여자의 응답으로 가장 적절한 것을 고르시오. [3점]

Woman: _____

① Not yet. I like to sleep in late on weekends.
② I don't know. I prefer to exercise in the mornings.
③ Interesting. I may have to give your suggestions a try.
④ That's great. I'm glad you signed me up for your gym.
⑤ Good idea. I'll put my phone in silent mode before I sleep.

15 다음 상황 설명을 듣고, Carl이 Brenda에게 할 말로 가장 적절한 것을 고르시오. [3점]

Carl: _____

① Please show me where your parking space is located.
② How come you parked your car in my space the other day?
③ You should ask the building manager for a new parking space.
④ I don't think it is safe for you to drive while your foot is injured.
⑤ Why don't we trade parking spaces until you are feeling better?

[16~17] 다음을 듣고, 물음에 답하시오.

16 남자가 하는 말의 주제로 가장 적절한 것은?

① features of the first human societies
② types of residences used by early humans
③ reasons that people used caves as shelters
④ benefits of stone as a construction material
⑤ spread of prehistoric people around the world

17 언급된 주거지가 <u>아닌</u> 것은?

① caves   ② tents   ③ igloos
④ log houses   ⑤ stone buildings

이제 듣기 문제가 끝났습니다. 채점을 마친 후 다음 페이지에서 방송을 다시 들으며 딕테이션 연습을 하시기 바랍니다.

* 채점 결과: 맞은 개수 _____ 개 / 17개   정답 및 해설 p.134

Dictation 정답 p.134

22회 고난도 영어듣기 모의고사 Dictation 음성을 들으며 빈칸에 알맞은 단어를 채워 넣으시기 바랍니다.

1

M Good morning, residents. I'm John Miller, the president of the Lexton Apartment Committee. As you know, we'll hold our annual food donation event soon. However, we are going to 1)_____ _____ _____ of participation from this year. To make sure the donations include a good variety of items, we've set up a new online sign-up sheet this year. You can 2)_____ _____ _____ for donation, such as canned meat, frozen vegetables, and dried fish. The link is in the text message we sent you this morning. We are 3)_____ _____ _____ the event, and we hope everyone joins us in helping out our community.

↘ 듣기 필수 표현
· sign-up sheet 참가 신청서

2

W Are you going somewhere, Liam?

M I'm meeting some classmates at the library, Mom.

W Oh, are you 1)_____ _____ _____ _____ _____ together?

M Yeah. We're supposed to write a report about a famous person in history.

W That sounds interesting. Group projects are a great way to learn 2)_____ _____ _____ with others.

M To be honest, it's not going well. Everyone keeps arguing about the topic.

W That must be hard, but you'll end up resolving the arguments.

M Hmm... Why are you so sure about that?

W Well, you have 3)_____ _____ _____ of writing a good report. So as you try to accomplish that goal, you'll learn how to work together.

M That sounds like a good lesson, but it's a difficult one.

W I know, but 4)_____ _____!

M Okay. I will, Mom.

↘ 듣기 필수 표현
· to be honest 솔직히 말해서
· go well 잘 되어가다
· end up 결국 ~하게 되다

3

M Welcome to *Weekend Sports*, Ms. Davis.

W Thanks. I am a long-time fan of your show.

M I appreciate that. I'm sure many of my listeners are excited to cheer for your team in the international soccer tournament that starts tomorrow. How 1)_____ _____ _____ for it?

W Well, I've organized practices for the players on my team every day for the last two months.

M Isn't that schedule tiring?

W Sure. But the players know they 2)_____ _____ _____ _____ to win difficult matches.

M Your star player Nancy Aston injured her leg recently. Is it serious?

W No. The team doctor expects it to heal in about a week.

M Will she be able to play well in the tournament?

W Yes, I believe so. Everyone is feeling confident that we can 3)_____ _____ _____ _____ at the end of the tournament.

M Great. Best of luck to you.

↘ 듣기 필수 표현
· cheer for ~를 응원하다
· Best of luck to you. 행운을 빌어요.

4

M Honey, we finally finished redecorating the guestroom.

W I think it looks amazing. What do you think?

M I agree. 1)_____ _____ _____ the checked rug on the floor.

W Me too. I'm not sure if the wardrobe next to the window is big enough, though.

M It's fine. Hmm, do you think we need to put in another lamp?

W No. The floor lamp 2)_____ _____ _____ is actually quite bright.

M Good. I want to make sure the painting you hung above the bed is easy to see.

W The flowers in that painting are beautiful. I hope our guests like it.

M I'm sure they will. Oh, maybe we should move the round table 3)_____ _____ _____ _____.

W I don't think that's necessary. I like the table on the rug where it is now.

M Great. Then, I guess we don't need to change anything.

↘ 듣기 필수 표현
· make sure ~을 확실히 하다

5

W Hey, Eric. Do you want to head over to the studio to record our video about woodworking?

M Just a moment. Let's make sure everything is ready.

W Right. I don't want to find out that we forgot something after we start filming.

M Exactly. I 1)_____ _____ _____ on my phone.

W Thanks. What is the first thing we should confirm?

M Do we have the wood and the power tools for 2)_____ _____ _____ _____ ?

W All of the equipment is packed into the van.

M What about the camera and the microphones?

W I brought those over to the studio earlier. They're all set up.

M Great. We still need to 3)_____ _____ _____ _____ to play in the video, right?

W Yeah. I can pick a song now.

M Perfect. I'll put the song in the video when editing it.

↘ 듣기 필수 표현
· head over to ~로 가다, 향하다

6

M Welcome to the Grand Canyon Souvenir Shop. How can I help you?

W Hi. I want to get some T-shirts for 1)_____ _____ _____ _____.

M What about these? The one with the cactus on it is $15, and the one with the picture of the Grand Canyon is $20.

W I'll take two with the cactus and one with the picture of the Grand Canyon.

M Here you go. Is there anything else you need?

W I was also thinking of buying some magnets.

M Well, this one is very popular, and it's only $10.

W Perfect. I'll 2)_____ _____, please.

M So you want two T-shirts with the cactus, one with the picture of the canyon, and four of these magnets, right?

W Yes. That's everything.

M Okay. Oh, I 3)_____ _____ _____ that we are having a sale today. Every item is 10% off.

W Wonderful. Here's my credit card.

↘ 듣기 필수 표현
· have a sale 세일하다

7

W Brandon, are you excited about our class field trip on Friday?

M Yes. I'm really looking forward to hiking in the national park. But I think I need a new backpack. Mine is pretty old.

W I want to 1)_____ _____ _____ _____, too. Do you want to go shopping with me this afternoon?

M I'd love to, but I have plans.

W Oh, you have a piano lesson today, right?

M No. My lesson is tomorrow, actually.

W Really? Then, are you supposed to 2)_____ _____ _____ your family?

M No. I have to visit the dentist at 2 p.m. this afternoon. It's time for 3)_____ _____ _____.

W I see. I'll ask Jenna to go to the mall with me instead. Will you have time to study for history class with me tomorrow?

M Of course. See you then.

↘ 듣기 필수 표현
· look forward to ~을 기대하다
· be supposed to ~하기로 되어 있다

8

M Gina, are you busy on Saturday? I'd like to visit the art museum with you.

W I appreciate the invitation, but I can't go. I'm taking the Emergency First Aid Course. It starts ¹)_____ _____ _____ on Saturday.

M What about ²)_____ _____ _____ in the afternoon?

W It's a four-hour class. I'll be too tired to do anything afterward.

M I understand. That sounds exhausting. Where are you taking the course?

W At the Robertson Community Center. It's just ³)_____ _____ _____ _____ from my home.

M That's convenient. It won't take you long to walk there. By the way, who is the instructor?

W The course is being taught by Evan Williams. He's ⁴)_____ _____ _____ who teaches classes at the center.

M That sounds great. I'm sure you'll learn a lot.

W Thanks! And I hope you have fun at the museum.

↘ 듣기 필수 표현
· take a course 수업을 듣다
· by the way 그런데

9

M Good morning. You are listening to *Around Town*. If you enjoy watching fireworks, don't miss the sixth annual Summer Fireworks Festival on Sunday. The event will begin at 9 p.m. and end at 11 p.m. It ¹)_____ _____ _____ in Harbor Park. Teams from four countries will compete to put on the best fireworks display. You are sure to have a great time. And if you get hungry during the festival, don't worry. There will be many vendors selling snacks and drinks. Parking ²)_____ _____ _____ in the lot on the east side of the park and will cost $15 for three hours. However, space is limited, so attendees are advised to ³)_____ _____ _____. For more information, visit www.summerfireworks.com.

↘ 듣기 필수 표현
· put on ~을 공연하다

10

W Honey, have you ¹)_____ _____ _____ _____ for our ski trip to Denver?

M I'm just looking at the agency's website. What about this one?

W It only has seats for two people.

M I didn't notice that. That will be too small. There will be four of us traveling together.

W And it is going to ²)_____ _____ _____ _____, so we will need a vehicle that's fuel efficient.

M Yeah. It should get at least 12 kilometers to the liter.

W Right. And I don't want to spend more than $50 per day on the rental.

M Me neither. Oh, look! One of ³)_____ _____ _____ has a ski rack.

W We definitely need one to hold the skis.

M I agree. I guess we should reserve this car, then.

↘ 듣기 필수 표현
· fuel efficient 연료 효율이 좋은

11

M Mom, have you called a taxi yet? We need to leave for the airport soon.

W Oh, I ¹)_____ _____. Can you do that?

M Sure. *[Pause]* I just ²)_____ _____ _____ with an app! Hopefully, it won't take too long to get here.

↘ 듣기 필수 표현
· leave for ~으로 떠나다

12

W Honey, ¹)_____ _____ _____ stopping at the supermarket on your way home from work tonight?

M Of course not. What do you need me to pick up from the store?

W I'm planning on baking a cake tomorrow. Could you ²)_____ _____ _____ _____?

13

[Phone rings.]

W You've reached the front desk at the Sunset Hotel.

M Hi. This is Steve Harris in Room 303.

W Good evening, Mr. Harris. How can I help you?

M The people in 1)_____ _____ _____ _____ _____ are very noisy.

W Oh, I see. Is the noise disturbing you?

M Yes. Would it be possible to get a different room?

W I'll check if there are any rooms available now, Mr. Harris. [Typing sound] I'm very sorry, but we are 2)_____ _____ _____. I can have you moved to another one tomorrow.

M But that doesn't help me now. I'm trying to prepare for an important meeting tomorrow, but I can't focus on my work.

W I'll ask the guests in that room to be quiet.

M Thanks. I really 3)_____ _____ _____.

W No problem. Could you tell me which room the noise is coming from?

↘ 듣기 필수 표현
· focus on ~에 집중하다

14

W I can't believe how tired I am today, David.

M Did you stay up late last night?

W Yeah. I've been having trouble sleeping lately.

M That's unfortunate. I used to have the same problem as well.

W Really? Did you figure out a way to deal with it?

M Well, one thing that is very important is to avoid using your computer or phone 1)_____ _____ _____.

W I've heard people say that. But I don't understand why it's so important.

M 2)_____ _____ _____ _____ from these devices can make you feel more alert.

W I see what you mean. Did you change anything else?

M I'd also suggest exercising every day. I read that it 3)_____ _____ _____.

W Did that work for you?

M Yes. I joined a gym, and I've been sleeping better ever since.

↘ 듣기 필수 표현
· stay up late 늦은 시간까지 깨어있다
· figure out ~을 알아내다
· deal with ~을 해결하다
· feel alert 정신이 깨다
· ever since 그 이후로 계속

15

W Carl and Brenda live in the same apartment building. Their building provides each resident with an individual parking space. Carl's parking space is 1)_____ _____ _____ _____ of the building, but Brenda's is about 30 meters away from the door. Last week, Brenda slipped on the icy pavement and sprained her ankle. When Carl came home from work today, he noticed that she was 2)_____ _____ _____ from her car to the building's entrance. Therefore, Carl wants to tell Brenda that she can use his parking space and he will use hers while 3)_____ _____ _____. In this situation, what would Carl most likely say to Brenda?

↘ 듣기 필수 표현
· sprain one's ankle 발목을 삐다

16~17

M Good afternoon. Last class, we started talking about how people in early societies lived. Today, I want to focus on the various types of shelters that they used. First, caves were one of the 1)_____ _____ _____. In fact, one cave in Eastern Europe was inhabited about 54,000 years ago. Second, tents were best for people who moved from place to place in search of food. These 2)_____ _____ were usually made with animal skins and wooden poles. Some of them were large enough for 10 to 15 people to live in comfortably. Third, igloos have been made for thousands of years by people living in the Arctic. These are built using blocks of snow, and they provide excellent 3)_____ _____ _____ _____ _____ of this region. Lastly, prehistoric people also constructed stone buildings. The oldest known example is on an island in the Middle East. It is believed to be over 8,500 years old. Now, let's look at some photos of these shelters.

↘ 듣기 필수 표현
· from place to place 여기저기로
· in search of ~을 찾아서

1번부터 17번까지는 듣고 답하는 문제입니다. 1번부터 15번까지는 한 번만 들려주고, 16번부터 17번까지는 두 번 들려줍니다. 방송을 잘 듣고 답을 하시기 바랍니다.

1 다음을 듣고, 여자가 하는 말의 목적으로 가장 적절한 것을 고르시오.

① 체육관 개관을 홍보하려고
② 단체 운동의 장점을 설명하려고
③ 개인 트레이너 비용을 안내하려고
④ 최신 운동 기구 이용을 권장하려고
⑤ 체육관 주별 수업 일정을 공지하려고

2 대화를 듣고, 남자의 의견으로 가장 적절한 것을 고르시오.

① 할 수 있을 때마다 글쓰기 연습을 해야 한다.
② 단순하고 간결하게 쓰인 글이 이해하기 쉽다.
③ 만화책은 어휘력을 키우는 데 도움이 되지 않는다.
④ 뛰어난 작가는 다양한 문체를 구사할 줄 알아야 한다.
⑤ 다양한 책을 많이 읽는 것만으로 작문 실력이 향상될 수 있다.

3 대화를 듣고, 두 사람의 관계를 가장 잘 나타낸 것을 고르시오.

① 편집장 — 시청 공무원
② 역사학자 — 박물관 직원
③ 건축가 — 행사 기획자
④ 정치인 — 방송 기자
⑤ 대학 교수 — 조교

4 대화를 듣고, 그림에서 대화의 내용과 일치하지 않는 것을 고르시오.

5 대화를 듣고, 남자가 할 일로 가장 적절한 것을 고르시오.

① 욕실 청소하기
② 빨래 돌리기
③ 생선 조리하기
④ 디저트 준비하기
⑤ 반려견 산책시키기

6 대화를 듣고, 여자가 지불할 금액을 고르시오. [3점]

① $60   ② $90   ③ $100   ④ $120   ⑤ $190

7 대화를 듣고, 여자가 피아노 반주를 대신해 줄 수 없는 이유를 고르시오.

① 은퇴 기념 파티에 참석해야 해서
② 곡을 연습할 시간이 부족해서
③ 가족 여행을 가야 해서
④ 손가락을 다쳐서
⑤ 어머니 선물을 준비해야 해서

8 대화를 듣고, International Sand Sculpture Competition에 관해 언급되지 않은 것을 고르시오.

① 날짜   ② 장소   ③ 예상 관중 수
④ 조각 주제   ⑤ 티켓 가격

9 Westbrook Cultural Exchange Program에 관한 다음 내용을 듣고, 일치하지 않는 것을 고르시오.

① 선발된 참가자들은 스페인으로 여행을 떠난다.
② 프로그램은 9일에 걸쳐 진행된다.
③ 참가자들은 프로그램 기간에 맞춰 출국해야 한다.
④ 참가 신청을 할 수 있는 세 자리가 남아 있다.
⑤ 참가하고 싶은 이유를 제출해야 한다.

10 다음 표를 보면서 대화를 듣고, 여자가 구매할 커피 머그잔 세트를 고르시오.

Coffee Mug Sets

	Set	Price	Size	Color	Free Gift
①	A	$35	Small	Blue	Coffee Beans
②	B	$40	Medium	White	Tea Spoons
③	C	$43	Large	Brown	Coffee Beans
④	D	$52	Medium	Black	Tea Spoons
⑤	E	$60	Large	Green	Coffee Beans

11 대화를 듣고, 여자의 마지막 말에 대한 남자의 응답으로 가장 적절한 것을 고르시오.

① I see. But he talks too much.
② No, thanks. I had a big lunch today.
③ Really? I thought he was quite popular.
④ Don't worry. You'll like your new classmates.
⑤ Okay. I'll start a conversation when I see him.

12 대화를 듣고, 남자의 마지막 말에 대한 여자의 응답으로 가장 적절한 것을 고르시오.

① I see. We'd prefer to book a table for 7 p.m.
② It's all right. We'll just come back another day.
③ That's fine. We can just sit at the table over there.
④ Never mind. The system seems to be working again.
⑤ Of course. I'll call the restaurant for a reservation now.

13 대화를 듣고, 남자의 마지막 말에 대한 여자의 응답으로 가장 적절한 것을 고르시오.

Woman:

① I can't. It doesn't turn on anymore.
② I'm not sure. You might need a smaller size.
③ No worries. The repairman is coming tomorrow.
④ That's great. This deal is too good to pass up.
⑤ Definitely! The delivery will be made today.

14 대화를 듣고, 여자의 마지막 말에 대한 남자의 응답으로 가장 적절한 것을 고르시오. [3점]

Man:

① Sure. I might be able to help carry some light items.
② Yes. I'm starting to feel much better after the surgery.
③ That's not possible. I'll be hospitalized for the next few weeks.
④ Don't worry. This wheelchair is easy to move around in.
⑤ No. The doctor says I can't go because of my knee injury.

15 다음 상황 설명을 듣고, Emily가 Carl에게 할 말로 가장 적절한 것을 고르시오. [3점]

Emily:

① You should check the prices of these pictures.
② How about choosing pictures of unique animals?
③ I've already looked up different galleries in the area.
④ You'd better reconsider where to hang your photos.
⑤ Why don't we visit the exhibition this afternoon?

[16~17] 다음을 듣고, 물음에 답하시오.

16 여자가 하는 말의 주제로 가장 적절한 것은?

① how germs lead to diseases
② why public spaces are so dirty
③ benefits of cleaning your home often
④ ways that bacteria transfer to new places
⑤ household objects that contain many germs

17 언급된 물건이 <u>아닌</u> 것은?

① door knobs   ② smartphones
③ remote controls   ④ light switches
⑤ kitchen sponges

이제 듣기 문제가 끝났습니다. 채점을 마친 후 다음 페이지에서 방송을 다시 들으며 딕테이션 연습을 하시기 바랍니다.

* 채점 결과: 맞은 개수 _____ 개 / 17개   정답 및 해설 p.140

▲ Dictation
음성 바로 듣기

Dictation 정답 p.140

23회 고난도 영어듣기 모의고사 Dictation 음성을 들으며 빈칸에 알맞은 단어를 채워 넣으시기 바랍니다.

1

W Are you trying to exercise more often? Do you find it hard ¹)_____ _____ _____ while working out alone? If so, we have some great news for you. The Center Street Gym will have its ²)_____ _____ on May 15th. We encourage everyone to come check it out! Conveniently located near the Bayside Subway Station, our facility will include state-of-the-art equipment. Best of all, each member ³)_____ _____ _____ to personal trainers and a wide variety of group classes including yoga and aerobics. There will always be someone to ⁴)_____ _____ _____ to meet your fitness goals. Visit www.centergym.com for more information about our gym.

↘ 듣기 필수 표현
· work out 운동하다
· conveniently located 교통이 편리한 곳에 자리잡은
· best of all 무엇보다도
· meet a goal 목표를 달성하다

2

M What are you doing, Emma?

W I'm writing an essay about Shakespeare.

M You seem frustrated. Are you ¹)_____ _____ _____ _____ ?

W Well, it's not the topic but the writing. I think my writing is too simple, and I keep using the same words.

M There's an easy way to fix that.

W Really? What's that?

M You should read a lot of different books, ²)_____ _____, _____, and even comics, whenever you can.

W I don't see how that can help.

M The books are all written in different styles and ³)_____ _____ _____ _____ _____ and phrases. You would become familiar with many types of writing.

W But ⁴)_____ _____ _____ writing.

M That doesn't matter. Just by reading a lot, your vocabulary naturally increases and your writing improves.

W I get it. I'll give it a try!

3

[Cell phone rings.]

W Hello? You've reached Audrey Jones.

M Hi. This is Ronald Stein from the Kenwood History Museum. I'm calling to invite you to our museum's event.

W Oh? What's the event?

M It's a 150th celebration of the founding of our city. We're ¹)_____ _____ _____ _____ about its history.

W That sounds wonderful. Is there anything specific you'd like me to talk about?

M Your research on what happened in our city during the 1980s is renowned. We would be honored if you could speak about that time period.

W I'd love to. ²)_____ _____ _____ ?

M It's on May 7th at 4 p.m. It'll be held in the museum's lecture hall.

W I'll be there. And is it possible for me to bring my assistant?

M Of course. That's absolutely fine.

W Thank you. She usually ³)_____ _____ _____ _____ public speeches.

M That won't be a problem. I look forward to seeing you!

↘ 듣기 필수 표현
· look forward to ~을 기대하다

4

M Katie, there you are! Are you doing your painting for the art contest here?

W Yeah. Isn't this spot perfect?

M This maple tree you're sitting under is so beautiful!

W I know! It inspired me to paint here.

M I thought you would bring the checkered mat, but the one you ¹)_____ _____ _____ .

W Yeah. I prefer to sit on this because it's more comfortable, and it's also big enough. I put all of my paints and sketchbook here, too.

M Did you see those ²)_____ _____ _____ by the corner of the mat?

W Actually, I already put those flowers in my painting.

M Oh, look at that! There's 3)_____ _____ _____.

W How cute! It's eating some grass. Maybe I should add that to my painting.

M That's a good idea. Anyway, do you mind if I work on my painting here?

W No problem. Have a seat.

↘ 듣기 필수 표현
· Do you mind if ~? ~해도 될까?
· Have a seat. 자리에 앉아.

5

W Good morning, honey. How did you sleep?

M Great. You must be tired from our dinner party last night.

W I'm fine. Thanks again for 1)_____ _____ _____ for our guests. They really enjoyed it.

M I'm glad. I also loved the dessert you prepared.

W Thank you. I 2)_____ _____ _____ _____.

M Well, it's time for us to do some housework. I'll get started on the laundry.

W That's okay. I did that earlier this morning.

M That's so sweet of you. Then, what's left? Let me know 3)_____ _____ _____ _____.

W You could take the dog for a walk or clean the bathroom. It's up to you.

M I'll 4)_____ _____ _____. Why don't you get some fresh air with the dog?

W Great. Then, we can get coffee together afterwards.

↘ 듣기 필수 표현
· do housework 집안일을 하다
· It's up to you. 당신 선택에 달렸어.
· get some fresh air 바람을 쐬다

6

M Hello. Can I take your order?

W Hi. We're thinking of ordering the Set Menu Special.

M Okay. We have two options. Would you like me 1)_____ _____ _____ _____ _____ _____?

W That would be great.

M Set A includes a salad, chicken dish, and dessert. Set B includes a salad, pasta, steak, and dessert.

W What's the price difference?

M Set A is $30, and Set B is $50.

W Well, we are pretty hungry, so we'll 2)_____ _____ _____ _____ of Set B.

M Oh, that might be too much for two of you.

W Actually, our friends will be joining us soon, so there will be 3)_____ _____ _____ _____ _____.

M That should be perfect, then. Also, we're offering 10% off your total if you post a picture and mention us on social media.

W Oh, great. I'll 4)_____ _____ _____ _____.

7

M Christine, I have a favor to ask.

W Sure. How can I help?

M My school choir has a performance this weekend, but 1)_____ _____ _____ _____ her finger and can't play for us.

W I'm sorry to hear that. 2)_____ _____ _____ _____ to fill in?

M Could you do it? There isn't much time to practice, but you're such a great pianist. I'm sure you'll be able to learn the songs.

W Well... When is it?

M It's this Saturday afternoon at 3.

W I'm sorry. 3)_____ _____ _____ _____.

M Oh, I forgot. You're going on a family trip.

W That's not the problem. We canceled our trip.

M Then, why not?

W My 4)_____ _____ _____ is that day. Her coworkers have been preparing it as a surprise for her.

M I see. Then, I'll find someone else.

↘ 듣기 필수 표현
· fill in 대신하다, 채우다

8

W What's that, Tyler?

M I'm looking at a post online about the International Sand Sculpture Competition. It sounds like a lot of fun.

W Why don't we 1)_____ _____ _____ _____? When is it?

M It begins on September 29th, and the competitors' pieces will be available for public viewing for one week.

W Great. Isn't it being held at Logan Beach?

M That's right. Apparently 2)_____ _____ _____ from all over the world are competing.

W Wow. I wonder what kind of sculptures they will make.

M It says the competition is about 3)_____ _____ _____. So I'm guessing there will be things like mermaids and sea dragons!

W That sounds amazing. How much does it cost?

M Tickets are only $8 for adults, and kids are free.

W Great. Then, let's buy them now. I'm sure it'll be a unique experience.

9

W Okay, class. Before you leave, I'd like to remind you about the Westbrook Cultural Exchange Program that the city 1)_____ _____ _____ _____. As you know, all selected participants will travel to Spain. The program will take place over nine days. However, participants who would like to explore the country on their own 2)_____ _____ _____ or stay longer. There are still three spaces left in the program. If you're interested in going, please visit the program's website, whose address I've written 3)_____ _____ _____ _____ _____. Please note that you'll have to submit an essay about why you want to participate. The deadline for applications is next Monday. I encourage you all 4)_____ _____ _____ this wonderful opportunity.

↘ 듣기 필수 표현
· on one's own 스스로, 개별적으로
· be interested in ~할 의향이 있다

10

M Hey, Rose. What are you doing?

W I'm trying to buy a set of coffee mugs online. 1)_____ _____ _____ _____ _____ _____?

M Okay. [Pause] They all look nice. But this set is pretty expensive.

W Yeah. I want to stick to a price under $60.

M What about size? How big do you want the mugs to be?

W I prefer 2)_____ _____ _____ _____. I drink a lot of coffee, so those small cups aren't big enough.

M Now, you have to consider the colors. Do any of them stand out to you?

W I don't really like 3)_____ _____ _____. They will get stained easily.

M Then, these two are your last options. They both come with a free gift, too.

W Oh, that's great. I love coffee of course, but I think 4)_____ _____ would be pretty useful. I'll go with that one.

M Great. Looks like you've made your choice.

↘ 듣기 필수 표현
· stick to 고수하다, 지키다
· stand out 눈에 띄다
· come with ~이 딸려 나오다
· make one's choice 결정을 내리다, 선택하다

11

W Are you okay, Marcus? You've barely touched your dinner.

M Sorry, Mom. I 1)_____ _____ _____ my classmate. He just transferred from another school, and he always 2)_____ _____ _____.

W That's tough. I know you're shy, but why don't you try talking to him?

12

M Hello. I'm the restaurant manager. Did you 1)_____ _____ _____ for dinner tonight?

W No, I didn't. Hmm... I didn't know I could make reservations here.

M Oh, you can find the booking system on our website. Unfortunately, we are 2)_____ _____ _____ tonight.

13

W Excuse me. Do you mind helping me?

M I'd be happy to. What do you need?

W I'm 1)_____ _____ _____ a new television, but I can't decide which one to get. How about this one?

M Well, it is our best-selling model. But it's 2)_____ _____ _____.

W Then, could you recommend a more affordable model?

M There's this one. You 3)_____ _____ _____ a few weeks for it to be delivered, though. It's currently sold out everywhere.

W Oh, really? That's too bad.

M Or if you don't want to wait, we do have one in the back. But the box is open. A customer returned it for a refund.

W Are there any problems with it?

M No. It's perfectly fine. He decided to buy a bigger one.

W I see. Can you 4)_____ _____ _____ _____ on it?

M We can offer you 20% off the regular price.

↘ 듣기 필수 표현
· regular price 정가

14

W Honey, what did the doctor say at the hospital?

M He recommended knee surgery.

W I'm not surprised... Is it a serious procedure?

M No. It's a pretty minor one. I'll be in and out of the hospital 1)_____ _____ _____ _____.

W Good. When is it scheduled?

M It'll be next Thursday.

W Okay. I'll 2)_____ _____ _____. What is the recovery time?

M It'll take a few weeks. The doctor also advised me not to walk for at least a week after leaving the hospital.

W Oh, will we need to get you a wheelchair?

M Just for that first week. I think the hospital can lend us one.

W Then, maybe I should 3)_____ _____ _____ so that it's easier for you to move around in the wheelchair.

M That would be great. Thank you.

W No problem. Should I start preparing the house today?

↘ 듣기 필수 표현
· advise A to B A에게 B할 것을 조언하다

15

M Carl is a photographer and will have his photos exhibited at a gallery soon. His work mainly focuses on rare plants and animals. Carl is excited because it's 1)_____ _____ _____ his photographs will be hung up in a gallery. However, he's having a difficult time selecting the photographs for his exhibition. He knows that his friend Emily 2)_____ _____ _____ _____ with photography exhibits than he does. Carl asks her for advice about which pictures to select. Because the gallery already features a lot of plant photographs, Emily believes Carl should show pictures of animals to stand out. So Emily wants to suggest that Carl select photographs 3)_____ _____ _____. In this situation, what would Emily most likely say to Carl?

↘ 듣기 필수 표현
· focus on ~에 초점을 두다
· hang up ~을 걸다
· have a difficult time 어려움을 겪다

16~17

W Hi, everyone. Last time, we talked about why it is so important to keep public spaces clean. Today, I want to talk about objects in your home where 1)_____ _____ _____ _____ _____ live. Door knobs are the first example I should mention. Bacteria on our hands transfer to these every time we open or close a door. And what's more, 2)_____ _____ _____ _____ because they don't appear to be dirty. Second up are smartphones. Disease-causing germs are able to grow quickly on their glass surfaces because we're constantly touching them throughout the day. Third, we have light switches. We use them often, and hardly wash our hands before touching them. And because they 3)_____ _____ _____ _____, viruses can survive on them for a long time. Finally, kitchen sponges are one of the dirtiest objects in our houses. Sponges provide a favorable humid environment for bacteria, and 4)_____ _____ _____ _____ _____ that feeds the germs. Okay. Now, I'll show you a video about properly cleaning these things.

↘ 듣기 필수 표현
· what's more 게다가

정답 및 해설 p.146

1번부터 17번까지는 듣고 답하는 문제입니다. 1번부터 15번까지는 한 번만 들려주고, 16번부터 17번까지는 두 번 들려줍니다. 방송을 잘 듣고 답을 하시기 바랍니다.

1 다음을 듣고, 여자가 하는 말의 목적으로 가장 적절한 것을 고르시오.

① 쇼핑몰 환불 정책 변경을 공지하려고
② 고객 문의 처리 지연을 사과하려고
③ 고객 만족도 조사 참여를 요청하려고
④ 쇼핑몰 할인 행사 종료일을 안내하려고
⑤ 우수 고객 선정 기준을 설명하려고

2 대화를 듣고, 남자의 의견으로 가장 적절한 것을 고르시오.

① 로봇은 일자리 감소 문제를 일으킬 수 있다.
② 로봇의 주된 사용처는 제조 공장이 될 것이다.
③ 유독한 산업 폐기물로 오염 사고가 늘고 있다.
④ 로봇은 사람들의 삶에 긍정적인 영향을 줄 것이다.
⑤ 로봇은 아직 사람을 완전히 대체할 수 없다.

3 대화를 듣고, 두 사람의 관계를 가장 잘 나타낸 것을 고르시오.

① 스포츠 기자 — 대학 교수
② 농구 선수 — 코치
③ 환자 — 재활 치료사
④ 스포츠 관람객 — 심판
⑤ 학생 — 프로 선수

4 대화를 듣고, 그림에서 대화의 내용과 일치하지 않는 것을 고르시오.

5 대화를 듣고, 여자가 할 일로 가장 적절한 것을 고르시오.

① 여동생 데리러 가기
② 아마추어 대회 준비하기
③ 도서관에 책 반납하기
④ 드럼 수업 등록하기
⑤ 수학 시험 준비하기

6 대화를 듣고, 여자가 지불할 금액을 고르시오. [3점]

① $48   ② $50   ③ $63   ④ $66   ⑤ $70

7 대화를 듣고, 남자가 동창회에 참석할 수 <u>없는</u> 이유를 고르시오.

① 대학교 수업을 들어야 해서
② 할머니가 오시기로 해서
③ 바비큐 파티에 참석하기로 해서
④ 운전면허 시험을 봐야 해서
⑤ 게임 대회에 출전해야 해서

8 대화를 듣고, 자선 기부 행사에 관해 언급되지 <u>않은</u> 것을 고르시오.

① 주최 기관   ② 행사 목적   ③ 행사 날짜
④ 기부 방법   ⑤ 기부 제한 품목

9 Applewood Play Night에 관한 다음 내용을 듣고, 일치하지 <u>않는</u> 것을 고르시오.

① 다음 주 금요일 저녁에 열릴 예정이다.
② 학교 강당에서 진행된다.
③ 학생당 최대 3명의 손님을 초대할 수 있다.
④ 지각 입장은 허용되지 않는다.
⑤ 공연 전에 무료 다과가 제공될 것이다.

10 다음 표를 보면서 대화를 듣고, 여자가 구매할 스탠딩 책상을 고르시오.

Standing Desks

	Model	Price	Adjustment Method	Width	Color
①	A	$270	Manual	90 cm	White
②	B	$280	Electric	85 cm	Black
③	C	$285	Electric	95 cm	White
④	D	$295	Electric	105 cm	Black
⑤	E	$305	Manual	100 cm	White

11 대화를 듣고, 남자의 마지막 말에 대한 여자의 응답으로 가장 적절한 것을 고르시오.

① I can't. The launch event is on Friday.

② Why not? Everyone loves beauty products.

③ Me too. I was thinking of buying a bottle of it.

④ You're right. We should listen to her song again.

⑤ Definitely. I just bought a copy of her new album.

12 대화를 듣고, 여자의 마지막 말에 대한 남자의 응답으로 가장 적절한 것을 고르시오.

① I have some cuts on my arm.

② I took some medicine last night.

③ The park was really crowded today.

④ Why weren't you wearing a helmet?

⑤ You can rent skateboards at the park.

13 대화를 듣고, 여자의 마지막 말에 대한 남자의 응답으로 가장 적절한 것을 고르시오.

Man: _____

① I love making campfires at night.

② Maybe we should go another weekend.

③ The forecast said it will be mostly sunny.

④ Let's go to the store down the street.

⑤ Why don't we buy some bug spray?

14 대화를 듣고, 남자의 마지막 말에 대한 여자의 응답으로 가장 적절한 것을 고르시오. [3점]

Woman: _____

① I know. People need to recycle more.

② Really? Are you sure he would let us use it?

③ Of course. Plastic waste harms many animals.

④ Exactly. The clean-up event was a big success.

⑤ Great. I'll have the posters ready for you soon.

15 다음 상황 설명을 듣고, Vanessa가 Matt에게 할 말로 가장 적절한 것을 고르시오. [3점]

Vanessa: _____

① I think you may want to check the mirror.

② It's important to make a good impression.

③ I can see that you ate spinach before class.

④ You probably didn't have time to get breakfast.

⑤ I'm glad we got the chance to introduce ourselves.

[16~17] 다음을 듣고, 물음에 답하시오.

16 남자가 하는 말의 주제로 가장 적절한 것은?

① decline in human labor due to AI

② risks associated with the use of AI

③ ways different industries utilize AI

④ potential of AI to alter the economy

⑤ process of developing an AI system

17 언급된 분야가 <u>아닌</u> 것은?

① agriculture　② education　③ transportation

④ healthcare　⑤ finance

이제 듣기 문제가 끝났습니다. 채점을 마친 후 다음 페이지에서 방송을 다시 들으며 딕테이션 연습을 하시기 바랍니다.

* 채점 결과: 맞은 개수 _____ 개 / 17개　　　　정답 및 해설 p.146

24회 Dictation

Dictation 정답 p.146

24회 고난도 영어듣기 모의고사 Dictation 음성을 들으며 빈칸에 알맞은 단어를 채워 넣으시기 바랍니다.

1

W Dear shoppers. I'm Chelsea Anderson from the Galleria Mall. I'd like to let you know about our 1)_____ _____ _____ _____. The deadline for this feedback is December 8th. However, with just a week left, we have only received a small number of replies. So I'd like to encourage everyone 2)_____ _____ _____ this survey. It's a great opportunity for you to help us improve. Please let us know what we're doing right and what we can do better. In particular, we'd like to hear your opinions on the recent changes to 3)_____ _____ _____. We hope you take the time to help us make our mall a better place for our valued customers. Thank you.

↘ 듣기 필수 표현
· in particular 특히

2

W Hey, Adam. Did you watch that TV documentary on robots I mentioned?

M Yeah, I saw it last night.

W Didn't you think the technology was scary?

M Actually, I think robots are going to have an 1)_____ _____ _____ on human lives.

W I'm surprised you feel that way.

M Robots are already useful. They are used to 2)_____ _____ _____ _____.

W But aren't you worried that people will lose their jobs to robots in the future?

M Not really. Robots will mostly be used for tasks that people don't want to do.

W What do you mean?

M For instance, robots can be used to stop wildfires or 3)_____ _____ _____ _____.

W Ah, I see. So they will let humans avoid dangerous situations.

M Exactly. That's why I think robots will be a good thing for people.

↘ 듣기 필수 표현
· lose A to B B 때문에 A를 잃다

3

W I feel like I let everyone down tonight, Mr. Campbell.

M We all have good days and bad days. Don't be so hard on yourself, Rebecca.

W I missed 1)_____ _____ _____, even when the basket was wide open.

M I'll tell you a story. During my first game in college, I was so nervous that I could 2)_____ _____ _____ _____.

W Really? But you were voted MVP for three years, and then you became a professional player.

M Exactly. If I had 3)_____ _____ _____ _____ after that first game, I wouldn't be where I am today.

W I see. Do you miss playing?

M Sometimes. But 4)_____ _____ _____ like you is my greatest joy these days.

W That's good. But I don't know how I can recover from this.

M Trust me. Just pick yourself up and get back out there.

W Okay, thank you. I won't give up.

↘ 듣기 필수 표현
· let ~ down ~를 실망시키다
· be hard on ~를 심하게 대하다
· pick oneself up (마음 등을) 다잡다

4

M Hey, Collette. What are you looking at?

W It's a photo of a hotel room in Paris. I might book this one for my vacation.

M Oh, the bed looks so 1)_____ _____ _____.

W I know. And the painting of the lily on the wall is beautiful.

M Look at that crystal chandelier 2)_____ _____ _____ _____. That's so luxurious!

W Yes. But the best part is the nice view through the window.

M Wow, you can see the Eiffel Tower from the room.

W Yeah, that's amazing.

M Oh, there's a round table with ³)_____ _____ _____ _____ _____. Do you think you'll use it?

W Yes. I can't wait to have my coffee and baguette there every morning.

M I think you should go ahead and book it.

W Yes, I agree.

↘ 듣기 필수 표현
· go ahead 실행에 옮기다

5

M Hi, Grace. Are you walking over to the library?

W No. Why do you ask? Is something going on?

M Some of our classmates are going there now ¹)_____ _____ _____ for the math exam.

W Oh, I didn't know. Are you going?

M Yes. I ²)_____ _____ _____ _____ I can get.

W Well, I won't be able to join you. I have a drum lesson this afternoon.

M Oh, do you play the drums? When did you start to learn?

W I just started six months ago. I'm planning to sign up for an amateur drummer contest next year.

M Sounds great! Then, are you ³)_____ _____ _____ _____ now for your lesson?

W No. My mom asked me to walk my sister home. I have to ⁴)_____ _____ _____ _____ her kindergarten first.

M All right. See you tomorrow.

↘ 듣기 필수 표현
· sign up for ~에 참가하다

6

M Welcome to the Orlando Pottery Museum. Can I help you?

W Hello. I want to buy some tickets.

M All right. They're ¹)_____ _____ _____ and $10 for children.

W Great. I'll take two adult tickets for me and my friend. Also, we are students. Is there a discount?

M Yes. You can get 10% off of the tickets. May I see your student IDs?

W Sure. [Pause] Here you go.

M Thanks. And I should ²)_____ _____ _____ _____ we are offering a pottery-making experience for visitors today.

W That sounds fun. How much is it?

M It's $15 per person. But there isn't a student discount for it.

W That's okay. We'll ³)_____ _____ _____ as well.

M So you want two admission tickets with a student discount and two pottery session passes, right?

W That's correct. Here's my card.

7

W Noah, is that you? You've ¹)_____ _____ so much since I last saw you.

M Hi, Ms. Murphy! I haven't seen you since I graduated from middle school. But I've really missed you.

W I'm so glad to run into you. How are you?

M Great. I'm going to be a sophomore in college next year.

W Wow, ²)_____ _____ _____. It seems like yesterday that you were in my class.

M I just got my driver's license, too.

W That's wonderful. Are you coming to the ³)_____ _____ _____ on Saturday? We're planning a barbecue.

M No. I can't make it.

W That's too bad. There will be lots of fun games with small prizes.

M I know. But my grandmother is ⁴)_____ _____ that day.

W Oh, that's so nice. Have a great time with her.

M Thanks, Ms. Murphy.

↘ 듣기 필수 표현
· graduate from ~을 졸업하다
· run into ~를 우연히 만나다

8

M Katie, have you seen that letter I was reading earlier?

W Is this it, Dad? It's from the Canadian Cancer Foundation.

M Yeah! That's the one. It has some details about that organization's 1)_____ _____.

W What kind of event is it?

M It's a sale. The foundation sells new and used items that people donate to them. The purpose is to 2)_____ _____ _____ _____ _____.

W Oh, that sounds like a good cause. When is it?

M Let me check. *[Pause]* It's on June 17th.

W How can we donate items?

M They will 3)_____ _____ _____ _____ whenever it's convenient for us. I just have to call them the day before.

W I have some toys that I don't play with anymore.

M Great. Should I have them stop by tomorrow afternoon, then?

W Sure. I'll get everything ready tonight.

↘ 듣기 필수 표현
· stop by 들르다

9

W Good morning, students of Applewood High School. I'm Ms. Barnes, the advisor for the school drama club. Our club will have an event called Applewood Play Night next Friday evening. We'll perform brief plays 1)_____ _____ _____ _____. All students are encouraged to attend. Each student is permitted to invite 2)_____ _____ _____ _____ guests. The performance will begin at 7 p.m., but the doors to the auditorium will be closed at 6:55 p.m. Those who arrive after that time will not be allowed to enter. So make sure that your guests arrive no later than that. 3)_____ _____ _____, free refreshments will be served in the hall outside of the auditorium. I hope all of you enjoy our event. Thank you.

10

W Hi, Derek. Can I get your opinion on something?

M Of course. What is it?

W I want to buy a standing desk, but I can't decide which model to choose.

M How much can you spend?

W I 1)_____ _____ a standing desk over $300.

M We can cross one off the list, then. What type of adjustment method do you want?

W I want 2)_____ _____ _____, not a manual one.

M Good idea. Then, you just have to push a button to make it go up and down.

W Also, my computer screen is really wide. So the desk should be 3)_____ _____ _____ centimeters.

M In that case, you're down to these two models. What about the color?

W I'm looking for something to 4)_____ _____ _____ _____ _____. So I shouldn't pick the black one.

M You should get this one, then.

↘ 듣기 필수 표현
· cross A off B B에서 A를 지우다
· be down to ~밖에 남지 않다

11

M Where are you going, Taylor?

W I'm 1)_____ _____ _____ to a pop-up event. My favorite singer, Serena Tillman, has launched her own beauty brand.

M Oh, I heard her perfume 2)_____ _____ _____ _____.

12

W Max, are you okay? Did something happen at the park today?

M Well, I was skateboarding with my friends. But I 1)_____ _____ _____ myself, Mom.

W Oh, no! Let me have a look. 2)_____ _____ _____ _____?

13

W Joshua! There you are.

M Hey, Rachel. Are you ready for the 1)_____ _____ tomorrow?

W Not even close. We have so much to prepare!

M Let's 2)_____ _____ _____ of what we all need. Then, I can go to the store and pick up some things.

W Yes, please! Could we add marshmallows to the list? It was so nice to roast them on our last camping trip.

M Definitely. I also might buy handheld electric fans 3)_____ _____ _____ _____.

W Is it going to be really hot?

M Yes, so we better pack lots of shorts and T-shirts.

W I'm a little worried about bugs, then.

M Me too. I think there will be lots of mosquitoes.

W Well, how can we 4)_____ _____?

↘ 듣기 필수 표현
· Not even close. 전혀 아니야.

14

M What are you making, Crystal?

W Hi, Pete. It's a poster for the beach clean-up event I'm organizing.

M That's a great idea. What is involved in this event?

W We'll 1)_____ _____ _____ at Turtle Beach.

M Great. I saw so much garbage the last time I went there. I didn't want to swim.

W Yeah. And when trash gets into the ocean, it 2)_____ _____ _____.

M I've read that many sea turtles have died from eating plastic bags. It's really sad.

W But we can do something about the problem.

M You're right. I'd love to volunteer for your event. How can I help?

W Well... I need someone 3)_____ _____ _____ _____, and I still need to figure out how to take care of the collected trash.

M I have a suggestion. Let's 4)_____ _____ _____ _____ for that.

↘ 듣기 필수 표현
· figure out ~을 생각해 내다

15

W Vanessa and Matt are high school freshmen who have never met before. Today is their first day at their new school. Both of them are assigned to the same homeroom class, and they happen to sit down 1)_____ _____ _____ _____. When class begins, their teacher asks everyone to introduce themselves to their new classmates. When Matt greets Vanessa, she immediately notices that he has a big piece of 2)_____ _____ _____ _____ _____. Vanessa knows that Matt is about to meet everyone else in the class for the first time, and she doesn't want him to embarrass himself. So Vanessa wants to tell him that he should go look at 3)_____ _____ _____ _____. In this situation, what would Vanessa most likely say to Matt?

↘ 듣기 필수 표현
· happen to 우연히 ~하다
· be about to 곧 ~할 참이다

16~17

M Hello, students. Last time, we talked about the development of artificial intelligence. As we make new progress in technology, AI is 1)_____ _____ _____ all over the world. So today, we'll discuss how AI is applied in various fields. First, AI has become essential to agriculture. Not only do farmers use AI to monitor drones and drive tractors, but this technology can also 2)_____ _____ _____ _____. Next, AI is being heavily incorporated into transportation. AI is needed for the smooth operation of self-driving buses and cars. With the help of this technology, these vehicles can actually understand their surroundings in order to navigate. Another developing AI industry is healthcare. AI is revolutionizing how patients are diagnosed, analyzed, and monitored. In addition, it's enabling scientists to discover new treatments. Finally, AI has led to changes in finance. 3)_____ _____ _____ _____ financial experts, people can use AI investors. These virtual assistants analyze market trends and provide advice on which stocks to buy or sell. Now, let's watch a video about how AI accomplishes these feats.

↘ 듣기 필수 표현
· enable A to B A가 B할 수 있게 하다

수능 1등급을 위한 **완벽한 실전 대비서**

해커스

수능영어듣기 모의고사 20+4회

기본

초판 3쇄 발행 2024년 4월 1일

초판 1쇄 발행 2023년 5월 9일

지은이	해커스 어학연구소
펴낸곳	㈜해커스 어학연구소
펴낸이	해커스 어학연구소 출판팀

주소	서울특별시 서초구 강남대로61길 23 ㈜해커스 어학연구소
고객센터	02-537-5000
교재 관련 문의	publishing@hackers.com
	해커스북 사이트(HackersBook.com) 고객센터 Q&A 게시판
동영상강의	star.Hackers.com

ISBN	978-89-6542-587-8 (53740)
Serial Number	01-03-01

저작권자 ⓒ 2023, 해커스 어학연구소

이 책 및 음성파일의 모든 내용, 이미지, 디자인, 편집 형태에 대한 저작권은 저자에게 있습니다.
서면에 의한 저자와 출판사의 허락 없이 내용의 일부 혹은 전부를 인용, 발췌하거나 복제, 배포할 수 없습니다.

중고등영어 1위,
해커스북 HackersBook.com

· 여러 가지 버전으로 실전에 대비할 수 있는 **기본 속도 MP3, 고속 버전 MP3, 고사장 버전 MP3**
· 복습이 간편해지는 **딕테이션 MP3 및 문항별 MP3**
· 학습한 단어의 암기 여부를 쉽게 점검할 수 있는 **어휘 리스트** 및 **어휘 테스트**

한경비즈니스 선정 2020 한국품질만족도 교육(온·오프라인 중·고등영어) 부문 1위 해커스

중·고등영어도 역시 **1위** 해커스

중·고등

해커스 young star

중·고등영어의 압도적인 점수 상승,
해커스 영스타 중·고등에서 현실이 됩니다.

해커스 영스타 중·고등 **강의 무료체험**

내게 맞는 공부법 체크! **학습전략검사**

해커스 중·고등교재 **무료 학습자료**

보카 강의 수강생 수
1위 박가은

[중고등영어 1위] 한경비즈니스 선정 2020 한국품질만족도 교육(온·오프라인 중·고등영어) 부문 1위 해커스
[수강생 수 1위] 해커스인강 보카 강의 담당 선생님 누적 수강생 수 비교 결과(2017.01.~2021.04.)

수능 1등급을 위한
완벽한 실전 대비서

해커스

수능영어듣기
모의고사 20+4 회 고난도

기본

정답 및 해설

해커스

수능영어듣기 모의고사 20+4회 고난도

기본

정답 및 해설

해커스 어학연구소

기출유형 01 목적 파악   정답 ③

M Hello, Lockwood High School students. This is your school librarian, Mr. Wilkins. I'm sure you're aware that our school library is hosting a bookmark design competition. **I encourage students of all grades to participate in the competition.** The winning designs will be made into bookmarks, which will be distributed to library visitors. We're also giving out a variety of other prizes. **So don't let this great opportunity slip away.** Since the registration period for the bookmark design competition ends this Friday, make sure you visit our school library to submit your application. **Come and participate to display your creativity and talents.**	남 안녕하십니까, 록우드 고등학교 학생 여러분. 저는 학교 사서인 Wilkins 선생님입니다. 우리 학교 도서관에서 책갈피 디자인 대회를 개최한다는 것을 여러분들은 분명 알고 있을 겁니다. 저는 모든 학년의 학생들이 이 대회에 참가하기를 독려합니다. 우승작 디자인은 책갈피로 만들어져, 도서관 방문자들에게 배부될 것입니다. 또한 다양한 다른 상들도 시상할 예정입니다. 그러니 이런 좋은 기회를 놓치지 마세요. 책갈피 디자인 대회 접수 기간은 이번 주 금요일에 끝나므로, 지원서를 내러 학교 도서관을 꼭 방문하십시오. 참가하러 오셔서 여러분의 창의력과 재능을 발휘해보세요.

남자가 록우드 고등학교 도서관에서 개최하는 책갈피 디자인 대회에 모든 학생이 참가하기를 독려한다고 하면서, 우승작 특전 및 접수 기간을 안내하고 있다. 따라서, 남자가 하는 말의 목적으로 ③ '책갈피 디자인 대회 참가를 독려하려고'가 가장 적절하다.

어휘 aware ⑱ 알고 있는 distribute ⑧ 배부하다, 나눠주다 slip away 사라지다, 떠나다 registration ⑲ 접수, 등록 make sure 꼭 ~하다 submit ⑧ 제출하다
application ⑲ 지원서; 신청 display ⑧ 드러내다; 전시하다

기출유형 02 의견 파악   정답 ②

M Honey, do you want some apples with breakfast? W Sounds great. **Can you save the apple peels for me?** M Why? What do you want them for? W I'm going to use them to make a face pack. **Apple peels are effective for improving skin condition.** M Where did you hear about that? W I recently read an article about their benefits for our skin. M Interesting. What's in them? W It said apple peels are rich in vitamins and minerals, so they moisturize our skin and enhance skin glow. M That's good to know. W Also, they remove oil from our skin and have a cooling effect. M Wow! Then I shouldn't throw them away. W Right. **Apple peels can help improve our skin condition.** M I see. I'll save them for you.	남 여보, 아침으로 사과 좀 먹을래? 여 좋아. 날 위해 사과 껍질을 좀 남겨 줄 수 있어? 남 왜? 그걸 어디에 사용하려고? 여 얼굴 팩을 만드는 데 사용할 거야. 사과 껍질은 피부 상태를 개선하는 데 효과적이야. 남 그걸 어디에서 들었어? 여 최근에 그게 피부에 주는 이로움에 관한 기사를 읽었어. 남 흥미롭군. 사과 껍질에 뭐가 들어있지? 여 사과 껍질은 비타민과 미네랄이 풍부해서, 피부에 수분을 공급하고 윤기를 증진한다고 쓰여 있었어. 남 알아두면 좋은 내용이네. 여 또한, 그것은 피부에서 기름기를 제거하고 피부 온도를 낮춰주는 효과가 있어. 남 우와! 그러면 그것을 버리지 말아야겠어. 여 맞아. 사과 껍질은 피부 상태 개선에 도움이 될 수 있어. 남 알았어. 당신을 위해 남겨 둘게.

여자가 남자에게 사과를 먹은 뒤 껍질을 남겨 달라고 부탁하면서 사과 껍질이 피부 상태를 개선하는 데 효과적이라고 했다. 따라서, 여자의 의견으로 ② '사과 껍질은 피부 상태 개선에 도움이 된다.'가 가장 적절하다.

어휘 peel ⑲ 껍질 article ⑲ 기사, 글 moisturize ⑧ 수분을 공급하다 enhance ⑧ 증진하다, 강화하다 glow ⑲ 윤기, 광채 throw away ~을 버리다

기출유형 03 관계 파악   정답 ③

W Hello, Mr. Roberts. I appreciate you taking the time to share your experience and knowledge. M My pleasure, Ms. Lee. **I've enjoyed all your bestselling books.** So, I'm excited to help you. W Thanks. **Since I'm writing about world-class athletes, I wanted to hear how you've trained children who became Olympic swimming champions.** M Then we should start with what I observe on the first day of my swimming classes. W Do some children stand out right away? M Yes. **Some kids are able to pick up my instructions quickly and easily.** W I see. So did many of those kids go on to become Olympic champions? M Well, practicing is much more important. Those who consistently practiced made great improvements and ultimately became champions.	여 안녕하세요, Roberts 씨. 당신의 경험과 지식을 공유해주려 시간을 내주셔서 감사합니다. 남 천만에요, Lee 씨. 저는 당신의 베스트셀러 책을 모두 잘 읽었어요. 그래서, 당신을 돕게 되어 기쁩니다. 여 감사합니다. 제가 세계적인 운동선수들에 관해 글을 쓰고 있어서, 당신이 올림픽 수영 챔피언이 된 아이들을 어떻게 훈련시켰는지 듣고 싶었어요. 남 그럼 제가 수영 수업 첫날 무엇을 관찰하는지부터 시작해야겠네요. 여 일부 아이들은 눈에 바로 띄나요? 남 네. 몇몇 아이들은 제 지도 사항을 빠르고 쉽게 익힐 수 있어요. 여 그렇군요. 그래서 그 아이들 중 다수가 나중에 올림픽 챔피언이 되었나요? 남 음, 연습이 훨씬 더 중요합니다. 꾸준히 연습한 아이들이 큰 발전을 이루었고 결국 챔피언이 되었어요.

| W **This is good insight I can use in my book.**
M I hope it helps. | 여 이건 제 책에 쓸 수 있는 훌륭한 통찰력이네요.
남 도움이 되길 바랍니다. |

두 사람이 남자의 수영 코칭 경험에 관해 이야기하고 있다. 여자는 베스트셀러가 된 책을 출간한 적이 있으며 현재 세계적인 운동선수들에 관해 글을 쓰고 있다고 했고, 남자는 올림픽 수영 챔피언이 된 아이들을 어떻게 훈련시켰는지 설명하는 것으로 보아 두 사람의 관계로 ③ '작가 — 수영 코치'가 가장 적절하다.

어휘 appreciate 통 감사하다 athlete 명 운동선수 observe 통 관찰하다 stand out 눈에 띄다, 두드러지다 pick up ~을 익히다, 배우다 instruction 명 지도 사항, 가르침
go on to 나중에 ~하다, 이어서 ~하다 consistently 부 꾸준히, 지속적으로 ultimately 부 결국, 궁극적으로

기출유형 **04** 그림 내용 불일치 파악   정답 ④

| M Hi, Jane. What are you looking at on your phone?
W Hi, Brian. It's a picture I took at Grand Boulder National Park. I went hiking there last weekend.
M Let me see. I like the bear statue wearing the check pattern jacket.
W It's cute, right?
M Yeah. There's a park map between the lights. It seems to include useful information.
W It helps me pick a different trail each time I go hiking. Do you see the two flowerpots in front of the cabin?
M Yes. They look beautiful. **Oh, there's a round table by the path.**
W I had lunch there.
M What a nice place to enjoy lunch! Look at the bird on the tree branch.
W Isn't it lovely? I love going there and being close to nature. | 남 안녕, Jane. 휴대폰으로 뭘 보고 있니?
여 안녕, Brian. 이건 그랜드 볼더 국립공원에서 내가 찍은 사진이야. 지난 주말에 그곳으로 하이킹하러 갔었어.
남 어디 봐. 난 체크무늬 재킷을 입은 곰 조각상이 마음에 들어.
여 귀엽지, 그렇지?
남 그러게. 가로등 사이에는 공원 지도가 있구나. 유용한 정보를 담은 것 같아.
여 그건 내가 하이킹하러 갈 때마다 다른 길을 선택하는 걸 도와줘. 오두막집 앞에 두 개의 화분 보이지?
남 응. 아름다워 보이는걸. 오, 길가에 둥근 테이블이 있네.
여 나는 거기서 점심을 먹었어.
남 점심을 즐기기에 정말 좋은 곳이야! 나뭇가지 위에 새 좀 봐.
여 사랑스럽지 않니? 나는 그곳에 가서 자연과 가까이 있는 것을 좋아해. |

대화에서 남자가 길가에 둥근 테이블이 있다고 말했는데, ④에는 사각 테이블이 그려져 있다.

어휘 statue 명 조각상 trail 명 길, 산길 flowerpot 명 화분 cabin 명 오두막집

기출유형 **05** 할 일 파악   정답 ②

| W Honey, I'm so excited for our restaurant's reopening event tomorrow.
M So am I. Let's see. We've ordered enough ingredients, right?
W I think so. We need to remind our loyal customers of the event.
M I already sent text messages.
W Good. I hope people like the new menu items that we added.
M Don't worry. We have a great chef. So I'm sure the new dishes will be a hit.
W What about the live music? Did you confirm the song list with the band?
M Not yet. **And we also need to wrap wine glasses to give as gifts for the customers.**
W Okay. **Could you wrap them?**
M **Sure. I'll do it now.**
W Great! Then I'll contact the band. | 여 여보, 내일 우리 식당 재개업 행사가 너무 기대돼.
남 나도 그래. 어디 보자. 재료는 충분히 주문했어, 그렇지?
여 그런 것 같아. 단골손님들에게 행사를 다시 한번 알려줘야 해.
남 내가 이미 문자 메시지를 보냈어.
여 좋아. 사람들이 우리가 추가한 신메뉴를 좋아하면 좋겠다.
남 걱정하지 마. 우리에게는 훌륭한 요리사가 있잖아. 그러니 새로운 요리는 분명 인기를 끌 거야.
여 라이브 음악은 어때? 곡 목록을 밴드와 확인했어?
남 아직이야. 그리고 손님들에게 선물로 줄 와인 잔도 포장해야 해.
여 알았어. 당신이 그것들을 포장해 줄 수 있어?
남 물론이지. 지금 할게.
여 좋아! 그럼 내가 밴드와 연락해 볼게. |

식당 재개업 행사를 앞두고 준비 상황을 점검하고 있다. 여자가 손님에게 선물할 와인 잔을 포장해 줄 수 있는지 묻자, 남자가 지금 하겠다고 했으므로 남자가 할 일로 ② '와인 잔 포장하기'가 가장 적절하다.

어휘 remind A of B A에게 B를 다시 한번 알려주다, 상기시키다 loyal customer 단골손님 be a hit 인기를 끌다 wrap 통 포장하다

M	Welcome to Daisy Valley Restaurant.
W	Hi. I'd like to order some food to go. How much is the shrimp pasta and the chicken salad?
M	**The shrimp pasta is $20, and the chicken salad is $10.**
W	**I'll take two shrimp pastas and one chicken salad, please.**
M	Sure. Would you like some dessert, too?
W	Yes. What do you recommend?
M	**The mini cheese cake is one of the best sellers in our restaurant. It's $5 each.**
W	Great! **I'll order two of them.**
M	Okay. Let me confirm your order. Two shrimp pastas, one chicken salad, and two mini cheese cakes. Is that correct?
W	Yes. And I have a birthday coupon here. Can I use it?
M	Let me see. *[Pause]* Yes. **You can get a 10% discount off the total.**
W	Terrific. I'll use this coupon. Here's my credit card.

남	Daisy Valley Restaurant에 오신 걸 환영합니다.
여	안녕하세요. 포장해 갈 음식을 주문하고 싶어요. 새우 파스타와 치킨 샐러드는 얼마인가요?
남	새우 파스타는 20달러이고, 치킨 샐러드는 10달러입니다.
여	새우 파스타 둘, 치킨 샐러드 하나 주세요.
남	그럼요. 디저트도 드시겠어요?
여	네. 어떤 걸 추천하시나요?
남	미니 치즈 케이크가 저희 식당에서 가장 잘 팔리는 것 중 하나예요. 한 조각에 5달러예요.
여	좋아요! 두 조각 주문할게요.
남	알겠습니다. 주문을 확인해드릴게요. 새우 파스타 둘, 치킨 샐러드 하나, 미니 치즈 케이크 두 조각입니다. 맞나요?
여	네. 그리고 여기 생일 쿠폰이 있어요. 이걸 쓸 수 있나요?
남	어디 볼게요. *[잠시 멈춤]* 네. 총액에서 10% 할인받으실 수 있어요.
여	아주 좋군요. 이 쿠폰을 쓸게요. 여기 제 신용 카드요.

여자가 새우 파스타 둘($20×2=$40), 치킨 샐러드 하나($10), 미니 치즈 케이크 둘($5×2=$10)을 구매했고, 10% 할인($60×0.9=$54)을 받았으므로 정답은 ④ '$54'이다.

어휘 | food to go 포장해 갈 음식 confirm 통 확인하다 terrific 형 아주 좋은, 대단한

W	Sam, do you want to go to the K-Trend Festival with me this Saturday?
M	Hi, Olivia. Is that the festival held at Central Square?
W	Yeah, that's it. There'll be many attractions including Taekwondo performances that incorporate K-pop dance moves.
M	Really? Sounds cool! What time does it start?
W	It starts at 5 p.m. Will you be working at the movie theater at that time?
M	No, I'm not working this Saturday. But I can't come to the festival.
W	Too bad. Do you have to study for your economics exam?
M	Actually, I already took the exam yesterday.
W	Then, what's the matter?
M	**I have to take my younger sister to the airport on Saturday evening.**
W	Where's she going?
M	She's going to Canada to study abroad.
W	That's awesome. I hope she has a good experience there.

여	Sam, 이번 주 토요일에 나랑 K-Trend Festival에 가지 않을래?
남	안녕, Olivia. 그거 센트럴 광장에서 열리는 축제니?
여	응, 맞아. K-pop 안무를 결합한 태권도 공연을 포함해서 볼거리가 많을 거야.
남	정말? 멋질 것 같다! 몇 시에 시작해?
여	오후 5시에 시작해. 그 시간에 영화관에서 일하는 거야?
남	아니, 이번 주 토요일에는 근무 안 해. 하지만 나는 그 축제에 갈 수 없어.
여	안됐다. 경제학 시험공부를 해야 해?
남	사실, 어제 이미 그 시험을 봤어.
여	그럼, 무슨 일이야?
남	토요일 저녁에 여동생을 공항에 데려다줘야 해.
여	여동생이 어디 가는데?
남	캐나다로 유학을 갈 거야.
여	멋지다. 그녀가 그곳에서 좋은 경험을 하길 바랄게.

남자는 토요일에 열리는 K-Trend Festival에 못 간다고 하면서 그날 저녁 여동생을 공항에 데려다줘야 한다고 말했으므로, 남자가 축제에 갈 수 없는 이유는 ⑤ '동생을 공항에 데려다줘야 해서'이다.

어휘 | attraction 형 볼거리; 끌림 incorporate 통 결합하다, 합체시키다 economics 형 경제학 study abroad 유학하다, 외국에서 공부하다 awesome 형 멋진

	[Telephone rings.]
W	Hello, Jennifer Porter speaking.
M	Hi, Ms. Porter. This is Steve Jackson from Lifetime Photo Studio.
W	Oh, how are you?
M	Good. I'm scheduled to shoot your school's graduation photos on Wednesday, **November 23rd**. So, I'm calling to confirm the details.
W	Sure. As we previously discussed, the place will be **Lily Pond Park**.
M	Okay. Could you tell me the exact number of students taking part in the photo session?
W	Let me check. *[Pause]* Well, it'll be **180 students**.
M	I see. The same as you said before.
W	That's right. How long will it take to shoot the photos?
M	It'll take **almost three hours**. We should finish by noon.
W	Great. Is there any other information you need?
M	No, I'm all set. Bye.

	[전화기가 울린다.]
여	여보세요, Jennifer Porter입니다.
남	안녕하세요, Porter 씨. 저는 Lifetime Photo Studio의 Steve Jackson입니다.
여	오, 어떻게 지내세요?
남	잘 지내요. 제가 11월 23일 수요일에 선생님의 학교 졸업 사진을 찍기로 되어 있습니다. 그래서 세부 사항을 확인하려고 전화했어요.
여	그래요. 우리가 전에 논의했던 것처럼, 장소는 릴리 호수 공원이 될 거예요.
남	알겠습니다. 사진 촬영 시간에 참가할 정확한 학생 수를 알려 주시겠어요?
여	확인해 볼게요. *[잠시 멈춤]* 음, 180명일 거예요.
남	그렇군요. 전에 말씀하신 것과 같네요.
여	맞아요. 사진을 찍는 데 얼마나 걸릴까요?
남	약 3시간이 걸릴 겁니다. 정오까지는 끝날 거예요.
여	좋군요. 필요한 다른 정보가 있으신가요?
남	아니요, 다 됐습니다. 안녕히 계세요.

날짜(11월 23일), 장소(릴리 호수 공원), 참여 학생 수(180명), 소요 시간(약 3시간)에 대해 언급했고, ③ '복장'은 언급하지 않았다.

어휘 be scheduled to ~하기로 되어 있다　shoot 통 (사진이나 영화를) 찍다, 촬영하다; 쏘다　graduation 명 졸업　detail 명 세부 사항　previously 분 전에　take part in ~에 참가하다
session 명 (활동) 시간　be all set (준비가) 다 되다

기출유형 **09** 내용 불일치 파악 정답 ②

W Hello, listeners. I'm Melinda Jones from the organizing committee of the Greenville Houseplant Expo. I'm here to announce that the expo will run for three days starting on March 17th, 2023. **Just on the opening day, there'll be a lecture on plant care methods.** This lecture will be given by Dr. Evans, host of the TV show *Plants Love You*. Most importantly, you can buy a variety of plants, including rare species, exhibited in the expo. Due to its popularity, you'd better get your tickets early. Tickets are available through online purchase only. If you're a plant lover, come to the expo, which will take place at the Emerald Convention Center, and refresh your houseplant collection.	여 안녕하십니까, 청취자 여러분. 저는 Greenville Houseplant Expo 조직위원회의 Melinda Jones입니다. 박람회는 2023년 3월 17일부터 3일 동안 진행된다는 점을 알려드리고자 합니다. 개막일에만 식물 관리 방법에 관한 강의가 있을 것입니다. 이 강의는 TV 쇼 <Plants Love You>의 진행자인 Evans 박사님이 진행할 예정입니다. 가장 중요한 것은, 여러분이 희귀종을 포함하여 박람회에 전시된 다양한 식물들을 구입할 수 있다는 점입니다. 박람회는 인기가 많기 때문에 입장권을 일찍 구입하시는 편이 좋겠습니다. 입장권은 온라인 구매를 통해서만 구할 수 있습니다. 식물 애호가라면 에메랄드 컨벤션 센터에서 열리는 박람회에 오셔서, 여러분의 화초 수집 컬렉션을 새롭게 꾸며보세요.

화초 박람회에 대한 안내 방송이다. 여자가 개막일에만 식물 관리 방법에 관한 강의가 있을 것이라고 했으므로 ② '식물 관리 방법에 관한 강의가 매일 있을 것이다.'는 내용과 일치하지 않는다.

어휘 organizing committee 조직위원회　lecture 명 강의　rare species 희귀종　exhibit 통 전시하다　houseplant 명 화초

기출유형 **10** 도표 정보 파악 정답 ①

M Welcome to Uptown Music Shop. How can I help you?	남 Uptown Music Shop에 어서 오십시오. 무엇을 도와드릴까요?
W Hi, I'm looking for a hard cello case.	여 안녕하세요, 첼로 하드 케이스를 찾고 있어요.
M All right. Here's our catalog. These are the ones we have in stock. How much are you willing to spend?	남 알겠습니다. 여기 저희 카탈로그가 있습니다. 이것들이 저희가 재고로 가지고 있는 것들이죠. 얼마를 쓰실 의향이신가요?
W **I can spend up to $200.**	여 200달러까지 쓸 수 있어요.
M Okay. How about the interior material? Do you have a preference?	남 알겠습니다. 안감은 어떤가요? 선호하시는 것이 있나요?
W **Well, I don't want the velvet one.** It seems difficult to take care of.	여 음, 벨벳으로 된 것은 원하지 않습니다. 관리하기 힘들어 보여요.
M Right. Then how about the length?	남 그렇군요. 그럼 길이는 어떤가요?
W I have a full-size cello, **so I want a case that's at least 50 inches long.**	여 저는 보통 크기의 첼로를 가지고 있어서, 길이가 최소한 50인치인 케이스를 원해요.
M Now you have two options left. **Do you need wheels on your case?**	남 이제 고르실 수 있는 것이 두 개 남았습니다. 케이스에 바퀴가 달린 것이 필요하신가요?
W **No, I don't need them.** I won't carry it around a lot.	여 아니요, 필요 없어요. 그리 많이 갖고 다니지는 않을 거예요.
M Then this is the one for you.	남 그러면 이게 손님을 위한 거군요.
W Thank you. I'll take it.	여 고마워요. 그걸로 할게요.

여자는 200달러까지 쓸 수 있는 것 중에서, 안감이 벨벳이 아니고, 길이는 최소 50인치이며, 바퀴가 달리지 않은 첼로 케이스를 골랐다.

어휘 in stock 재고로　be willing to ~할 의향이 있다, 기꺼이 ~하다　interior material 안감　full-size 형 보통 크기의　at least 최소한

기출유형 **11** 짧은 대화의 응답 파악 정답 ②

M **Mom, I'd like to get a new bicycle helmet.** Can you buy me one?	남 엄마, 새 자전거 헬멧을 갖고 싶어요. 사 주실 수 있으세요?
W I'll buy you a new helmet if you need it. But what's the problem with the one you have now?	여 필요하면 새 헬멧을 하나 사 줄게. 그런데 지금 가지고 있는 것에 무슨 문제라도 있니?
M **My helmet feels too tight. It hurts my head.**	남 헬멧이 너무 꽉 끼는 것 같아요. 머리가 아파요.
W All right. I'll buy a bigger one that fits you.	여 <u>알겠어. 네게 맞는 더 큰 것을 사 줄게.</u>
	선택지 ① 신경 쓰지 마. 오래된 내 헬멧을 팔게. ② 알겠어. 네게 맞는 더 큰 것을 사 줄게. ③ 절대로 안 돼. 밤에는 자전거를 타면 안 된단다. ④ 좋아. 그게 네 자전거와 완벽하게 어울리는 것 같구나. ⑤ 아니. 우리는 빡빡한 일정에 대해 걱정할 필요가 없단다.

남자가 새 자전거 헬멧을 갖고 싶다면서 그 이유로 기존 헬멧이 너무 꽉 끼어 아프다고 했으므로, 이에 대한 응답으로는 더 큰 헬멧을 사주겠다는 ② 'All right. I'll buy a bigger one that fits you.'가 가장 적절하다.

어휘 tight 형 꽉 끼는; 빡빡한　fit 통 (크기·모양이) 맞다　match 통 어울리다

기출유형 12 — 긴 대화의 응답 파악

정답 ④

M Can I come in, Professor Rossini?	남 들어가도 될까요, Rossini 교수님?
W Of course. Come on in, Ben. What brings you here?	여 물론이지. 어서 들어오렴, Ben. 여기는 어쩐 일로 온 거니?
M I came to ask for advice on studying Italian.	남 이탈리아어 공부에 대해 조언을 구하러 왔어요.
W Is there anything specific you're having trouble with?	여 특별히 곤란한 점이 있니?
M Yes. I'm experiencing difficulty using words properly. Could I get some tips?	남 네. 단어를 적절하게 사용하는 데 어려움을 겪고 있어요. 조언을 좀 받을 수 있을까요?
W Sure. First, let me ask how you use your dictionary.	여 물론이지. 먼저, 네가 사전을 어떻게 사용하는지 물어볼게.
M Well, I use it to look up words that I don't know the meanings of.	남 음, 의미를 모르는 단어를 찾기 위해 그것을 사용해요.
W Dictionaries provide example sentences for most words. Do you read them, too?	여 사전은 대부분의 단어에 대해 예문을 제공해. 그것들도 읽는 거지?
M No, I don't pay attention to the example sentences.	남 아니요, 예문은 신경 쓰지 않아요.
W Knowing the meaning of words is important, but you should also understand the context in which the words are properly used.	여 단어의 의미를 아는 것은 중요하지만, 단어들이 적절하게 사용되는 맥락도 이해해야 한단다.
M I see. So you're suggesting that I study the example sentences as well, right?	남 그렇군요. 그러니까 제게 예문도 공부하라고 제안하시는 거군요, 그렇죠?
W Exactly. That way you can use the proper words in context.	여 정확해. 그런 식으로 해서 문맥에 맞는 적절한 단어를 사용할 수 있단다.

선택지 ① 그렇지 않아. 간단한 문장으로 말하는 게 더 낫단다.
② 그래. 어근 단어를 학습해서 단어를 암기하려고 노력해 보렴.
③ 그게 맞단다. 네가 적절한 사례를 공부했다니 다행이구나.
④ 정확해. 그런 식으로 해서 문맥에 맞는 적절한 단어를 사용할 수 있단다.
⑤ 난 그렇게 생각하지 않는단다. 항상 이탈리아 단어를 이탈리아어로 설명하는 사전을 사용하렴.

이탈리아어 공부 방법에 대해 조언을 구하는 상황이다. 남자가 여자의 말을 되풀이하면서 예문도 공부하라고 제안한 것인지 물었으므로, 이에 대한 응답으로는 제안한 공부법을 재확인해주는 ④ 'Exactly. That way you can use the proper words in context.'가 가장 적절하다.

어휘 specific 형 특별한, 구체적인 properly 부 적절하게 (proper 형 적절한) look up (사전에서) ~을 찾다 example sentence 예문 context 명 맥락 root word 어근 단어

기출유형 13 — 상황에 적절한 말 파악

정답 ③

M Jacob just started volunteering at a nursing home and is planning his next visit. He recalls that not every resident in the nursing home enjoyed the activity he had prepared last time. To avoid this situation, he tries to find an activity that all residents in the nursing home can enjoy. But he can't come up with one that everyone would like. He asks his friend Katie for advice because she has lots of experience volunteering at a nursing home. Katie thinks there's no single activity that can interest all the residents. So Katie wants to suggest to Jacob that next time he should plan more than one activity. In this situation, what would Katie most likely say to Jacob?	남 Jacob은 요양원에서 자원봉사를 막 시작했고 다음 방문을 계획 중입니다. 그는 지난번에 준비했던 활동을 요양원의 모든 거주자가 즐긴 것은 아니었다는 점을 떠올립니다. 이러한 상황을 피하기 위해, 그는 요양원의 모든 거주자가 즐길 수 있는 활동을 찾으려 노력합니다. 그러나 그는 모든 사람이 좋아할 만한 활동을 생각해내지 못합니다. 그는 친구 Katie가 요양원에서 자원봉사를 한 경험이 많기 때문에, 그녀에게 조언을 구합니다. Katie는 모든 거주자의 흥미를 끌 수 있는 단 하나의 활동은 없다고 생각합니다. 그래서 Katie는 Jacob에게 다음번에는 그가 한 가지 이상의 활동을 계획해야 한다고 제안하고 싶습니다. 이러한 상황에서, Katie가 Jacob에게 가장 할 것 같은 말은 무엇입니까?

선택지 ① 넌 요양원이 얼마나 많은지 확인해야 해.
② 네가 지난번에 준비했던 활동을 다시 사용하지 않을래?
③ 다음 방문 때에는 여러 개의 활동을 준비하는 게 어때?
④ 넌 간호 업무에 대해서 더 실용적인 지식을 얻어야 해.
⑤ 네가 이웃 주민들에게 말을 하는 게 좋겠어.

Jacob이 다음 요양원 자원봉사 때 어떤 활동을 준비해야 할지 고민하는 것을 보고, Katie가 한 가지 이상의 활동을 계획하라고 제안하려 한다. 따라서, Katie가 할 말로 ③ 'How about preparing multiple activities for your next visit?'가 가장 적절하다.

어휘 volunteer 동 자원봉사하다 nursing home 요양원 recall 동 떠올리다, 상기하다 resident 명 거주자, 주민 come up with ~을 생각해내다

W Hello, students. Perhaps no material on earth has been more important in human history than metal. **Today, we're going to discuss the contribution of metals to the development of civilization.** First, **gold** was considered the most valuable metal due to its beauty and scarcity. Because of its visual appeal and ability to be easily shaped, it's been used to decorate religious places and objects. Second, **silver** was mainly prized for being the shiniest of all metals. It's been one of the main forms of currency since it was the chief metal used for making coins. Next, **iron** became widely used once humans discovered techniques to strengthen it. This metal was fashioned into tools that revolutionized farming, and later, machines that industrialized the world. Finally, **aluminum** is the most abundant metal in the world and is also lightweight. That's why it's been essential to countless industries in modern society from automotive to aerospace to household products. Now, let's watch a short related video.

여 안녕하세요, 학생 여러분. 아마도 인류 역사에서 지구상의 어떤 물질도 금속보다 더 중요하지는 않았을 것입니다. 오늘, 우리는 금속이 문명의 발전에 기여한 바에 대해 논의할 것입니다. 첫째, 금은 그것의 아름다움과 희소성 때문에 가장 가치 있는 금속으로 여겨졌습니다. 시각적 매력과 쉽게 모양을 만들 수 있는 특성 때문에, 그것은 종교적인 장소와 사물을 장식하는 데 사용되어 왔습니다. 둘째, 은은 주로 모든 금속 중에서 가장 빛나는 금속으로 귀하게 여겨졌습니다. 그것은 동전을 만드는 데 사용된 주요 금속이었기 때문에 주요한 화폐 종류 중 하나였습니다. 다음으로, 철은 인류가 그것을 강화하는 기술을 발견하자 널리 사용되었습니다. 이 금속은 농업에 혁명을 일으킨 도구로, 나중에는 세계를 산업화시킨 기계로 만들어졌습니다. 마지막으로, 알루미늄은 세계에서 가장 풍부한 금속이며 또한 무게가 가볍습니다. 그 이유로 그것은 자동차 부품에서 항공 우주 제품, 가정용품까지 현대 사회의 수많은 산업에 필수적인 요소가 되어 왔습니다. 이제, 관련된 짧은 영상을 보겠습니다.

선택지 **01** ① 금속이 어떻게 인류 문명을 발전시켰는지
② 금속에 적용된 기술이 어떻게 개선되었는지
③ 대부분의 귀금속이 어디에서 기원했는지
④ 금속이 왜 패션 산업에 사용되었는지
⑤ 고대 문명이 왜 금속을 두고 경쟁했는지
02 ① 금 ② 은 ③ 철 ④ 알루미늄 ⑤ 니켈

01 금속이 문명의 발전에 기여한 바에 대해 논의하고 있으므로 여자가 하는 말의 주제로 ① 'how metals advanced human civilization'이 가장 적절하다.

02 금, 은, 철, 알루미늄은 언급했지만 ⑤ 'nickel'은 언급하지 않았다.

어휘 material 명 물질   contribution 명 기여, 이바지   civilization 명 문명   scarcity 명 희소성   appeal 명 매력   shape 통 모양을 만들다 명 모양   prize 통 귀하게 여기다 명 상   currency 명 화폐   strengthen 통 강화하다   fashion 통 만들다 명 유행   revolutionize 통 혁명을 일으키다   industrialize 통 산업화하다   abundant 형 풍부한   lightweight 형 (무게가) 가벼운   countless 형 수많은   automotive 형 자동차의   aerospace 형 항공 우주의   household 형 가정용의; 가정의   related 형 관련된   advance 통 발전시키다 명 진전

영어듣기 모의고사

1	②	2	①	3	③	4	②	5	⑤	6	③	7	⑤	8	③	9	①	10	⑤
11	④	12	③	13	⑤	14	①	15	②	16	②	17	④						

• 각 문제의 정답 근거는 굵은 글씨로, Dictation 정답은 밑줄로 표시되어 있습니다.

---

1 목적 파악 　　　　　　　　　　　　　　　　　　　　　　　정답 ②

W	Good afternoon, Grenville High School students. This is Ms. Reynolds, your music teacher. **I'm excited to announce that we will be** ¹⁾holding auditions **for our school talent show on November 7th and 8th.** All students are welcome to audition. The performances will be divided into three categories, which are music, dance, and comedy. Auditions will be held after school from 5 to 6:30 p.m. You may sign up on the sheet posted ²⁾on the bulletin board. Please bring any special equipment you need, such as costumes or ³⁾musical instruments. We will provide a microphone. We hope to see you there!

여 안녕하세요, 그렌빌 고등학교 학생 여러분. 여러분의 음악 선생님 Reynolds입니다. 11월 7일과 8일에 학교 장기자랑 오디션을 개최하는 것을 알리게 되어 기쁩니다. 모든 학생들은 오디션에 참가하여도 좋습니다. 공연은 노래, 춤, 그리고 코미디의 세 가지 분야로 나뉠 것입니다. 오디션은 방과 후 5시부터 6시 30분까지 열릴 예정입니다. 게시판에 게시된 용지에 신청하면 됩니다. 의상이나 악기와 같이 필요한 특별한 장비를 가지고 오시기 바랍니다. 마이크는 제공할 예정입니다. 거기서 뵙기를 바라겠습니다!

여자가 학교 장기자랑 오디션을 개최하는 것을 알리게 되어 기쁘다고 하면서, 오디션 일정, 신청 방법 등 세부 사항에 대해 말하고 있다. 따라서, 여자가 하는 말의 목적으로 ② '장기자랑 오디션을 공지하려고'가 가장 적절하다.

어휘 announce 통 알리다; 발표하다 audition 명 오디션 통 오디션을 보다 divide into ~으로 나누다 sign up 신청하다 post 통 게시하다 bulletin board 게시판 equipment 명 장비

---

2 의견 파악 　　　　　　　　　　　　　　　　　　　　　　　정답 ①

W	Honey, what's wrong? Your face is so pale.
M	My stomach really hurts. I don't know why.
W	What ¹⁾did you eat yesterday?
M	We had pasta for dinner. And I ate a tuna sandwich for lunch.
W	Where did you get the tuna sandwich?
M	It was ²⁾in the back of the refrigerator.
W	Oh, no. I made that sandwich two weeks ago. It should have been thrown out last week.
M	It did smell strange. But I was so hungry that I just ate it.
W	**I think we should** ³⁾clean out the refrigerator **at least once a week.**
M	Yeah. Maybe we can do it every Sunday when we clean the house.
W	Good idea. Do you need to ⁴⁾go see a doctor?
M	No. I'll be fine if I lie down for a while.

여 여보, 무슨 일이야? 당신 얼굴이 너무 창백해.
남 배가 너무 아파. 왜 그런지 모르겠네.
여 어제 뭐 먹었어?
남 저녁으로 파스타를 먹었잖아. 그리고 점심으로는 참치 샌드위치를 먹었어.
여 참치 샌드위치는 어디서 가져왔어?
남 냉장고 뒤쪽에 있었어.
여 오, 이런. 그 샌드위치는 내가 2주 전에 만들었어. 지난주에 버렸어야 했는데.
남 냄새가 정말 이상했어. 그런데 너무 배가 고파서 그냥 먹었어.
여 적어도 일주일에 한 번은 냉장고를 청소해야 할 것 같아.
남 맞아. 매주 일요일에 집을 청소할 때 할 수 있을 거야.
여 좋은 생각이야. 당신 병원에 가야 할까?
남 아니. 잠시 누워 있으면 괜찮을 거야.

오래된 샌드위치를 먹고 배탈이 난 남자에게 여자가 적어도 일주일에 한 번은 냉장고를 청소해야 할 것 같다고 했다. 따라서, 여자의 의견으로 ① '냉장고를 적어도 일주일에 한 번 청소해야 한다.'가 가장 적절하다.

어휘 tuna 명 참치 refrigerator 명 냉장고 throw out ~을 버리다 clean out 청소하다, 깨끗이 치우다 at least 적어도 lie down 눕다

---

3 관계 파악 　　　　　　　　　　　　　　　　　　　　　　　정답 ③

	[Telephone rings.]
M	Hello. This is Forever Fashion. How can I help you?
W	Hi. **I ordered a pair of pants online.** I wanted the small size, but they ¹⁾arrived in a large.
M	Okay. Would you like to return them or exchange them?
W	**I'd like a full refund, please.**
M	Can you ²⁾tell me your order number, please?
W	Yes. It's 10456. My name is Michelle Linton.

[전화기가 울린다.]
남 안녕하세요. Forever Fashion입니다. 무엇을 도와드릴까요?
여 안녕하세요. 인터넷으로 바지 한 벌을 주문했는데요. 저는 스몰 사이즈를 원했는데, 라지 사이즈가 도착했어요.
남 알겠습니다. 반품하시겠어요, 아니면 교환하시겠어요?
여 전액 환불해 주세요.
남 주문 번호를 말씀해 주시겠어요?
여 네. 10456입니다. 제 이름은 Michelle Linton이고요.

M Hmm... You purchased this item two weeks ago. **But according to our return policy, you can only return items ³⁾within a week of the purchase date.**	남 흠... 이 물건을 2주 전에 구매하셨네요. 하지만 저희 환불 정책에 따르면, 구매일로부터 일주일 이내에만 반품이 가능해요.
W I was away on a business trip, so I didn't get to ⁴⁾open the package until today. I hope you understand.	여 출장 중이어서 오늘까지 택배를 열지 못했어요. 이해 부탁 드려요.
M All right. Let me talk to my manager and call you right back.	남 알겠습니다. 매니저와 상의하고 바로 전화 드리겠습니다.
W Thank you.	여 감사합니다.

두 사람이 잘못 배송된 바지의 환불에 대해 이야기하고 있다. 남자는 여자의 요청사항에 대해 응대하면서 환불 정책을 설명하고 있고, 여자는 구매한 바지 사이즈가 잘못 배송되었다며 환불을 요청하고 있는 것으로 보아 두 사람의 관계로 ③ '고객 상담원 ― 구매자'가 가장 적절하다.

어휘 return 통 반품하다; 돌아오다 (full refund 전액 환불) exchange 통 교환하다 purchase 통 구매하다 according to ~에 따르면 policy 명 정책 a business trip 출장 package 명 택배, 소포

---

4 그림 내용 불일치 파악   정답 ②

W What are you doing, James?	여 뭐 하는 중이야, James?
M Hi, Melissa. I'm looking at this photo from last weekend.	남 안녕, Melissa. 지난 주말에 찍은 사진을 보고 있어.
W Where was it taken?	여 어디서 찍은 거야?
M This was at my aunt's house in the countryside.	남 시골에 있는 이모 집에서 찍은 사진이야.
W That must be your aunt. Who's that girl in the ¹⁾polka dot dress?	여 저분이 이모님이겠구나. 물방울무늬 드레스를 입은 저 소녀는 누구야?
M That's my cousin, Emily. She just turned three.	남 내 사촌 Emily야. 이제 막 세 살이 됐어.
W She's adorable. Those ²⁾two little dogs are cute, too.	여 사랑스럽다. 저 작은 개 두 마리도 귀여워.
M Their names are Coco and Peanut. They're really friendly.	남 이름은 Coco와 Peanut이야. 정말 다정해.
W There's even a picnic table in the yard.	여 마당에 피크닉 테이블도 있네.
M Yes. We had lunch there.	남 응. 거기서 점심을 먹었어.
W It sounds like you had a great time. Oh, what is that basket ³⁾under the tree for?	여 즐거운 시간을 보낸 것 같네. 아, 나무 밑에 있는 저 바구니는 뭐에 쓰는 거야?
M We put apples in it when we pick them from the tree. Do you see the flowers in the pot in front of the house? I gave her the flowers to thank her for hosting me.	남 나무에서 사과를 따면 거기에 담아둬. 집 앞 화분에 있는 꽃 보여? 나를 초대해 주신 것이 감사해서 저 꽃을 드렸어.
W That's very sweet of you.	여 너 정말 다정하다.

대화에서 여자가 작은 개 두 마리도 귀엽다고 말했는데, ②에는 개가 한 마리만 그려져 있다.

어휘 countryside 명 시골 cousin 명 사촌 turn 통 (나이가) 되다; 돌다 pick 통 따다; 고르다 host 통 초대하다

---

5 할 일 파악   정답 ⑤

W That's a cool T-shirt, Sam. Where did you get it?	여 멋진 티셔츠네, Sam. 어디서 샀어?
M It ¹⁾used to be a regular T-shirt, but I dyed it at home.	남 보통 티셔츠였는데, 내가 집에서 염색했어.
W Oh, yeah? Was it hard to make that pattern?	여 아, 그래? 무늬 만드는 건 어려웠니?
M No. It was actually really easy.	남 아니. 사실 정말 쉬웠어.
W How did you do it?	여 어떻게 했어?
M First, I mixed ²⁾different colored dyes, and then I tied up the T-shirt with rubber bands.	남 먼저, 다른 색깔의 염료들을 섞고, 그리고 나서 티셔츠를 고무줄로 묶었어.
W Okay. I can do that.	여 알겠어. 나도 할 수 있겠다.
M Then, I poured the dyes onto it. After waiting for 24 hours, I ³⁾washed it really well. That's all.	남 그다음, 그 위에 염료를 부었어. 24시간을 기다린 후에, 정말 철저히 씻었어. 그게 다야.
W Where can you buy the dyes? I want to try this.	여 염료는 어디서 살 수 있니? 이거 해보고 싶어.
M The art supply store on Main Street sells them. **Do you want me to ⁴⁾take you there?**	남 메인가에 있는 미술용품 가게에서 그것들을 팔아. 그곳에 데려다줄까?
W **That would be great.** Thank you.	여 그러면 정말 좋겠어. 고마워.

티셔츠 염색에 대해 이야기하고 있다. 여자가 염료를 어디서 살 수 있는지 묻자, 남자가 미술용품 가게에서 판다면서 그곳에 데려다줄지 물었고 여자가 좋다고 했으므로 남자가 할 일로 ⑤ '가게에 데려다주기'가 가장 적절하다.

어휘 used to (예전에는) ~였다 regular 형 보통의 dye 통 염색하다 명 염료, 염색제 pattern 명 무늬, 패턴 tie up ~을 묶다 rubber band 고무줄 pour 통 붓다

6 금액 정보 파악   정답 ③

M Welcome to V Mart's grand opening sale. Please let me know if I can help you with anything.	남 V Mart의 개업 기념 특별 세일에 오신 것을 환영합니다. 제가 도와드릴 일이 있으면 알려주세요.
W Hello. How much are these blueberries?	여 안녕하세요. 이 블루베리들은 얼마인가요?
M Each pack is $3. If you ¹⁾buy two packs, you can get both for $5.	남 한 팩에 3달러예요. 두 팩을 구매하시면 두 팩을 5달러에 구매하실 수 있어요.
W Sure. I'll get two packs of blueberries, then.	여 그래요. 그럼 블루베리 두 팩 주세요.
M Do you like grapes? These ones are really sweet. Each bag is $5.	남 포도 좋아하시나요? 정말 달콤하거든요. 한 봉지에 5달러입니다.
W Okay. I'll take ²⁾three bags of grapes, too.	여 네. 포도도 세 봉지 주세요.
M Would you like anything else today?	남 오늘은 더 필요한 것은 없으세요?
W No, that will be everything.	여 아뇨, 그게 전부예요.
M All right. And because today is our grand opening day, we are offering 10% off the total.	남 좋아요. 그리고 오늘은 개업일이기 때문에 총액에서 10% 할인을 제공하고 있습니다.
W That's great. I'll ³⁾put everything on my credit card, please.	여 잘됐네요. 전부 신용 카드로 계산해 주세요.

여자가 블루베리 두 팩($5)과 포도 세 봉지($5×3=$15)을 구매했고, 총액에서 10% 할인($20×0.9=$18)을 받았으므로 정답은 ③ '$18'이다.

어휘 grand opening sale 개업 기념 특별 세일   let ~ know ~에게 알려주다   offer 통 제공하다

7 이유 파악   정답 ⑤

W Martin! I've been calling you, but I guess you couldn't ¹⁾hear me.	여 Martin! 계속 불렀는데, 내 말을 못 들었나 봐.
M Sorry, Jen. I was listening to the new song by The Twinkles.	남 미안해, Jen. The Twinkles의 신곡을 듣고 있었어.
W I didn't know you liked them. I have two tickets to their concert next month.	여 네가 그들을 좋아하는 줄 몰랐어. 나한테 다음 달 그들의 콘서트 표 두 장 있어.
M Really? Those tickets are expensive.	남 정말? 그 표는 비싸잖아.
W My mom ²⁾got them for me for my birthday.	여 엄마가 생일 선물로 사주셨어.
M You're lucky. I'd love to go to that concert.	남 운이 좋네. 나는 그 콘서트에 가고 싶어.
W Well, do you want to go with me? It's on the 14th.	여 음, 나랑 같이 갈래? 14일에 해.
M I wish I could, but I'm busy that day.	남 그럴 수 있으면 좋겠지만, 그날은 바빠.
W Why? Do you have to ³⁾practice piano?	여 왜? 피아노 연습을 해야 하니?
M It's not that. I have to take my midterm test that night.	남 그게 아니야. 그날 밤에 중간고사를 쳐야 하거든.
W What test? I haven't heard about this.	여 무슨 시험? 이것에 대해 들어본 적이 없는데.
M Oh, I'm taking ⁴⁾an online coding course.	남 아, 내가 온라인 코딩 강의를 듣고 있거든.
W I see. Then, good luck with your test.	여 그렇구나. 그럼, 시험 잘 봐.

남자는 콘서트에 못 간다고 하면서 그날 밤에 중간고사를 쳐야 한다고 말했으므로, 남자가 콘서트에 갈 수 없는 이유는 ⑤ '중간고사를 쳐야 해서'이다.

어휘 practice 통 연습하다   take one's midterm test 중간고사를 치다   course 명 강의

8 언급 유무 파악   정답 ③

W Dad, can you sign this permission form?	여 아빠, 이 허가서에 서명해 주시겠어요?
M What's it for, Cathy?	남 이게 뭐니, Cathy?
W Actually, I'm competing at the Youth Regional Tennis Championship.	여 사실은, 저 청소년 지역 테니스 선수권 대회에 참가할 거예요.
M That's wonderful. When is it?	남 정말 멋지네. 그게 언제니?
W It ¹⁾runs from June 20th to 21st. It's on a weekend.	여 6월 20일부터 21일까지 진행돼요. 주말이에요.
M Maybe your mom and I can go watch you. Where ²⁾is it being held?	남 네 엄마랑 내가 보러 갈 수도 있겠구나. 어디서 열리니?
W It will be at Riverford High School.	여 리버포드 고등학교에서 열릴 거예요.
M Perfect. That's only a 20-minute drive from here.	남 완벽하네. 여기서 차로 20분 거리야.
W I'm so glad you'll be there. Oh, and there's a registration fee. It's $50.	여 대회에 오실 거라니 정말 기뻐요. 아, 그리고 등록비가 있어요. 50달러에요.
M Okay. How do I pay for it?	남 알겠다. 어떻게 내면 되니?
W Can you give it to me in cash? I have to ³⁾register by tomorrow. I can submit the permission form and the payment together.	여 현금으로 주실 수 있나요? 내일까지 등록해야 해요. 허가서와 함께 돈을 제출하면 돼요.
M Great. I'll get my wallet, then.	남 좋아. 그럼 지갑을 가져오마.
W Thanks, Dad.	여 감사해요, 아빠.

대회 기간(6월 20일부터 21일까지), 대회 장소(리버포드 고등학교), 등록비(50달러), 등록 마감일(내일)에 대해 언급했고, ③ '대회 상금'은 언급하지 않았다.

어휘 permission 명 허가, 허락   compete 통 참가하다; 경쟁하다   registration fee 등록비   register 통 등록하다   submit 통 제출하다

9 내용 불일치 파악

정답 ①

M Welcome to our New Year's celebration. I'm David Allen, the mayor of Rockville, and I'm thrilled to be here with you on the last day of the year. **This evening, many of our** [1)]talented local musicians **will be performing live music.** Additionally, we have food from all over the world. Please visit one of our 20 food trucks for a delicious meal. An ice-skating rink has also been set up in front of city hall, so please [2)]go ahead and enjoy yourselves! We'll be ringing the bell at midnight to celebrate the start of the New Year. We will finish the night with a spectacular fireworks display. You won't want to miss that, so be sure to stick around [3)]until the very end.	남 저희 새해 축하 행사에 오신 것을 환영합니다. 저는 록빌의 시장 David Allen이고, 올해의 마지막 날에 여러분과 함께하게 되어 정말 감격스럽습니다. 오늘 저녁, 재능 있는 많은 지역 음악가들이 라이브 음악을 공연할 것입니다. 게다가, 전 세계 각국의 음식도 준비되어 있습니다. 20대의 푸드트럭 중 한 곳을 방문하여 맛있는 식사를 즐기세요. 시청 앞에 아이스 스케이트장도 마련되어 있으니, 가서 마음껏 즐기십시오! 새해의 시작을 축하하기 위해 자정에 종을 울릴 것입니다. 장관을 이루는 불꽃놀이로 밤을 마무리하겠습니다. 그것을 놓치고 싶지 않으실 테니, 마지막까지 꼭 머물러 주세요.

새해 축하 행사에 대한 환영 연설이다. 남자가 재능 있는 많은 지역 음악가들이 라이브 음악을 공연할 것이라고 했으므로 ① '전 세계의 음악가들이 공연할 예정이다.'는 내용과 일치하지 않는다.

[어휘] mayor 몡 시장 thrilled 혱 감격한 talented 혱 재능 있는 local 혱 지역의 additionally 튀 게다가 all over the world 전 세계에 spectacular 혱 장관을 이루는 stick around 머무르다

10 도표 정보 파악

정답 ⑤

W Gary, did you buy a clock for your living room?	여 Gary, 거실에 둘 시계 샀어?
M No, not yet. I want to order one from this website. Can you help me pick one?	남 아니, 아직. 이 웹사이트에서 하나 주문하고 싶어. 고르는 것 좀 도와줄래?
W Of course. How much are you willing to spend?	여 물론이지. 얼마를 쓸 의향이 있어?
M I don't want to spend [1)]more than $30.	남 30달러 이상은 쓰고 싶지 않아.
W All right. Which material do you like, plastic or wood?	여 좋아. 플라스틱과 나무 중 어떤 소재가 좋아?
M I like these ones [2)]made of wood. What do you think?	남 나무로 만든 것이 좋아. 어떻게 생각해?
W I agree. They look nicer than the plastic ones. What about the size?	여 동의해. 플라스틱으로 만들어진 것들보다 더 좋아 보이네. 사이즈는?
M I should get a [3)]large one. That way, I can read it from across the room.	남 라지 사이즈로 사야겠어. 그러면 방 맞은편에서도 볼 수 있어.
W That makes sense. Do you want to get an analog or a digital clock?	여 말이 되네. 아날로그 시계를 원하니, 아니면 디지털시계를 원하니?
M I prefer the look of [4)]analog clocks.	남 아날로그 시계 모양이 더 좋아.
W Then, that only leaves this one.	여 그럼, 이것만 남네.

남자는 30달러 이하인 것 중에서, 나무로 만들어졌고, 라지 사이즈인 아날로그 시계를 골랐다.

[어휘] be willing to ~할 의향이 있다 material 몡 소재 made of ~으로 만든 make sense 말이 되다 look 몡 모양, 외관

11 짧은 대화의 응답 파악

정답 ④

M Sarah, can you help the customer who just [1)]walked into the bank? I'm going to take my lunch break.	남 Sarah, 방금 은행에 들어온 손님 좀 도와줄래요? 저는 점심을 먹으러 갈 거라서요.
W Sorry, I don't think I can. I have to [2)]copy these documents right now.	여 죄송해요, 못 할 것 같아요. 이 서류들을 지금 당장 복사해야 해서요.
M I understand. I can do it.	남 이해해요. 제가 할게요.
W Sorry. I'll be right back to cover for you.	여 죄송해요. 당신을 대신하기 위해 곧 돌아올게요.

[선택지] ① 걱정하지 마세요. 제가 복사해 드릴게요.
② 아뇨, 괜찮습니다. 저는 점심으로 샌드위치를 먹을 거예요.
③ 물론이죠. 저희는 오늘 많은 고객을 도왔어요.
④ 죄송해요. 당신을 대신하기 위해 곧 돌아올게요.
⑤ 괜찮아요. 은행은 오후 6시에 문을 닫아요.

점심을 먹으러 간다며 손님 응대를 부탁한 남자에게 여자가 지금 당장 복사할 서류가 있어서 손님을 못 도와준다고 하자 남자가 알겠다면서 본인이 하겠다고 했으므로, 이에 대한 응답으로는 미안하다고 말하는 ④ 'Sorry. I'll be right back to cover for you.'가 가장 적절하다.

[어휘] take one's a lunch break 점심을 먹다 copy 통 복사하다 document 몡 서류, 문서 cover 통 (자리를 비운 사람의 일을) 대신하다; 가리다

12 짧은 대화의 응답 파악

정답 ③

W	Dad, I want to get a part-time job this summer. What do you think?
M	That's ¹⁾a good idea. **The owner of the convenience store is looking for someone.**
W	But I don't have ²⁾any work experience. **Would she hire a student?**
M	Why don't you go and ask her?

여	아빠, 전 이번 여름에 아르바이트하고 싶어요. 어떻게 생각하세요?
남	좋은 생각이야. 편의점 주인이 사람을 구하고 있더구나.
여	하지만 저는 근무 경험이 전혀 없잖아요. 그분이 학생을 고용할까요?
남	가서 그녀에게 물어보는 게 어떠니?

[선택지]
① 내가 이미 그 일에 지원했어.
② 그녀와 함께 일하는 것은 수월했어.
③ 가서 그녀에게 물어보는 게 어떠니?
④ 언제부터 여기서 일할 수 있니?
⑤ 길 아래에 있는 편의점이야.

남자가 편의점 주인이 사람을 구하는 중이라고 하자 여자가 학생을 고용할지 의문을 가졌으므로, 이에 대한 응답으로는 가서 물어보라고 조언하는 ③ 'Why don't you go and ask her?'이 가장 적절하다.

[어휘] part-time job 아르바이트   owner 명 주인   convenience store 편의점   look for ~를 구하다   work experience 근무 경험, 경력   hire 통 고용하다   apply for ~에 지원하다

13 긴 대화의 응답 파악

정답 ⑤

W	**John, I heard that your family is ¹⁾moving next week! Is that true?**
M	That's right, Britney. My dad got a new job in Springton.
W	I guess that means you'll have to change schools, right?
M	Yes, but I'm going to be here until December.
W	Really? How is that possible? Springton is so far away from here.
M	I'm going to live with my uncle nearby. My parents want me to ²⁾finish the semester here. It's only a couple of months.
W	Oh, I'm so happy to hear that! But I'll miss you when you move.
M	I'll miss you, too. We have phones, though. We can talk or send messages any time we want.
W	**You'd better ³⁾call me often and keep me posted.**
M	I promise. I'll tell you about everything that happens.

여	John, 너희 가족이 다음 주에 이사 간다고 들었어! 진짜야?
남	맞아, Britney. 아빠가 스프링턴에서 새 직장을 구하셨거든.
여	그러면 전학 가야 할 것 같은데, 맞니?
남	응, 하지만 12월까지는 여기 다닐 거야.
여	정말? 어떻게 그게 가능한 거야? 스프링턴은 여기서 너무 멀잖아.
남	근처에 계신 삼촌과 함께 살 거야. 부모님께서는 내가 여기서 이번 학기를 마치길 원하시거든. 두어 달밖에 안 되는걸.
여	아, 그 말을 들으니 정말 기쁘다! 하지만 네가 이사 가면 보고 싶을 거야.
남	나도 보고 싶을 거야. 그래도 전화가 있잖아. 우리가 원할 때 언제든지 대화하거나 메시지를 보낼 수 있어.
여	자주 전화해서 계속 내게 소식을 전해주면 좋겠어.
남	약속할게. 일어나는 모든 일에 대해 말해 줄게.

[선택지]
① 물론이지. 새로운 친구를 사귀는 것이 너무 신나.
② 동의해. 아빠에게 좋은 기회인 것 같아.
③ 괜찮아. 어쨌든 전학가고 싶었어.
④ 알아. 나도 이사 안 가면 좋겠어.
⑤ 약속할게. 일어나는 모든 일에 대해 말해 줄게.

남자가 이사 가게 된 상황에서 여자가 자주 전화해서 계속 소식을 전해주는 것이 좋겠다고 했으므로, 이에 대한 응답으로는 그렇게 하겠다고 대답하는 ⑤ 'I promise. I'll tell you about everything that happens.'가 가장 적절하다.

[어휘] move 통 이사 가다; 움직이다   get a job 직장을 구하다   change schools 전학 가다   far away from ~에서 먼   nearby 부 근처에   keep ~ posted ~에게 계속 소식을 전하다

14 긴 대화의 응답 파악

정답 ①

M	Honey, what else do we have to do for our son's birthday party?
W	Let's see. We've taken care of the guest list, the food, and the decorations.
M	Okay. What about ¹⁾some small gift bags for the kids to take home?
W	Oh, right. But what should we put inside them?
M	How about some candy?
W	I don't think that's a good idea. Sugar is bad for their teeth.
M	Then, how about ²⁾art supplies? We could get some crayons and small sketchbooks.
W	I like that idea. [Pause] Oh, no!
M	What's the matter?
W	I ³⁾forgot to buy his birthday gift. He wanted a bicycle.
M	No worries. We still have some time. **Let me go to the store right now and see what's in stock.**
W	Thank you. I've been so forgetful these days.

남	여보, 우리 아들 생일 파티에 또 뭘 해야 할까?
여	어디 보자. 손님 명단, 음식, 장식을 처리했어.
남	알겠어. 아이들이 집에 가져갈 작은 선물 가방은 어때?
여	아, 맞아. 그런데 그 안에 무엇을 넣어야 할까?
남	사탕은 어때?
여	그건 좋은 생각이 아닌 것 같아. 설탕은 치아에 나쁘잖아.
남	그럼 미술용품은 어때? 크레용과 작은 스케치북을 줘도 돼.
여	그 아이디어 마음에 드네. [잠시 멈춤] 오, 이런!
남	무슨 일이야?
여	아들 생일 선물을 사는 걸 깜빡했어. 그가 자전거를 원했거든.
남	걱정 마. 아직 시간이 좀 남았어. 내가 지금 당장 매장에 가서 재고가 있는 걸 확인해 볼게.
여	고마워. 요즘 내가 건망증이 심해.

[선택지]
① 고마워. 요즘 내가 건망증이 심해.
② 괜찮아. 내가 미술용품을 벌써 다 샀어.
③ 미안해. 자전거 재고가 없네.
④ 천만에. 내가 준비한 선물 가방이 여기 있어.
⑤ 안됐네. 아이들이 사탕을 얼마나 좋아하는지 알잖아.

두 사람이 아들의 생일 파티를 준비하는 상황이다. 여자가 생일 선물을 사는 것을 깜빡했다고 하자 남자가 아직 시간이 좀 남았으니 지금 당장 매장에 가서 재고가 있는 것을 확인해 본다고 했으므로, 이에 대한 응답으로 고맙다고 하는 ① 'Thank you. I've been so forgetful these days.'가 가장 적절하다.

어휘 take care of ~을 처리하다 decoration 명 장식 bad for ~에 나쁜 art supplies 미술용품 No worries. 걱정 마. in stock 재고가 있는 forgetful 형 건망증이 있는, 잘 잊어버리는

15 상황에 적절한 말 파악   정답 ②

M Mia and Patrick are working on a science presentation together. They [1]made a list of the tasks that needed to be done for the presentation. They then divided up these tasks equally. Mia began [2]working on her tasks right away. She finished everything, and now it is two days before the day of the presentation. But Patrick still has not completed any of his tasks. Mia is worried that he will not [3]be able to finish on time. **So Mia wants to tell Patrick that she can assist him in completing his tasks.** In this situation, what would Mia most likely say to Patrick?

남 Mia와 Patrick은 과학 발표를 함께 준비하고 있습니다. 그들은 발표를 위해 수행해야 할 일 목록을 만들었습니다. 그러고 나서 그들은 이 일들을 균등하게 나눴습니다. Mia는 즉시 그녀의 일을 시작했습니다. 그녀는 모든 것을 마쳤고, 이제 발표 이틀 전이 되었습니다. 하지만 Patrick은 여전히 어떤 일도 완수하지 못했습니다. Mia는 그가 제시간에 끝내지 못할 것을 걱정하고 있습니다. 그래서, Mia는 Patrick에게 자신이 그의 일을 완수하는 것을 도울 수 있다고 말하고 싶습니다. 이러한 상황에서, Mia가 Patrick에게 가장 할 것 같은 말은 무엇입니까?

선택지 ① 난 나쁜 점수를 받고 싶지 않아.
② 네 일을 끝낼 수 있도록 도와줄게.
③ 그냥 혼자서 모든 것을 끝낼 수 있어.
④ 아직 발표 전에 시간이 있어.
⑤ 네가 제시간에 모든 것을 끝낼 수 있으면 좋겠어.

Patrick이 주어진 일을 제시간에 끝내지 못할 것이 걱정되어서, Mia는 그녀가 그의 일을 완수하는 것을 도울 수 있다고 말하려 한다. 따라서, Mia가 할 말로 ② 'I will help you finish your tasks.'가 가장 적절하다.

어휘 presentation 명 발표 divide up ~을 분배하다 task 명 일, 임무 equally 부 균등하게 complete 동 완수하다, 끝내다 on time 제시간에 assist 동 돕다, 지원하다 by oneself 혼자서

16-17 세트 문항   정답 16 ② 17 ④

W Hello, *Morning Show* listeners. Staying healthy is important, and it becomes even more important [1]as we get older. **Today, we'll discuss ways our older listeners can take care of their mental health.** First, **drawing** is a relaxing activity, especially for those of you who can no longer walk that well. It's an enjoyable way to express your feelings and stay creative. Another activity that's good for our elderly listeners is **writing**. Writing in a journal can [2]help you organize your thoughts and improve your memory. Next, **gardening** is a great way to get fresh air and enjoy the outdoors. It also provides gentle exercise. Lastly, **volunteering** is a wonderful way to connect with the community. It can also prevent feelings of loneliness. I hope you [3]found these tips helpful. Please visit our website for more wellness tips!

여 안녕하세요, <Morning Show> 청취자 여러분. 건강을 유지하는 것은 중요하고, 나이가 들수록 더욱 중요해집니다. 오늘은, 나이가 있는 우리 청취자들이 정신 건강을 챙길 수 있는 방법에 대해 알아보겠습니다. 첫째, 그림 그리기는 특히 더 이상 잘 걸을 수 없는 분들에게 편안한 활동입니다. 그것은 여러분의 감정을 표현하고 창의적으로 지낼 수 있는 즐거운 방법입니다. 우리의 나이 든 청취자들에게 좋은 또 다른 활동은 글쓰기입니다. 일기를 쓰는 것은 여러분의 생각을 정리하고 기억력을 향상시키는 데 도움을 줄 수 있습니다. 다음으로, 정원 가꾸기는 신선한 공기를 마시며 야외에서 즐길 수 있는 좋은 방법입니다. 그것은 또한 가벼운 운동을 제공합니다. 마지막으로, 자원봉사는 지역사회와 가까워지는 훌륭한 방법입니다. 그것은 또한 외로움의 감정을 예방할 수 있습니다. 이 조언들이 도움이 되었기를 바랍니다. 더 많은 건강 조언을 원하시면 저희 웹사이트를 방문해주세요!

선택지 16 ① 나이 드신 조부모님과 함께 즐거운 시간을 보내는 방법
② 노인들이 정신 건강을 유지할 수 있는 방법
③ 노인들을 위한 신체 활동 종류
④ 이웃의 노인들이 외로움을 느끼는 징후
⑤ 노인들의 기억 상실 원인
17 ① 그림 그리기 ② 글쓰기 ③ 정원 가꾸기 ④ 노래 부르기
⑤ 자원봉사 하기

16 나이가 있는 청취자들이 정신 건강을 챙길 수 있는 방법에 대해 알아보고 있으므로 여자가 하는 말의 주제로 ② 'how seniors can maintain their mental health'가 가장 적절하다.
17 그림 그리기, 글쓰기, 정원 가꾸기, 자원봉사 하기는 언급했지만 ④ 'singing'은 언급하지 않았다.

어휘 especially 부 특히 no longer 더 이상 ~않다 enjoyable 형 즐거운 express 동 표현하다 creative 형 창의적인 journal 명 일기 organize 동 정리하다 gentle 형 가벼운; 부드러운 connect with ~와 가까워지다 community 명 지역사회 wellness 명 건강

1	①	2	⑤	3	①	4	④	5	②	6	③	7	②	8	⑤	9	④	10	③
11	⑤	12	①	13	④	14	②	15	⑤	16	①	17	②						

• 각 문제의 정답 근거는 굵은 글씨로, Dictation 정답은 밑줄로 표시되어 있습니다.

---

1 목적 파악

정답 ①

M Attention, students. This is Principal Carson. As you know, a ¹⁾<u>severe typhoon passed</u> through this area last night. After we checked our buildings, we found that the ²⁾<u>auditorium was damaged</u>. The high winds weakened the building's roof. Obviously, this could be a serious safety threat. **So we would like to ask you to keep away from the auditorium.** We ³⁾<u>plan to start repairing</u> the auditorium soon. We will inform you when we have a set schedule. Thank you for your cooperation.

남 주목해 주십시오, 학생 여러분. 저는 Carson 교장입니다. 아시다시피, 어젯밤 심한 태풍이 이 지역을 통과했습니다. 건물들을 확인한 결과, 강당이 손상된 것을 발견했습니다. 강풍으로 건물 지붕이 약해졌습니다. 분명히, 이것은 안전에 심각한 위협이 될 수 있습니다. 따라서 여러분에게 강당에 가까이 가지 말 것을 요청하고자 합니다. 곧 강당 수리를 시작할 계획입니다. 일정이 정해지면 알려드리겠습니다. 협조해 주어서 고맙습니다.

남자가 태풍으로 인해 강당 건물 지붕이 손상된 것을 발견하여, 학생들에게 강당에 가까이 가지 말라고 요청하고 있다. 따라서, 남자가 하는 말의 목적으로 ① '강당에 접근하지 말 것을 요청하려고'가 가장 적절하다.

어휘 severe 형 심한 auditorium 명 강당 weaken 동 약화시키다 obviously 부 분명히 threat 명 위협 keep away from ~에 가까이 가지 않다 set 형 정해진 동 놓다 cooperation 명 협조

---

2 의견 파악

정답 ⑤

M Do you usually drive to work, Mia?
W Yeah. What about you?
M I take the subway instead.
W I didn't realize that. Do you find the subway more convenient?
M Not really. I have to ¹⁾<u>transfer twice</u>, and both transfer stations are pretty crowded at rush hour.
W Why don't you just drive, then? You have a car.
M Well, using public transportation is ²⁾<u>better for the environment.</u>
W What do you mean?
M Cars and trucks release many harmful materials into the air. If everyone used public transportation, ³⁾<u>the air quality</u> would be a lot better.
W Hmm... I never considered that. I might start taking the subway as well.
M I'm glad to hear that.

남 넌 보통 차로 출근하니, Mia?
여 응. 넌?
남 난 그 대신 지하철을 타.
여 그건 몰랐네. 지하철이 더 편리한 것 같아?
남 그렇지는 않아. 두 번 갈아타야 하는데, 두 환승역 모두 출퇴근 시간에는 꽤 붐비거든.
여 그러면 그냥 운전하지 그래? 너 차도 있잖아.
남 글쎄, 대중교통을 이용하는 게 환경에 더 좋잖아.
여 무슨 뜻이야?
남 자동차와 트럭은 많은 해로운 물질을 대기로 배출해. 만약 모두가 대중교통을 이용한다면, 대기질이 훨씬 더 좋아질 텐데 말이야.
여 흠... 그건 생각 안 해봤네. 나도 지하철 타는 걸 시작해야 할 수도 있겠어.
남 그 말을 들으니 기쁘다.

지하철 대신 차로 운전해서 출근하는 것을 제안하는 여자에게 남자가 대중교통을 이용하는 것이 환경에 더 좋다고 했다. 따라서, 남자의 의견으로 ⑤ '환경을 위해 대중교통을 이용해야 한다.'가 가장 적절하다.

어휘 transfer 동 갈아타다, 환승하다 명 환승 pretty 부 꽤, 어느 정도 형 예쁜 crowded 형 붐비는 at rush hour 출퇴근 시간에 public transportation 대중교통 environment 명 환경 release 동 배출하다; 해방하다 material 명 물질 quality 명 질, 품질

---

3 관계 파악

정답 ①

[Cell phone rings.]
M Hi. Is this Janet Patterson?
W Yes. Who's calling, please?
M I'm with Express Shipping Company. I'm having ¹⁾<u>problems finding your house</u>. Is your address 1278 Oak Drive?
W No. It's 1078 Oak Drive.
M Got it. I'll ²⁾<u>deliver your package</u> in about 30 minutes.
W I was just on my way out. **Could you leave it by my front door?**
M Actually, that won't work. I need you to sign for the package.
W In that case, would you be able to come after 4 p.m.? I have to take my daughter to the dentist right now.
M That's fine. I also have some boxes to ³⁾<u>drop off</u> at an apartment building across town.
W Thanks so much. I really appreciate it.

남 안녕하세요. Janet Patterson 씨 되시나요?
여 네. 전화하신 분은 누구신가요?
남 Express Shipping Company에서 전화 드렸습니다. 고객님의 집을 찾는 데 어려움을 겪고 있어요. 주소가 오크 도로 1278번지인가요?
여 아뇨. 오크 도로 1078번지예요.
남 알겠습니다. 약 30분 후에 고객님의 택배를 배달해 드리겠습니다.
여 제가 막 외출하려던 참이었어요. 그걸 저희 집 현관문 옆에 놓고 가시겠어요?
남 사실, 그렇게는 안 됩니다. 택배를 받았다는 고객님의 서명이 필요해요.
여 그렇다면, 오후 4시 이후에 오실 수 있으세요? 제가 지금 당장 딸을 치과로 데려가야 해서요.
남 좋습니다. 마을 건너편에 있는 아파트로 배달해야 할 상자 몇 개도 있거든요.
여 정말 고마워요. 진짜로 감사드립니다.

두 사람이 택배 배달에 관해 이야기하고 있다. 남자는 여자의 집 주소를 확인하며 택배를 배달해 주겠다고 하고 있고, 여자는 택배를 집 현관문 앞에 놓고 가 달라고 하는 것으로 보아 두 사람의 관계로 ① '택배 기사 — 고객'이 가장 적절하다.

어휘 deliver 통 배달하다 package 명 택배, 소포 drop off ~을 배달하다

4 그림 내용 불일치 파악

정답 ④

M	What are you looking at, honey?	남	뭘 보고 있어, 여보?
W	It's a picture of my childhood home.	여	내 어릴 적 집 사진이야.
M	Wow. It's really nice. Why are there ¹⁾three chairs in the front yard?	남	우와. 정말 좋다. 왜 앞마당에 의자가 세 개 있어?
W	My parents and I liked to sit there and watch the sunset.	여	우리 부모님과 난 거기 앉아서 일몰을 보는 걸 좋아했어.
M	Is that your bicycle next to the front door?	남	현관 옆에 있는 건 당신 자전거야?
W	Yeah. I used to ride my bike every day.	여	응. 난 매일 자전거를 타곤 했어.
M	Sounds fun. Oh, the flowers in the pot ²⁾hanging by the door are really pretty.	남	재밌었겠다. 아, 문 옆에 걸려 있는 화분의 꽃들이 정말 예뻐.
W	I agree. My mom put them there.	여	동감이야. 우리 어머니가 그걸 거기에 두셨어.
M	Where was your bedroom?	남	당신 침실은 어디였어?
W	**You see the three square windows on the second floor?** The middle one was my room.	여	2층에 있는 세 개의 네모난 창문이 보여? 가운데가 내 방이었어.
M	I see. Oh, the house ³⁾has a chimney. Does that mean you had a fireplace?	남	그렇구나. 아, 집에 굴뚝이 있네. 벽난로가 있었다는 뜻인가?
W	Yes. In the living room.	여	응. 거실에 있었어.
M	You are lucky to have grown up in such a wonderful home.	남	이렇게 근사한 집에서 성장했다니 운이 좋았네.

대화에서 여자가 2층에 세 개의 네모난 창문이 보이는지 물으면서 창문의 모양을 언급했는데, ④에는 타원형 창문 세 개가 그려져 있다.

어휘 childhood 명 어릴 적, 어린 시절 sunset 명 일몰 used to ~하곤 했다 pot 명 화분 chimney 명 굴뚝 fireplace 명 벽난로 grow up 성장하다, 자라다

5 할 일 파악

정답 ②

M	Amy, are we almost ready for the grand opening of our café tomorrow?	남	Amy, 우리 내일 카페 개업 준비가 거의 다 된 걸까?
W	I think so. I just ¹⁾mopped the floors.	여	그런 것 같아. 내가 방금 바닥을 닦았어.
M	What about the tables and chairs? Should I finish setting them up?	남	탁자와 의자는 어때? 내가 배치를 끝마쳐야 할까?
W	I took care of that this morning.	여	오늘 아침에 내가 처리했어.
M	Thanks. And I've already washed all the dishes, so they are ready to use.	남	고마워. 그리고 이미 설거지를 다 했으니까, 접시는 사용할 준비가 돼 있어.
W	Great. Hmm... do we need to ²⁾order any more fruit to make juice?	여	좋아. 흠... 주스로 만들 과일을 더 주문해야 해?
M	No. We received a shipment this morning with everything we need.	남	아니. 필요한 물건들은 오늘 아침에 모두 배송받았어.
W	**Then, I will hand out ³⁾some flyers in the area around our café.**	여	그러면 내가 우리 카페 주변에 광고지를 좀 나눠줄게.
M	Good plan. The more people know about our café, the busier we will be tomorrow.	남	좋은 계획이야. 더 많은 사람이 우리 카페를 알수록, 내일 더 붐빌 거야.

카페 개업 준비에 관해 이야기하고 있다. 여자가 카페 주변에 광고지를 나눠주겠다고 했으므로 여자가 할 일로 ② '광고지 나눠주기'가 가장 적절하다.

어휘 mop 통 (걸레로) 닦다 명 대걸레 wash the dishes 설거지를 하다 shipment 명 배송, 수송 hand out ~을 나눠주다 flyer 명 광고지, 전단

6 금액 정보 파악

정답 ③

M	Welcome to Super Cinema.	남	Super Cinema에 오신 것을 환영합니다.
W	Thanks. Are there still seats available for the 3 p.m. showing of *Jungle Adventure*?	여	감사해요. 오후 3시에 상영하는 <Jungle Adventure>의 좌석이 아직 있나요?
M	Yes. How many tickets do you need?	남	네. 표가 몇 장 필요하세요?
W	**I need tickets for two adults and one child.** How much do the tickets cost?	여	어른 2명과 어린이 1명 표가 필요해요. 얼마죠?
M	It's ¹⁾$15 for adults and $10 for children 12 and under.	남	어른은 15달러, 12세 이하의 어린이는 10달러입니다.
W	That's good. My kid is 11.	여	잘 됐네요. 제 애는 11살이에요.
M	Okay. Will you be paying with cash or credit card?	남	알겠습니다. 결제는 현금으로 하시겠습니까, 아니면 신용 카드로 하시겠습니까?
W	Credit card. Could you check if I get a 20% discount with this credit card?	여	신용 카드로요. 이 신용 카드로 하면 제가 20% 할인을 받을 수 있는지 확인해 주실래요?
M	Let me see. *[Pause]* Actually, no. **You qualify for ²⁾a 10% discount.**	남	어디 볼게요. *[잠시 멈춤]* 사실, 아니에요. 10% 할인을 받으실 수 있습니다.
W	Oh, okay. Thanks for checking.	여	아, 알았어요. 확인해 주셔서 감사합니다.
M	No problem. I'll ³⁾process your payment now.	남	천만에요. 지금 결제를 처리해 드리겠습니다.

여자는 어른 2명과 어린이 1명이 볼 영화표($15×2+$10=$40)를 구매했고, 10% 할인($40×0.9=$36)을 받았으므로 정답은 ③ '$36'이다.

어휘 showing 명 상영; 전시 qualify for ~을 받다, ~자격을 얻다 process 통 처리하다 명 과정

영어듣기 모의고사 해커스 수능영어듣기 모의고사 20+4회 기본

7 이유 파악 정답 ②

W Hi, Mike. I heard you're planning to move to Chicago next month.	여 안녕, Mike. 너 다음 달에 시카고로 이사할 계획이라고 들었어.
M That's right. I'm moving there on May 1st.	남 맞아. 5월 1일에 그곳으로 이사할 거야.
W Why did you make that decision? Does your family live there?	여 왜 그런 결정을 내렸어? 너희 가족이 거기 살아?
M Actually, I ¹⁾don't know anyone in Chicago right now.	남 사실, 난 당장은 시카고에 아는 사람이 없어.
W Then, I guess it must be for work. Did you ²⁾get a new job?	여 그럼, 틀림없이 직장 때문이겠구나. 새 직장 구했니?
M No. That's not it. I'm taking some time off from work.	남 아니. 그게 아냐. 난 일을 좀 쉴 거야.
W Then, you will have lots of time to visit all the art galleries there.	여 그러면, 넌 거기의 모든 미술관을 방문할 수 있을 정도로 시간이 많겠다.
M Well, I think I'll be too busy for that.	남 글쎄, 그러기엔 너무 바쁠 것 같아.
W Really? Why?	여 정말? 왜?
M **I'm going to enter graduate school. I plan on ³⁾getting my master's degree.** That's why I'm relocating to Chicago.	남 난 대학원에 입학할 거야. 석사 학위를 딸 계획이거든. 그게 바로 내가 시카고로 이사하는 이유야.
W Wow, that's very impressive.	여 우와, 그거 정말 인상적인데.

남자가 시카고로 이사할 계획이라면서 대학원에 입학하여 석사 학위를 따려고 가는 것이라고 했으므로, 남자가 이사를 결심한 이유는 ② '대학원에 입학할 예정이어서'이다.

어휘 make a decision 결정을 내리다 take time off from work 일을 쉬다, 휴직하다 graduate school 대학원 master's degree 석사 학위 relocate 통 이사하다, 이전하다

8 언급 유무 파악 정답 ⑤

M What are you doing on the computer, honey?	남 컴퓨터로 뭐 하는 중이야, 여보?
W I'm ¹⁾purchasing tickets for the Midtown Music Festival. I'm planning to go with my best friend.	여 Midtown Music Festival 티켓을 사려고. 내 절친과 함께 갈 계획이야.
M That sounds like fun. Where will the event be held?	남 재미있겠다. 그 행사는 어디서 열려?
W It will take place at **the Warren Performing Arts Center.**	여 워런 공연 예술 센터에서 열릴 거야.
M That's convenient. There's a subway station right across the street.	남 접근이 편리하겠어. 길 바로 건너편에 지하철역이 있잖아.
W I think I might drive, though. The center ²⁾offers free parking for special events.	여 그렇지만 난 운전해서 갈 것 같아. 센터에서 특별 행사 때는 무료 주차를 제공하거든.
M Great. When is the festival?	남 좋네. 축제가 언제야?
W It's on Saturday, **July 15th.** It's an all-day event.	여 7월 15일 토요일에 해. 온종일 하는 행사야.
M Are tickets expensive?	남 티켓이 비싸?
W They're only **$15** each.	여 한 장에 겨우 15달러야.
M Wow. That's quite cheap.	남 우와. 꽤 싸네.
W I know. I think the event organizers received funding from the city government. So they aren't ³⁾charging too much for attendance.	여 그러니까. 행사 주관사가 시 정부로부터 자금을 받은 것 같아. 그래서 입장료를 많이 부과하지 않는 거지.
M That's great to hear.	남 잘됐다.

개최 장소(워런 공연 예술 센터), 주차 비용(무료 주차), 개최 날짜(7월 15일), 티켓 가격(15달러)에 대해 언급했고, ⑤ '참여 가수'는 언급하지 않았다.

어휘 purchase 통 사다, 구매하다 convenient 형 접근이 편리한 all-day 형 온종일 하는 organizer 명 주관사, 주최자 funding 명 자금, 기금 charge 통 부과하다, 청구하다 attendance 명 입장, 참석, 출석

9 내용 불일치 파악 정답 ④

W You're listening to *About Town* on Radio KR100. I'm your host Diane Ramsey with a special announcement. The Pineville Cooking School is holding its fifth annual Community Baking Contest on July 5th. The contest will be held at the school, and all ¹⁾kitchen tools will be provided. There will be three categories of competition, which are cakes, pies, and bread. Those who wish to participate must sign up on the school's website. There is no entry fee, but all competitors must bring their own ingredients. **The five judges are ²⁾all instructors at the school.** Also, prizes of $1,000 will be awarded to the winner of ³⁾each category. The deadline to sign up is this Friday, so visit the website soon!	여 여러분은 지금 라디오 KR100의 <About Town>을 듣고 계십니다. 저는 특별한 소식을 가지고 온 진행자 Diane Ramsey입니다. 파인빌 요리 학교에서 7월 5일 5번째 연례 Community Baking Contest를 개최합니다. 대회는 학교에서 열리며, 모든 주방 도구가 제공될 것입니다. 세 가지 부문으로 대회가 열리는데, 케이크, 파이, 그리고 빵으로 나뉩니다. 참여를 원하는 사람들은 학교 웹사이트에서 신청해야 합니다. 참가비는 없지만, 모든 참가자가 각자 자신의 재료를 가져와야 합니다. 다섯 명의 심사위원은 모두 이 학교의 강사들입니다. 또한, 각 부문의 우승자에게 1,000달러의 상금이 수여될 것입니다. 신청 마감일은 이번 주 금요일이니, 빨리 웹사이트를 방문하세요!

파인빌 요리 학교에서는 열리는 베이킹 대회에 대한 안내 방송이다. 여자가 다섯 명의 심사위원은 모두 파인빌 요리 학교의 강사들이라고 했으므로 ④ '외부의 유명 강사를 심사위원으로 초빙했다.'는 내용과 일치하지 않는다.

어휘 category 명 부문, 구분 competitor 명 참가자, 경쟁자 ingredient 명 재료 instructor 명 강사, 지도자 award 통 수여하다 명 상 deadline 명 마감일, 기한

10 도표 정보 파악 정답 ③

M	Excuse me. Could you help me find a new suitcase?	남	실례합니다. 새 여행 가방 찾는 걸 도와주시겠어요?
W	Of course. Are you planning on ¹⁾taking a trip soon?	여	물론이죠. 곧 여행을 떠날 계획이신가요?
M	Yeah. I'll be visiting Spain for a family vacation next month.	남	네. 저는 다음 달에 가족 휴가로 스페인을 방문할 예정입니다.
W	Sounds like fun. Then, how much are you looking to spend?	여	재미있겠군요. 그럼, 얼마를 쓰실 생각이신가요?
M	²⁾No more than $65.	남	65달러 이하요.
W	Got it. We have a number of models in that price range.	여	알겠습니다. 그 가격대에는 많은 모델이 있어요.
M	Oh, I should mention that I don't want a small suitcase. A small one won't be ³⁾big enough to carry all my clothes.	남	아, 작은 여행 가방은 원하지 않는다고 말씀드려야겠군요. 작은 건 제 옷을 다 담기에 충분히 크지 않을 거예요.
W	Okay. And what about a front pocket?	여	그래요. 그리고 앞주머니는 어떠신가요?
M	Oh, I definitely want one with a front pocket.	남	아, 저는 꼭 앞주머니가 있는 걸 원해요.
W	Then, these two models ⁴⁾meet your requirements.	여	그러면, 이 두 모델이 손님의 요구 사항에 들어맞아요.
M	Both of those look good. But I prefer the blue one.	남	둘 다 좋아 보이네요. 하지만 저는 파란색이 더 좋아요.
W	That's a great choice.	여	좋은 선택이에요.

남자는 가격이 65달러 이하이며, 크기가 작지 않고, 앞주머니가 있으며, 파란색인 여행 가방을 골랐다.

어휘 **look to** ~할 생각이다, ~할 것을 고려하다 **a number of** 많은 **price range** 가격대 **meet** 통 들어맞다, 충족하다; 만나다 **requirement** 명 요구 사항 **prefer** 통 더 좋아하다, 선호하다

11 짧은 대화의 응답 파악 정답 ⑤

W	Honey, ¹⁾did you notice that our car has been making a strange noise?	여	여보, 우리 차에서 이상한 소리가 나는 거 알았어?
M	No. But I haven't driven it for a few days. What does the noise sound like?	남	아니. 그런데 난 며칠 동안 운전을 안 했어. 소리가 어떻게 들리는데?
W	I hear ²⁾a grinding noise every time I turn the car on.	여	차에 시동을 걸 때마다 삐걱거리는 소리가 나.
M	I guess we should get it checked by a mechanic.	남	내 생각엔 정비사에게 점검받아야 할 것 같아.

선택지 ① 언제 차에서 그런 소리가 나는데?
② 그 자동차를 사는 걸 고려해야 해.
③ 시동이 걸리지 않아서 걱정이야.
④ 교통사고를 당하지 않도록 조심해.
⑤ 내 생각엔 정비사에게 점검받아야 할 것 같아.

여자가 차에 시동을 걸 때마다 삐걱거리는 이상한 소리가 난다고 했으므로, 이에 대한 응답으로는 점검을 받아야겠다는 ⑤ 'I guess we should get it checked by a mechanic.'이 가장 적절하다.

어휘 **make a noise** 소리를 내다 **grind** 통 삐걱거리다; 갈다 **turn on** 시동을 걸다, ~을 켜다 **mechanic** 명 정비사

12 짧은 대화의 응답 파악 정답 ①

M	Karen, you upgraded your cell phone to ¹⁾the latest model, right?	남	Karen, 너 휴대폰을 최신형으로 바꾼 거지, 그렇지?
W	Yes, I did. It takes great photographs and videos. It can prevent camera shake.	여	응, 바꿨어. 사진과 동영상이 잘 찍혀. 카메라가 흔들리는 걸 방지할 수 있거든.
M	Wow, that sounds cool! I was also thinking of buying one. Can ²⁾I try taking pictures with your phone?	남	와, 그거 멋진데! 나도 하나 살까 생각 중이었어. 네 휴대폰으로 한번 사진을 찍어봐도 될까?
W	Why not? I don't mind at all.	여	왜 안 되겠어? 전혀 상관없어.

선택지 ① 왜 안 되겠어? 전혀 상관없어.
② 물론이지. 여기 카메라 받아.
③ 정말? 그 스마트폰을 사야겠어.
④ 좋아. 이건 네 가족사진이야?
⑤ 미안해. 사진 찍을 때 손이 떨렸어.

남자가 여자의 최신형 휴대폰으로 사진을 한번 찍어봐도 될지 물었으므로, 이에 대한 응답으로는 요청에 대해 허락하는 ① 'Why not? I don't mind at all.'이 가장 적절하다.

어휘 **upgrade** 통 (상급으로) 바꾸다, 변경하다 **latest** 형 최신의 **shake** 명 흔들림 통 떨다, 흔들리다 **not ~ at all** 전혀 ~이 아닌 **mind** 통 상관하다, 언짢아하다

13 긴 대화의 응답 파악

정답 ④

[Telephone rings.]	[전화기가 울린다.]
W Thank you for calling Jackson Steakhouse. How can I help you today?	여 Jackson Steakhouse에 전화해 주셔서 감사합니다. 오늘 무엇을 도와드릴까요?
M Hi. **I would like to make a dinner reservation for tomorrow night.**	남 안녕하세요. 내일 저녁 식사 예약을 하고 싶습니다.
W Of course. How many people will be ¹⁾in your party?	여 그럼요. 일행이 몇 분이신가요?
M There will be eight in total.	남 총 8명일 거예요.
W And what time would you like to book a table for?	여 그리고 몇 시에 자리를 예약하고 싶으세요?
M Hmm... would it be ²⁾possible to get a private room?	남 흠... 개인실을 얻을 수 있을까요?
W One of our private dining rooms will be available at 8 p.m. tomorrow. Does that work?	여 내일 저녁 8시에 개인실 중 하나를 이용하실 수 있습니다. 괜찮으실까요?
M Could we come at 7 instead?	남 대신 7시에 와도 될까요?
W Unfortunately, there's no private room available at that time. They're ³⁾all booked.	여 안타깝게도, 그 시간에는 개인실이 없어요. 예약이 다 찼어요.
M In that case, 8 p.m. is fine. And my name is Jason Sutherland.	남 그렇다면 오후 8시도 괜찮아요. 그리고 제 이름은 Jason Sutherland입니다.
W Thanks, Mr. Sutherland. **Will you ⁴⁾bring any young kids?** **We can provide special chairs for them if necessary.**	여 감사합니다, Sutherland 씨. 아이들을 데려오실 건가요? 필요하다면 아이들용 의자를 제공해 드릴 수 있어요.
M Everyone in my group is an adult.	남 저희 일행은 모두 성인이에요.

선택지 ① 몇 시에 그 개인실을 이용할 수 있나요?
② 하지만 저는 이미 예약했는데요.
③ 그곳은 아이들에게 매우 인기가 많아요.
④ 저희 일행은 모두 성인이에요.
⑤ 부디 환불해 주세요.

식당에 예약 전화를 하는 상황에서 여자가 아이들을 데려올 것인지 물었으므로, 이에 대한 응답으로는 일행의 연령을 언급하는 ④ 'Everyone in my group is an adult.'가 가장 적절하다.

어휘 make a reservation 예약하다 party 몡 일행, 동료; 파티 private 휑 개인의, 사적인 available 휑 이용할 수 있는 unfortunately 튀 안타깝게도 bring 통 데려오다, 가져오다
necessary 휑 필요한 refund 몡 환불

14 긴 대화의 응답 파악

정답 ②

M Denise, do you ¹⁾have any plans for Saturday? There's a science-fiction movie playing that I really want to watch.	남 Denise, 토요일에 약속 있어? 내가 꼭 보고 싶은 공상과학 영화가 상영 중인데.
W I'd love to, Jim. But I'm going to be busy all weekend.	여 나도 보고 싶어, Jim. 하지만 난 주말 내내 바쁠 거야.
M What plans do you have?	남 무슨 일이 있는데?
W **I think I mentioned before that my family will be ²⁾hosting an exchange student.**	여 우리 가족이 교환학생을 초대할 거라고 예전에 말했던 것 같은데.
M Oh, right. She's from Vietnam, right?	남 아, 맞다. 베트남에서 온다고 했었어, 맞지?
W Yes. She will be arriving on Friday evening. I'm going to spend the weekend showing her around.	여 응. 그녀는 금요일 저녁에 도착할 거야. 주말에는 그녀에게 주변을 구경시켜 주며 보내려고 해.
M That's nice of you.	남 너 정말 친절한걸.
W Well, I want to make sure she feels comfortable here.	여 음, 그녀가 여기서 편안하다고 느끼게 해주고 싶어.
M **Why don't we do some sightseeing with her together?**	남 우리가 함께 그녀와 관광하는 건 어때?
W **Good idea.** She would probably enjoy ³⁾making another friend here.	여 좋은 생각이야. 아마 여기서 다른 친구를 사귀는 걸 좋아할 거야.
M I'm free all day on Saturday.	남 난 토요일에 온종일 한가해.
W All right. Let's meet together if she wants to.	여 그래. 그녀가 원한다면 같이 만나자.

선택지 ① 알았어. 일요일 아침에 전화 줄게.
② 그래. 그녀가 원한다면 같이 만나자.
③ 고마워. 구경시켜 줘서 고마워.
④ 미안해. 하지만 다음 주말은 안 되겠어.
⑤ 좋아. 그녀는 토요일 오후에 여기 도착할 거야.

여자네 집에서 초대한 교환학생과 함께 관광하는 것을 제안한 남자에게 여자가 좋은 생각이라고 하자 남자가 토요일에 한가하다고 했으므로, 이에 대한 응답으로는 그 교환학생도 좋다고 하면 같이 만나자고 말하는 ② 'All right. Let's meet together if she wants to.'가 가장 적절하다.

어휘 science-fiction movie 공상과학 영화 host 통 초대하다 exchange student 교환학생 show ~ around ~를 구경시켜 주다 do sightseeing 관광하다

15 상황에 적절한 말 파악

정답 ⑤

M Isabella is shopping at a department store for ¹⁾<u>a new pair of sneakers</u>. She has tried on several pairs, and there is one that she really likes. The sneakers ²⁾<u>fit her well</u> and are very comfortable. However, they are black, and she would prefer white. She asks Gordon, who works at the store, to bring her the sneakers in white. Unfortunately, that color is very popular, and there are none left. **Gordon has to tell Isabella that there are no shoes in ³⁾<u>her preferred color</u> available right now.** In this situation, what would Gordon most likely say to Isabella?

여 Isabella는 백화점에서 새 운동화를 사려고 쇼핑 중입니다. 그녀는 여러 켤레를 신어 보았는데, 그녀 마음에 꼭 든 것이 하나 있습니다. 그 운동화는 그녀에게 잘 맞고 매우 편안합니다. 하지만, 그건 검은색이고, 그녀는 흰색을 선호합니다. 그녀는 그 가게에서 근무하는 Gordon에게 그 운동화를 흰색으로 가져다 달라고 부탁합니다. 안타깝게도, 그 색상은 매우 인기가 많아서, 남아있는 게 없습니다. Gordon은 Isabella에게 그녀가 선호하는 색상의 신발이 지금은 없다고 말해야 합니다. 이러한 상황에서, Gordon이 Isabella에게 가장 할 것 같은 말은 무엇입니까?

선택지 ① 이 신발은 극도로 편안합니다.
② 어떤 색상을 선호하시는지 알려주시겠어요?
③ 손님께서 선택하신 브랜드는 매우 인기가 많습니다.
④ 대신 흰색을 신어 보시겠어요?
⑤ 죄송하지만, 원하시는 것이 현재 품절입니다.

Isabella가 흰색 운동화를 가져다 달라고 부탁하는 것을 듣고, 신발 가게 직원인 Gordon은 그 색상의 신발이 지금 가게에 없다고 말하려 한다. 따라서, Gordon이 할 말로 ⑤ 'I'm afraid the ones you want are currently out of stock.'이 가장 적절하다.

어휘 try on ~을 신어보다 fit 통 맞다 extremely 부 극도로 select 통 선택하다 currently 부 현재 out of stock 품절인

16-17 세트 문항

정답 16 ① 17 ②

W Good morning. Last class, we talked about languages that were at risk of disappearing. **Today, I want to discuss some languages that are ¹⁾<u>widely used these days</u>.** The first of these is **English**, and there are over 1.5 billion speakers of this language worldwide. Interestingly, many of these people have learned it ²⁾<u>as a second language</u>. Next, I'd like to mention **French**. It has about 300 million speakers. Most of them live in Europe and Africa. It is also an official language of ³⁾<u>many international organizations</u>, including the United Nations. Thirdly, there is **Hindi**, with around 600 million speakers. Most of the people who live in India use this language. Finally, there are about 550 million **Spanish** speakers. In fact, this is the official language of much of Central and South America. Now, let's watch a video that shows how to say ⁴⁾<u>some common expressions</u> in each of these languages.

여 안녕하십니까. 지난 수업에서, 우리는 사라질 위험에 처한 언어들에 대해 이야기 했습니다. 오늘은, 요즘에 널리 쓰이는 언어들에 관해 논의하고 싶습니다. 그 중 첫 번째는 영어이고, 전 세계적으로 15억 명 이상의 영어 사용자가 있습니다. 흥미롭게도, 이러한 사람 중 많은 이들이 영어를 제2외국어로 배우고 있습니다. 다음으로 프랑스어를 언급하겠습니다. 그것은 약 3억 명의 사용자가 있습니다. 그들 중 대부분은 유럽과 아프리카에 삽니다. 그것은 또한 유엔을 포함한 많은 국제기구의 공용어입니다. 세 번째로, 힌디어가 있는데, 약 6억 명의 사용자가 있습니다. 인도에 사는 대부분의 사람들이 이 언어를 사용합니다. 마지막으로, 약 5억 5천만 명의 스페인어 사용자가 있습니다. 사실, 이것은 중앙아메리카와 남아메리카에 속한 많은 지역에서 공용어입니다. 이제, 각 언어에서 쓰이는 몇 가지 흔한 표현을 어떻게 말하는지 보여주는 동영상을 시청하겠습니다.

선택지 16 ① 흔하게 쓰이는 언어들
② 여러 다른 언어들이 공유하는 특성
③ 두 개 이상의 공식 언어를 사용하는 국가들
④ 왜 일부 언어들이 사라지기 시작하는지
⑤ 무엇이 일부 언어가 더 인기 있게 만드는지
17 ① 영어 ② 중국어 ③ 프랑스어 ④ 힌디어 ⑤ 스페인어

16 요즘에 널리 쓰이는 언어들에 관해 논의하고 있으므로 여자가 하는 말의 주제로 ① 'languages which are commonly spoken'이 가장 적절하다.
17 영어, 프랑스어, 힌디어, 스페인어는 언급했지만 ② 'Chinese'는 언급하지 않았다.

어휘 at risk of ~의 위험에 처한 disappear 통 사라지다 widely 부 널리 worldwide 부 전 세계적으로 interestingly 부 흥미롭게도 second language 제2외국어 official language 공용어 common 형 흔한; 공통의 trait 명 특징, 특성

1	②	2	③	3	①	4	④	5	⑤	6	②	7	⑤	8	④	9	④	10	③
11	①	12	②	13	③	14	⑤	15	③	16	②	17	④						

• 각 문제의 정답 근거는 굵은 글씨로, Dictation 정답은 밑줄로 표시되어 있습니다.

---

1 목적 파악
정답 ②

W Attention, football fans. I'm Kerry Platt, host of SBH Sports Network. Would you like to ¹⁾get free tickets to a football game? **If so, enter our special prize-drawing event by following these simple steps.** First, download the SBH Sports Network application on your phone. Next, fill out ²⁾a short survey, and enter your contact information. Then, watch our Friday night game of the week on SBH. During the live broadcast, one lucky person who filled out a survey will be selected at random. We'll give them two tickets to see ³⁾a game of their choice. This is an amazing opportunity, so don't miss this chance!	여 주목해주세요, 축구 팬 여러분. 저는 SBH Sports Network의 진행자 Kerry Platt입니다. 축구 경기 무료입장권을 얻고 싶으신가요? 그렇다면, 간단한 절차에 따라 특별 경품 추첨 행사에 참가하세요. 먼저 휴대폰으로 SBH Sports Network 앱을 다운로드하세요. 다음으로 간단한 설문조사를 작성하고 연락처 정보를 기입하세요. 그다음에, SBH에서 저희의 금요일 밤 경기를 시청해주세요. 생방송 중, 설문지를 작성한 행운의 인물 1명을 무작위로 선정합니다. 경기를 선택해서 볼 수 있도록 입장권 두 장을 드리겠습니다. 이건 굉장한 기회이니, 이 기회를 놓치지 마세요!

여자가 축구 경기 무료입장권을 경품으로 주는 특별 경품 추첨 행사에 대해 안내하면서, 이 기회를 놓치지 말라고 참여를 독려하고 있다. 따라서, 여자가 하는 말의 목적으로 ② '특별 경품 추첨 행사를 홍보하려고'가 가장 적절하다.

어휘 enter ⑧ 참가하다; 들어가다 prize-drawing event 경품 추첨 행사 follow ⑧ 따르다 fill out ~을 기입하다 survey ⑲ 설문조사 contact information 연락처 정보 select ⑧ 선정하다 at random 무작위로 opportunity ⑲ 기회 chance ⑲ 기회; 가능성

---

2 의견 파악
정답 ③

W What are you doing, Justin?	여 뭐 하고 있어, Justin?
M Hi, Kate. I'm doing a personality test.	남 안녕, Kate. 성격 검사를 하고 있어.
W That sounds like a fun way to ¹⁾learn about yourself.	여 그건 스스로에 대해 배울 수 있는 재미있는 방법 같아.
M Yeah. The results will also show what jobs fit my personality.	남 맞아. 결과는 어떤 직업이 내 성격에 맞는지도 보여줄 거야.
W Oh, are you looking for a new job? I thought you enjoyed working at the bank.	여 오, 너 새로운 직장을 찾고 있어? 네가 은행에서 일하는 것을 즐긴다고 생각했는데.
M I do. But I've worked there ²⁾for so long, and I really want to learn some different skills.	남 즐기고 있어. 그런데 나는 거기서 너무 오랫동안 일했고, 다른 기술들을 정말 배우고 싶어.
W You are taking a big step.	여 크게 도약하려는구나.
M Maybe so. **But I think it's important to ³⁾keep learning and trying new things.**	남 그럴지도 모르지. 하지만 새로운 것을 계속 배우고 시도하는 게 중요하다고 생각해.
W Yeah. I guess that will help you prepare for unexpected changes.	여 맞아. 예상치 못한 변화에 대비하는 데 도움이 될 것 같아.
M Also, it will help me feel confident in myself to succeed in learning something new.	남 그리고, 새로운 것을 배우는 데 성공해서 내 자신에 대해 더 자신감을 느끼도록 도와줄 거야.
W I see. That makes sense.	여 그렇구나. 그것도 일리가 있어.

새로운 기술을 배우려는 남자에게 여자가 크게 도약하려는 것이라고 평하자 남자는 새로운 것을 계속 배우고 시도하는 것이 중요하다고 생각한다고 했다. 따라서, 남자의 의견으로 ③ '새로운 것을 계속 배우고 시도하는 것은 중요하다.'가 가장 적절하다.

어휘 personality ⑲ 성격 result ⑲ 결과 fit ⑧ 맞다 skill ⑲ 기술 take a big step 크게 도약하다 unexpected ⑱ 예상치 못한 confident ⑱ 자신감 있는 succeed ⑧ 성공하다 make sense 일리가 있다, 말이 되다

---

3 관계 파악
정답 ①

M **Thanks for agreeing to the interview, Captain Simone.**	남 인터뷰에 응해 주셔서 감사합니다, Simone 기장님.
W It's my pleasure, Mr. Roberts. **I always enjoy reading your articles in Harrisburg Magazine.**	여 천만에요, Roberts 씨. 전 항상 <Harrisburg Magazine>에 실린 당신의 기사를 즐겨 읽고 있어요.
M Thanks. Now, I understand that you ¹⁾originally worked as a flight attendant.	남 감사합니다. 자, 제가 알기로 기장님은 원래 승무원으로 근무하셨죠.
W That's correct. I wanted to fly, but there weren't many opportunities for women.	여 맞습니다. 저는 비행을 하고 싶었지만, 여성들에게 기회가 많지 않았거든요.
M Even now, there are few women who fly planes.	남 지금도 비행기를 조종하는 여성은 거의 없어요.
W Right. Back then, I couldn't even imagine being in charge of my own plane.	여 맞아요. 그 당시에 제 비행기를 담당하는 것은 상상조차 할 수 없었죠.
M But you ²⁾eventually went back to flight school. What inspired you to do that?	남 하지만 결국 비행 학교로 돌아가셨죠. 무엇이 그렇게 하게끔 영감을 주었나요?
W Well, I realized that I could pass the flight tests if I worked hard. And I wanted to follow my dream.	여 글쎄요, 열심히 노력하면 비행 시험을 통과할 수 있다는 것을 깨달았어요. 그리고 저는 제 꿈을 따르고 싶었답니다.

M But was it difficult being the ³⁾first female captain for NW Airlines?	남 그렇지만, NW 항공의 첫 여성 기장이 되는 것은 어려웠나요?
W It was lonely sometimes, but I had to do it.	여 가끔은 외롭기도 했지만, 해야만 했어요.
M Well, I think our readers will be inspired by your story. Thank you.	남 음, 우리 독자들이 기장님의 이야기에 영감을 받을 거라고 생각해요. 감사합니다.

두 사람은 잡지 인터뷰를 하고 있다. 남자는 여자에게 인터뷰에 응해 줘서 고맙다고 하고, 여자는 어떻게 항공사의 첫 여성 기장이 될 수 있었는지 이야기하는 것으로 보아 두 사람의 관계로 ① '잡지 기자 — 조종사'가 가장 적절하다.

[어휘] agree to ~에 응하다 originally 閈 원래 flight attendant 승무원 fly 图 비행을 하다 imagine 图 상상하다 be in charge of ~을 담당하다 eventually 閈 결국
inspire 图 영감을 주다

4 그림 내용 불일치 파악

정답 ④

M Mom, are you finished with the preparations for the party to celebrate Dad's promotion?	남 엄마, 아빠 승진 축하 파티 준비 다 하셨나요?
W Yes. What do you think?	여 응. 어떻니?
M I like the flowers in the basket. They look fresh.	남 바구니 안에 있는 꽃이 좋네요. 신선해 보여요.
W Thanks. I ¹⁾ordered them this morning. What about the picture of your dad on the wall?	여 고마워. 오늘 아침에 주문했거든. 벽에 있는 네 아빠 사진은 어때?
M Dad is all smiles in that picture. It looks great.	남 아빠는 저 사진에서 아주 행복해 보여요. 좋아 보이는걸요.
W I thought so, too.	여 나도 그렇게 생각했단다.
M And those two gift boxes ²⁾on the couch must be for Dad. What did you get for him?	남 그리고 소파 위 선물 상자 두 개는 아빠를 위한 것이 틀림없겠네요. 무엇을 사셨어요?
W One of the boxes has chocolates in it, and the other one has a new watch.	여 상자 중 하나에는 초콜릿이 들어 있고, 다른 하나에는 새 시계가 들어 있어.
M I also like the star-shaped balloons in the corner.	남 구석에 있는 별 모양의 풍선들도 맘에 들어요.
W Yeah, they are cute. And I moved the side table in front of them. That's where the cake will be.	여 응, 귀엽지. 그리고 그것들 앞으로 사이드 테이블을 옮겼어. 케이크를 거기에 놓을 거란다.
M Good idea. You did a great job ³⁾organizing everything.	남 좋은 생각이에요. 모든 걸 잘 준비하셨네요.
W Thanks. I hope your dad likes it.	여 고맙다. 너희 아빠가 좋아했으면 좋겠네.

대화에서 남자가 구석에 있는 별 모양의 풍선들이 맘에 든다고 말했는데, ④에는 하트 모양 풍선들이 그려져 있다.

[어휘] preparation 圐 준비 promotion 圐 승진; 홍보 be all smiles 아주 행복해 보이다 couch 圐 소파 star-shaped 圀 별 모양의 organize 图 준비하다

5 할 일 파악

정답 ⑤

W Mr. Evans, how are the preparations for the school musical going?	여 Evans 선생님, 학교 뮤지컬 준비는 잘 되어 가고 있나요?
M They're taking longer than we expected, Ms. Bennett. We still need ¹⁾to paint the set.	남 예상했던 것보다 시간이 더 걸리고 있네요, Bennett 선생님. 아직 세트장에 페인트칠해야 해요.
W I see. I'll ask the art students to help paint the set. What else needs to be done?	여 그렇군요. 미술부 학생들에게 세트장에 페인트칠하는 걸 도와달라고 부탁하게요. 그 밖에 무엇을 해야 할까요?
M The posters and flyers have already been printed out. So we need to pick them up from the printing center.	남 포스터와 광고지는 이미 인쇄했어요. 그래서, 인쇄소에서 그것들을 가져와야 해요.
W I'll call and ²⁾have them delivered to the school.	여 제가 전화해서 학교로 배송되게 할게요.
M Great. Also, we need to promote the musical. I'd like to put an announcement in the local newspaper.	남 좋아요. 또, 뮤지컬을 홍보할 필요가 있어요. 지역 신문에 공고를 내고 싶은데요.
W Good idea. We should also see if the local radio station can run an advertisement.	여 좋은 생각이에요. 지역 라디오 방송국에 광고를 낼 수 있는지도 알아봐야겠어요.
M That would be awesome. Should I call the station?	남 그러면 정말 굉장할 거예요. 제가 방송국에 전화할까요?
W No. Let me do it. You should ³⁾contact the newspaper.	여 아니요. 제가 할게요. 선생님께서는 신문사에 연락해주세요.
M Okay, I'll do that now.	남 알겠어요, 지금 할게요.

학교 뮤지컬 홍보에 대해 이야기하고 있다. 여자가 남자에게 지역 신문사에 연락해달라고 하자, 남자가 지금 하겠다고 했으므로 남자가 할 일로 ⑤ '지역 신문사에 연락하기'가 가장 적절하다.

[어휘] flyer 圐 광고지, 전단 print out ~을 인쇄하다 deliver 图 배송하다 announcement 圐 공고 run an advertisement 광고를 내다 contact 图 연락하다 圐 연락처

6 금액 정보 파악   정답 ②

M	Welcome to Bamboo Garden Restaurant.
W	Hi. We 1)have a reservation for six people at 6 p.m.
M	Right this way. *[Pause]* Are you here for the buffet?
W	Yes. It's $15 per person on weekdays, right?
M	I'm sorry, but that's only until 4 p.m. **After that, it's $20 per person for the dinner buffet.**
W	Oh, okay. Is it 2)the same price for kids?
M	How old is your child? Kids under five can eat for free.
W	That's good. He's just four.
M	Okay. **So, that will be five adults having the dinner buffet.**
W	That's correct. And is there a way I can get any additional discounts?
M	Yes. **If you sign up for a membership card, we will give you** 3)$5 off the total.
W	**All right. I'll do that right now.**

남	Bamboo Garden Restaurant에 오신 것을 환영합니다.
여	안녕하세요. 오후 6시에 6명 예약했는데요.
남	이쪽으로 오세요. *[잠시 멈춤]* 뷔페 드시러 오신 건가요?
여	네. 평일에는 1인당 15달러죠?
남	죄송하지만, 그건 오후 4시까지만 가능합니다. 그 후에, 저녁 뷔페는 1인당 20달러입니다.
여	오, 알겠습니다. 아이들도 같은 가격인가요?
남	자녀분이 몇 살인가요? 5세 미만의 어린이들은 무료로 먹을 수 있어요.
여	잘됐네요. 그는 겨우 네 살이에요.
남	알겠습니다. 그럼, 어른 다섯 명이 저녁 뷔페를 드시는 거죠.
여	네. 그리고 제가 추가 할인을 받을 수 있는 방법이 있나요?
남	네. 멤버십 카드에 등록하시면 총액에서 5달러를 할인해 드립니다.
여	좋아요. 지금 바로 그렇게 할게요.

여자가 뷔페에서 어른 다섯 명($20×5=$100)의 식사를 지불하려고 하고, 멤버십 카드 등록으로 5달러 할인을 받았으므로($100-$5=$95) 정답은 ② '$95'이다.

어휘 reservation 명 예약 weekday 명 평일 price 명 가격 for free 무료로 additional 형 추가의 sign up 등록하다, 가입하다

7 이유 파악   정답 ⑤

	[Cell phone rings.]
W	Hello, Dad?
M	Hi, Elena. I'm really sorry, but I can't 1)drive you to your violin lesson today.
W	That's okay. I can take the bus. Are you working late tonight?
M	No. I actually finished work early today.
W	Then, are you meeting Grandmother?
M	No. I'm not meeting anyone tonight.
W	It must be because you're 2)still not feeling well.
M	I'm feeling fine. **I can't drive you because I'm stuck in traffic right now. I won't be able to get home in time.**
W	Oh, I see. Don't worry about it, Dad. Just 3)get home safe.
M	Thanks, sweetie.

	[휴대폰이 울린다.]
여	여보세요, 아빠?
남	안녕, Elena. 정말 미안하지만, 오늘은 바이올린 수업에 차로 데려다줄 수가 없겠구나.
여	괜찮아요. 버스를 타도 돼요. 오늘 밤늦게까지 일하세요?
남	아니. 오늘 일은 사실 일찍 끝났단다.
여	그럼, 할머니를 만나시나요?
남	아니. 오늘 밤엔 아무도 안 만날 거란다.
여	아직도 몸이 안 좋아서 그러시군요.
남	몸은 괜찮단다. 지금 차가 막혀서 태워다 줄 수가 없어. 제시간에 집에 도착할 수 없을 거야.
여	아, 그렇군요. 걱정하지 마세요, 아빠. 집에 조심히 들어가세요.
남	고맙구나, 얘야.

남자가 여자에게 오늘은 바이올린 수업에 차로 데려다 줄 수가 없다고 하면서 지금 차가 막혀서 태워다 줄 수 없다고 말했으므로, 남자가 여자를 바이올린 수업에 데려다 줄 수 없는 이유는 ⑤ '차가 너무 막혀서'이다.

어휘 drive 통 차로 데려다주다 work late 늦게까지 일하다 stuck in traffic 차가 막히는

8 언급 유무 파악   정답 ④

M	What do you want to do tomorrow, Luna? It's finally the weekend.
W	Hi, Jack. Well... the Modern Sculpture Exhibition is going on.
M	That sounds interesting. Where is 1)it being held?
W	It's at **the Fantasia Art Gallery**. We can take the bus to get there.
M	Perfect! Do you know who is participating?
W	I don't know, but I'll look it up online now. *[Pause]* Oh, there will be statues by **Jamie Adams and Kelly Peterson**.
M	I've 2)heard of them. They're quite famous, so we should go.
W	Exactly! Also, the entrance fee is very cheap. It costs only **$5**.
M	When 3)does the gallery close? I think I can go after 2 p.m.
W	That's fine. It is open until **5 p.m.** Let's meet at 2:30 in front of the gallery.
M	Sure. See you then!

남	Luna, 내일 뭐 하고 싶어? 드디어 주말이야.
여	안녕, Jack. 글쎄... 현대 조각 전시회가 열리고 있어.
남	그거 재미있겠는데. 어디서 열려?
여	판타지아 미술관이야. 거기에 가려면 버스를 타면 돼.
남	완벽해! 누가 참여하는지 알고 있어?
여	잘은 모르겠지만, 지금 인터넷으로 찾아볼게. *[잠시 멈춤]* 아, Jamie Adams와 Kelly Peterson의 조각상이 있을 거야.
남	들어본 적 있어. 그들은 꽤 유명하잖아, 그러니 가봐야겠어.
여	맞아! 또, 입장료가 매우 저렴해. 5달러밖에 안 하거든.
남	그 미술관은 언제 닫아? 나는 오후 2시 이후에 갈 수 있을 것 같아.
여	괜찮아. 오후 5시까지 열어. 미술관 앞에서 2시 30분에 만나자.
남	그래. 그때 봐!

장소(판타지아 미술관), 참여 작가(Jamie Adams, Kelly Peterson), 입장료(5달러), 종료 시각(오후 5시)에 대해 언급했고, ④ '할인 정보'는 언급하지 않았다.

어휘 finally 부 드디어 exhibition 명 전시회 participate 통 참여하다 look up ~을 찾아보다 statue 명 조각상 quite 부 꽤 entrance fee 입장료

9 내용 불일치 파악

정답 ④

M Good morning, listeners. This spring, the Wild Plant Expo will be here in Golden City. The expo will 1)run for a week starting May 3rd. It'll be held in the Central Convention Center. Visitors can enjoy a wide variety of wild flowers and 2)rare plants. **Also, there will be special lectures every day by Dr. Garret, who is a 3)leading plant specialist.** The tickets are $15 a person, but residents of our city can participate for just $5. If you're interested in plants or gardening, 4)be sure to come. Thank you.	남 좋은 아침입니다, 청취자 여러분. 올봄, 야생 식물 엑스포가 이곳 골든시에서 열릴 예정입니다. 엑스포는 5월 3일부터 일주일 동안 열립니다. 센트럴 컨벤션 센터에서 개최됩니다. 방문객들은 매우 다양한 야생화와 희귀한 식물들을 즐길 수 있습니다. 또한, 일류 식물 전문가 Garret 박사의 특별 강의가 매일 있을 예정입니다. 입장권은 1인당 15달러이지만, 우리 도시 주민들은 단돈 5달러에 참여하실 수 있습니다. 만약 여러분이 식물이나 원예에 관심이 있으시면, 꼭 오십시오. 감사합니다.

야생 식물 엑스포에 대한 안내 방송이다. 남자가 일류 식물 전문가 Garret 박사의 특별 강의가 매일 있을 예정이라고 했으므로 ④ '여러 전문가의 특별 강연이 매일 있을 것이다.'는 내용과 일치하지 않는다.

어휘 wild 휑 야생의 run 통 열리다; 달리다 a variety of 다양한 rare 휑 희귀한 lecture 뎽 강의 leading 휑 일류의, 뛰어난 specialist 뎽 전문가 resident 뎽 주민 gardening 뎽 원예

10 도표 정보 파악

정답 ③

M Hello. Can I help you with anything? **W** Yes. I want to buy a treadmill. **M** Okay. Will you use it for running or walking? **W** I want it for running. The weather is too cold for me to 1)run outside these days. **M** In that case, I'd recommend a track that's wider than 45 centimeters. It'll be more comfortable when you run. **W** Got it. Is there anything else I should consider? **M** The maximum speed should be at least 2)16 kilometers an hour. **W** Hmm... All right. **M** How much are you willing to spend? **W** I want to keep it under $700. **M** Then, you can choose from these two. Do you need one that folds up to save space? **W** No, I don't. I have 3)plenty of space. **M** Then, I recommend this one. **W** Perfect. I'll take it.	남 안녕하세요. 무엇을 도와드릴까요? 여 네. 러닝머신을 사고 싶은데요. 남 알겠습니다. 달리기에 사용하실 건가요, 아니면 걷기에 사용하실 건가요? 여 달리기용으로 주세요. 요즘 날씨가 너무 추워서 밖에서 뛰기가 힘들어요. 남 그렇다면 폭이 45cm 이상 되는 트랙을 추천할게요. 달릴 때 더 편하실 거예요. 여 알겠습니다. 제가 더 고려해야 할 것이 있나요? 남 최고 속도는 적어도 시속 16km는 되어야 해요. 여 흠... 좋아요. 남 얼마를 쓰실 의향이 있으신가요? 여 700달러 미만으로 하고 싶어요. 남 그럼, 이 두 가지 중에서 선택하실 수 있어요. 공간 절약을 위해 접히는 것이 필요하신가요? 여 아니요. 저한테는 충분한 공간이 있어요. 남 그럼, 전 이것을 추천해요. 여 완벽하네요. 그걸 살게요.

여자는 트랙 폭이 45cm 이상이고, 최고 속도는 시속 16km 이상이며, 700달러 미만인 것 중에서, 접히지 않는 러닝머신을 골랐다.

어휘 treadmill 뎽 러닝머신 recommend 통 추천하다 comfortable 휑 편안한 maximum 휑 최고의 be willing to ~할 의향이 있다 fold up 접히다 save 통 절약하다; 구하다 space 뎽 공간

11 짧은 대화의 응답 파악

정답 ①

W Michael, why are you 1)at home? You're supposed to go to a drum lesson. **M** Actually, my teacher canceled today's lesson, Mom. **W** Really? 2)Did something happen to him? **M** He called to tell me he has the flu.	여 Michael, 왜 집에 있니? 너 드럼 레슨 가기로 되어 있잖아. 남 사실, 우리 선생님이 오늘 레슨을 취소하셨어요, 엄마. 여 정말? 선생님에게 무슨 일이 생기셨니? 남 독감에 걸렸다고 제게 전화하셨어요. 선택지 ① 독감에 걸렸다고 제게 전화하셨어요. ② 드럼을 배우는 건 너무 어려워요. ③ 방과 후에 선생님을 만날 거예요. ④ 제 드럼 세트는 수리가 필요해요. ⑤ 수업은 오늘 오후 3시에 끝났어요.

남자가 오늘 선생님이 드럼 레슨을 취소했다고 하자 여자가 선생님에게 무슨 일이 생겼는지 물었으므로, 이에 대한 응답으로는 선생님의 취소 사유를 설명하는 ① 'He called to tell me he has the flu.'가 가장 적절하다.

어휘 be supposed to ~하기로 되어 있다 cancel 통 취소하다 flu 뎽 독감 repair 통 수리하다

12 짧은 대화의 응답 파악　　　　　　　　　정답 ②

M Honey, what are you doing?	남 여보, 뭐 하고 있어?
W I'm going to ¹⁾make some pancakes for breakfast. Do you want some?	여 아침 식사로 팬케이크를 좀 만들려고 해. 당신도 좀 먹을래?
M Sure! But ²⁾do we have any maple syrup?	남 물론이지! 그런데 메이플 시럽은 있어?
W I think so. Check inside the refrigerator.	여 <u>그런 것 같아. 냉장고 안을 확인해봐.</u>

선택지 ① 응. 메이플 시럽이 다 떨어졌어.
② 그런 것 같아. 냉장고 안을 확인해봐.
③ 나도. 정말 달콤하고 맛있었어.
④ 아니, 괜찮아. 이미 아침을 많이 먹었어.
⑤ 전혀. 팬케이크 마음껏 먹어.

여자가 아침 식사로 팬케이크를 만들 것이라고 말하면서 남자에게 팬케이크를 권하자 남자가 메이플 시럽이 있는지 물었으므로, 이에 대한 응답으로는 냉장고 안을 확인해보라고 하는 ② 'I think so. Check inside the refrigerator.'가 가장 적절하다.

어휘 for breakfast 아침 식사로　run out of ~이 다 떨어지다, 다 써버리다　feel free to 마음껏 ~하다

13 긴 대화의 응답 파악　　　　　　　　　정답 ③

W Nate, what's that sound?	여 Nate, 저 소리 뭐지?
M I think it's a puppy. Oh, it's over there by the bushes.	남 강아지인 것 같아. 오, 저기 덤불 옆에 있어.
W He ¹⁾looks lost and scared.	여 강아지가 길을 잃고 겁먹은 것 같아.
M Yeah, he must be somebody's pet. Do you have anything to feed him?	남 응, 누군가의 반려견임이 틀림없어. 강아지 먹이를 줄 것 좀 갖고 있니?
W Yes. I have some sausage snacks in my bag. Here you go.	여 응. 내 가방에 소시지 간식이 좀 있어. 여기 있어.
M Wow, he was so hungry! By the way, doesn't the puppy ²⁾look familiar?	남 우와, 배가 정말 고팠나 봐! 그런데, 이 강아지가 낯이 익지 않니?
W Yeah. I think you're right! Wasn't there a poster in the neighborhood?	여 응. 네 말이 맞는 것 같아! 동네에 포스터가 있지 않았어?
M Right. One of our neighbors was looking for their lost puppy. But I can't remember who.	남 맞아. 우리 이웃 중 한 명이 잃어버린 강아지를 찾고 있었어. 그런데 누군지 기억이 안 나네.
W We should ³⁾check the poster again. Then, we can contact the owner.	여 포스터를 다시 확인해 봐야겠어. 그러면, 주인에게 연락할 수 있을 거야.
M I think I saw it on the building next to our house.	남 <u>그걸 우리 집 옆 건물에서 본 것 같아.</u>

선택지 ① 내 친구네 강아지와 똑같이 생겼어.
② 공공장소에 포스터를 붙여야 해.
③ 그걸 우리 집 옆 건물에서 본 것 같아.
④ 강아지에게 다른 먹을 것을 갖다주자.
⑤ 지금 당장 아버지께 전화해서 확인해 볼게.

길을 잃은 강아지를 발견한 상황에서 남자가 이웃이 잃어버린 강아지를 찾고 있었는데 누군지 기억이 안 난다고 하자 여자가 포스터를 다시 확인해 봐야겠다고 했으므로, 이에 대한 응답으로는 포스터의 위치를 언급하는 ③ 'I think I saw it on the building next to our house.'가 가장 적절하다.

어휘 bush 圕 덤불　lost 圕 길을 잃은　feed 圕 먹이를 주다　snack 圕 간식　by the way 그런데　familiar 圕 낯이 익은, 익숙한　neighborhood 圕 동네, 이웃　owner 圕 주인
public place 공공장소

14 긴 대화의 응답 파악　　　　　　　　　정답 ⑤

M Oh, it's nice to run into you at this café, Aletha. Are you ¹⁾waiting for your coffee?	남 오, 이 카페에서 널 우연히 만나다니 반가워, Aletha. 커피가 나오는 걸 기다리고 있어?
W Yeah. I ordered a latte. Oh, here it is.	여 응. 라테를 주문했거든. 오, 여기 나왔네.
M Why did they serve your latte in a tumbler?	남 왜 네 라테는 텀블러에 담겨서 나왔니?
W I always ask them to ²⁾put it in my tumbler.	여 나는 항상 내 텀블러에 담아달라고 부탁해.
M Isn't that inconvenient?	남 불편하지 않니?
W It's a little annoying to always carry a tumbler. But this way, I don't throw away a cup whenever I get coffee.	여 텀블러를 항상 들고 다니는 건 좀 귀찮아. 하지만 이렇게 하면, 커피를 마실 때마다 컵을 버리지 않게 돼.
M Oh, so using your tumbler is a way of protecting the environment, right?	남 오, 텀블러를 사용하는 것이 환경을 보호하는 한 방법인 거네?
W Yeah. This one simple thing ³⁾prevents a lot of waste.	여 응. 이 간단한 것 하나면 많은 쓰레기를 방지할 수 있어.
M That's pretty smart. What else do you do to protect the earth?	남 꽤 현명하다. 너는 지구를 보호하기 위해 또 무엇을 하니?
W I use old towels to clean instead of wet tissue.	여 <u>나는 물티슈 대신 낡은 수건을 써서 청소해.</u>

선택지 ① 나는 보통 커피에 우유를 넣어 마시는 것을 좋아해.
② 이 카페는 환경 보호를 돕고 있어.
③ 가능한 한 많은 컵을 재활용해야 해.
④ 텀블러를 가져오는 것을 기억해야 해.
⑤ 나는 물티슈 대신 낡은 수건을 써서 청소해.

카페에서 두 사람이 환경 보호 방법에 대해 이야기하는 상황이다. 여자가 텀블러를 사용하면 많은 쓰레기를 방지할 수 있다고 하자 남자가 여자에게 지구를 보호하기 위해 또 무엇을 하는지 물었으므로, 이에 대한 응답으로는 다른 환경 보호 방법을 언급하는 ⑤ 'I use old towels to clean instead of wet tissue.'가 가장 적절하다.

어휘 run into ~를 우연히 만나다 serve 통 (음식을) 내다 inconvenient 형 불편한 annoying 형 귀찮은, 짜증 나는 throw away ~을 버리다 protect 통 보호하다 environment 명 환경
prevent 통 막다 waste 명 쓰레기; 낭비 recycle 통 재활용하다 wet tissue 물티슈

15 상황에 적절한 말 파악

정답 ③

W Alex and Susan are close friends who enjoy spending time together. They both like swimming, but there are no beaches nearby. So when Susan recently got her driver's license, they made plans to ¹⁾take a road trip to the beach during summer vacation. They found a good place to stay and made reservations. However, a week before the trip, Susan started to ²⁾feel a minor pain in her back. Now, Susan is worried that she can't drive safely because the pain distracts her while she is driving. **So she wants to suggest to Alex that they should ³⁾travel there by train instead.** In this situation, what would Susan most likely say to Alex?

여 Alex와 Susan은 함께 시간을 보내는 것을 즐기는 친한 친구입니다. 그들은 둘 다 수영하는 것을 좋아하지만, 근처에는 해변이 없습니다. 그래서 Susan이 최근에 운전 면허증을 땄을 때, 그들은 여름휴가 동안 해변으로 자동차 여행을 갈 계획을 세웠습니다. 그들은 머물기 좋은 장소를 찾았고 예약을 했습니다. 하지만, 여행을 일주일 앞두고 Susan은 허리에 가벼운 통증을 느끼기 시작했습니다. 이제, Susan은 운전 중 통증으로 인해 주의가 산만해져 안전하게 운전할 수 없을까 봐 걱정하고 있습니다. 그래서, 그녀는 Alex에게 대신 기차로 그곳까지 이동할 것을 제안하고 싶습니다. 이러한 상황에서, Susan이 Alex에게 가장 할 것 같은 말은 무엇입니까?

선택지 ① 그럼 방문할 다른 해변을 찾아보자.
② 거기까지 운전해서 가기에는 너무 비싼 것 같아.
③ 기차를 타고 해변에 가는 게 어때?
④ 허리 엑스레이를 찍어보는 건 어때?
⑤ 같이 자동차 여행을 가지 않을래?

Alex와 함께 떠날 여행을 앞두고, Susan은 허리 통증으로 안전하게 운전하지 못할 것을 걱정하여 대신 기차로 그곳까지 이동할 것을 제안하려고 한다. 따라서, Susan이 할 말로 ③ 'Why don't we take a train to the beach?'가 가장 적절하다.

어휘 spend 통 (시간을) 보내다 nearby 부 근처에 recently 부 최근에 driver's license 운전 면허증 road trip 자동차 여행 make a reservation 예약을 하다 minor 형 가벼운; 작은
pain 명 통증 distract 통 주의를 산만하게 하다, 집중이 안 되게 하다 travel 통 이동하다; 여행하다

16-17 세트 문항

정답 16 ② 17 ④

M Hello. This is Dr. Matthew Ashland. Previously, I told you about foods that can give you more energy, like chocolate. **Today, I want to talk about some ¹⁾common foods that have the power to help cure illnesses.** First, people have been using **ginger** for hundreds of years to treat stomachaches. You can ease an upset stomach or ²⁾digest better with a cup of ginger tea. Similarly, **garlic** is good for your immune system. Many people eat it to get better from a cold. Another food that helps when you're sick is **honey**. This sweet liquid can be ³⁾effective in soothing a sore throat. Finally, **mushrooms** are full of nutrients. Studies have even found that certain types of mushrooms can help patients with cancer. So try consuming these foods when you're not feeling well to ⁴⁾recover more quickly. Now, let's watch a short video about some other healing foods.

남 안녕하세요. Matthew Ashland 박사입니다. 이전에, 초콜릿과 같은 더 많은 에너지를 여러분에게 줄 수 있는 음식에 대해 말씀드렸습니다. 오늘은 질병 치료를 도울 힘이 있는 몇 가지 흔한 식품에 대해 이야기하고 싶습니다. 첫째, 사람들은 복통을 치료하기 위해 수백 년 동안 생강을 사용해 왔습니다. 여러분은 생강차 한 잔으로 배탈을 완화시키거나 소화가 더 잘 되게 할 수 있습니다. 비슷하게, 마늘은 면역 체계에 좋습니다. 많은 사람들이 감기를 낫게 하기 위해 마늘을 먹습니다. 아플 때 도움이 되는 또 다른 음식은 꿀입니다. 이 달콤한 액체는 인후통을 진정시키는 데 효과적일 수 있습니다. 마지막으로, 버섯은 영양분으로 가득 차 있습니다. 연구들은 심지어 특정한 종류의 버섯들이 암 환자들을 도울 수 있다는 것을 발견했습니다. 그러니, 몸이 좋지 않을 때 더 빨리 회복할 수 있도록 이 식품들을 한번 먹어보십시오. 이제 치유에 좋은 몇몇 다른 식품에 대한 짧은 영상을 보도록 하겠습니다.

선택지 16 ① 에너지를 증진시킬 수 있는 음식
② 질병을 치료하는 데 좋은 음식
③ 면역 체계를 강화하기 위한 요리법
④ 감기에 걸렸을 때 피해야 할 음식
⑤ 암 치료에 대한 연구 결과
17 ① 생강 ② 마늘 ③ 꿀 ④ 양파 ⑤ 버섯

16 질병 치료를 도울 힘이 있는 몇 가지 흔한 식품에 대해 이야기하고 있으므로 남자가 하는 말의 주제로 ② 'foods that are good for healing diseases'가 가장 적절하다.
17 생강, 마늘, 꿀, 버섯은 언급했지만 ④ 'onions'는 언급하지 않았다.

어휘 previously 부 이전에 common 형 흔한 cure 통 치료하다 illness 명 질병 ginger 명 생강 treat 통 치료하다; 다루다 ease 통 완화하다 upset stomach 배탈 digest 통 소화하다
similarly 부 비슷하게 be good for ~에 좋다 immune system 면역 체계 liquid 명 액체 effective 형 효과적인 soothe 통 진정시키다 sore throat 인후통
be full of ~으로 가득 차 있다 nutrient 명 영양분 consume 통 먹다; 소비하다 recover 통 회복하다 boost 통 증진시키다

1	①	2	③	3	⑤	4	④	5	④	6	②	7	⑤	8	③	9	④	10	⑤
11	①	12	②	13	④	14	④	15	③	16	①	17	②						

• 각 문제의 정답 근거는 굵은 글씨로, Dictation 정답은 밑줄로 표시되어 있습니다.

1 목적 파악
정답 ①

W Attention, students and job seekers. Are you unsure about your career path? Would you like the chance to meet professionals ¹⁾working in different fields? **Then, come to the career fair at Centerville College!** The fair will run from 9 a.m. to 5 p.m. on April 15th. Companies in a variety of industries, including travel, medicine, and technology, ²⁾will participate. Their booths will be set up so visitors can experience job interviews and learn more about possible careers. Please check the school website for the complete list of participants. Attendees should ³⁾come prepared with a résumé and questions! We hope to see you there.

여 주목해주세요, 학생 및 구직자 여러분. 여러분의 진로에 대해 확신하지 못하시나요? 다양한 분야에서 일하는 전문가들을 만날 기회를 원하시나요? 그렇다면, 센터빌 대학교에서 열리는 채용 박람회에 오세요! 박람회는 4월 15일 오전 9시부터 오후 5시까지 열립니다. 여행, 의료, 기술 등을 포함한 다양한 업계의 기업들이 참여할 예정입니다. 방문객들이 구직 면접을 경험하고 가능한 진로에 대해 더 알아 갈 수 있도록 부스가 설치될 예정입니다. 전체 참가 기업 명단은 학교 웹사이트에서 확인하세요. 참석자들께서는 이력서와 질문을 준비해 오셔야 합니다! 그곳에서 뵙기를 바랍니다.

여자가 채용 박람회에 오라고 하면서, 개최 날짜, 참여 기업, 부스 설치 등에 대한 정보를 주고 있다. 따라서, 여자가 하는 말의 목적으로 ① '채용 박람회를 홍보하려고'가 가장 적절하다.

[어휘] unsure 휑 확신하지 못하는 career path 진로 field 휑 분야 fair 휑 박람회 run 통 열리다; 뛰다 industry 휑 업계; 산업 set up ~을 설치하다 interview 휑 면접 attendee 휑 참석자 résumé 휑 이력서

2 의견 파악
정답 ③

M Jean, what's the matter? You look upset.

W I'm concerned about my daughter. She's nine, but she still doesn't ¹⁾have any manners.

M Oh, really? What happened?

W Her uncle visited us yesterday, but she didn't greet him. And she made rude comments during dinner.

M Oh, she can't do that. **In my opinion, kids need to learn that** ²⁾proper etiquette **is important.**

W I told her not to behave rudely. But she kept saying it was just a joke.

M I think you need to explain how her uncle felt. She should know that ³⁾being rude is different from being playful.

W Okay, I'll do that. I'll let her know the importance of having good manners.

M Good luck. I hope you can ⁴⁾persuade her to change her attitude.

남 Jean, 무슨 일이야? 기분이 안 좋아 보여.
여 나는 우리 딸이 걱정돼. 그녀는 아홉 살인데도 여전히 예의가 없어.
남 오, 정말? 무슨 일이 있었어?
여 그녀의 삼촌이 어제 우리 집에 방문했는데, 그에게 인사하지 않더라. 그리고 저녁 식사 중에 무례한 말을 했어.
남 오, 그러면 안 되지. 내 생각에, 아이들은 적절한 예절이 중요하다는 걸 배울 필요가 있어.
여 나는 그녀에게 무례하게 행동하지 말라고 했어. 그런데 그냥 농담이었다고 계속 말하더라.
남 그녀의 삼촌이 어떤 기분이었을지 설명해줘야 할 것 같아. 무례한 것과 장난치는 것은 다르다는 걸 알아야 해.
여 알겠어, 그렇게 할게. 예의를 잘 지키는 것의 중요성을 알려줘야겠어.
남 행운을 빌어. 그녀가 태도를 바꾸도록 설득할 수 있기를 바랄게.

딸이 예의가 없어서 걱정하는 여자에게 남자가 아이들은 적절한 예절이 중요하다는 것을 배울 필요가 있다고 말했다. 따라서, 남자의 의견으로 ③ '아이들은 예절의 중요성을 배워야 한다.'가 가장 적절하다.

[어휘] be concerned about ~을 걱정하다 manners 휑 예의 greet 통 인사하다 make a comment 말하다 rude 휑 무례한 in one's opinion ~의 생각에 proper 휑 적절한 etiquette 휑 예절 behave 통 행동하다 different from ~과 다른 playful 휑 장난치는 persuade 통 설득하다 attitude 휑 태도

3 관계 파악
정답 ⑤

W **So now you've seen all of the apartments on our list.** Do you have any questions?

M Actually, I have a few about the last apartment we saw. **First, how much is the rent?**

W **It's $1,000 a month.** It's much ¹⁾cheaper than most apartments in the area.

M Okay. How many parking spots would I get?

W ²⁾Each unit comes with two underground parking spots.

M That's good. Lastly, isn't Pomona High School nearby? My son goes there.

W Yes. It's just a 10-minute walk from here.

여 자, 이제 저희 목록에 있는 모든 아파트를 보셨어요. 질문 있으신가요?
남 사실, 마지막으로 본 아파트에 대해 몇 가지 질문이 있어요. 먼저, 임대료는 얼마인가요?
여 한 달에 1,000달러예요. 이 지역의 웬만한 아파트보다 훨씬 저렴합니다.
남 알겠습니다. 주차 공간은 몇 개나 되나요?
여 각 가구에 두 개의 지하 주차 공간이 딸려 있어요.
남 잘됐네요. 마지막으로 포모나 고등학교가 근처에 있지 않나요? 제 아들이 거기에 다니거든요.
여 네. 여기서 걸어서 딱 10분 거리예요.

M	That's perfect. All the places you've shown me were great, but I can really ³⁾imagine living here.	남	완벽해요. 보여주신 모든 곳이 훌륭한데, 여기서 사는 것이 정말 그려지네요.
W	That's wonderful. Do you think you'll take the apartment?	여	잘됐네요. 이 아파트로 하시겠어요?
M	I think so. **I'm excited to move in!**	남	그럴 것 같아요. 입주할 생각에 신나네요!

두 사람이 새로운 아파트를 둘러보고 있다. 여자는 남자에게 자신의 목록에 있는 모든 아파트를 봤다면서 임대료 등을 설명하고 있고, 남자는 아파트에 대한 질문을 마친 뒤 입주할 생각을 하고 있는 것으로 보아 두 사람의 관계로 ⑤ '부동산 중개업자 — 고객'이 가장 적절하다.

[어휘] rent 몡 임대료, 집세 area 몡 지역 spot 몡 공간, 장소 unit 몡 한 가구; 구성 단위 come with ~이 딸려 있다 underground 혱 지하의 move in 입주하다, 이사 오다

---

4 그림 내용 불일치 파악   정답 ④

M	Emily, how are the preparations going for your wedding?	남	Emily, 결혼 준비는 잘 돼가?
W	The wedding planner just sent me this picture of the wedding hall.	여	웨딩 플래너가 방금 결혼식장 사진을 보냈어.
M	Wow. That three-layer wedding cake looks incredible!	남	우와. 저 3단 웨딩 케이크 정말 멋져 보여!
W	Thanks! But is the ¹⁾large vase of flowers at the front of the stage too big?	여	고마워! 그런데 무대 앞에 있는 대형 꽃병이 너무 큰 것 같니?
M	Not at all. It will look nice in the photos.	남	전혀. 사진으로 보면 멋질 거야.
W	I'm glad you think so. The curtains will make a pretty background for photos, too.	여	그렇게 생각한다니 다행이네. 저 커튼은 사진에서 예쁜 배경이 될 것 같아.
M	I agree. The leaf patterns on the curtains are beautiful. **And I see ²⁾two microphone stands on the left side of the stage. Will that be enough?**	남	동의해. 커튼에 그려진 나뭇잎 무늬가 멋지다. 그리고 무대 왼편에 있는 마이크 스탠드가 두 개 보이네. 그걸로 충분할까?
W	Yes. One is for the wedding host, and the other is for the singer.	여	응. 하나는 결혼식 사회자를 위한 것이고, 다른 하나는 가수를 위한 거야.
M	Got it. But is it a good idea to ³⁾have those two candles on either side of the aisle?	남	알겠어. 그런데 통로 양쪽에 초 두 개를 두는 것이 좋은 생각일까?
W	Oh... Those could be dangerous.	여	오... 그건 위험할 수도 있겠어.
M	Maybe you should mention that to the wedding planner.	남	웨딩 플래너에게 그 말을 하는 게 좋을 것 같아.
W	I will.	여	그럴게.

대화에서 남자가 무대 왼편에 마이크 스탠드 두 개가 보인다고 했는데, ④에는 마이크 스탠드 한 개만 그려져 있다.

[어휘] layer 몡 단, 층 on either side 양쪽에 mention 통 말하다

---

5 할 일 파악   정답 ④

W	Hi, Coach Wilson. How are things going with the school volleyball team?	여	안녕하세요, Wilson 코치님. 학교 배구팀은 어떻게 되어 가고 있나요?
M	Good, Principal Smith. The team ¹⁾has a tournament in Boston next month.	남	잘되고 있습니다, Smith 교장 선생님. 다음 달에 보스턴에서 시합이 있어요.
W	Okay. Have you made all the arrangements?	여	네. 모든 준비를 다 하셨나요?
M	Almost. I've booked hotel rooms for the athletes and arranged transportation. Now, I just ²⁾need to organize a team-building event.	남	거의 다 됐어요. 선수들 호텔 방을 예약하고 교통편을 마련했습니다. 이제 팀워크 행사만 준비하면 됩니다.
W	Do you have any ideas?	여	아이디어가 있으세요?
M	I can't think of anything yet.	남	아직 아무것도 생각이 나질 않네요.
W	How about an escape room? There's one near the school that the teachers went to last year.	여	방 탈출은 어때요? 작년에 선생님들이 갔었던 곳이 학교 근처에 한 군데 있어요.
M	Oh, that would be perfect. The players will have to work together to ³⁾solve the puzzles to escape.	남	오, 완벽할 것 같네요. 선수들은 탈출하기 위해 퍼즐을 풀려면 힘을 합쳐야 할 거예요.
W	**I can look up the phone number of that place if you like.**	여	원하시면 그곳 전화번호를 찾아볼게요.
M	**Sure. I'd appreciate that.**	남	물론이죠. 그렇게 해주시면 감사하겠습니다.

학교 배구팀의 시합 준비에 대해 이야기하고 있다. 여자가 남자에게 원한다면 방 탈출 가게의 전화번호를 찾아보겠다고 하자, 남자가 그렇게 해주면 감사하겠다고 했으므로 여자가 할 일로 ④ '가게 전화번호 찾아보기'가 가장 적절하다.

[어휘] tournament 몡 시합, 토너먼트 make an arrangement 준비를 하다 book 통 예약하다 몡 책 athlete 몡 (운동)선수 transportation 몡 교통편 team-building event 팀워크 행사 escape room 방 탈출 work together 힘을 합치다 look up ~을 찾아보다

6 금액 정보 파악

정답 ②

M Welcome to the Pine City Christmas Light Festival.	남 파인시 크리스마스 빛 축제에 오신 것을 환영합니다.
W Hello. How much is ¹⁾the entrance fee?	여 안녕하세요. 입장료는 얼마인가요?
M It's $10 for adults and $5 for children under the age of 12.	남 어른은 10달러이고, 나이가 12세 미만인 어린이는 5달러입니다.
W I need tickets for four adults and four children.	여 어른 네 명과 어린이 네 명의 표가 필요합니다.
M Sure. Also, we are ²⁾offering a chance to take pictures with Santa Claus.	남 알겠습니다. 저희는 산타클로스와 함께 사진을 찍을 기회도 제공하고 있어요.
W Oh, great. How much does it cost?	여 오, 좋아요. 비용이 얼마나 드나요?
M It's ³⁾$20 per photo.	남 사진 한 장에 20달러예요.
W Can I get one with all of the kids in it?	여 한 장에 모든 아이들이 들어가게 찍어도 되나요?
M Certainly. That would be fine.	남 물론이죠. 괜찮을 거예요.
W Okay. **I'll take one of those.** Also, I'm ⁴⁾a citizen of Pine City. Do I get a discount?	여 네. 한 장 할게요. 그리고, 저는 파인시 시민인데요. 할인되나요?
M Yes. **Residents get $10 off the total.**	남 네. 주민은 총액에서 10달러 할인받을 수 있어요.
W Great. I'm glad I asked.	여 좋군요. 여쭤보길 잘했네요.
M So that's four adult tickets, four child tickets, one photo with Santa, with the discount.	남 그럼 어른 4장, 어린이 4장, 산타와 함께 찍는 사진 1장을 하시고, 할인도 받으시게 되네요.
W That's right. I'll pay in cash.	여 맞습니다. 현금으로 계산할게요.

여자가 크리스마스 빛 축제에서 어른 입장권 4장($10×4=$40), 어린이 입장권 4장($5×4=$20)과 산타클로스와 함께 찍는 사진 1장($20)을 구매했고, 총액에서 10달러 할인($80-$10=$70)을 받았으므로 정답은 ② '$70'이다.

어휘 under the age of 나이가 ~ 미만의 offer 통 제공하다 cost 통 비용이 들다 citizen 명 시민

7 이유 파악

정답 ⑤

W Hi, Robert. Is your finger feeling better? It ¹⁾looked pretty bad when you cut it on that guitar string.	여 안녕, Robert. 손가락은 좀 괜찮아졌니? 기타 줄에 베였을 때 꽤 심해 보였어.
M Hey, Jenny. It's much better now. I've been playing again.	남 안녕, Jenny. 지금은 많이 좋아졌어. 나는 다시 연주하고 있어.
W That's great. Do you think you can ²⁾come to band practice on Thursday night?	여 잘됐네. 목요일 밤에 밴드 연습하러 올 수 있을 것 같니?
M I'm sorry, but I can't.	남 미안하지만, 그럴 수 없어.
W Why not? Do you have to work on your English homework?	여 왜? 영어 숙제를 해야 해?
M No. I ³⁾already finished that.	남 아니. 그건 이미 다 했어.
W I see. Maybe you have to help your mom at her store, then.	여 그렇구나. 그때 너희 어머니 가게에서 도와드려야 할지도 모르나 보네, 그럼.
M No, my brother will help my mom at that time. **Actually, I have to** ⁴⁾study for the math quiz.	남 아니, 그때는 형이 엄마를 도와줄 거야. 사실, 수학 시험공부를 해야 해.
W Got it. But I will see you at chess club tomorrow, right?	여 알겠어. 그래도 내일 체스 동아리에서 만날 거야, 그렇지?
M For sure. See you there.	남 물론이지. 거기서 봐.

남자는 밴드 연습하러 갈 수 없을 것 같다고 하면서 수학 시험공부를 해야 한다고 말했으므로, 남자가 밴드 연습에 참여할 수 없는 이유는 ⑤ '수학 시험공부를 해야 해서'이다.

어휘 bad 형 심한; 나쁜 cut 통 베다 string 명 줄 at that time 그때 For sure. 물론이지.

8 언급 유무 파악

정답 ③

M What should we do with the kids today, honey?	남 여보, 오늘 아이들과 뭘 할까?
W The weather is so nice. I thought we could visit a place called Applewood Farm. The entrance fee is only **$2** a person.	여 날씨가 너무 좋아. 애플우드 농장이라는 곳을 방문할 수 있겠다고 생각했어. 입장료는 1인당 단돈 2달러야.
M That's a great idea. But is it ¹⁾far from here? Traffic might be bad because it's the weekend.	남 좋은 생각이야. 그런데 그곳은 여기서 멀어? 주말이라 교통 상황이 안 좋을 수도 있어.
W It's not too far. It only takes **30 minutes** to drive there.	여 그리 멀지 않아. 거기까지 차로 30분밖에 안 걸려.
M All right. And are you sure they're open today?	남 좋아. 거기 오늘 영업하는 게 확실해?
W Yes. I just ²⁾checked their website. They're open **from 9 a.m. to 6 p.m.**	여 응. 방금 웹사이트를 확인했어. 오전 9시부터 오후 6시까지 영업해.
M Then, we'll have plenty of time. Do you know what kinds of activities they have?	남 그럼, 시간은 충분하겠네. 그곳에 어떤 종류의 활동이 있는지 알아?
W We can **pick apples** there. Also, ³⁾they offer **pony rides**.	여 거기서 사과를 딸 수 있어. 그리고, 조랑말 타기도 제공해.
M Oh, I bet the kids will love that. Let's go!	남 오, 아이들이 틀림없이 좋아할 거야. 가자!
W Sure. I'll get the kids ready.	여 물론이지. 아이들을 준비시킬게.

입장료(2달러), 이동 시간(30분), 운영 시간(오전9시부터 오후6시), 체험 활동 종류(사과 따기, 조랑말 타기)에 대해 언급했고, ③ '주차 가능 여부'는 언급하지 않았다.

어휘 traffic 명 교통 plenty of 충분한, 많은 activity 명 활동 pony 명 조랑말 I bet ~. 틀림없이 ~하다.

9 내용 불일치 파악   정답 ④

W	Attention, Palmas High School students. This is your principal, Ms. Garcia. I have a very exciting announcement to make. The Global Science Olympiad is [1]being held in Rome, Italy this spring. This event only happens once every four years. This year, it will run from April 22nd to 28th. **More than 200 students [2]from around the world will take part in competitions that will test their knowledge of various scientific fields, such as physics and chemistry.** I am extremely proud to say that [3]two of our students have been selected to attend this important event. Stephanie Kane and Michael Park will compete in the chemistry category. Congratulations to Stephanie and Michael, and good luck in Rome!	여 주목해주세요, 팔마스 고등학교 학생 여러분. Garcia 교장 선생님입니다. 아주 흥미로운 소식을 전합니다. Global Science Olympiad가 올봄에 이탈리아 로마에서 개최될 예정입니다. 이 행사는 4년마다 단 한 번만 열립니다. 올해는 4월 22일부터 28일까지 열릴 것입니다. 전 세계에서 온 200명 이상의 학생들이 물리학과 화학 같은 다양한 과학 분야에 대한 지식을 테스트하는 대회에 참가할 것입니다. 우리 학생들 중 두 명이 이 중요한 행사에 참석할 수 있게 선발된 것이 매우 자랑스럽습니다. Stephanie Kane과 Michael Park이 화학 부문에 참가할 것입니다. Stephanie와 Michael에게 축하를 보내며, 로마에서 행운이 있길 빕니다!

Global Science Olympiad 대회 출전자를 알리는 교내 방송이다. 여자가 전 세계에서 온 200명 이상의 학생들이 대회에 참가할 것이라고 했으므로 ④ '전 세계에서 100명의 학생이 출전한다.'는 내용과 일치하지 않는다.

어휘 announcement 명 소식   hold 통 개최하다   take part in ~에 참가하다   physics 명 물리학   chemistry 명 화학   attend 통 참석하다   compete 통 참가하다; 경쟁하다

10 도표 정보 파악   정답 ⑤

M	Welcome to Office Buddy.	남 Office Buddy에 오신 것을 환영합니다.
W	Hello. I need a planner, but I can't decide which one to buy.	여 안녕하세요. 플래너가 필요한데, 어떤 것을 사야 할지 결정을 못 하겠어요.
M	Do you want separate pages for each day? Or do you prefer to make weekly or even monthly plans?	남 매일마다 별도의 페이지가 있는 것을 원하시나요? 아니면 주 단위 또는 월 단위의 계획을 세우는 것을 선호하시나요?
W	**I don't like ones with [1]daily pages.**	여 일일 페이지가 있는 것은 별로 좋아하지 않아요.
M	Then, you'll want to look at our weekly or monthly planners. How much would you like to spend?	남 그렇다면 주간 또는 월간 플래너를 살펴보세요. 얼마를 지출하고 싶으신가요?
W	**I'd rather spend less than $15.**	여 15달러 이하로 지출하는 게 낫겠어요.
M	All right. Would you prefer one [2]with extra blank pages at the back?	남 좋아요. 뒷면에 여분의 빈 페이지가 있는 것을 선호하시나요?
W	Yes. I like to write out my thoughts. **So a planner with many blank pages would be good.**	여 네. 저는 제 생각을 자세히 쓰는 걸 좋아해요. 그래서 빈 페이지가 많은 플래너가 좋을 것 같아요.
M	Okay. What colors do you like [3]for the cover?	남 알겠습니다. 표지는 어떤 색을 좋아하세요?
W	**I like dark colors like navy and black.**	여 저는 남색이나 검은색 같은 어두운색이 좋아요.
M	Then, I think you should get this planner.	남 그럼 이 플래너를 구입하시는 게 좋을 것 같네요.

여자는 일일 페이지 구성이 아니고, 15달러 이하인 것 중에서, 뒷면에 빈 페이지가 추가로 있으며, 표지 색상은 남색이나 검은색인 플래너를 골랐다.

어휘 decide 통 결정하다   separate 형 별도의, 분리된   daily 형 일일의   would rather ~하는 게 낫다   extra 형 추가의   blank 형 빈   write out ~을 자세히 쓰다

11 짧은 대화의 응답 파악   정답 ①

W	[1]What should we have for dinner tonight, honey?	여 여보, 오늘 저녁 식사로 뭘 먹을까?
M	We have prime beef [2]in the fridge. **I can cook some steaks on the grill.**	남 냉장고에 최고급 소고기가 있어. 그릴에 스테이크를 구워도 돼.
W	That would be nice. **Why don't we invite the neighbors over?**	여 그거 좋겠다. 우리 이웃들을 초대하는 게 어때?
M	Why not? We'll have great time together.	남 왜 안 되겠어? 함께 즐거운 시간을 보낼 거야.
		선택지 ① 왜 안 되겠어? 함께 즐거운 시간을 보낼 거야.
		② 확실해? 냉장고를 확인해 보는 게 어때?
		③ 맞아. 최근에 이웃들을 보지 못했어.
		④ 완벽해. 새 석쇠를 사고 싶어.
		⑤ 됐어. 아직 저녁 먹은 걸로 너무 배불러.

남자가 냉장고에 최고급 소고기가 있다면서 그릴에 스테이크를 굽겠다고 하자 여자가 이웃들을 초대하는 것을 제안했으므로, 이에 대한 응답으로는 제안을 수락하는 ① 'Why not? We'll have great time together.'가 가장 적절하다.

어휘 for dinner 저녁 식사로   prime beef 최고급 소고기   fridge 명 냉장고   grill 명 그릴, 석쇠   invite ~ over ~를 초대하다

12 짧은 대화의 응답 파악

정답 ②

[Cell phone rings.] **M** Hey, Marie. **I'm sorry, but I** ¹⁾can't meet you at the theater. **W** Really? But I'm almost there. We're supposed to meet in 10 minutes. **M** I'm so sorry. **I've been** ²⁾feeling really sick since I woke up this morning. **W** Would you like to meet next weekend instead?	[휴대폰이 울린다.] 남 안녕, Marie. 미안하지만, 극장에서 만날 수 없을 것 같아. 여 정말? 하지만 난 거의 다 왔는걸. 우리 10분 후에 만나기로 되어 있었잖아. 남 정말 미안해. 오늘 아침에 일어난 이후로 몸이 너무 안 좋아. 여 대신 다음 주말에 만날래? 선택지 ① 오늘 오후에 어떤 영화를 보고 싶니? ② 대신 다음 주말에 만날래? ③ 표가 매진되었는지 확인해 봤니? ④ 몇 시에 여기에 도착할 수 있어? ⑤ 내가 아직도 아픈지 어떻게 알았어?

10분 후에 만나기로 되어 있는 상황에서 남자가 여자에게 만날 수 없다면서 몸이 너무 안 좋다고 했으므로, 이에 대한 응답으로는 대신 다음에 만날 날을 제안하는 ② 'Would you like to meet next weekend instead?'가 가장 적절하다.

어휘 almost 뮈 거의   be supposed to ~하기로 되어 있다   sold out 매진된

---

13 긴 대화의 응답 파악

정답 ④

M Hi, Mom. Did you have a good day? **W** Yes, I did. What are you doing, Paul? **M** I just finished cleaning the electric kettle. You ¹⁾told me to clean it this morning. **W** Oh, I see. Thank you for doing that, sweetie. **M** No problem. **Now, I just need to plug it in.** **W** Wait. Your hands are wet, aren't they? You shouldn't ²⁾touch the plug. **M** I already shook all the water off my hands. **W** That's not enough. **It's dangerous to touch cords and plugs while** ³⁾your hands are wet. **M** Okay. I'll get a towel and dry them completely.	남 안녕하세요, 엄마. 좋은 하루 보내셨나요? 여 응, 그랬단다. 뭐 하는 중이니, Paul? 남 방금 전기 전자 세척을 마쳤어요. 오늘 아침에 씻어두라고 말씀하셨잖아요. 여 오, 그렇구나. 그렇게 해줘서 고맙구나, 얘야. 남 문제없어요. 이제 전원을 연결하기만 하면 돼요. 여 잠깐만. 네 손이 젖었잖아, 그렇지 않니? 플러그를 만지면 안 돼. 남 이미 손에 묻은 물은 다 털어냈어요. 여 그걸로는 충분하지 않아. 손이 젖은 상태에서 전기 코드와 플러그를 만지는 건 위험해. 남 알겠어요. 수건을 가져와서 완전히 닦을게요. 선택지 ① 맞아요. 저는 커피보다 녹차를 더 좋아해요. ② 알아요. 지난주에도 주전자를 세척했거든요. ③ 어디 봐요. 먼저 비누와 물로 그것들을 씻으세요. ④ 알겠어요. 수건을 가져와서 완전히 닦을게요. ⑤ 아니요, 괜찮아요. 전 차를 더 이상 마시고 싶지 않아요.

손에 묻은 물을 털어내고 플러그를 만지려고 하는 남자에게 여자가 손이 젖은 상태에서 전기 코드와 플러그를 만지는 것은 위험하다고 했으므로, 이에 대한 응답으로는 손을 완전히 닦겠다고 대답하는 ④ 'Okay. I'll get a towel and dry them completely.'가 가장 적절하다.

어휘 kettle 몡 주전자   plug ~ in ~에 전원을 연결하다   wet 혱 젖은   touch 통 만지다   shake off ~을 털어내다   cord 몡 전기 코드; 줄   prefer A to B B보다 A를 선호하다
dry 통 닦다, 말리다 혱 건조한

---

14 긴 대화의 응답 파악

정답 ④

[Telephone rings.] **M** Hello. This is the security desk at River Valley Mall. How can I help you? **W** Hi. Do you have a ¹⁾lost and found center there? **M** We do. Did you lose something at the mall? **W** I might have. **I think I lost my necklace there yesterday.** **M** Can you ²⁾describe it in detail? **W** Yes. It's silver with a round locket pendant. **M** What else can you tell me about it? **W** You can open the locket. Inside, there is ³⁾a picture of my hamster. **M** Okay. I'll call you again if I find it. **W** Wait. There's one more thing. The letter J is stamped on the back of the pendant. **M** **Oh, I think I see your necklace here. You can** ⁴⁾come pick it up now if you like.** **W** Thank you so much. I'll be there in 20 minutes.	[전화기가 울린다.] 남 여보세요. River Valley Mall 보안 데스크입니다. 무엇을 도와드릴까요? 여 안녕하세요. 거기 분실물 취급 센터가 있나요? 남 있습니다. 쇼핑몰에서 물건을 잃어버리셨나요? 여 그랬을지도 몰라요. 어제 거기서 목걸이를 잃어버린 것 같아요. 남 그것을 상세하게 설명해 주시겠어요? 여 네. 은으로 되어 있고 동그란 모양의 펜던트가 있어요. 남 그 밖에 또 말씀해주실 게 있나요? 여 그 펜던트를 열 수 있거든요. 안에는 제 햄스터 사진이 있어요. 남 알겠습니다. 찾으면 다시 전화하겠습니다. 여 잠깐만요. 한 가지 더 있어요. J라는 글자가 펜던트 뒷면에 각인되어 있어요. 남 오, 여기 손님의 목걸이가 보이는 것 같네요. 원하시면 지금 찾으러 오셔도 됩니다. 여 정말 감사합니다. 20분 후에 도착할 거예요. 선택지 ① 걱정하지 마세요. 찾아드리겠다고 약속할게요. ② 좋습니다. 은목걸이를 착용할게요. ③ 신경 쓰지 마세요. 내내 제 지갑 안에 있었어요. ④ 정말 감사합니다. 20분 후에 도착할 거예요. ⑤ 유감이네요. 다음에는 더 운이 좋기를 바랄게요.

잃어버린 물건이 쇼핑몰 분실물 취급 센터에 있는지 전화해서 물어보는 상황이다. 여자가 목걸이에 대한 자세한 설명을 하자 목걸이를 찾아낸 남자가 원하면 지금 찾으러 와도 된다고 했으므로, 이에 대한 응답으로는 예상 도착 시간을 언급하는 ④ 'Thank you so much. I'll be there in 20 minutes.'가 가장 적절하다.

[어휘] security 명 보안, 경비 lost and found 분실물 취급소 describe 통 설명하다 in detail 상세하게 stamp on ~을 각인시키다 Don't bother. 신경 쓰지 마세요. purse 명 지갑 all along 내내, 계속

15 상황에 적절한 말 파악

정답 ③

W Milo is a rock musician, and Anna is his manager. Milo is making his second album. Last night, Anna went to Milo's studio to listen ¹⁾to his new song. She was surprised to find out that it's a ballad, which is different from his other songs. Anna thinks he ²⁾should not put it on his new album because his fans might be disappointed. However, Milo wants to show them that he can play more than just rock music. **So Milo wants to tell Anna that ³⁾she should trust him because he thinks his fans will like his new style of music.** In this situation, what would Milo most likely say to Anna?

여 Milo는 록 뮤지션이고, Anna는 그의 매니저입니다. Milo는 그의 두 번째 음반을 만들고 있습니다. 어젯밤 Anna는 Milo의 신곡을 듣기 위해 그의 스튜디오에 갔습니다. 그녀는 그 노래가 그의 다른 노래들과는 다르게, 발라드라는 사실을 알게 되어 놀랐습니다. Anna는 팬들이 실망할 수 있기 때문에 새 음반에 그것을 넣지 말아야 한다고 생각합니다. 하지만 Milo는 자신이 록 음악 외에도 다양한 음악을 할 수 있다는 것을 보여주고 싶습니다. 그래서 Milo는 Anna에게 팬들이 그의 새로운 음악 스타일을 좋아할 것이라고 생각하므로 자신을 믿어보라고 말하고 싶습니다. 이러한 상황에서, Milo가 Anna에게 가장 할 것 같은 말은 무엇입니까?

[선택지]
① 말도 안 돼요. 음악에 대해 아무것도 모르시잖아요.
② 동의해요. 이 노래가 크게 히트할 것 같아요.
③ 절 믿어보세요. 팬들이 제 새로운 음악 스타일을 정말 좋아할 거예요.
④ 당신이 맞아요. 이 발라드곡에서 제 목소리가 좋게 들리네요.
⑤ 제 실수예요. 팬들이 제게 실망할 거예요.

Milo의 기존 노래 스타일과는 다른 발라드 음악이 팬들을 실망시킬 수 있다고 생각하는 Anna에게, Milo는 팬들이 자신의 새로운 음악 스타일을 좋아할 것이므로 그를 믿어보라고 설득하려 한다. 따라서, Milo가 할 말로 ③ 'Believe me. My fans will love my new music style.'이 가장 적절하다.

[어휘] find out ~을 알다 disappointed 형 실망한 trust 통 믿다

16-17 세트 문항

정답 16 ① 17 ②

M Hello, everybody. Previously, we talked about how technology changed the fashion industry. **Today, I want to talk about the advantages of ¹⁾some common fabrics.** First, **cotton** is one of the most popular fabrics. Clothing made from the cotton plant is soft and comfortable. This material is good at absorbing moisture, so it is often used to make towels. Next, there is **wool**, which comes from sheep. Because it ²⁾traps heat well, it is used to make winter clothing, such as coats, sweaters, and scarves. Additionally, **silk** from the silkworm has been used to make clothing for hundreds of years. It is light, smooth, and shiny, but also very strong. Another strong fabric is **nylon**. This is a fabric that is cheap and easy to wash. Moreover, it does not ³⁾get wrinkled easily, so it is used to make all kinds of clothing. Now, let's look at page 105 in our textbook for more information on these fabrics.

남 안녕하세요, 여러분. 이전에, 우리는 기술이 패션 산업을 어떻게 변화시켰는지에 대해 이야기했습니다. 오늘은, 몇 가지 일반적인 직물의 장점에 대해 이야기하려고 합니다. 첫째, 면은 가장 인기 있는 직물 중 하나입니다. 목화로 만든 옷은 부드럽고 편안합니다. 이 소재는 수분을 잘 흡수해서, 수건을 만드는 데 자주 사용됩니다. 다음으로, 양에서 나오는 양모가 있습니다. 이것은 열을 잘 가두기 때문에 코트, 스웨터, 목도리와 같은 겨울 의류를 만드는 데 사용됩니다. 또한, 누에에서 나오는 비단은 수백 년 동안 옷을 만드는 데 사용되어 왔습니다. 이것은 가볍고, 매끄럽고, 반짝거릴 뿐만 아니라 매우 튼튼합니다. 또 다른 튼튼한 직물은 나일론입니다. 이것은 싸고 세탁하기 쉬운 직물입니다. 게다가, 구김이 쉽게 생기지 않아 모든 종류의 옷을 만드는 데 사용됩니다. 이제, 이 직물들에 대한 더 많은 정보를 위해 교과서의 105페이지를 살펴보도록 하겠습니다.

[선택지]
16 ① 일반적으로 사용되는 직물들의 이점
② 인기 있는 직물들의 숨겨진 문제
③ 동물에서 나오는 직물의 종류
④ 천연 직물과 인공 직물의 비교
⑤ 기술이 패션 산업을 변화시킨 방법
17 ① 면 ② 리넨 ③ 양모 ④ 비단 ⑤ 나일론

16 몇 가지 일반적인 직물의 장점에 대해 이야기하고 있으므로 남자가 하는 말의 주제로 ① 'benefits of commonly used fabrics'가 가장 적절하다.
17 면, 양모, 비단, 나일론은 언급했지만 ② 'linen'은 언급하지 않았다.

[어휘] technology 명 기술 advantage 명 장점, 이점 common 형 일반적인 fabric 명 직물 made from ~으로 만든 cotton plant 목화 absorb 통 흡수하다 moisture 명 수분, 습기 come from ~에서 나오다 trap 통 가두다 heat 명 열 light 형 가벼운 smooth 형 매끄러운, 부드러운 wrinkle 통 구김이 생기다 명 주름 comparison 명 비교 man-made 형 인공의

1	⑤	2	③	3	②	4	④	5	③	6	④	7	①	8	⑤	9	②	10	④
11	②	12	③	13	⑤	14	②	15	④	16	①	17	③						

• 각 문제의 정답 근거는 굵은 글씨로, Dictation 정답은 밑줄로 표시되어 있습니다.

1   목적 파악   정답 ⑤

W Good morning, Bluetech Company employees. This is Dana Brand from the marketing department. As you know, we ¹⁾will be celebrating the company's 50th anniversary next month. In honor of this, we have decided to design a new company logo, and we need your help! **We are ²⁾holding a logo design contest, and all employees are welcome to enter.** The winning logo will be chosen based on the quality and originality of the design. All entries must ³⁾include the color blue to match our company's name. Please send me your work by e-mail. I look forward to seeing your designs!

여 좋은 아침입니다, Bluetech Company 직원 여러분. 마케팅 부서의 Dana Brand입니다. 아시다시피, 우리는 다음 달에 회사 창립 50주년 기념식을 거행할 예정입니다. 이를 기념하여, 새로운 회사 로고를 디자인하기로 결정했고, 여러분의 도움이 필요합니다! 로고 디자인 공모전을 열 예정으로, 모든 직원들의 참여를 환영합니다. 우승 로고는 디자인의 품질과 독창성에 근거하여 선정될 것입니다. 모든 출품작은 우리 회사의 이름과 어울리게끔 파란색을 포함해야 합니다. 여러분의 작품을 이메일로 보내주세요. 여러분의 디자인을 볼 수 있기를 기대하겠습니다!

여자가 Bluetech Company에서 새로운 회사 로고 디자인 공모전을 진행하고 있다고 하면서, 심사 기준과 출품작의 조건을 알려주고 있다. 따라서, 여자가 하는 말의 목적으로 ⑤ '회사 로고 디자인 공모전을 안내하려고'가 가장 적절하다.

어휘   employee 몡 직원   department 몡 부서   in honor of ~을 기념하여   enter 동 참여하다; 들어가다   based on ~에 근거하여   quality 몡 품질   originality 몡 독창성   entry 몡 출품작   include 동 포함하다   match 동 어울리다   look forward to ~을 기대하다

2   의견 파악   정답 ③

W Have you ¹⁾submitted your university application, Tony?
M Not yet, Mom. I can't decide what to major in. I'm interested in computer science, but I think I should study business.
W Well, let's talk about it. What do you like about computer science?
M I love computers. My dream is to ²⁾develop computer programs that improve people's lives.
W That's great. Now, why do you think you should study business?
M I also want to make lots of money. CEOs are usually paid very well.
W I see. **I think you should choose to do what you love ³⁾as a career.**
M But money is important, too.
W Of course. But if you enjoy what you do, you'll have a greater ⁴⁾chance of success. The money will come later.
M That makes sense. Then, I should study computer science.

여 Tony, 대학 지원서 제출했니?
남 아직이요, 엄마. 무엇을 전공해야 할지 모르겠어요. 전 컴퓨터 공학에 관심이 있는데, 경영학을 공부해야 할 것 같아요.
여 음, 이야기해보자꾸나. 컴퓨터 공학의 어떤 점이 좋니?
남 전 컴퓨터를 정말 좋아해요. 제 꿈은 사람들의 삶을 향상시키는 컴퓨터 프로그램을 개발하는 거예요.
여 좋네. 자, 왜 경영학을 공부해야 한다고 생각하니?
남 돈도 많이 벌고 싶거든요. CEO들은 보통 보수가 좋으니까요.
여 그렇구나. 나는 네가 좋아하는 일을 직업으로 선택해야 한다고 생각한단다.
남 하지만 돈도 중요하잖아요.
여 물론이지. 하지만 네가 하는 일을 즐긴다면, 성공할 가능성이 더 클 거야. 돈은 나중에 따라올 거란다.
남 말이 되네요. 그럼, 컴퓨터 공학을 공부해야겠어요.

대학 전공을 고민하고 있는 남자에게 여자가 좋아하는 일을 직업으로 선택해야 한다고 생각한다고 했다. 따라서, 여자의 의견으로 ③ '좋아하는 일을 직업으로 선택해야 한다.'가 가장 적절하다.

어휘   submit 동 제출하다   application 몡 지원서; 지원   major in ~을 전공하다   business 몡 경영학; 사업   develop 동 개발하다   be paid well 보수가 좋다   make sense 말이 되다

3 관계 파악
정답 ②

W	It's great to meet you, Mr. Cooper.
M	You too, Ms. Harris. I've heard so much about you from my son.
W	**Derek is a wonderful student. He's doing well in class.**
M	That's good to hear. I ¹⁾was concerned because we had to move right in the middle of the school year.
W	He was a bit shy when he first entered my class, but he's making friends and getting used to the new environment.
M	Is there anything he ²⁾needs help with?
W	Well, I think he's having trouble reading the board from the back of the class.
M	Oh, really? I should take him to ³⁾get his eyes checked.
W	Yes. I think that would be a good idea.
M	Thank you for letting me know.

여	만나서 반갑습니다, Cooper 씨.
남	저도요, Harris 선생님. 제 아들에게서 말씀 많이 들었습니다.
여	Derek은 훌륭한 학생이에요. 수업을 잘 듣고 있어요.
남	다행이네요. 학년 중간에 바로 이사를 와야 해서 걱정했거든요.
여	반에 처음 들어왔을 때는 좀 수줍어했지만, 친구들을 사귀고 새로운 환경에 익숙해지고 있어요.
남	아이에게 도움이 필요한 게 있을까요?
여	음, 제 생각에 아이가 교실 뒤에서 칠판을 읽는 데 어려움을 겪고 있는 것 같아요.
남	오, 정말요? 시력 검사를 받으러 데려가야겠네요.
여	네. 그게 좋을 것 같습니다.
남	알려주셔서 감사합니다.

두 사람이 남자의 아들의 학교생활에 대해 이야기하고 있다. 여자는 남자의 아들이 훌륭한 학생이며 수업을 잘 듣고 있다고 했고, 남자는 학년 중간에 이사를 와야 해서 걱정했었다면서 아들의 새 학교 적응에 대해 여자에게 묻는 것으로 보아 두 사람의 관계로 ② '교사 — 학부모'가 가장 적절하다.

어휘 concerned 형 걱정하는 school year 학년 make a friend 친구를 사귀다 get used to ~에 익숙해지다 environment 명 환경 board 명 칠판

4 그림 내용 불일치 파악
정답 ④

M	Hi, Aunt Tina. It looks like you did some remodeling here in the living room.
W	Yeah, we changed a few things this summer. What do you think?
M	Oh, I love the new L-shaped sofa.
W	Thanks! We wanted to get one that ¹⁾more people could sit on.
M	It's perfect for that. It was a good idea to install a new shelf above the fireplace, too.
W	I thought so. I wanted the room to look more modern.
M	And you moved that plant ²⁾into the corner, right?
W	Yeah! Good eye. **What do you think about the round coffee table?**
M	I much prefer it to the old one.
W	We're thinking about replacing the polka dot rug, too.
M	Really? I think it makes the room more fun.
W	The dots are ³⁾too distracting.
M	Hmm... Maybe you're right.

남	안녕하세요, Tina 이모. 여기 거실에 리모델링을 좀 하신 것 같네요.
여	응, 이번 여름에 몇 가지를 바꿨어. 어떻게 생각하니?
남	오, 새로 사신 L자형 소파가 마음에 들어요.
여	고마워! 더 많은 사람들이 앉을 수 있는 것을 사고 싶었거든.
남	그 용도로 딱 좋네요. 벽난로 위에 새 선반을 설치한 것도 좋은 생각인 것 같아요.
여	나도 그렇게 생각한다. 공간이 좀 더 현대적으로 보이기를 원했어.
남	그리고 식물을 구석으로 옮기신 거죠?
여	응! 잘 알아보는구나. 둥근 커피 테이블은 어떻니?
남	예전 것보다 훨씬 더 좋아요.
여	물방울무늬 러그도 교체할까 생각 중이야.
남	정말요? 이게 공간을 더 유쾌하게 만드는 것 같은데요.
여	물방울무늬가 너무 산만해.
남	흠... 그 말이 맞을 수도 있겠네요.

대화에서 여자가 둥근 커피 테이블은 어떤지 물었는데, ④에는 사각형 모양의 커피 테이블이 그려져 있다.

어휘 fireplace 명 벽난로 move A into B A를 B로 옮기다 prefer A to B A를 B보다 더 좋아하다 replace 통 교체하다 polka dot 물방울무늬 distracting 형 산만한

5 할 일 파악
정답 ③

M	Hi, Erin. I'm Joseph. I'm in charge of the volunteers here at the hospital.
W	Nice to meet you. Is there some kind of orientation I need to go through?
M	Yes. I'll ¹⁾take you on a tour of the hospital. But before that, we need to do a couple of things. Here's your vest.
W	Thanks. Do I need to wear this while I'm volunteering?
M	Exactly. You should ²⁾keep it on at all times.
W	Got it. Oh, is there anywhere to store my coat and bag?
M	There's a locker area down the hall. **But please sign ³⁾this volunteer agreement first.**
W	**No problem.** Oh, do you have a pen I can borrow?
M	Sure. Here you go.
W	Thanks.

남	안녕하세요, Erin. 저는 Joseph입니다. 이 병원에서 자원봉사자들을 담당하고 있어요.
여	만나서 반가워요. 제가 거쳐야 할 오리엔테이션 같은 것이 있나요?
남	네. 병원 구경을 시켜 드릴게요. 하지만 그 전에, 우리는 두어 개의 일들을 해야 해요. 여기 조끼 받으세요.
여	감사합니다. 봉사활동을 하는 동안 이걸 입어야 하나요?
남	맞아요. 항상 입고 있어야 해요.
여	알겠습니다. 아, 제 코트와 가방을 보관할 곳이 있나요?
남	복도 끝에 개인 물품 보관함 구역이 있어요. 하지만 먼저 이 자원봉사 동의서에 서명해 주세요.
여	그럼요. 아, 펜 좀 빌릴 수 있을까요?
남	물론이죠. 여기 있어요.
여	고마워요.

병원의 자원봉사 담당자가 신규 자원봉사자에게 설명을 해주고 있다. 남자가 먼저 자원봉사 동의서에 서명해달라고 하자, 여자가 그러겠다고 했으므로 여자가 할 일로 ③ '동의서 서명하기'가 가장 적절하다.

어휘 in charge of ~을 담당하는 go through ~을 거치다, 겪다 vest 명 조끼 at all times 항상 store 통 보관하다 명 가게 locker 개인 물품 보관함 agreement 명 동의서; 동의

6 금액 정보 파악 　　　　　　　　　　　　　　　정답 ④

M	Welcome to HC Telecom.
W	Hi. I'd like to change my phone plan.
M	Sure. **Our Basic Plan is $25 a month, and the Premium Plan is $35 a month.** They're the most popular plans.
W	Can you ¹⁾tell me more about the Basic Plan?
M	It includes unlimited phone calls and text messages, and two gigabytes of data.
W	Hmm... That isn't enough data for me.
M	**Then, I recommend the Premium Plan.** You can use ²⁾as much data as you want.
W	Great. **I'll change my plan to that one. I'd also like to add a ringtone service.**
M	Certainly. **That will be an extra $5 a month.**
W	Okay. **I have this 10% off coupon ³⁾for the first month. Can I use it?**
M	**Yes.** Here is your total for the first month.

남　HC Telecom에 오신 것을 환영합니다.
여　안녕하세요. 휴대폰 요금제를 바꾸고 싶은데요.
남　물론이죠. 기본 요금제는 월 25달러이고, 프리미엄 요금제는 월 35달러입니다. 가장 인기 있는 요금제들이에요.
여　기본 요금제에 대해 좀 더 말씀해 주시겠어요?
남　무제한 전화와 문자 메시지, 2GB의 데이터가 포함되어 있어요.
여　흠... 저한테는 데이터가 충분하지 않네요.
남　그럼 프리미엄 요금제를 추천해요. 원하시는 만큼 데이터를 사용하실 수 있어요.
여　좋아요. 그걸로 요금제를 바꿀게요. 벨소리 서비스도 추가하고 싶어요.
남　물론입니다. 한 달에 5달러가 추가되겠습니다.
여　알겠습니다. 첫 달 10% 할인 쿠폰을 가지고 있는데요. 이걸 쓸 수 있나요?
남　네. 여기 첫 달 총액입니다.

여자가 프리미엄 요금제($35)에 벨소리 서비스($5)를 추가하고, 첫 달 10% 할인($40×0.9=$36)을 받았으므로 정답은 ④ '$36'이다.

[어휘] plan 阌 요금제; 계획　popular 阍 인기 있는　unlimited 阍 무제한의　add 阋 추가하다, 더하다　ringtone 阌 벨소리　extra 阍 추가의

7 이유 파악 　　　　　　　　　　　　　　　　　정답 ①

M	Can I talk to you, Ms. Wallace? It's about the history report.
W	Sure, Kevin. What is it?
M	I won't be able to finish it ¹⁾by the deadline.
W	How come? Are you having trouble thinking of a topic?
M	No. I've decided to write about the Korean War.
W	Okay. Then, is it because you can't find enough information on it?
M	That's not a problem. There are a lot of books about it at the library.
W	Then, it must be because you're busy with ²⁾student council activities.
M	**Actually, it's because my mother ³⁾just had surgery. I'm going to care for her in the hospital for a few days.**
W	Oh, I see. In that case, I'll give you an extra three days to work on it. And ⁴⁾take good care of your mother.
M	I will. Thank you.

남　Wallace 선생님, 말씀 좀 드릴 수 있을까요? 역사 보고서에 관해서요.
여　물론이지, Kevin. 무엇이니?
남　제가 이걸 마감일까지 끝낼 수 없을 것 같아요.
여　왜? 주제를 생각해내는 데 어려움을 겪고 있니?
남　아니요. 전 한국 전쟁에 대해 쓰기로 했어요.
여　알겠다. 그렇다면, 그에 대한 충분한 정보를 찾을 수 없어서 그러니?
남　그건 문제가 아니에요. 도서관에는 관련 서적이 많이 있어요.
여　그럼, 학생회 활동 때문에 바쁜 게 틀림없겠구나.
남　사실, 저희 어머니가 막 수술을 받으셔서요. 며칠 동안 병원에서 병간호를 할 거예요.
여　아, 그렇구나. 그렇다면, 3일 더 작업할 수 있는 시간을 주마. 그리고 어머니를 잘 돌봐드리렴.
남　그럴게요. 감사해요.

남자는 역사 보고서를 마감일까지 끝낼 수 없을 것 같다고 하면서 어머니가 막 수술을 받아서 며칠 동안 병원에서 병간호를 할 것이라고 했으므로, 남자가 보고서 마감일을 맞출 수 없는 이유는 ① '어머니 간호를 해야 해서'이다.

[어휘] deadline 阌 마감일　How come? 왜?, 어째서?　be busy with ~으로 바쁘다　student council 학생회　activity 阌 활동　surgery 阌 수술　care for ~를 병간호하다
in that case 그렇다면, 이 경우에는

8 언급 유무 파악 　　　　　　　　　　　　　　　정답 ⑤

W	Leo, are you going to the Green Planet Special Lecture tonight?
M	Oh, what's that?
W	It's an event at **the Harborside Public Library**. The famous environmental scientist Bill Jensen is giving a talk.
M	Wow, I'm ¹⁾a big fan of his. Do I need to buy a ticket?
W	Yes, but you can buy it at the library. Tickets are **$5 each**.
M	Okay. What's the lecture about?
W	He will talk about **how to use less plastic ²⁾in our daily lives.**
M	That sounds interesting. What time does it start?
W	It starts at **7 p.m.** But I'm going early so that I can get a seat ³⁾near the front.
M	That's a good idea. Do you want to sit together?
W	Sure. Meet me in front of the library at 6:30.
M	All right. See you there.

여　Leo, 오늘 밤 Green Planet Special Lecture에 갈 거야?
남　오, 그게 뭐야?
여　하버사이드 공공 도서관에서 열리는 행사야. 유명한 환경학자 Bill Jensen이 강연할 거야.
남　우와, 난 그의 열렬한 팬이야. 티켓을 사야 하니?
여　응, 그런데 도서관에서 살 수 있어. 티켓은 한 장에 5달러야.
남　알겠어. 강의 내용이 뭐야?
여　그는 우리의 일상생활에서 플라스틱을 덜 사용하는 방법에 대해 말할 거야.
남　재미있겠는데. 몇 시에 시작해?
여　저녁 7시에 시작해. 그런데 나는 앞쪽에 자리를 잡으려고 일찍 갈 거야.
남　좋은 생각이야. 같이 앉을래?
여　물론이지. 6시 30분에 도서관 앞에서 만나.
남　좋아. 거기서 봐.

강연 장소(하버사이드 공공 도서관), 티켓 가격(5달러), 강연 주제(일상생활에서 플라스틱을 덜 사용하는 방법), 시작 시각(저녁 7시)에 대해 언급했고, ⑤ '참가 가능 인원'은 언급하지 않았다.

[어휘] environmental scientist 환경학자　give a talk 강연하다　daily life 일상생활

W What about :
M That works f

두 사람이 여자가 기자
면서 원하는 메이크업을

어휘 makeup 몡 메이

---

4 그림 내

M Hey, Kelly. V
W Hi, Ralph. It'
M Wow, that's
W I baked suga
the roof to n
M It almost loo
on the hous
W Yes, and do
M Yeah. That's
W You're right.
M The dog in f
W Thank you.

대화에서 여자가 문에

어휘 type 몡 종류 a

---

5 할 일 ㅍ

[Cell phone ring
M Hi, Jessica.
W Yeah. I'm lc
M Did you ma
W Don't worry
M That's a rel
W Good. She'
M What abou
W I've got tha
M Sounds go
sunny tod
W Okay, thar
M Then, see y

두 사람이 친구의 테니
으므로 여자가 할 일로

어휘 tournament
be supposec

---

9 내용 불일치 파악 정답 ②

W Attention, students. This is your English teacher, Ms. Rose. Our field trip will be on February 23rd. On that day, we will be ¹⁾attending a performance of Shakespeare's *Romeo and Juliet* at the New Classic Theater. **The bus to the theater will ²⁾leave the school at exactly 9:30 a.m.** So you must make sure that you are not late. We'll have lunch together ³⁾after the play ends. The fee for the field trip is $15, including the ticket and lunch. Please take one of these ⁴⁾permission forms, and bring it back to me by Friday with a parent's signature. Thank you.

여 주목해주세요, 학생 여러분. 여러분의 영어 선생님인 Rose 선생님입니다. 현장 학습이 2월 23일에 있을 예정입니다. 그날, 우리는 뉴클래식 극장에서 열리는 셰익스피어의 <로미오와 줄리엣> 공연에 참석할 것입니다. 극장으로 가는 버스는 정확히 오전 9시 30분에 학교에서 출발할 것입니다. 그러므로 반드시 늦지 않도록 하세요. 연극이 끝난 후에 함께 점심을 먹을 예정입니다. 현장 학습 비용은 티켓과 점심 식사 비용을 포함하여 15달러입니다. 이 허가서를 한 장 가지고 가서 금요일까지 부모님의 서명과 함께 제게 가져다주세요. 감사합니다.

현장 학습에 대한 안내 방송이다. 여자가 극장으로 가는 버스가 오전 9시 30분에 학교에서 출발할 것이라고 했으므로 ② '오전 9시 30분에 극장에 도착하는 일정이다.'는 내용과 일치하지 않는다.

어휘 field trip 현장 학습 performance 몡 공연 leave 동 출발하다, 떠나다 exactly 튄 정확히 make sure 반드시 ~하다 play 몡 연극 fee 몡 비용 permission form 허가서 signature 몡 사인

---

10 도표 정보 파악 정답 ④

W Hey, Tom. How about getting Martin a calendar for his birthday?
M Good idea. I remember he wanted one last year.
W I was looking at these photo calendars. We ¹⁾could include photos of the three of us together.
M They look good. But the small one is a little hard to read.
W **Let's get a medium or large calendar.**
M Okay, **but I don't think we should ²⁾spend more than $50.**
W That's fine. **What about the number of photos?**
M We need more than one picture per month.
W Yeah, but I don't think we'll find 36 photos to use.
M **Then, 24 will be perfect.**
W There are still ³⁾two to choose from.
M Hmm... One of them takes longer to process.
W **Let's get the one with ⁴⁾the shorter processing time, then.**
M That works for me!

여 안녕, Tom. Martin에게 생일 선물로 달력을 사주는 게 어때?
남 좋은 생각이야. 작년에 하나 갖고 싶어 했던 걸로 기억해.
여 내가 이 포토 달력들을 보고 있었어. 우리 셋이 함께 찍은 사진도 포함시킬 수 있어.
남 좋아 보인다. 하지만 작은 것은 읽기가 조금 어려워.
여 중간 또는 큰 달력으로 하자.
남 좋아, 그런데 50달러 이상은 쓰면 안 될 것 같아.
여 그게 좋겠어. 사진의 수는 어떻게 하지?
남 한 달에 한 장 이상의 사진이 필요해.
여 응, 하지만 쓸 수 있는 36장의 사진을 찾을 수 있을 것 같진 않아.
남 그럼, 24장이면 되겠네.
여 아직 선택할 수 있는 것이 두 가지가 있어.
남 흠... 그중 하나는 처리하는 데 시간이 더 오래 걸려.
여 처리 시간이 더 짧은 걸로 하자, 그럼.
남 나는 좋아!

두 사람은 중간 또는 큰 사이즈면서, 50달러 미만인 것 중에서, 24장의 사진이 들어가며, 처리 시간이 더 짧은 포토 달력을 골랐다.

어휘 calendar 몡 달력 the number of ~의 수 take long 오래 걸리다 process 동 처리하다

---

11 짧은 대화의 응답 파악 정답 ②

W Jack, what happened? Why do you have a cast on your leg?
M I ¹⁾slipped on the stairs and fell down. **My ankle is broken.**
W Oh, no! **Will it ²⁾take a long time to heal?**
M Yes. I can't walk on it for at least six weeks.

여 Jack, 무슨 일이야? 왜 다리에 깁스를 했어?
남 계단에서 미끄러져서 넘어졌어. 발목이 부러졌어.
여 오, 이런! 낫는 데 시간이 오래 걸려?
남 응, 적어도 6주는 걸을 수가 없어.

선택지 ① 그렇지 않아. 깁스할 필요조차 없어.
② 응. 적어도 6주는 걸을 수가 없어.
③ 물론이지. 엑스레이를 보니 발목이 멀쩡해.
④ 아닌 것 같아. 어제 아침에 일어난 일이거든.
⑤ 괜찮아. 의사 선생님이 당장 네게 외주실 거야.

남자가 발목이 부러졌다고 하자 여자가 낫는 데 시간이 오래 걸리는지 물었으므로, 이에 대한 응답으로는 회복 시간을 말하는 ② 'Yes. I can't walk on it for at least six weeks.'가 가장 적절하다.

어휘 have a cast 깁스를 하다 slip 동 미끄러지다 fall down 넘어지다 ankle 몡 발목 heal 동 낫다

1 목적

W Attention...
some m...
Cyber M...
of produ...
including...
toaster, ...
40% off.

여자가 TechStop...
가장 적절하다.

어휘 miss out o...
mark 통 표...

2 의견

M What we...
W I was ¹⁾h...
I hope y...
Well... I ...
M You shou...
W But he...
assignm...
M Yes, **but**...
them.
W That's tr...
M I underst...
W You're ri...

아들의 숙제를 도와...
요하다.'가 가장 적...

어휘 correct an...

3 관계

[Cell phone...

W Hello, N...
M Hi, Shar...
M I'm doin...
event or...
M What kir...
W **It's a pr...**
M **Oh, I he...**
W Thank y...
M Don't w...
or woul...
W I'd like a...
M No prob...

---

6 금액 정보 파악   정답 ④

M Welcome to Echo Bay Aquarium. How can I help you?	남 Echo Bay Aquarium에 오신 것을 환영합니다. 무엇을 도와드릴까요?
W Hello. ¹⁾**I'd like tickets for two adults and two students, please.**	여 안녕하세요. 어른 두 명과 학생 두 명 표 주세요.
M **Tickets are $30 each for adults and $25 for students.**	남 어른은 한 장에 30달러, 학생은 25달러입니다.
W Okay. Can we watch a movie at the Ocean Theater with these tickets?	여 알겠습니다. 이 표로 오션 극장에서 영화를 볼 수 있나요?
M No. You have to pay extra. **It's $10 for adults and $5 for students.**	남 아니요. 추가 요금을 내셔야 해요. 어른은 10달러, 학생은 5달러예요.
W I see. What's ²⁾playing right now?	여 그렇군요. 지금 뭘 상영하고 있나요?
M It's a documentary called *Reef Adventure*.	남 <Reef Adventure>라는 다큐멘터리예요.
W All right. **Can I get tickets for that, too?**	여 알겠습니다. 그 표도 살 수 있나요?
M **Sure.** So that's ³⁾admission and movie tickets for two adults and two students.	남 물론이죠. 그럼 어른 2명과 학생 2명의 입장권과 영화표이신 거죠.
W That's correct. **Can I use this coupon I found online? It's for $10 off the total.**	여 맞아요. 온라인에서 찾은 이 쿠폰을 쓸 수 있나요? 총액에서 10달러 할인돼요.
M **Yes, you can.** How ⁴⁾would you like to pay?	남 네, 쓸 수 있으세요. 계산은 어떻게 하시겠어요?
W I'll pay in cash.	여 현금으로 계산할게요.

여자는 수족관 입장권 어른 2장($30×2=$60), 학생 2장($25×2=$50)과 영화표 어른 2장($10×2=$20), 학생 2장($5×2=$10)을 구매했고, 10달러 할인($140-$10=$130)을 받았으므로 정답은 ④ '$130'이다.

어휘 pay extra 추가 요금을 내다 play 통 상영하다; 놀다 admission 명 입장권; 입장

---

7 이유 파악   정답 ②

W Hey, Michael. Why are you loading that fan into your car?	여 안녕, Michael. 왜 차에 선풍기를 싣고 있어?
M It's the one I bought yesterday. I'm taking it back ¹⁾for a refund.	남 이건 내가 어제 산 거야. 환불받기 위해서 반품할 거야.
W Oh, really? Did you finally find an air conditioner for a good price?	여 오, 그래? 마침내 좋은 가격의 에어컨을 찾은 거야?
M No. Those were still too expensive.	남 아니. 그것들은 아직 너무 비싸더라.
W I remember you wanted a black fan. Was the fan ²⁾the wrong color?	여 네가 검은색 선풍기를 원했던 걸로 기억해. 선풍기 색깔이 잘못됐어?
M That's not it. This one looks fine.	남 그게 아니야. 이건 괜찮아 보여.
W Is there any problem with it?	여 선풍기에 무슨 문제라도 있는 거야?
M No. It works perfectly.	남 아니. 이건 완벽하게 작동해.
W I know that the weather is supposed to get cooler soon. Maybe you don't need a fan anymore.	여 내가 알기로 날씨가 곧 선선해질 예정이야. 더 이상 선풍기가 필요 없나 보다.
M Summer is almost over, but it's still hot. **Actually, I just thought the fan ³⁾was too loud.**	남 여름이 거의 끝나가는데도, 여전히 더워. 사실, 선풍기 소리가 너무 큰 것 같아.
W Oh, yeah. That can be annoying.	여 오, 그래. 그게 짜증 날 수도 있지.
M Seriously. I just want to get my money back.	남 정말이야. 난 그냥 돈을 돌려받고 싶어.
W Good luck!	여 행운을 빌어!

남자는 어제 산 선풍기를 반품할 것이라면서 선풍기 소리가 너무 큰 것 같다고 말했으므로, 남자가 선풍기를 반품하려는 이유는 ② '소리가 너무 커서'이다.

어휘 take back ~을 반품하다 refund 명 환불 price 명 가격 work 통 작동하다; 일하다 perfectly 부 완벽하게 over 부 끝나서, 지나서 annoying 형 짜증나는 get back ~을 돌려받다

---

8 언급 유무 파악   정답 ②

W Do you want to hang out this weekend, Kyle?	여 이번 주말에 놀러 갈래, Kyle?
M I'd love to, but I can't. I'll be ¹⁾volunteering at a charity concert called Water for Life.	남 그러고 싶지만, 못 가. Water for Life라는 자선 콘서트에서 자원봉사를 할 거라서 말이야.
W That sounds interesting. When is it?	여 그거 재미있겠는데. 언젠데?
M It's on Saturday at **8 p.m.**	남 토요일 저녁 8시에 해.
W Luckily, I'll be free at that time. Can you tell me more about it?	여 운 좋게도, 난 그때 한가할 거야. 그것 관련해서 좀 더 말해 줄래?
M We're raising money to ²⁾provide clean water in Africa.	남 아프리카에 깨끗한 물을 공급하기 위해 돈을 모금할 거야.
W That sounds like a great cause.	여 좋은 목적인 것 같네.
M It is! And the tickets are only **$10 per person.**	남 맞아! 그리고 표는 1인당 10달러밖에 안 해.
W That's ³⁾not much at all. I'll definitely be there. Where is it being held?	여 전혀 비싸지 않네. 꼭 갈게. 어디서 열려?
M It will be at **Stanville Park.**	남 스탠빌 공원에서 열릴 거야.
W Okay. See you there.	여 알았어. 그럼 거기서 봐.

시작 시각(저녁 8시), 모금 목적(아프리카에 깨끗한 물을 공급하기 위해), 입장료(10달러), 행사 장소(스탠빌 공원)에 대해 언급했고, ② '수용 인원'은 언급하지 않았다.

어휘 hang out 놀다 charity 명 자선; 자선 단체 raise money 돈을 모금하다 provide 통 공급하다 cause 명 목적, 명분; 이유 definitely 부 꼭, 확실히

9 내용 불일치 파악

정답 ⑤

M Good afternoon, Lakefield High School students. This is your principal, Mr. Morris. I'd like to announce that we will have Yearbook Picture Day on October 12th. The photo shoots will start at 9:15 a.m. We'll call classes into the gym ¹⁾one by one starting then. After the photographer finishes with the individual pictures, we'll have group photo shoots. Your photos will be available on the ²⁾school website. To access them, you just need to log in to the website. **For students who will be absent from school on the 12th, there will be ³⁾a photo retake day on October 26th.** Thank you.	남 안녕하세요, 레이크필드 고등학교 학생 여러분. Morris 교장 선생님입니다. 10월 12일에 졸업 사진 촬영일이 예정되어 있음을 알려드립니다. 사진 촬영은 오전 9시 15분에 시작됩니다. 그때부터 한 학급씩 체육관으로 부르겠습니다. 사진작가님이 개인 사진을 다 찍은 후에는 단체 사진 촬영을 할 겁니다. 여러분의 사진은 학교 웹사이트에서 볼 수 있습니다. 사진을 입수하려면, 웹사이트에 로그인하기만 하면 됩니다. 12일 학교에 결석하는 학생들을 위해, 10월 26일에 재촬영일이 있습니다. 감사합니다.

졸업 사진 촬영일에 대한 안내 방송이다. 남자가 10월 26일에 사진 재촬영일이 있다고 했으므로 ⑤ '10월 12일에 재촬영이 있을 예정이다.'는 내용과 일치하지 않는다.

어휘 announce 통 알리다, 발표하다 photo shoot 사진 촬영 access 통 입수하다 명 접근 be absent from ~에 결석하다 retake 명 재촬영 통 탈환하다

10 도표 정보 파악

정답 ④

W Are you busy, Oliver?	여 바쁘니, Oliver?
M No, Susan. Do you need help with something?	남 아니, Susan. 뭐 도와줄까?
W I want to buy a new blanket, but there are ¹⁾too many options. Can you help me decide?	여 새 이불을 사고 싶은데, 선택지가 너무 많아. 결정하는 것 좀 도와줄래?
M Sure. What's your budget?	남 물론이지. 예산이 어떻게 돼?
W I can't spend more than $150.	여 난 150달러 이상은 못 써.
M Then, this one is too expensive. How big is your bed?	남 그럼 이건 너무 비싸네. 침대는 얼마나 크니?
W I have a queen-size bed, so ²⁾either a queen or king would fit.	여 퀸사이즈 침대가 있어서, 퀸이나 킹 둘 다 맞을 거야.
M That leaves these three options. What about washing it? Is it okay if the blanket can only be dry cleaned?	남 그러면 세 가지 선택지가 남네. 세탁은 어때? 이불을 드라이클리닝만 해야 한대도 괜찮아?
W It has to be machine washable. I don't want to spend time taking it to the cleaners.	여 세탁기로 세탁할 수 있어야 해. 세탁소에 가져가느라 시간을 쓰고 싶지 않아.
M Okay. What ³⁾kind of material would you like?	남 알겠어. 어떤 종류의 소재를 원해?
W I prefer cotton over wool.	여 양모보다는 면이 더 좋아.
M Great. Then, you should get this one.	남 좋아. 그러면, 너는 이걸 사야겠다.

여자는 150달러 미만인 것 중에서, 크기는 퀸이나 킹사이즈이고, 세탁기로 세탁할 수 있어야 하며, 소재는 면으로 된 이불을 골랐다.

어휘 option 명 선택지 budget 명 예산 fit 통 맞다 machine washable 세탁기로 세탁할 수 있는 material 명 소재, 재료 cleaner 명 세탁소 prefer A over B B보다 A를 더 좋아하다 wool 명 양모

11 짧은 대화의 응답 파악

정답 ①

W Honey, I'm going to ¹⁾the grocery store now.	여 여보, 나 지금 식료품점에 가려고 해.
M Okay. **Can you stop by the library, too?** Our library books are ²⁾due today.	남 그래. 도서관에도 들러줄 수 있어? 도서관 책이 오늘 만기야.
W I have to pick up the kids from school, so I won't have time. Can you ³⁾return the books?	여 학교에 아이들을 데리러 가야 해서 시간이 없을 거야. 당신이 책을 반납해줄 수 있어?
M No problem. I will go do that right now.	남 문제없어. 지금 바로 가서 할게.
	선택지 ① 문제없어. 지금 바로 가서 할게.
	② 물론이지. 언제든지 나랑 같이 가도 돼.
	③ 확실해. 아이들은 그곳에서 우리를 보고 기뻐할 거야.
	④ 그래? 오늘 도서관이 문을 닫은 줄 몰랐어.
	⑤ 알겠어. 식료품점에서 뭐 필요한 거 있어?

남자가 책을 반납하러 도서관에 들를 수 있는지 묻자 여자는 학교에 아이들을 데리러 가야 해서 시간이 없으니 남자에게 직접 반납해달라고 요청했으므로, 이에 대한 응답으로는 요청을 수락하는 ① 'No problem. I will go do that right now.'가 가장 적절하다.

어휘 grocery store 식료품점 stop by 들르다 due 형 만기인; ~하기로 되어 있는 pick up ~를 데리러 가다 return 통 반납하다

12 짧은 대화의 응답 파악

정답 ⑤

[Telephone rings.] **M** Hi. This is Dr. Miller's office. **W** Hi. My name is Elsa Peterson. **Is Dr. Miller** 1)<u>available</u> <u>today</u>? **My back really hurts.** **M** I'm afraid he's booked all day. 2)<u>The earliest he can see</u> you is tomorrow at 9:30 a.m. **W** That's fine. Please book an appointment for me.	[전화기가 울린다.] 남 여보세요. Miller 의원입니다. 여 안녕하세요. 제 이름은 Elsa Peterson이에요. Miller 의사 선생님 오늘 진료 가능하신가요? 허리가 너무 아파서요. 남 하루 종일 예약이 꽉 찼어요. 진료 보실 수 있는 가장 빠른 시간은 내일 오전 9시 30분이에요. 여 <u>괜찮아요. 제 예약을 잡아주세요.</u> 선택지 ① 맞아요. 그는 항상 일 때문에 너무 바빠요. ② 그래요? 저는 다음 주는 안 돼요. ③ 맞아요. 저는 집에 있어야 할 것 같아요. ④ 아니, 괜찮습니다. 진료받을 필요가 없어요. ⑤ 괜찮아요. 제 예약을 잡아주세요.

여자가 허리 때문에 오늘 진료가 가능한지 문의하는 상황에서 남자가 하루 종일 예약이 꽉 찼다며 내일 오전 시간 진료를 제안했으므로, 이에 대한 응답으로는 예약을 잡아달라고 하는 ⑤ 'That's fine. Please book an appointment for me.'가 가장 적절하다.

어휘 available 혱 시간이 있는; 이용 가능한   back 혱 허리   all day 하루 종일   book an appointment 예약을 잡다

13 긴 대화의 응답 파악

정답 ④

W What's wrong, Coach Stevens? You seem concerned. **M** I am, Principal Klein. **I'm worried about how I'll manage this year's soccer team.** **W** But you told me we have 1)<u>some talented new players</u>. **M** We do, but they don't work together on the field. They have trouble 2)<u>passing the ball around</u>. **W** Oh, no. What do you think the problem is? **M** **The players don't seem** 3)<u>comfortable with each other</u>. Some of them don't even celebrate when their teammates score a goal. **W** It sounds like you need to teach them the importance of team spirit. **M** You're right. I have to plan 4)<u>some training programs</u> to bring them together and strengthen their bond. **W** What about organizing a team meal so they can become friends off the field? **M** Good idea. The team should have dinner together.	여 왜 그러세요, Stevens 코치님? 걱정하시는 것처럼 보여요. 남 맞아요, Klein 교장 선생님. 올해 축구팀을 어떻게 관리할지 걱정이에요. 여 하지만 재능 있는 새로운 선수들이 있다고 하셨잖아요. 남 있죠, 그런데 그들은 경기장에서 협력하지 않아요. 공을 패스하며 돌리는 데 어려움을 겪고 있죠. 여 오, 이런. 문제가 뭐라고 생각하세요? 남 선수들이 서로 편하지 않은 것 같아요. 그들 중 몇몇은 심지어 팀원이 골을 넣었을 때도 축하해주지 않아요. 여 코치님께서 단체정신의 중요성을 가르쳐주셔야 할 것 같네요. 남 맞아요. 그들을 하나로 묶고 유대감을 강화하기 위한 몇 가지 훈련 프로그램을 계획해야겠어요. 여 경기장 밖에서 친구가 될 수 있도록 팀 식사를 준비하는 건 어때요? 남 <u>좋은 생각입니다. 우리 팀은 함께 저녁을 먹어야겠어요.</u> 선택지 ① 맞아요. 그들 대부분은 친한 친구들이에요. ② 아쉽네요. 우리에겐 가장 재능 있는 선수들이 있는데요. ③ 모르겠어요. 그들은 아마 다음 경기에서 질 거예요. ④ 좋은 생각입니다. 우리 팀은 함께 저녁을 먹어야겠어요. ⑤ 동의해요. 추가 훈련 시간을 마련할게요.

축구팀 선수들의 사이가 편하지 않아 어떻게 관리할지 걱정하는 상황에서 여자가 경기장 밖에서 선수들이 친구가 될 수 있도록 팀 식사를 준비하는 것은 어떤지 물었으므로, 이에 대한 응답으로는 좋은 생각이라고 답하는 ④ 'Good idea. The team should have dinner together.'가 가장 적절하다.

어휘 concerned 혱 걱정하는   manage 통 관리하다   talented 혱 재능 있는   work together 협력하다   celebrate 통 축하하다   score a goal 골을 넣다   team spirit 단체정신   bring ~ together ~를 하나로 묶다   bond 혱 유대감

14 긴 대화의 응답 파악

정답 ①

M Where have you been, Stacy? Our drama club's play is starting in 10 minutes. **W** I'm sorry, Mr. James. I 1)<u>don't feel very good</u> right now. **M** What's wrong? Do you need some medicine? **W** No. **I just don't think I can go on stage tonight.** My knees 2)<u>feel shaky</u>. **M** Ah, it sounds like you're a little nervous. I know what will help you. **You need to go to the dressing room and take deep breaths for five minutes.** **W** Okay. But what if I'm still nervous after that? **M** Once you get onto the stage, don't 3)<u>look at the audience</u>. **W** Then, where do I keep my eyes? **M** **You can stare at the back wall. Trust me. If you do these things, you'll** 4)<u>feel much better</u>. **W** Okay. I'll try to do what you've suggested.	남 어디 있었니, Stacy? 우리 동아리 연극이 10분 후에 시작해. 여 죄송해요, James 선생님. 지금 별로 상태가 좋지 않아요. 남 왜 그러니? 약 좀 줄까? 여 아뇨. 오늘 밤에는 무대에 못 나갈 것 같아요. 무릎이 떨려요. 남 오, 약간 긴장한 것 같구나. 무엇이 네게 도움이 될지 알고 있단다. 탈의실에 가서 5분 동안 숨을 깊이 들이쉬렴. 여 알겠어요. 하지만 그 후에도 제가 여전히 긴장하면 어떡하죠? 남 일단 무대에 오르면, 관객들을 쳐다보지 마. 여 그럼, 어디에 눈을 둬요? 남 뒤쪽 벽을 쳐다봐도 돼. 선생님을 믿으렴. 이렇게 하면 기분이 훨씬 나아질 거란다. 여 <u>좋아요. 제안하신 대로 해볼게요.</u>

① 좋아요. 제안하신 대로 해볼게요.

② 알겠습니다. 무대에서 더 많이 눈을 마주칠게요.

③ 걱정하지 마세요. 정말 잘 하실 거라는 걸 알아요.

④ 감사합니다. 조언이 정말 효과가 있었어요.

⑤ 그럴지도 몰라요. 탈의실 안을 다시 한번 볼게요.

무대에 서기 전 긴장한 여자에게 남자가 긴장감을 완화하는 방법을 알려주는 상황이다. 남자가 숨을 깊게 들이마시고 무대 위에서는 뒤쪽 벽을 쳐다보는 등의 방법을 해보라고 제안했으므로, 이에 대한 응답으로는 제안한 대로 해보겠다고 말하는 ① 'Okay. I'll try to do what you've suggested.'가 가장 적절하다.

어휘 medicine 명 약 knee 명 무릎 shaky 형 떨리는 nervous 형 긴장한 dressing room 탈의실 take deep breaths 숨을 깊이 들이쉬다 What if ~? ~이라면 어떡하지? audience 명 관객, 청중 stare at ~을 쳐다보다 make eye contact 눈을 마주치다

15 상황에 적절한 말 파악 정답 ④

W Eddie and Jessica are siblings. They have agreed to ¹⁾watch a film together on Saturday night. Eddie has been looking forward to watching this movie for a long time. But one hour before it is ²⁾about to start, Jessica calls to tell him that she cannot come to the theater. She forgot that she had dinner plans with her friends. This is ³⁾not the first time Jessica has canceled on Eddie at the last minute. **So Eddie wants to tell her that she should ⁴⁾manage her schedule more carefully.** In this situation, what would Eddie most likely say to Jessica?

여 Eddie와 Jessica는 남매입니다. 그들은 토요일 밤에 함께 영화를 보는 것에 대해 서로 동의했습니다. Eddie는 오랫동안 이 영화를 보기를 기대해 왔습니다. 하지만 영화가 막 시작되기 약 한 시간 전에, Jessica는 그에게 전화를 해서 극장에 올 수 없다고 말합니다. 그녀는 친구들과 저녁 약속이 있다는 것을 잊어버렸습니다. Jessica가 마지막 순간에 Eddie를 바람맞히는 것은 이번이 처음이 아닙니다. 그래서, Eddie는 그녀에게 일정을 좀 더 신중하게 관리해야 한다고 말하고 싶습니다. 이러한 상황에서, Eddie가 Jessica에게 가장 할 것 같은 말은 무엇입니까?

선택지 ① 오늘 내가 극장에 너무 늦게 도착해서 미안해.

② 네가 저녁을 다 먹고 나면 영화를 보러 가자.

③ 같이 내 친구들 보러 가지 않을래?

④ 네 일정을 철저히 확인해야 한다고 생각해.

⑤ 약속을 취소한 것에 대해 네 친구에게 사과해야 해.

Jessica가 친구들과의 저녁 약속이 있다는 것을 잊어버렸다가 마지막 순간에 Eddie를 바람맞히자, Eddie는 그녀에게 일정을 좀 더 신중하게 관리해야 한다고 말하려 한다. 따라서, Eddie가 할 말로 ④ 'I think you need to check your schedule thoroughly.'가 가장 적절하다.

어휘 sibling 명 남매, 형제자매 be about to 막 ~하려 하다 cancel on ~를 바람맞히다 at the last minute 마지막 순간에 thoroughly 부 철저히

16-17 세트 문항 정답 16 ① 17 ③

M Hello, everybody. Welcome to another episode of the *Planet Rangers* podcast. I'm your host Ken Thompson. **Today, I want to tell you about some simple ways to ¹⁾conserve resources and help the planet.** First, saving **water** is easy to do. Never ²⁾leave it running while you brush your teeth, and take short showers. You can also preserve **trees** by using less paper. For example, you can use mobile tickets instead of printed ones. Additionally, it's not hard to save **electricity**. Switch off the lights whenever you leave a room, and ³⁾use rechargeable batteries as much as possible. Finally, you can cut down on **gasoline** use by leaving your car at home and taking public transportation instead. Walking and cycling are other great ways to save on fuel while also getting exercise. These small actions can have ⁴⁾a big impact over time. Thank you for listening, and have a great day!

남 안녕하세요, 여러분. <Planet Rangers> 팟캐스트의 또 다른 에피소드를 들으러 오신 것을 환영합니다. 저는 진행자 Ken Thompson입니다. 오늘, 여러분께 자원을 보존하고 지구를 도울 수 있는 몇 가지 간단한 방법에 대해 말씀드리려고 합니다. 첫째, 물을 절약하기는 쉽습니다. 이를 닦는 동안 절대 물을 틀어놓은 채로 두지 마시고, 샤워를 짧게 하세요. 그리고 종이를 덜 사용함으로써 나무를 보존할 수 있습니다. 예를 들어, 모바일 티켓을 인쇄된 것 대신에 사용할 수 있습니다. 게다가, 전기를 절약하는 것은 어렵지 않습니다. 방을 나갈 때마다 불을 끄고, 가능한 한 재충전할 수 있는 건전지를 주로 사용하세요. 마지막으로, 여러분은 차를 집에 두고 대신 대중교통을 이용함으로써 휘발유 사용을 줄일 수 있습니다. 걷기와 자전거 타기는 운동도 하면서 연료를 절약할 수 있는 또 다른 좋은 방법입니다. 이런 작은 행동들이 시간이 지나면서 큰 영향을 끼칠 수 있습니다. 들어주셔서 감사하고, 좋은 하루 보내세요!

선택지 16 ① 자원을 절약하기 위한 방법

② 가정에서 쓰레기를 줄이는 쉬운 방법

③ 지구에서 자원을 얻는 방법

④ 지구가 직면한 환경 문제

⑤ 천연자원의 중요성

17 ① 물 ② 나무 ③ 석탄 ④ 전기 ⑤ 휘발유

16 자원을 보존하고 지구를 도울 수 있는 몇 가지 간단한 방법에 대해 말하고 있으므로 남자가 하는 말의 주제로 ① 'tips for conserving resources'가 가장 적절하다.

17 물, 나무, 전기, 휘발유는 언급했지만 ③ 'coal'은 언급하지 않았다.

어휘 conserve 동 보존하다 resource 명 자원 planet 명 지구; 행성 brush one's teeth 이를 닦다 take a shower 샤워를 하다 preserve 동 보존하다 instead of ~ 대신에 switch off ~을 끄다 rechargeable 형 재충전할 수 있는 as ~ as possible 가능한 한 ~하게 cut down on ~을 줄이다 public transportation 대중교통 fuel 명 연료 impact 명 영향 over time 시간이 지나면서 obtain 동 얻다 face 동 직면하다 명 얼굴

1	④	2	①	3	①	4	④	5	④	6	③	7	①	8	②	9	⑤	10	④
11	③	12	⑤	13	①	14	②	15	③	16	②	17	③						

• 각 문제의 정답 근거는 굵은 글씨로, Dictation 정답은 밑줄로 표시되어 있습니다.

---

1 목적 파악   정답 ④

W Greetings, patients! This is Allison from Princeton Hospital. **I'd like to inform you that we have a** <u>¹⁾new online booking system</u>**. You can now visit our website to make a doctor's appointment. The system is simple to use.** First, ²⁾<u>create an account</u> and log in. Then, click on "Manage My Appointments." On the next screen, select your doctor to check availability. Choose your preferred date and time. Lastly, type the reason for your appointment, and ³⁾<u>confirm your reservation</u>. You can also reschedule or cancel your appointments online. We hope this system will make scheduling appointments more convenient. Thank you.

여 안녕하세요, 환자 여러분! 프린스턴 병원의 Allison입니다. 새로운 온라인 예약 시스템이 생겼음을 알려드립니다. 이제 저희 웹사이트를 방문하셔서 진료 예약을 하실 수 있습니다. 시스템은 사용하기 쉽습니다. 먼저, 계정을 만들고 로그인합니다. 그런 다음, '내 예약 관리'를 누릅니다. 다음 화면에서, 의사를 선택하여 예약 가능 여부를 확인합니다. 원하는 날짜와 시간을 선택합니다. 마지막으로, 예약 사유를 입력하고, 예약을 확정합니다. 온라인으로 예약을 변경하거나 취소하실 수도 있습니다. 이 시스템이 예약을 잡으시는 데 더 편리하기를 바랍니다. 감사합니다.

여자가 프린스턴 병원에 새로운 온라인 예약 시스템이 생겼다면서, 온라인 진료 예약 방법을 차례대로 알려주고 있다. 따라서, 여자가 하는 말의 목적으로 ④ '온라인 진료 예약 방법을 설명하려고'가 가장 적절하다.

어휘 inform 통 알리다 booking 명 예약 make a doctor's appointment 진료 예약을 하다 create 통 만들다 account 명 계정, 계좌 select 통 선택하다 type 통 입력하다 명 종류 confirm 통 확정하다 reservation 명 예약 convenient 형 편리한

---

2 의견 파악   정답 ①

M Andrea, don't you have to ¹⁾<u>submit your essay</u> tomorrow morning?
W Yes, Dad. I'll work on it after I watch this TV program.
M How much more do you have left?
W Honestly... I haven't started writing it yet.
M It's already 5 p.m. You don't have much time.
W It's just a short essay, so it ²⁾<u>won't take long</u>.
M That's not a good idea. **You should not put off your work** ³⁾<u>until the last minute</u>.
W But I usually do better under pressure.
M Didn't you make the same mistake last time you had an essay assignment?
W You're right. I turned that one in late, and I got a bad grade.
M That's the point. ⁴⁾<u>Never wait until</u> **the last minute to do your work.** You can relax and watch TV after finishing the essay.

남 Andrea, 너 내일 아침에 에세이를 제출해야 하지 않니?
여 네, 아빠. 이 TV 프로그램을 보고 나서 할 거예요.
남 남은 양이 얼마나 되니?
여 솔직히... 아직 쓰는 걸 시작하지 않았어요.
남 벌써 오후 5시란다. 시간이 많지 않아.
여 짧은 에세이니까, 오래 걸리지 않을 거예요.
남 그건 좋은 생각이 아니야. 너의 일을 마지막 순간까지 미루면 안 돼.
여 하지만 저는 보통 압박감을 느끼면 더 잘해요.
남 지난번에 에세이 과제를 했을 때도 같은 실수를 하지 않았니?
여 맞아요. 늦게 제출해서 형편없는 점수를 받았어요.
남 바로 그거야. 일을 하기 위해 마지막 순간까지 기다리지 말렴. 에세이를 다 쓴 후에는 편안하게 TV를 볼 수 있잖니.

에세이 쓰기를 미루고 있는 여자에게 남자가 일을 마지막 순간까지 미루면 안 된다고 했다. 따라서 남자의 의견으로 ① '해야 할 일을 마지막 순간까지 미뤄서는 안 된다.'가 가장 적절하다.

어휘 submit 통 제출하다 put off ~을 미루다 last minute 마지막 순간, 막판 under pressure 압박감을 느끼는 make a mistake 실수를 하다 turn in ~을 제출하다

3 관계 파악

정답 ①

[Cell phone rings.] **W** Hello? This is Lynn Sawyer. **M** Hi. It's Donald Porter from *Science for Life*. **W** Ah, Mr. Porter. It's nice to hear from you again. **I liked ¹⁾<u>your last article on</u> the future of robotics.** **M** Thank you. **Now, I'm writing an article on artificial intelligence, and I know you're an expert in that field.** **W** Sure. I'd be happy to discuss my work on AI with you. **M** Great! When ²⁾<u>are you available</u>? **W** I'm busy this week, but I have some time the week after that. **M** Okay. Are you free next Tuesday at 10 a.m.? **W** Yes. That's fine. If you ³⁾<u>come to my lab</u>, I can show you around and answer any questions you have. **M** Thank you. See you then.	*[휴대폰이 울린다.]* 여 여보세요? Lynn Sawyer입니다. 남 안녕하세요. <Science for Life>의 Donald Porter입니다. 여 아, Porter 씨. 또 연락을 받게 되어 기쁘네요. 로봇 공학의 미래에 대한 당신의 지난 기사는 아주 좋았어요. 남 감사합니다. 지금, 저는 인공지능에 대한 기사를 쓰고 있고, 선생님께서 그 분야의 전문가이신 것을 알고 있어요. 여 그럼요. AI에 대한 제 연구에 대해 기꺼이 이야기하고 싶군요. 남 좋습니다! 언제 시간이 되시나요? 여 이번 주는 바쁘지만, 그다음 주에는 시간이 좀 있어요. 남 알겠습니다. 다음 주 화요일 오전 10시에 시간 있으세요? 여 네. 괜찮아요. 제 연구실로 오시면, 구경시켜 드리고 어떤 질문이든 대답해 드릴게요. 남 감사합니다. 그때 봬요.

두 사람이 인공지능에 대해 이야기하기 위해 약속을 잡고 있다. 여자는 남자의 지난 기사가 마음에 들었다고 했고, 남자는 여자가 인공지능 분야의 전문가인 것을 알고 있다고 하는 것으로 보아 두 사람의 관계로 ① '인공지능 전문가 — 기자'가 가장 적절하다.

어휘 hear from ~로부터 연락을 받다 article 뗑 기사 artificial intelligence 인공 지능 expert 뗑 전문가 field 뗑 분야; 들판 discuss 통 이야기하다, 논의하다 show ~ around ~를 구경시켜 주다

4 그림 내용 불일치 파악

정답 ④

M Hi, Mandy. I rearranged my bedroom. Do you want to see a picture? **W** Okay. *[Pause]* That's ¹⁾<u>a cool car poster</u> on the wall. **M** Thanks. I just bought it last week. **W** Did you get a new blanket, too? This blanket has a star pattern on it. **M** Yeah. My mom got it for me. It's really warm. **W** That's awesome. I see your dog sleeping ²⁾<u>next to the bed</u>. **M** Yeah, he likes to sleep in my room sometimes. **That's why I put the two heart-shaped cushions ³⁾<u>in the corner</u>.** They're for him. **W** That's so sweet. **M** Do you notice anything else that's new? **W** Is that ⁴⁾<u>plant by the window</u> the one I gave you? It grew so much! **M** That's right. I had to change the pot. Thanks again. **W** You're welcome.	남 안녕, Mandy. 내 침실을 재배치했거든. 사진 볼래? 여 그래. *[잠시 멈춤]* 벽에 멋진 자동차 포스터가 붙어 있네. 남 고마워. 지난주에 막 샀어. 여 이불도 새로 샀어? 이불에 별 무늬가 그려져 있네. 남 응. 엄마가 사주셨어. 정말 따뜻해. 여 좋네. 침대 옆에서 자고 있는 너희 개가 보여. 남 응, 가끔씩 내 방에서 자는 걸 좋아하거든. 그래서 하트 모양의 쿠션 두 개를 구석에 두었어. 그 녀석을 위한 거야. 여 정말 다정하네. 남 또 다른 새로운 것은 못 알아차리겠어? 여 창가에 있는 저 식물이 내가 줬던 거야? 정말 많이 자랐어! 남 맞아. 화분을 갈아야 했어. 다시 한번 고마워. 여 천만에.

대화에서 남자가 하트 모양의 쿠션 두 개를 구석에 두었다고 말했는데, ④에는 원형 쿠션 두 개가 그려져 있다.

어휘 rearrange 통 재배치하다 blanket 뗑 이불, 담요 notice 통 알아차리다 pot 뗑 화분; 냄비

5 할 일 파악

정답 ④

W Scott, did you hang the laundry? **M** Yes, Mom. I ¹⁾<u>vacuumed the whole house</u>, too. **W** Thanks, dear. You've been a big help while I've been busy with work. **M** Well, it's winter vacation, so I have lots of time to help out. **W** Okay, but I still want you to enjoy your vacation. Is there anything you'd be interested in doing? **M** Yes. I want to go to a sports camp. **W** **My friend's son is going to a ski camp. Should I ²⁾<u>call her</u> and get more information about it?** **M** **Sure!** That sounds like fun. Oh, I'm ³⁾<u>making some hot chocolate</u>. Do you want some? **W** Of course. Thank you.	여 Scott, 빨래는 다 널었니? 남 네, 엄마. 진공청소기로 집 전체를 청소하기도 했어요. 여 고맙다, 얘야. 내가 일 때문에 바쁜 동안 큰 도움이 되었어. 남 음, 겨울 방학이라서, 도와 드릴 수 있는 시간이 많아요. 여 좋아, 하지만 그래도 네가 방학을 즐기면 좋겠구나. 하고 싶은 일이 있니? 남 네. 스포츠 캠프에 가고 싶어요. 여 내 친구 아들이 스키 캠프에 갈 거란다. 그녀에게 전화해서 그에 대한 정보를 더 얻어볼까? 남 당연하죠! 재미있겠는데요. 아, 저 지금 핫초코를 만들 건데요. 좀 드릴까요? 여 물론이지. 고맙다.

겨울 방학에 할 일에 대해 이야기하고 있다. 여자가 친구의 아들이 스키 캠프에 갈 것이라면서 그녀에게 전화해서 정보를 더 얻어볼지 묻자, 남자가 물론이라고 했으므로 여자가 할 일로 ④ '친구에게 전화하기'가 가장 적절하다.

어휘 laundry 뗑 빨래 vacuum 통 진공청소기로 청소하다 whole 헝 전체의 help out 돕다

6   금액 정보 파악   정답 ③

W Welcome to the Lotus Valley Music Festival. Can I help you?	여 Lotus Valley Music Festival에 오신 것을 환영합니다. 도와드릴까요?
M Hi. How much are the tickets?	남 안녕하세요. 티켓이 얼마예요?
W Standard tickets are $55. ¹⁾<u>Reserved seating tickets</u> are $80.	여 일반 티켓은 55달러입니다. 지정석 티켓은 80달러이고요.
M So... with the standard tickets, I wouldn't have a seat?	남 그러니까... 일반 티켓을 사면 좌석에 앉을 수 없나요?
W No. **And with reserved seats, you can watch the performances in a section closer to the stage.**	여 못 하세요. 그리고 지정석을 받으시면, 무대에 가까운 구역에서 공연을 관람할 수 있습니다.
M Great. I'll take two of those.	남 좋네요. 그걸로 두 장 살게요.
W Sure. **And for just $20 extra, you can buy a VIP Pass.** It will let you get ²⁾<u>free food and drinks</u> in the VIP Lounge.	여 네. 그리고 20달러만 더 내시면, VIP 패스를 구매하실 수 있어요. 그것으로 VIP 라운지에서 무료 음식과 음료를 이용하실 수 있습니다.
M Oh, that would be nice. **I'll get ³⁾<u>two passes</u>, please.**	남 오, 그거 좋겠네요. 패스 두 장 주세요.
W No problem. So that's two reserved seat tickets and two VIP Passes.	여 알겠습니다. 그럼 지정석 티켓 두 장과 VIP 패스 두 장이시지요.
M That's right. **And can I use this 10% discount coupon?**	남 맞아요. 그리고 이 10% 할인 쿠폰을 사용할 수 있나요?
W **Sure.** How would you like to pay?	여 물론이죠. 결제는 어떻게 하시겠습니까?
M I'll pay by credit card.	남 신용 카드로 결제하겠습니다.

남자가 지정석 티켓 두 장($80×2=$160)과 VIP 패스 두 장($20×2=$40)을 구매했고, 10% 할인($200×0.9=$180)을 받았으므로 정답은 ③ '$180'이다.

[어휘] standard 휑 일반의, 보통의 몡 표준, 기준   reserved seat 지정석   performance 몡 공연   section 몡 구역   close to ~에 가까운

---

7   이유 파악   정답 ①

W Hey, Oscar. Do you want to go running after school? The marathon is in a week.	여 안녕, Oscar. 방과 후에 달리기하러 갈래? 마라톤이 일주일 후야.
M I'm sorry, but I'm not participating in this year's marathon after all.	남 미안하지만, 난 올해 마라톤에는 결국 참가하지 않으려고.
W Why not? We've ¹⁾<u>been training for months</u>. Is it because you have to study for exams?	여 왜? 우리 몇 달 동안 훈련해 왔잖아. 시험공부를 해야 해서 그래?
M No. I'm already prepared for them.	남 아니. 그건 이미 준비가 되었어.
W Are you still hurt? You ²⁾<u>injured your knee</u> a while ago.	여 아직도 아파? 너 얼마 전에 무릎을 다쳤잖아.
M No. It's perfectly fine now.	남 아니. 이제 완전히 괜찮아.
W I don't understand why you'd drop out a week before the race.	여 왜 경기 일주일 전에 빠지려는 건지 모르겠어.
M Do you remember ³⁾<u>the photo contest</u> I entered last month?	남 내가 지난달에 참가했던 사진 대회 기억나?
W Yeah. You sent a photograph of a kangaroo.	여 응. 넌 캥거루 사진을 보냈었잖아.
M **Well, I won the grand prize! The reward for winning was a free trip to Australia. I'll leave tomorrow and stay there for nine days.**	남 음, 나 대상을 받았어! 우승에 대한 포상은 무료 호주 여행이었어. 내일 떠나서 9일 동안 거기에 머물 거야.
W No way! Congratulations!	여 말도 안 돼! 축하해!

남자는 올해 마라톤에는 결국 참가하지 않으려고 한다면서 사진 대회에서 우승하여 포상으로 무료 호주 여행을 가게 됐다고 했으므로, 남자가 마라톤에 불참하려는 이유는 ① '호주로 여행을 가게 돼서'이다.

[어휘] after all 결국   train 통 훈련하다 몡 기차   injure 통 다치다   drop out 빠지다, 손을 떼다   contest 몡 대회   enter 통 참가하다; 들어가다   grand prize 대상   reward 몡 포상, 보상
       No way! 말도 안 돼!

---

8   언급 유무 파악   정답 ②

W Dad, I'm so excited for Grandpa's 70th birthday party.	여 아빠, 할아버지의 칠순 잔치가 너무 기대돼요.
M Yeah, it will be great to see everyone. I haven't seen your aunt and uncle in a long time.	남 그래, 모두를 보게 되어 정말 좋을 거야. 네 이모와 삼촌을 한동안 보지 못했잖니.
W I know. We're meeting at **the Chinese restaurant downtown**, right?	여 그러게요. 시내에 있는 중식당에서 만나는 게 맞죠?
M That's right. I ¹⁾<u>booked the largest room</u> so that there will be enough space for everyone.	남 맞아. 모두에게 충분한 공간이 되도록 가장 큰 방으로 예약했단다.
W Good. When does the party begin?	여 좋아요. 파티는 언제 시작해요?
M The reservations are for **5 p.m.** next Sunday.	남 예약은 다음 주 일요일 오후 5시에 해두었어.
W Perfect. I also remember you saying that there will be ²⁾<u>eight different dishes served</u>.	여 완벽해요. 여덟 가지 다양한 요리가 제공될 것이라고 말씀하셨던 걸 기억해요.
M Yes, with barbecue duck as the main dish.	남 응, 바비큐 오리가 메인 요리지.
W Wow, I love barbecue duck! And do you think Grandpa will like my gift? I **painted a picture of him.**	여 우와, 전 바비큐 오리를 정말 좋아해요! 그런데 할아버지가 제 선물을 좋아하실까요? 할아버지 그림을 그렸는데요.
M It's ³⁾<u>a very thoughtful present</u>. He'll love it.	남 정말 사려 깊은 선물이네. 좋아하실 거야.
W I hope so.	여 그러시면 좋겠어요.

장소(시내에 있는 중식당), 시작 시각(오후 5시), 음식 가짓수(여덟 가지), 준비한 선물(할아버지를 그린 그림)에 대해 언급했고, ② '참석 인원수'는 언급하지 않았다.

어휘 in a long time 한동안 downtown 凰 시내에 space 똉 공간 dish 뗑 요리; 접시 serve 통 제공하다 thoughtful 뼹 사려 깊은

9 내용 불일치 파악   정답 ⑤

W	Good morning, everyone. I'm Karen Moon, the owner of Moon Yoga Studio. I'm happy to announce that we're offering a Summer Yoga Program. The classes will take place every Saturday here 1)at the community center. The first class is scheduled for next Saturday at 7 a.m. We'll accept both beginner and advanced students, so anyone can attend. However, attendees should bring their own yoga mat. **There is 2)no fee to take this class.** But I encourage all of you to become members of my studio so you can 3)get additional practice. If you enjoy the class, you can purchase a membership on my website. I hope to see you all soon!	여	안녕하세요, 여러분. 저는 Moon Yoga Studio의 사장 Karen Moon입니다. 저희가 여름 요가 프로그램을 제공한다는 것을 알려드리게 되어 기쁩니다. 수업은 매주 토요일 이곳 주민센터에서 진행될 예정입니다. 첫 수업은 다음 주 토요일 오전 7시로 예정되어 있습니다. 초급자와 상급자 모두 받고 있으니, 누구나 참석 가능합니다. 하지만, 참석자들은 각자 요가 매트를 가져오셔야 합니다. 이 수업을 듣는 것에는 수업료가 없습니다. 하지만 여러분들이 추가적으로 연습하실 수 있도록 제 스튜디오의 회원이 되시는 것을 권장합니다. 수업이 즐거우시면 저희 홈페이지에서 회원권을 구매하셔도 됩니다. 곧 여러분 모두를 만나길 바랍니다!

여름 요가 프로그램에 대한 안내 방송이다. 여자가 이 수업을 듣는 것에는 수업료가 없다고 했으므로 ⑤ '회원이 아니면 수강료를 지불해야 한다.'는 내용과 일치하지 않는다.

어휘 owner 뗑 사장; 주인 offer 통 제공하다 take place 진행되다, 열리다 be scheduled for ~로 예정되어 있다 advanced 뼹 상급의; 전진한 attendee 뗑 참석자 fee 통 수업료; 수수료 additional 뼹 추가적인 purchase 통 구매하다

10 도표 정보 파악   정답 ④

M	Welcome to Sports Stop. Please let me know if you need anything.	남	Sports Stop에 오신 것을 환영합니다. 필요한 게 있으면 말씀해 주세요.
W	Hi. Can you help me choose a water bottle?	여	안녕하세요. 물병 고르는 것 좀 도와주시겠어요?
M	Sure. These are our most popular water bottles. They come in many sizes.	남	물론이죠. 이것들이 가장 인기 있는 물병이에요. 다양한 크기로 나옵니다.
W	It has to 1)fit in my bag. **So anything over 700 milliliters would be too large.**	여	제 가방 안에 들어가야 해요. 그래서, 700ml가 넘는 것은 너무 클 거예요.
M	Okay. How much do you want to spend on it?	남	알겠습니다. 여기에 얼마를 쓰고 싶으신가요?
W	**I think $25 and under is reasonable.** I don't want to spend more than that.	여	25달러 이하가 합리적이라고 생각해요. 그보다 많이는 쓰고 싶지 않아요.
M	And 2)what about the material? We have plastic, stainless steel, and glass.	남	그리고 소재는 어떠세요? 플라스틱, 스테인리스, 유리가 있습니다.
W	I don't want a plastic bottle. **Either glass or stainless steel would be fine.**	여	플라스틱병은 원하지 않아요. 유리나 스테인리스 중 하나가 좋겠어요.
M	**Do you want it to come with 3)its own straw?**	남	빨대가 딸려 나오는 것을 원하시나요?
W	Sure. I'd like that. It'll be easier to drink from that way.	여	그럼요. 그게 좋죠. 그럼 마시기가 더 수월할 거예요.
M	Then, I recommend you get this one.	남	그렇다면, 이것을 사는 걸 추천해요.

여자는 용량이 700ml가 넘지 않는 것 중에서, 25달러 이하의 가격대이며, 유리나 스테인리스 소재로 되어 있고, 빨대가 딸려 나오는 물병을 골랐다.

어휘 choose 통 고르다 popular 뼹 인기 있는 come in ~으로 나오다, 출시되다 fit in ~안에 들어가다, ~에 맞다 spend on ~에 (돈, 시간을) 쓰다 reasonable 뼹 합리적인 material 뗑 소재 come with ~이 딸려 나오다 straw 뗑 빨대; 짚 recommend 통 추천하다

11 짧은 대화의 응답 파악   정답 ③

W	Ted, do you know a good place to get a men's haircut in our neighborhood?	여	Ted, 우리 동네에서 남자들 머리 자르기에 좋은 곳을 아니?
M	Yes. **Amigo Hair 1)is located across from our school. I'm a regular customer there.**	남	응. Amigo Hair는 우리 학교 건너편에 있어. 나는 거기 단골손님이야.
W	**That's good. My brother wants to 2)try a different hair salon.**	여	잘됐네. 내 남동생이 다른 미용실에 가보고 싶어 하거든.
M	I'm sure he will like the hairdresser there.	남	분명히 거기 미용사를 마음에 들어 할 거야.
		선택지	① 난 이번 주말에 머리를 자를 거야.
			② 너를 위해 미용실을 예약했어.
			③ 분명히 거기 미용사를 마음에 들어 할 거야.
			④ 네 머리를 염색하려면 그곳에 가야 해.
			⑤ 거기는 요즘 단골손님을 잃고 있어.

남자가 한 미용실을 추천해주며 자신이 그곳의 단골이라고 하자 여자가 잘됐다면서 그녀의 남동생이 다른 미용실에 가보고 싶어 한다고 말했으므로, 이에 대한 응답으로는 여자의 남동생이 그곳의 미용사를 마음에 들어 할 것이라고 말하는 ③ 'I'm sure he will like the hairdresser there.'가 가장 적절하다.

어휘 get a haircut 머리를 자르다 neighborhood 뗑 동네 regular customer 단골손님 hair salon 미용실 hairdresser 뗑 미용사

12 짧은 대화의 응답 파악

정답 ⑤

[Telephone rings.]

M This is King Toys. How can I help you?

W I'm looking for a nutcracker doll. Do you 1)have any in stock?

M Wait a second. [Typing sound] Yes, but there's 2)only one left. Should I set it aside for you?

W Yes, please. I'll be right there.

[전화기가 울린다.]

남 King Toys입니다. 무엇을 도와드릴까요?

여 호두까기 인형을 찾고 있어요. 재고가 있나요?

남 잠깐만요. [타자 치는 소리] 네, 그런데 하나밖에 안 남았어요. 챙겨둘까요?

여 네, 부탁합니다. 금방 갈게요.

선택지 ① 아니요, 괜찮습니다. 필요 없어요.

② 죄송해요. 당신을 도울 수 있으면 좋을 텐데요.

③ 어쨌든 고마워요. 나중에 다시 전화할게요.

④ 아니요. 모든 곳에서 품절이에요.

⑤ 네, 부탁합니다. 금방 갈게요.

여자가 호두까기 인형 재고가 있는지 묻자 남자가 하나밖에 안 남았다면서 챙겨둘지 물었으므로, 이에 대한 응답으로는 그렇게 해달라고 부탁하는 ⑤ 'Yes, please. I'll be right there.'가 가장 적절하다.

어휘 look for ~을 찾다 nutcracker doll 호두까기 인형 in stock 재고가 있는 set aside ~을 챙겨두다, 따로 떼어 두다 sold out 품절인

13 긴 대화의 응답 파악

정답 ①

W Honey, are we still going to 1)visit your parents for Thanksgiving this weekend?

M I want to, but I'm not sure if we can anymore.

W The car isn't fixed yet?

M No. The repairman says it won't be ready in time. I thought maybe we could 2)take a bus instead, but there are no tickets available.

W Yeah, Thanksgiving is just around the corner.

M I don't know what to do.

W Well, we could 3)rent a car.

M Won't that be expensive?

W But we don't have any other choice. Let's pick it up the day before we leave and start driving really early in the morning.

M That's a good idea. Then, we can beat the traffic.

W Exactly. It'll 4)be worth it to enjoy the holiday with family.

M You're right. I'll start researching rentals now.

여 여보, 이번 주말 추수감사절에 당신 부모님 댁에 가기로 한 거 맞지?

남 그러고 싶지만, 이제 그럴 수 있을지 모르겠어.

여 차가 아직 고쳐지지 않은 거야?

남 안 고쳐졌지. 정비사 말로는 제시간에 준비가 안 될 거래. 대신 버스를 탈 수 있을 거라고 생각했는데, 표가 없어.

여 응, 추수감사절이 곧이잖아.

남 어떻게 해야 할지 모르겠네.

여 음, 차를 빌리면 되지.

남 비싸지 않을까?

여 하지만 다른 선택의 여지가 없잖아. 출발하기 전날 차를 찾아와서 진짜 아침 일찍부터 운전해서 가자.

남 좋은 생각이야. 그러면, 교통체증을 피할 수 있겠어.

여 바로 그거야. 가족과 함께 연휴를 즐기려면 그럴 가치가 있을 거야.

남 맞아. 지금부터 대여를 알아보기 시작할게.

선택지 ① 맞아. 지금부터 대여를 알아보기 시작할게.

② 안됐네. 수리비가 비쌀 거야.

③ 확인해 보자. 우리가 탈 수 있는 버스가 있을지도 몰라.

④ 괜찮아. 차를 가지러 일찍 그곳에 갈 거야.

⑤ 스트레스 받지 마. 가지 않아도 당신 부모님께서 이해하실 거야.

추수감사절에 부모님 댁에 가기로 했으나 차 수리가 늦어져서 곤란해진 상황이다. 여자가 차를 빌리는 것을 제안하면서 비싸긴 하지만 그럴 가치가 있을 것이라고 말했으므로, 이에 대한 응답으로는 제안을 수락하며 대여를 알아보겠다고 대답하는 ① 'You're right. I'll start researching rentals now.'가 가장 적절하다.

어휘 anymore 图 이제, 더 이상 repairman 图 정비사, 수리공 around the corner 곧, 임박하여 rent 图 빌리다 pick up ~을 찾아오다, 가져오다 beat the traffic 교통체증을 피하다 worth 图 가치가 있는

14 긴 대화의 응답 파악

정답 ②

M Jenna, what are you doing on your laptop?

W I'm about to 1)join a virtual meeting, Dad. I recently joined an online book club.

M I 2)used to be in a book club, too. But we met at the local library.

W Oh, I didn't know that. Well, my book club meets online every Wednesday.

M That sounds convenient. What kind of books 3)do you discuss?

W All of the members are great fans of Ernest Hemingway. So we mostly read and talk about his books.

M Really? Are all the other members students like you?

W No. It's 4)a very mixed group. There's even one old woman from India.

M That's great. Are you enjoying the discussions with such a diverse group?

W Definitely. I love hearing various opinions and ideas.

남 Jenna, 노트북으로 뭐 하고 있니?

여 막 화상 회의에 참석하려는 참이에요, 아빠. 최근에 온라인 독서 모임에 가입했거든요.

남 나도 독서 모임을 했단다. 하지만 우리는 지역 도서관에서 만났지.

여 오, 그건 몰랐네요. 음, 저희 독서 모임은 매주 수요일마다 온라인으로 모임을 해요.

남 편할 것 같네. 어떤 종류의 책에 대해 토론하니?

여 모든 회원들은 어니스트 헤밍웨이의 열렬한 팬들이에요. 그래서 우리는 주로 그의 책을 읽고 이야기해요.

남 정말? 다른 회원들도 모두 너와 같은 학생들이니?

여 아뇨. 각양각색의 사람들이 모인 집단이에요. 심지어 인도 출신의 할머니도 한 분 계세요.

남 잘됐네! 이렇게 다양한 집단과의 토론을 즐기고 있니?

여 물론이죠. 저는 여러 의견과 생각을 듣는 것을 좋아해요.

선택지 ① 감사해요. 하지만 저는 헤밍웨이의 모든 책을 가지고 있어요.
② 물론이죠. 저는 여러 의견과 생각을 듣는 것을 좋아해요.
③ 네. 토론만이 문제를 해결할 수 있는 유일한 방법이에요.
④ 괜찮아요. 매주 새로운 책을 읽어도 괜찮아요.
⑤ 왜요? 저는 나이가 다른 친구들이 있다는 것이 좋다고 생각해요.

여자가 참여하고 있는 독서 모임에는 각양각색의 사람들이 모여 있고, 남자가 이러한 다양한 집단과의 토론을 즐기고 있는지 물었으므로, 이에 대한 응답으로 여러 의견과 생각을 듣는 것을 좋아한다고 대답하는 ② 'Definitely. I love hearing various opinions and ideas.'가 가장 적절하다.

어휘 be about to 막 ~하려는 참이다 virtual meeting 화상 회의 local 형 지역의 convenient 형 편한, 편리한 mixed 형 각양각색의; 혼합된 diverse 형 다양한 How come? 왜요?

15 상황에 적절한 말 파악

정답 ③

W Nicole and Nathan are classmates in high school. They are working on a group science project together. Nicole 1)suggests light pollution as their topic, and they agree to research it. But Nicole catches the flu and ends up missing a week of school. During this time, Nathan searches for some materials, but it isn't easy 2)to find anything useful. He also hears that another group is working on the same topic. **So when Nicole comes back to school, Nathan wants to tell her that they should** 3)change their topic. In this situation, what would Nathan most likely say to Nicole?

여 Nicole과 Nathan은 고등학교 반 친구입니다. 그들은 과학 조별 과제를 함께 수행하고 있습니다. Nicole은 빛 공해를 주제로 제안했고, 그들은 그것을 조사하기로 합의했습니다. 하지만 Nicole은 독감에 걸려서 결국 일주일 동안 학교를 결석하게 됩니다. 이 기간 동안, Nathan은 몇몇 자료들을 찾지만, 유용한 것을 찾기가 쉽지 않습니다. 그는 다른 조가 같은 주제를 수행하고 있다는 것 또한 들었습니다. 그래서 Nicole이 학교로 돌아오면, Nathan은 그녀에게 주제를 바꿔야 한다고 말하고 싶습니다. 이러한 상황에서, Nathan이 Nicole에게 가장 할 것 같은 말은 무엇입니까?

선택지 ① 다른 조에 도움을 요청하자.
② 도서관에서 더 많은 자료를 찾을 수 있어.
③ 우리가 다른 주제를 수행해야 한다고 생각해.
④ 내가 빛 공해에 대한 많은 정보를 찾았어.
⑤ 우리 과제를 끝낼 시간을 더 달라고 하는 게 어때?

Nathan은 빛 공해에 대한 유용한 자료를 찾는 것이 쉽지 않고 다른 조도 같은 주제라는 것을 알게 되어서, 조원인 Lucy에게 주제를 바꿔야 한다고 말하려 한다. 따라서, Nathan이 할 말로 ③ 'I think we should work on a different topic.'이 가장 적절하다.

어휘 light pollution 빛 공해 agree to ~하기로 합의하다 catch the flu 독감에 걸리다 end up 결국 ~하게 되다 useful 형 유용한

16-17 세트 문항

정답 16 ② 17 ③

M Good afternoon. In yesterday's session, we discussed how to build a shelter and find food if you are ever trapped on a mountain. **Today, we will look at what equipment you might need to** 1)keep yourself alive **on a deserted island.** First, it is important to have a **lighter.** That way, you can start a fire to keep warm and cook food. Next, a **knife** is necessary. It can be used to 2)cut sticks and vines, as well as to make a spear to catch fish. A **blanket** is also very useful. You can wrap yourself in it while you sleep, and it can 3)provide a comfortable place to sit during the day. Finally, a long piece of **rope** is another necessity. It can be used to tie up materials, which is useful for collecting items or building a shelter. I hope today's talk has given you some tips that will be helpful if you ever find yourself alone on 4)an isolated island.

남 안녕하십니까. 어제 수업에서는 산에 갇혔을 경우 대피소를 짓고 식량을 찾는 방법에 대해 논의했습니다. 오늘은, 무인도에서 생존해 있기 위해 필요한 장비가 무엇인지 살펴보겠습니다. 첫째, 라이터를 소지하는 것이 중요합니다. 그렇게 하면, 온기를 유지하고 음식을 요리하기 위해 불을 피울 수 있습니다. 다음으로, 칼이 필요합니다. 그것은 물고기를 잡기 위한 작살을 만드는 데 사용될 수 있을 뿐만 아니라, 나뭇가지와 덩굴을 자르는 데도 쓰일 수 있습니다. 담요 또한 매우 유용합니다. 잠자는 동안 담요를 몸에 걸칠 수 있고, 낮 동안에는 담요가 편히 앉을 장소를 제공할 수 있습니다. 마지막으로, 긴 밧줄은 또 다른 필수품입니다. 그것은 재료들을 묶는 데 사용될 수 있는데, 이는 물건을 모으거나 피난처를 짓는 데 유용합니다. 오늘의 논의가 여러분에게 외딴섬에서 홀로 됐다면 도움이 될 몇 가지 조언을 드렸기를 바랍니다.

선택지 16 ① 특정 지역에서 식량을 찾기가 어려운 이유
② 무인도에서 살아남기 위해 필요한 것
③ 고립된 지역에서 탈출하는 가장 좋은 방법
④ 유사시에 대비하는 것의 중요성
⑤ 산에 대피소를 짓는 방법
17 ① 라이터 ② 칼 ③ 텐트 ④ 담요 ⑤ 밧줄

16 무인도에서 생존해 있기 위해 필요한 장비가 무엇인지 살펴보고 있으므로 남자가 하는 말의 주제로 ② 'what is needed to survive on a deserted island'가 가장 적절하다.
17 라이터, 칼, 담요, 밧줄은 언급했지만 ③ 'tent'는 언급하지 않았다.

어휘 session 명 수업; (활동) 시간 trap 통 가두다 명 덫 alive 형 생존한, 살아 있는 deserted 형 사람이 살지 않는; 버림받은 start a fire 불을 피우다 vine 명 덩굴
as well as ~뿐만 아니라 spear 명 작살; 창 wrap oneself in ~을 몸에 걸치다 necessity 명 필수품 tie up ~을 묶다 isolated 형 외딴, 고립된
region 명 지역 escape from ~에서 탈출하다 prepare for emergencies 유사시에 대비하다

1	⑤	2	④	3	①	4	③	5	①	6	④	7	①	8	③	9	⑤	10	③
11	①	12	④	13	⑤	14	②	15	②	16	①	17	③						

• 각 문제의 정답 근거는 굵은 글씨로, Dictation 정답은 밑줄로 표시되어 있습니다.

1 목적 파악

정답 ⑤

W Attention, all passengers. Thank you for choosing the Lyon Bus Line for your trip. We want to 1)make sure that everyone has a comfortable trip on our buses. **That is why we would like to remind everyone of a new rule about food.** Recently, we've 2)received complaints about strong-smelling snacks and spilled beverages. **So passengers are no longer 3)allowed to bring food and drinks on the bus.** But don't worry! Your driver will make regular stops, so you will have a chance to eat during your trip. Thank you.

여 탑승객 여러분께 알려드립니다. 여행을 위해 Lyon Bus Line을 선택해 주셔서 감사합니다. 저희는 여러분 모두가 버스를 타고 편안한 여행을 하시게 하고 싶습니다. 그런 이유로 여러분에게 음식물에 관한 새로운 규칙을 다시 한번 알려드리려고 합니다. 최근 저희는 냄새가 심한 간식거리와 엎질러진 음료에 관한 불만 사항을 받았습니다. 그래서 탑승객들은 더 이상 음식과 음료를 가지고 버스에 탈 수 없습니다. 하지만 걱정하지 마십시오! 기사님이 정기적으로 정차하시니, 여행 중에 식사하실 기회가 있을 것입니다. 감사합니다.

여자가 Lyon Bus Line 탑승객들에게 더 이상 음식과 음료를 가지고 버스에 탈 수 없다는 새로운 규칙을 안내하고 있다. 따라서, 여자가 하는 말의 목적으로 ⑤ '버스 음식물 반입 금지를 당부하려고'가 가장 적절하다.

어휘 passenger 몡 탑승객 remind 통 다시 한번 알려주다, 상기시키다 complaint 몡 불만 사항, 불평 spill 통 엎지르다 beverage 몡 음료 no longer 더 이상 ~이 아닌 make a stop 정차하다, 멈추다

2 의견 파악

정답 ④

M What are you doing this weekend, Mandy?
W I'm going to a concert with my friends.
M Lucky you. That sounds like a lot of fun.
W What about you?
M I'm 1)doing some volunteer work on Saturday.
W Really? What exactly will you do?
M I belong to a student group that picks up trash in local parks.
W That 2)must be exhausting.
M It is, honestly. I am always surprised by how much garbage we see.
W Hasn't our city banned throwing trash on the ground in parks?
M Yeah, but the laws are not strict. **The city really needs to 3)increase the fine for this.**
W I agree. But until that happens, it is good that there are people like you to keep our parks clean.

남 이번 주말에 뭐 할 거야, Mandy?
여 친구들과 콘서트에 갈 거야.
남 잘됐네. 그거 정말 재미있을 것 같아.
여 너는?
남 토요일에 봉사활동을 할 거야.
여 정말? 정확히 뭘 할 거니?
남 나는 우리 지역 공원에서 쓰레기를 줍는 학생 모임에 소속되어 있거든.
여 그건 분명히 진 빼는 일이겠어.
남 솔직히, 그래. 우리가 얼마나 많은 쓰레기를 보게 되는지 항상 놀라.
여 우리 시에서 공원 땅바닥에 쓰레기 버리는 걸 금지하지 않았어?
남 맞아, 하지만 법이 엄격하지 않아. 시에서 이에 대한 벌금을 정말로 인상해야 해.
여 동의해. 하지만 그렇게 되기까지, 너처럼 공원을 깨끗하게 유지하려는 사람들이 있어서 다행이야.

시에서 공원 땅바닥에 쓰레기 버리는 것을 금지하지 않았는지 묻는 여자에게 남자가 법이 엄격하지 않다면서 벌금을 정말로 인상해야 한다고 했다. 따라서, 남자의 의견으로 ④ '쓰레기 투기에 대한 벌금을 인상해야 한다.'가 가장 적절하다.

어휘 Lucky you. 잘됐네. volunteer work 봉사활동 belong to ~에 소속되다, 속하다 pick up ~을 줍다 exhausting 혱 진을 빼는 garbage 몡 쓰레기 ban 통 금지하다 strict 혱 엄격한 fine 몡 벌금 혱 좋은

3 관계 파악

정답 ①

W	Thanks for meeting with me today.
M	No problem. I'm really excited to work with you on this project.
W	Great. **I think your art style will be perfect for** 1)**my new children's book**.
M	I hope so. **All of the characters you want me to draw are animals, right?**
W	That's correct. The story is about a group of animals living in the zoo.
M	Interesting. 2)How many illustrations will you need in total?
W	The book is 20 pages long. I want to include at least 10 pictures in it.
M	Okay. 3)When is the deadline?
W	I'd like you to finish everything by June 10th at the latest. Does that work for you?
M	That should be fine.

여	오늘 저를 만나주셔서 감사합니다.
남	천만에요. 당신과 이 프로젝트를 함께 하게 되어 정말 기쁜걸요.
여	좋네요. 제 생각에 당신의 화풍이 제 아동 도서 신작에 딱 맞을 것 같아요.
남	그러면 좋겠군요. 그려주길 바라시는 캐릭터는 모두 동물이죠, 맞나요?
여	정확해요. 그 이야기는 동물원에 사는 한 무리의 동물들에 관한 거예요.
남	흥미롭군요. 총 몇 개의 삽화가 필요합니까?
여	그 책은 20페이지 길이예요. 적어도 열 개의 그림을 담고 싶고요.
남	알겠습니다. 마감일은 언제죠?
여	늦어도 6월 10일까지는 모두 끝내 주셨으면 해요. 괜찮으실까요?
남	괜찮을 거 같네요.

두 사람이 아동 도서 프로젝트에 대해 이야기하고 있다. 여자는 자신의 아동 도서 신작에 남자의 화풍이 딱 맞을 것 같다고 했고, 남자는 여자에게 그려줄 삽화 캐릭터에 대해 물어보는 것으로 보아 두 사람의 관계로 ① '아동문학 작가 — 삽화가'가 가장 적절하다.

어휘 illustration 명 삽화 at least 적어도, 최소한 deadline 명 마감일 at the latest 늦어도

4 그림 내용 불일치 파악

정답 ③

M	Honey, I just finished setting up the backyard for the summer.
W	Wow. It looks great.
M	What about the 1)three lanterns hanging on the fence? Do you think they will provide enough light?
W	I do. If not, we can always add more. And the table with the two chairs in the middle of the yard looks really cozy.
M	I agree. We can have dinner there on summer nights.
W	**And the** 2)**striped umbrella above the table is very eye-catching.**
M	Yeah. It's also practical. It will keep the rain off us.
W	Oh, I see you moved the barbecue grill 3)next to the table.
M	Right. I thought that would be a good spot.
W	Good idea. The big tree beside it will provide shade while we cook.
M	Exactly. We need to stay cool.

남	여보, 내가 여름을 대비해 뒷마당 준비를 끝마쳤어.
여	우와. 멋져 보이는걸.
남	울타리에 걸려있는 세 개의 랜턴은 어때? 충분한 빛을 줄 수 있을까?
여	그렇다고 생각해. 그렇지 않다면, 언제든 더 추가할 수 있어. 그리고 마당 한가운데에 놓인 테이블과 의자 두 개가 정말 아늑해 보여.
남	동감이야. 우리는 여름밤에 저기에서 저녁을 먹을 수 있어.
여	그리고 테이블 위의 줄무늬 파라솔이 매우 눈길을 끄네.
남	응. 그건 실용적이기도 해. 비를 막아줄 거야.
여	오, 당신 바비큐 그릴을 테이블 옆으로 옮겼구나.
남	맞아. 거기가 좋은 자리인 것 같았어.
여	좋은 생각이야. 우리가 요리하는 동안 옆에 있는 큰 나무가 그늘을 드리울 테니까.
남	그러니까. 시원하게 있어야지.

대화에서 여자가 테이블 위에 줄무늬 파라솔이 눈길을 끈다고 말했는데, ③에는 물방울무늬 파라솔이 그려져 있다.

어휘 backyard 명 뒷마당, 뒤뜰 fence 명 울타리 umbrella 명 파라솔, 우산 eye-catching 형 눈길을 끄는 practical 형 실용적인 keep ~ off (비, 태양 등을) 막다 spot 명 자리, 장소 shade 명 그늘

5 부탁한 일 파악

정답 ①

W	Chris, what are you doing this afternoon?
M	Nothing special. Why are you asking, Miranda?
W	Do you 1)remember my host family in Korea?
M	Of course! You stayed with Minyoung and her parents. You told me they were very nice.
W	Yes. Well, Minyoung is going to stay with my family for three weeks. I 2)promised to teach her English.
M	Wow, you seem thrilled.
W	Yes. But there's an unexpected issue.
M	Is it anything I can give you a hand with?
W	**Actually, I am supposed to** 3)**pick her up at the airport this afternoon.** But I haven't finished a report that I need to hand in today.
M	**And you need someone to meet Minyoung at the airport.**
W	**Could you please do it for me?**
M	Sure. Why not? But you will have to 4)buy me dinner sometime.

여	Chris, 오늘 오후에 뭐 할 거야?
남	특별한 건 없어. 왜 물어보는 거야, Miranda?
여	한국의 내 주인집 가족을 기억하니?
남	물론이지! 넌 민영이랑 그녀의 부모님과 함께 지냈잖아. 그들이 매우 친절했다고 말해줬어.
여	그래. 음, 민영이가 3주 동안 우리 가족과 지내러 올 거야. 내가 영어를 가르쳐주기로 약속했어.
남	와, 너 신나 보인다.
여	응. 그런데 예상치 못한 문제가 하나 있어.
남	내가 도와줄 수 있는 거야?
여	사실, 난 오늘 오후에 공항으로 그녀를 데리러 가기로 했어. 그런데 오늘 제출해야 하는 보고서를 다 못 끝냈어.
남	그러면 넌 민영이를 공항에 마중 나갈 사람이 필요하겠네.
여	나 대신 해 줄 수 있어?
남	물론이지. 왜 안 되겠어? 하지만 언젠가 나한테 저녁 사줘야 해.

한국에서 오는 친구를 맞이할 계획에 대해 얘기하고 있다. 여자가 오늘 오후에 공항으로 그녀를 데리러 가기로 했으나 보고서를 아직 다 못 끝냈다면서 자기 대신 해 줄 수 있는지 부탁했으므로 여자가 남자에게 부탁한 일로 ① '공항으로 마중 가기'가 가장 적절하다.

어휘 promise 동 약속하다 thrilled 형 신이 난 unexpected 형 예상치 못한 give ~ a hand ~를 도와주다 be supposed to ~하기로 하다 hand in ~을 제출하다

6 금액 정보 파악

정답 ④

M Do you need help with anything today?	남 오늘은 무엇을 도와드릴까요?
W Yes. I want to 1)buy my nephews skateboards for Christmas.	여 네. 크리스마스를 맞이해서 조카들에게 스케이트보드를 사주고 싶어요.
M Well, what do you think of this model? It is our best one, **and it only costs $50.**	남 음, 이 모델은 어떠세요? 가장 좋은 것이고, 가격은 50달러밖에 안 해요.
W I guess my nephews will like it. **I'll take two.**	여 조카들이 좋아할 것 같네요. 두 개 주세요.
M Great. Do they have helmets already? **This helmet is $25.**	남 좋아요. 조카분들이 헬멧은 이미 가지고 있나요? 이 헬멧은 25달러예요.
W **I'll take two of those as well.**	여 그것도 두 개 주세요.
M Oh, I almost forgot. We are 2)having a sale on helmets this week.	남 아, 깜빡할 뻔했네요. 이번 주에는 헬멧을 할인하고 있어요.
W That's wonderful. How much of a discount will I get?	여 정말 잘됐네요. 얼마나 할인이 되나요?
M **You will 3)get 10% off the helmets.** Is there anything else you need today?	남 헬멧에서 10% 할인됩니다. 오늘 더 필요하신 건 없으신가요?
W No. That's everything. Thank you so much for your help.	여 아뇨. 그게 전부예요. 도와주셔서 감사해요.

여자가 스케이트보드 두 개($50×2=$100)와, 헬멧 두 개($25×2=$50)를 구매했고, 헬멧은 10% 할인($50×0.9=$45)을 받았으므로 정답은 ④ '$145'이다.

어휘 nephew 명 (남자) 조카 as well ~도, 역시 discount 명 할인

7 이유 파악

정답 ①

W Mark, why are you still at home? I thought you had soccer practice this afternoon.	여 Mark, 왜 아직도 집에 있니? 오늘 오후에 축구 연습이 있는 줄 알았는데.
M I'm not going today, Mom.	남 오늘은 안 갈 거예요, 엄마.
W Oh, that's right. You have history homework 1)due tomorrow.	여 아, 맞다. 내일까지 해야 하는 역사 숙제가 있구나.
M I finished it already.	남 그건 벌써 끝냈어요.
W Then, are you sick? Should I take you to the doctor's office?	여 그럼, 어디 아프니? 병원에 데려다줄까?
M No. I had a cold last week, but I feel fine now.	남 아니요. 지난주에 감기에 걸렸지만, 지금은 괜찮아요.
W 2)Are you planning to go to a movie or something with your friends?	여 친구들이랑 영화 같은 걸 보러 갈 계획이니?
M I don't have time for anything like that today.	남 오늘은 그런 걸 할 시간 없어요.
W Then, why are you not going to practice today?	여 그럼, 오늘 왜 연습 안 할 거니?
M **One of my classmates has to give a speech in front of our class tomorrow.**	남 저희 반 친구 중 한 명이 내일 반 애들 앞에서 발표를 해야 해요.
W What does that have to do with soccer practice?	여 그게 축구 연습이랑 무슨 상관이니?
M **I promised that I would 3)help him prepare for it.**	남 발표 준비하는 걸 돕겠다고 약속했거든요.
W I see. That is nice of you.	여 그렇구나. 정말 착하네.

남자는 오늘 오후에 있는 축구 연습을 하지 않을 것이라면서 반 친구가 내일 할 발표 준비를 돕기로 약속했다고 말했으므로, 남자가 축구 연습에 가지 않는 이유는 ① '친구의 발표 준비를 도와야 해서'이다.

어휘 due 형 (~까지) 하기로 되어 있는 have a cold 감기에 걸리다 give a speech 발표하다, 연설하다 in front of ~의 앞에서 have to do with ~과 상관이 있다

8 언급 유무 파악

정답 ③

M Denise, have you found a new job yet?	남 Denise, 새 직장 구했니?
W No. I'm getting 1)a little stressed about it.	여 아니. 그것 때문에 스트레스를 좀 받고 있어.
M Well, the Dolman Job Fair is coming up soon. Maybe you should check it out.	남 음, 곧 Dolman Job Fair가 열릴 거야. 어쩌면 네가 한번 확인해 보는 게 좋겠어.
W Really? When is it taking place?	여 정말? 언제 개최되는데?
M It will be 2)on **May 25th.**	남 5월 25일에 열릴 거야.
W Do you know where I should go?	여 어디로 가야 하는지 알아?
M It'll be at **the Star Hotel downtown.**	남 시내에 있는 스타 호텔에서 열릴 거야.
W That's convenient. How many companies will 3)be participating?	여 가까운걸. 몇 개의 회사가 참여할 예정이야?
M **Around 50.** And many of them are in your field of work.	남 50개 정도. 그리고 그중 많은 회사가 네 업무 분야에 있어.
W Great. Oh, I just remembered that I have a doctor's appointment that day. I won't be free until 5 p.m.	여 좋다. 아, 내가 그날 병원 예약이 있다는 게 방금 생각났어. 오후 5시는 돼야 시간이 날 텐데.
M That's fine. The fair will 4)run **until 9.**	남 괜찮아. 박람회는 9시까지 진행될 거야.
W Then, I'll definitely go. Thanks for letting me know about it.	여 그러면 꼭 가야겠다. 알려줘서 고마워.

행사 일자(5월 25일), 행사 장소(시내에 있는 스타 호텔), 참가 기업 수(50개 정도), 종료 시각(9시)에 대해 언급했고, ③ '주최 기관'은 언급하지 않았다.

어휘 find a job 직장을 구하다 come up 열리다, 생기다 check out ~을 확인하다 take place 개최되다 convenient 형 (~에) 가까운; 편리한 field 명 분야; 들판
not A until B B는 되어야 A하다 definitely 부 꼭, 분명히

9 내용 불일치 파악　　　　　　　　　　　　　　　　　　정답 ⑤

W　Welcome to the opening of the James Harper Exhibit at the Museum of Modern Architecture. Mr. Harper was one of the [1])most important architects of the 1990s. He designed around 240 buildings during his lifetime. The exhibit includes photographs of his most famous buildings. But the models of the houses that Mr. Harper designed are [2])the main attraction. These are incredibly detailed. If you would prefer a guided tour of the exhibit, speak to one of the staff members at the information desk. **This service is not included in the admission fee, so there will be** [3])an additional $10 charge. I hope all of you enjoy the exhibit.	여　현대 건축 박물관에서 열리는 James Harper Exhibit 개막식에 오신 것을 환영합니다. Harper 씨는 1990년대의 가장 뛰어난 건축가 중 한 명이었습니다. 그는 생전에 약 240채의 건물을 설계했습니다. 전시회에는 그의 가장 유명한 건축물의 사진들이 포함됩니다. 하지만 Harper 씨가 설계한 주택 모형들이 가장 주요한 볼거리입니다. 이것들은 믿을 수 없을 정도로 정밀합니다. 전시회 해설 관람을 원하신다면, 안내 데스크의 직원 중 한 명에게 이야기하십시오. 이 서비스는 입장료에 포함되지 않아서, 10달러의 추가 요금이 발생합니다. 여러분 모두 전시회를 즐기시기를 바랍니다.

현대 건축 박물관에서 열리는 전시회에 대한 안내 방송이다. 여자가 전시회 해설 관람 서비스는 입장료에 포함되지 않아서 10달러의 추가 요금이 발생한다고 했으므로 ⑤ '입장료에는 해설 관람 비용이 포함되어 있다.'는 내용과 일치하지 않는다.

어휘　architect 몡 건축가　during one's lifetime 생전에, 일생 동안　attraction 몡 볼거리; 매력　incredibly 몜 믿을 수 없을 정도로　detailed 혱 정밀한, 상세한　admission fee 입장료
additional 혱 추가의　charge 몡 요금 톰 청구하다

10 도표 정보 파악　　　　　　　　　　　　　　　　　　정답 ③

M　What are you doing, Tara?	남　뭐 하는 중이야, Tara?
W　I'm looking at computer monitors online. I need to buy a new one.	여　컴퓨터 모니터를 온라인으로 보고 있어. 새 걸 사야 하거든.
M　Have you [1])decided on a model yet?	남　모델은 정했어?
W　No. **But I definitely want one with a screen size of at least 22 inches.**	여　아니. 하지만 나는 화면 크기가 적어도 22인치는 되는 걸 꼭 원해.
M　That's a good size. What about cost? How much are you willing to spend?	남　괜찮은 크기네. 비용은 어때? 얼마를 쓸 의향이 있어?
W　I have [2])a budget of $200. I can't go over that amount.	여　200달러의 예산이 있어. 그 금액은 넘길 수 없어.
M　Well, that seems to leave two models to choose from.	남　음, 두 가지 모델 중에서 선택할 수 있는 것 같네.
W　I know. But I am having a hard time [3])picking a color.	여　그러게. 그런데 난 색깔을 고르는 데 어려움을 겪고 있어.
M　**The black one seems best to me.**	남　내겐 검은색이 제일 좋아 보여.
W　**You're right. I'll get that one.** Thanks for your help.	여　네 말이 맞아. 그걸로 할게. 도와줘서 고마워.
M　No problem.	남　천만에.

여자가 화면 크기가 적어도 22인치는 되고, 200달러의 예산을 넘지 않으며, 검은색인 컴퓨터 모니터를 골랐다.

어휘　be willing to ~할 의향이 있다　budget 몡 예산　amount 몡 금액, 양　have a hard time ~하는 데 어려움을 겪다

11 짧은 대화의 응답 파악　　　　　　　　　　　　　　　정답 ①

W　What's the matter, Brad? You look really worried.	여　무슨 일이야, Brad? 걱정이 많아 보여.
M　**I just noticed that** [1])my wallet isn't in my pocket!	남　지갑이 주머니에 없다는 걸 방금 알아차렸어!
W　Did you leave it at the restaurant where we [2])had lunch?	여　우리가 점심 먹었던 식당에 두고 온 거야?
M　Possibly. I'll call there now to check.	남　그럴 수도 있어. 지금 확인하러 전화할게.
	선택지　① 그럴 수도 있어. 지금 확인하러 전화할게.
	② 당연하지. 예약하자.
	③ 모르겠어. 지금은 배가 안 고파.
	④ 미안해. 네가 점심값을 내야겠어.
	⑤ 고마워. 내 지갑을 찾아줘서 정말 다행이야.

지갑이 없어진 것을 방금 알아차린 남자에게 여자가 식당에 두고 왔던 것인지 물었으므로, 이에 대한 응답으로는 그럴 수도 있으니 확인해보겠다고 하는 ① 'Possibly. I'll call there now to check.'가 가장 적절하다.

어휘　notice 톰 알아차리다　wallet 몡 지갑　leave 톰 두고 오다; 떠나다　make a reservation 예약하다　pay for ~의 값을 내다, 지불하다

12 짧은 대화의 응답 파악

정답 ④

M Mom, could you ¹⁾drive me to the movie theater?	남 엄마, 영화관까지 태워다 주실 수 있어요?

M Mom, could you <u>1)drive me to</u> the movie theater?
W Sure. What time do you need to be there?
M Actually, in about 30 minutes. We <u>2)should hurry</u>.
W <u>We had better leave right away, then.</u>

남 엄마, 영화관까지 태워다 주실 수 있어요?
여 물론이란다. 몇 시에 거기 도착해야 하니?
남 실은, 30분 정도 후에요. 서둘러야 해요.
여 <u>그럼 바로 출발하는 게 좋겠구나.</u>

[선택지] ① 거기까지 가는 데 30분이 걸렸어.
② 하지만 내가 어제 그 영화를 예매했단다.
③ 내 티켓 어디서 본 적 있니?
④ 그럼 바로 출발하는 게 좋겠구나.
⑤ 오늘 나를 태워다 주겠니?

남자가 여자에게 영화관까지 태워달라고 부탁하면서 30분 후에는 도착하게끔 서둘러야 한다고 했으므로, 이에 대한 응답으로는 그러면 바로 출발하는 것이 좋겠다고 말하는 ④ 'We had better leave right away, then.'이 가장 적절하다.

[어휘] drive 통 태워다 주다; 운전하다   hurry 통 서두르다   give ~ a ride ~를 태워다 주다

13 긴 대화의 응답 파악

정답 ⑤

M Cindy, are you planning to attend the school's science festival next week?
W Yes, Mr. Parker. It sounds like fun.
M We need some student volunteers for the event. **I thought maybe you would be interested in** ¹⁾helping out.
W What would I have to do?
M Well, the volunteers will assist the presenters.
W **Could I** ²⁾choose which presenter to help?
M Do you have one in mind?
W Yeah. The school's website says that there will be a presentation about flight.
M Oh, the one about airplane design.
W Right. I'd like to be a pilot someday, so that's a topic I follow closely.
M **You should speak to Ms. Clarkson about this. She's in charge of** ³⁾assigning the volunteers **for the event.**
W I'll ask her about it in the afternoon.

남 Cindy, 다음 주에 있을 학교 과학 축제에 참석할 계획이니?
여 네, Parker 선생님. 그건 재미있을 것 같아요.
남 그 행사를 위해 학생 자원봉사자들이 좀 필요하단다. 내 생각에 네게 도와줄 의향이 있을 수도 있겠어.
여 제가 뭘 해야 하나요?
남 음, 자원봉사자들은 발표자들을 보조할 거야.
여 도와드릴 발표자를 제가 고를 수 있나요?
남 염두에 둔 발표자가 있니?
여 네. 학교 웹사이트에 비행에 관한 발표가 있을 거라고 나와 있어요.
남 아, 비행기 디자인에 관한 거 말이구나.
여 맞아요. 저는 언젠가 조종사가 되고 싶어서, 그건 제가 관심 있게 지켜보는 주제예요.
남 Clarkson 선생님에게 얘기해 보렴. 행사에 자원봉사자들을 배정하는 일을 담당하고 있거든.
여 <u>오후에 그분에게 그것에 관해 물어볼게요.</u>

[선택지] ① 그녀는 과학 축제를 준비하는 것에 동의했어요.
② 비행에 관한 발표는 취소됐어요.
③ 저는 축제가 성공할 것이라고 확신해요.
④ 비행기는 매우 흥미로운 주제예요.
⑤ 오후에 그분에게 그것에 관해 물어볼게요.

남자가 여자에게 학교 과학 축제에 자원봉사자로 참가할 것을 권유하는 상황에서, 비행 관련 발표자를 돕고 싶어 하는 여자에게 남자가 배정 담당 선생님을 소개해 주었으므로, 이에 대한 응답으로는 담당 선생님과 이야기할 계획을 말하는 ⑤ 'I'll ask her about it in the afternoon.'이 가장 적절하다.

[어휘] be interested in ~할 의향이 있다   assist 통 보조하다   presenter 명 발표자   have ~ in mind ~을 염두에 두다   pilot 명 조종사   be in charge of ~을 담당하다   assign 통 배정하다
organize 통 준비하다; 조직하다   certain 형 확신하는; 특정한

14 긴 대화의 응답 파악

정답 ②

[Telephone rings.]
M You've reached Benson Catering.
W Hi. I'm planning ¹⁾a graduation party for my daughter. One of my friends recommended your company to provide the food.
M That's wonderful. How many people will be attending?
W I'm expecting 35 guests.
M Okay. What kind of food would you ²⁾like to serve?
W My daughter really likes Italian food, so pasta and pizza would be great.
M We can do that. I'll send you a list of dishes you can choose from. Then, you can just pick what you want.
W Perfect. I was planning to hold the event next Saturday.
M Let me check my schedule. *[Pause]* Oh, no. **We are** ³⁾already booked **for another event on that day.**

[전화기가 울린다.]
남 Benson Catering입니다.
여 안녕하세요. 저는 딸의 졸업 파티를 계획하고 있어요. 제 친구 중 한 명이 음식 제공 업체로 당신의 회사를 추천했어요.
남 좋은 일이네요. 몇 명이 참석할 예정입니까?
여 35명의 손님을 예상하고 있어요.
남 알겠습니다. 어떤 종류의 음식을 제공하고 싶으세요?
여 제 딸이 이탈리아 음식을 정말 좋아해서, 파스타와 피자가 좋을 것 같아요.
남 그렇게 할 수 있습니다. 손님이 고르실 수 있는 요리 목록을 보내드릴게요. 그럼, 원하시는 것을 그냥 골라주시면 됩니다.
여 완벽해요. 저는 다음 주 토요일에 행사를 열 계획이었어요.
남 제 일정을 확인해 보겠습니다. *[잠시 멈춤]* 오, 안 되겠네요. 이미 그날 다른 행사 예약이 잡혀 있어요.

W Then, what about next Friday? 4)Would that work?

M We have nothing else scheduled for that day.

여 그러면 다음 주 금요일은 어때요? 그날은 괜찮을까요?

남 그날에는 다른 일정이 없네요.

선택지 ① 따님의 졸업을 축하드립니다.
② 그날에는 다른 일정이 없네요.
③ 저희는 매우 다양한 이탈리아 요리들을 제공합니다.
④ 손님분들이 저희 음식을 맛있게 드셨기를 바랍니다.
⑤ 죄송하지만 신용 카드는 받지 않습니다.

음식 제공 업체에 예약 전화를 하는 상황에서 여자가 원하는 날에 이미 예약이 잡혀있다고 남자가 말하자, 대안으로 여자가 다음 주 금요일은 괜찮은지 물었으므로, 이에 대한 응답으로는 일정을 확인해서 대답하는 ② 'We have nothing else scheduled for that day.'가 가장 적절하다.

어휘 graduation 명 졸업 serve 통 제공하다 dish 명 요리; 접시 book 통 예약하다 명 책 a wide variety of 매우 다양한 credit card 신용 카드

15 상황에 적절한 말 파악

정답 ②

W Samantha is studying for the final exam in her 1)biology class. She finds the subject difficult, and she is having a hard time focusing on her lecture notes. To make things worse, her younger brother, Neal, 2)keeps distracting her. He is playing video games in the living room, and the volume is very loud. In addition, he keeps shouting and laughing while he plays. Unfortunately, her bedroom is right next to the living room, so she can't ignore him. **So Samantha wants to ask Neal to go to another room in the house while she 3)studies for the exam.** In this situation, what would Samantha most likely say to Neal?

여 Samantha는 생물 수업 기말고사 공부를 하고 있습니다. 그녀는 이 과목이 어렵다고 생각하고, 강의 노트에 집중하는 데 어려움을 겪고 있습니다. 설상가상으로, 남동생 Neal은 계속해서 그녀의 주의를 산만하게 합니다. 그는 거실에서 비디오 게임을 하고 있는데, 소리가 매우 큽니다. 게다가, 그는 노는 동안 계속 소리를 지르고 웃습니다. 안타깝게도, 그녀의 방은 거실 바로 옆에 있어서, 그녀가 무시할 수는 없습니다. 그래서 Samantha는 Neal에게 그녀가 시험공부를 하는 동안 집에 있는 다른 방에 가 있으라고 부탁하고 싶습니다. 이러한 상황에서, Samantha가 Neal에게 가장 할 것 같은 말은 무엇입니까?

선택지 ① TV 소리를 줄여줄까?
② 내가 공부하는 동안 다른 곳에서 놀아줄래?
③ 얼마나 오랫동안 비디오 게임을 할 거니?
④ 네 침실에서 시험을 준비해도 될까?
⑤ 거실에서 책을 읽는 게 어때?

남동생 Neal이 계속 시끄럽게 놀고 있어 기말고사 공부를 방해받는 상황에서, Samantha는 Neal에게 시험공부 하는 동안 집에 있는 다른 방에 가 있으라고 부탁한다. 따라서, Samantha가 할 말로 ② 'Could you play somewhere else while I study?'가 가장 적절하다.

어휘 biology 명 생물학 subject 명 과목; 주제 focus on ~에 집중하다 to make things worse 설상가상으로 distract 통 주의를 산만하게 하다 ignore 통 무시하다
turn down (소리를) 줄이다

16-17 세트 문항

정답 16 ① 17 ③

M Good morning. Yesterday, we talked about the 1)various causes of natural disasters. **Today, I want to discuss what we must do to survive when these disasters happen.** First, the key to keeping safe 2)during an earthquake is to protect yourself from falling objects. You should get under something sturdy like a table or a desk. In the case of a **tsunami**, you must go to high ground as quickly as possible. Move away from the beach, and 3)climb the nearest hill. Next, be sure to stay indoors during a **hurricane**. The high winds and heavy rains make it unsafe to be outside. Finally, if 4)a flood occurs, it is dangerous to be in an underground parking lot or on one of the lower floors of a building. Go to a higher floor or even the roof of the building. I hope this lesson has given you a better understanding of what to do in these situations.

남 좋은 아침입니다. 어제, 우리는 자연재해의 다양한 원인에 대해 이야기했습니다. 오늘은, 이러한 재해가 발생했을 때 살아남으려면 우리가 무엇을 해야 하는지 논하고 싶습니다. 첫 번째로, 지진 동안 안전을 유지하는 비결은 떨어지는 물건들로부터 여러분 자신을 보호하는 데 있습니다. 여러분은 탁자나 책상 같은 튼튼한 것 아래로 들어가야 합니다. 쓰나미의 경우에는, 가능한 한 빨리 높은 지대로 가야 합니다. 해변에서 멀리 떨어져서, 가장 가까운 언덕으로 올라가십시오. 다음으로, 허리케인 동안에는 반드시 실내에 있도록 하십시오. 강한 바람과 폭우는 야외에 있는 것을 안전하지 않게 합니다. 마지막으로, 홍수가 발생하면, 지하 주차장이나 건물의 낮은 층에 있는 것은 위험합니다. 더 높은 층이나 혹은 건물 지붕 위로 가십시오. 이 수업을 통해 이러한 상황에서 무엇을 해야 하는지 여러분이 더 잘 이해할 수 있게 되었길 바랍니다.

선택지 16 ① 자연재해 때 안전을 유지하는 방법
② 쓰나미가 발생하기 쉬운 장소
③ 지진해일가 더 흔해지는 이유
④ 허리케인의 위험이 가장 큰 지역
⑤ 역사상 가장 심각했던 자연재해
17 ① 지진 ② 쓰나미 ③ 토네이도 ④ 허리케인 ⑤ 홍수

16 자연재해가 발생했을 때 살아남으려면 무엇을 해야 하는지에 대해 논하고 있으므로 남자가 하는 말의 주제로 ① 'how to stay safe during natural disasters'가 가장 적절하다.
17 지진, 쓰나미, 허리케인, 홍수는 언급했지만 ③ 'tornado'는 언급하지 않았다.

어휘 cause 명 원인 통 일으키다 natural disaster 자연재해 key 명 비결; 열쇠 earthquake 명 지진 protect A from B A를 B로부터 보호하다 sturdy 형 튼튼한, 견고한
as ~ as possible 가능한 한 ~하게 indoors 부 실내에 flood 명 홍수 underground 형 지하의 be likely to ~하기 쉽다 risk 명 위험

1	④	2	③	3	②	4	④	5	⑤	6	②	7	④	8	⑤	9	③	10	②
11	①	12	⑤	13	③	14	②	15	④	16	②	17	④						

• 각 문제의 정답 근거는 굵은 글씨로, Dictation 정답은 밑줄로 표시되어 있습니다.

1　목적 파악　　　　　　　　　　　　　　　　정답 ④

M　Attention, please. I have an update regarding this year's spring computer course. As you may already know, Riverview High School offers a ¹⁾spring computer course every year. Students have a chance to learn basic coding and create simple computer programs. Originally, the last date that you could apply was March 30th. **However, due to the ²⁾large number of applicants, we've decided to close the application period early. Therefore, I need to inform you that the ³⁾new deadline to apply will be March 15th.** If you have any questions about the application process, please visit the school's website. Thank you for understanding.

남　주목해 주세요. 올해 춘계 컴퓨터 강좌에 관한 최신 소식을 가져왔습니다. 여러분이 이미 알고 있는 것처럼, 리버뷰 고등학교는 매년 춘계 컴퓨터 강좌를 제공합니다. 학생들은 기본적인 코딩을 배우고 간단한 컴퓨터 프로그램을 만들 기회를 갖습니다. 원래, 여러분이 신청할 수 있는 마지막 날짜는 3월 30일이었습니다. 하지만, 많은 수의 신청자들로 인해 신청 기간을 앞당겨 마감하기로 했습니다. 따라서, 저는 여러분께 새로운 신청 마감일이 3월 15일이라는 것을 알려드려야 합니다. 신청 과정에 대해 궁금한 점이 있으시면 학교 웹사이트를 방문해 주세요. 이해해 주셔서 감사합니다.

남자가 올해 춘계 컴퓨터 강좌의 신청 기간을 기존에 공지한 날보다 앞당겨 마감하기로 했다면서, 새로운 신청 마감일을 알려주고 있다. 따라서 남자가 하는 말의 목적으로 ④ '강좌 참가 신청 마감일 변경을 안내하려고'가 가장 적절하다.

어휘　regarding 쩐 ~에 관한　due to ~으로 인해, 때문에　apply 통 신청하다 (applicant 몡 신청자, 지원자)　inform 통 알리다　deadline 몡 마감일

2　의견 파악　　　　　　　　　　　　　　　　정답 ③

M　What's the matter, Tory? You're frowning.
W　My friend Anna said something rude to me earlier. She really ¹⁾hurt my feelings.
M　Oh, no. I'm sorry to hear that. Did she apologize for it?
W　No. She doesn't even know I'm upset.
M　Well, maybe you should tell her how you feel. **I think you need to have an honest conversation with her so you can ²⁾resolve the conflict.**
W　No. It'll be too uncomfortable. I'll just try to forget about it.
M　But if she doesn't know what she did wrong, she will probably do it again. ³⁾Honest communication is important for keeping relationships healthy.
W　Hmm... I think you're right. Maybe I'll message her about it.
M　That's a good idea, but you shouldn't wait too long.
W　Okay. I'll send her a text now. Thanks for your advice!

남　무슨 일이야, Tory? 눈살을 찌푸리고 있네.
여　내 친구 Anna가 아까 나한테 무례한 말을 했어. 그녀는 정말 내 마음에 상처를 줬어.
남　오, 저런. 유감이야. 그녀가 그것에 대해 사과했어?
여　아니. 그녀는 내가 화난 줄도 몰라.
남　음, 네가 어떤 기분인지 말해야 할 것 같아. 갈등을 해결할 수 있도록 그녀와 솔직한 대화를 해 볼 필요가 있다고 생각해.
여　아니. 그건 너무 불편할 거야. 그냥 잊어버리려고 노력해야겠어.
남　하지만 만약 그녀가 자신이 무엇을 잘못했는지 모른다면, 그녀는 아마 다시 또 그렇게 할 거야. 정직한 의사소통은 관계를 건강하게 유지하는 데 있어 중요해.
여　흠... 네 말이 맞는 것 같아. 이에 대해 그녀에게 메시지를 보내볼 수도 있겠어.
남　좋은 생각이지만, 너무 오래 주저하면 안 돼.
여　알았어. 지금 문자 보낼게. 충고 고마워!

여자는 친구 Anna의 심한 말로 마음이 상했고, 남자는 이러한 갈등을 해결하려면 솔직한 대화를 해야 한다고 여자에게 조언하고 있다. 따라서, 남자의 의견으로 ③ '갈등 해결을 위해서는 솔직한 대화가 필요하다'가 가장 적절하다.

어휘　frown 통 눈살을 찌푸리다, 성난 표정을 짓다　rude 형 무례한　apologize 통 사과하다　upset 형 화난, 기분 나쁜　honest 형 솔직한, 정직한　resolve 통 해결하다　conflict 통 갈등, 마찰　relationship 몡 관계

3　관계 파악　　　　　　　　　　　　　　　　정답 ②

M　Hi, Dana. **My chief editor mentioned that you could help with the article ¹⁾I'm writing.**
W　Sure. Is this for that story you're reporting on about the Brentwood Museum?
M　Right. The museum got a big donation from an anonymous person.
W　That's interesting. **Do you need pictures ²⁾from my photo collection for the article?**
M　Actually, we need new ones.
W　**I can go over there and take some pictures.** What do you need me to do?
M　This story is going on the front page of the newspaper. So I'd like a photo of the new sculpture by the main entrance. A few paintings were also donated. Let's get those, too.

남　안녕하세요, Dana. 저희 편집장님께서 그러시길 당신이 제가 쓰고 있는 기사를 도와주실 수 있다고 하셔서요.
여　물론이죠. 브렌트우드 박물관에 대해 취재 중인 기사를 위한 건가요?
남　맞아요. 그 박물관은 익명의 한 사람으로부터 많은 기증을 받았거든요.
여　흥미롭군요. 제 사진 컬렉션에서 그 기사에 쓸 사진이 필요하신가요?
남　사실, 새것들이 필요해요.
여　제가 그곳에 가서 사진을 찍어드릴 수 있어요. 어떻게 해드리면 될까요?
남　이 기사는 신문의 1면에 실릴 거예요. 그래서 저는 정문 옆에 놓인 새로운 조각품의 사진이 필요해요. 몇몇 그림들도 기증되었어요. 그것들의 사진도 찍읍시다.

W	No problem. When do you need my photos?	여	문제없어요. 제 사진이 언제 필요하세요?
M	**The article will be** ³⁾published on April 15th.	남	그 기사는 4월 15일에 발행될 거예요.
W	Will we make the deadline if I send you the photos in three days?	여	3일 후에 사진을 보내드리면 마감일을 맞출 수 있을까요?
M	Yeah. That would be perfect. Thanks!	남	네. 그럼 완벽해요. 감사합니다!

남자는 자신이 쓰고 있는 기사에 쓸 사진을 여자에게 부탁하고 있다. 남자가 어떤 사진이 언제까지 필요한지 이야기해주고 있으며, 여자는 부탁을 들어주며 사진을 찍어주겠다고 하는 것으로 보아 두 사람의 관계로 ② '기자 — 사진사'가 가장 적절하다.

어휘 chief editor 편집장 article 명 기사 donation 명 기증, 기부 anonymous 형 익명의 sculpture 명 조각품 main entrance 정문 publish 동 발행하다, 출판하다
make the deadline 마감일을 맞추다

4 그림 내용 불일치 파악   정답 ④

W	Honey, this market is really amazing. I'm glad our tour guide brought us here.	여	여보, 이 시장 정말 끝내준다. 우리 여행 가이드가 우리를 여기로 데려와 줘서 다행이야.
M	I think so, too. Let's visit that stall over there.	남	나도 그렇게 생각해. 저기에 있는 노점에 가 보자.
W	You mean the one with the banner that says "Handmade Goods"?	여	'Handmade Goods'라고 쓰인 현수막이 있는 곳 말하는 거지?
M	Right. It caught my eye because of ¹⁾that striped roof. It looks like an interesting place to shop.	남	응. 저 줄무늬 지붕 때문에 내 눈길이 사로잡혔어. 저기는 쇼핑하기에 재미있는 장소처럼 보여.
W	Look at those three jars on the counter. They would be perfect for storing spices.	여	계산대 위에 있는 저 세 개의 병을 봐. 저것들은 향신료를 보관하기에 완벽할 거야.
M	I agree. **What's that hanging on the wall behind the counter?**	남	나도 같은 생각이야. 계산대 뒤의 벽에 걸려 있는 것은 뭘까?
W	**It looks like a large,** ²⁾round clock. It seems to be carved out of wood.	여	크고 둥근 시계인 것 같아. 나무로 조각한 것처럼 보여.
M	It's beautiful. What do you think of that lantern ³⁾next to the rabbit doll?	남	아름답네. 토끼 인형 옆에 있는 저 랜턴은 어떤 것 같아?
W	I like it. Maybe we should get it for our garden.	여	마음에 들어. 우리 정원에 두게 그걸 사야 할 것 같아.
M	That's a great idea. It will make our garden more cheerful.	남	좋은 생각이야. 저건 우리 정원에 생기를 더 불어넣어 줄 거야.

대화에서 여자가 계산대 뒤의 벽에 걸려 있는 것이 크고 둥근 시계인 것 같다고 했는데, ④에는 네모난 시계가 그려져 있다.

어휘 stall 명 노점 banner 명 현수막, 배너 catch one's eye ~의 눈길을 사로잡다 striped 형 줄무늬의 spice 명 향신료 carve 동 조각하다, 깎다 cheerful 형 생기를 불어넣는, 쾌활한

5 할 일 파악   정답 ⑤

W	Hey, Shawn. Good job with your fundraising booth yesterday. You sold so many cookies.	여	안녕, Shawn. 어제 모금 부스를 잘 해냈더구나. 쿠키를 정말 많이 팔았어.
M	Thanks, Ms. Henderson. I was happy to raise a lot of money for ¹⁾the animal shelter.	남	고마워요, Henderson 선생님. 동물 보호소를 위한 많은 돈을 모을 수 있어서 기뻤어요.
W	You must have been very busy, though.	여	그런데, 틀림없이 무척 바빴겠던걸.
M	I was. I think I'll need some help when I go back to the booth today.	남	그랬죠. 아마도 오늘 제가 부스로 돌아갈 때는 도움이 좀 필요할 것 같아요.
W	I would lend a hand, but I have a meeting in an hour.	여	도와주려 했지만, 난 한 시간 후에 회의가 있단다.
M	I see. Well, is there anyone else who can work at the booth with me?	남	그렇군요. 음, 저와 함께 부스에서 일할 수 있는 다른 사람이 있을까요?
W	I can ask! I'll ²⁾send out a text message to the other volunteers right away.	여	내가 물어봐 줄 수 있단다! 지금 바로 다른 자원봉사자들에게 문자 메시지를 보낼게.
M	Thanks for doing that.	남	그렇게 해주신다니 감사합니다.
W	No problem. Oh, could you send me ³⁾the location of your booth?	여	별일 아니란다. 아, 부스 위치 좀 보내줄 수 있겠니?
M	Sure. I saved a map that shows where the booth is. You can send the image if you want.	남	물론이죠. 부스 위치가 표시된 지도를 저장해놨어요. 원하신다면 이 이미지를 보내셔도 돼요.

모금 부스 행사에 대해 이야기하고 있다. 남자가 자신과 함께 일할 수 있는 다른 사람이 필요하다고 하자, 여자가 지금 바로 다른 자원봉사자들에게 문자를 보내겠다고 했으므로, 여자가 할 일로 ⑤ '문자 보내기'가 가장 적절하다.

어휘 fundraising 명 모금 raise money 돈을 모으다 go back to ~로 돌아가다 lend a hand 도와주다 send out ~을 보내다 volunteer 명 자원봉사자 location 명 위치, 장소

6 금액 정보 파악

정답 ②

W Welcome to Bay Area Amusement Park. How can I help you?	여 베이 에어리어 놀이공원에 오신 것을 환영합니다. 무엇을 도와드릴까요?
M Hi. How much is a day pass to the park?	남 안녕하세요. 하루짜리 탑승권은 얼마예요?
W For adults it's $30, and for children it's $20.	여 어른은 30달러, 어린이는 20달러입니다.
M Okay. Then, I'd like tickets for 1)two adults and one child.	남 네. 그럼 어른 두 명과 어린이 한 명 표 부탁드려요.
W All right. And would you like to buy fast passes with that?	여 알겠습니다. 그리고 신속 탑승권을 함께 구매하실 건가요?
M What is a fast pass?	남 신속 탑승권이 뭐예요?
W It allows you to move to the front of the line of some rides. They're $10 each.	여 그건 몇몇 놀이 기구들의 대기 줄 맨 앞으로 갈 수 있게 해줘요. 한 장당 10달러입니다.
M That's okay. I 2)don't need any.	남 괜찮아요. 필요 없어요.
W Okay, so you need two adult tickets and one child ticket.	여 알겠습니다, 그러면 어른 표 두 장과 어린이 표 한 장이 필요하신 거죠.
M That's correct. I also have a coupon. Can I use it with this purchase?	남 맞아요. 저한테 쿠폰도 있어요. 이번 구매 때 함께 사용할 수 있나요?
W Let me see. [Pause] 3)Yes, you can. I'll take 20% off of your total.	여 어디 볼게요. [잠시 멈춤] 네, 가능합니다. 총액에서 20% 할인해 드리겠습니다.
M Great! Here's my card.	남 좋아요! 여기 제 카드요.

남자가 어른 두 명($30×2=$60)과 어린이 1명($20)의 표를 구매했고, 20% 할인($80×0.8=$64)을 받았으므로, 정답은 ② '$64'이다.

어휘 amusement park 놀이공원 pass 圏 탑승권 图 통과하다 line 圏 대기 줄; 선 ride 圏 놀이 기구 图 타다 purchase 圏 구매 图 구매하다

7 이유 파악

정답 ④

M Hey, Kelly. How was your weekend?	남 안녕, Kelly. 주말 잘 보냈어?
W It wasn't very fun. I had to stay home and do homework.	여 그렇게 재미있지는 않았어. 집에 있으면서 숙제를 해야 했거든.
M Oh, no. So you didn't get to enjoy the lovely weather?	남 오, 저런. 그래서 이 멋진 날씨를 즐기지 못했다고?
W No. It's a shame. The weather was so nice all weekend.	여 못했지. 아쉬워. 주말 내내 날씨가 너무 좋았잖아.
M Well, I have two tickets for a sunset cruise this Saturday. Would you like 1)to join me?	남 음, 이번 주 토요일에 석양을 볼 수 있는 유람선 티켓이 두 장 있는데. 나랑 같이 갈래?
W That sounds wonderful, but I can't go.	여 정말 좋은데, 난 갈 수가 없어.
M Is it 2)because of your homework? Will you still be working on it?	남 숙제 때문이니? 그때도 계속 그걸 하고 있을 예정이야?
W No. It's finished. I submitted it yesterday.	여 아니. 그건 마무리했어. 어제 제출했거든.
M Then, it must be because you get sick on boats.	남 그렇다면, 넌 배를 타면 속이 메스꺼워져서 그렇겠구나.
W Actually, I love going on boat rides. But I already have 3)plans to go camping this weekend.	여 사실, 난 배 타는 걸 좋아해. 하지만 이번 주말에는 이미 캠핑 갈 계획이 있어.
M I see. Well, let's grab dinner sometime this week instead.	남 그렇구나. 음, 대신 이번 주 중에 저녁이나 같이 먹자.
W Sure, I'd love to.	여 그래, 얼마든지.

여자는 남자의 유람선 여행 제안을 거절하면서 이번 주말에는 이미 캠핑 계획이 있다고 말했으므로, 여자가 유람선 여행을 갈 수 없는 이유는 ④ '캠핑을 가야 해서'이다.

어휘 It's a shame. 아쉬워. cruise 圏 유람선 여행 submit 图 제출하다 sick 圏 속이 메스꺼운, 속이 안 좋은; 아픈 grab dinner 저녁을 먹다

8 언급 유무 파악

정답 ⑤

W Henry, have you heard about the winter trip the French club is taking?	여 Henry, 프랑스어 동아리에서 겨울 여행을 떠나는 것에 대해 들어본 적 있어?
M No, I haven't. Can you tell me more about it?	남 아니, 못 들어봤어. 그것에 대해 좀 더 말해 줄래?
W There's some information on their website. It sounds really fun.	여 웹사이트에 정보가 좀 있어. 정말 재미있을 것 같아.
M Let's see. [Pause] So they're 1)going to Canada for five days.	남 어디 보자. [잠시 멈춤] 그러니까 5일 동안 캐나다에 가는구나.
W Yeah. They're leaving on November 22nd.	여 응. 11월 22일에 떠난대.
M It says here that they'll be visiting some famous landmarks.	남 여기에 사람들이 유명한 랜드마크들을 방문할 거라고 쓰여 있어.
W They're 2)going skiing, too.	여 스키도 타러 간대.
M That's awesome. How much is the trip?	남 굉장하네. 여행 비용은 얼마야?
W It says down here that it's $750, and that includes transportation, food, and accommodations.	여 여기 아래에 750달러라고 쓰여 있는데, 여기에는 교통비, 식비, 숙박비가 포함되어 있어.
M Wow, that's really fair. Is it only for 3)French club members?	남 우와, 정말 괜찮네. 이건 프랑스어 동아리 회원들 전용인가?
W I think so. But if not enough people sign up, they'll let others join, too.	여 그런 것 같아. 하지만 사람들이 충분히 많이 신청하지 않으면, 다른 사람들도 함께 가게 해줄 거야.
M Okay. I'll ask my parents about it.	남 알았어. 우리 부모님께 여쭤볼게.

목적지(캐나다), 출발일(11월 22일), 활동(유명한 랜드마크 방문, 스키 타기), 경비(750달러)에 대해 언급했고, ⑤ '인솔자'는 언급하지 않았다.

어휘 Have you heard about ~? ~에 대해 들어본 적 있어? It says here that ~. 여기에 ~라고 쓰여 있다. landmark 圏 랜드마크, 주요 지형지물 transportation 圏 교통 accommodation 圏 숙박 시설, 숙소 fair 圏 괜찮은, 정당한

9 내용 불일치 파악   정답 ③

W	Attention, students. This is Ms. Nelson, the biology teacher. I'd like to remind you all about the Clean Marine Poster Contest. The contest is ¹⁾open to all Pinewood High School students, so I highly encourage everyone to participate. The theme this year is "Save Our Seas." We are now accepting entries, and the submission deadline is ²⁾May 31st. Contestants' posters will be hung up in the cafeteria, and students will ³⁾vote on the best ones. **The first-, second-, and third-place winners will receive cash prizes of $50, $30, and $15, respectively.** The winners will be announced on World Oceans Day, which is June 8th. The first-place poster's design will be ⁴⁾printed on the T-shirts given to beach-cleaning volunteers.	여 주목해 주세요, 학생 여러분. 생물 선생님인 Nelson 선생님입니다. 저는 여러분 모두에게 Clean Marine Poster Contest에 대해 상기시켜 드리고자 합니다. 이 대회는 파인우드 고등학교 학생들 모두에게 열려 있기 때문에, 저는 여러분 모두에게 참여할 것을 강력히 권합니다. 올해 주제는 '우리의 바다를 구하자'입니다. 현재 접수를 받고 있으며, 제출 마감일은 5월 31일입니다. 참가자들의 포스터는 식당에 걸릴 예정이고, 학생들이 최고의 포스터에 투표할 것입니다. 1등, 2등, 3등은 각각 50달러, 30달러, 15달러의 상금을 받게 됩니다. 수상자들은 6월 8일 세계 해양의 날에 발표될 것입니다. 1등 포스터 디자인은 해변 청소 봉사자들에게 주어지는 티셔츠에 인쇄될 것입니다.

포스터 대회에 대한 안내 방송이다. 여자가 1등, 2등, 3등이 각각 50달러, 30달러, 15달러를 받는다고 했으므로, ③ '대회 3위는 상금 30달러를 받는다.'는 내용과 일치하지 않는다.

어휘 remind 동 상기시키다 theme 명 주제, 테마 entry 명 접수, 참가 submission 명 제출; 항복 contestant 명 참가자 respectively 부 각각 announce 동 발표하다

10 도표 정보 파악   정답 ②

W	Honey, don't you think we should change the espresso machine? Ours is too old.	여 여보, 우리 에스프레소 기계를 바꿔야 하지 않을까? 우리 것은 너무 낡았어.
M	Actually, I was already looking at some new ones on Webmart.	남 사실, 내가 이미 Webmart에서 신상품들을 보고 있었어.
W	Hmm... *[Pause]* These look great, but I ¹⁾don't want to spend more than $400 on an espresso machine.	여 흠... *[잠시 멈춤]* 이것들이 좋아 보이는데, 에스프레소 기계에 400달러 이상을 쓰고 싶지는 않아.
M	Fair enough. How long should the brewing time be?	남 좋아. 추출 시간은 얼마나 걸리는 게 좋을까?
W	I'm happy with anything that makes espresso in ²⁾less than 50 seconds.	여 50초 이하로 에스프레소를 추출하는 것이라면 무엇이든 만족해.
M	What about the cleaning function? Is that necessary?	남 청소 기능은 어때? 그게 필수일까?
W	I do think ³⁾we need that. Espresso machines are pretty hard to clean.	여 그건 정말 필요할 것 같아. 에스프레소 기계는 청소하기 꽤 어렵거든.
M	It looks like we have two colors to choose from, then.	남 그럼 선택할 색상이 두 가지 남은 것 같네.
W	I really like that shade of blue.	여 나는 저 파란색 색조가 정말 마음에 들어.
M	I like it, but it doesn't go with the color of the kitchen.	남 나도 마음에 들지만, 부엌 색깔과는 어울리지 않아.
W	You're right. Let's ⁴⁾buy the other one.	여 네 말이 맞아. 다른 걸 사자.
M	Perfect. I'll order it now.	남 완벽해. 지금 주문할게.

두 사람은 400달러 미만인 것 중에서, 추출 시간은 50초 이하이고, 청소 기능이 탑재되어 있으며, 파란색이 아닌 에스프레소 기계를 골랐다.

어휘 Fair enough. (생각이나 제안에 대해) 좋아, 타당해. brew 동 (커피 원액을) 추출하다, (차를) 우리다 function 명 기능 necessary 형 필수적인, 필요한 shade 명 색조; 그늘
go with ~과 어울리다

11 짧은 대화의 응답 파악   정답 ①

M	Ma'am, here is your water. Would you like ¹⁾some more time with the menu?	남 손님, 여기 물 드리겠습니다. 메뉴 고르실 시간을 좀 더 드릴까요?
W	No, thanks. I've already decided what I want to order.	여 아뇨, 괜찮습니다. 이미 주문하고 싶은 것을 결정했어요.
M	Okay. Then, ²⁾what can I get you?	남 알겠습니다. 그럼, 무엇으로 드릴까요?
W	Can I get the pasta salad, please?	여 파스타 샐러드로 주시겠어요?

선택지 ① 파스타 샐러드로 주시겠어요?
② 온라인으로 주문할 것 같아요.
③ 채소를 충분히 씻어주세요.
④ 저희 예약은 오늘 저녁 6시 30분입니다.
⑤ 스테이크를 어떻게 해드릴까요?

남자가 여자의 주문을 받는 상황에서, 여자가 주문하고 싶은 것을 결정했다고 하자 남자가 무엇으로 줄지 물어봤으므로, 이에 대한 응답으로는 결정한 메뉴를 이야기하는 ① 'Can I get the pasta salad, please?'가 가장 적절하다.

어휘 thoroughly 부 충분히, 철저하게 reservation 명 예약

12 짧은 대화의 응답 파악
정답 ⑤

W	Hey, John. I thought you would be at the school fair. What are you doing 1)in the library?
M	I'm printing out flyers for the jazz band's concert.
W	Could I 2)use the computer after you? I need to print my English class essay.
M	Sure. I'll be done in five minutes.

여	안녕, John. 네가 학교 박람회에 있을 거라고 생각했는데. 도서관에서 뭐 하는 중이야?
남	재즈 밴드 콘서트 광고지를 출력하고 있어.
여	너 다음에 컴퓨터를 써도 될까? 영어 수업 에세이를 인쇄해야 하거든.
남	물론이지. 5분이면 끝나.

선택지 ① 정확해. 우리 콘서트는 다음 주 토요일이야.
② 좋아. 네 에세이를 읽는 것이 즐거웠어.
③ 미안해. 하지만 그 책은 이용할 수 없어.
④ 아니. 박람회 표는 어린이들에게는 무료야.
⑤ 물론이지. 5분이면 끝나.

도서관 컴퓨터로 출력 중인 남자에게 여자가 영어 수업 에세이를 인쇄해야 한다면서 다음 순서로 컴퓨터를 써도 되는지 물었으므로, 이에 대한 응답으로는 써도 된다고 말하는 ⑤ 'Sure. I'll be done in five minutes.'가 가장 적절하다.

어휘 fair 뗑 박람회 print out ~을 출력하다 flyer 뗑 광고지, 전단

13 긴 대화의 응답 파악
정답 ③

W	I love that photo, David. Did you take it for our photography class?
M	Yeah, I did. Thanks. Actually, I'm entering it in an amateur photography contest.
W	I didn't know there was a contest!
M	It's being sponsored by *Art of Our Times*.
W	Oh, I love that magazine.
M	You should 1)enter the contest, too. Anyone who is not a professional photographer can participate.
W	Interesting. So is there 2)a particular theme?
M	It's people in nature.
W	Oh, so I would need to have a model in the photo?
M	Well, there needs to be at least one person.
W	Hmm... I usually just take photos of natural settings. I don't think I'll 3)join after all.
M	Okay, but you should know that the winner will get a free trip to Thailand.
W	Really? Maybe I should submit a photo, then.

여	저 사진 너무 마음에 든다, David. 우리 사진 수업 때 찍은 거야?
남	응, 맞아. 고마워. 사실, 아마추어 사진 대회에 저걸 출품하려고 해.
여	대회가 있는 줄 몰랐어!
남	<Art of Our Times>에서 후원받는 대회야.
여	아, 그 잡지 정말 좋아하는데.
남	너도 콘테스트에 참가해야 해. 전문 사진작가가 아닌 사람이라면 누구나 참여할 수 있어.
여	흥미롭네. 그러면, 특정한 주제가 있어?
남	자연 속의 사람들이 주제야.
여	아, 그럼 사진 속에 모델이 있어야겠네?
남	음, 적어도 한 명은 있어야 해.
여	흠... 나는 주로 자연환경의 사진만 찍어. 어쨌든 난 참가하지는 않을 것 같아.
남	알겠어, 하지만 우승자는 태국으로 무료 여행을 가게 된다는 점을 알아두는 게 좋을걸.
여	정말? 그럼 사진을 제출하는 게 좋겠네.

선택지 ① 동의해. 정말 좋은 잡지야.
② 잠깐만. 카메라를 조금만 조정해 볼게.
③ 정말? 그럼 사진을 제출하는 게 좋겠네.
④ 미안해. 너는 그 대회에 참가할 자격이 안 돼.
⑤ 아니. 차라리 나는 사람들의 사진을 찍는 게 낫겠어.

아마추어 사진 대회에 참가할 것을 권유하는 상황이다. 여자가 자신이 주로 찍는 사진과는 다른 주제의 대회라서 참가하지 않을 것 같다고 하자 남자가 대회 우승자에게는 무료 여행 기회가 주어진다는 점을 강조했으므로, 이에 대한 응답으로는 생각을 바꿔 말하는 ③ 'Really? Maybe I should submit a photo, then.'이 가장 적절하다.

어휘 amateur 뗑 아마추어, 비전문가 sponsor 뙝 후원하다 professional 혱 전문의, 전문적인 particular 혱 특정한 after all 어쨌든 adjust 뙝 조정하다 qualify 뙝 자격이 있다

14 긴 대화의 응답 파악
정답 ②

M	Which movie should we watch at the theater tonight, Elena?
W	Here's a list of what's playing right now. Do any of them interest you?
M	Hmm... What about this one? It's a 1)science-fiction movie.
W	You know I'm not a big fan of science fiction.
M	That's right. *[Pause]* Maybe we can watch this one. It's a romantic comedy.
W	That one got a lot of negative reviews, so I 2)don't think we should watch it.
M	You should choose the movie, then. I'm not as picky as you are.
W	All right. Then, let's watch this one! It's a horror movie.
M	Are you sure about that? It looks pretty scary.
W	Do you think it's a bad idea 3)to watch it?
M	Yeah. Horror movies give me nightmares.

남	오늘 밤에 영화관에서 어떤 영화 볼래, Elena?
여	지금 상영하고 있는 것들의 목록이 여기 있어. 이 중에 흥미를 끄는 게 있니?
남	흠... 이건 어때? 공상 과학 영화야.
여	내가 공상 과학을 별로 좋아하지 않는다는 거 알잖아.
남	그랬지. *[잠시 멈춤]* 아마 이건 볼 수 있을 것 같아. 로맨틱 코미디야.
여	그 영화는 부정적인 평가를 많이 받아서, 보지 않는 게 좋을 것 같아.
남	그럼 네가 영화를 골라. 난 너만큼 까다롭지 않으니까.
여	그래. 그럼, 이걸 보자! 공포 영화야.
남	진심이야? 꽤 무서워 보여.
여	그 영화를 보는 게 좋지 않다고 생각해?
남	응. 공포 영화는 날 악몽을 꾸게 해.

선택지 ① 그러게. 그러니까 우리가 그걸 안 봤잖아.
② 응. 공포 영화는 날 악몽을 꾸게 해.
③ 맞아. 우리는 다른 영화를 골랐어야 했어.

④ 딱히. 나는 영화 비평가들의 의견에 항상 동의하지는 않거든.

⑤ 좋아. 공상 과학 영화 재미있을 것 같아!

영화관에서 영화를 고르고 있는 상황이다. 공포 영화를 보자는 제안에 남자가 꽤 무서워 보인다고 하자 여자가 그 영화를 보는 것이 좋지 않다고 생각하는지 물었으므로, 이에 대한 응답으로는 그렇다고 답하며 이유를 말하는 ② 'Yeah. Horror movies give me nightmares.'가 가장 적절하다.

어휘 science-fiction movie 공상 과학 영화 negative 형 부정적인 picky 형 까다로운 nightmare 명 악몽 critic 명 비평가

---

15 상황에 적절한 말 파악   정답 ④

M Gina is a member of the school soccer team. She is a talented player, but she has difficulty scoring goals. During games, she frequently misses good chances to score because her shots are inaccurate. As a result, she has been ¹⁾training more and more. These days, Gina often continues to practice even when she feels tired or sore. Her coach, Mr. Penn, has ²⁾started to worry about Gina. He thinks that her training habits are harmful. He believes that Gina should let her body recover more. **So Mr. Penn wants to tell Gina that practicing so hard may cause her ³⁾to get injured.** In this situation, what would Mr. Penn most likely say to Gina?

남 Gina는 학교 축구팀의 일원입니다. 그녀는 재능 있는 선수이지만, 골을 넣는 데 어려움을 겪고 있습니다. 경기 중에, 그녀는 슛이 부정확해서 득점할 좋은 기회를 자주 놓칩니다. 결과적으로, 그녀는 점점 더 많은 훈련을 하고 있습니다. 요즘에, Gina는 피곤하거나 근육이 아플 때도 종종 연습을 계속합니다. 그녀의 코치인 Penn 선생님은 Gina에 대해 걱정하기 시작했습니다. 그는 그녀의 훈련 습관이 해롭다고 생각합니다. 그는 Gina가 그녀의 몸을 더 회복하게 둬야 한다고 생각합니다. 그래서, Penn 선생님은 Gina에게 너무 심하게 연습하는 것은 그녀가 부상을 입게 만들 수도 있다고 말하고 싶습니다. 이러한 상황에서, Penn 선생님이 Gina에게 가장 할 것 같은 말은 무엇입니까?

선택지 ① 정확하게 패스하는 것이 슈팅보다 더 중요하지.
② 연습 동안 몇 가지 기술을 보여줄 수 있어.
③ 제대로 낫고 싶다면 휴식이 필요하단다.
④ 너무 많은 훈련은 부상의 원인이 될 수 있단다.
⑤ 득점하는 것은 고된 노력을 필요로 하지.

Gina가 휴식도 없이 연습을 계속하는 것을 보고, Penn 선생님은 너무 심하게 연습하는 것은 부상을 입게 만들 수도 있다고 조언하려 한다. 따라서, Mr. Penn이 할 말로 ④ 'Too much training can cause an injury.'가 가장 적절하다.

어휘 talented 형 재능 있는, 타고난 score a goal 골을 넣다, 득점하다 frequently 부 자주, 흔히 miss a chance 기회를 놓치다 inaccurate 형 부정확한 as a result 결과적으로
sore 형 (근육 등이) 아픈 habit 명 습관 harmful 형 해로운 get injured 부상을 입다 properly 부 제대로

16-17 세트 문항   정답 16 ② 17 ④

W Hello, students. In class last week, we talked about why countries have certain symbols on their flags. **Today, we'll learn about ¹⁾national flags that have animals on them.** The first is the flag of **Mexico**. It shows a golden eagle, which is a character in a famous Aztec legend. The second flag is that of **Sri Lanka**. It ²⁾includes a golden lion holding a sword. The lion is the symbol of Sri Lanka because the country's first king had this animal on his flag. Another flag with an animal on it is that of **Moldova**. This small country, ³⁾located in Eastern Europe, used to have an unusual animal on its flag. Until the 1800s, it displayed the head of a bull. Finally, the flag of **Dominica** shows a ⁴⁾green parrot. This country is the only one with this type of bird on its flag. Now, let's look at some pictures of these flags.

여 안녕하세요, 학생 여러분. 지난주 수업에서, 우리는 왜 국가들이 국기에 특정한 상징을 두었는지에 대해 이야기했습니다. 오늘은, 동물이 그려진 국기에 대해 배워보겠습니다. 첫 번째는 멕시코의 국기입니다. 이것은 황금 독수리를 보여주는데, 이것은 유명한 아스텍 전설 속 캐릭터입니다. 두 번째 국기는 스리랑카의 것입니다. 그것은 검을 들고 있는 황금 사자를 포함하고 있습니다. 스리랑카의 초대 왕이 이 동물을 국기에 넣었기 때문에 사자는 스리랑카의 상징입니다. 동물이 그려진 또 다른 국기는 몰도바의 것입니다. 동유럽에 위치한 이 작은 나라는 국기에 특이한 동물을 담고 있었습니다. 1800년대까지, 그것은 황소의 머리를 보여주었습니다. 마지막으로, 도미니카 공화국의 국기는 녹색 앵무새를 보여줍니다. 이 나라는 국기에 이런 종류의 새가 있는 유일한 나라입니다. 이제, 이 국기들의 사진을 몇 장 봅시다.

선택지 **16** ① 다양한 국가들이 세워진 방법
② 국기에 동물이 있는 국가
③ 왕들이 동물을 그들의 상징으로 한 이유
④ 다양한 국가들의 상징 동물
⑤ 시간에 따른 국기 디자인의 변화
17 ① 멕시코 ② 스리랑카 ③ 몰도바 ④ 페루 ⑤ 도미니카 공화국

16 동물이 그려진 국기에 대해 배우고 있으므로 여자가 하는 말의 주제로 ② 'nations that have animals on their flags'가 가장 적절하다.
17 멕시코, 스리랑카, 몰도바, 도미니카 공화국은 언급했지만 ④ 'Peru'는 언급하지 않았다.

어휘 certain 형 특정한 symbol 명 상징 national flag 국기 legend 명 전설 sword 명 검 located in ~에 위치한 used to (과거에) ~했다 display 동 보여주다, 드러내다 bull 명 황소
found 동 세우다, 설립하다

1	②	2	⑤	3	①	4	③	5	⑤	6	②	7	④	8	⑤	9	②	10	③
11	④	12	①	13	②	14	③	15	①	16	④	17	③						

• 각 문제의 정답 근거는 굵은 글씨로, Dictation 정답은 밑줄로 표시되어 있습니다.

---

1 목적 파악

정답 ②

W Attention, listeners! When you're busy, do you have trouble ¹⁾keeping your tasks organized? **Then, the new smartphone app, List Keeper, can help!** With List Keeper, you can keep your task list, shopping list, and reading list in one place. It also helps you finish the most ²⁾important tasks first. You can set alarms for reminders of what you have to do. You can even share your to-do lists with others, so List Keeper is great for ³⁾managing group projects. **Sign up now for a free 14-day trial, and then ⁴⁾subscribe for only $2 per month.**

여 주목해주세요, 청취자 여러분! 바쁘실 때 할 일을 정리하는 데 어려움을 겪으시나요? 그렇다면, 새로운 스마트폰 앱인 List Keeper가 도움이 될 수 있습니다! List Keeer를 사용하면 할 일 목록, 쇼핑 목록 및 독서 목록을 한곳에 보관할 수 있습니다. 또한 가장 중요한 일을 먼저 마칠 수 있도록 도와줍니다. 수행해야할 일을 미리 알려주는 알림을 맞출 수 있습니다. 다른 사용자와 할 일 목록을 공유할 수도 있으므로, List Keeper는 그룹 프로젝트를 관리하는 데 유용합니다. 지금 14일 무료 체험판에 가입하시고, 이후에는 단 2달러로 매월 구독하세요.

여자가 새로운 스마트폰 앱인 List Keeper가 할 일을 정리하는 데 도움이 될 것이라고 하면서, 체험판 가입과 매월 구독할 것을 권유하고 있다. 따라서, 여자가 하는 말의 목적으로 ② '새로운 스마트폰 앱을 홍보하려고'가 가장 적절하다.

어휘 have trouble ~하는 데 어려움을 겪다 organize 통 정리하다 set an alarm 알람을 맞추다 share 통 공유하다 manage 통 관리하다 sign up 가입하다 subscribe 통 구독하다

---

2 의견 파악

정답 ⑤

W How was your weekend, Mark?
M Great. My daughter got a new computer, so I helped her set it up.
W I bet she was happy that you bought her a computer.
M Actually, she ¹⁾bought it herself. She's been saving up for years.
W That's amazing. Did you teach her how to save?
M Yes. **I believe kids need to learn ²⁾the value of money from a young age.**
W How did you do it? I want to teach my kids, too.
M My wife and I pay her to do chores. For example, she gets $1 every time she cleans her room, and it ³⁾goes straight into her piggy bank.
W I see. That sounds like a great way for children to learn about the value of money.
M Yeah, it worked for us.

여 주말 잘 보냈니, Mark?
남 잘 보냈어. 우리 딸이 새 컴퓨터를 사서, 설치하는 것을 도와줬어.
여 네가 컴퓨터를 사줘서 그녀가 행복했을 것이 분명해.
남 사실, 딸이 직접 샀어. 몇 년 동안 저축해 왔거든.
여 정말 놀랍네. 저축하는 법을 가르쳤어?
남 응. 난 아이들이 어릴 때부터 돈의 가치를 배워야 한다고 생각하거든.
여 어떻게 했어? 나도 내 아이들을 가르치고 싶어.
남 아내와 나는 딸이 집안일을 하는 것에 돈을 지불해. 예를 들어, 방을 청소할 때마다 1달러를 받고, 그 돈은 바로 그녀의 돼지 저금통으로 들어가.
여 그렇구나. 아이들이 돈의 가치에 대해 배울 수 있는 좋은 방법 같네.
남 응, 우리한테는 효과가 있었어.

딸에게 저축하는 법을 가르쳤는지 묻는 여자에게 남자는 그렇게 했다면서 아이들은 어릴 때부터 돈의 가치를 배워야 한다고 생각한다고 했다. 따라서, 남자의 의견으로 ⑤ '아이들은 어릴 때부터 돈의 가치를 배워야 한다.'가 가장 적절하다.

어휘 set up ~을 설치하다 bet 통 분명하다, 틀림없다; 돈을 걸다 save up 저축하다 value 명 가치 pay 통 지불하다 straight 부 곧바로 piggy bank 돼지 저금통 work 통 효과가 있다; 일하다

---

3 관계 파악

정답 ①

W Hello. How can I help you?
M Hi. My name is Terry Lee. **I called this morning and made an appointment.**
W Okay, just one moment. [Typing sound] Yes, you told me ¹⁾you hurt your ankle, right?
M That's right. I fell off a ladder while replacing a ceiling light. **I think I sprained my left ankle.**
W Do you have any other injuries?
M No, that's it.
W ²⁾Have you visited our clinic before?
M No. It's my first time.
W Then, please show me your ID card.
M Here it is.

여 안녕하세요. 무엇을 도와드릴까요?
남 안녕하세요. 제 이름은 Terry Lee입니다. 오늘 아침에 전화해서 예약했는데요.
여 네, 잠시만요. [타자 치는 소리] 네, 발목 다쳤다고 하셨죠?
남 맞아요. 천장 조명을 교체하다가 사다리에서 떨어졌어요. 왼쪽 발목을 삐었나 봐요.
여 다른 부상은 없으세요?
남 네, 그게 다예요.
여 전에 저희 병원에 방문하신 적이 있나요?
남 아니요. 처음이에요.
여 그럼, 신분증을 보여주세요.
남 여기 있습니다.

W	Okay. **Registration** ³⁾is complete. We'll give you an X-ray first. Then, you'll be able to see the doctor.	여	알겠습니다. 접수가 완료되었어요. 먼저 엑스레이를 찍어드릴게요. 그다음에, 의사 선생님께 진찰받으실 거예요.
M	All right. Thanks.	남	좋아요. 감사해요.

두 사람이 남자의 부상에 대해 이야기하고 있다. 여자는 증상을 물어보고 전에 이 병원에 방문한 적이 있는지 확인하면서 진료 접수를 해주고 있고, 남자는 진료 예약을 했으며 왼쪽 발목을 삐었다고 하는 것으로 보아 두 사람의 관계로 ① '정형외과 직원 — 환자'가 가장 적절하다.

어휘 make an appointment 예약하다 ankle 명 발목 fall off ~에서 떨어지다 ladder 명 사다리 replace 동 교체하다 ceiling 명 천장 sprain 동 삐다 injury 명 부상 clinic 명 병원 ID card 신분증 complete 형 완료된

4 그림 내용 불일치 파악

정답 ③

W	Hey, Luke. I went to the new café near our school to study last night.	여	안녕, Luke. 나 어젯밤에 공부하러 학교 근처에 새로 생긴 카페에 갔었어.
M	How was it? I haven't ¹⁾been there yet.	남	어땠어? 난 아직 가본 적이 없어.
W	I'll show you a picture. [Pause] Doesn't it look nice?	여	사진을 보여줄게. [잠시 멈춤] 좋아 보이지 않아?
M	Yes. It looks cozy. Look at the sleeping cat on the counter.	남	응. 아늑해 보이네. 계산대 위에 잠자고 있는 고양이를 봐.
W	It's so cute. And the bookshelf on the right made the café feel ²⁾like a library.	여	너무 귀여워. 그리고 오른쪽에 있는 책장은 카페를 도서관처럼 느끼게 해줬어.
M	It looks like a great place for studying. **I like those striped curtains.**	남	공부하기 좋은 곳 같아. 저 줄무늬 커튼이 마음에 들어.
W	I thought they were stylish. And isn't that a cool lamp on the table?	여	그게 스타일리시하다고 생각했어. 그리고 테이블 위에 있는 램프 멋지지 않아?
M	Yeah. That square clock on the wall is beautiful, too.	남	응. 벽에 있는 네모난 시계도 아름답네.
W	Oh, yes. It was useful for keeping track of the time.	여	아, 맞아. 그건 시간을 관리하는 데 유용했어.
M	Let me know if you ³⁾plan to go again. I want to join you.	남	또 갈 계획이 있으면 알려줘. 나도 합류하고 싶어.
W	Sounds good.	여	좋아.

대화에서 남자가 줄무늬 커튼이 마음에 든다고 말했는데, ③에는 무늬가 없는 커튼이 그려져 있다.

어휘 counter 명 계산대 cool 형 멋진; 시원한 useful 형 유용한 keep track of ~을 관리하다, 기록하다

5 할 일 파악

정답 ⑤

W	Hi, Aaron. I can't wait for Irene's surprise birthday party on Sunday.	여	안녕, Aaron. 일요일에 Irene의 깜짝 생일 파티가 너무 기대돼.
M	Me neither. She's going to be shocked. Did you ¹⁾decide on a restaurant?	남	나도. 그녀가 깜짝 놀랄 거야. 식당은 정했어?
W	Irene loves seafood, so I booked a room at the Seaside Kitchen.	여	Irene이 해산물을 좋아해서, Seaside Kitchen에 방을 예약했어.
M	Perfect. How many of us will there be?	남	완벽해. 우리 몇 명이나 가?
W	There will be 10 people in total.	여	총 10명일 거야.
M	Great. Have you found a present for her yet?	남	좋아. 그녀에게 줄 선물은 찾아봤어?
W	Actually, I ²⁾made her a bracelet during my jewelry-making class. It has her initials on it.	여	사실, 액세서리 만들기 수업에서 그녀를 위해 팔찌를 만들었어. 그녀의 이니셜이 적혀 있어.
M	What a special gift! I got her some of her favorite jasmine tea.	남	정말 특별한 선물이다! 나는 그녀가 가장 좋아하는 재스민차를 샀어.
W	She'll love that.	여	걔가 정말 좋아할 거야.
M	I hope so. **Oh, should we order a cake for her?** There's a great bakery near my house.	남	그랬으면 좋겠어. 아, 우리 케이크를 주문할까? 우리 집 근처에 맛있는 빵집이 있어.
W	Okay. **Do you mind ³⁾taking care of it?**	여	알겠어. 괜찮다면 그 일을 좀 맡아 줄래?
M	**Not at all. I'll drop by soon.**	남	물론이지. 곧 들를게.

친구를 위한 깜짝 생일 파티 계획에 대해 이야기하고 있다. 여자가 남자에게 케이크 주문하는 일을 맡아줄 수 있는지 묻자, 남자가 물론이라면서 곧 들르겠다고 했으므로 남자가 할 일로 ⑤ '케이크 주문하러 가기'가 가장 적절하다.

어휘 shocked 형 깜짝 놀란 seafood 명 해산물 in total 총, 통틀어 bracelet 명 팔찌 Do you mind ~? 괜찮다면 ~해줄래? take care of ~을 맡아서 하다 drop by 들르다

6   금액 정보 파악 정답 ②

M	Welcome to Wild Water World. Are you here to enjoy our outdoor pools and water slides?
W	Yes. How much are tickets?
M	It's ¹⁾$30 <u>for adults</u> and $20 for children.
W	Okay. **We have two adults and two children in our group.**
M	All right. Also, we have a special promotion going on this weekend. **Our lunch buffet tickets are $10 for adults and** ²⁾<u>free for all children</u>.
W	**That sounds good.** Can I pay for those now, too?
M	Certainly. So you want admission and lunch tickets for two adults and two children.
W	Right. And I have this coupon. Is it ³⁾<u>still valid</u>?
M	You're lucky. Today's the last day you can use it. **So you'll get 10% off the total.**
W	Great. I'll pay with my credit card.

남	Wild Water World에 오신 것을 환영합니다. 야외 수영장과 워터 슬라이드를 즐기러 오셨나요?
여	네. 입장권은 얼마인가요?
남	어른은 30달러, 어린이는 20달러입니다.
여	네. 저희 그룹에는 어른 두 명과 아이 두 명이 있어요.
남	알겠습니다. 그리고, 이번 주말에는 특별 프로모션을 진행해요. 저희 점심 뷔페 이용권이 어른은 10달러, 어린이는 모두 무료입니다.
여	그거 좋네요. 그것들도 지금 계산할 수 있나요?
남	물론이죠. 그럼 어른 두 명과 어린이 두 명의 입장권과 점심 이용권을 원하시는 거군요.
여	맞아요. 그리고 이 쿠폰을 가지고 있어요. 아직 유효한가요?
남	운이 좋으시네요. 오늘이 사용하실 수 있는 마지막 날이에요. 그럼 총액에서 10%를 할인해 드릴게요.
여	좋아요. 신용 카드로 지불할게요.

여자는 Wild Water World의 어른 입장권 두 장($30×2=$60)과 어린이 입장권 두 장($20×2=$40)을 구매하고, 추가로 점심 이용권 두 장($10×2=$20)을 구매했다. 이후 총액에서 10% 할인($120×0.9=$108)을 받았으므로 정답은 ② '$108'이다.

[어휘] outdoor 휑 야외의　admission 뗑 입장　valid 휑 유효한　pay with one's credit card 신용 카드로 지불하다

---

7   이유 파악 정답 ④

W	How was baseball practice, Jay? I'm looking forward to watching you play tomorrow.
M	Hi, Cindy. Practice was good, but I ¹⁾<u>won't be playing</u> tomorrow.
W	Really? That's too bad.
M	I know. But it's out of my control.
W	Is it because you're still not ²⁾<u>fully recovered from</u> your cold?
M	No. I'm much better now, except for the occasional cough.
W	I remember your cousin is visiting from Calgary. You must be busy showing him around our town, right?
M	No. That's not why. **I'm** ³⁾<u>auditioning for</u> the school play tomorrow.
W	Oh, that's cool. Good luck with that.
M	Thanks. See you later in math class.
W	Okay. See you.

여	야구 연습은 어땠니, Jay? 내일 네 경기를 보는 걸 기대하고 있어.
남	안녕, Cindy. 연습은 좋았는데 내일은 경기에 나가지 않을 거야.
여	정말? 유감이야.
남	그러게. 하지만 그건 내가 제어할 수가 없어.
여	감기가 아직 완전히 낫지 않아서 그런 거야?
남	아니. 가끔 기침을 하는 것을 제외하고는 지금 많이 좋아졌어.
여	캘거리에서 온 사촌이 방문 중인 걸로 기억하는데. 우리 동네를 구경시켜 주느라 바쁘구나, 그렇지?
남	아니야. 그 이유가 아니야. 나 내일 학교 연극 오디션을 봐.
여	오, 멋지다. 행운을 빌어.
남	고마워. 나중에 수학 시간에 봐.
여	알겠어. 나중에 봐.

남자는 내일 야구 경기에 나가지 않을 거라고 하면서 내일 학교 연극 오디션을 본다고 말했으므로, 남자가 경기에 출전할 수 없는 이유는 ④ '학교 연극 오디션을 봐야 해서'이다.

[어휘] play 통 경기에 나가다; 놀다 뗑 연극　out of one's control 제어할 수 없는　recover 통 낫다, 회복되다　except for ~을 제외하고는　occasional 휑 가끔의
show A around B A에게 B를 구경시켜 주다　audition 통 오디션을 보다 뗑 오디션

---

8   언급 유무 파악 정답 ⑤

M	Helen, what are you looking at?
W	It's a pamphlet ¹⁾<u>for winter activities</u> at the community center, Dad.
M	Is there anything that looks interesting?
W	Yeah. I'm interested in the ice-skating program.
M	Let's see here. *[Pause]* They offer **beginner and intermediate classes for speed skating**. There's also **a figure-skating class for advanced skaters**.
W	Well... I've only skated a few times before, so I should ²⁾<u>take the beginner</u> class.
M	It's every Wednesday evening at **7 p.m.**
W	That works for me. When does it start?
M	It starts on **January 4th** and runs for eight weeks.
W	Okay. Is there anything I need to bring?
M	You just need **a pair of ice skates**. They also ³⁾<u>recommend bringing</u> **a helmet**.
W	Great. I can't wait to start!

남	Helen, 뭘 보고 있어?
여	지역 주민센터에 있는 겨울 활동에 대한 팸플릿이에요, 아빠.
남	재미있어 보이는 게 있니?
여	네. 아이스 스케이팅 프로그램에 관심이 있어요.
남	여기 좀 보자. [잠시 멈춤] 스피드 스케이팅에는 초급반과 중급반을 제공하는구나. 상급 스케이터들을 위한 피겨 스케이팅 수업도 있어.
여	음... 저는 스케이트를 몇 번밖에 안 타봐서, 초급반을 들어야겠어요.
남	그건 매주 수요일 저녁 7시에 있구나.
여	제 일정에 맞아요. 언제 시작하나요?
남	1월 4일에 시작해서 8주간 운영하네.
여	네. 가져가야 할 것이 있나요?
남	스케이트화 한 켤레만 있으면 돼. 헬멧을 가지고 가는 것도 추천하고 있구나.
여	좋아요. 빨리 시작하고 싶어요!

수업 종류(스피드 스케이팅 초급반과 중급반, 피겨 스케이팅 고급반), 수업 시각(저녁 7시), 시작 날짜(1월 4일), 준비물(스케이트화, 헬멧)에 대해 언급했고, ⑤ '강사 이름'은 언급하지 않았다.

[어휘] look at ~을 보다　activity 뗑 활동　community center 지역 주민센터　be interested in ~에 관심이 있다　intermediate 휑 중급의　advanced 휑 상급의, 고급의; 전진한
run 통 운영하다　recommend 통 추천하다

9 내용 불일치 파악
정답 ②

W Good morning, students. This is your principal Ms. Crawley with a special announcement. We are now accepting submissions for the Voices of Youth Literary Competition. All students ¹⁾<u>are invited to submit</u> one of their best short stories, poems, or essays. **The first-place winner in each of the three categories will be awarded** ²⁾**a cash prize of $500.** The winners will also ³⁾<u>have their work published</u> in the Glendale County newspaper. Submissions will be accepted online until midnight on March 31st. Please check the Voices of Youth website for full contest rules and ⁴⁾<u>previous winners</u> in each category.	여 좋은 아침입니다, 학생 여러분. 특별 발표를 가지고 온 Crawley 교장입니다. 우리는 Voices of Youth Literary Competition에 지원을 받고 있습니다. 모든 학생들에게 각자 최고의 단편 소설, 시 또는 수필 중 하나를 제출하기를 요청합니다. 세 가지 부문에서 1등을 차지한 각 수상자는 500달러의 상금을 받을 것입니다. 또한 수상자들의 작품은 글렌데일 카운티 신문에 실릴 것입니다. 지원은 3월 31일 자정까지 온라인으로 접수됩니다. 전체 대회 규정과 부문별 이전 수상자는 Voices of Youth 웹사이트에서 확인하세요.

문학 공모전 지원에 대한 독려 방송이다. 여자가 세 가지 부문에서 1등을 차지한 각 수상자는 500달러의 상금을 받을 것이라고 했으므로 ② '부문별 1등에게 300달러의 상금이 주어진다.'는 내용과 일치하지 않는다.

어휘 announcement 명 발표 submission 명 지원, 제출; 항복 invite 통 요청하다; 초대하다 submit 통 제출하다 be awarded (상을) 받다 publish 통 싣다, 게재하다; 출판하다 rule 명 규칙 previous 형 이전의

10 도표 정보 파악
정답 ③

M Amy, we need to book a practice room for tonight. Our dance performance is tomorrow.	남 Amy, 오늘 밤 연습실을 예약해야 해. 우리 내일 댄스 공연이 있잖아.
W I know. There aren't many available now. We should have booked it earlier.	여 맞아. 지금은 이용할 수 있는 곳이 많지 않아. 더 일찍 예약했어야 했어.
M But there are still ¹⁾<u>a few rooms left</u>. **It just needs to be large enough for the three of us.**	남 하지만 아직 연습실이 몇 개 남아 있어. 우리 세 명에게 충분할 정도로 크기만 하면 돼.
W Right. How long do we need to practice for?	여 그래. 얼마나 오래 연습해야 해?
M We need it for at least two hours.	남 적어도 두 시간은 필요해.
W Okay. How much money can we spend?	여 알겠어. 우리 돈은 얼마나 쓸 수 있어?
M ²⁾<u>Anything under $25</u> per hour is fine.	남 시간당 25달러 미만이면 좋겠어.
W All right. That leaves us with two options. Oh, it looks like only this one has air conditioning.	여 좋아. 그럼 두 가지 선택지가 남아. 아, 에어컨은 이곳에만 있는 것 같네.
M We definitely ³⁾<u>need air conditioning</u>. It'll be so hot.	남 에어컨이 꼭 필요해. 너무 더울 거야.
W Then, we should book that one.	여 그럼 그 연습실로 예약해야겠네.
M Perfect. Let me call right now.	남 완벽해. 지금 바로 전화해 볼게.

두 사람은 세 명에게 충분한 크기이면서, 적어도 두 시간은 사용할 수 있고, 시간당 25달러 미만인 곳 중에서, 에어컨이 있는 연습실을 골랐다.

어휘 practice room 연습실 performance 명 공연 available 형 이용할 수 있는 at least 적어도 option 명 선택지 definitely 부 꼭, 분명히 capacity 명 수용력, 용량 minimum 형 최소의

11 짧은 대화의 응답 파악
정답 ④

W Honey, I skipped lunch today. Now, I'm ¹⁾<u>really hungry</u>.	여 여보, 난 오늘 점심을 걸렀어. 이제 정말 배가 고파.
M I'm making spaghetti and meatballs for dinner. Can you ²⁾<u>wait until it's done</u>?	남 저녁으로 스파게티와 미트볼을 만들고 있어. 다 될 때까지 기다려 줄래?
W Of course. **Will it take a long time?**	여 물론이지. 오래 걸려?
M It will be ready in about 10 minutes.	남 약 10분 후에 준비될 거야.
	선택지 ① 식사 시간은 충분해.
	② 지금은 전혀 배가 고프지 않아.
	③ 당신이 점심을 많이 먹었다고 했잖아.
	④ 약 10분 후에 준비될 거야.
	⑤ 난 이미 아까 저녁을 다 먹었어.

남자가 저녁으로 스파게티와 미트볼을 만들고 있다며 다 될 때까지 기다려달라고 하자 여자가 물론이라면서 오래 걸릴지 물었으므로, 이에 대한 응답으로는 약 10분 후에 준비될 것이라고 말하는 ④ 'It will be ready in about 10 minutes.'가 가장 적절하다.

어휘 skip lunch 점심을 거르다 take a long time 오래 걸리다 plenty of 충분한, 많은

12 짧은 대화의 응답 파악 정답 ①

M	Nancy, do you 1)have any plans for Saturday evening?
W	No. I was just going to stay home and watch TV. Why?
M	**There's a free pop concert in Oak Park. We 2)should go together.**
W	Definitely. That sounds like a lot of fun.

남 Nancy, 토요일 저녁에 계획 있어?
여 아니. 그냥 집에 머물면서 TV를 보려고 했어. 왜?
남 오크 공원에서 무료 가요 콘서트가 있어. 우리 같이 가야 해.
여 꼭 갈래. 정말 재미있을 것 같아.

선택지
① 꼭 갈래. 정말 재미있을 것 같아.
② 말도 안 돼. 오늘 공원이 너무 붐비네.
③ 물론이지. 인터넷으로 표 두 장을 샀어.
④ 미안해. 오늘 밤에는 이미 약속이 있어.
⑤ 그래? 콘서트는 재미있었어?

남자가 여자에게 오크 공원에서 무료 가요 콘서트가 있다면서 같이 갈 것을 제안했으므로, 이에 대한 응답으로는 제안을 수락하는 ① 'Definitely. That sounds like a lot of fun.'이 가장 적절하다.

어휘 stay home 집에 머물다 free 형 무료의; 자유로운 pop 명 가요 crowded 형 붐비는

13 긴 대화의 응답 파악 정답 ②

W	Jordan, I'm so glad I found you.
M	Hey, Amber. What's up?
W	I need help putting up these signs.
M	I can help. What are the signs for?
W	Our 1)student council is holding a flea market next Saturday. We are donating the money that we raise to the children's hospital.
M	Wow, cool. What time is the flea market?
W	It'll start at 10 a.m. and finish at 4 p.m.
M	Then, I can participate. Where did you 2)get the items you are selling?
W	We're collecting them from our teachers and other students. **Do you have 3)anything we could sell? We would really appreciate it.**
M	Sure. I have some old books I can donate.

여 Jordan, 널 찾아서 정말 기뻐.
남 안녕, Amber. 무슨 일이야?
여 이 표지판을 세우는 데 도움이 필요해.
남 내가 도와줄게. 이 표지판들은 뭘 위한 거야?
여 다음 주 토요일에 학생회에서 벼룩시장을 열거든. 모금한 돈을 어린이 병원에 기부할 거야.
남 우와, 멋지다. 벼룩시장은 몇 시에 해?
여 오전 10시에 시작해서 오후 4시에 끝날 거야.
남 그럼, 내가 참여할 수 있겠다. 팔 물건들은 어디서 구했어?
여 선생님들과 다른 학생들로부터 모으고 있어. 우리가 팔 수 있는 물건이 있을까? 그럼 정말 고맙겠어.
남 물론이지. 기부할 수 있는 오래된 책이 몇 권 있어.

선택지
① 미안해. 그 물건은 다 팔렸어.
② 물론이지. 기부할 수 있는 오래된 책이 몇 권 있어.
③ 좋아. 학교 주변에 표지판을 몇 개 세워 놓을게.
④ 아니, 괜찮아. 지금은 아무것도 필요 없어.
⑤ 놀라워! 돈을 많이 모으는 데 성공했네.

어린이 병원 기부를 위한 벼룩시장을 준비 중인 여자가 남자에게 벼룩시장에서 팔 수 있는 물건이 있는지 물었으므로, 이에 대한 응답으로는 기부할 수 있는 오래된 책이 있다고 대답하는 ② 'Sure. I have some old books I can donate.'가 가장 적절하다.

어휘 put up ~을 세우다, 설치하다 sign 명 표지판 student council 학생회 flea market 벼룩시장 donate 동 기부하다 raise 동 모금하다; 올리다 item 명 물건
collect 동 모으다, 수집하다 appreciate 동 고마워하다

14 긴 대화의 응답 파악 정답 ③

M	Hi, Bailey. I haven't seen you 1)in a while!
W	Hey, Jake. I know! I've been so busy. **I started a part-time job a few weeks ago.**
M	How is it going?
W	It's been pretty good. I'm a tour guide.
M	Oh, that sounds like a nice job. Where are you 2)leading the tours?
W	I work at the Plant Museum.
M	Isn't that located next to Lake Park downtown?
W	Right. It's 3)pretty far from my house.
M	Tell me about it. **So what is your commute like?**
W	It takes me an hour to get there by subway.

남 안녕, Bailey. 널 못 본 지 꽤 됐는걸!
여 안녕, Jake. 그러니까! 너무 바빴어. 몇 주 전부터 아르바이트를 시작했거든.
남 어떻게 되고 있어?
여 꽤 괜찮아. 나 여행 가이드야.
남 오, 멋진 직업인 것 같아. 어디에서 가이드를 하고 있어?
여 나 식물 박물관에서 일해.
남 그건 시내에 있는 호수 공원 옆에 있지 않아?
여 맞아. 우리 집에서 꽤 멀어.
남 얘기 좀 해봐. 그래서 출퇴근 어때?
여 지하철로 한 시간이 걸려.

선택지
① 식물 박물관의 관람은 오전 10시에 시작해.
② 일이 내가 생각했던 것보다 더 재미있어.
③ 지하철로 한 시간이 걸려.
④ 공부하면서 아르바이트하는 것은 어려워.
⑤ 박물관에서 귀중한 경험을 쌓고 있어.

두 사람이 근황을 묻고 있는 상황이다. 여자가 일하는 곳이 집에서 꽤 멀다고 하자 남자가 출퇴근은 어떤지 물었으므로, 이에 대한 응답으로는 출퇴근 시간을 언급하는 ③ 'It takes me an hour to get there by subway.'가 가장 적절하다.

어휘 part-time job 아르바이트 pretty 부 꽤 형 예쁜 tour guide 여행 가이드 commute 명 출퇴근, 통근 valuable 형 귀중한

15 상황에 적절한 말 파악

정답 ①

W Ava is taking a German language class this semester at her high school. Ava's father worked in Germany for a long time, so he [1]offered to tutor her. Ava accepted, believing that the lessons would help her get a good grade in the class. Today, however, Ava found out that she [2]failed an exam for the German class. Ava seems very disappointed and says that she is surprised that she failed. **In response, Ava's father wants to tell her to [3]look over the test paper so she can find out what mistakes she made.** In this situation, what would Ava's father most likely say to Ava?

여 Ava는 이번 학기에 고등학교에서 독일어 과목을 수강하고 있습니다. Ava의 아버지는 독일에서 오랫동안 근무했기 때문에, Ava에게 개인 교습을 해주겠다고 제안했습니다. Ava는 이 교습 시간이 학교 수업 때 좋은 성적을 받을 수 있게 도움을 줄 것이라고 생각하면서, 제안을 수락했습니다. 하지만 오늘, Ava는 자신이 독일어 과목 시험에서 낙제했다는 사실을 알게 되었습니다. Ava는 매우 실망한 기색이었고, 시험에 낙제한 것에 놀랐다고 말했습니다. 이에 대해 Ava의 아버지는 그녀에게 어떤 실수를 했는지 확인할 수 있도록 시험지를 살펴보라고 말하고 싶습니다. 이러한 상황에서, Ava의 아버지가 Ava에게 가장 할 것 같은 말은 무엇입니까?

선택지 ① 잘못을 통해 배울 수 있도록 네 시험지를 검토해야 해.
② 네 독일어 실력이 이렇게 빠르게 향상된 것에 감명받았단다.
③ 내가 너에게 공부할 과목을 잘못 추천했나 보구나.
④ 넌 더 높은 수준의 독일어 과정에 등록하는 것이 좋겠어.
⑤ 실수를 피하기 위해서는 답안을 다시 확인하는 것이 중요해.

Ava가 독일어 과목 시험에서 낙제를 한 것을 보고, Ava의 아버지는 어떤 실수를 했는지 확인할 수 있도록 시험지를 살펴보라고 조언하려고 한다. 따라서, Ava의 아버지가 할 말로 ① 'You should review the test paper to learn from your errors.'가 가장 적절하다.

어휘 semester 명 학기 offer 동 제안하다; 제공하다 tutor 동 개인 교습을 하다 get a good grade 좋은 성적을 받다 fail an exam 시험에서 낙제하다 disappointed 형 실망한, 낙담한 in response 이에 대해 look over ~을 살펴보다

16-17 세트 문항

정답 16 ④ 17 ③

M Good evening, everyone. I'm Damien Grey, founder of the Roseberry Art Institute. Art [1]has existed for thousands of years. **Today in our lecture series, we'll be discussing how doctors can use art activities when they treat mental problems.** First, they can use **painting** to [2]better understand patients who don't speak out about their difficulties. Second, **sculpting** can be helpful. For example, patients with depression show improvement when they participate in this activity. Third, **acting** can be [3]an effective treatment as well. Acting therapy involves role play and storytelling to help people recognize their problems and solve them. Lastly, **singing** is used because it lets people express their feelings through lyrics and sound. In these ways, it allows people to communicate their thoughts and emotions when words alone fail, and this can [4]be incredibly healing. I hope you found today's talk interesting. Please join us again next week. Thank you.

남 안녕하십니까, 여러분. 저는 로즈베리 예술 협회의 설립자 Damien Grey입니다. 예술은 수천 년 동안 존재해 왔습니다. 오늘 우리의 강연에서는, 의사들이 정신적인 문제를 치료할 때 어떻게 예술 활동을 이용할 수 있는지에 대해 논의할 것입니다. 첫째, 어려움에 대해 밝히지 않는 환자들을 더 잘 이해하기 위해 그림 그리기를 사용할 수 있습니다. 둘째, 조각하기가 도움이 될 수 있습니다. 예를 들어, 우울증 환자는 이런 활동에 참여할 때 개선된 모습을 보입니다. 셋째, 연기도 효과적인 치료가 될 수 있습니다. 연기 치료는 사람들이 그들의 문제를 인식하고 해결하는 것을 돕기 위해 역할극과 이야기하는 것을 포함합니다. 마지막으로, 노래는 사람들이 가사와 소리를 통해 그들의 감정을 표현할 수 있게 하기 때문에 사용됩니다. 이런 식으로, 사람들이 말만으로는 잘 안 될 때 그들의 생각과 감정을 전달할 수 있게 해주고, 이것은 믿을 수 없을 정도로 치유가 될 수 있습니다. 오늘 강연이 재미있으셨기를 바랍니다. 다음 주에 또 와 주세요. 감사합니다.

선택지 16 ① 다양한 예술 형태의 특징
② 명확한 의사소통의 중요성
③ 역사를 통틀어 예술이 변화된 방식
④ 정신 건강을 개선시키기 위해 예술을 이용하는 방법
⑤ 그림 그리기가 더 인기를 끌게 된 이유
17 ① 그림 그리기 ② 조각하기 ③ 글쓰기 ④ 연기하기 ⑤ 노래하기

16 의사들이 정신적인 문제를 치료할 때 어떻게 예술 활동을 이용할 수 있는지에 대해 논의하고 있으므로 남자가 하는 말의 주제로 ④ 'ways art is used to improve mental health'가 가장 적절하다.

17 그림 그리기, 조각하기, 연기하기, 노래하기는 언급했지만 ③ 'writing'은 언급하지 않았다.

어휘 founder 명 설립자 exist 동 존재하다 lecture 명 강연 treat 동 치료하다; 다루다 mental 형 정신적인 speak out 밝히다, 말하다 sculpt 동 조각하다 depression 명 우울증 improvement 명 개선, 향상 participate in ~에 참여하다 therapy 명 치료 recognize 동 인식하다 lyrics 명 가사 emotion 명 감정 incredibly 부 믿을 수 없을 정도로

1	①	2	⑤	3	④	4	⑤	5	②	6	③	7	④	8	④	9	②	10	②
11	①	12	⑤	13	④	14	②	15	④	16	②	17	③						

• 각 문제의 정답 근거는 굵은 글씨로, Dictation 정답은 밑줄로 표시되어 있습니다.

---

1 목적 파악　　　　　　　　　　　　　　　　　　　　　　　　정답 ①

M Good morning. This is Chief Anthony Walker of the Brownsville Police Department. **With winter approaching, I wanted to give everyone some tips for** ¹⁾driving on icy roads. To begin with, make sure that you have proper winter tires on your vehicle. This will greatly reduce your chances of ²⁾being in an accident. Also, take care when approaching intersections. Follow the traffic lights, and watch for any ³⁾pedestrians on the crosswalk. Finally, do not speed. Drive slowly and carefully because you never know when the road will become slippery. I hope all of you have a safe winter on the road.

남 안녕하십니까. 브라운스빌 경찰서의 Anthony Walker 서장입니다. 겨울이 다가옴에 따라, 저는 여러분에게 빙판길에서 운전하는 것에 관한 몇 가지 조언을 드리고자 합니다. 우선, 차량에 적절한 겨울용 타이어가 장착되어 있는지 확인하십시오. 이것은 사고를 당할 가능성을 크게 줄여줄 것입니다. 또한, 교차로에 접근할 때 주의하십시오. 신호등을 따르고, 횡단보도에 보행자가 없는지 살펴보십시오. 마지막으로, 속도를 내지 마십시오. 길이 언제 미끄러워질지 모르기 때문에 천천히 조심해서 운전하십시오. 여러분 모두 도로에서 안전한 겨울을 보내시기 바랍니다.

남자가 겨울철 빙판길을 안전하게 운전할 수 있는 방법 몇 가지를 알려주고 있다. 따라서, 남자가 하는 말의 목적으로 ① '빙판길 안전 운전 방법을 설명하려고'가 가장 적절하다.

어휘　approach 통 다가오다, 접근하다　to begin with 우선　proper 형 적절한　vehicle 명 차량　chance 명 가능성　take care 주의하다　intersection 명 교차로　traffic light 신호등　pedestrian 명 보행자　crosswalk 명 횡단보도

---

2 의견 파악　　　　　　　　　　　　　　　　　　　　　　　　정답 ⑤

M Hi, Samantha. I haven't seen you in a while. How are you doing?
W I'm fine, Dale. But I don't have much time to chat right now. I'm in a bit of a hurry.
M Where are you going?
W I need to vote for the ¹⁾city's new mayor. I have plans tonight, so I want to do this during my lunch break.
M Oh, I forgot that was today. Honestly, voting is too ²⁾much of a bother.
W Don't tell me you're not planning to vote today. **You have to cast your vote.**
M It doesn't matter if I do or not. One vote won't ³⁾make a difference.
W **But it's the responsibility of all citizens to vote.**
M I guess you're right. Could I come with you?
W Of course. Let's go now.

남 안녕, Samantha. 오랜만에 보네. 어떻게 지내?
여 잘 지내, Dale. 하지만 지금은 수다 떨 시간이 별로 없어. 좀 급하거든.
남 어디 가는 중이야?
여 새로운 시장을 뽑아야 해. 오늘 밤에 약속이 있어서, 점심시간에 하고 싶어.
남 아, 그게 오늘이라는 걸 깜빡했어. 솔직히, 투표는 너무 성가셔.
여 설마 오늘 투표할 계획이 없었다는 건 아니겠지. 넌 투표해야 해.
남 내가 하든지 말든지 중요하지 않잖아. 한 표로는 차이가 안 날 거야.
여 하지만 투표하는 것은 모든 시민의 의무야.
남 네 말이 맞는 것 같아. 너랑 같이 가도 될까?
여 물론이지. 지금 가자.

투표를 성가셔하는 남자에게 여자가 투표는 모든 시민의 의무이므로 투표해야 한다고 했다. 따라서, 여자의 의견으로 ⑤ '모든 시민은 반드시 투표에 참여해야 한다.'가 가장 적절하다.

어휘　in a hurry 급하게, 서둘러　vote for ~를 뽑다, ~에게 투표하다　mayor 명 시장　honestly 부 솔직히　bother 명 성가심 통 괴롭히다　Don't tell me ~. 설마 ~이라는 건 아니겠지.　cast one's vote 투표하다, 한 표를 행사하다　responsibility 명 의무, 책임

---

3 관계 파악　　　　　　　　　　　　　　　　　　　　　　　　정답 ④

M Good morning. I'm sorry I'm late. The traffic was quite heavy.
W No problem. I'm just glad you came.
M You said you were having a problem with your kitchen sink?
W **Actually, it's the one in my bathroom. It** ¹⁾keeps leaking.
M When did this start?
W Last week. I tried fixing it myself, but it began leaking again yesterday. So I decided to ²⁾call a professional.
M I see. **It sounds like I will need to replace the pipe under the sink.**
W Will that take very long?
M It will depend on the type of pipe. If I have to ³⁾order a replacement, you will need to wait a couple of days.
W Got it. I'll show you where the bathroom is.

남 좋은 아침입니다. 늦어서 죄송해요. 차가 꽤 막혔어요.
여 괜찮습니다. 와주신 것만으로 다행인걸요.
남 부엌 싱크대에 문제가 있다고 하셨던가요?
여 실은, 화장실의 세면대가 문제예요. 계속 물이 새요.
남 언제부터 시작됐죠?
여 지난주에요. 제가 직접 고치려고 한번 해봤는데, 어제 다시 물이 새기 시작했어요. 그래서 전문가를 부르기로 했죠.
남 그렇군요. 세면대 아래 파이프를 교체해야 할 것 같네요.
여 아주 오래 걸릴까요?
남 파이프 종류에 따라 달라요. 만약 제가 교체품을 주문해야 한다면, 며칠 기다리셔야 해요.
여 알겠습니다. 화장실이 어디 있는지 안내해드릴게요.

두 사람이 고장 난 화장실 세면대에 관해 이야기하고 있다. 남자는 세면대 아래 파이프를 교체해야 할 것 같다고 하고 있고, 여자는 세면대에 물이 새는 문제를 고쳐 달라고 의뢰하는 것으로 보아 두 사람의 관계로 ④ '배관 수리공 — 의뢰인'이 가장 적절하다.

어휘　sink 명 싱크대, 세면대　leak 통 물이 새다　professional 명 전문가 형 프로의　depend on ~에 따라 다르다, ~에 달려 있다　replacement 명 교체(품)

4 그림 내용 불일치 파악

M Anna, what do you think of my new home office?	남 Anna, 내 새 홈 오피스에 대해 어떻게 생각해?
W You ¹⁾set it up really well, Brian. I like the two plants on your desk.	여 너 정말 잘 꾸며놨다, Brian. 책상 위에 있는 두 개의 식물이 마음에 들어.
M Thanks. What about the painting of the mountain above the desk?	남 고마워. 책상 위쪽의 산 그림은 어때?
W It looks great. What is in the ²⁾cabinet next to the desk?	여 멋져 보여. 책상 옆에 있는 캐비닛에는 뭐가 들었어?
M That's where I keep all my important work documents.	남 중요한 업무 문서를 모두 보관하는 곳이야.
W How convenient! I'm not sure about the curtains on the window, though. The ³⁾star pattern is too distracting.	여 정말 편리하겠다! 하지만 창문에 걸린 커튼은 잘 모르겠어. 별 무늬가 너무 정신 사나워.
M I know. But they were a gift from a friend, so I don't want to take them down.	남 나도 알아. 하지만 그건 친구가 준 선물이라서, 떼고 싶지 않아.
W That's understandable. **Why did you hang ⁴⁾two lamps from the ceiling?**	여 이해할 만해. 왜 천장에 등을 두 개나 달았어?
M It's because I like a bright room so I don't strain my eyes.	남 그건 내가 눈에 무리가 가지 않도록 밝은 방을 좋아하기 때문이야.
W Good idea. Well, I think you have an amazing workspace.	여 좋은 생각이야. 음, 네게 아주 멋진 업무 공간이 생긴 것 같아.
M Thanks!	남 고마워!

대화에서 여자가 왜 천장에 등을 두 개나 달았는지 물었는데, ⑤에는 등이 하나만 그려져 있다.

어휘 cabinet 명 캐비닛, 진열장 document 명 문서, 서류 convenient 형 편리한 take ~ down ~을 떼다, 치우다 understandable 형 이해할 만한, 이해할 수 있는 ceiling 명 천장 strain 통 무리를 주다; 잡아당기다

5 할 일 파악

W Greg, are you ready to work at the library? It's your first day.	여 Greg, 도서관에서 일할 준비는 됐나요? 오늘이 첫 근무일이잖아요.
M I am, Ms. Denson.	남 준비됐어요, Denson 선생님.
W Great. Usually, new staff members have to put away ¹⁾returned books. But we have already finished that today.	여 좋아요. 보통, 새로운 직원은 반납 도서를 치워야 해요. 하지만 오늘은 이미 그걸 끝내놨어요.
M I see. Maybe I could help visitors find the books they need, then.	남 그렇군요. 그렇다면 제가 방문객들이 필요한 책을 찾으시도록 도울 수 있을지도 몰라요.
W Actually, I have something else for you to do. We are setting up a children's reading room on the second floor.	여 사실, 당신이 해야 할 다른 일이 있어요. 우리는 2층에 어린이 열람실을 설치하고 있거든요.
M What should I do, specifically?	남 구체적으로 제가 뭘 해야 하죠?
W The tables and chairs were moved there yesterday, **but we still need to ²⁾install the bookshelves. Could you help with that?**	여 탁자와 의자는 어제 그곳으로 옮겨졌지만, 아직 책장은 설치해야 해요. 그걸 도와줄래요?
M **Of course. I'd be happy to.**	남 물론이죠. 기꺼이 하겠습니다.
W Wonderful. Let's ³⁾head to the second floor now so I can show you what to do.	여 훌륭해요. 이제 2층으로 가서 뭘 해야 하는지 보여줄게요.

도서관에서의 첫 근무에 관해 이야기하고 있다. 여자가 2층 어린이 열람실에 책장 설치하는 것을 도와달라고 부탁하자, 남자가 기꺼이 하겠다고 했으므로 남자가 할 일로 ② '책장 설치하기'가 가장 적절하다.

어휘 put away ~을 치우다, 정리하다 return 통 반납하다; 돌아오다 visitor 명 방문객, 손님 specifically 부 구체적으로 install 통 설치하다 bookshelf 명 책장 head to ~로 가다

6 금액 정보 파악

M Hello. Are you looking for anything in particular today?	남 안녕하세요. 오늘 특별히 찾고 계신 물건이 있으신가요?
W Yeah. I'm going on a camping trip with some friends next week, so I need to buy a tent.	여 네. 다음 주에 친구들이랑 캠핑하러 가기 때문에, 텐트를 사야 해요.
M This model is one of our most popular tents. It's ¹⁾completely waterproof and very easy to set up.	남 이 모델은 가장 인기 있는 저희 텐트 중 하나입니다. 완전히 방수되고 설치가 매우 쉬워요.
W How much is it?	여 얼마예요?
M **The ²⁾two-person model is $100, and the four-person model is $120.**	남 2인용 모델은 100달러이고, 4인용 모델은 120달러예요.
W **The one for two people should be fine.**	여 2인용이면 될 거예요.
M Okay. Oh, I forgot to mention that we are having a sale, **so you'll ³⁾receive a 10% discount on the tent.**	남 알겠습니다. 아, 할인하고 있다는 말을 깜빡해서요, 텐트에 10% 할인을 받으실 거예요.
W Great! Also, do you sell camping lanterns?	여 잘됐네요! 그리고 캠핑용 랜턴도 파시나요?
M We do. **These lanterns are $10 each.**	남 팔죠. 이 랜턴들은 한 개에 10달러입니다.
W Perfect. **I'll take two of them.**	여 딱 좋네요. 그걸로 두 개 주세요.
M Do you need anything else?	남 더 필요한 게 있으실까요?
W No. That's it.	여 아뇨. 그게 다예요.

여자가 2인용 텐트 하나를 10% 할인받아($100×0.9=$90) 구매했고, 캠핑용 랜턴 두 개($10×2=$20)도 구매했으므로 정답은 ③ '$110'이다.

어휘 in particular 특별히 completely 부 완전히 waterproof 형 방수의 That's it. 그게 다예요.

7 이유 파악

정답 ④

W Hi, Paul. How do you think you did on the math test today?	**여** 안녕, Paul. 오늘 수학 시험은 어떻게 본 것 같아?
M Pretty good. I studied a lot for it.	**남** 꽤 잘했어. 공부 많이 했거든.
W Me too. I was thinking of going to a movie tonight to relax. Do you want to come?	**여** 나도. 오늘 밤에 쉴 겸 영화 보러 갈까 생각 중이었어. 너도 갈래?
M I'm sorry, but I can't.	**남** 미안하지만, 그럴 수 없어.
W Oh, you have ¹⁾band practice on Friday evenings, right?	**여** 아, 금요일 저녁마다 밴드부 연습이 있구나, 맞지?
M Actually, that's on Thursdays.	**남** 사실, 그건 목요일마다 해.
W Then, are you ²⁾spending time with your family?	**여** 그러면 가족과 함께 시간을 보낼 거니?
M No. **I'm going to see a musical tonight.** It's a very popular show, so I'm happy that I managed to get a ticket.	**남** 아니. 오늘 밤 뮤지컬을 보러 갈 거야. 인기 있는 공연이라서, 간신히 표를 구해서 다행이야.
W Great. I hope you ³⁾enjoy the musical.	**여** 잘됐네. 뮤지컬 즐기고 오길 바랄게.
M Thank you. I'll tell you all about it on Monday.	**남** 고마워. 월요일에 다 말해줄게.

남자가 함께 영화를 보러 갈 수 없다고 하면서 오늘 밤 뮤지컬을 보러 갈 것이라고 말했으므로, 남자가 함께 영화를 보러 갈 수 없는 이유는 ④ '뮤지컬을 보러 가야 해서'이다.

어휘 relax 통 쉬다 manage to 간신히 ~하다

8 언급 유무 파악

정답 ④

M What are you looking at, Denise?	**남** 뭘 보고 있니, Denise?
W It's a brochure for the Eastwood Comics Fair.	**여** 이건 Eastwood Comics Fair의 안내 책자야.
M Interesting. Are you planning on going?	**남** 흥미로운걸. 넌 갈 계획이야?
W Yeah. It's being held in **New York City**. I'll be visiting friends there the same day.	**여** 응. 그건 뉴욕에서 열려. 난 같은 날에 그곳에 있는 친구들도 만날 거야.
M That's great. When will it ¹⁾take place?	**남** 잘됐네. 언제 열리는데?
W It starts on **June 12th**. I'll probably only go on the first day.	**여** 6월 12일에 시작해. 아마 나는 첫날에만 갈 것 같아.
M Are tickets expensive?	**남** 표가 비싸니?
W Not really. ²⁾A one-day pass is **$35**.	**여** 그렇지 않아. 1일 입장권은 35달러야.
M That's reasonable. Who is ³⁾organizing the event?	**남** 적당하네. 누가 그 행사를 주최하는데?
W A company called **New Horizons**. It operates a chain of comic-book stores across the country.	**여** New Horizons라는 회사야. 거긴 전국적으로 만화책 전문 서점 가맹점을 운영하고 있어.
M Well, I hope you have a great time at the fair.	**남** 음, 박람회에서 즐거운 시간 보내길 바랄게.
W Thanks a lot.	**여** 정말 고마워.

개최 장소(뉴욕), 개최일(6월 12일), 입장료(35달러), 주관사(New Horizons)에 대해 언급했고, ④ '참여 만화가'는 언급하지 않았다.

어휘 brochure 명 안내 책자, 소책자 pass 명 입장권, 통행증 통 통과하다 reasonable 형 (가격이) 적당한; 합리적인 operate 통 운영하다 chain 명 가맹점, 체인점; 쇠사슬 across the country 전국적으로

9 내용 불일치 파악

정답 ②

W If you don't have ¹⁾anything on your calendar this autumn, why don't you attend the Young Musicians Concert Series? Every week, Milton Hall will be ²⁾holding a concert with young musicians from the city. **The first concert will ³⁾be held on October 2nd.** For the last concert, the pianist Matthew Livingston will be performing. A list of performers and their show dates will be posted on our website. Tickets are only sold online. You can get a ticket at a discounted price if you are ⁴⁾a local resident. Thank you.	**여** 만약 이번 가을에 아무 계획도 없으시다면, Young Musicians Concert Series에 참석하는 건 어떠십니까? 매주, 밀턴 회관은 이 도시의 젊은 음악가들과 함께 공연을 열 것입니다. 첫 번째 공연은 10월 2일에 열립니다. 마지막 공연에서는, 피아니스트 Matthew Livingston이 연주할 예정입니다. 공연자 명단과 공연 날짜는 저희 웹사이트에 올라갈 것입니다. 입장권은 온라인으로만 판매됩니다. 지역 주민이시라면 할인된 가격에 입장권을 구하실 수 있습니다. 감사합니다.

밀턴 회관에서 개최하는 콘서트 시리즈에 대한 안내 방송이다. 여자가 첫 번째 공연이 10월 2일에 열린다고 했으므로 ② '마지막 공연은 10월 2일에 열린다.'는 내용과 일치하지 않는다.

어휘 autumn 명 가을 performer 명 공연자 post 통 올리다, 게시하다 discount 통 할인하다 명 할인 local 형 지역의 resident 명 주민

10 도표 정보 파악
정답 ②

[Telephone rings.]	[전화기가 울린다.]
M Thank you for calling Workout World. How can I help you today?	남 Workout World에 전화해 주셔서 감사합니다. 오늘 제가 무엇을 도와드릴까요?
W Hi. I'm ¹⁾interested in taking a yoga class.	여 안녕하세요. 요가 수업 듣는 것에 관심이 있는데요.
M Well, we have a beginner class that is very popular.	남 음, 매우 인기 있는 초급반 수업이 있어요.
W Oh, I've been doing yoga for a while, so I don't want to take a low-level class.	여 아, 한동안 요가를 해본 적이 있어서, 낮은 수준의 수업은 듣고 싶지 않아요.
M Okay. We also offer ²⁾intermediate and advanced classes.	남 네. 중급반과 상급반 수업도 있습니다.
W Great. **I'll take an intermediate class. But I can't join a morning class because I'm busy before noon.**	여 좋아요. 중급반 수업을 들을게요. 하지만 저는 정오 전에는 바빠서 오전 수업은 들을 수 없어요.
M All right. Um, all of our classes meet two days a week. Either on Mondays and Thursdays or Tuesdays and Fridays.	남 알겠습니다. 음, 수업은 모두 일주일에 이틀씩 열려요. 월요일과 목요일이거나 화요일과 금요일이죠.
W **Tuesdays and Fridays will work for me.** I have a ³⁾pretty busy schedule on Mondays.	여 화요일과 금요일이 좋겠어요. 월요일에는 일정이 꽤 바쁘거든요.
M In that case, there is one class that meets your requirements.	남 그렇다면, 요구 사항에 맞는 수업이 하나 있네요.
W Great. I'd like to sign up for it now.	여 좋아요. 지금 신청하고 싶어요.

여자는 중급반 수업이면서, 오전 수업이 아니고, 화요일과 금요일에 열리는 요가 강좌를 골랐다.

어휘 beginner 명 초급(자) intermediate 형 중급의, 중간의 advanced 형 상급의; 전진한 either A or B A거나 B인 in that case 그렇다면, 그런 경우에는 requirement 명 요구 사항

11 짧은 대화의 응답 파악
정답 ①

W Pardon me. **I'm looking for Delight Rice Cakes.** Its website says it's ¹⁾located next to the bookstore, but I can't see it.	여 실례합니다. Delight Rice Cakes를 찾고 있어요. 웹사이트에는 서점 옆에 있다고 나와 있는데, 안 보이네요.
M Oh, that store has moved to another place.	남 아, 그 가게는 다른 곳으로 옮겼어요.
W Really? **Can you give me directions if you ²⁾know where it is?**	여 정말요? 그게 어디 있는지 아신다면 제게 길을 알려주실 수 있나요?
M Sure. It's on the corner of Main Street.	남 물론이죠. 거긴 메인가 모퉁이에 있어요.
	선택지 ① 물론이죠. 거긴 메인가 모퉁이에 있어요.
	② 신경 쓰지 마세요. 제가 직접 가게를 방문할게요.
	③ 맞습니다. 그곳은 다양한 종류의 떡을 팝니다.
	④ 괜찮습니다. 서점은 오전 10시에 열어요.
	⑤ 고마워요. 이전했다는 걸 알게 되어 다행이네요.

여자가 가게로 가는 길을 알려달라고 했으므로, 이에 대한 응답으로는 가게의 위치를 말해주는 ① 'Sure. It's on the corner of Main Street.'가 가장 적절하다.

어휘 Pardon me. 실례합니다. give directions 길을 알려주다 Never mind. 신경 쓰지 마세요. in person 직접 relocation 명 이전, 이주

12 짧은 대화의 응답 파악
정답 ⑤

M **Louise, you're going to ¹⁾take swimming lessons, right?**	남 Louise, 너 수영 수업 들을 거지, 맞지?
W Yes. I'm really looking forward to them. I already bought a swimsuit and goggles.	여 응. 정말 기대하고 있어. 벌써 수영복과 수경도 샀어.
M That's good. **Maybe I should ²⁾register for the same lessons as you.**	남 잘됐다. 나도 너랑 같은 수업을 등록하는 건 어떨까 싶어.
W Great plan. We'll have a lot of fun together.	여 멋진 계획이야. 우린 함께 정말 즐거운 시간을 보낼 거야.
	선택지 ① 알겠어. 수영복을 반품할게.
	② 미안해. 오늘은 수영하고 싶지 않아.
	③ 맞아. 넌 등록 날짜를 놓쳤어.
	④ 딱 좋아. 해변에 가서 정말 즐거웠거든.
	⑤ 멋진 계획이야. 우린 함께 정말 즐거운 시간을 보낼 거야.

남자가 여자와 같은 수영 수업을 등록하는 것이 어떨까 한다면서 고민의 뜻을 비치고 있으므로, 이에 대한 응답으로는 멋진 계획이라면서 같이 듣는 것을 찬성하는 ⑤ 'Great plan. We'll have a lot of fun together.'가 가장 적절하다.

어휘 look forward to ~을 기대하다 goggles 명 수경, 보안경 register 통 등록하다 (registration 명 등록) return 통 반품하다 feel like ~하고 싶다

13 긴 대화의 응답 파악　　　　　　　　　　　　　　　정답 ④

W Honey, do you have any plans today?	여 여보, 오늘 약속 있어?
M No. Why?	남 아니. 왜?
W **I want to do some spring cleaning.** It would be great if you could help me.	여 봄맞이 대청소를 좀 하고 싶어. 당신이 날 도와주면 좋겠어.
M Sure. What do you want me to do?	남 물론이지. 내가 뭘 하면 좋겠어?
W Well, I was going to begin by washing the windows. **Maybe you could** ¹⁾clean out the garage.	여 음, 난 창문부터 닦으려고 했어. 당신이 차고를 청소할 수도 있겠어.
M Of course. We have a lot of stuff stored in there.	남 그래. 거기에 보관된 물건들 진짜 많잖아.
W Right. There is ²⁾barely enough room for the car, now.	여 맞아. 지금 차를 댈 공간도 거의 충분하지 않아.
M I agree. But I'm not sure where to put everything.	남 동감이야. 하지만 그것들을 전부 어디에 둬야 할지 잘 모르겠어.
W **What do you think about having a yard sale?**	여 야드 세일을 하는 건 어때?
M You mean we should sell the items in the garage?	남 차고에 있는 물건들을 팔자는 말이야?
W That's it! **You need to figure out** ³⁾what to sell while cleaning.	여 바로 그거야! 당신은 청소하면서 뭘 팔아야 할지 알아내야 해.
M Got it. There should be many items for a yard sale.	남 알았어. 거기엔 야드 세일에 내놓을 물건이 많을 거야.
	선택지 ① 정말? 난 살 만한 걸 못 찾았어.
	② 물론이지. 창문만 마저 다 닦을게.
	③ 잘 모르겠어. 그럼, 어디에 주차할까?
	④ 알았어. 거기엔 야드 세일에 내놓을 물건이 많을 거야.
	⑤ 이해해. 그건 당신 혼자 하기엔 너무 많은 일이야.

봄맞이 대청소를 하며 야드 세일을 계획하는 상황이다. 여자가 차고를 청소하면서 야드 세일에서 팔 물건을 알아내라고 했으므로, 이에 대한 응답으로는 그러겠다고 대답하는 ④ 'Got it. There should be many items for a yard sale.'이 가장 적절하다.

어휘 spring cleaning 봄맞이 대청소　stuff 뎽 물건　store 통 보관하다 뎽 가게　barely 뿐 거의 ~않다　figure out ~을 알아내다

14 긴 대화의 응답 파악　　　　　　　　　　　　　　　정답 ②

M **Mom, can I go to Thrill Land with my friends this weekend?**	남 엄마, 이번 주말에 친구들이랑 Thrill Land에 가도 돼요?
W Is that the ¹⁾new amusement park that opened last month?	여 지난달에 문을 연 놀이공원 말이니?
M Right. Michael got three tickets from his parents, so he invited Miles and me.	남 맞아요. Michael이 부모님께 세 장의 입장권을 받아서, Miles와 절 초대했어요.
W How will you get there?	여 거기에 어떻게 갈 건데?
M By bus. It should ²⁾take about an hour.	남 버스로요. 한 시간 정도 걸릴 거예요.
W I see. What time will you be home?	여 그렇구나. 집에는 몇 시에 올 거니?
M We are planning to leave there at 5 p.m., so I should be back before dinner.	남 오후 5시에는 거기서 나올 거니까, 저녁 식사 전에는 돌아올 거예요.
W That's fine, then. Just make sure to call me if you are going to be late.	여 그러면 괜찮아. 늦을 것 같으면 꼭 전화하렴.
M Thanks, Mom. **Um, could I have some money to** ³⁾spend on snacks that day?	남 고마워요, 엄마. 음, 그날 간식 사는데 쓸 돈을 좀 받을 수 있을까요?
W Sure. Remind me before you leave.	여 물론이지. 떠나기 전에 한 번 더 알려주렴.
	선택지 ① 아니. 입장권은 한 장에 15달러란다.
	② 물론이지. 떠나기 전에 한번 더 알려주렴.
	③ 알았어. 내가 돌아올 때 꼭 저녁 식사 준비해두렴.
	④ 당연하지. 거기서 놀이기구를 탈 생각에 너무 기대되는구나.
	⑤ 미안하구나. 간식에 그렇게 많은 돈을 쓰지 말았어야 했는데.

놀이공원에 놀러 갈 것을 엄마인 여자에게 허락받는 상황에서 남자가 놀이공원에서 간식 사는 데 쓸 돈을 받을 수 있을지 물었으므로, 이에 대한 응답으로는 알겠다고 대답하는 ② 'Sure. Remind me before you leave.'가 가장 적절하다.

어휘 amusement park 놀이공원　invite 통 초대하다　make sure to 꼭 ~하다　spend on ~에 (돈을) 쓰다　remind 통 다시 한번 알려주다, 상기하다　ride 뎽 놀이기구, 탈것 통 타다

15 상황에 적절한 말 파악　　　　　　　　　　　　　　정답 ④

M Josh and Emma live in the same apartment building. Josh's apartment is ¹⁾directly below Emma's. Emma is watching a TV program with a friend late at night. Unfortunately, the TV is very loud, and Josh hears it easily in his apartment. He has to wake up early in the morning for ²⁾a job interview, but he cannot sleep because of the noise. **So Josh wants to ask Emma to** ³⁾make the TV quieter. In this situation, what would Josh most likely say to Emma?	남 Josh와 Emma는 같은 아파트 건물에 살고 있습니다. Josh의 집은 Emma의 바로 아래입니다. Emma는 밤늦게 친구와 같이 TV 프로그램을 보고 있습니다. 불행히도, TV는 매우 시끄러웠고, Josh의 집에서는 그 소리가 잘 들립니다. 그는 면접을 보기 위해 아침 일찍 일어나야 하는데, 소음 때문에 잠을 잘 수가 없습니다. 그래서, Josh는 Emma에게 텔레비전 소리를 더 조용하게 해달라고 부탁하고 싶습니다. 이러한 상황에서, Josh가 Emma에게 가장 할 것 같은 말은 무엇입니까?
	선택지 ① 당신의 친구에게 떠나라고 요청해야 합니다.
	② 당신 집에서 제 TV 소리가 들리시나요?
	③ 소음을 많이 내지 않도록 노력할게요.
	④ 소리 좀 줄여 주시겠어요?
	⑤ 당신이 보고 있는 TV 프로그램이 뭔가요?

Emma가 밤늦게 텔레비전을 시끄럽게 틀어놓은 것을 듣고, Josh는 텔레비전 소리를 더 조용하게 해달라고 부탁하려 한다. 따라서, Josh가 할 말로 ④ 'Would you mind turning down the volume?'이 가장 적절하다.

어휘 directly 분 바로, 곧장 unfortunately 분 불행하게도 wake up 일어나다 try one's best 노력하다, 최선을 다하다 turn down ~을 줄이다

16-17 세트 문항

정답 16 ② 17 ③

W Hello, everyone. In our class last week, I explained why global warming is happening. **This afternoon, I want to look at its** 1)effects on wildlife. The most typical example of this is the **polar bear.** As the Arctic sea ice melts, it becomes hard for polar bears to 2)travel and find prey. The **sea turtle** is another creature facing great hardship. Global warming has caused sea levels to rise, destroying sea turtles' nesting areas on beaches. Next, the **African cheetah** is particularly vulnerable to climate change. It lives in areas with little water, so the droughts resulting from higher temperatures 3)threaten its existence. Finally, the **giant panda** is another animal that is at risk. The problem is that bamboo, its main source of food, is sensitive to changes in the climate. The plant may die off if 4)temperatures get too high, and then the panda won't have anything to eat. Now, let's watch a brief video about these animals.	여 안녕하십니까, 여러분. 지난주 우리 수업에서, 저는 왜 지구 온난화가 일어나고 있는지 설명했습니다. 오늘 오후에는, 그것이 야생동물에 끼치는 영향을 살펴보고 싶습니다. 이것의 가장 전형적인 사례는 북극곰입니다. 북극의 해빙이 녹으면서, 북극곰이 이동하여 먹이를 찾기가 어려워지고 있습니다. 바다거북은 큰 어려움에 직면한 또 다른 동물입니다. 지구 온난화로 인해 해수면이 상승하여, 해변에 있는 바다거북의 보금자리가 파괴되었습니다. 다음으로, 아프리카 치타는 기후 변화에 특히 취약합니다. 그것은 물이 거의 없는 지역에 살기 때문에, 높아진 기온에서 비롯한 가뭄은 생존을 위협합니다. 마지막으로, 자이언트 판다는 위험에 처한 또 다른 동물입니다. 문제는 자이언트 판다의 주요 식량인 대나무가 기후 변화에 민감하다는 것입니다. 온도가 너무 높아지면 그 식물은 차례로 죽어갈 수 있고, 그러면 판다가 먹을 것이 없을 것입니다. 이제, 이 동물들에 관한 짧은 동영상을 보겠습니다.

선택지 16 ① 지구 온난화에 책임이 있는 대상
② 기후 변화가 동물에 끼치는 영향
③ 온도 상승을 막을 수 있는 방법
④ 해수면 상승이 식물에 끼치는 영향
⑤ 야생동물을 보호하면 좋은 점
17 ① 북극곰 ② 바다거북 ③ 북극여우 ④ 아프리카 치타
⑤ 자이언트 판다

16 지구 온난화가 야생동물에 끼치는 영향을 살펴보고 있으므로 여자가 하는 말의 주제로 ② 'the impact of climate change on animals'가 가장 적절하다.

17 북극곰, 바다거북, 아프리카 치타, 자이언트 판다는 언급했지만 ③ 'Arctic fox'는 언급하지 않았다.

어휘 wildlife 명 야생동물 typical 형 전형적인 Arctic 형 북극의 melt 통 녹다 prey 명 먹이 face 통 직면하다 얼굴 hardship 명 어려움, 고난 destroy 통 파괴하다
nesting area 보금자리, 둥지를 트는 영역 vulnerable to ~에 취약한 drought 명 가뭄 result from ~에서 비롯하다, ~이 원인이다 threaten 통 위협하다 existence 명 생존; 존재
at risk 위험에 처한 sensitive to ~에 민감한 die off (하나도 남지 않을 때까지) 차례로 죽어가다 be responsible for ~에 책임이 있다

1	②	2	⑤	3	③	4	⑤	5	④	6	④	7	①	8	④	9	③	10	④
11	②	12	⑤	13	③	14	②	15	⑤	16	④	17	③						

• 각 문제의 정답 근거는 굵은 글씨로, Dictation 정답은 밑줄로 표시되어 있습니다.

1 목적 파악

정답 ②

W May I have your attention, please? Kenwood High School is celebrating its 15th anniversary next month. We have a lot of ¹⁾activities scheduled, **and I'd like to add one more, an essay writing contest.** The topic of the essay is helping others, and it should be 500 to 700 words in length. The ²⁾deadline is February 28th. The judges will be our three English teachers and a special guest. I bet some of you are fans of this guest. We will ³⁾reveal this guest's name before the winners are announced. The grand prize is $200. Thank you.

여 주목해주시겠습니까? 켄우드 고등학교는 다음 달에 개교 15주년을 기념할 예정입니다. 많은 활동이 예정되어 있는데, 한 가지 더, 글짓기 대회를 추가하고 싶습니다. 작문 주제는 다른 사람을 돕는 것이고, 길이는 500자에서 700자여야 합니다. 마감일은 2월 28일입니다. 심사위원들은 세 명의 영어 선생님과 특별 객원 위원이 맡아주시겠습니다. 여러분 중 일부는 분명 이 객원 위원의 팬일 것입니다. 수상자가 발표되기 전에 이 객원 위원의 성함을 공개할 예정입니다. 최우수 수상 상금은 200달러입니다. 감사합니다.

여자가 켄우드 고등학교에서 개교기념일을 맞아 열리는 글짓기 대회 개최 사실을 알리면서, 주제 및 마감일 등의 정보를 주고 있다. 따라서, 여자가 하는 말의 목적으로 ② '글짓기 대회 개최에 대해 공지하려고'가 가장 적절하다.

[어휘] celebrate 图 기념하다 anniversary 圆 주년; 기념일 length 圆 길이 deadline 圆 마감일 judge 圆 심사위원; 판사 reveal 图 공개하다, 밝히다 announce 图 발표하다

2 의견 파악

정답 ⑤

M Hi, Sarah. Joel and I are going to a café after school today. Do you want to come with us?
W I'd love to, but I can't.
M Why not?
W I joined the school's ¹⁾volleyball team. I have practice this afternoon.
M That's great. You've always wanted to play on the volleyball team.
W To be honest, I'm ²⁾thinking of quitting. The coach is really demanding, and we practice four times a week. It's a lot ³⁾harder than I expected.
M **You shouldn't give up on something you enjoy just because it's difficult.**
W You really think so?
M Of course. Overcoming difficulties can make you ⁴⁾feel more confident.
W I guess you're right. Thanks for the advice.

남 안녕, Sarah. Joel과 나는 오늘 방과 후에 카페에 갈 거야. 너도 함께 갈래?
여 그러고 싶지만, 갈 수 없어.
남 왜 못 가?
여 학교 배구팀에 들어갔거든. 오늘 오후에 연습이 있어.
남 잘됐네. 넌 항상 배구팀에서 뛰고 싶어 했잖아.
여 솔직히 말하면, 그만둘 생각이야. 코치님이 정말 요구 사항이 많으시고, 우리는 일주일에 네 번 연습해. 내가 예상했던 것보다 훨씬 힘들어.
남 단지 힘들다는 이유로 네가 좋아하는 일을 포기하면 안 돼.
여 정말 그렇게 생각해?
남 물론이지. 어려움을 극복하는 건 널 더 자신감 있게 만들어 줄 수 있어.
여 네 말이 맞는 것 같아. 조언해 줘서 고마워.

배구부 연습이 힘들어서 그만둘 것을 고민하는 여자에게 남자가 단지 힘들다는 이유로 좋아하는 일을 포기하면 안 된다고 했다. 따라서, 남자의 의견으로 ⑤ '힘들다는 이유로 좋아하는 일을 포기해서는 안 된다.'가 가장 적절하다.

[어휘] volleyball 圆 배구 to be honest 솔직히 말하면 quit 图 그만두다 demanding 圈 요구가 많은 give up on ~을 포기하다 overcome 图 극복하다 confident 圈 자신감 있는

3 관계 파악

정답 ③

M Do you have a question?
W Yes. Could you tell me ¹⁾when we'll leave this art gallery?
M We'll leave in about 30 minutes. We're going to listen to the artist talk about his paintings first.
W And we'll be going to the National Museum after this?
M That's right. Why? Is there a problem?
W **I checked the schedule you handed out on the tour bus this morning.** But I couldn't find information ²⁾about a meal break.
M **Oh, we'll get some lunch after I finish showing the group around the museum.**
W Where will we be eating?
M I made a reservation at a famous local restaurant. I'm sure everyone will enjoy their seafood.
W Great. Thanks for all your effort. **You've really ³⁾made our trip enjoyable.**

남 질문 있으신가요?
여 네. 언제 이 미술관을 떠날지 알려주시겠어요?
남 약 30분 후에 떠날 거예요. 우선은 화가가 그의 그림에 관해 이야기하는 것을 듣겠습니다.
여 그리고 그게 끝나고 나면 국립 박물관에 갈 거죠?
남 맞습니다. 왜 그러시죠? 무슨 문제가 있나요?
여 오늘 아침 관광버스에서 나눠주신 일정을 확인했어요. 그런데 식사 시간에 관한 정보를 찾을 수 없었어요.
남 아, 박물관을 다 구경시켜 드린 후에 점심을 좀 먹을 거예요.
여 식사는 어디서 하죠?
남 유명한 현지 식당을 예약했어요. 분명 모든 분들께서 그곳의 해산물 요리를 좋아하실 거예요.
여 좋아요. 노력해주셔서 감사합니다. 저희 여행을 정말 즐겁게 해주시네요.

두 사람이 여행 일정에 관해 이야기하고 있다. 남자는 아침에 관광버스에서 여행 일정을 나눠줬고 여자가 묻는 세부 일정, 식사 장소 등에 대해 답변을 하고 있고, 여자는 남자에게 즐거운 여행을 만들어주어 고맙다고 하는 것으로 보아 두 사람의 관계로 ③ '여행 가이드 — 관광객'이 가장 적절하다.

어휘 hand out ~을 나눠주다 show A around B A에게 B를 구경시켜 주다 local 형 현지의; 지역의 effort 명 노력

4 그림 내용 불일치 파악

정답 ⑤

M	Natalie, are you done setting up your booth for our school's science fair?
W	I just finished, Mr. Parker. What do you think?
M	It looks great. Are those models of volcanoes on the two tables ¹⁾in the middle of the booth?
W	Right. And the poster on the wall to the left shows a volcano erupting.
M	That's very interesting. And I see you put a big banner that says "Volcanoes" on the wall behind the table.
W	That's correct. I want to make sure everyone knows my topic.
M	What is the ²⁾square map underneath the banner for?
W	Oh, I marked where several famous volcanoes are located.
M	Wonderful. **What is that ³⁾rock sculpture in the picture on the right wall?**
W	**It's called a dol hareubang.** It's a traditional Korean sculpture made from volcanic rock.

남	Natalie, 우리 학교 과학 박람회 부스는 다 설치했니?
여	방금 끝냈어요, Parker 선생님. 어떻게 생각하세요?
남	멋져 보이는구나. 화산 모형들은 부스 중앙에 있는 두 탁자 위에 놓인 거니?
여	맞아요. 그리고 왼쪽 벽의 포스터는 화산이 폭발하는 것을 보여줘요.
남	아주 흥미롭구나. 그리고 보아하니 탁자 뒤쪽 벽에 'Volcanoes'라고 쓰인 큰 현수막을 걸어뒀구나.
여	정확해요. 모두에게 제 주제를 분명히 알게 하고 싶어서요.
남	현수막 아래에 있는 네모난 지도는 무얼 위한 거니?
여	아, 여러 유명한 화산들이 위치한 곳을 표시했어요.
남	훌륭하구나. 오른쪽 벽에 있는 사진 속 돌로 만든 조각품은 무엇이니?
여	그건 돌하르방이라고 해요. 화산암으로 만들어진 한국의 전통 조각이에요.

대화에서 남자가 오른쪽 벽에 있는 사진 속 돌로 만든 조각품이 무엇인지 묻자 여자가 그것을 돌하르방이라고 설명했는데, ⑤에는 섬 사진이 그려져 있다.

어휘 fair 명 박람회 model 명 모형 volcano 명 화산 (volcanic rock 화산암) erupt 통 폭발하다, 분출하다 banner 명 현수막 underneath 전 ~ 아래에 mark 통 표시하다 locate 통 위치시키다 sculpture 명 조각

5 할 일 파악

정답 ④

W	Honey, we still have a lot to do before we leave for Paris.
M	But we've already ¹⁾packed our suitcases. I think we're almost ready to go.
W	Well, I want to contact our hotel to ²⁾confirm our reservation.
M	Oh, I didn't think about that. Good idea.
W	When I do that, I'll also book us seats on the hotel's airport shuttle bus.
M	What can I do to help?
W	**Could you visit the airport website and find out how ³⁾much long-term parking costs?**
M	**Of course. I'll take care of that now.**
W	Did you remember to exchange some money? We'll need euros in Paris.
M	Don't worry. I did that already.

여	여보, 우리 파리로 떠나기 전에 아직 할 일이 많아.
남	하지만 이미 여행 가방은 다 쌌잖아. 떠날 준비는 거의 다 된 것 같아.
여	음, 난 호텔에 연락해서 예약을 확인하고 싶어.
남	아, 그건 생각 못 했어. 좋은 생각이야.
여	그 일을 할 때 내가 호텔의 공항 셔틀버스 좌석도 예약할게.
남	난 뭘 도우면 될까?
여	공항 웹사이트를 방문해서 장기주차료가 얼마인지 알아봐 줄래?
남	물론이지. 그건 지금 처리할게.
여	환전하는 건 잊지 않았지? 파리에서는 유로화가 필요해.
남	걱정하지 마. 벌써 했어.

파리로 출발하기 전 할 일에 관해 이야기하고 있다. 여자가 공항 웹사이트를 방문해서 장기주차료가 얼마인지 알아봐 달라고 부탁하자, 남자가 지금 처리하겠다고 했으므로 남자가 할 일로 ④ '공항 장기주차료 알아보기'가 가장 적절하다.

어휘 pack 통 싸다, 챙기다 suitcase 명 여행 가방 confirm 통 확인하다 find out ~을 알아보다 long-term 형 장기의 take care of ~을 처리하다 exchange money 환전하다

6 금액 정보 파악

정답 ④

M	Welcome to Food Express. How can I help you today?
W	I'd ¹⁾like three orders of French fries, please.
M	Of course. Which size would you like? **A large is $6, and a small is $5.**
W	**I'll get two large fries and one small.**
M	Sure. And would you like ²⁾anything to drink with that?
W	Yes. **How much is a large cola?**
M	**That'll be $3.**
W	**I'll get one of those, then.**
M	Would you like to pay with cash or a credit card?
W	Cash, please. Oh, I almost forgot. **I have ³⁾this coupon for 10% off.**
M	Okay. I'll ring your order up now.

남	Food Express에 오신 것을 환영합니다. 오늘 무엇을 도와드릴까요?
여	감자튀김 세 개를 주문하고 싶어요.
남	물론이죠. 어떤 사이즈를 원하세요? 큰 것은 6달러이고 작은 것은 5달러입니다.
여	감자튀김 큰 것 두 개랑 작은 것 하나 주세요.
남	그럼요. 그리고 함께 마실 것도 원하시나요?
여	네. 큰 콜라는 얼마예요?
남	3달러입니다.
여	그러면, 그걸로 하나 할게요.
남	현금으로 하시겠어요, 아니면 신용 카드로 하시겠어요?
여	현금으로요. 아, 까먹을 뻔했네요. 이 10% 할인 쿠폰이 있어요.
남	알겠습니다. 주문하신 것을 지금 계산해 드리겠습니다.

여자가 감자튀김 큰 것 둘($6×2=$12), 작은 것 하나($5), 그리고 콜라 큰 것 하나($3)를 주문했고, 10% 할인($20×0.9=$18)을 받았으므로 정답은 ④ '$18'이다.

어휘 order 명 주문; 순서 cash 명 현금 credit card 신용 카드 ring ~ up ~을 계산해주다

7 이유 파악

정답 ①

W Billy, Walton's Department Store is ¹⁾having a big sale. All of its winter jackets are 40% off.	여 Billy, 월턴즈 백화점에서 대규모 할인을 하고 있어. 겨울 재킷이 모두 40% 할인돼.
M That's good to hear. I need to buy a new coat.	남 좋은 소식이네. 난 새 코트를 한 벌 사야 해.
W Do you want to go shopping together on Sunday?	여 일요일에 같이 쇼핑하러 갈래?
M I'd love to, but I'm going to be busy that day.	남 그러고 싶지만, 그날은 바쁠 예정이야.
W Too bad. Will you be ²⁾working at your part-time job?	여 안됐다. 아르바이트하는 거야?
M No. I only work on Saturdays.	남 아니. 난 토요일에만 일해.
W I see. I guess you need to prepare for the big math test on Monday, then.	여 그렇구나. 그러면, 월요일에 있을 중요한 수학 시험을 준비해야 하나 본데.
M Actually, I'm ready for that. **My dad got tickets for the ³⁾championship basketball game on Sunday. We're going together.**	남 사실, 그건 준비됐어. 우리 아빠가 일요일에 있을 농구 경기 결승전 티켓을 구하셨거든. 함께 갈 거야.
W Lucky you. I heard tickets were really hard to get.	여 잘됐네. 티켓 구하기가 정말 힘들다고 들었어.
M Yeah. There will be a lot of people at the game.	남 응. 경기장에 사람들이 많을 거야.
W Okay. Have fun.	여 알았어. 즐겁게 봐.

남자는 일요일에 같이 쇼핑하러 갈 수 없다고 하면서 남자의 아버지가 일요일 농구 경기 결승전 티켓을 구해서 함께 보러 갈 것이라고 말했으므로, 남자가 함께 쇼핑하러 갈 수 없는 이유는 ① '농구 경기를 보러 가야 해서'이다.

어휘 Too bad. 안됐다. part-time job 아르바이트, 시간제 근무 championship 명 결승전; 선수권 대회 Lucky you. 잘됐네.

8 언급 유무 파악

정답 ④

M Nora, you enjoy gardening, right?	남 Nora, 넌 정원 가꾸는 거 좋아하지, 그렇지?
W Yeah. It's been my hobby for several years now. Why?	여 응. 지금까지 몇 년째 내 취미생활이야. 왜?
M The third annual Landford Garden Show is on **May 15th.** ¹⁾I was wondering if you'd like to go with me.	남 제3회 연례 Landford Garden Show가 5월 15일에 열려. 나랑 같이 가고 싶은지 궁금해서.
W That sounds like fun. Where is it being held?	여 재미있겠다. 어디서 열리는데?
M At **the Linden Conference Center**. We can get there by subway.	남 린든 콘퍼런스 센터에서. 지하철로 갈 수 있어.
W Great. How much are the tickets?	여 좋아. 입장권은 얼마야?
M They are ²⁾$12 each. But I got a couple of free tickets from my company, so you don't have to pay anything.	남 한 장에 12달러야. 하지만 우리 회사에서 공짜 표를 두 장 얻었으니까, 넌 돈을 낼 필요가 없어.
W Wow. Thank you so much.	여 와. 정말 고마워.
M No problem. This year's event should be really amazing. ³⁾**Over 200 companies** are participating.	남 천만에. 올해 행사는 정말 멋질걸. 200개가 넘는 회사가 참여할 거야.
W I can't wait. Thanks again for inviting me.	여 너무 기대돼. 날 초대해 줘서 다시 한번 고마워.

날짜(5월 15일), 장소(린든 콘퍼런스 센터), 입장료(12달러), 참여업체 수(200개가 넘음)에 대해 언급했고, ④ '행사 순서'는 언급하지 않았다.

어휘 annual 형 연례의, 매년 열리는 wonder 동 궁금해하다 a couple of 둘의, 두어 개의 I can't wait. 너무 기대돼.

9 내용 불일치 파악

정답 ③

W Welcome to our center's *Topics of Interest* series of lectures. As you know, we will be ¹⁾meeting three times a week to attend a lecture. After each lecture, there will be a question-and-answer session. **You each have a brochure that** ²⁾**provides the particulars** on the 12 lectures for this month. Our topic for today is climate change. Rising global temperatures pose a significant threat to all life on our planet. We will look at the causes of this problem and ³⁾efforts to address them. We hope you will enjoy today's lecture. Now, I'd like to present Anne Johnson, our lecturer.	여 저희 센터의 <Topics of Interest> 강연 시리즈에 오신 것을 환영합니다. 아시다시피, 저희는 강연을 듣기 위해 일주일에 세 번 모일 것입니다. 각 강연이 끝난 후에는 질의응답 시간이 있을 예정입니다. 여러분은 각자 이번 달에 있을 12개 강연에 관한 상세한 내용을 제공하는 소책자를 받으셨습니다. 오늘의 주제는 기후 변화입니다. 지구의 온도 상승은 지구상의 모든 생명체에 중대한 위협이 됩니다. 저희는 이 문제의 원인과 이를 해결하기 위한 노력을 살펴볼 것입니다. 여러분이 오늘의 강연을 즐겁게 들으시길 바랍니다. 이제, 강연자인 Anne Johnson을 소개하겠습니다.

센터에서 열리는 강연에 대한 안내 방송이다. 여자가 각 참석자는 이번 달에 있을 12개 강연에 관한 소책자를 받았다고 했으므로 ③ '참석자들은 다음 달 강연에 관한 소책자를 받았다.'는 내용과 일치하지 않는다.

어휘 meet 동 모이다; 만나다 question-and-answer session 질의응답 시간 brochure 명 소책자, 안내서 particular 명 상세한 내용 형 특정한 global 형 지구의, 세계적인 pose a threat to ~에 위협이 되다 significant 형 중대한 address 동 해결하다 명 주소 present 동 소개하다; 증정하다 형 현재의

10 도표 정보 파악

정답 ④

W	Honey, have you decided what Christmas present to get your nephew Craig yet?
M	He mentioned that he needs a new pair of headphones for his computer. I was just looking at some models online.
W	Let me see... Some of those are quite expensive.
M	Yeah, I guess I shouldn't ¹⁾spend more than $50. We have a lot of gifts to buy this year.
W	Right. And don't get a pair made of plastic. That material breaks very easily.
M	That's a good point.
W	Do you think he will ²⁾need a microphone?
M	Absolutely. He likes to chat with his friends while they play games together.
W	Well, that leaves you with a couple of options to choose from.
M	I think I'll ³⁾go for the purple headphones. That's his favorite color.

여	여보, 당신 조카 Craig에게 크리스마스 선물로 뭘 사줄지 정했어?
남	그가 컴퓨터용 새 헤드셋이 필요하다고 했어. 온라인에서 모델 몇 개를 막 보고 있었지.
여	어디 보자... 그것들 중 일부는 꽤 비싸네.
남	응, 50달러 이상 쓰면 안 될 것 같아. 우리는 올해 사야 할 선물이 많아.
여	맞아. 그리고 플라스틱으로 된 건 사지 마. 그 재질은 아주 잘 부서져.
남	좋은 지적이야.
여	그에게 마이크가 필요할까?
남	물론이지. 그는 친구들과 함께 게임을 하면서 수다 떠는 걸 좋아해.
여	음, 그러면 선택할 수 있는 게 두 개 남게 돼.
남	보라색 헤드셋으로 할게. 그가 가장 좋아하는 색이야.

남자는 가격대가 50달러 미만인 것 중에서, 재질이 플라스틱으로 되어 있지 않으며, 마이크가 있고, 보라색인 컴퓨터용 헤드셋을 골랐다.

어휘 nephew 명 남자 조카 quite 분 꽤, 상당히 made of ~으로 만들어진 material 명 재질, 재료 break 동 부서지다 Absolutely. 물론이지. chat 동 수다 떨다 metal 명 금속

11 짧은 대화의 응답 파악

정답 ②

W	Mr. Baker, I saw on a poster that the City Choir is ¹⁾recruiting new members.
M	Oh, right. We'll ²⁾have an audition this Friday to pick four sopranos. Are you interested?
W	Yes. I'd like to participate in it.
M	Fill out this application form, then.

여	Baker 선생님, 시 합창단에서 새로운 합창단원을 모집한다는 포스터를 봤어요.
남	아, 맞아. 이번 주 금요일에 소프라노 네 명을 뽑는 오디션을 볼 거야. 관심 있니?
여	네. 거기 참여하고 싶어요.
남	그럼 이 신청서를 작성해 주렴.

선택지 ① 포스터 거는 것 좀 도와주겠니?
② 그럼 이 신청서를 작성해 주렴.
③ 네가 합창단에 합류하게 되어 정말 기쁘구나.
④ 이번 주 토요일 오디션장에서 보자.
⑤ 우린 정말로 피아노를 연주해 줄 사람이 필요해.

남자가 금요일에 소프라노를 뽑는 오디션이 있다고 하자 여자가 참여하고 싶다고 했으므로, 이에 대한 응답으로는 참여 방법을 알려주는 ② 'Fill out this application form, then.'이 가장 적절하다.

어휘 choir 명 합창단 recruit 동 모집하다 participate in ~에 참여하다 fill out ~을 작성하다 application form 신청서

12 짧은 대화의 응답 파악

정답 ⑤

M	Is that a new backpack, Beth?
W	Yeah. I got it on sale yesterday. It only ¹⁾cost me $35.
M	I need one as well. Could you tell me ²⁾where you bought it?
W	I'll send you the store's name and address.

남	그거 새 배낭이야, Beth?
여	응. 어제 할인가에 샀어. 겨우 35달러였어.
남	나도 하나 필요한데. 어디서 샀는지 알려줄래?
여	내가 가게 이름과 주소를 보내줄게.

선택지 ① 왜 그걸 사기로 한 거야?
② 네 것을 하루 동안 빌려줄 수 있을까?
③ 최종 가격에서 10% 할인해 줄 수 있어.
④ 그건 내 예상보다 훨씬 더 비쌌어.
⑤ 내가 가게 이름과 주소를 보내줄게.

남자가 어디에서 배낭을 샀는지 알려달라고 부탁했으므로, 이에 대한 응답으로는 가게 정보를 알려주겠다는 ⑤ 'I'll send you the store's name and address.'가 가장 적절하다.

어휘 backpack 명 배낭 as well ~도, 역시 borrow 동 빌리다 final 형 최종의

13 긴 대화의 응답 파악　　　　　　　　　　　　　정답 ③

W	Next in line, please.
M	Hi. Could you tell me what time the train for London departs?
W	Well, we have one scheduled for 1 p.m. However, it's ¹⁾already fully booked.
M	Are there any more today?
W	Yes. **There is one train departing at 2 p.m. and another at 3 p.m.**
M	I see. I need to get to London by 5 p.m., so I guess I'd better take the earlier train.
W	**Actually, you should consider the train that leaves at 3 p.m.**
M	Really? Why?
W	It's the ²⁾express train, so it takes just under two hours.
M	What about the other train?
W	**The earlier train stops several times between here and London. It won't** ³⁾get you there on time.
M	Then, I'll take one ticket for the 3 p.m. train.

여	다음 분 와 주세요.
남	안녕하세요. 런던행 열차가 몇 시에 출발하는지 알려주시겠어요?
여	음, 오후 1시로 예정되어 있어요. 하지만, 그건 이미 예약이 꽉 찼습니다.
남	오늘 열차가 더 있나요?
여	네. 오후 2시에 출발하는 열차와 3시에 출발하는 게 또 한 대 있습니다.
남	그렇군요. 저는 오후 5시까지 런던에 도착해야 해서, 더 이른 열차를 타는 게 좋을 것 같아요.
여	사실은, 오후 3시에 출발하는 열차를 고려해보세요.
남	정말요? 왜요?
여	급행열차라서, 두 시간도 채 안 걸려요.
남	남은 다른 열차는요?
여	더 이른 열차는 이곳과 런던 사이에서 여러 번 정차해요. 손님께서 제시간에 도착하시지 못할 거예요.
남	그러면 오후 3시 열차표로 한 장 주세요.

선택지 ① 저는 1시에 출발하는 열차를 타는 게 더 좋아요.
② 제 좌석 번호를 확인해 주시겠어요?
③ 그러면 오후 3시 열차표로 한 장 주세요.
④ 예상치 못한 지연의 이유가 뭔가요?
⑤ 일정이 정확하지 않을 수도 있다고 생각해요.

열차표를 구매하는 상황이다. 여자가 오후 3시에 출발하는 급행열차를 추천하면서 남은 다른 열차로는 제시간에 도착하지 못한다고 했으므로, 이에 대한 응답으로는 3시 열차표를 사겠다고 답하는 ③ 'Then, I'll take one ticket for the 3 p.m. train.'이 가장 적절하다.

어휘 depart 图 출발하다 consider 图 고려하다 express 휑 급행의, 고속의 图 표현하다 delay 冏 지연 图 연기하다 accurate 휑 정확한

---

14 긴 대화의 응답 파악　　　　　　　　　　　　　정답 ②

M	Hazel, why weren't you at school yesterday?
W	I had a really bad cold, so my mother told me to stay home.
M	That's unfortunate. Are you ¹⁾feeling better today?
W	Yeah. I'm just kind of tired. But I'm also a little stressed.
M	Why? What's ²⁾bothering you?
W	**I'm supposed to hand in the book report for English class today, but I didn't finish it. I was too sick.**
M	I'm sure Ms. Kingston will understand if you ³⁾explain the situation to her.
W	Do you think so? She is pretty strict.
M	Of course. **Why don't you see her and ask for** ⁴⁾a later deadline?
W	Okay. I'll go to the teachers' office right now.

남	Hazel, 어제 왜 학교 안 왔니?
여	심한 독감에 걸려서, 엄마가 집에 있으라고 하셨어.
남	안 됐네. 오늘은 좀 나아졌어?
여	응. 그냥 약간 피곤할 뿐이야. 하지만 나는 스트레스도 조금 받고 있어.
남	왜? 뭐가 문제야?
여	오늘 영어 수업 시간에 독후감을 제출하기로 했는데, 다 못 끝냈어. 너무 아팠거든.
남	Kingston 선생님은 분명 상황을 설명해 드리면 이해해 주실 거야.
여	그렇게 생각해? 그분은 꽤 엄격하시잖아.
남	물론이지. 선생님을 찾아뵙고 마감일을 더 늦춰달라고 부탁하는 게 어때?
여	알았어. 지금 바로 교무실로 갈게.

선택지 ① 걱정하지 마. 난 이미 보고서를 제출했어.
② 알았어. 지금 바로 교무실로 갈게.
③ 네 말이 맞아. 나으려면 더 쉬어야겠어.
④ 잘 모르겠어. 그녀가 어제 왜 수업에 빠졌을까?
⑤ 동의해. 넌 출석 기록을 확인해야 해.

독후감 제출 마감일을 걱정하는 상황이다. 여자가 아파서 오늘 제출해야 하는 독후감을 다 못 끝냈다고 하자 남자가 선생님을 찾아뵙고 마감일을 늦춰달라고 부탁할 것을 제안했으므로, 이에 대한 응답으로는 제안을 수락하는 ② 'Okay. I'll go to the teachers' office right now.'가 가장 적절하다.

어휘 have a bad cold 독감에 걸리다 That's unfortunate 안 됐네. kind of 약간의 book report 독후감 strict 휑 엄격한 ask for ~을 부탁하다 turn in ~을 제출하다 teachers' office 교무실 rest 图 쉬다 attendance 冏 출석, 참석

15 상황에 적절한 말 파악 정답 ⑤

W Noah and Chloe are classmates. Their class will put on a play at the school festival in two months. Last night, Noah made ¹⁾a rehearsal schedule. Before making the schedule, Noah asked Chloe for her opinion. She said that she wanted the play to be a success, so rehearsing often was important. However, when Chloe read Noah's schedule this morning, she saw that it included rehearsals five nights a week. Chloe is worried that practicing so much will ²⁾interfere with their studies. **So Chloe wants to suggest that Noah ³⁾reduce the number of rehearsals each week.** In this situation, what would Chloe most likely say to Noah?

여 Noah와 Chloe는 반 친구입니다. 그들의 반은 두 달 후에 학교 축제에서 연극 공연을 할 것입니다. 어젯밤, Noah는 리허설 일정을 잡았습니다. Noah는 일정을 잡기 전에 Chloe에게 의견을 구했습니다. 그녀는 연극이 성공적이기를 원하니 자주 리허설하는 것이 중요하다고 말했습니다. 하지만, Chloe가 오늘 아침 Noah가 짠 일정을 읽었을 때, 그녀는 일주일에 다섯 번씩 저녁 리허설이 잡힌 것을 보았습니다. Chloe는 너무 많이 연습하는 것이 그들의 공부를 방해할까 봐 걱정됩니다. 그래서 Chloe는 Noah에게 매주 하는 리허설 횟수를 줄여야 한다고 제안하고 싶습니다. 이러한 상황에서, Chloe가 Noah에게 가장 할 것 같은 말은 무엇입니까?

선택지 ① 주말 말고 평일에 리허설하는 게 어때?
② 공연 준비할 시간이 충분하다고 생각해?
③ 우리 반의 리허설 일정을 짜줘서 고마워.
④ 원래 계획했던 것보다 더 일찍 연극을 공연하고 싶어.
⑤ 매주 리허설하러 만나는 횟수를 줄여야 해.

Noah가 일주일에 다섯 번씩 모이도록 연극 리허설 일정을 짠 것을 보고, Chloe는 리허설 횟수를 줄여야 한다고 제안하려 한다. 따라서, Chloe가 할 말로 ⑤ 'We should meet fewer times a week for rehearsals.'가 가장 적절하다.

어휘 put on ~을 공연하다 play 명 연극 통 놀다 rehearsal 명 리허설 opinion 명 의견 interfere 통 방해하다 reduce 통 줄이다 originally 부 원래

16-17 세트 문항 정답 16 ④ 17 ③

M Hello, everyone. As you probably already know, millions of people have heart attacks every year. **Today, I'd like to talk about ¹⁾types of food that reduce the risk of heart disease.** Most importantly, you need to ²⁾consume lots of fruits and vegetables. **Broccoli**, for example, contains vitamin A, which prevents heart problems. Similarly, whole grains like **brown rice** are ³⁾known to improve the health of the heart. At the same time, you should avoid eating too much **beef** and other types of red meat. Most meat is a source of cholesterol, a substance that can lead to heart attacks. Finally, ⁴⁾limit the amount of unhealthy fats you consume, such as those found in **butter**. Now, let's watch a brief video about how to plan and prepare healthy meals.

남 안녕하십니까, 여러분. 아마도 이미 알고 계시겠지만, 매년 수백만 명의 사람들이 심장마비를 겪습니다. 오늘은 심장 질환의 위험을 줄이는 음식의 종류에 대해 말씀드리고자 합니다. 가장 중요한 것은, 여러분이 과일과 채소를 많이 섭취해야 한다는 것입니다. 예를 들어, 브로콜리는 비타민 A를 함유하고 있는데, 이것은 심장 질환을 예방해 줍니다. 비슷하게, 현미와 같은 통곡물은 심장 건강을 증진하는 것으로 알려져 있습니다. 동시에, 여러분은 소고기와 다른 종류의 붉은 고기를 너무 많이 먹는 것을 피해야 합니다. 대부분의 육류는 심장마비를 일으킬 수 있는 물질인 콜레스테롤의 공급원입니다. 마지막으로, 버터에서 발견되는 지방처럼, 건강에 좋지 않은 지방의 섭취량을 제한하십시오. 이제 건강한 식단을 짜고 준비하는 방법에 관한 짧은 동영상을 보도록 하겠습니다.

선택지 16 ① 일반적인 콜레스테롤 공급원
② 심장병에 대한 자연적인 치료법
③ 음식 알레르기로 유발되는 증상
④ 심장 문제를 예방하는 음식
⑤ 건강한 음식 조리 방법
17 ① 브로콜리 ② 현미 ③ 설탕 ④ 소고기 ⑤ 버터

16 심장 질환의 위험을 줄이는 음식의 종류에 대해 말하고 있으므로 남자가 하는 말의 주제로 ④ 'foods that prevent heart problems'가 가장 적절하다.

17 브로콜리, 현미, 소고기, 버터는 언급했지만 ③ 'sugar'는 언급하지 않았다.

어휘 heart attack 심장마비 consume 통 섭취하다 contain 통 함유하다 similarly 부 비슷하게, 유사하게 whole grain 통곡물 brown rice 현미 substance 명 물질 lead to ~을 일으키다, 초래하다 limit 통 제한하다 fat 명 지방 형 뚱뚱한 allergy 명 알레르기

| 1 | ⑤ | 2 | ① | 3 | ③ | 4 | ④ | 5 | ③ | 6 | ④ | 7 | ③ | 8 | ④ | 9 | ⑤ | 10 | ② |
| 11 | ② | 12 | ⑤ | 13 | ④ | 14 | ① | 15 | ② | 16 | ③ | 17 | ④ | | | | | | | | |

• 각 문제의 정답 근거는 굵은 글씨로, Dictation 정답은 밑줄로 표시되어 있습니다.

1 목적 파악

정답 ⑤

M Good morning, Martin's Department Store customers. **As you know, hundreds of people** 1)lost their homes **due to the recent tornado in Pike City.** We would like to help them rebuild their lives. **So for today only, we will donate one dollar to the victims for each dollar you spend at the store.** The funds 2)will be delivered directly to the Pike City Volunteer Group. This charity group will use the money to help those most in need. In other words, your donations 3)will help pay for temporary housing, home repairs, and medical care. Thank you in advance for your help and cooperation.	남 좋은 아침입니다, 마틴즈 백화점 고객 여러분. 아시다시피, 최근 파이크시에서 발생한 토네이도로 인해 수백 명의 사람들이 집을 잃었습니다. 저희는 그들이 삶을 재건하는 것을 돕고자 합니다. 그래서, 오늘 하루만, 여러분께서 매장에서 1달러를 쓰실 때마다 1달러씩 이재민들에게 기부할 것입니다. 기금은 파이크시 자원봉사단에 직접 전달될 것입니다. 이 자선 단체는 가장 큰 어려움에 처한 사람들을 돕기 위해 그 돈을 사용할 것입니다. 다시 말해, 여러분의 기부금은 임시 주택, 집수리, 그리고 의료비를 지불하는 데 도움이 될 것입니다. 여러분의 도움과 협조에 미리 감사드립니다.

남자가 파이크시에서 발생한 토네이도로 수백 명의 사람들이 집을 잃었다고 하면서, 피해자들을 돕기 위해 백화점에서 진행하는 기부 행사에 대해 안내하고 있다. 따라서, 남자가 하는 말의 목적으로 ⑤ '재해 복구 기금 모금 행사를 안내하려고'가 가장 적절하다.

어휘 customer 명 고객 due to ~으로 인해 recent 형 최근의 rebuild 동 재건하다 donate 동 기부하다 victim 명 이재민, 피해자 deliver 동 전달하다 directly 부 직접, 바로 charity group 자선 단체 in need 어려움에 처한 in other words 다시 말해 temporary housing 임시 주택 repair 명 수리 in advance 미리 cooperation 명 협조

2 의견 파악

정답 ①

M Honey, I heard they're going to provide healthier lunches at the elementary school.	남 여보, 내가 듣기로 초등학교에서 더 건강한 점심을 제공할 거래.
W Why? Aren't they 1)pretty good already?	여 왜? 이미 꽤 괜찮지 않아?
M Yes, but there will be more fresh fruits and vegetables now.	남 응, 하지만 이제 신선한 과일과 채소가 더 나올 거야.
W I don't think the kids will like that.	여 아이들이 좋아할 것 같지 않은데.
M Maybe not at first. **But I think serving healthy lunches will improve** 2)their eating habits.	남 처음엔 안 좋아할 수도 있어. 하지만 건강한 점심을 제공하는 것이 아이들의 식습관을 개선할 거라고 생각해.
W Hmm... Kids 3)can be very picky.	여 흠... 아이들은 매우 까다로울 수도 있는데.
M If they eat fresh fruits and vegetables every day, they'll learn to enjoy the taste.	남 만약 매일 신선한 과일과 채소를 먹는다면, 그 맛을 즐기는 법을 배우게 될 거야.
W I guess that's true.	여 그건 사실인 것 같아.
M And I like that the school is setting a good example.	남 그리고 학교가 좋은 본보기가 된다는 점이 좋아.
W What do you mean?	여 무슨 뜻이야?
M They will have a positive example of 4)healthy eating choices.	남 아이들이 건강한 식사를 선택할 수 있는 긍정적인 본보기를 갖게 될 거라는 말이야.
W That's true. Maybe they'll be more likely to choose healthier foods later in life.	여 맞아. 나중에 그들이 살면서 더 건강에 좋은 음식을 선택할 가능성을 더 높일지도 몰라.
M I hope so!	남 그랬으면 좋겠어!

초등학교에서 더 건강한 점심을 제공한다고 들은 남자가 아이들이 처음에는 이것을 안 좋아할 수도 있지만 건강한 점심을 제공하는 것이 아이들의 식습관을 개선할 것이라고 했다. 따라서 남자의 의견으로 ① '건강한 급식을 제공하면 아이들의 식습관이 개선된다.'가 가장 적절하다.

어휘 provide 동 제공하다 at first 처음에는 improve 동 개선하다, 향상시키다 eating habit 식습관 picky 형 까다로운 set a good example 좋은 본보기가 되다 positive 형 긍정적인

3 관계 파악

정답 ③

M	Hi. **I'd like to know if the DVD I reserved is available now.**
W	**May I have your student ID?** Just a second, please. *[Typing sound]* You reserved *Early American History*, right? **It's available.**
M	Yes. That's the one. What a relief! I need to ¹⁾watch it before my exam this week.
W	Would you like to take it home or watch it in the library's media room?
M	I think I'd ²⁾better watch it here because other students will need it, too.
W	All right. We have one media room that's free, and the film is about an hour long.
M	Sounds good. **Oh, could I check out these books first?**
W	**Sure. I can** ³⁾help you with that.
M	Thanks!

남 안녕하세요. 제가 예약한 DVD가 지금 이용 가능한지 알고 싶은데요.
여 학생증 좀 주시겠어요? 잠시만 기다려주세요. *[타자 치는 소리]* 예약하신 게 <Early American History>가 맞나요? 그건 이용 가능합니다.
남 네. 바로 그거예요. 정말 다행이네요! 이번 주 시험 전에 봐야 하거든요.
여 집에 가져가시겠어요, 아니면 도서관 미디어실에서 보시겠어요?
남 다른 학생들도 필요할 테니까 여기서 보는 게 좋을 것 같아요.
여 알겠습니다. 비어 있는 미디어실이 하나 있고, 영화는 약 1시간 길이에요.
남 좋아요. 아, 먼저 이 책들을 대출할 수 있을까요?
여 물론이죠. 제가 도와드릴게요.
남 감사합니다!

두 사람이 도서관에서 DVD와 책 대여에 관해 이야기하고 있다. 남자는 여자에게 자신이 예약한 DVD가 지금 이용 가능한지 물어보고 있고, 여자는 학생증을 요구하며 대여 가능 여부를 확인해 주고 있는 것으로 보아 두 사람의 관계로 ③ '학생 — 사서'가 가장 적절하다.

어휘 reserve 통 예약하다 available 형 이용 가능한 What a relief! 정말 다행이네요! check out ~을 대출하다

4 그림 내용 불일치 파악

정답 ④

M	How was your Christmas, Martha?
W	It was wonderful. Here's a photo my mother took.
M	Oh, did you ¹⁾decorate the tree? It's beautiful with that star on top.
W	Yes, my family and I did. We do it every year.
M	And under the tree, there's a gift ²⁾wrapped with striped paper. Whose gift was that?
W	That one was for me. It was a winter coat.
M	Ah, that's why the box is so big. Those must be your grandparents ³⁾sitting on the couch by the window.
W	Yeah! You can see that they were happy.
M	**The three socks on the wall look so cute.**
W	Yeah, they were filled with candy.
M	Was this photo taken in the morning? You're ⁴⁾holding a mug with a reindeer on it.
W	Right. I was still drinking my coffee.
M	It looks like you had the perfect Christmas.

남 크리스마스 어떻게 보냈어, Martha?
여 정말 좋았어. 여기 우리 엄마가 찍은 사진이야.
남 오, 네가 트리를 장식했어? 별이 꼭대기에 있어서 아름답다.
여 응, 우리 가족과 내가 했어. 우리는 매년 이걸 하거든.
남 그리고 나무 아래에, 줄무늬 종이로 포장된 선물이 있네. 누구 선물이야?
여 나를 위한 거였어. 겨울 코트였지.
남 아, 그래서 상자가 되게 큰 거구나. 창가의 소파에 앉아 계신 분들은 너희 조부모님이실 것 같아.
여 맞아! 행복해하시는 게 보이지.
남 벽에 있는 양말 세 개가 너무 귀여워.
여 응, 사탕으로 가득 차 있었어.
남 이 사진은 아침에 찍은 사진이니? 너는 순록이 그려진 머그잔을 들고 있네.
여 맞아. 아직 커피를 마시는 중이었어.
남 네가 완벽한 크리스마스를 보낸 것 같네.

대화에서 남자가 벽에 있는 양말 세 개가 귀엽다고 말했는데, ④에는 양말이 두 개만 그려져 있다.

어휘 decorate 통 장식하다 wrap 통 포장하다 be filled with ~으로 가득 차 있다 hold 통 들다, 잡다 reindeer 명 순록

5 할 일 파악

정답 ③

W	Hi. May I help you?
M	I bought this gift card here at the outlet mall, but it didn't work at some of the shops.
W	I'm sorry about that. Can you tell me where the card didn't work?
M	I ¹⁾tried using it at Papa's Pizza and Norman's Boutique.
W	Hmm... I don't know what the problem is. Can I take a look at it?
M	Here you go.
W	*[Typing sound]* I've checked it, and it still has $45 on it. I don't see anything wrong with the card.
M	**Could you** ²⁾refund the money in cash?
W	**Sorry, but I can't. Instead, I'll** ³⁾replace the card with a new one.
M	What if I have the same problem?
W	You can come back here, and we'll ⁴⁾look for a solution.

여 안녕하세요. 도와드릴까요?
남 제가 여기 아웃렛 몰에서 이 기프트 카드를 샀는데, 몇몇 매장에서 작동하지 않았어요.
여 죄송합니다. 어디에서 카드가 작동하지 않았는지 말해주실 수 있나요?
남 Papa's Pizza와 Norman's Boutique에서 사용하려고 했어요.
여 흠... 문제가 뭔지 모르겠네요. 제가 한번 봐도 될까요?
남 여기 있어요.
여 *[타자 치는 소리]* 확인해 봤는데, 아직 45달러가 들어있네요. 카드에 문제가 있는 것 같지 않아요.
남 현금으로 돈을 환불해주실 수 있나요?
여 죄송하지만, 그럴 수가 없습니다. 대신 카드를 새것으로 교체해 드릴게요.
남 같은 문제가 생기면 어떡하죠?
여 여기로 다시 오시면, 저희가 해결책을 찾아보겠습니다.

기프트 카드의 오류에 대해 이야기하고 있다. 남자가 현금으로 돈을 환불해줄 수 있는지 묻자, 여자가 그럴 수 없다면서 대신 카드를 새것으로 교체해준다고 했으므로 여자가 남자를 위해 할 일로 ③ '새 카드로 교체해 주기'가 가장 적절하다.

어휘 gift card 기프트 카드, 선불카드 work 통 작동하다; 일하다 take a look at ~을 보다, 점검하다 replace 통 교체하다 What if ~? ~하면 어떡하죠? solution 명 해결책

6 금액 정보 파악 정답 ④

W	Can I help you find anything, sir?	여	찾으시는 것을 좀 도와 드릴까요?
M	Yes, thanks. **I'm looking for two pairs of warm gloves.**	남	네, 고마워요. 저는 따뜻한 장갑 두 켤레를 찾고 있어요.
W	Certainly. All our winter accessories are over this way.	여	알겠습니다. 저희 겨울 액세서리들은 모두 이쪽에 있습니다.
M	Ah, okay. *[Pause]* How much are these gloves?	남	아, 네. *[잠시 멈춤]* 이 장갑은 얼마예요?
W	**That pair is $25. We also** ¹⁾have a waterproof version **for $35.**	여	한 켤레에 25달러예요. 35달러짜리 방수 버전도 있습니다.
M	**Oh, I need the waterproof ones.** They'll keep my hands warm and dry when I'm removing snow from my driveway.	남	오, 저는 방수가 되는 것이 필요해요. 도로에서 눈을 치울 때 제 손을 따뜻하고 마른 상태로 유지할 수 있도록요.
W	Do you need anything else?	여	더 필요한 건 없으세요?
M	I suppose I should get a scarf, too. How about this one?	남	목도리도 사야 할 것 같아요. 이건 어때요?
W	²⁾The wool scarves cost **$20. But if you buy two, the second will be $10.**	여	울 목도리는 20달러입니다. 하지만 두 개를 구매하시면, 두 번째 것은 10달러예요.
M	That won't be necessary. **Just one wool scarf, please.**	남	그럴 필요는 없어요. 울 목도리 하나만 주세요.
W	Okay. So that's ³⁾two pairs of waterproof gloves and a wool scarf.	여	알겠습니다. 그러니까 방수 장갑 두 켤레와 울 목도리 하나인 거군요.
M	That's correct.	남	맞아요.
W	Perfect. The cash register is right over here.	여	완벽하네요. 계산대는 바로 이쪽에 있습니다.

남자가 방수가 되는 장갑 두 켤레($35×2=$70)와 울 목도리 하나($20)를 구매했으므로 정답은 ④ '$90'이다.

어휘 a pair of 한 켤레의, 한 쌍의 waterproof 형 방수의 remove A from B A를 B에서 치우다, 제거하다 driveway 명 도로 cash register 계산대

7 이유 파악 정답 ③

W	Hi, Nathan. I just read your message about the beach trip tomorrow. I was busy studying for my exam last night.	여	안녕, Nathan. 내일 바다 여행에 관한 메시지를 방금 읽었어. 어젯밤에는 시험공부를 하느라 바빴거든.
M	I understand. You must be disappointed that we ¹⁾had to cancel the trip.	남	이해해. 우리가 여행을 취소해야 해서 실망스럽지.
W	Yeah. I was really looking forward to it. Is it canceled because of the weather?	여	응. 나 정말 기대하고 있었거든. 날씨 때문에 취소된 거야?
M	No. It's actually supposed to be sunny and warm.	남	아니. 사실 그날 날씨는 좋을 거라고 되어 있어.
W	Oh, did our friends ²⁾make other plans?	여	아, 우리 친구들이 다른 계획을 세운 거니?
M	Not at all. Everyone is available.	남	전혀 아니야. 모두 시간이 있어.
W	Is the trip too expensive?	여	여행에 돈이 너무 많이 드니?
M	No. **There's a** ³⁾problem with transportation.	남	아니야. 이동 수단에 문제가 있어.
W	What's wrong?	여	무슨 일인데?
M	**Well, all the bus and train tickets for that day are sold out.**	남	음, 그날 버스와 기차표가 모두 매진됐어.
W	Oh, I see. We should have ⁴⁾reserved tickets earlier.	여	아, 그렇구나. 우리 더 일찍 표를 예매했어야 했어.
M	Right. We'll have to make our plans earlier next time.	남	맞아. 다음번에는 좀 더 일찍 계획을 세워야 할 것 같아.

내일의 바다 여행이 취소된 상황에서 남자가 그날 버스와 기차표가 모두 매진되는 이동 수단 문제가 있다고 말했으므로, 두 사람이 내일 바다 여행을 갈 수 없는 이유는 ③ '버스와 기차표가 매진되어서'이다.

어휘 look forward to ~을 기대하다 be supposed to ~하기로 되어 있다 Not at all. 전혀 아니야. transportation 명 이동 수단; 수송 sold out 매진된

8 언급 유무 파악 정답 ④

M	Megan, you like acting, right?	남	Megan, 너 연기하는 거 좋아하지, 그렇지?
W	Yeah. I'm in the drama club.	여	응. 나는 연극 동아리에 있잖아.
M	Did you see this flyer? They're ¹⁾having auditions for a new television show at **Grandview Theater.**	남	이 광고지 봤어? 그랜드뷰 극장에서 새 텔레비전 쇼 오디션을 할 거야.
W	Really? Oh, it's next Sunday!	여	정말? 아, 다음 주 일요일이네!
M	Yes. The auditions start at **7 a.m.** You should go!	남	응. 오디션은 오전 7시에 시작해. 넌 꼭 가야 해!
W	What's the show about?	여	그 쇼는 무엇에 관한 거야?
M	It says here that it's a crime show. They need a few young actors and actresses ²⁾for different parts.	남	여기에 범죄 프로그램이라고 쓰여 있어. 각종 역할을 맡을 젊은 남자 배우와 여자 배우가 몇 명 필요하대.
W	That's perfect!	여	완벽해!
M	To sign up for the audition, you just have to **email them a photograph and your name.** They'll put you on the audition list.	남	오디션을 보기 위해서는, 사진과 네 이름을 이메일로 보내기만 하면 돼. 너를 오디션 명단에 올려줄 거야.
W	What's the email address?	여	이메일 주소가 뭐야?
M	It's **grandview@softmail.com.** You can see it here on the flyer.	남	grandview@softmail.com이야. 여기 광고지에서 볼 수 있어.
W	Thank you ³⁾for letting me know. I can't wait to audition!	여	알려줘서 고마워. 빨리 오디션 보고 싶어!

장소(그랜드뷰 극장), 시간(오전 7시), 신청 방법(사진과 이름을 이메일로 보내기), 이메일 주소(grandview@softmail.com)에 대해 언급했고, ④ '담당자 이름'은 언급하지 않았다.

어휘 drama club 연극 동아리 flyer 명 광고지, 전단 crime 명 범죄 part 명 역할; 부분 put ~ on the list ~를 명단에 올리다

9 내용 불일치 파악

정답 ⑤

W Attention, viewers. Do you love traveling? Wouldn't you love to go on a guided tour for free? Well, thanks to Peer Tours, you can. Peer Tours ¹⁾<u>connects you with experts</u> who can recommend special places you'll like. These expert guides are all people who live in the cities you'll be visiting. Because they are locals, they will bring you to restaurants that ²⁾<u>only local people know</u> about. Also, if you don't know the local language, our guides can interpret for you. **To book your free tour,** ³⁾<u>call us at</u> **555-1990.** Then, we'll connect you with a guide in ⁴⁾<u>the city of your choice</u>! If you're interested in leading a tour of your own area, please register on our website.	여 주목해주세요, 시청자 여러분. 여행하는 것을 좋아하시나요? 무료로 가이드 투어를 하고 싶지 않나요? 자, Peer Tours 덕분에 하실 수 있습니다. Peer Tours는 여러분이 좋아할 만한 특별한 장소를 추천해 줄 수 있는 전문가들과 여러분을 연결해 줍니다. 이 전문 가이드들은 모두 여러분이 방문할 도시에 사는 사람들입니다. 그들은 현지인이기 때문에, 현지인들만 아는 식당으로 여러분을 데려가 줄 것입니다. 또한, 현지 언어를 모르신다면 저희 가이드들이 통역해 드릴 수 있습니다. 무료 투어 예약을 위해서 555-1990으로 전화 주세요. 그러면, 원하는 도시의 가이드와 연결해 드리겠습니다! 만약 여러분 지역의 투어를 주도하는 것에 관심이 있다면, 저희 웹사이트에 등록하세요.

무료 가이드 투어 서비스에 대한 홍보 방송이다. 여자가 무료 투어 예약을 위해서는 전화해 달라고 했으므로, ⑤ '투어 예약은 웹사이트를 통해 신청해야 한다.'는 내용과 일치하지 않는다.

어휘 for free 무료로 expert 몡 전문가 local 몡 현지인 혱 지역의, 현지의 interpret 동 통역하다; 해석하다 lead 동 주도하다, 이끌다

10 도표 정보 파악

정답 ②

M Honey, did you check out house cleaning services?	남 여보, 집 청소 서비스는 확인해 봤어?
W I'm looking at some now. Do you want to see?	여 지금 몇 개 보고 있어. 당신도 볼래?
M Sure. ¹⁾<u>What time do you think</u> they should come to clean the house?	남 물론이지. 당신은 그들이 몇 시에 집을 청소하러 와야 한다고 생각해?
W **I'd like them to be finished before 12 p.m.**	여 오후 12시 전에 끝내 주면 좋겠어.
M I agree. We're rarely home in the morning anyway, so those times are ²⁾<u>more convenient</u>.	남 동의해. 아침에는 우리가 집에 거의 없으니까, 그 시간대가 더 편리하겠어.
W What about the price?	여 가격은 어때?
M **I think anything over $150 is too much.**	남 150달러가 넘는 것은 무리인 것 같아.
W Okay. So we won't choose this one.	여 좋아. 그럼 이건 선택하지 않겠어.
M ³⁾<u>How often</u> do we want them to come?	남 얼마나 자주 오는 게 좋을까?
W I think every two weeks would be good. Since we have a dog and a cat, once a month is not enough.	여 2주에 한 번이면 좋을 것 같아. 우리가 개와 고양이를 기르고 있으니까, 한 달에 한 번으로는 충분하지 않아.
M That's true. **So let's go with** ⁴⁾<u>a biweekly one</u>. **Do we want laundry service, too?**	남 맞아. 그럼 격주로 오는 것으로 선택하자. 세탁 서비스도 원해?
W **Of course.** That would be a big help.	여 물론이지. 큰 도움이 될 거야.
M Then, let's go with this one!	남 그럼 이걸로 선택하자!

두 사람은 오후 12시 전에 청소가 끝나면서, 150달러를 넘지 않는 가격대의, 격주로 방문하는 것 중에서, 세탁 서비스가 제공되는 청소 서비스를 골랐다.

어휘 rarely 뿐 거의 ~않는 convenient 혱 편리한 go with ~을 선택하다 biweekly 혱 격주의 frequency 몡 빈도

11 짧은 대화의 응답 파악

정답 ②

M It's good to be back at the weekend farm, Jane. How are the ¹⁾<u>cucumbers that we planted</u>?	남 주말농장에 돌아와서 좋다, Jane. 우리가 심은 오이는 어떻니?
W They're doing well, Dad. **We should be able to** ²⁾<u>pick them soon</u>.	여 잘 자라고 있어요, 아빠. 곧 딸 수 있을 거예요.
M Great. **When do you think we should do that?**	남 좋아. 우리가 그걸 언제 해야 한다고 생각하니?
W I think we can pick them next weekend.	여 다음 주말에 따면 될 것 같아요.
	선택지 ① 그 농부는 일요일에 돌아올 거예요.
	② 다음 주말에 따면 될 것 같아요.
	③ 제가 그것들을 금방 심을 수 있어요.
	④ 내년 봄에 주말농장을 하나 마련해요.
	⑤ 그냥 오이를 샐러드에 넣었어요.

여자가 오이를 곧 딸 수 있을 것이라고 하자 남자가 언제 해야 한다고 생각하는지 물었으므로, 이에 대한 응답으로는 오이를 딸 시기를 말해주는 ② 'I think we can pick them next weekend.'가 가장 적절하다.

어휘 be back 돌아오다 cucumber 몡 오이 plant 동 심다 몡 식물 pick 동 (채소, 과일 등을) 따다, 뽑다

12 짧은 대화의 응답 파악   정답 ⑤

W Paul, are you ready for your flight tomorrow?
 M Yes. I've ¹⁾<u>packed</u> <u>everything</u>. I'm just feeling a little worried. **I can't find the external battery I bought last week.**
 W Well, I have one that I don't need. You can ²⁾<u>borrow</u> <u>it</u> <u>from</u> <u>me</u> if you want.
 M Perfect. I'll give it back to you later.
	여 Paul, 내일 비행기 탈 준비 다 됐어?
	 남 응. 모든 걸 다 챙겼어. 그냥 걱정이 좀 되는 것뿐이야. 지난주에 산 보조 배터리를 못 찾겠어.
	 여 음, 나한테 필요 없는 게 하나 있어. 네가 원한다면 나에게 빌려도 돼.
	 <u>남 완벽해. 나중에 돌려줄게.</u>
	
	 선택지 ① 응. 스웨터, 바지, 코트를 챙겼어.
	     ② 괜찮아. 그냥 택시를 타고 공항으로 갈게.
	     ③ 그렇지 않아. 최근에 산 것이 더 좋아.
	     ④ 걱정 마. 네가 그걸 곧 찾을 거라고 확신해.
	     ⑤ 완벽해. 나중에 돌려줄게.

지난주에 산 보조 배터리를 찾지 못해서 걱정하는 남자에게 여자가 자신에게 필요 없는 것이 하나 있다면서 빌려줄 수 있다고 했으므로, 이에 대한 응답으로는 나중에 그것을 돌려주겠다고 말하는 ⑤ 'Perfect. I'll give it back to you later.'가 가장 적절하다.

어휘 be ready for ~을 할 준비가 되다   pack 통 (짐을) 챙기다 명 묶음, 꾸러미   external battery 보조 배터리   prefer 통 ~을 더 좋아하다, 선호하다

13 긴 대화의 응답 파악   정답 ④

[Telephone rings.]
 M Hi. Are you Mindy Miller? I'm Brian from the animal shelter.
 W Yes. I called earlier ¹⁾<u>about</u> <u>your</u> <u>advertisement</u>.
 M Right. **So you saw the pictures of the puppies we just rescued.**
 W They look so cute. **I was thinking ²⁾<u>about</u> <u>adopting</u> one of them.**
 M That's great, but have you ever owned a dog before?
 W Well, my parents had dogs growing up. So I have some experience.
 M Having your own dog ³⁾<u>requires</u> <u>a</u> <u>lot</u> <u>more</u> <u>responsibility</u>.
 W Oh, I'm aware of that. I know I can do a good job.
 M That's good. But keep in mind, these guys love to play.
 W I'm a pretty active person, so that's perfect for me.
 M Okay. Let's ⁴⁾<u>arrange</u> <u>a</u> <u>time</u> for you to come and see them.
 W What if I come by later today?
 M That's fine. I'll be at the shelter until 5 p.m.
	[전화기가 울린다.]
	 남 안녕하세요. Mindy Miller이신가요? 저는 동물 보호소의 Brian입니다.
	 여 네. 아까 광고 보고 전화했어요.
	 남 그래요. 그러니까 저희가 방금 구조한 강아지들의 사진을 보셨군요.
	 여 너무 귀여워 보여요. 그중 한 마리를 입양할까 생각 중이었어요.
	 남 좋습니다만, 전에 개를 키워본 적이 있으신가요?
	 여 음, 저희 부모님이 개들을 키우셨어요. 그래서 저는 경험이 좀 있어요.
	 남 선생님만의 개를 키우는 것은 훨씬 더 많은 책임감을 요구해요.
	 여 아, 알고 있어요. 제가 잘할 수 있다는 것도 알고요.
	 남 잘됐네요. 그런데 명심하세요, 이 아이들은 노는 것을 정말 좋아한다는 것을요.
	 여 저는 꽤 활동적인 사람이라서, 저한테 딱 맞아요.
	 남 알겠습니다. 당신이 그들을 보러 올 수 있는 시간을 조정합시다.
	 여 오늘 늦게 들르면 어떨까요?
	 <u>남 괜찮아요. 저는 오후 5시까지 보호소에 있을 거예요.</u>
	
	 선택지 ① 죄송해요. 지금 사진을 올릴게요.
	     ② 그렇게 해요. 세게 밀어붙이시네요.
	     ③ 전적으로 동의합니다. 일이 너무 많아요.
	     ④ 괜찮아요. 저는 오후 5시까지 보호소에 있을 거예요.
	     ⑤ 그럴 필요 없어요. 강아지들을 볼 수 있습니다.

강아지를 입양하기 위해 동물 보호소에 전화한 여자가 오늘 늦게 보호소에 들려도 되는지 물었으므로, 이에 대한 응답으로는 오후 5시까지 보호소에 있을 예정이라서 괜찮다고 대답하는 ④ 'That's fine. I'll be at the shelter until 5 p.m.'이 가장 적절하다.

어휘 advertisement 명 광고   rescue 통 구조하다   adopt 통 입양하다   require 통 요구하다   responsibility 명 책임감   be aware of ~을 알다   keep in mind 명심하다
active 형 활동적인   arrange 통 조정하다   come by 들르다   strike a hard bargain (흥정 등을) 세게 밀어붙이다

14 긴 대화의 응답 파악   정답 ①

M Christine, you seem stressed. What's wrong? **W** **I'm planning to surprise my grandmother this weekend for her birthday, but it's not going well.** **M** How so? **W** All the train tickets are sold out, and the present I bought online ¹⁾<u>hasn't</u> <u>been</u> <u>delivered</u> yet. **M** What are you going to do, then? **W** Well, I managed to get a bus ticket, and I might send the present by mail later. But I'm still pretty upset about it all. **M** I'm sorry you're having so many problems. **W** It's okay. I'm just glad I'll ²⁾<u>get</u> <u>to</u> <u>see</u> <u>her</u>. **M** Well, is there anything else you need to figure out? **W** **Actually, I need to find someone to ³⁾<u>collect</u> <u>my</u> <u>newspaper</u> while I'm gone.**	남 Christine, 너 스트레스 받는 것 같아 보여. 무슨 일이야? 여 이번 주말에 할머니 생신을 위해 깜짝 놀라게 해드릴 계획인데, 잘 되어 가고 있지 않아. 남 어떤데? 여 기차표가 매진됐고, 인터넷에서 산 선물도 아직 안 왔어. 남 그럼 어떻게 할 거야? 여 음, 간신히 버스표는 구했는데 선물은 나중에 우편으로 보내야 할지도 몰라. 하지만 이 모든 것에 대해 아직 꽤 속상해. 남 그렇게 많은 문제를 겪고 있다니 유감이야. 여 괜찮아. 난 그저 할머니를 뵈러 갈 수 있다는 게 기뻐. 남 음, 더 해결해야 할 것이 있니? 여 사실, 내가 없는 동안 신문을 모아놔 줄 사람을 찾아야 해. 남 내가 해줄 수 있어. 다른 걱정은 하지 않아도 돼. 여 확실해?

M **I can do it.** You shouldn't have to ⁴⁾worry about anything else.

W Are you sure?

M Yes. **Just enjoy your visit with your grandmother.**

W I really appreciate your help.

남 응. 넌 그냥 할머니와 함께 즐겁게 시간을 보내도록 해.

여 도와줘서 정말 고마워.

선택지 ① 도와줘서 정말 고마워.

② 난 다른 주말에 가야 할 것 같아.

③ 배송은 토요일로 예정되어 있어.

④ 그녀에게 다른 것을 사드릴 수 있을지 몰라.

⑤ 짐만 싸고 나면 준비가 다 될 거야.

할머니 생신을 위해 준비한 여자의 계획이 잘 되어가지 않는 상황이다. 여자가 본인이 없는 동안 신문을 모아놔 줄 사람을 찾아야 한다고 하자 남자가 자신이 해줄 수 있으니 할머니와 함께 보내는 시간을 즐기라고 했으므로, 이에 대한 응답으로는 도움에 대한 고마움을 표현하는 ① 'I really appreciate your help.'가 가장 적절하다.

어휘 go well 잘 되어가다 manage to 간신히 ~하다 upset 혱 속상한 figure out ~을 해결하다 collect 통 모으다 one's visit with ~와 함께 보내는 시간

---

15 상황에 적절한 말 파악 　　　　　　　　정답 ②

W Arthur and Lisa are members of a high school music club. The club is holding a concert soon, so they are ¹⁾helping to promote it. Arthur and Lisa are in charge of posting flyers throughout the school. The club president also asked them to ²⁾make a larger poster to place on the main bulletin board by the school's entrance. **Originally, Arthur agreed to make the poster by himself.** Lisa was going to make the flyers. However, Arthur has ³⁾recently gotten busy with school work. Now, Lisa thinks she should make the poster instead of Arthur because she has more free time than him. **So Lisa wants to suggest to Arthur that she take on his job.** In this situation, what would Lisa most likely say to Arthur?

여 Arthur와 Lisa는 고등학교 음악 동아리의 회원입니다. 동아리에서 곧 콘서트를 열 예정이라서, 그들은 홍보를 돕고 있습니다. Aruther와 Lisa는 학교 곳곳에 광고지를 붙이는 일을 맡았습니다. 또한 동아리 회장은 그들에게 학교 입구에 있는 메인 게시판에 놓을 더 큰 포스터를 만들라고 요청했습니다. 원래, Arthur는 포스터를 그가 혼자서 만드는 것에 동의했습니다. Lisa가 광고지를 만들려고 했습니다. 하지만, Arthur는 최근 학교 공부로 바빠졌습니다. 이제, Lisa는 Arthur보다 더 많은 자유 시간이 있기 때문에 Arthur 대신 포스터를 만들어야겠다고 생각합니다. 그래서 Lisa는 Arthur에게 그의 일을 맡겠다고 제안하고 싶습니다. 이러한 상황에서, Lisa가 Arthur에게 가장 할 것 같은 말은 무엇입니까?

선택지 ① 나는 내일 동아리 회장을 만날 거야.

② 내가 너를 위해 포스터 작업을 하는 게 어때?

③ 콘서트는 오후 7시에 강당에서 시작해.

④ 나는 할 일이 너무 많아서 널 도와줄 수가 없어.

⑤ 포스터가 좀 더 화려해져야 하지 않을까?

Arthur가 학교 공부로 바빠진 것을 보고, Lisa는 그가 하기로 했던 큰 포스터 만드는 일을 자신이 맡겠다고 제안하려 한다. 따라서, Lisa가 할 말로 ② 'Why don't I work on the poster for you?'가 가장 적절하다.

어휘 promote 통 홍보하다 in charge of ~을 맡아서 bulletin board 게시판 entrance 혱 입구 take on (일을) 맡다

16-17 세트 문항 　　　　　　　　정답 16 ③ 17 ④

M Good afternoon. Yesterday, we talked about animal parenting techniques. **Today, I'd like to discuss how animals get home ¹⁾after long journeys.** First, there's **salmon**. These fish are born in rivers and swim to the ocean when they are young. As adults, the fish return to the same place to lay eggs, guided by their sense of smell. **Sea turtles** ²⁾follow a similar pattern. They hatch on the beach but live in the sea mostly. By sensing the earth's magnetic fields, they can find their way home, even from across the ocean. Next, some **seagulls** from the Arctic go even farther. They can fly from Canada to South Africa. By watching the sun and the stars, they ³⁾return to nests in the north every year. **Whales** also go home to breed. They get there thanks to their sense of hearing. They make clicking sounds that ⁴⁾reflect back to them, so they always know where they are in the sea. Let's take a look at a video.

남 안녕하세요. 어제, 우리는 동물들의 양육 기술에 대해 이야기했습니다. 오늘은, 동물들이 긴 여정 후 집에 돌아가는 방법에 대해 논의하고 싶습니다. 먼저, 연어가 있습니다. 이 물고기들은 강에서 태어나 어릴 때 바다로 헤엄쳐 갑니다. 어른이 되면, 그 물고기들은 후각에 이끌려 같은 장소로 돌아가 알을 낳습니다. 바다거북도 비슷한 패턴을 따릅니다. 그들은 해변에서 부화하지만 대부분 바다에서 삽니다. 지구의 자기장을 감지함으로써, 그들은 바다 건너에서도 집으로 돌아가는 길을 찾을 수 있습니다. 다음으로, 북극에서 온 몇몇 갈매기들은 훨씬 더 멀리 갑니다. 그들은 캐나다에서 남아프리카까지 날 수 있습니다. 태양과 별들을 관찰함으로써, 그들은 매년 북쪽에 있는 둥지로 돌아옵니다. 고래들도 번식을 위해 집으로 갑니다. 그들은 청각 덕분에 그곳에 도착합니다. 그들은 반사되어 돌아오는 딸깍거리는 소리를 내기 때문에, 항상 그들이 바다 어디쯤에 있는지 알고 있습니다. 영상을 한번 보겠습니다.

선택지 16 ① 동물들이 같은 장소에서 번식하는 이유

② 종마다 다른 양육 방식을 가지는 이유

③ 동물들이 장거리 여정 후에 집으로 돌아오는 방법

④ 바다 동물들이 후각을 사용하는 방법

⑤ 물고기가 먹이를 얻기 위해 먼 거리를 이동할 수 있는 방법

17 ① 연어 ② 바다거북 ③ 갈매기 ④ 거위 ⑤ 고래

16 동물들이 긴 여정 후 집에 돌아가는 방법에 대해 논의하고 있으므로 남자가 하는 말의 주제로 ③ 'how animals return home after long distance travel'이 가장 적절하다.

17 연어, 바다거북, 갈매기, 고래는 언급했지만, ④ 'geese'는 언급하지 않았다.

어휘 parent 통 양육하다 명 부모 get home 집에 돌아가다 journey 명 여정, 여행; 이동 ocean 명 바다 lay egg 알을 낳다 sense 명 감각 통 감지하다 hatch 통 부화하다 magnetic field 명 자기장 nest 명 둥지 breed 통 번식하다 thanks to ~ 덕분에 reflect 통 반사하다

1	⑤	2	①	3	②	4	⑤	5	②	6	③	7	⑤	8	④	9	②	10	③
11	⑤	12	①	13	①	14	②	15	③	16	⑤	17	①						

• 각 문제의 정답 근거는 굵은 글씨로, Dictation 정답은 밑줄로 표시되어 있습니다.

1 목적 파악

정답 ⑤

M Attention, all customers. We hope you are enjoying your time at the Plaza Shopping Center and are finding everything you need in our stores. **We would like to notify everyone that our** ¹⁾closing time will be changed **for today. We will close two hours earlier than usual to perform an** ²⁾annual safety check **on this building.** This includes making sure that the fire alarm and sprinkler system are working. We ³⁾apologize for any inconvenience this may cause, but it is necessary to ensure the safety of our customers. The shopping center will return to its regular hours of operation tomorrow. Thank you.

남 모든 고객님께 안내 말씀드립니다. 플라자 쇼핑센터에서 즐거운 시간을 보내시면서 저희 매장에서 필요하신 모든 것을 찾으시길 바랍니다. 고객님들께 오늘 저희 폐점 시간이 변경되었음을 알려드립니다. 연례 건물 안전 점검을 시행하기 위해 평소보다 2시간 일찍 문을 닫을 예정입니다. 이 점검에는 화재 경보 및 스프링클러 소화 장치가 작동하는지 확인하는 작업이 포함됩니다. 이로 인해 발생할 수 있는 불편에 대해 사과드리오나, 이는 고객님들의 안전을 보장하는 데 필요한 일입니다. 내일부터는 쇼핑센터의 정상적인 운영 시간으로 돌아갈 것입니다. 감사합니다.

남자가 건물 안전 점검 때문에 플라자 쇼핑센터의 폐점 시간이 변경되어, 평소보다 2시간 일찍 문을 닫겠다고 안내하고 있다. 따라서, 남자가 하는 말의 목적으로 ⑤ '쇼핑센터 영업 종료 시각 변경을 공지하려고'가 가장 적절하다.

어휘 notify ⑧ 알리다 perform ⑧ 시행하다, 실시하다 annual ⑲ 연례의, 매년 하는 apologize ⑧ 사과하다 inconvenience ⑲ 불편 ensure ⑧ 보장하다 operation ⑲ 운영

2 의견 파악

정답 ①

W What's the matter, honey?
M I'm a little concerned about our son.
W Really? Did something happen?
M You know he is ¹⁾giving a science presentation in class next week. He seems really worried about it.
W Well, it will be ²⁾his first time speaking in front of an audience. He must be nervous.
M I know. But he is really stressed out about it.
W I think it's okay. **In fact, stress can sometimes be** ³⁾beneficial for **children.**
M What do you mean?
W When children learn to deal with stress on their own, they become better at overcoming difficult situations.
M Interesting. So this could actually be a ⁴⁾positive experience for him.
W Exactly. Of course, if he asks for our advice, we should give it. But we shouldn't just offer to help because he looks stressed.

여 무슨 일이야, 여보?
남 우리 아들이 좀 걱정돼서.
여 정말? 무슨 일 있었어?
남 우리 아들이 다음 주 수업에서 과학 발표할 거라는 거 알잖아. 그가 그걸 정말 걱정하는 것 같아.
여 음, 청중 앞에서 발표하는 것은 이번이 처음일 거야. 긴장한 게 분명해.
남 그러게. 하지만 그것 때문에 진짜로 스트레스를 받고 있어.
여 괜찮을 것 같아. 사실, 때로는 아이들에게 스트레스가 이로울 수 있어.
남 무슨 뜻이야?
여 아이들이 스스로 스트레스 다루는 법을 배우면, 어려운 상황을 더 잘 극복하게 돼.
남 흥미롭네. 그래서 이게 실제로는 긍정적인 경험이 될 수 있겠구나.
여 정확해. 물론, 아들이 우리의 조언을 구한다면, 조언해줘야겠지. 하지만 그냥 스트레스를 받는 것처럼 보인다고 도와주겠다고 하는 건 안 돼.

과학 수업 발표 때문에 스트레스를 많이 받는 아들을 걱정하는 남자에게 여자가 때로는 아이들에게 스트레스가 이로울 수 있다고 했다. 따라서, 여자의 의견으로 ① '때로는 아이들에게 스트레스가 이로울 수 있다.'가 가장 적절하다.

어휘 presentation ⑲ 발표 audience ⑲ 청중 beneficial ⑲ 이로운, 유익한 deal with ~을 다루다 on one's own ~ 스스로 overcome ⑧ 극복하다 positive ⑲ 긍정적인
ask for advice 조언을 구하다

3 관계 파악

정답 ②

W	How are you doing, Mr. Williams?
M	Not very good. I slipped on the ice while ¹⁾<u>clearing</u> <u>snow</u> from the sidewalk near my house.
W	I guess that is why you came to see me today.
M	Right. I ²⁾<u>hurt</u> <u>my</u> <u>back</u> when I fell. I want you to check it.
W	When did this injury occur?
M	Two days ago. I thought it would get better, but it seems to have gotten worse.
W	I see. **Well, you probably pulled a muscle. But we should take an X-ray to be sure.**
M	Okay. Will it ³⁾<u>take</u> <u>very</u> <u>long</u>? I have to bring my kids to soccer practice.
W	No. It won't take more than 20 minutes.
M	Great. Thanks so much.

여	어떻게 지내셨어요, Williams 씨?
남	별로 좋지 않아요. 집 근처 인도에 쌓인 눈을 치우다가 빙판길에서 미끄러졌어요.
여	그래서 오늘 저를 보러 오셨겠군요.
남	맞아요. 넘어질 때 허리를 다쳤어요. 그걸 확인해주시면 좋겠어요.
여	그 부상이 언제 생긴 건가요?
남	이틀 전에요. 나아질 줄 알았는데, 더 악화된 것 같아요.
여	그렇군요. 아마 근육이 결렸을 거예요. 하지만 확실히 하려면 엑스레이를 찍어야겠어요.
남	알겠습니다. 엄청 오래 걸릴까요? 제 아이들을 축구 연습에 데려줘야 해서요.
여	아뇨. 20분 이상 걸리지 않을 거예요.
남	좋아요. 정말 감사합니다.

두 사람이 남자의 허리 부상에 관해 이야기하고 있다. 여자는 남자의 부상을 근육 결림으로 진단하고 엑스레이를 찍어보자고 하고 있고, 남자는 넘어질 때 허리를 다쳤다면서 여자가 확인해주길 바란다고 하는 것으로 보아 두 사람의 관계로 ② '정형외과 의사 — 환자'가 가장 적절하다.

어휘 slip on the ice 빙판길에서 미끄러지다　sidewalk 명 인도, 보도　injury 명 부상　pull a muscle 근육이 결리다

4 그림 내용 불일치 파악

정답 ⑤

M	Is everything ready for Dad's birthday party, Mom?
W	I just finished setting up the dining room. What do you think?
M	I like the big banner on the wall that says, "Happy Birthday"!
W	Thanks. I made it myself.
M	Did you also ¹⁾<u>bake</u> <u>the</u> <u>cake</u> on the table?
W	No. I ordered that from the bakery this morning.
M	And there are ²⁾<u>three</u> <u>different</u> <u>main</u> <u>dishes</u> on the table, too. That's a lot of food!
W	I wanted to have all of your father's favorites. Oh, do you see the ³⁾<u>two</u> <u>presents</u> on the cabinet? Those are the ones we got him.
M	Great. **And I really like the** ⁴⁾<u>star-shaped</u> <u>balloons</u> **to the right of the presents.** They look really cute.
W	I think so, too.

남	아빠 생신 파티 준비는 다 됐나요, 엄마?
여	방금 식사 공간을 다 꾸몄단다. 어떠니?
남	벽에 걸린 'Happy Birthday'라고 쓰여 있는 큰 배너가 마음에 들어요!
여	고맙구나. 그건 내가 직접 만들었단다.
남	식탁 위에 있는 케이크도 엄마가 구운 거예요?
여	아니. 오늘 아침에 빵집에서 주문했어.
남	그리고 식탁에 세 가지 메인 요리도 있네요. 음식이 정말 많군요!
여	네 아빠가 좋아하는 음식을 다 차려놓고 싶었어. 아, 진열장 위에 있는 두 개의 선물이 보이니? 그것들이 우리가 준비한 거란다.
남	좋네요. 그리고 전 선물 오른편에 있는 별 모양 풍선들이 정말 마음에 들어요. 진짜 귀여워 보여요.
여	나도 그렇게 생각한단다.

대화에서 남자가 선물 오른편의 별 모양 풍선들이 정말 마음에 든다고 말했는데, ⑤에는 동그란 풍선들이 그려져 있다.

어휘 set up ~을 꾸미다, 설치하다　back 통 굽다　cabinet 명 진열장, 캐비닛

5 할 일 파악

정답 ②

W	Honey, I can't wait for our family camping trip tomorrow.
M	I'm really excited, too. We still have a lot of ¹⁾<u>preparations</u> <u>to</u> <u>make</u>, though.
W	That's true. I'm going to the supermarket this afternoon to buy the food we need.
M	Great. I've ²⁾<u>already</u> <u>loaded</u> our tents and sleeping bags into the car.
W	Okay. Did you also pack some warm clothes for the kids?
M	I took care of that this morning. Um, could you put gas in the car after you go shopping?
W	No problem. **And while I'm out, why don't you** ³⁾<u>look</u> <u>for</u> the lanterns? I checked in the garage earlier, but I didn't see them.
M	Hmm... I think they are somewhere ⁴⁾<u>in</u> <u>the</u> <u>basement</u>. Don't worry. **I'll find them.**
W	I hope so. We'll need the lanterns at night.

여	여보, 내일 우리 가족의 캠핑 여행이 너무 기대돼.
남	나도 정말 신나. 하지만 아직 준비해야 할 것들이 많아.
여	맞아. 나는 오늘 오후에 필요한 음식을 사러 슈퍼마켓에 갈 거야.
남	좋아. 내가 텐트와 침낭은 이미 차에 실었어.
여	알았어. 아이들이 입을 따뜻한 옷도 몇 벌 챙겼어?
남	오늘 아침에 했어. 음, 쇼핑하고 나서 차에 기름 좀 넣어 줄래?
여	문제없어. 그리고 내가 외출해 있는 동안, 랜턴을 찾아보는 게 어때? 내가 아까 차고 안을 확인해봤는데, 못 찾았어.
남	흠... 내 생각에 그건 지하실 어딘가에 있는 것 같아. 걱정 마. 내가 찾아 놓을게.
여	그러면 좋겠다. 밤에 랜턴이 필요할 거야.

가족 캠핑 여행을 앞두고 준비해야 할 것들을 이야기하고 있다. 여자가 차고 안에서 랜턴을 찾지 못했다면서 자기가 외출해 있는 동안 랜턴을 찾아보는 것이 어떨지 묻자, 남자가 찾아 놓겠다고 했으므로 남자가 할 일로 ② '랜턴 찾아보기'가 가장 적절하다.

어휘 can't wait for ~이 너무 기대되다　preparation 명 준비　load 통 싣다 명 짐　sleeping bag 침낭　put gas in a car 차에 기름을 넣다　garage 명 차고　basement 명 지하실

6 금액 정보 파악

정답 ③

M	Welcome to Java Café. What can I get for you?
W	Hi. Do you sell green tea?
M	Of course. **A small cup is $2, and a large is $3.**
W	Great. **I'll get two large cups of tea and** 1)one small cup to go, please.
M	Okay. Would you like anything else?
W	**Oh, how much are these blueberry muffins?**
M	**They are $4 each.**
W	I'll take 2)three of them, please.
M	So you want two large green teas, one small green tea, and three blueberry muffins to go.
W	Right. **And I think I can get** 3)$2 off the total **with this coupon.**
M	**That's correct.** Would you like to pay with cash or by card?
W	Here's my credit card.

남	Java Café에 오신 것을 환영합니다. 뭘 드릴까요?
여	안녕하세요. 녹차 파시나요?
남	물론이죠. 작은 컵은 2달러, 큰 컵은 3달러입니다.
여	좋아요. 녹차 큰 것으로 두 잔이랑 작은 것 한 잔 테이크아웃해 갈게요.
남	알겠습니다. 더 필요한 게 있으실까요?
여	아, 이 블루베리 머핀은 얼마예요?
남	한 개에 4달러예요.
여	세 개 주세요.
남	그럼, 녹차 큰 것 두 잔, 작은 것 한 잔, 그리고 블루베리 머핀 세 개를 테이크아웃 하시려는군요.
여	맞아요. 그리고 이 쿠폰으로 총액에서 2달러를 할인받을 수 있을 것 같아요.
남	맞습니다. 현금으로 하시겠습니까, 아니면 카드로 하시겠습니까?
여	여기 제 신용 카드요.

여자가 큰 녹차 두 잔($3×2=$6), 작은 녹차 한 잔($2), 블루베리 머핀 세 개($4×3=$12)를 구매했고, 2달러 할인($20-$2=$18)을 받았으므로 정답은 ③ '$18'이다.

어휘 to go 테이크아웃하는, 포장해가는

7 이유 파악

정답 ⑤

W	Hi, Greg. Did you hear about Jenna's housewarming party on Thursday evening?
M	Yes. But I 1)don't think I can make it.
W	Do you have to work late that night?
M	No, I don't.
W	Then, is it because you have a 2)book club meeting? You usually meet with the other members on Thursdays.
M	I no longer belong to that club.
W	I see. Have you already made dinner plans with other friends, then?
M	No. **The problem is that I'm scheduled to go on a business trip abroad.**
W	How long will you be gone?
M	I leave tomorrow, and I'll 3)get back on Saturday.
W	Then, why don't you visit Jenna next week? She would love to 4)show you her new apartment.
M	I'll talk to her about it today.

여	안녕, Greg. 목요일 저녁에 있을 Jenna의 집들이 소식 들었어?
남	응. 그런데 난 못 갈 것 같아.
여	그날 밤늦게까지 일해야 해?
남	아니, 그렇지 않아.
여	그럼, 독서회 모임이 있어서 그래? 넌 보통 목요일마다 다른 회원들과 만나잖아.
남	난 더 이상 그 동호회 소속이 아니야.
여	그렇구나. 그러면 다른 친구들과 이미 저녁 약속을 잡았니?
남	아니. 문제는 내가 해외 출장을 갈 예정이라는 거야.
여	얼마나 오래 가 있는 건데?
남	내일 출발해서, 토요일에 돌아올 거야.
여	그러면 다음 주에 Jenna를 방문하는 게 어때? Jenny가 너에게 새 아파트를 보여 주고 싶어 할 거야.
남	오늘 그녀와 그 점에 대해 얘기해 볼게.

남자가 목요일에 있을 Jenna의 집들이에 못 간다고 하면서 해외 출장을 가서 토요일에 돌아올 예정이라고 말했으므로, 남자가 친구의 집들이에 갈 수 없는 이유는 ⑤ '해외 출장을 다녀와야 해서'이다.

어휘 housewarming party 집들이 no longer 더 이상 ~이 아닌 belong to ~의 소속이다 be scheduled to ~할 예정이다 go on a business trip 출장 가다 abroad 图 해외로

8 언급 유무 파악

정답 ④

M	Long time no see, Grace! How are you doing?
W	I've been really busy lately. I'm organizing the Greenville Book Fair.
M	That sounds interesting. 1)When will it be held?
W	On Saturday, **June 23rd.** It's a one-day event.
M	I'll definitely go.
W	Great. Then, come to **Maple Park** on that day.
M	Okay. What time does the fair start?
W	It 2)begins at **10 a.m.** But if you're driving, you should come early. Parking is limited.
M	Got it. I was planning to take the subway, anyway. And how much is 3)the admission fee?
W	It's **$10**, but I'll send you a free ticket.
M	Thanks. I really appreciate that.

남	오랜만이야, Grace! 어떻게 지냈어?
여	요즘 정말 바빴어. Greenville Book Fair를 준비 중이거든.
남	재미있겠는데. 언제 열려?
여	6월 23일, 토요일에. 하루 동안의 행사야.
남	내가 꼭 갈게.
여	좋아. 그러면 그날 메이플 공원으로 와.
남	알겠어. 박람회는 몇 시에 시작해?
여	오전 10시에 시작해. 하지만 운전해서 올 거면, 일찍 와야 해. 주차가 제한되어 있어.
남	알겠어. 어쨌든 난 지하철을 탈 계획이었어. 그리고 입장료는 얼마야?
여	10달러지만, 내가 공짜 표를 보내줄게.
남	고마워. 진짜로 고마워.

날짜(6월 23일), 장소(메이플 공원), 개장 시각(오전 10시), 입장료(10달러)에 대해 언급했고, ④ '주차 요금'은 언급하지 않았다.

어휘 Long time no see. 오랜만이야. lately 图 요즘에, 최근에 organize 图 준비하다, 조직하다 limit 图 제한하다 Got it. 알겠어. admission fee 입장료 appreciate 图 고마워하다

9 내용 불일치 파악

정답 ②

W	Hello, everyone. I'm pleased to announce the third annual Paper Folding Design Competition. This competition is open to ¹⁾youth and adults. For the youth group, we accept participants aged 12 to 18 years. The adult group participants should be 19 or older. **You should turn in your design with a ²⁾short explanation by e-mail.** The deadline is May 13th. But keep in mind that you should not submit designs that you have used in other contests. We will choose ³⁾10 winners and hold an exhibition with these designs. We hope many of you participate.	여	안녕하십니까, 여러분. 제3회 연례 Paper Folding Design Competition을 발표하게 되어 기쁩니다. 이 대회는 청소년과 성인이 참가할 수 있습니다. 청소년 부문의 경우, 12세에서 18세 사이의 참가자를 받습니다. 성인 부문 참가자는 19세 이상이어야 합니다. 간단한 설명과 함께 이메일로 여러분의 디자인을 제출해야 합니다. 마감일은 5월 13일입니다. 하지만 다른 대회에서 사용했던 디자인은 제출해서는 안 된다는 것을 명심하세요. 10명의 수상자를 선정하여 그 디자인들을 가지고 전시회를 열 것입니다. 여러분의 많은 참여를 바랍니다.

종이접기 디자인 대회에 대한 안내 방송이다. 여자가 이메일로 디자인을 제출해야 한다고 했으므로 ② '디자인은 우편으로 제출해야 한다.'는 내용과 일치하지 않는다.

어휘 youth 몡 청소년; 젊음 turn in ~을 제출하다 explanation 몡 설명 keep in mind ~을 명심하다 submit 통 제출하다 exhibition 몡 전시회; 전시

10 도표 정보 파악

정답 ③

M	Can I help you find anything?	남	뭐 찾으시는 걸 도와드릴까요?
W	Yes. My coffee machine ¹⁾stopped working, so I want to buy a new one.	여	네. 제 커피 머신이 작동을 안 해서, 새 걸 사고 싶어요.
M	We have a number of models available. Which capacity do you need?	남	구매하실 수 있는 모델이 많이 있습니다. 어떤 용량으로 필요하신가요?
W	**It has to make ²⁾at least four cups of coffee at one time.**	여	한 번에 적어도 네 잔의 커피를 만들어야 해요.
M	I see. Does the length of the warranty matter to you?	남	알겠습니다. 보증기간이 중요할까요?
W	**I'd prefer one with a two-year warranty or longer.**	여	보증기간이 2년 이상인 게 좋겠어요.
M	Okay. What about ³⁾your price range?	남	네. 가격대는 어떠세요?
W	**The maximum I want to spend is $40.**	여	제가 쓰고 싶은 최대 금액은 40달러예요.
M	Got it. And are there any special features you are interested in?	남	알겠어요. 그리고 관심 있는 특별한 기능이 있으신가요?
W	**It has to ⁴⁾have a timer.** I like to set up the coffee machine before I go to sleep and then wake up to the smell of fresh coffee.	여	타이머가 있어야 해요. 저는 잠들기 전에 커피 머신을 설정하고 나서, 신선한 커피 향으로 잠에서 깨는 걸 좋아해요.
M	I think we have just what you are looking for.	남	손님이 찾고 계신 게 바로 여기 있는 것 같군요.

여자는 적어도 네 잔 이상의 용량을 가지고 있고, 보증기간이 2년 이상이며, 최대 금액 40달러를 넘지 않는 것 중에서, 타이머가 있는 커피 머신을 골랐다.

어휘 a number of 많은 capacity 몡 용량; 수용력 warranty 몡 보증(기간) matter to ~에게 중요하다, 문제가 되다 price range 가격대 maximum 몡 최대 feature 몡 기능, 특징

11 짧은 대화의 응답 파악

정답 ⑤

W	**Brett, I heard you won a prize in an ¹⁾art contest.** Congratulations!	여	Brett, 미술 대회에서 상을 받았다는 얘기 들었어. 축하해!
M	Thanks. I was really surprised. I only started drawing last year.	남	고마워. 나 진짜 놀랐어. 작년에서야 그림을 그리기 시작했거든.
W	Wow. You must be really talented. **Can I ²⁾see your artwork?**	여	우와. 넌 재능이 정말 뛰어난 게 틀림없어. 네 작품 좀 볼 수 있을까?
M	Why not? I'll show it to you tomorrow.	남	물론 좋지. 내일 보여줄게.

선택지	① 어서! 그 대회에 참가해야 해.
	② 멋지다! 그림 그린 지 얼마나 됐어?
	③ 어쩌면. 그런데 심사위원들이 좋아했는지는 모르겠어.
	④ 물론이지. 널 위해서라면 하나 그려주는 것도 괜찮겠어.
	⑤ 물론 좋지. 내일 보여줄게.

미술 대회에서 상을 받은 남자를 축하해주는 상황에서 여자가 남자의 작품을 볼 수 있을지 물었으므로, 이에 대한 응답으로는 여자에게 보여주겠다고 대답하는 ⑤ 'Why not? I'll show it to you tomorrow.'가 가장 적절하다.

어휘 win a prize 상을 받다 talented 혱 재능이 뛰어난 artwork 몡 작품 Come on! 어서!, 서둘러! enter 통 참가하다; 들어가다 awesome 혱 멋진, 굉장한 Why now? 물론 좋지.

12 짧은 대화의 응답 파악 정답 ①

M Excuse me. Do you ¹⁾sell notebooks here?	남 실례합니다. 여기서 공책 파나요?
W Unfortunately, no. But there is a stationery store just down the street.	여 유감스럽게도, 안 팝니다. 하지만 길 바로 아래에 문구점이 있습니다.
M I'd like to know ²⁾how far it is from here.	남 여기서 얼마나 먼지 알고 싶어요.
W It's no more than two blocks away.	여 두 블록도 안 되는 거리에 있습니다.

선택지 ① 두 블록도 안 되는 거리에 있습니다.
② 제가 급해서, 택시를 타고 거기로 가겠습니다.
③ 그 가게의 모든 품목이 지금 할인 중입니다.
④ 그 공책은 학생들에게 인기가 좋습니다.
⑤ 도로명 주소를 적어주셔야 합니다.

남자가 문구점이 여기에서 얼마나 먼지 알고 싶다고 했으므로, 이에 대한 응답으로는 문구점까지의 거리를 알려주는 ① 'It's no more than two blocks away.'이다.

어휘 stationery store 문구점 no more than ~도 안 되는, 고작해야 be in a rush 급하다, 서두르다 be on sale 할인 중이다

---

13 긴 대화의 응답 파악 정답 ①

[Doorbell rings.]	[초인종이 울린다.]
W Come in. Thank you for coming here on such short notice.	여 들어오세요. 이렇게 갑작스러운 요청에도 와주셔서 감사합니다.
M No problem. **You said there's ¹⁾a problem with your hot water heater, right?**	남 천만에요. 온수기에 문제가 있다고 하셨어요, 그렇죠?
W Yes. We have only had cold water in the house since yesterday.	여 네. 어제부터 집에서 찬물만 나와요.
M Is your water heater making any unusual noises?	남 온수기에서 이상한 소리가 나나요?
W Hmm... Now that you mention it, yes. It ²⁾makes a loud noise once in a while.	여 흠... 그 말을 듣고 보니, 그렇네요. 가끔 큰 소음을 내요.
M Do you know how old the water heater is?	남 온수기가 몇 년 됐는지 아시나요?
W I think it was ³⁾installed about 10 years ago.	여 10년 정도 전에 설치됐던 것 같아요.
M Most water heaters need to be replaced after 10 years. **You probably need a new one.**	남 대부분의 온수기는 10년이 지나면 교체해야 해요. 아마 새것이 필요할 거예요.
W I really hope not. A new one would be expensive. It would be great if you ⁴⁾could fix it.	여 아니면 좋겠네요. 새것은 비쌀 테니까요. 그걸 고쳐주실 수 있다면 정말 좋겠어요.
M I'll look at it now and see what I can do.	남 제가 지금 살펴보고 뭘 할 수 있을지 알아볼게요.

선택지 ① 제가 지금 살펴보고 뭘 할 수 있을지 알아볼게요.
② 바로 하나 사실 계획이세요?
③ 온수기는 오늘 늦게 설치될 것입니다.
④ 당신이 구매한 모델은 정말 믿을 만합니다.
⑤ 고쳐드릴 수 있어서 참 다행이에요.

남자가 여자의 온수기를 고치러 온 상황이다. 여자가 새것은 비싸니 온수기를 고쳐줄 수 있다면 정말 좋겠다고 했으므로, 이에 대한 응답으로는 고칠 수 있을지 알아보겠다고 답하는 ① 'I'll look at it now and see what I can do.'가 가장 적절하다.

어휘 on such short notice 이렇게 갑작스러운 요청에도 hot water heater 온수기, 온수난방 장치 Now that you mention it 그 말을 듣고 보니 once in a while 가끔 install 통 설치하다 replace 통 교체하다 plan on ~할 계획이다 immediately 부 바로, 즉시 purchase 통 구매하다 reliable 형 믿을 만한, 믿을 수 있는

---

14 긴 대화의 응답 파악 정답 ②

M Hey, Sandra! What did you do last weekend?	남 안녕, Sandra! 지난 주말에 뭐 했어?
W Hi, James. I just stayed home. How about you?	여 안녕, James. 그냥 집에 있었어. 너는?
M I went to an international food festival at the Stanford Cultural Center. It was really fun.	남 스탠포드 문화 센터에서 열린 세계 음식 축제에 갔었어. 정말 재밌었어.
W That sounds great! ¹⁾What types of foods did you try there?	여 좋았겠다! 거기서 어떤 종류의 음식을 먹어봤어?
M I ate some Mexican, Vietnamese, and Russian foods. Everything was delicious.	남 멕시코 음식, 베트남 음식, 그리고 러시아 음식을 먹었어. 모두 다 맛있었어.
W I'm so jealous. I wish I had gone to the festival.	여 정말 부럽다. 나도 축제에 갔으면 좋았을 텐데.
M Don't worry. **It will be held again this weekend.** I'm ²⁾planning to go one more time myself.	남 걱정하지 마. 이번 주말에 또 열릴 거야. 난 한 번 더 갈 계획이야.
W Really? **Why don't we check it out together?**	여 정말? 우리 같이 보러 가는 게 어때?
M I was just going to suggest that.	남 내가 마침 그걸 제안하려던 참이었어.
W Which day were you thinking of going?	여 무슨 요일에 갈 생각이었어?
M I have a dentist appointment on Saturday, so Sunday would be best. Does ³⁾that work for you?	남 토요일에는 치과 예약이 있어서, 일요일이 가장 좋을 것 같아. 넌 그날 괜찮아?
W That's fine. I don't have any plans that day.	여 괜찮아. 그날은 아무 계획도 없어.

선택지 ① 미안해. 난 주말 내내 동네에 없을 거야.
② 괜찮아. 그날은 아무 계획도 없어.
③ 재밌게 놀아. 나도 이번 주말에 갈 수 있으면 좋을 텐데.
④ 걱정하지 마. 그냥 정기 치과 검진이야.
⑤ 물론이지! 토요일 아침에 데리러 갈게.

주말에 열리는 세계 음식 축제에 함께 놀러 갈 약속을 정하는 상황이다. 남자가 일요일에 가는 것이 가장 좋다면서 여자도 그날이 괜찮은지 물었으므로, 이에 대한 응답으로는 괜찮다고 답하는 ② 'That's fine. I don't have any plans that day.'가 가장 적절하다.

어휘 jealous 형 부러워하는, 질투하는 check out ~을 보러 가다 regular 형 정기의, 규칙적인 checkup 명 (건강)검진 pick up ~를 데리러 가다

15 상황에 적절한 말 파악

정답 ③

W Matthew has a pet lizard that he loves very much. However, he will be ¹⁾going on vacation with his parents next month. They will be away from home for two weeks, and he cannot leave his lizard alone for that long. The pet hotels in his city are very expensive, and he does not want his parents to ²⁾pay for one. **So Matthew wants to ask his friend Beth if she would be willing to look after his lizard while ³⁾he is away.** In this situation, what would Matthew most likely say to Beth?

여 Matthew에겐 몹시 아끼는 반려동물 도마뱀이 있습니다. 하지만, 그는 다음 달에 부모님과 함께 휴가를 갈 예정입니다. 그들은 2주 동안 집을 비울 것이고, 그는 그의 도마뱀을 그렇게 오랫동안 혼자 내버려 둘 수 없습니다. 그의 도시에 있는 반려동물 호텔은 매우 비싸고, 그는 부모님이 그 값을 치러주는 것을 원치 않습니다. 그래서, Matthew는 그의 친구 Beth에게 그가 없는 동안 그녀가 그의 도마뱀을 돌봐줄 의향이 있는지 묻고 싶습니다. 이러한 상황에서, Matthew가 Beth에게 가장 할 것 같은 말은 무엇입니까?

선택지 ① 넌 어디로 휴가를 갈 계획이야?
② 도마뱀을 어떻게 돌봐줘야 하는지 알려줄래?
③ 내가 여행 간 동안 내 도마뱀을 돌봐줄 수 있어?
④ 저렴한 반려동물 호텔을 추천해 줄래?
⑤ 네 도마뱀에게 매일 뭘 먹이니?

Matthew는 친구 Beth에게 그가 휴가를 떠나 있는 동안 그의 반려동물 도마뱀을 돌봐줄 의향이 있는지 물어보려고 한다. 따라서, Matthew가 할 말로 ③ 'Could you take care of my lizard during my trip?'이 가장 적절하다.

어휘 lizard 몡 도마뱀 go on vacation 휴가 가다 leave ~ alone ~를 혼자 내버려 두다 be willing to ~할 의향이 있다 look after ~를 돌봐주다 inexpensive 톙 저렴한 feed 통 (먹이를) 먹이다

16-17 세트 문항

정답 16 ⑤ 17 ①

M Good morning. As I mentioned in the last class, ¹⁾commuting by car is a major cause of traffic jams. **Today, I want to look at some of the other ²⁾options people can choose for commuting in cities.** First, **buses** are popular because they go almost everywhere. However, they use roads, so they might not ³⁾reduce traffic jams. Next, **trains** are a better option because they run on their own tracks. But there isn't always land available in a city to construct train tracks. That is why **subways** are often built in major cities. Their tracks go underground in tunnels. But perhaps the best option is **bicycles**. They take up less room. Plus, they ⁴⁾produce no pollution and provide a way to get regular exercise. I hope this lesson has given you some ideas about how we can reduce the amount of traffic on the roads.

남 좋은 아침입니다. 지난 수업에서 언급했듯이, 차로 출퇴근하는 것은 교통 체증의 주요 원인입니다. 오늘은, 사람들이 도시에서 통근하기 위해 택할 수 있는 다른 선택지들 중 몇 가지를 살펴보고 싶습니다. 첫째, 버스는 거의 모든 곳을 가기 때문에 인기가 많습니다. 하지만, 그건 도로를 이용하기 때문에 교통 체증을 줄일 수 없을지도 모릅니다. 다음으로, 기차는 그것만의 철도 위를 달리기 때문에 더 나은 선택입니다. 하지만 도시에 철도를 건설할 수 있는 땅이 항상 있는 것은 아닙니다. 그것이 주로 대도시에서 지하철이 건설되는 이유입니다. 지하철의 선로는 지하의 터널 속으로 뻗어나갑니다. 하지만 아마 가장 좋은 선택지는 자전거일 것입니다. 그것은 더 적은 공간을 차지합니다. 게다가 오염을 일으키지 않고, 규칙적인 운동을 할 수 있는 방법을 제공합니다. 저는 여러분이 이 수업으로 도로의 교통량을 줄일 수 있는 방법에 대한 아이디어를 얻으셨기를 바랍니다.

선택지 **16** ① 차를 운전하는 것의 이점
② 지하철 타기를 장려하는 방법
③ 환경오염을 일으키는 요인
④ 도시 생활의 흔한 문제
⑤ 대체 가능한 출근 방법
17 ① 오토바이 ② 버스 ③ 기차 ④ 지하철 ⑤ 자전거

16 사람들이 도시에서 통근하기 위해 택할 수 있는 다른 선택지들을 몇 가지 살펴보고 있으므로 남자가 하는 말의 주제로 ⑤ 'alternative methods to go to work'가 가장 적절하다.

17 버스, 기차, 지하철, 자전거는 언급했지만 ① 'motorcycles'는 언급하지 않았다.

어휘 commute 통 통근하다 major 톙 주요한, 큰 traffic jam 교통 체증 reduce 통 줄이다 construct 통 건설하다 underground 뷔 지하에 take up ~을 차지하다 pollution 몡 오염 encourage 통 장려하다 factor 몡 요인 alternative 톙 대체 가능한, 대안의

1	④	2	①	3	⑤	4	③	5	④	6	③	7	③	8	④	9	⑤	10	②
11	①	12	③	13	①	14	①	15	⑤	16	③	17	②						

• 각 문제의 정답 근거는 굵은 글씨로, Dictation 정답은 밑줄로 표시되어 있습니다.

1　목적 파악

정답 ④

W Attention, passengers traveling on Flight 118 to Seattle. **This announcement is an** 1)update about your departure time. As you know, the flight was originally scheduled to leave at 9:30 a.m. **However, the flight has been delayed because of strong winds and ice. Your new departure time will be 1 p.m.** Depending on the weather, there could be 2)further delays. We apologize for the inconvenience. If you have any questions or concerns about this matter, please talk to our staff at the information desk. Thank you for flying with us, and we hope to 3)get you to your destination soon.

여 시애틀행 118편 비행기를 이용하시는 승객 여러분께 안내 말씀드립니다. 여러분의 출발 시각에 관한 최신 알림 공지입니다. 아시다시피, 그 비행기는 원래 오전 9시 30분에 출발할 예정이었습니다. 하지만, 강풍과 결빙 때문에 비행이 지연되었습니다. 새로운 출발 시각은 오후 1시가 되겠습니다. 날씨에 따라, 그 이상의 지연이 있을 수도 있습니다. 불편을 드려 죄송합니다. 이 문제에 대해 질문이나 우려 사항이 있으시면, 안내 데스크의 저희 직원에게 말씀해주십시오. 저희와 함께 비행해 주셔서 감사드리며, 곧 목적지로 모실 수 있기를 바랍니다.

여자가 시애틀행 비행기가 강풍과 결빙 때문에 지연되었다면서, 새로운 출발 시각을 알려주고 있다. 따라서, 여자가 하는 말의 목적으로 ④ '비행기 출발 지연에 대해 공지하려고'가 가장 적절하다.

어휘 departure 명 출발　be scheduled to ~할 예정이다　delay 통 지연시키다　depending on ~에 따라　destination 명 목적지

2　의견 파악

정답 ①

W Honey, I think we should make our son, Ben, read more.
M Really? He's only six years old.
W Sure, but he'll start school soon. We need to make sure his reading skills are improving.
M I disagree. **I don't think young children should be** 1)forced to read.
W Why is that?
M Well, I've read that it's better for them to do things that they are naturally interested in. If we make him read when he doesn't want to, he might 2)start disliking it.
W Hmm... that makes sense.
M This could cause him to avoid books in the future and fall behind in school.
W So we should not 3)stress over how much he is reading.
M No. But let's encourage him to be creative when he does. He could draw pictures or keep a diary about what he reads.
W Okay. Let's try that.

여 여보, 우리 아들 Ben에게 책을 더 읽게 해야 할 것 같아.
남 정말? 그는 겨우 여섯 살이야.
여 그렇긴 한데, 곧 입학할 거잖아. 그의 읽기 능력이 향상되고 있는지 확인할 필요가 있어.
남 난 의견이 달라. 난 어린아이들에게 책을 읽도록 강요해서는 안 된다고 생각해.
여 왜 그래?
남 음, 애들이 자연스럽게 흥미를 갖게 된 일을 하는 게 더 좋다는 걸 읽었어. 만약 우리가 그가 원하지 않을 때 읽게 한다면, 그는 독서를 싫어하기 시작할 수도 있어.
여 흠... 일리 있는 말이야.
남 이건 미래에 그가 책을 피하고 학교에서 뒤처지게 만들 수도 있어.
여 그러니까, 그에게 얼마나 많이 읽고 있는지에 대해 스트레스를 주면 안 되겠구나.
남 안 되지. 하지만 그가 독서할 때는 창의적이 되도록 격려하자. 읽은 것에 대해 그림을 그리거나 일기를 쓸 수도 있어.
여 알았어. 한번 해보자.

아들에게 입학 전에 책을 더 읽게 하자는 여자에게 남자가 어린아이들에게 책을 읽도록 강요해서는 안 된다고 했다. 따라서, 남자의 의견으로 ① '아이들에게 책을 억지로 읽게 해서는 안 된다.'가 가장 적절하다.

어휘 start school 입학하다　disagree 통 의견이 다르다　force 통 강요하다　dislike 통 싫어하다　fall behind in school 학교에서 뒤처지다　encourage 통 격려하다　creative 형 창의적인　keep a diary 일기를 쓰다

3　관계 파악

정답 ⑤

M Ms. Smith, I'm here with your order.
W These are lovely, Mr. Anderson. **The tulips are perfect.**
M Thanks. I wanted to design something special for the awards ceremony.
W I appreciate that. **I can tell that you and your staff** 1)worked hard on these flower arrangements.
M Should we go ahead and set these up in the banquet hall?
W Yes, please. I've got the rest of the decorations ready to go. I'll show you where to put everything.
M Oh, and when would you like us to come back with 2)the special bouquets for the winners?

남 Smith 씨, 주문하셨던 것 가지고 왔습니다.
여 그거 정말 사랑스럽네요, Anderson 씨. 튤립이 완벽해요.
남 고맙습니다. 시상식을 위해 특별한 걸 디자인하고 싶었어요.
여 그 점은 감사해요. 당신과 직원분들이 꽃꽂이에 공을 들이신 걸 알겠어요.
남 연회장으로 가서 이것들을 설치할까요?
여 네, 부탁드립니다. 나머지 장식품들도 가져가실 준비가 되게 해 두었어요. 전부 어디에 둬야 할지 보여드릴게요.
남 아, 그리고 수상자들을 위한 특별 꽃다발은 언제 다시 가져다드릴까요?

W Please be here at 5. The caterer is coming with the food at 5:30, so I'll be busy then.	여 5시에 여기로 와 주세요. 5시 30분에는 케이터링 업체가 음식을 가지고 올 거라서, 그때는 바쁠 것 같아요.
M No problem. **This is such a big ceremony. Who are you** 3)organizing it for?	남 문제없습니다. 이건 정말 큰 시상식이잖아요. 누구를 위해 이걸 기획하셨나요?
W It's for an advertising company. They hold it every year.	여 광고 회사를 위한 거예요. 매년 열고 있어요.
M Well, I'm sure it'll be a success.	남 음, 틀림없이 성공할 거예요.

두 사람이 연회장에 놓을 꽃장식 및 꽃다발에 관해 이야기하고 있다. 남자는 시상식을 위해 특별한 튤립 꽃장식을 디자인했고, 여자는 광고 회사를 위해 시상식을 기획했다고 하는 것으로 보아 두 사람의 관계로 ⑤ '플로리스트 — 행사 기획자'가 가장 적절하다.

어휘 flower arrangement 꽃꽂이 banquet 몡 연회 bouquet 몡 꽃다발 advertising 몡 광고

---

4 그림 내용 불일치 파악 정답 ③

M Angela, is that a picture of your kitchen?	남 Angela, 저거 너희 부엌 사진이야?
W Yeah. We just renovated it. What do you think?	여 응. 이제 막 부엌을 수리했어. 어떻게 생각해?
M I really like it. That's a cool 1)teapot on the counter.	남 정말 마음에 들어. 조리대 위에 저건 멋진 찻주전자네.
W Yeah, we drink a lot of tea. And that's our new blender next to the sink. We make fruit smoothies every morning.	여 응, 우린 차를 많이 마시거든. 그리고 싱크대 옆에 있는 게 새 믹서기야. 매일 아침 과일 스무디를 만들어.
M I see. **I like that basket you have** 2)beside the blender. **What's that for?**	남 그렇구나. 믹서기 옆에 있는 바구니가 맘에 든다. 그건 뭐에 쓰는 거야?
W Oh, that's where we'll put our fruit. It's empty now, though.	여 아, 저기가 과일을 두는 곳이야. 하지만 지금은 비어 있어.
M And what about that jar on the microwave? What's inside?	남 그리고 전자레인지 위의 저 병은? 안에 뭐가 있어?
W I love to bake cookies, and I usually put them in there.	여 내가 쿠키 굽는 걸 좋아해서, 보통 쿠키를 거기에 둬.
M I hope I get to try some.	남 한번 먹어 볼 수 있으면 좋겠다.
W You will. Do you like this cloud-shaped whiteboard on the wall?	여 그럴 거야. 벽에 걸린 구름 모양의 화이트보드는 괜찮니?
M Yes. That'll be useful for 3)writing down any ingredients you need.	남 응. 네게 필요한 재료를 적어두는 데 유용하겠네.

대화에서 여자가 믹서기 옆에 과일을 두는 용도의 바구니가 있지만 지금은 비어 있다고 말했는데, ③에는 과일이 들어 있는 바구니가 그려져 있다.

어휘 renovate 통 수리하다 blender 몡 믹서기 jar 몡 병, 항아리 microwave 몡 전자레인지 ingredient 몡 재료

---

5 할 일 파악 정답 ④

M Hi, Grace. How is the magazine going?	남 안녕, Grace. 잡지 어떻게 되고 있어?
W Hey, Phil. Here, take a look at the layout.	여 안녕, Phil. 여기, 레이아웃을 한번 봐.
M Wow, it looks amazing. Is there anything else we have to do?	남 와, 정말 멋지다. 우리가 더 해야 할 일은 없니?
W Some of the articles aren't finished yet. So I'll email the writers and tell them to 1)send their articles before the end of the week.	여 몇몇 기사가 아직 안 끝났어. 그래서 작가들에게 이메일을 보내서 이번 주 마지막 날 전에 기사를 보내라고 할 거야.
M Great. I told the photographers to take more photos for the articles, too. They'll send their photos to you by then.	남 좋아. 내가 사진사들에게 기사에 쓸 사진도 더 찍으라고 말해뒀어. 그들이 그때까지는 너에게 사진을 보낼 거야.
W Okay. I already 2)finished the cover. And I told the printer that our copies need to be ready by Tuesday morning.	여 알았어. 내가 표지는 이미 끝냈어. 그리고 인쇄소에 화요일 오전까지 인쇄물이 준비되어야 한다고 말했어.
M Who will be 3)picking up the copies from the printer?	남 누가 인쇄소에서 인쇄물을 가져올 거야?
W We haven't figured it out yet. **But we need someone with a car.**	여 그건 아직 생각해보지 못했어. 하지만 차를 가진 사람이 필요해.
M Well, I can do it.	남 음, 내가 할 수 있어.
W Are you sure?	여 확실해?
M Of course. You're so busy with other things anyway.	남 물론이지. 어쨌든 넌 다른 일로 너무 바쁘잖아.
W Thank you. I'll send the address soon.	여 고마워. 내가 곧 주소를 보내줄게.

잡지 출간을 앞두고 상황을 점검하고 있다. 여자가 인쇄소에서 인쇄물을 가져오려면 차를 가진 사람이 필요하다고 하자, 남자가 본인이 할 수 있다고 했으므로 남자가 할 일로 ④ '인쇄물 가져오기'가 가장 적절하다.

어휘 article 몡 기사 cover 몡 표지 통 덮다 printer 몡 인쇄소; 프린터기 copy 몡 인쇄물, 사본 통 복사하다 figure out ~을 생각해보다 address 몡 주소

6 금액 정보 파악

정답 ③

W Welcome to Jackie's Art Shop. How may I help you?	여 Jackie's Art Shop에 오신 것을 환영합니다. 무엇을 도와드릴까요?
M Hi. I'm ¹⁾looking for some paints.	남 안녕하세요. 물감을 좀 찾고 있는데요.
W Okay. Here's our paint section. As you can see, we have many paints to choose from. But these two sets are the most popular.	여 알겠습니다. 여기가 물감 코너입니다. 보시다피, 선택하실 수 있는 물감이 많이 있어요. 하지만 이 두 세트가 가장 인기가 많죠.
M How much are they?	남 얼마인가요?
W This paint set is $30. **The other set comes with ²⁾larger quantities of the paints, so it's $40.**	여 이 물감 세트는 30달러예요. 나머지 다른 세트에는 더 많은 양의 물감이 딸려 있어서, 40달러입니다.
M **I'll take the bigger one.**	남 더 큰 걸로 하나 할게요.
W Okay. Do you need any brushes?	여 네. 붓은 필요하지 않으세요?
M I have some, but they're very old. So I need some new ones.	남 붓이 몇 개 있긴 한데, 아주 오래됐어요. 그래서 새것이 필요해요.
W **Well, this brush set is highly rated. It's usually $15, but it's ³⁾on sale for $10 right now.**	여 음, 이 붓 세트는 높이 평가받고 있어요. 보통 15달러인데, 지금은 할인해서 10달러예요.
M **Then, I'll get that one, too.**	남 그러면 그것도 하나 살게요.
W Okay. So you want the large paint set and the brush set.	여 알겠습니다. 그러니까, 큰 물감 세트와 붓 세트를 원하시는 거군요.
M Yes, **and I have this coupon here for 10% off.**	남 네, 그리고 여기 10% 할인 쿠폰이 있어요.
W All right. I'll ring everything up for you.	여 좋습니다. 계산해 드릴게요.

남자가 큰 물감 세트 하나($40)와 할인 중인 붓 세트 하나($10)를 구매했고, 10% 할인($50×0.9=$45)을 받았으므로 정답은 ③ '$45'이다.

어휘 come with ~이 딸려 있다 quantity 명 양, 수량 brush 명 붓 rate 통 평가하다 명 속도 ring ~ up ~을 계산해주다

7 이유 파악

정답 ③

M Hey, Rose. How was your birthday?	남 안녕, Rose. 생일 어땠어?
W It was great! My parents took me to a nice place for dinner.	여 정말 좋았어! 우리 부모님이 날 좋은 저녁 식사 장소에 데려가 주셨어.
M Did you get any presents?	남 선물은 받았어?
W I did. They gave me a sweater, but I'm going to ¹⁾exchange it.	여 받았지. 스웨터를 주셨는데, 교환할 거야.
M Is it because you don't like it?	남 그게 마음에 안 들어서 그래?
W That's not it. I've wanted to buy a sweater from this brand for a while.	여 그런 게 아니야. 한동안 이 브랜드의 스웨터를 사고 싶었어.
M Is it because of the size? It's difficult to guess someone's size when you're buying them clothes.	남 사이즈 때문이야? 누군가에게 옷을 사 줄 때 그 사람의 사이즈를 추측하는 건 어렵잖아.
W Well, it ²⁾fits me perfectly.	여 글쎄, 그건 내 몸에 딱 맞아.
M Then, why are you exchanging it?	남 그러면 왜 교환하려는 거야?
W **This one is black, but I really want the blue one.**	여 이건 검은색인데, 파란색이 정말 갖고 싶거든.
M Oh, I see. So are you going to the mall now?	남 아, 그렇구나. 그래서, 지금 쇼핑몰에 갈 거야?
W Yeah. I just hope they ³⁾aren't sold out.	여 그래. 그게 다 팔리지 않았길 바랄 뿐이야.

여자가 부모님께 선물 받은 스웨터를 교환할 것이라고 하면서 검은색이 아닌 파란색이 갖고 싶다고 말했으므로, 여자가 스웨터를 교환하려는 이유는 ③ '다른 색상을 원해서'이다.

어휘 exchange 통 교환하다 guess 통 추측하다 fit 통 (크기 등이) 맞다

8 언급 유무 파악

정답 ④

W Hey, David. Are you busy this Friday?	여 안녕, David. 이번 주 금요일에 바쁘니?
M No. I don't ¹⁾have any plans. Why?	남 아니. 아무 계획도 없어. 왜?
W Our movie club is going to hold the first Lakeshore Movie Night at **school**, and I'd like you to come.	여 우리 영화 동아리에서 처음으로 Lakeshore Movie Night를 학교에서 열 건데, 네가 와주면 좋겠어.
M That sounds fun. Who is going?	남 재미있겠다. 누구누구 가?
W **Jack, Emma, and Nicole** will also be there. And we've decided to ²⁾screen that horror film, *Midnight Scream*.	여 Jack, Emma, 그리고 Nicole도 올 거야. 그리고 공포 영화인 <Midnight Scream>을 상영하기로 했어.
M Oh, I wanted to watch that.	남 아, 그거 보고 싶었어.
W Do you think you'll come to the event, then?	여 그러면 그 행사에 올 생각이니?
M I'd love to. What time does it start?	남 그러고 싶어. 몇 시에 시작해?
W ³⁾At 7 p.m., after all the classes finish.	여 모든 수업이 끝나고 나서 저녁 7시에.
M Okay. And should I bring anything with me?	남 알았어. 그리고 내가 뭔가 가져가야 해?
W I don't think so, but I'll message you if we need something.	여 그럴 것 같지 않지만, 필요한 게 있으면 문자 보낼게.
M Sure. I can't wait!	남 그래. 정말 기대된다!

장소(학교), 참석자(Jack, Emma, Nicole), 영화 제목(<Midnight Scream>), 시작 시각(저녁 7시)에 대해 언급했고, ④ '제공 간식'은 언급하지 않았다.

어휘 hold 통 열다; 잡다 screen 통 상영하다 명 화면 message 통 문자 보내다 명 메시지 I can't wait! 정말 기대된다!

9 내용 불일치 파악 정답 ⑤

M Good afternoon, listeners! This is Chris Lee from *Afternoon Tunes*. I want to tell you all about an exciting event ¹⁾<u>coming up next week</u>. The Los Angeles Santa Claus Parade is finally returning to the city after being canceled last year ²⁾<u>due to bad weather</u>. The event will be held on December 12th at 1 p.m. The parade will take place along Pine Street beginning at the police station. Some highlights of the parade include Santa and his reindeer, a marching band, and professional dancers. There will also be a concert featuring live music from local musicians. **Because many of the main roads in this area will be ³⁾closed until 3 p.m., we recommend that you take public transportation to attend this event.**	남 안녕하십니까, 청취자 여러분! <Afternoon Tunes>의 Chris Lee입니다. 다음 주에 있을 흥미로운 행사에 관한 모든 것을 말씀드리고 싶습니다. Los Angeles Santa Claus Parade가 작년에 악천후로 취소된 이후 마침내 이 도시로 돌아올 것입니다. 행사는 12월 12일 오후 1시에 열립니다. 퍼레이드는 경찰서에서 시작하여 파인가를 따라 진행될 것입니다. 퍼레이드의 하이라이트에는 산타와 순록, 행진 악단, 그리고 전문 무용수들이 포함됩니다. 또한 현지 음악가들의 라이브 음악을 특징으로 하는 콘서트도 있을 것입니다. 이 구역의 많은 주요 도로들이 오후 3시까지 폐쇄될 것이기 때문에, 여러분에게 이 행사에 참석하려면 대중교통을 타시기를 추천합니다.

시에서 열리는 퍼레이드에 대한 안내 방송이다. 남자가 퍼레이드가 열리는 구역의 많은 주요 도로가 오후 3시까지 폐쇄될 것이라고 했으므로 ⑤ '주요 도로는 오후 3시부터 폐쇄될 예정이다.'는 내용과 일치하지 않는다.

어휘 cancel 동 취소하다 reindeer 명 순록 marching band 행진 악단 feature 동 ~을 특징으로 하다

10 도표 정보 파악 정답 ②

M Do you want to book a city tour for tomorrow, Erica?	남 내일 시티 투어를 예약할래, Erica?
W Yeah! I was already looking at a few different tour options online.	여 그래! 내가 벌써 온라인으로 몇 가지 다른 투어 선택지를 찾고 있었어.
M Okay, let's pick one together.	남 좋아, 같이 골라보자.
W First of all, I don't want to do it ¹⁾<u>late in the day</u>.	여 우선, 그날 늦게 투어를 하고 싶지는 않아.
M Me neither. **Let's choose one that starts in the morning, then.**	남 나도 그래. 그러면 아침에 시작하는 걸로 고르자.
W **I also want to avoid the boat tour.** I don't think we'd get ²⁾<u>close enough to the sights</u> on the boat.	여 난 또 보트 투어는 피하고 싶어. 보트 위에서는 관광지에 충분히 가까이 가지 못할 것 같아.
M Good point. What's our budget for the tour?	남 좋은 지적이야. 투어에 쓸 예산이 어떻지?
W **Well, I'd like to keep it under $40.**	여 음, 난 40달러 미만으로 하고 싶어.
M Sounds good. That still leaves us with a couple of options. Another thing to consider is the size of the tour group.	남 좋아. 여전히 우리에게 두 가지 선택지가 남아 있어. 또 하나 고려해야 할 건 투어 그룹의 규모야.
W **Oh, don't you think that it's best to go with as small a group as possible?**	여 아, 가능한 작은 그룹으로 하는 게 최선이라고 생각하지 않니?
M ³⁾**I totally agree.** Then, we're all set!	남 전적으로 동의해. 그러면, 다 됐다!

두 사람은 아침에 시작하면서, 보트 투어가 아니며, 40달러 미만인 것 중에서, 가능한 작은 그룹으로 된 투어 프로그램을 골랐다.

어휘 sights 명 관광지 Good point. 좋은 지적이야. as ~ as possible 가능한 ~한 be all set 다 되다

11 짧은 대화의 응답 파악 정답 ①

W Honey, I'm going to do some laundry before we ¹⁾<u>pack for our trip</u>.	여 여보, 여행 갈 짐을 싸기 전에 빨래를 좀 하려 해.
M Oh, great. I'll help you. I need to wash some clothes, too.	남 오, 좋아. 내가 도울게. 나도 옷을 좀 빨아야 하거든.
W **We'd better run to the store first. It looks like we're out of ²⁾laundry detergent.**	여 먼저 가게로 달려가는 게 좋겠어. 세탁 세제가 다 떨어진 것 같아.
M Okay. Let's go buy some now.	남 알겠어. 지금 사러 가자.

선택지 ① 알겠어. 지금 사러 가자.
② 아니. 이 옷은 깨끗해 보이지 않아.
③ 물론이지. 바지 좀 챙겨야겠어.
④ 완벽해. 우리는 이제 여행 갈 준비가 됐어.
⑤ 응. 우리 기차는 내일 아침 출발이야.

여자가 세탁 세제가 다 떨어져서 가게로 가자고 제안했으므로, 이에 대한 응답으로는 제안을 수락하는 ① 'Okay. Let's go buy some now.'가 가장 적절하다.

어휘 do laundry 빨래하다 be out of ~이 다 떨어지다 detergent 명 세제

12 짧은 대화의 응답 파악

M Welcome to the Burger Hut drive-through. What can I 1)get for you today?

W Hi. I'd like a cheeseburger combo, but I want to replace the fries with onion rings.

M We can do that. **Would you also like to** 2)add more toppings **to your burger?**

W Can I get extra lettuce on it?

정답 ③

남 Burger Hut의 드라이브스루에 오신 것을 환영합니다. 오늘은 무엇을 드릴까요?

여 안녕하세요. 치즈버거 세트를 사고 싶은데, 감자튀김을 양파튀김으로 바꾸고 싶어요.

남 그렇게 해드릴 수 있어요. 햄버거에 토핑도 더 추가하시겠습니까?

여 양상추를 더 얹어 주실 수 있나요?

[선택지] ① 신용카드도 받나요?

② 얼마나 기다려야 하나요?

③ 양상추를 더 얹어 주실 수 있나요?

④ 차를 어디에 주차해야 하나요?

⑤ 탄산음료는 어떤 게 있나요?

햄버거를 주문하는 상황에서 남자가 토핑을 더 추가할 것인지 물었으므로, 이에 대한 응답으로는 추가하고 싶은 토핑 재료를 말하는 ③ 'Can I get extra lettuce on it?'이 가장 적절하다.

[어휘] replace A with B A를 B로 바꾸다 lettuce 몡 양상추 soft drink 탄산음료

13 긴 대화의 응답 파악

W Richard, I heard that you're moving soon.

M Yes, Elizabeth. **My parents both** 1)got new jobs, **so we have to move to a different city.**

W Oh, I'm sorry to hear it. Everyone at school will miss you.

M I'll miss everyone, too. We've had some great times over the years.

W Definitely. Do you know when you'll start at your new school?

M Yes. I'll start there next week.

W Really? Are you nervous?

M A little bit. **But I** 2)like making friends, **so I'm looking forward to getting to know my classmates.** Plus, I'll meet people through sports teams.

W That's true. You'll have friends in no time, then.

M I hope so. But I'll always 3)cherish my friendships here, too. I still want to keep in touch with everyone.

W I think that's great. **I wish you the best of luck at your new school.**

M Thanks. I'm excited about this new chapter in life.

정답 ①

여 Richard, 너 곧 이사 간다고 들었어.

남 응, Elizabeth. 우리 부모님 두 분 다 새로운 일자리를 얻으셔서, 다른 도시로 이사 가야 해.

여 아, 유감이야. 학교에 있는 모두가 널 그리워할 거야.

남 나도 다들 그리울 거야. 지난 몇 년간 좋은 시간을 보냈잖아.

여 물론이지. 새 학교에서 언제 시작할 건지 아니?

남 응. 다음 주에 거기서 시작할 거야.

여 진짜? 긴장돼?

남 아주 약간만. 그런데 난 친구 사귀는 걸 좋아하니까, 반 친구들을 알아가는 게 기대돼. 게다가, 스포츠팀을 통해 사람들을 만날 거야.

여 맞아. 그러면 곧 친구가 생기겠다.

남 그러면 좋겠어. 하지만 난 이곳에서의 우정도 항상 소중히 간직할 거야. 나는 계속 모두와 연락하고 지내고 싶어.

여 그러면 좋을 것 같아. 새 학교에서의 행운을 빌게.

남 고마워. 인생의 새로운 장이 기대돼.

[선택지] ① 고마워. 인생의 새로운 장이 기대돼.

② 나도 그래. 새로운 학교로 전학 가는 건 정말 두려울 수 있지.

③ 알았어. 어쩌면 넌 친구들에게 곧 만나자고 전화하는 게 좋겠어.

④ 걱정하지 마. 결국 모든 게 잘 풀릴 거야.

⑤ 그럴지도 몰라. 하지만 지금 당장은 운동할 시간이 있을지 모르겠어.

이사 때문에 전학을 가게 되는 친구를 응원하는 상황이다. 남자가 새 친구 사귀는 것을 좋아해서 기대된다고 했고 여자는 새 학교에서의 행운을 빌어주었으므로, 이에 대한 응답으로는 응원에 고마워하는 ① 'Thanks. I'm excited about this new chapter in life.'가 가장 적절하다.

[어휘] miss 통 그리워하다; 놓치다 in no time 곧, 당장에 cherish 통 소중히 하다 friendship 몡 우정 keep in touch with ~와 연락하고 지내다 wish ~ luck 행운을 빌다 in the end 결국

14 긴 대화의 응답 파악

M Hello, Ms. Garner. What can I help you with?

W Well, I'm having vision problems lately.

M Can you describe them?

W When I drive at night, I can't see the 1)road signs clearly. And in meetings, I haven't been able to read anything on the board since last month.

M Do you have any issues reading books or magazines?

W No. I can see things clearly when they're close.

M It sounds like you need glasses. **We'll have to** 2)give you a vision test **today.**

W Oh, I see. How long will the test take?

M It only takes 10 minutes, but I think you should take some additional tests since this is your first time.

W It sounds like it'll take a long time. I need to go back to work in 20 minutes.

M Why don't you 3)come by after work? We're open until 8 p.m.

W No problem. I'll stop by later, then.

정답 ①

남 안녕하세요, Garner 씨. 무엇을 도와 드릴까요?

여 음, 요즘 시력에 문제가 있어요.

남 문제가 어떤지 말해주실 수 있나요?

여 밤에 운전할 때, 도로 표지판이 선명하게 안 보여요. 그리고 회의에서는, 지난달 이후로 칠판에 적힌 어떤 것도 읽지 못하겠어요.

남 책이나 잡지를 읽는 데는 문제가 없나요?

여 없어요. 가까이 있으면 사물이 선명하게 보여요.

남 안경이 필요하신 것 같네요. 오늘 시력 검사를 해야겠어요.

여 아, 그렇군요. 검사에 시간이 얼마나 걸릴까요?

남 그건 10분밖에 안 걸리지만, 이번이 처음이시니까 추가적인 검사를 좀 해야 할 것 같군요.

여 긴 시간이 걸릴 것 같네요. 전 20분 후에 다시 일하러 가야 해요.

남 퇴근 후에 들르시는 건 어때요? 저녁 8시까지 영업하거든요.

여 문제없어요. 그러면 나중에 들르겠습니다.

① 문제없어요. 그러면 나중에 들르겠습니다.

② 알겠습니다. 표지판에 여기서 우회전하라고 쓰여 있네요.

③ 잠시만요. 발표가 곧 시작될 거예요.

④ 감사합니다. 이걸 읽기를 기대하고 있었어요.

⑤ 물론이죠. 지금 검사실로 저를 따라오세요.

여자가 겪는 시력 문제에 관해 이야기하는 상황이다. 여자가 긴 검사를 받기엔 곧 일하러 가야 한다고 하자 남자가 퇴근 후에 들르는 것을 제안했으므로, 이에 대한 응답으로는 제안을 수락하는 ① 'No problem. I'll stop by later, then.'이 가장 적절하다.

[어휘] vision 명 시력 lately 부 요즘 describe 통 어떤지 말하다; 묘사하다 additional 형 추가적인 shortly 부 곧 exam 명 검사; 시험

15 상황에 적절한 말 파악

정답 ⑤

M Evelyn and Charlie are helping to organize their annual school festival. The day before the event, Charlie says that he is not feeling well. The next day, Evelyn notices that Charlie is ¹⁾coughing and sneezing, and his cheeks are red. But when she asks him how he is feeling, he says he feels fine. Evelyn thinks he is saying that because he would feel bad about ²⁾missing the festival and giving her more work. However, Evelyn is concerned that his health will get worse if he does not take care of himself. **So she wants to suggest to Charlie that he ³⁾go back home to rest.** In this situation, what would Evelyn most likely say to Charlie?

남 Evelyn과 Charlie는 매년 열리는 학교 축제를 기획하는 것을 돕고 있습니다. 축제 전날, Charlie는 몸이 좋지 않다고 말합니다. 다음날, Evelyn은 Charlie가 기침과 재채기를 하고 있고, 그의 뺨이 빨갛다는 것을 알아차립니다. 하지만 그녀가 그에게 상태가 어떤지 물으니, 그는 괜찮다고 말합니다. Evelyn은 그가 축제에 빠져서 그녀에게 더 많은 일을 주는 것에 대해 죄책감을 느끼게 될까 봐 그렇게 말한다고 생각합니다. 하지만, Evelyn은 그가 자신을 돌보지 않으면 건강이 더 나빠질까 봐서 걱정입니다. 그래서, 그녀는 Charlie에게 집으로 돌아가서 쉬라고 제안하고 싶습니다. 이러한 상황에서, Evelyn이 Charlie에게 가장 할 것 같은 말은 무엇입니까?

① 오늘 학교 축제에 빠지지 않는 게 좋겠어.

② 네가 없었다면 이 모든 것이 불가능했을 거야.

③ 네가 빨리 낫도록 도울 방법을 좀 생각해 보자.

④ 왜 진료 예약을 안 잡았어?

⑤ 너는 집에 가서 쉬어야 할 것 같아.

축제 준비 중에 Charlie가 아픈데도 미안함에 괜찮다고 하는 것을 보고, Evelyn은 집에 가서 쉬라고 제안하려 한다. 따라서, Evelyn이 할 말로 ⑤ 'I think you should go home and relax.'가 가장 적절하다.

[어휘] annual 형 매년 열리는, 연례의 cough 통 기침하다 sneeze 통 재채기하다 cheek 명 뺨 feel bad about ~에 대해 죄책감을 느끼다 concerned 형 걱정인 take care of ~를 돌보다 rest 통 쉬다

16-17 세트 문항

정답 16 ③ 17 ②

W Good afternoon, class. Last week, we started discussing the many ways that humans are changing the planet. **Today, I want to talk about the things humans are doing that harm animals.** Animals such as **elephants** are negatively affected by the first activity, which is ¹⁾illegal hunting. Because people break the law and hunt species they shouldn't, animals like elephants are close to disappearing forever. Next, **orangutans** and other animals are harmed by deforestation, which is the ²⁾destruction of forests. This activity has caused countless animals to lose their homes. Animals like **whales** can be killed by plastic pollution. It's ³⁾a major threat to the health of animals in general because they often eat it. Lastly, birds that fly in large groups like **sparrows** die because of tall buildings in cities. They don't perceive windows as barriers and hit them while flying. Now, let's look at some ways that we can help save these animals from ⁴⁾vanishing forever.

여 안녕하십니까, 학급 여러분. 지난주에, 우리는 인류가 지구를 변화시키고 있는 많은 방식에 대해 논의하기 시작했습니다. 오늘은, 인류가 동물들에 해를 끼치고 있는 행동에 관해 이야기하고 싶습니다. 코끼리와 같은 동물들은 첫 번째 행위인 불법 사냥으로 부정적인 영향을 받습니다. 사람들이 법을 어기고 사냥해서는 안 되는 종을 사냥하기 때문에, 코끼리와 같은 동물들은 금방이라도 영원히 사라질 것 같습니다. 다음으로, 오랑우탄과 다른 동물들은 삼림 벌채, 즉 삼림 파괴로 인해 피해를 봅니다. 이 행위는 수많은 동물들이 그들의 서식지를 잃도록 만들었습니다. 고래와 같은 동물은 플라스틱 오염으로 죽을 수 있습니다. 그것은 동물들이 자주 플라스틱을 먹게 되기 때문에 일반적으로 동물들의 건강에 큰 위협이 됩니다. 마지막으로, 참새처럼 떼를 지어 날아다니는 새들은 도시의 높은 건물들 때문에 죽습니다. 그것들은 창문을 장벽으로 인식하지 못하고 날다가 창문에 부딪힙니다. 이제, 이 동물들이 영원히 사라지는 것을 막는 데 도움이 될 몇 가지 방법을 알아보겠습니다.

16 ① 야생 조류 불법 사냥의 결과
  ② 해양 플라스틱 오염을 줄이는 방법
  ③ 사람들이 동물들에 부정적인 영향을 끼치는 방식
  ④ 멸종 위기에 처한 종이 멸종되는 것을 막는 방법
  ⑤ 지구에서 사라진 동물들의 사례
17 ① 코끼리 ② 악어 ③ 오랑우탄 ④ 고래 ⑤ 참새

16 인류가 동물들에 해를 끼치고 있는 행동에 관해 이야기하고 있으므로 여자가 하는 말의 주제로 ③ 'ways people are negatively affecting animals'가 가장 적절하다.
17 코끼리, 오랑우탄, 고래, 참새는 언급했지만 ② 'crocodiles'는 언급하지 않았다.

[어휘] harm 통 해를 끼치다 illegal 형 불법의 break the law 법을 어기다 deforestation 명 삼림 벌채 destruction 명 파괴 countless 형 수많은 threat 명 위협 in general 일반적으로 perceive 통 인식하다 barrier 명 장벽 save A from B A가 B하는 것을 막다 vanish 통 사라지다 endangered 형 멸종 위기에 처한 extinction 명 멸종

| 1 | ① | 2 | ⑤ | 3 | ① | 4 | ④ | 5 | ③ | 6 | ② | 7 | ⑤ | 8 | ③ | 9 | ② | 10 | ④ |
| 11 | ④ | 12 | ② | 13 | ③ | 14 | ⑤ | 15 | ④ | 16 | ② | 17 | ④ | | | | | | | | |

• 각 문제의 정답 근거는 굵은 글씨로, Dictation 정답은 밑줄로 표시되어 있습니다.

---

1 목적 파악
정답 ①

W Hello, museum visitors. May I have your attention please? Thank you for visiting the Denver Museum of Natural History. **Unfortunately, we need to notify you that our *Frozen in Time* event ¹⁾<u>has been canceled</u>** for the rest of the day. This is ²⁾<u>due to a problem</u> with a projector system in the conference hall that will require a replacement part. If you purchased tickets to the event, you are welcome to attend a future showing. If you would ³⁾<u>prefer to return</u> your event ticket, a full refund will be provided. We apologize for any inconvenience this causes and hope that you enjoy the rest of your visit to the museum.

여 안녕하세요, 박물관 방문객 여러분. 주목해 주시겠습니까? 덴버 자연사 박물관에 방문해 주셔서 감사드립니다. 안타깝게도, 오늘 남은 시간 동안 저희의 <Frozen in Time> 행사가 취소되었음을 여러분들께 알려드려야 합니다. 이는 회의장의 프로젝터 시스템의 문제로 인한 것이며 대체 부품이 필요하게 되었기 때문입니다. 만약 행사 티켓을 구매하셨다면, 다음번 행사에 자유롭게 참석하실 수 있습니다. 만약 행사 티켓 환불을 원하신다면, 전액 환불해 드리겠습니다. 이로 인해 발생한 불편에 대해 사과드리며, 나머지 박물관 관람도 즐겁게 하시기 바랍니다.

여자가 박물관 행사가 취소되었음을 알리면서, 그 이유를 방문객들에게 설명하고 있다. 따라서, 여자가 하는 말의 목적으로 ① '박물관 행사 취소를 공지하려고'가 가장 적절하다.

[어휘] unfortunately 🔢 안타깝게도, 유감스럽게도 notify 🔢 알리다, 발표하다 projector 🔢 프로젝터, 투사기 conference hall 회의장 replacement 🔢 대체 purchase 🔢 구매하다 welcome to 자유롭게 ~할 수 있는 inconvenience 🔢 불편, 민폐

---

2 의견 파악
정답 ⑤

W Honey, did you hear that Jackie is ¹⁾<u>going on a walking tour</u> across Spain this summer? Doesn't that sound great?
M That sounds a little hard to me.
W **I think walking tours are the best way to travel.**
M Why not just drive to places? It's much faster.
W Well, when you're walking, you enjoy the scenery more.
M I guess you do notice more things when you're moving slower.
W And it's ²⁾<u>a healthier way to travel</u>. You get to move around instead of just sitting inside a car.
M Yeah, it would be nice to get some exercise while we're on vacation.
W Exactly. **That's why a walking tour is ³⁾<u>a good vacation idea</u>.**
M I see what you mean. Maybe we should try it.
W Yeah! Let's make a list of places we can go.

여 여보, Jackie가 이번 여름에 스페인을 횡단하는 도보 여행을 한다는 것을 들었어? 그거 정말 멋지지 않아?
남 나한테는 조금 힘들 것 같은데.
여 내 생각엔 도보 여행이야말로 여행하기에 가장 좋은 방법 같아.
남 그냥 운전해서 다니는 게 어때? 이게 훨씬 빨라.
여 글쎄, 걸어다니면 경치를 더 즐기게 될 거야.
남 당신은 천천히 이동할 때 확실히 더 많은 것들을 알아차리는 것 같긴 해.
여 그리고 이게 더 건강한 여행 방식인걸. 당신도 차 안에 그냥 앉아 있는 대신 돌아다니게 될 거야.
남 그래, 휴가 중에도 조금씩 운동을 하는 것은 좋을 테니까 말이야.
여 바로 그거야. 이래서 도보 여행이 좋은 휴가 아이디어라는 거야.
남 무슨 말인지 알겠어. 우리도 도전해 봐야 할 것 같아.
여 좋아! 우리가 갈 수 있는 곳의 목록을 만들어 보자.

자동차로 여행을 하고 싶어 하는 남자에게 여자는 도보 여행이 여행하기 가장 좋은 방법이라면서 도보 여행의 장점을 설명하고 있다. 따라서, 여자의 의견으로 ⑤ '도보 여행은 최고의 여행 방식이다.'가 가장 적절하다.

[어휘] across 🔢 횡단하는 scenery 🔢 경치, 풍경 get to ~하게 되다 instead of ~ 대신 exercise 🔢 운동

---

3 관계 파악
정답 ①

W The restaurant is busier than usual today! How's everything going in the kitchen?
M So many orders have come in all at once. But we're keeping up!
W Great. **Well, the customer at Table 4 ordered a chicken salad, but she has a peanut allergy.** Are there any peanuts in the salad?
M No. We don't put peanuts in the salads.
W Okay. I'll go out to her table and let her know.
M **By the way, ¹⁾<u>are the customers enjoying</u> today's special? It's the first time we've made salmon steaks.**
W They love it. I think ²⁾<u>you should serve</u> more seafood dishes.
M I'm glad to hear that. And I'll keep that in mind when I update the menu.
W Sounds good. **Oh, how much longer will the roast beef take? It's for Table 6.**

여 오늘은 식당이 평소보다 더 정신없네요! 주방 일은 잘 되어 가나요?
남 한꺼번에 너무 많은 주문이 들어왔어요. 하지만 따라잡고 있어요!
여 좋아요. 음, 4번 테이블 손님이 치킨 샐러드를 주문했는데, 이분은 땅콩 알레르기가 있어요. 샐러드에 땅콩이 들어있나요?
남 아뇨. 우리는 샐러드에 땅콩을 넣지 않아요.
여 알았어요. 제가 그녀의 테이블로 가서 알려줄게요.
남 그런데, 손님들이 오늘의 특선 요리를 즐기고 있나요? 연어 스테이크를 만든 건 이번이 처음이잖아요.
여 정말 좋아하세요. 제 생각엔 더 많은 해산물 요리를 제공하는 것이 좋겠어요.
남 다행이네요. 메뉴를 업데이트할 때 참고할게요.
여 좋아요. 아, 로스트비프는 얼마나 더 걸리나요? 6번 테이블로 갈 거예요.

M I just ³⁾took it out of the oven. Let me put it on a plate.	남 방금 오븐에서 꺼냈어요. 접시에 담을게요.
W Alright. I'll be right back.	여 알았어요. 금방 다시 올게요.

두 사람이 식당의 메뉴와 손님 접대에 관해 이야기하고 있다. 여자는 손님의 알레르기 특이사항과 주문받은 음식의 상태에 관해 묻고 있고, 남자는 그에 대해 답변하면서 자신이 만든 메뉴에 대한 손님의 반응을 살피는 것으로 보아 두 사람의 관계로 ① '식당 종업원 — 주방장'이 가장 적절하다.

[어휘] order ⑲ 주문 all at once 한꺼번에, 동시에 keep up 따라잡다 peanut ⑲ 땅콩 allergy ⑲ 알레르기 today's special 오늘의 특선 요리 salmon ⑲ 연어 serve ⑧ 제공하다
keep in mind ~을 참고하다, 명심하다

4 그림 내용 불일치 파악 　　　　　　　　　　　　정답 ④

M Check out my living room, Chloe. I just redecorated it recently.	남 우리 집 거실을 좀 봐, Chloe. 최근에 내가 다시 꾸며봤어.
W It's amazing. I love ¹⁾that square table. Where did you get it?	여 정말 근사하다. 저 사각형 테이블이 마음에 들어. 어디서 구했어?
M I actually made it myself.	남 사실 내가 직접 만들었어.
W Wow, I'm impressed. It looks great.	여 우와, 정말 대단하다. 보기 좋아.
M Thanks. I think it matches the new checked sofa well.	남 고마워. 새로 산 체크무늬 소파와 잘 어울리는 것 같아.
W I see you put a bookcase in the corner of the room.	여 방 한구석에는 책장을 두었구나.
M Right. That's where I keep all my board games.	남 맞아. 그곳이 내 모든 보드게임들을 보관해두는 곳이야.
W I love board games. **And there's a ²⁾guitar against the wall.** I didn't know you played guitar.	여 나 보드게임 정말 좋아해. 그리고 기타가 벽에 기대어져 있네. 네가 기타 치는 줄 몰랐어.
M I just started learning on my own. I'm not very good at it yet.	남 이제 막 혼자 배우기 시작했어. 아직 잘하진 못해.
W I'm sure you'll get better with practice.	여 연습하면 더 잘할 수 있을 거야.
M What do you think of ³⁾this framed photo on the wall?	남 벽에 걸린 이 액자 사진은 어떻게 생각해?
W Oh, that's a cool picture. Did you take it yourself?	여 오, 멋진 사진인걸. 네가 직접 찍은 거야?
M Yes, I used a special zoom lens for it.	남 응, 그걸 찍으려고 특수 줌 렌즈를 사용했어.

여자가 벽에 기타가 기대어져 있다고 했는데, ④에는 피아노가 세워져 있다.

[어휘] redecorate ⑧ 다시 꾸미다, 다시 장식하다 recently ⑨ 최근에 match ⑧ 어울리다 ⑲ 성냥 bookcase ⑲ 책장 keep ⑧ 보관하다 against ㉟ 기대어서; 반대로
be good at ~을 잘하다 framed ㉺ 액자의, 액자에 넣은

5 할 일 파악 　　　　　　　　　　　　정답 ③

M I'm looking forward to working on the garden, honey!	남 나는 정원 일을 하는 게 기대돼, 여보!
W Me, too! We have a lot to do today, so I made a plan. First, ¹⁾we need some seeds.	여 나도! 오늘 할 일이 많다 보니, 내가 계획을 세워봤어. 먼저, 우리는 씨앗이 좀 필요해.
M I already bought some flower and vegetable seeds. I got them when I went to buy the small trees.	남 내가 이미 꽃과 채소 씨앗을 좀 사 두었어. 작은 나무들을 사러 갔을 때 그것들도 샀어.
W Great. Now, we need to fill the garden with new soil.	여 좋아. 이제, 우리는 정원을 새 흙으로 채워야 해.
M ²⁾Are you sure? The soil we have now seems good enough.	남 진짜로? 지금 우리가 가지고 있는 흙도 충분히 좋아 보이는데.
W Oh, really? Well, you have more gardening experience than me, so I trust your judgment.	여 아, 그래? 음, 나보다 당신이 정원을 가꾼 경험이 더 많으니까 당신의 판단을 믿을게.
M Okay. What else do we have to do?	남 알았어. 우리가 해야 할 일이 또 뭐가 있을까?
W We have to ³⁾plant the seeds and small trees.	여 씨앗과 작은 나무들을 심어야 해.
M Sounds good. Let's do that now.	남 좋아. 지금 바로 하자.
W Wait. **We need ⁴⁾some gardening tools for that.** Do you know where they are?	여 잠깐만. 그 일을 하기 위해 원예 도구들이 필요해. 그것들이 어디에 있는지 알아?
M **They're in the garage. I'll go get them.**	남 차고에 있어. 내가 가서 가져올게.
W All right. I'll start bringing these trees to the garden.	여 알겠어. 난 이 나무들을 정원에 가져다 놓기 시작할게.

정원 가꾸는 일을 하려는 상황이다. 씨앗과 작은 나무들을 심기 위해 여자가 원예 도구가 필요하다고 하자, 남자가 차고에 있으니 본인이 가서 가져오겠다고 했으므로 남자가 할 일로 ③ '원예 도구 가져오기'가 가장 적절하다.

[어휘] look forward to ~을 기대하다 seed ⑲ 씨앗 soil ⑲ 흙, 토양 judgment ⑲ 판단, 평가 plant ⑧ 심다 ⑲ 식물 gardening tool 원예 도구 garage ⑲ 차고

6 금액 정보 파악

정답 ②

M Hello. How can I help you?	남 안녕하세요. 무엇을 도와드릴까요?
W Hi. Do you still have seats available for the musical *Chicago Nights*?	여 안녕하세요. 뮤지컬 <Chicago Nights>의 이용 가능한 좌석이 아직 있나요?
M ¹⁾How many do you need?	남 몇 자리 필요하세요?
W Four, please.	여 네 자리요.
M I see. Just a moment. *[Typing sound]* Okay, I found a row where ²⁾you can all sit together.	남 알겠습니다. 잠시만요. *[타자 치는 소리]* 네, 다 같이 앉으실 수 있는 열을 찾았어요.
W Great.	여 좋아요.
M Are those all adult tickets?	남 모두 성인 티켓인가요?
W **Actually, we have two adults and ³⁾two children.**	여 사실, 성인 두 명과 어린이 두 명이에요.
M Got it. **It's $30 for adults and $20 for children.**	남 알겠습니다. 성인은 30달러, 어린이는 20달러입니다.
W Oh, I saw an advertisement that said ⁴⁾I could get a discount with a theater membership card. Is that right?	여 아, 극장 회원 카드로 할인을 받을 수 있다는 광고를 봤어요. 맞나요?
M Yes. **You can get a 10% discount.**	남 네. 10% 할인을 받으실 수 있습니다.
W Here's my membership card and my credit card, then.	여 그럼, 여기 제 멤버십 카드와 신용 카드요.
M Okay. Let me just ring everything up.	남 네. 전부 계산해드리겠습니다.

여자는 성인 티켓 2장($30×2=$60)과 어린이 티켓 2장($20×2=$40)을 구매했고, 멤버십 카드로 10% 할인($100×0.9=$90)을 받았으므로 정답은 ② '$90'이다.

어휘 available 형 이용 가능한, 유효한 row 명 열, 줄 advertisement 명 광고 discount 명 할인 theater 명 극장 ring ~ up ~을 계산해주다

7 이유 파악

정답 ⑤

M Hey, Elizabeth. Did you enjoy science class today?	남 안녕, Elizabeth. 오늘 과학 수업 재미있었어?
W Yeah. It was interesting. I'm a little nervous about ¹⁾the test next week, though.	여 응. 흥미로웠어. 그렇지만, 난 다음 주 시험 때문에 조금 불안해.
M But you're so good at science. I was actually wondering if you could ²⁾help me study what we learned because it sounds a bit confusing.	남 하지만 너는 과학을 엄청 잘 하잖아. 사실 우리가 배운 것이 조금 아리송해서 네가 내 공부를 도와줄 수 있을지 궁금해.
W Oh, I'm sorry, but I can't today.	여 아, 미안하지만, 오늘은 안 돼.
M Really? Do you have an art club meeting?	남 그래? 미술 동아리 모임이 있는 거야?
W No. I decided to skip it this week.	여 아니. 이번 주는 모임을 건너뛰기로 했어.
M I see. I guess you're hanging out with some friends?	남 그렇구나. 아마도 몇몇 친구들이랑 시간을 보낼 건가 보네?
W I usually don't see them until the weekend. **Today, I have to ³⁾go to the eye doctor.**	여 보통 주말이 되어서야 만나. 오늘은 안과에 가야 해.
M Oh, is everything okay?	남 이런, 괜찮은 거지?
W Yes. **I just need a regular checkup.** I'm feeling fine.	여 응. 그냥 정기 검진이 필요한 거야. 난 괜찮아.
M All right. I'll see you later, then.	남 알겠어. 그럼 나중에 보자.

공부를 도와줄 수 있는지 묻는 남자에게 여자는 오늘은 정기 검진을 받으러 안과에 가야 한다고 거절했으므로, 여자가 공부를 도와줄 수 없는 이유는 ⑤ '안과에서 검진을 받아야 해서'이다.

어휘 nervous 형 불안한, 긴장되는 wonder 동 궁금하다 confusing 형 아리송한, 혼란스러운 skip 동 건너뛰다 hang out 시간을 보내다, 놀다 not A until B B가 되어서야 A하다
checkup 명 검진, 진단

8 언급 유무 파악

정답 ③

M Linda, do you have any plans this weekend?	남 Linda, 이번 주말에 무슨 계획 있어?
W No. I'm free. Why?	여 아니. 한가해. 왜 그러니?
M I'm participating in a charity soccer game. You should ¹⁾come see the match!	남 내가 자선 축구 경기에 참여하게 되었거든. 너도 이 경기를 보러 와야 해!
W Oh, that sounds fun. When is it?	여 오, 재미있겠는데. 언제 하는데?
M The game is on Saturday at **11 a.m.** It's taking place at the high school's soccer field.	남 경기는 토요일 오전 11시에 있어. 고등학교 축구 경기장에서 열려.
W Good. I can ²⁾walk there from my house.	여 좋아. 집에서 걸어가면 되겠다.
M You should bring **$5** in cash for the ticket.	남 티켓값으로 현금 5달러를 가져와야 해.
W Okay. What charity will the money be given to?	여 알겠어. 그 돈은 어떤 자선단체에 기부될 예정이야?
M It's **an organization that helps the homeless.**	남 노숙자들을 돕는 단체야.
W That's a great cause.	여 정말 좋은 목적이네.
M Yes. And you might want to bring some extra money for some of ³⁾the other activities.	남 응. 그리고 다른 활동들을 위해 추가로 돈을 좀 가지고 오는 게 좋을 거야.
W Oh, really? Like what?	여 오, 그래? 어떤 게 있는데?
M For instance, you can pay to have ⁴⁾a photo shoot with the school mascot.	남 예를 들어, 돈을 내고 학교 마스코트와 사진 촬영을 할 수 있어.
W Great. I can't wait!	여 진짜 좋다. 정말 기대돼!

시작 시간(오전 11시), 입장료(5달러), 수익금 기부처(노숙자들을 돕는 단체), 부대 행사(마스코트와 사진 촬영)에 대해 언급했고, ③ '상대 팀'은 언급하지 않았다.

어휘 charity 圐 자선 take place 열리다, 일어나다 organization 圐 단체, 조직 cause 圐 목적, 명분; 원인 I can't wait! 정말 기대돼!

9 내용 불일치 파악   정답 ②

M Good evening, everyone. I'm Graham Bowman, the president of the Pittsburgh Film Federation. This year is 1)the 13th anniversary of the Steel City Film Festival. This festival attracts a lot of international attention. **In fact, the opening ceremony will be broadcast live in cities 2)around the world.** This year's festival will be the biggest one so far, with about 350 films playing at theaters across the city. Tickets will go on sale starting 3)next Friday. They can be purchased online through the festival's official website. Special group tickets for eight or more people will also be available at a 15% discount. Don't miss out on the most exciting event of the year! Thank you for your attention.	남 안녕하십니까, 여러분. 저는 피츠버그 영화 연맹의 회장 Graham Bowman입니다. 올해는 스틸시 영화제의 13주년입니다. 이 축제는 많은 국제적인 관심을 끌고 있습니다. 실제로, 개막식은 전 세계의 도시에 생중계될 예정입니다. 약 350편의 영화를 도시 전역의 극장에서 상영하면서, 올해의 축제는 역대 가장 큰 규모의 행사가 될 것입니다. 티켓은 다음 주 금요일부터 판매될 예정입니다. 티켓은 축제의 공식 웹사이트를 통해 온라인으로 구매하실 수 있습니다. 또한 8인 이상을 위한 특별 단체 티켓은 15% 할인된 가격에 구매하실 수 있습니다. 올해의 가장 흥미로운 행사를 놓치지 마시기 바랍니다! 경청해 주셔서 감사합니다.

영화제에 대한 안내 방송이다. 남자는 개막식이 전 세계 도시에 생중계될 예정이라고 했으므로 ② '개막식은 국내에서만 생중계될 것이다.'는 내용과 일치하지 않는다.

어휘 federation 圐 연맹 international 圐 국제적인 attention 圐 관심, 이목, 경청 in fact 실제로, 사실 opening ceremony 개막식 so far 역대, 지금까지 go on sale 판매하다 miss out on ~을 놓치다

10 도표 정보 파악   정답 ④

W Honey, can you help me choose some winter boots for our daughter? M Of course. The Northern Shoe Company is having a sale on all winter boots right now. *[Typing sound]* Here are the most popular models for girls. W Okay. **She wears 1)a size 6.** M All right. What's our budget? W She needs a new coat and gloves, too. **So let's not spend more than $60 on boots.** M We should be able to find a nice pair for less than that. How about the color? W **I think she would like 2)anything except black.** M Then, we need to decide between these ones. W Well, it gets pretty wet in the winter. **The boots we buy 3)should be waterproof.** M Then, we should get this pair. W Great. I think those are perfect.	여 여보, 우리 딸에게 줄 겨울 부츠 고르는 것 좀 도와줄래? 남 물론이지. Northern Shoe Company에서 지금 모든 겨울 부츠를 할인하고 있어. *[타자 치는 소리]* 여자아이들에게 가장 인기 있는 모델들이 여기에 있네. 여 좋아. 우리 애는 6사이즈를 신어. 남 알겠어. 우리 예산이 얼마지? 여 새 코트와 장갑도 필요해. 그러니 부츠에 60달러보다 많이는 쓰지 말자. 남 그것보다 싼 가격에 괜찮은 한 켤레를 찾을 수 있을 거야. 색깔은 어때? 여 검은색 빼고는 다 좋아할 것 같아. 남 그럼, 우리는 이것들 중에서 정해야 해. 여 음, 겨울에는 꽤 축축해지잖아. 우리가 살 부츠는 방수가 되어야 해. 남 그럼, 이 한 켤레를 사야겠네. 여 좋아. 완벽한 것 같아.

두 사람은 사이즈가 6이면서, 가격은 60달러를 넘지 않고, 검은색을 제외한 색깔 중에서, 방수가 되는 겨울 부츠를 골랐다.

어휘 have a sale 할인하다 budget 圐 예산 spend 圄 쓰다, 소비하다 more than ~보다 많이, ~ 이상의 pair 圐 켤레, 짝 except 圙 ~을 빼고는, 제외하고는 waterproof 圐 방수의

11 짧은 대화의 응답 파악   정답 ④

W This cookie is delicious, Henry. 1)Where did you get it? M **It's from a new bakery that just opened downtown.** They have a wide selection of cakes, too. W I'd love to 2)contact them about ordering a cake for my son's birthday party. M Good idea. I'll send you their information.	여 이 쿠키 맛있다, Henry. 이거 어디서 났어? 남 시내에 새로 문을 연 빵집에서 산 거야. 다양한 종류의 케이크도 있더라. 여 우리 아들 생일 파티에 놓을 케이크를 주문하는 것에 대해 연락해보고 싶어. 남 좋은 생각이야. 내가 정보를 보내줄게. 선택지 ① 잠깐만. 그곳에 어떻게 갈 수 있는지 좀 볼게. ② 알아. 딸기가 들어간 바닐라 케이크잖아. ③ 맞아. 난 주문을 하고 싶어. ④ 좋은 생각이야. 내가 정보를 보내줄게. ⑤ 그런 것 같아. 거긴 오전 9시부터 오후 4시까지 열어.

여자가 아들 생일 파티에 놓을 케이크를 주문하는 것에 대해 남자가 쿠키를 산 빵집과 연락해보고 싶다고 했으므로, 이에 대한 응답으로는 그 빵집의 정보를 보내주겠다고 하는 ④ 'Good idea. I'll send you their information.'이 가장 적절하다.

어휘 downtown 圉 시내에 would love to ~하고 싶다 contact 圄 연락하다, 접촉하다 Hold on. 잠깐만. make an order 주문하다

12 짧은 대화의 응답 파악　　　　　　　　　정답 ②

M Honey, I just ¹⁾called the repair shop about your broken laptop screen. It's fixed now, so we can pick it up any time.	남 여보, 화면이 고장 난 당신의 노트북에 관해서 방금 수리점에 전화해 봤어. 이제 다 고쳐져서, 언제든지 가지러 가면 돼.
W Oh, that's great news. **Let's walk over there now.**	여 오, 좋은 소식이네. 걸어서 지금 거기로 가자.
M Okay, but why are you ²⁾bringing an umbrella?	남 알겠어, 그런데 당신 왜 우산을 챙기고 있어?
W It's supposed to rain soon.	여 곧 비가 올 거거든.
	선택지 ① 공원을 통과해서 가자.
	② 곧 비가 올 거거든.
	③ 여기 그들의 전화번호가 있어.
	④ 다음 주면 가져갈 준비가 될 거야.
	⑤ 노트북 화면이 심하게 파손되었어.

외출하려는 상황에서 남자가 여자에게 왜 우산을 챙기고 있는지 물어봤으므로, 이에 대한 응답으로는 곧 비가 올 것이라고 대답하는 ② 'It's supposed to rain soon.'이 가장 적절하다.

어휘 repair shop 수리점　broken 형 고장 난　laptop 명 노트북　badly 부 심하게

13 긴 대화의 응답 파악　　　　　　　　　정답 ③

M Hello. May I help you?	남 안녕하세요. 도와드릴까요?
W Yes. **I'd like to** ¹⁾get a refund for this skirt.	여 네. 이 치마를 환불받고 싶어서요.
M Is there a problem with it?	남 무슨 문제라도 있나요?
W It's just too tight for me.	여 저한테 너무 꽉 끼네요.
M I see. **Unfortunately, our store doesn't offer refunds. We** ²⁾only offer exchanges.	남 그렇군요. 유감스럽게도 저희 매장은 환불을 해 드리지는 않습니다. 저희는 교환만 해 드려요.
W Okay. Then, I'd like to try the skirt in a larger size. Do you have any in stock?	여 알았어요. 그럼 치마를 좀 더 큰 사이즈로 입어보고 싶어요. 재고가 있나요?
M I'll check. Just one moment, please. *[Typing sound]* I'm afraid we're all sold out.	남 확인해 볼게요. 잠시만 기다려주세요. *[타자 치는 소리]* 죄송하지만 다 팔렸네요.
W Hmm... Do you have any designs that ³⁾are similar to this one?	여 흠... 이것과 비슷한 디자인이 있나요?
M We do, actually. I recommend this skirt right here. It's one of our best-selling items.	남 사실, 있습니다. 바로 여기 있는 이 치마를 추천해 드려요. 저희 매장에서 가장 잘 팔리는 상품 중 하나입니다.
W Oh, I love it! How much is it?	여 오, 정말 맘에 들어요! 얼마인가요?
M This one is $30. The skirt you originally purchased was $20.	남 이건 30달러예요. 고객님이 원래 구매하신 치마는 20달러였습니다.
W So I ⁴⁾just have to pay the difference, right?	여 그러면, 저는 차액만 내면 되는 거죠?
M That's correct. You'll need to pay an additional $10.	남 맞습니다. 추가로 10달러를 지불하셔야 합니다.
	선택지 ① 잘 모르겠습니다. 좀 더 밝은색도 있나요?
	② 물론이죠. 그 스커트는 더 작은 사이즈로도 있습니다.
	③ 맞습니다. 추가로 10달러를 지불하셔야 합니다.
	④ 알겠습니다. 환불이 곧 처리될 것입니다.
	⑤ 죄송합니다. 저희 매장 정책상 그것을 허용하지 않습니다.

환불 대신 교환만 가능한 매장에서 다른 치마를 교환받으려는 상황이다. 새로 고른 치마의 가격은 30달러, 기존에 여자가 구매한 치마는 20달러로, 여자가 남자 직원에게 차액만 지불하면 되는지 물었으므로, 이에 대한 응답으로는 차액을 알려주는 ③ 'That's correct. You'll need to pay an additional $10.'가 가장 적절하다.

어휘 get a refund 환불받다　tight 형 꽉 끼는, 조이는　exchange 명 교환　have ~ in stock ~의 재고가 있다　originally 부 원래　difference 명 차액; 차이　go through 처리되다, 통과되다
policy 명 정책

14 긴 대화의 응답 파악　　　　　　　　　정답 ⑤

[Cell phone rings.]	*[휴대폰이 울린다.]*
W Hello, Uncle Adam.	여 여보세요, Adam 삼촌.
M Hi, Sweetie. Are you okay? I ¹⁾was trying to call earlier.	남 안녕, 귀염둥이. 너 괜찮니? 아까 전화하려고 했었는데.
W Oh, I'm fine. I didn't mean to make you worry. **My phone died during the storm.**	여 아, 전 괜찮아요. 삼촌 걱정하시게 만들 생각은 아니었어요. 폭풍 중에 휴대폰이 꺼졌어요.
M I understand. But I ²⁾was watching the news about the typhoon last night. It looked bad.	남 이해한다. 그런데 어젯밤 태풍에 대한 뉴스를 보고 있었거든. 심각해 보였어.
W Yeah, it was a powerful storm. The power went out for several hours, and my Internet wasn't working.	여 맞아요, 강력한 폭풍이었어요. 몇 시간 동안 전기가 나가서, 인터넷이 안 됐어요.
M No wonder I couldn't reach you! Well, that must have been scary.	남 연락이 안 된 게 당연하구나! 음, 무서웠겠어.
W It was! And the wind was so strong. I couldn't sleep at all.	여 정말요! 그리고 바람이 너무 강했어요. 잠을 전혀 못 잤어요.
M Was there much damage to your neighborhood?	남 동네에도 많은 피해가 있었니?
W ³⁾Many trees fell down. And some older buildings were damaged.	여 많은 나무들이 쓰러졌어요. 그리고 몇몇 오래된 건물들이 피해를 입었고요.
M That's terrible. Did anyone get hurt?	남 끔찍하구나. 다친 사람은 없었어?

W I heard that some people were injured, but not too badly.

M That's a relief. **You know, events like these show us** [4)]how powerful nature can be.

W Yeah. Storms like that one can do a great deal of damage.

여 몇몇 사람들이 다쳤다고 들었는데, 그렇게 심한 건 아니래요.

남 다행이네. 알잖니, 이런 사건들은 자연이 얼마나 강력할 수 있는지 보여주는구나.

여 네. 이런 폭풍은 엄청나게 큰 피해를 줄 수 있어요.

선택지 ① 맞아요. 폭풍에 대한 대비를 시작해야 해요.

② 저는 반대예요. 저는 자연에서 시간을 보내는 것을 정말 좋아해요.

③ 물론이죠. 전 매일 일기예보를 확인해요.

④ 그것은 사실이에요. 발전소는 우리 집 바로 옆에 있어요.

⑤ 네. 이런 폭풍은 엄청나게 큰 피해를 줄 수 있어요.

남자가 태풍으로 인해 연락이 두절됐던 조카와 통화를 하는 상황이다. 남자가 이런 사건들이 자연이 얼마나 강력할 수 있는지 보여준다고 말했으므로, 이에 대한 응답으로는 그 말에 동의하는 ⑤ 'Yeah. Storms like that one can do a great deal of damage.'가 가장 적절하다.

어휘 mean 통 의도하다; 의미하다 storm 명 폭풍 typhoon 명 태풍 power 명 전기, 전력; 힘 go out (불, 전기 등이) 나가다, 꺼지다 No wonder ~. ~한 것이 당연하다.
fall down 쓰러지다, 무너지다 terrible 형 끔찍한 injured 형 다친 power station 발전소 a great deal of 엄청 큰, 다량의

15 상황에 적절한 말 파악
정답 ④

M Liam and his mother are planning to spend the day [1)]hiking up a mountain. After finishing his breakfast, Liam begins to get ready for the hike. As the weather is warm and sunny, he decides to bring [2)]only a light jacket. He thinks he will get too hot if he wears a heavier one. However, his mother checks the forecast and discovers that the weather is going to be much cooler on the mountain. In fact, there may be some snow near the summit, even though spring is around the corner. She worries that he will [3)]feel too cold and might even get sick. **So she wants to tell him to bundle up during the hike.** In this situation, what would Liam's mother most likely say to him?

남 Liam과 그의 어머니는 하루 동안 등산을 할 계획입니다. 아침 식사를 마친 후, Liam은 등산 준비를 하기 시작합니다. 날씨가 따뜻하고 화창하기 때문에, 그는 가벼운 재킷만 가져가기로 합니다. 그는 더 두꺼운 재킷을 입으면 너무 더워질 것 같다는 생각입니다. 하지만 그의 어머니는 일기예보를 확인하고 산의 날씨가 훨씬 더 서늘할 것이라는 점을 알게 됩니다. 사실, 봄이 곧 다가오는데도 불구하고, 정상 부근에는 눈이 조금 있을 수 있습니다. 그녀는 그가 너무 추워서 심지어 아프게 되지는 않을까 걱정합니다. 그래서 그녀는 그에게 등산 동안 옷을 따뜻하게 입으라고 말하고 싶습니다. 이러한 상황에서, Liam의 어머니가 Liam에게 가장 할 것 같은 말은 무엇입니까?

선택지 ① 다른 날에 등산하러 가는 건 어떠니?

② 네가 지금 입고 있는 재킷은 너무 두꺼워 보이는구나.

③ 우리가 출발하기 전에 너는 일기예보를 확인해야 해.

④ 등산하는 동안에는 꼭 옷을 따뜻하게 입으렴.

⑤ 내가 다른 코트를 입어야 할 것 같니?

Liam이 등산을 앞두고 가벼운 재킷만 가져가기로 한 것을 보고, Liam의 어머니는 옷을 따뜻하게 입으라고 말하려 한다. 따라서, Liam의 어머니가 할 말로 ④ 'Make sure to wear warm clothes while hiking.'이 가장 적절하다.

어휘 heavy 형 (옷이) 두꺼운; 무거운 discover 통 알게 되다; 발견하다 summit 명 정상 around the corner 곧 다가오는, 임박하여 bundle up 옷을 따뜻하게 입다 put on ~을 입다, 착용하다

16-17 세트 문항
정답 16 ② 17 ④

W Hello, and welcome back to another episode of *What a Wonderful World*. I'm your host, Monica Pierce. **Today, I want to talk about New Year's Eve celebrations in different cities around the world.** First, there's the famous ball drop in **New York City**. A gigantic ball is lowered down a pole [1)]on the roof of a building in Times Square just before midnight. In **Sydney**, people go to the Sydney Harbour Bridge to [2)]enjoy the amazing fireworks. The first show takes place early in the evening, while the main show happens at midnight. Next, there is the bell-ringing ceremony at Bosingak Pavilion in **Seoul**. The bell is rung 33 times [3)]to mark the beginning of the New Year. Lastly, more than two million people celebrate New Year's Eve in **Rio de Janeiro**. The city hosts a large beach party that includes a fireworks display and lots of loud music. I hope this talk [4)]gives you some ideas of where to visit for New Year's Eve. Thanks for tuning in.

여 안녕하십니까, 그리고 <What a Wonderful World>의 또 다른 에피소드로 돌아오신 것을 환영합니다. 진행자 Monica Pierce입니다. 오늘은, 전 세계의 다양한 도시들에서의 새해 전야제에 대해 이야기하고자 합니다. 먼저, 뉴욕에서는 유명한 공 떨어트리기 행사가 있습니다. 자정 직전, 타임스퀘어의 한 건물 옥상에서 거대한 공이 장대 아래로 내려갑니다. 시드니에서는, 사람들이 멋진 불꽃놀이를 즐기기 위해 시드니 하버 브리지로 갑니다. 첫 번째 쇼는 이른 저녁에 열리며, 메인 쇼는 자정에 열립니다. 다음으로, 서울에서는 보신각의 종을 치는 행사가 있습니다. 이 종은 새해의 시작을 기념하기 위해 33번 울립니다. 마지막으로, 2백만 명 이상의 사람들이 리우데자네이루에서 새해 전날을 기념합니다. 그 도시는 불꽃놀이와 시끌벅적한 음악을 포함한 성대한 해변 파티를 개최합니다. 저는 이 이야기가 여러분께 새해 전날 어디를 방문해야 할지에 대한 아이디어를 드렸기를 바랍니다. 청취해 주셔서 감사합니다.

선택지 16 ① 불꽃놀이를 보기 위해 방문하기 가장 좋은 장소

② 다양한 도시에서 열리는 새해 전야제

③ 다른 나라들의 새해 전날에 대한 믿음

④ 젊은이들에게 인기 있는 여행지

⑤ 축제 개최가 가져오는 경제적 이익

17 ① 뉴욕 ② 시드니 ③ 서울 ④ 런던 ⑤ 리우데자네이루

16 전 세계의 다양한 도시들에서의 새해 전야제에 대해 이야기하고 있으므로 여자가 하는 말의 주제로 ② 'New Year's Eve celebrations in various cities'가 가장 적절하다.

17 뉴욕, 시드니, 서울, 리우데자네이루는 언급했지만, ④ 'London'은 언급하지 않았다.

어휘 host 명 진행자 통 개최하다 gigantic 형 거대한 firework 명 불꽃놀이 mark 통 기념하다, 축하하다; 표시하다 tune in 청취하다, 시청하다

1	④	2	③	3	①	4	③	5	③	6	⑤	7	②	8	④	9	④	10	④
11	①	12	④	13	⑤	14	③	15	④	16	⑤	17	⑤						

• 각 문제의 정답 근거는 굵은 글씨로, Dictation 정답은 밑줄로 표시되어 있습니다.

1 목적 파악

정답 ④

W	Hello, everyone! At Natural Beverage, our goal is to provide you with the best healthy fruit and vegetable juices. **We recently** ¹⁾<u>updated our menu</u> **after listening to customer feedback. We're excited to tell you about the new items, including Berry Burst, Mango Explosion, and Harvest Smoothie.** They ²⁾<u>are now available at</u> every shop where our juices are sold! These delicious new juices are all-natural and packed with nutrients to ³⁾<u>keep you energized</u> throughout the day. So be sure to check out our new flavors soon. Thank you for choosing Natural Beverage!	여 안녕하세요, 여러분! Natural Beverage에서는, 최고의 건강한 과일과 야채 주스를 공급하는 것이 목표입니다. 저희는 고객의 의견을 듣고 최근에 주스 메뉴를 업데이트했습니다. Berry Burst, Mango Explosion, 그리고 Harvest Smoothie를 포함한, 새로운 품목을 소개해 드리게 되어 기쁩니다. 이제 저희의 주스를 파는 모든 가게에서 이것들을 구입하실 수 있습니다! 이 맛있는 새로운 주스들은 모두 천연이고 하루 종일 여러분을 활기차게 해줄 영양분으로 가득합니다. 그러니, 조만간 새로운 맛을 꼭 확인해 보세요. Natural Beverage를 선택해 주셔서 감사합니다!

여자가 주스 공급 업체인 Natural Beverage에서 최근에 주스 메뉴를 업데이트했다고 말하면서, 새로운 메뉴 출시에 대해 자세히 알리고 있다. 따라서, 여자가 하는 말의 목적으로 ④ '새로운 메뉴의 출시를 홍보하려고'가 가장 적절하다.

어휘 goal 몡 목표 provide A with B A에게 B를 공급하다 feedback 몡 의견, 피드백 be packed with ~으로 가득하다 energize 통 활기차게 하다 check out ~을 확인하다 flavor 몡 맛

2 의견 파악

정답 ③

M	Honey, what should we give to our daughter Alice for her birthday?	남 여보, 우리 딸 Alice의 생일에 무엇을 선물해야 할까?
W	Well, why don't we ¹⁾<u>go to the mall</u> this weekend to look around?	여 글쎄, 이번 주말에 쇼핑몰에 가서 둘러보는 게 어때?
M	Hmm... But we always do that. I'd like to ²⁾<u>give her an experience</u> this year.	남 흠... 그렇지만 우리 매번 그렇게 하잖아. 올해는 그녀에게 경험을 선물해 주고 싶어.
W	Are you sure? She gets so excited over gifts.	여 확실해? 그녀는 선물을 받고서 매우 좋아하잖아.
M	**Getting a great experience as a gift is better than getting an object that will** ³⁾<u>become less exciting</u> over time.	남 선물로 좋은 경험을 주는 것이 시간이 지남에 따라 흥미가 떨어지는 물건을 주는 것보다 나아.
W	That's true. I also can't think of any items she wants.	여 그건 그래. 나는 딸이 원하는 물품이 잘 떠오르지도 않아.
M	An object just takes up space, and if she doesn't like it, we have to return or exchange it.	남 물건은 자리를 차지할 뿐이고, 만약 그녀가 좋아하지 않는다면, 반품하거나 교환해야 해.
W	You're right. Doing something ⁴⁾<u>together as a family</u> would be more special. How about going to the amusement park on her birthday?	여 당신 말이 맞아. 가족으로서 함께 무언가를 하는 것이 더 특별할 거야. 생일에 놀이공원을 가는 게 어때?
M	Great idea. I think such an experience will mean a lot more to her.	남 좋은 생각이야. 그런 경험이 그녀에게 훨씬 더 의미가 있을 거라고 생각해.

딸의 생일 선물을 쇼핑몰에서 고르려는 여자에게 남자가 선물로 좋은 경험을 주는 것이 시간이 지남에 따라 흥미가 떨어지는 물건을 주는 것보다 낫다고 했다. 따라서, 남자의 의견으로 ③ '물건보다 경험을 선물하는 것이 더 낫다.'가 가장 적절하다.

어휘 look around 둘러보다, 구경하다 object 몡 물건 take up space 자리를 차지하다

3 관계 파악

정답 ①

W	Hello. You must be Mr. Jacobs. I'm Olivia Roberts, **and I'll be interviewing you today.**	여 안녕하세요. 당신이 Jacobs 씨군요. 저는 오늘 인터뷰를 하게 될 Olivia Roberts입니다.
M	Welcome aboard. **I'm a** ¹⁾<u>huge fan of your show</u> Adventures Abroad.	남 탑승을 환영합니다. 저는 당신의 쇼 <Adventures Abroad>의 열렬한 팬이에요.
W	Thank you. **I've heard wonderful things about your boat tours.**	여 감사합니다. 당신의 보트 투어에 대해 멋진 이야기를 들었어요.
M	Well, I grew up here, **so it's easy** ²⁾<u>to show people around.</u>	남 음, 저는 여기서 자랐기 때문에, 사람들을 구경시켜 주는 것은 쉬워요.
W	**Do you ever get tired of taking people out on your boat?**	여 사람들을 배에 태우고 나가는 것에 싫증이 난 적 있나요?
M	Not at all. The islands here are beautiful, and I enjoy meeting people from all over the world.	남 전혀요. 이곳의 섬들은 아름답고, 저는 전 세계 사람들을 만나는 걸 즐기거든요.
W	That's great. So where will we be going today ³⁾<u>to shoot the show</u>?	여 좋습니다. 그럼 오늘은 어디로 가서 촬영을 할까요?
M	We'll sail over to an island which is about 30 minutes away.	남 약 30분 거리에 있는 섬으로 항해할 거예요.
W	Do you think ⁴⁾<u>the water will be rough</u>? One of the members of my film crew gets seasick.	여 물살이 거칠 것 같나요? 촬영진 중 한 명이 뱃멀미를 하거든요.
M	No. The water should be quite calm today.	남 아니요. 오늘은 물살이 꽤 잔잔할 거예요.
W	Okay, then. I think we're ready to go.	여 좋습니다, 그럼. 저희 갈 준비가 된 것 같아요.

두 사람이 선상에서 인터뷰에 대해 이야기하고 있다. 여자는 남자에게 오늘 인터뷰 촬영을 맡은 사람이라고 소개하고 있고, 남자는 탑승을 환영한다면서 자신의 배에 사람들을 태우고 구경시켜 주는 것에 대해 말하는 것으로 보아 두 사람의 관계로 ① '리포터 — 선장'이 가장 적절하다.

어휘 show ~ around ~를 구경시켜 주다 get tired of ~에 싫증이 나다 shoot 통 촬영하다; 쏘다 sail 통 항해하다 rough 형 거친 film crew 촬영진 get seasick 뱃멀미하다 calm 형 잔잔한

---

4 그림 내용 불일치 파악

정답 ③

M Hey, Lauren. Have you finished setting up the home office?	남 안녕, Lauren. 재택근무 사무실 준비를 마쳤니?
W Yeah, it's ¹⁾all done. What do you think?	여 응, 다 끝났어. 어떻게 생각해?
M It's very cozy. And I love that you put the desk by the window.	남 아주 아늑하다. 그리고 책상을 창가에 놓은 것이 좋아.
W Right? Then, I can look out at the view while I work.	여 그렇지? 그러면 일하면서 바깥 경치를 볼 수 있어.
M Is that a new lamp on the desk?	남 책상 위에 있는 저것은 새 램프야?
W Yeah. I just bought it.	여 응. 얼마 전에 샀어.
M I like how modern it looks.	남 현대적인 느낌이 좋다.
W The ²⁾fan on the floor is also new. I don't have air conditioning, so I thought it would be useful.	여 바닥에 있는 선풍기도 새것이야. 에어컨이 없어서, 유용할 것 같았어.
M Definitely. And I like that cushion with a flower on the chair.	남 물론이지. 그리고 나는 의자 위의 꽃이 그려진 쿠션이 마음에 들어.
W It makes the chair ³⁾a lot more comfortable.	여 그게 의자를 훨씬 더 편안하게 해줘.
M That makes sense. But what are in those two boxes next to the desk?	남 말이 되네. 그런데 책상 옆에 있는 두 개의 상자에는 무엇이 들어있니?
W Oh, those are just full of office supplies.	여 아, 사무용품들로 가득 차 있어.
M I see. Your home office looks great.	남 그렇구나. 네 재택근무 사무실이 멋져 보여.

대화에서 여자가 바닥에 있는 선풍기도 새것이라고 언급했는데, ③에는 선풍기가 책상 위에 그려져 있다.

어휘 set up ~을 준비하다, 설치하다 home office 재택근무 사무실 cozy 형 아늑한 modern 형 현대적인, 현대의 useful 형 유용한 be full of ~으로 가득 차 있다 office supplies 사무용품

---

5 할 일 파악

정답 ③

W Tyler, how is the planning going for the Student Film Festival?	여 Tyler, 학생 영화제 계획은 어떻게 되어 가고 있니?
M It's going well. I've ¹⁾already made the timetable for all of the movies.	남 잘되고 있어. 이미 모든 영화의 시간표를 짰어.
W That's good. Did you put up the flyers around campus?	여 잘됐네. 학교 주변에 광고지는 붙였어?
M I did that this morning, actually.	남 사실, 오늘 아침에 했어.
W Great. I'm thinking about sending an email out to all the students, too.	여 좋네. 난 모든 학생들에게 이메일도 보낼까 생각 중이야.
M Oh, I just sent one. I ²⁾included all of the information from the flyer.	남 오, 내가 방금 보냈어. 광고지에 있는 모든 정보를 포함시켰어.
W Amazing job. Also, maybe we should sell some popcorn and drinks for attendees. What do you think?	여 잘했네. 또, 참여자들을 위해 팝콘과 음료를 좀 팔아야 할 것 같아. 어떻게 생각해?
M Yeah. We could set up booths for tickets and snacks.	남 응. 표와 간식을 위한 부스를 마련할 수도 있겠어.
W Okay. I'll ³⁾buy some snacks from the store.	여 그래. 내가 가게에서 간식을 좀 사 올게.
M Let me do it. I have time this afternoon. How did the meeting with the directors go?	남 그건 내가 할게. 오늘 오후에 시간이 있어. 감독들과 회의는 어떻게 됐어?
W It went well. They accepted our invitation to attend the opening ceremony.	여 잘됐어. 개막식에 참석해달라는 우리의 초대를 받아들였어.

학생 영화제 준비에 대해 이야기하고 있다. 여자가 부스에서 팔 간식을 사 오겠다고 하자 남자가 본인이 하겠다고 했으므로 남자가 할 일로 ③ '간식 구매하기'가 가장 적절하다.

어휘 timetable 명 시간표 put up ~을 붙이다, 게시하다 flyer 명 광고지, 전단 include 통 포함하다 attendee 명 참석자 accept 통 받다

6 금액 정보 파악

정답 ⑤

M	Welcome to Wanda's Bakery. May I help you?
W	Hello. I'd like to order a wedding cake. What type of cake ¹⁾<u>do you recommend</u>?
M	Usually, people order a medium or large vanilla cake.
W	How much are they?
M	**Our medium cake is $100, and the large is $150.**
W	**I'll go with a medium, please.**
M	I also recommend ²⁾<u>adding fresh flowers</u> to the cake. Here are some example photos.
W	Oh, wow. These are beautiful.
M	**It's another $20 for the flowers. Would you like to add some?**
W	**Sure.** I'd like to ³⁾<u>put pink roses</u> on it.
M	So you want one medium wedding cake and some flower decorations.
W	That's right. **Also,** ⁴⁾<u>do you deliver</u>?
M	Yes. **It will be an additional $5.**
W	**Okay.** This is the address of the wedding hall. Here's my card.

남	Wanda's Bakery에 오신 것을 환영합니다. 무엇을 도와드릴까요?
여	안녕하세요. 웨딩 케이크를 주문하고 싶어요. 어떤 종류의 케이크를 추천하시나요?
남	보통, 사람들은 중간 또는 큰 크기의 바닐라 케이크를 주문해요.
여	얼마예요?
남	중간 크기의 케이크는 100달러이고 큰 케이크는 150달러예요.
여	중간 크기로 선택할게요.
남	케이크에 신선한 꽃을 추가하는 것도 추천해드려요. 여기 몇 가지 예시 사진이 있어요.
여	오, 우와. 아름답네요.
남	꽃은 20달러 추가돼요. 추가하시겠어요?
여	물론이죠. 분홍색 장미꽃을 올리고 싶어요.
남	그럼, 중간 크기의 웨딩 케이크 하나와 꽃장식이 필요하신 거군요.
여	맞아요. 그리고 배달도 되나요?
남	네. 추가로 5달러 되겠습니다.
여	알겠습니다. 이건 결혼식장의 주소예요. 그리고 여기 제 카드입니다.

여자가 중간 크기 웨딩 케이크 하나($100)에 꽃장식을 추가($20)했고, 배달비($5)도 추가했으므로 정답은 ⑤ '$125'이다.

어휘 type 몡 종류 recommend 통 추천하다 go with ~을 선택하다 decoration 몡 장식 additional 혱 추가의

7 이유 파악

정답 ②

M	Hi, Ms. Napa. I need to talk to you about the teacher's seminar.
W	Sure, Principal Kim. What's going on?
M	We can ¹⁾<u>no longer have the seminar</u> here at the school. Can you book a conference room at the Skymark Hotel instead?
W	Sure, but why is that? Is our meeting room too small?
M	No. There will be less than 20 teachers attending.
W	Is it because there is a ²⁾<u>basketball game scheduled</u> at the same time? It could be noisy.
M	That doesn't matter. The gymnasium is far from the meeting room.
W	Then, the teachers ³⁾<u>must have requested</u> the change.
M	**Actually, we can't have it here because** ⁴⁾<u>the projector is broken</u>. **It won't be repaired in time.**
W	Oh, I see! Let me call the hotel right now.
M	Thank you.

남	안녕하세요, Napa 선생님. 교사 세미나에 대해 얘기하고 싶어요.
여	그럼요, 김 교장 선생님. 무슨 일인가요?
남	더 이상 학교에서 세미나를 할 수 없어요. 대신 스카이마크 호텔에 회의실을 예약해주실 수 있나요?
여	물론이죠, 그런데 왜죠? 저희 회의실이 너무 작나요?
남	아니요. 20명 미만의 선생님들이 참석할 거예요.
여	농구 경기가 동시에 예정되어 있어서 그런가요? 시끄러울 수도 있긴 해요.
남	그건 중요하지 않아요. 체육관은 회의실에서 멀잖아요.
여	그렇다면, 선생님들이 변경을 요청했나 보군요.
남	사실, 프로젝터가 고장 나서 여기에서 할 수가 없어요. 제때 수리가 되지 않을 거예요.
여	오, 그렇군요! 지금 바로 호텔에 전화할게요.
남	고마워요.

남자는 더 이상 학교에서 교사 세미나를 할 수 없다면서, 프로젝터가 고장이 났는데 제때 수리가 되지 않을 것이라고 말했으므로, 남자가 세미나 장소를 변경하려는 이유는 ② '프로젝터가 고장 나서'이다.

어휘 conference room 회의실 attend 통 참석하다 at the same time 동시에 gymnasium 몡 체육관 repair 통 수리하다 in time 제때

8 언급 유무 파악

정답 ④

W	Hey, Josh. You like to write, don't you?
M	Yeah. I'm working on a few short stories. Why do you ask?
W	There's ¹⁾<u>a writing workshop</u> at **the local library** next week.
M	Really? That sounds interesting.
W	Yes. I have the brochure here. The theme is **crafting a story**, and it will focus on short stories and poetry.
M	Oh, that's perfect. I'd love to go.
W	Me too. It says we ²⁾<u>need to buy tickets</u> in advance. They're **$5** each.
M	That's fine. And how long is this workshop?
W	It's next Wednesday and Thursday from 6 to 9 p.m.
M	All right. Is there anything else we need to know?
W	It says we should bring ³⁾<u>any piece of writing</u> we want feedback on. But I think we'd better bring our laptops, too.
M	Then, let's buy our tickets today.
W	Sounds good!

여	안녕, Josh. 너 글 쓰는 것을 좋아하지, 그렇지 않니?
남	맞아. 몇 편의 단편 소설을 쓰고 있어. 왜 물어보는 거야?
여	음, 다음 주에 지역 도서관에서 글쓰기 워크숍이 있어.
남	정말? 그거 재미있겠다.
여	응. 여기 책자가 있어. 주제는 이야기를 정교하게 만들기이고, 특히 단편 소설과 시에 집중할 거야.
남	오, 아주 좋아. 가고 싶어.
여	나도. 사전에 표를 사야 한대. 한 장에 5달러야.
남	괜찮아. 그리고 이 워크숍은 얼마나 걸려?
여	다음 주 수요일과 목요일 저녁 6시부터 9시까지야.
남	알겠어. 우리가 알아야 할 다른 것이 있어?
여	피드백을 받고 싶은 글은 무엇이든 가져와야 한다고 쓰여 있어. 그런데 우리 노트북도 가져가는 게 좋을 것 같아.
남	그럼 오늘 표를 사자.
여	좋아!

장소(지역 도서관), 주제(이야기 정교하게 만들기), 참가비(5달러), 준비물(피드백 받고 싶은 글)에 대해 언급했고, ④ '강연자'는 언급하지 않았다.

[어휘] short story 단편 소설 brochure 몡 책자 theme 몡 주제 craft 통 정교하게 만들다 몡 공예 focus on ~에 집중하다 poetry 몡 시 in advance 사전에, 미리

---

9 내용 불일치 파악 정답 ④

M Hello, listeners! Are you looking for ¹⁾<u>a fun way to enjoy</u> the beautiful fall season with your family? Then, come to the Fall Family Carnival! This event, hosted by city hall, will feature ²⁾<u>a variety of games</u>, rides, and refreshments. It will also include a photo zone in the east garden where you can take pictures. The carnival will run from ³⁾<u>September 15th to 20th</u> at North Point Park. **Entrance to the event will be free for people of all ages, although food and rides require** ⁴⁾**<u>payment in cash</u>.** The money that is raised will go towards city development projects. For more information about the carnival, please visit www. fallfamilycarnival.com. We hope to see you there!	남 안녕하세요, 청취자 여러분! 가족과 함께 아름다운 가을을 즐길 수 있는 재미있는 방법을 찾고 있나요? 그렇다면, Fall Family Carnival에 오세요! 시청에서 주최하는 이 행사는 다양한 게임, 놀이기구, 간단한 음식 등을 선보일 예정입니다. 또한 동쪽 정원에 여러분이 사진을 찍을 수 있는 포토존이 포함됩니다. 카니발은 9월 15일부터 20일까지 노스포인트 공원에서 열립니다. 행사 입장료는 모든 연령대의 사람들에게 무료이나, 음식과 놀이기구는 현금으로 지불해야 합니다. 모인 돈은 도시 개발 프로젝트의 비용으로 쓰일 것입니다. 카니발에 대한 더 많은 정보를 원하시면, www.fallfamilycarnival.com을 방문해 보세요. 그곳에서 뵙기를 바랍니다!

시청에서 주최하는 Fall Family Carnival 행사에 대한 안내 방송이다. 남자가 음식과 놀이기구는 현금으로 지불해야 하지만 행사 입장료는 무료라고 했으므로, ④ '입장권은 현금으로 지불해야 한다.'는 내용과 일치하지 않는다.

[어휘] host 통 주최하다 a variety of 다양한 ride 몡 놀이기구 통 타다 refreshment 몡 간단한 음식, 다과 of all ages 모든 연령내의 go towards ~의 비용으로 쓰이다

---

10 도표 정보 파악 정답 ④

W Do you want to take a French course with me, Leo?	여 나랑 프랑스어 수업 들을래, Leo?
M Oh, I'd love to. I really need to ¹⁾<u>start practicing again</u>.	남 오, 좋아. 나는 정말 다시 연습을 시작해야 해.
W I just looked some up on my computer. Check them out.	여 방금 컴퓨터로 찾아봤어. 와서 확인해 봐.
M Okay. I don't think I can take this one. I'm too busy ²⁾<u>in the afternoons</u>.	남 그래. 나는 이건 못 들을 것 같아. 항상 오후에는 너무 바쁘거든.
W **Then, we should take one that ends at or before noon.** How much do you want to spend?	여 그럼 정오나 그 전에 끝나는 걸로 해야겠네. 얼마나 돈을 쓰고 싶어?
M I think ³⁾<u>keeping to a budget</u> of less than $300 is a good idea. What do you think?	남 300달러 이하로 예산을 유지하는 게 좋은 생각인 것 같아. 어떻게 생각해?
W I agree. And we've taken French classes before, **so let's not sign up for a beginner course.**	여 동의해. 그리고 우리는 전에 프랑스어 수업을 들은 적이 있으니까, 초보자 과정에는 등록하지 말자.
M Then, we just have to decide on the course topic.	남 그럼, 수업 주제만 정하면 되겠네.
W **We don't need to learn about French literature.**	여 프랑스 문학에 대해 배울 필요는 없어.
M No. **It'll be more helpful to learn how to use the** ⁴⁾<u>language in daily life</u>.	남 그럴 필요 없지. 일상생활에서 그 언어를 사용하는 방법을 배우는 것이 우리에게 더 도움이 될 거야.
W I guess we've made our selection, then.	여 그럼 다 선택한 것 같아.
M Great. Let's sign up now.	남 좋아. 지금 등록하자.

두 사람은 정오나 그 이전에 끝나면서, 300달러 이하인 것 중에서, 초보자 과정이 아니고, 일상 생활에서의 사용법을 배우는 프랑스어 수업을 골랐다.

[어휘] course 몡 수업, 강의 practice 통 연습하다 budget 몡 예산 sign up for ~에 등록하다 topic 몡 주제 daily life 일상생활 make a selection 선택하다
intermediate 혱 중급의; 중간의

---

11 짧은 대화의 응답 파악 정답 ①

W Jake, what a beautiful day for hiking!	여 Jake, 등산하기에 정말 좋은 날씨야!
M Yeah, the view is amazing. I'm getting a little hungry, though. **Should we** ¹⁾**<u>have our packed lunch</u> now?**	남 응, 경치가 정말 좋아. 배는 좀 고파지고 있지만 말이야. 이제 도시락을 먹을까?
W **We're almost at the top of the mountain. Let's** ²⁾<u>wait until we get there</u>.	여 우리 산 정상에 거의 다 왔어. 도착할 때까지 기다리자.
M Sure. I don't need to eat right away.	남 물론이지, 바로 먹을 필요는 없어.

[선택지] ① 물론이지, 바로 먹을 필요는 없어.
② 응. 너 내 떡 좀 먹어도 돼.
③ 아니. 네가 음식을 싸 오는 줄 알았어.
④ 맞아. 등산 가기 전에 점심을 먹자.
⑤ 난 그렇게 생각하지 않아. 우리는 이 아름다운 경치를 사진으로 찍어야 해.

남자가 등산 중에 도시락을 먹을지 묻자 여자가 산 정상에 거의 다 왔으니 도착할 때까지 기다리자고 했으므로, 이에 대한 응답으로는 여자의 의견에 수긍하는 ① 'Sure. I don't need to eat right away.'가 가장 적절하다.

[어휘] view 몡 경치 get hungry 배가 고파지다 packed lunch 도시락

12 짧은 대화의 응답 파악

정답 ④

M Are you okay, Jin? You seem really stressed out.	남 괜찮니, Jin? 정말 스트레스로 지친 것 같아 보여.
W **My laptop** 1)isn't working. I need it for a science assignment I'm doing right now.	여 내 노트북이 작동하지 않아. 지금 하고 있는 과학 과제에 그게 필요한데 말이야.
M **Do you** 2)want to use mine? I don't need it at the moment.	남 내 것을 쓸래? 나는 지금 필요 없어.
W Thank you! I'll give it back as soon as I'm done.	여 고마워! 끝나는 대로 돌려줄게.

선택지	① 여기 있어. 스트레스 해소에 도움이 될 거야.
	② 괜찮아. 오늘 안으로 고쳐질 거야.
	③ 모르겠어. 플러그를 꽂아도 충전이 되지 않아.
	④ 고마워! 끝나는 대로 돌려줄게.
	⑤ 맞아. 네가 해야 할 조사가 많아.

여자의 노트북이 작동하지 않는 상황에서 남자가 자신의 것을 쓰라고 제안했으므로, 이에 대한 응답으로는 제안에 고마워하는 ④ 'Thank you! I'll give it back as soon as I'm done.'이 가장 적절하다.

어휘 stressed out 스트레스로 지친 laptop 명 노트북 assignment 명 과제 at the moment 지금 plug in 플러그를 꽂다 as soon as ~하자마자 research 명 조사, 연구

13 긴 대화의 응답 파악

정답 ⑤

W Honey, why didn't you reply to my messages earlier?	여 여보, 아까 왜 내 메시지에 답하지 않았어?
M I'm sorry. My phone ran out of battery. Is everything okay?	남 미안해. 휴대폰 배터리를 다 써버렸어. 별일 없는 거지?
W **I got home earlier and noticed that our dog, Max, was** 1)acting strangely.	여 아까 집에 도착했는데 우리 개 Max가 이상하게 행동하고 있다는 걸 알아챘어.
M What do you mean?	남 무슨 말이야?
W **He won't eat his food, and he keeps whining.** He never does that.	여 그는 음식을 먹지도 않고 계속 칭얼거려. 절대 안 그러는데.
M Maybe it's because he's been alone a lot these days. We've both been 2)busier than usual, and dogs can get lonely.	남 아마 요즘 혼자 있는 시간이 많았어서 그런가 봐. 우리 둘 다 평소보다 더 바빴고, 그러면 개들은 외로워질 수도 있어.
W But I'm worried that he could be sick.	여 하지만 그가 아플까 봐 걱정돼.
M **Should we take him to the vet, then?**	남 그럼 수의사한테 데려갈까?
W I think so. I will feel better 3)if I know for sure that he's okay.	여 그래야 할 것 같아. 그가 괜찮다는 것을 확실히 알게 되면 내 기분이 훨씬 나아질 거야.
M You're right. We can take him tomorrow.	남 맞아. 내일 데려갈 수 있어.
W **Do you want me to make an appointment?**	여 내가 예약을 잡을까?
M Yes. Check if they can see him in the morning.	남 응. 아침에 진료할 수 있는지 확인해 봐.

선택지	① 알겠어. 내일 오후 4시쯤 데리고 오면 돼.
	② 좋은 생각이야. 그러면 우리는 좋은 시간을 가질 수 있어.
	③ 걱정하지 마. 며칠 지나면 나을 거야.
	④ 맞아. 그에게 다른 반려견 식품을 줘야겠어.
	⑤ 응. 아침에 진료할 수 있는지 확인해 봐.

키우는 개가 음식을 먹지 않고 칭얼거려 걱정이 되는 상황에서 여자가 내일 병원 예약을 잡을지 물었으므로, 이에 대한 응답으로는 아침에 진료가 가능한지 확인하라고 하는 ⑤ 'Yes. Check if they can see him in the morning.'이 가장 적절하다.

어휘 reply 동 답하다, 대답하다 run out of ~을 다 써버리다 notice 동 알아채다 whine 동 칭얼거리다 vet 명 수의사 make an appointment 예약을 잡다

14 긴 대화의 응답 파악

정답 ③

[Telephone rings.]	[전화기가 울린다.]
W Hello. Murray National Park. This is Gina speaking.	여 안녕하세요. 머레이 국립공원입니다. 저는 Gina입니다.
M Hi. **I'm calling to ask about** 1)the forest experience program for kids.	남 안녕하세요. 아이들을 위한 숲 체험 프로그램에 대해 여쭤보려고 전화 드려요.
W Oh, yes. How old is your child?	여 오, 네. 아이가 몇 살인가요?
M My son is five years old.	남 제 아들은 다섯 살이에요.
W Okay. We have many programs for children that age.	여 알겠습니다. 저희는 그 나이의 아이들을 위한 많은 프로그램이 있어요.
M Great. What kinds of activities do they do?	남 좋아요. 아이들이 어떤 종류의 활동을 하나요?
W We encourage them to explore the natural environment. So they 2)observe living things in the water, and they learn to identify plants.	여 저희는 그들에게 자연환경을 탐험할 것을 권장합니다. 그래서 그들은 물속의 생물들을 관찰하고, 식물을 식별하는 것을 배웁니다.
M I think my son would really enjoy that.	남 제 아들이 정말 좋아할 것 같아요.
W Yes, the kids love it. They also make artwork using leaves, rocks, and sticks.	여 네, 아이들이 좋아해요. 그들은 또한 나뭇잎, 바위, 잔가지를 사용해서 예술작품을 만듭니다.
M That's wonderful. Are there any fees to participate?	남 정말 멋지네요. 참가비가 있나요?
W No. But you'll need to 3)purchase certain materials, such as a plant identification booklet.	여 아니요. 하지만 식물 식별하기 책자와 같은 특정 자료를 구입하셔야 합니다.
M I see. **Can you send me a program schedule?**	남 그렇군요. 프로그램 일정을 보내주실 수 있나요?
W No problem. Just tell me your email address, and I'll send it to you.	여 문제없어요. 이메일 주소만 알려주시면 보내드릴게요.

① 그거참 좋겠네요. 가능한 한 빨리 가겠습니다.

② 물론이죠. 이 앱은 모든 국립공원의 위치를 보여줍니다.

③ 문제없어요. 이메일 주소만 알려주시면 보내드릴게요.

④ 감사합니다. 숲에서 본 식물들의 이름을 전혀 모르겠어요.

⑤ 천만에요. 당신의 아들이 오늘 즐거운 시간을 보냈기를 바랍니다.

국립공원에서 제공하는 아이들을 위한 숲 체험 프로그램에 대해 문의하는 상황이다. 남자가 프로그램 일정을 보내줄 수 있는지 물었으므로, 이에 대한 응답으로는 보내주겠다고 말하는 ③ 'No problem. Just tell me your email address, and I'll send it to you.'가 가장 적절하다.

[어휘] activity 몡 활동 encourage 동 권장하다, 독려하다 observe 동 관찰하다 identify 동 식별하다 (identification 몡 식별) artwork 몡 예술작품 stick 몡 잔가지
purchase 동 구입하다 certain 혱 특정한; 확실한 such as ~과 같은 booklet 몡 책자

15 상황에 적절한 말 파악

정답 ④

W Peter arrives at a resort for his vacation. As he is checking in, he sees a poster that advertises activities at the resort. Although there are many different options, he finds the scuba diving lesson the most interesting. According to the poster, lessons [1]must be booked in advance. Peter asks a staff member, Kylie, if he can book a spot during his stay. But when Kylie checks the computer system, she finds out that [2]the class is fully booked for the next few weeks. Nevertheless, other fun activities, such as kayaking, still have openings. **Therefore, Kylie wants to tell Peter that he can't join the class because it is full, though there are** [3]other activities available. In this situation, what would Kylie most likely say to Peter?

여 Peter는 휴가를 보낼 리조트에 도착합니다. 그가 체크인을 하고 있을 때, 리조트의 활동을 홍보하는 포스터를 봅니다. 많은 다양한 선택지들이 있지만, 그는 스쿠버 다이빙 수업이 가장 흥미롭다고 생각합니다. 포스터에 따르면, 수업은 미리 예약해야 합니다. Peter는 직원인 Kylie에게 그가 머무는 동안 자리를 예약할 수 있는지 물어봅니다. 하지만 Kylie가 컴퓨터 시스템을 확인했을 때, 그녀는 다음 몇 주 동안 그 수업의 예약이 꽉 찼다는 것을 알게 됩니다. 그럼에도 불구하고, 카약과 같은 다른 재미있는 활동들은 여전히 빈자리가 있습니다. 따라서 Kylie는 Peter에게 만석이기 때문에 그 수업에는 참여할 수 없지만, 다른 가능한 활동들이 있다고 말하고 싶습니다. 이러한 상황에서, Kylie가 Peter에게 가장 할 것 같은 말은 무엇입니까?

[선택지] ① 바쁘시면 제가 먼저 할게요.

② 저는 실내 활동보다 야외 활동을 더 선호해요.

③ 자리가 빨리 차니까 기다리지 말고 활동을 예약해 주세요.

④ 그건 예약이 꽉 찼지만, 여기 다른 선택지들이 있어요.

⑤ 돈을 절약할 수 있도록 지금 비행기 표를 사요.

Peter가 원하는 스쿠버 다이빙 수업이 만석이라 참여할 수 없는 것을 보고, 리조트 직원 Kylie는 다른 가능한 활동이 있다고 말하려 한다. 따라서, Kylie가 할 말로 ④ 'That one is fully booked, but here are some other options.'가 가장 적절하다.

[어휘] advertise 동 홍보하다 option 몡 선택지 according to ~에 따르면 book a spot 자리를 예약하다 nevertheless 閇 그럼에도 불구하고 opening 몡 빈자리, 공석

16-17 세트 문항

정답 16 ⑤ 17 ⑤

M Good morning, students. Let's continue our discussion of fruit from last class. **Today, I'd like to discuss several different fruits that have been** [1]transformed by humans. For example, **bananas** once were hard on the inside and difficult to eat. The modern banana is a hybrid of two wild species. Through selective breeding, people have created bananas that are much tastier than they used to be. Also, **watermelons** [2]have changed dramatically over time. In the past, they had more seeds and paler flesh. The watermelons we eat today look completely different due to human intervention. **Strawberries** are another fruit that has changed because of humans. Wild strawberries are tasty, but their shelf life is short. So humans bred strawberries that [3]could remain fresh for a longer time. Finally, ancient **peaches** were tiny fruits with a salty taste. But the peaches we buy at the supermarket today are much larger, sweeter, and juicier. Now, let's watch a short video about some of these fruits.

남 좋은 아침입니다, 학생 여러분. 지난 수업부터 진행한 과일에 대한 논의를 계속해보도록 하겠습니다. 오늘, 저는 인간에 의해 변형된 몇 가지 다양한 과일들에 대해 논의하고자 합니다. 예를 들어, 바나나는 한때 속이 딱딱해서 먹기 어려웠습니다. 현대의 바나나는 두 야생종의 결합체입니다. 선별적인 교배를 통해, 사람들은 예전보다 훨씬 더 맛있는 바나나를 만들어냈습니다. 또한, 수박은 시간이 지나면서 극적으로 변했습니다. 과거에, 그것들은 더 많은 씨앗과 더 옅은 색의 과육을 가지고 있었습니다. 오늘날 우리가 먹는 수박은 사람들의 개입에 의해 완전히 다르게 보입니다. 딸기는 인간 때문에 변한 또 다른 과일입니다. 야생 딸기는 맛있지만, 유통기한이 짧습니다. 그래서, 사람들은 더 오래 신선한 상태를 유지할 수 있는 딸기를 길렀습니다. 마지막으로, 고대 복숭아는 짠맛이 나는 작은 과일이었습니다. 하지만 오늘날 우리가 슈퍼마켓에서 사는 복숭아들은 훨씬 더 크고, 달콤하고, 과즙이 더 많습니다. 자, 이제 이 과일들에 대한 짧은 비디오를 봅시다.

[선택지] 16 ① 인공 식품이 신체에 끼치는 영향

② 과일 재배에 사용되는 농법

③ 오늘날의 기후에서 과일을 재배하는 것의 어려움

④ 몇몇 과일들이 인기가 줄어든 이유

⑤ 인간에 의해 변화된 과일들의 예시

17 ① 바나나 ② 수박 ③ 딸기 ④ 복숭아 ⑤ 사과

16 인간에 의해 변형된 몇 가지 다양한 과일들에 대해 논의하고 있으므로 남자가 하는 말의 주제로 ⑤ 'examples of fruits changed by humans'가 가장 적절하다.

17 바나나, 수박, 딸기, 복숭아는 언급했지만 ⑤ 'apples'는 언급하지 않았다.

[어휘] continue 동 계속하다 discussion 몡 논의; 토론 transform 동 변형하다 hybrid 몡 결합체 wild 혱 야생의 selective 혱 선별적인 breed 동 교배하다, 기르다 tasty 혱 맛있는
dramatically 閇 극적으로 over time 시간이 지나면서 pale 혱 옅은; 창백한 flesh 몡 과육; 살 intervention 몡 개입, 간섭 shelf life 유통기한 remain 동 유지하다
juicy 혱 과즙이 많은 artificial 혱 인공의 utilize 동 사용하다

1	②	2	④	3	②	4	②	5	⑤	6	③	7	②	8	⑤	9	⑤	10	③
11	④	12	⑤	13	①	14	③	15	⑤	16	③	17	④						

• 각 문제의 정답 근거는 굵은 글씨로, Dictation 정답은 밑줄로 표시되어 있습니다.

---

1 목적 파악

정답 ②

M Hello, everyone! My name is Mateo, **and I will be your tour guide for the week. To begin, let me** ¹⁾explain some safety rules **during the trip.** First of all, please keep all your belongings in a safe place. Your passport is the most important thing, so I ask that you always have it with you. Secondly, it is very dangerous ²⁾to walk alone at night. If you must go out at nighttime, I recommend bringing another tour member. Finally, the tap water here is not safe to drink. You should only drink bottled water. If you ³⁾follow these rules, you will have an enjoyable trip without any problems. Okay, shall we begin our trip?

남 안녕하세요, 여러분! 제 이름은 Mateo이고, 이번 주 동안 여러분의 여행 가이드를 해드리겠습니다. 먼저 여행 중 안전 수칙에 대해 설명하겠습니다. 우선, 여러분의 모든 소지품을 안전한 장소에 보관하세요. 여권이 가장 중요하니, 항상 가지고 다니시길 부탁드립니다. 두 번째로, 밤에 혼자 걷는 것은 매우 위험합니다. 밤에 꼭 나가야 한다면 다른 여행객을 대동하시는 것을 추천합니다. 마지막으로, 이곳의 수돗물은 마시기에 안전하지 않습니다. 여러분은 병에 든 생수만 마셔야 합니다. 이 규칙들을 따른다면, 여러분은 아무 문제 없이 즐거운 여행을 할 것입니다. 좋아요, 그럼 여행을 시작해볼까요?

남자가 본인을 여행 가이드라고 소개하면서 여행 중 안전 수칙에 대해 설명하고 있다. 따라서, 남자가 하는 말의 목적으로 ② '여행 안전 수칙을 설명하려고'가 가장 적절하다.

어휘 explain ⑧ 설명하다 safety rule 안전 수칙 belonging ⑲ 소지품 travel ⑧ 이동하다; 여행하다 tap water 수돗물 bottled water 병에 든 생수

---

2 의견 파악

정답 ④

M How is studying for your test, Jacky?
W It's fine, but I'm a little tired.
M Me too. I think I'll leave the library soon and go have dinner.
W I'll probably ¹⁾stay here for a while and get some coffee to help me stay awake.
M Didn't you already have a few cups today?
W Yeah. I need it to help me focus.
M I understand, **but drinking too much coffee will actually** ²⁾make it harder **for you to study.**
W Are you sure?
M Yes! After you drink a lot of coffee, you feel nervous and uncomfortable.
W Oh, I know that feeling.
M And when you stay up late drinking coffee, you are ³⁾exhausted the next day. So it's hard to remember what you studied.
W I see what you mean. I'll get some juice instead.

남 시험공부는 어떻게 돼 가니, Jacky?
여 괜찮아, 근데 좀 피곤하네.
남 나도 그래. 난 곧 도서관을 나와서 저녁 먹으러 가야겠어.
여 난 아마 여기 좀 더 있다가 커피나 마시면서 잠 좀 깨야겠어.
남 너 오늘 벌써 몇 잔 마시지 않았어?
여 응. 집중하려면 커피가 필요해.
남 이해는 하지만, 커피를 너무 많이 마시면 오히려 공부하기가 더 힘들어져.
여 정말이야?
남 응! 커피를 많이 마시고 나면, 긴장되고 불편한 기분이 들지.
여 오, 나 그 기분 알아.
남 그리고 밤늦게까지 커피를 마시면서 깨어 있으면, 다음날 피곤함을 느끼게 돼. 그래서 공부한 내용을 기억하기가 힘들지.
여 무슨 말인지 알겠어. 대신 주스 좀 마셔야겠다.

집중하기 위해서 커피를 더 마시려는 여자에게 남자가 커피를 너무 많이 마시면 오히려 공부하기가 더 힘들어진다고 했다. 따라서, 남자의 의견으로 ④ '커피를 많이 마시면 공부에 방해가 된다.'가 가장 적절하다.

어휘 stay awake (자지 않고) 깨어 있다 focus ⑧ 집중하다 nervous ⑲ 긴장한 uncomfortable ⑲ 불편한 stay up late 늦게까지 깨어 있다 exhausted ⑲ 피곤한, 지친

3 관계 파악   정답 ②

W	Hi, Mr. Hemmings. How are you today?
M	I've been pretty busy. I just 1)finished making some baguettes.
W	Great. Well... I wanted to ask whether you would be interested in a work-experience program for my class.
M	Oh, what is that?
W	Students would spend one day 2)getting work experience in your bakery.
M	That sounds good. Are the students interested in becoming bakers?
W	Yes. Some of my students want to open their own bakeries. So if you'd like to participate, these students can come here and spend a day with you.
M	What do I have to do? I can show them 3)what I do each day.
W	Yes. And you can answer any questions they ask. Also, they can help you out.
M	Sounds good. I'll sign up for it.
W	Thank you so much.

여	안녕하세요, Hemmings 씨. 오늘 하루 어떠신가요?
남	꽤 바빴어요. 방금 바게트 만드는 것을 마쳤답니다.
여	좋네요. 음... 저희 학급의 직업 체험 프로그램에 관심이 있으신지 묻고 싶었어요.
남	오, 그게 뭐죠?
여	학생들이 사장님의 제과점에서 직업 체험을 하면서 하루를 보내는 거예요.
남	재미있겠는데요. 학생들이 제빵사가 되는 것에 관심이 있나요?
여	네. 제 학생들 중 몇몇은 직접 제과점을 열고 싶어 해요. 그래서 사장님께서 참여하고 싶으시다면, 그 학생들이 여기에 와서 하루를 함께 보내게 될 거예요.
남	제가 뭘 해야 하죠? 매일 하는 일을 보여줄 수는 있어요.
여	네. 그리고 묻는 질문에 대답해주시면 돼요. 또, 아이들이 사장님 일을 도울 수 있어요.
남	좋아요. 신청할게요.
여	정말 감사합니다.

두 사람이 학급 직업 체험 프로그램에 대해 이야기하고 있다. 여자는 이 프로그램을 소개하면서 남자의 제과점에서 자신의 학생들이 직업 경험을 할 수 있을지 묻고 있고, 남자는 방금 바게트 만드는 것을 마쳤다고 하면서 학생들이 그의 제과점을 체험하도록 승낙하고 있는 것으로 보아 두 사람의 관계로 ② '선생님 — 제빵사'가 가장 적절하다.

어휘 be interested in ~에 관심이 있다 work experience 직업 체험 participate 통 참여하다 help out ~를 돕다 sign up for ~을 신청하다

4 그림 내용 불일치 파악   정답 ②

W	Is that a photo of the resort you stayed at last weekend, Sean?
M	Yeah. That waterslide in the pool was so fun.
W	That's your beach towel on the chair, right? I recognize 1)its striped pattern.
M	You're right. I spent a lot of time relaxing on that chair.
W	Did you get some snacks, too?
M	No. I just drank a glass of lemonade. You can see it on the table 2)between the two chairs.
W	It seems so peaceful.
M	It wasn't always peaceful. There was a big group of little kids. The resort staff kept warning them not to run.
W	That must be why there's a "No Running" sign posted.
M	Exactly. Those are 3)their three tubes in the pool.
W	Well, it looks like a really nice resort. Did you have a good time?
M	Definitely. You should go there soon.

여	저게 지난 주말에 네가 묵었던 리조트 사진이니, Sean?
남	맞아. 수영장에 있는 저 워터슬라이드 타는 거 정말 즐거웠어.
여	의자에 있는 것이 네 비치 타월 맞지? 저 줄무늬 패턴을 알아보겠어.
남	맞아. 그 의자에서 정말 오래 휴식을 취했어.
여	간식도 좀 먹었어?
남	아니. 그냥 레모네이드 한 잔 마셨어. 두 의자 사이의 테이블 위에 있는 게 보일 거야.
여	정말 평화로워 보인다.
남	항상 평화롭지는 않았어. 어린애들이 많았거든. 리조트 직원이 그 아이들에게 뛰지 말라고 계속 주의를 주더라.
여	그래서 '달리기 금지'라는 표지판이 세워져 있나 보다.
남	맞아. 수영장에 있는 튜브 3개도 그 아이들 거야.
여	음, 정말 좋은 리조트 같네. 즐거운 시간 보낸 거지?
남	물론이지. 너도 빨리 그곳에 가봐야 해.

대화에서 여자가 의자에 있는 비치 타월의 줄무늬 패턴을 알아보겠다고 말했는데, ②에는 물방울무늬의 비치 타월이 그려져 있다.

어휘 relax 통 휴식을 취하다 peaceful 형 평화로운 warn 통 주의를 주다, 경고하다 sign 명 표지판, 팻말 post 통 세우다; 게시하다

5 할 일 파악   정답 ⑤

W	Honey, your cousins from Germany arrive tomorrow. I can't wait to see them again.
M	I know. Is everything ready for their arrival?
W	Almost. I have to go to the store to buy some food for them.
M	I 1)made a list for you to take.
W	Thanks. Did you wash the blankets?
M	I did that earlier today while you cleaned the guest room.
W	Great. Did you move our storage boxes 2)out of the closet, too?
M	Yeah. They'll need lots of space for their luggage.
W	Okay. We need to figure out how they'll get here from the airport.
M	I can 3)arrange an airport taxi to pick them up.
W	Oh, leave it to me. I'll call right now.
M	No. You go to the store. I'll take care of it.

여	여보, 당신 사촌들이 독일에서 내일 도착해. 빨리 다시 그들을 만나고 싶어.
남	그래. 도착을 대비한 준비는 다 되었어?
여	거의. 난 그들에게 줄 음식을 좀 사러 가게에 가야 해.
남	난 당신이 가져갈 목록을 만들었어.
여	고마워. 이불은 빨았어?
남	당신이 손님 방을 청소하는 동안 오늘 아까 했어.
여	좋아. 보관 상자들도 옷장 밖으로 옮겼어?
남	응. 그들에게 짐을 넣을 공간이 많이 필요할 테니까.
여	알겠어, 공항에서 여기까지 그들이 어떻게 올지 알아내야겠어.
남	그들을 데리러 갈 공항택시를 준비해 줄 수 있어.
여	오, 그건 나한테 맡겨. 지금 바로 전화할게.
남	아니. 당신은 가게로 가. 내가 처리할게.

독일에서 방문하는 사촌들을 맞이할 준비를 하고 있다. 남자가 사촌들을 데리러 갈 공항택시를 준비해줄 수 있다고 하면서 재차 본인이 처리하겠다고 했으므로 남자가 할 일로 ⑤ '공항택시 예약하기'가 가장 적절하다.

어휘 arrival 명 도착 list 명 목록 blanket 명 이불, 담요 storage 명 보관 closet 명 옷장 figure out ~을 알아내다 arrange 통 준비하다, 마련하다 pick up ~를 데리러 가다
Leave it to me. 나한테 맡겨. take care of ~을 처리하다

6 금액 정보 파악

정답 ③

M Hello. May I help you?	남 안녕하세요. 도와드릴까요?
W Yes. **I'd like to buy a candle.**	여 네. 양초를 사고 싶은데요.
M What about this one? It's our [1]most popular scent, Vanilla Dream.	남 이건 어떠세요? 가장 인기 있는 향인 Vanilla Dream이에요.
W Oh, that smells great. How much is it?	여 오, 좋은 냄새가 나네요. 얼마인가요?
M Originally, it was $40. **But right now, it's $30.**	남 원래는 40달러였어요. 하지만 지금은 30달러예요.
W **I'll take one, please.** And do you have any room sprays?	여 하나 주세요. 그리고 룸 스프레이가 있나요?
M We do. What kind of scent are you looking for?	남 있죠. 어떤 향을 찾으세요?
W I'm looking for something that [2]smells really fresh.	여 정말 신선한 향기가 나는 것을 찾고 있어요.
M This lemon spray is perfect for that. It has a very clean smell, and it only costs $15.	남 이 레몬 스프레이를 써보세요. 매우 깨끗한 향이 나고, 가격은 15달러밖에 하지 않아요.
W Great. **I'll take [3]two bottles of it.**	여 좋아요. 그거 두 병 주세요.
M All right. So you want the candle and the two bottles of spray, right?	남 알겠습니다. 그럼, 양초랑 스프레이 두 병을 원하시는 거죠, 그렇죠?
W That's right. Can I [4]get a bag for all of this, please?	여 맞아요. 이 모든 것들을 넣을 가방을 하나 주시겠어요?
M Sure. Here are some free samples, too.	남 물론이죠. 여기 무료 샘플도 있습니다.
W Thanks. Here's my credit card.	여 고마워요. 여기 제 신용카드요.

여자가 양초 하나($30)와 레몬향 룸 스프레이 두 병($15×2=$30)을 구매했으므로 정답은 ③ '$60'이다.

어휘 popular 형 인기 있는 scent 명 향 look for ~을 찾다 fresh 형 신선한

7 이유 파악

정답 ②

W Hey, William. Our team's first soccer game is this weekend. Are you excited?	여 안녕, William. 우리 팀의 첫 번째 축구 경기가 이번 주말이야. 신나니?
M Actually, we have to cancel this Saturday's game.	남 사실, 이번 주 토요일 경기는 취소해야 해.
W Oh, no. I thought everyone on the team could make it.	여 오, 이런. 팀의 모든 사람들이 참석할 수 있다고 생각했는데.
M Yeah, we [1]are all free on that day.	남 맞아, 그날은 모두 한가해.
W Then, what's the reason? Is there heavy rain in the forecast?	여 그럼, 이유가 뭐야? 일기예보에 폭우가 올 거래?
M Not at all. It's going to be very sunny this weekend.	남 전혀. 이번 주말에는 날씨가 매우 맑을 거야.
W Hmm... Is it because we couldn't [2]find a referee for the game?	여 흠... 경기를 봐줄 심판을 찾지 못해서 그런 거야?
M No. I found one who is available. **The problem is that there's no field to play on.**	남 아니. 가능한 분을 한 명 찾았어. 문제는 축구할 경기장이 없다는 거야.
W Oh, are they [3]all booked for the day?	여 아, 그날 예약이 다 찼어?
M Yes. So we'll [4]have to wait until we can schedule a field.	남 응. 그래서 경기장 일정을 잡을 수 있을 때까지 기다려야 해.
W That's too bad. I was really looking forward to this game.	여 너무 유감이야. 난 이 경기를 정말 기대했는데.

남자는 이번 주 토요일 경기를 취소해야 한다면서 경기장 예약이 다 차서 없다고 말했으므로, 남자가 축구 시합을 취소해야 하는 이유는 ② '경기장 예약이 다 차서'이다.

어휘 make it 참석하다 free 형 한가한 heavy rain 폭우 forecast 명 일기예보 referee 명 심판 field 명 경기장; 들판 schedule 동 일정을 잡다 명 일정

8 언급 유무 파악

정답 ⑤

M Rebecca, have you seen the posters about the Green Haven Pottery Program?	남 Rebecca, Green Haven Pottery Program의 포스터 봤어?
W Oh, isn't that being held [1]at **the new studio** on Houston Street?	여 오, 그거 휴스턴가에 새로 생긴 스튜디오에서 열리는 거 아니야?
M Yeah, that's right. Would you like to sign up for it?	남 응, 맞아. 너도 참여하고 싶니?
W Definitely. It would be fun to make our own coffee mugs and plates.	여 물론이지. 우리만의 커피잔이나 접시를 만들면 재미있을 거야.
M I agree. The classes will take place [2]on Tuesday nights. They run **from 6 to 8 p.m.**	남 동감이야. 수업은 화요일 저녁마다 열릴 거야. 오후 6시부터 8시까지 진행돼.
W I'm free at that time. Let's sign up for it. But what about the fee for the program?	여 난 그 시간에 한가해. 그럼 등록하자. 그런데 프로그램 요금은 어떻게 돼?
M It's **$150**, but there are five classes in total.	남 150달러인데 총 5개의 클래스가 있어.
W That's fine with me. How do we enroll?	여 괜찮은데. 등록은 어떻게 하니?
M We have to [3]call the studio. But we should hurry before the class fills up.	남 스튜디오에 전화해야 해. 하지만 정원이 다 차기 전에 서둘러야겠어.
W Let's call today, then.	여 그럼, 오늘 전화하자.

장소(휴스턴가에 새로 생긴 스튜디오), 시간(오후 6시부터 8시까지), 비용(150달러), 신청 방법(스튜디오에 전화)에 대해 언급했고, ⑤ '수업 정원'은 언급하지 않았다.

어휘 plate 명 접시, 그릇 take place 열리다, 개최하다 run 동 진행하다, 운영하다 fee 명 요금; 수수료 in total 총, 통틀어 enroll 동 등록하다 fill up 다 차다, 가득 차다

9 내용 불일치 파악　　　　　　　　　　정답 ⑤

W Hello, students! Do you want to put your debate skills to the test? Then, we ¹⁾invite you to participate in the Riverside High School Debate this Thursday! The debate will take place from 9 to 10:30 a.m. in the auditorium. All students are welcome to compete. If you want to participate, you must ²⁾notify your teacher by Tuesday. Competitors will receive a free T-shirt and a certificate for participating. Each of the winners will receive a cash prize of $200. **They will also represent the school ³⁾in the regional debate competition.** Please join us, and show off your debate skills! For more information, please visit our school's website.	여 안녕하세요, 학생 여러분! 여러분의 토론 실력을 시험해 보고 싶으신가요? 그럼, 이번 주 목요일에 열리는 리버사이드 고등학교 토론회에 여러분이 참가하도록 초대합니다! 토론은 오전 9시부터 10시 30분까지 강당에서 개최됩니다. 모든 학생들의 출전을 환영합니다. 만약 참가하고 싶다면, 화요일까지 선생님께 알려야 합니다. 참가자들은 무료 티셔츠와 참가 증명서를 받을 것입니다. 우승자들은 각각 200달러의 상금을 받게 됩니다. 또한 지역 토론 대회에서 학교를 대표할 것입니다. 저희와 함께 토론 실력을 뽐내주세요! 더 많은 정보를 원하시면, 저희 학교 웹사이트를 방문해주세요.

고등학교 토론회 참가에 대한 안내 방송이다. 여자가 우승자들은 지역 토론대회에서 학교를 대표할 것이라고 했으므로 ⑤ '우승자들은 전국 토론 대회에 대표로 참가한다.'는 내용과 일치하지 않는다.

어휘　put ~ to the test ~을 시험해보다　auditorium 명 강당　compete 동 출전하다; 경쟁하다　notify 동 알리다　certificate 명 증명서　cash prize 상금　represent 동 대표하다
regional 형 지역의　show off ~을 뽐내다

10 도표 정보 파악　　　　　　　　　　정답 ③

M Welcome to Freeman's Department Store. W Hi. I'm looking for a new winter scarf. M Okay. You should ¹⁾take a look at our most popular options over here. We have all kinds of materials to choose from. W **I don't want a wool scarf because ²⁾that material itches my skin.** M I understand. So what's your price range? W **I don't want to spend more than $50.** M Got it. **And do you prefer one that you can ³⁾wash in a machine?** W **Yes.** I think that would be convenient. M Now, you just have to choose ⁴⁾which color you want. W **I like the gray one.** It'll go with my coat. M Excellent. Then, we've found the perfect scarf for you.	남 프리맨즈 백화점에 오신 것을 환영합니다. 여 안녕하세요. 새 겨울 스카프를 찾고 있는데요. 남 알겠습니다. 여기서 가장 인기 있는 선택지들을 보셔야 합니다. 선택하실 수 있는 모든 종류의 소재가 있어요. 여 울 스카프는 제 피부를 가렵게 해서 원하지 않아요. 남 알겠습니다. 그럼 가격대는 얼마를 생각하시나요? 여 50달러 이상은 쓰고 싶지 않아요. 남 알겠습니다. 그리고 세탁기로 세탁할 수 있는 것을 선호하시나요? 여 네. 그게 편할 것 같아요. 남 이제 원하는 색상을 선택하시면 됩니다. 여 회색이 좋아요. 제 코트와 잘 어울릴 거예요. 남 훌륭해요. 그럼, 저희가 손님에게 딱 맞는 스카프를 찾았네요.

여자는 울 소재가 아니면서, 50달러 미만인 것 중에서, 세탁기로 세탁할 수 있는, 회색 스카프를 골랐다.

어휘　option 명 선택지　material 명 소재, 재료　itch 동 가렵게 하다　price range 가격대　prefer 동 선호하다　convenient 형 편한, 편리한　go with ~과 잘 어울리다　cashmere 명 캐시미어

11 짧은 대화의 응답 파악　　　　　　　　　　정답 ④

M Hey, Chloe. What are you writing? W I'm ¹⁾writing a letter to my friend Alice. She lives in Amsterdam, and we exchange letters often. M Wow, that's cool. But Amsterdam is so far away. **You must have met her ²⁾when you were traveling.** W Actually, we went to the same summer camp.	남 안녕, Chloe. 무엇을 쓰고 있니? 여 내 친구 Alice에게 편지를 쓰고 있어. 그녀는 암스테르담에 살고 있고, 우리는 자주 편지를 주고받거든. 남 우와, 멋있어. 하지만 암스테르담은 너무 멀잖아. 틀림없이 여행 중에 그녀를 만났나 보구나. 여 사실, 우리는 같은 여름 캠프에 갔어. 선택지 ① 보통 편지는 일주일 안에 도착해. ② 불행하게도, 그녀는 나에게 답장을 보내지 않았어. ③ 아마 다음 주에 만나서 커피 한잔할 수 있을 거야. ④ 사실, 우리는 같은 여름 캠프에 갔어. ⑤ 바라건대 암스테르담에 갈 기회가 있으면 좋겠어.

여자가 암스테르담에 살고 있는 친구와 편지를 주고받는다고 하자 남자가 여행 중에 친구를 만난 것이 틀림없다고 단언했으므로, 이에 대한 응답으로는 친구를 어떻게 만났는지 언급하는 ④ 'Actually, we went to the same summer camp.'가 가장 적절하다.

어휘　exchange 동 주고받다; 교환하다　write back ~에게 답장하다

12 짧은 대화의 응답 파악

정답 ⑤

[Cell phone rings.]	*[휴대폰이 울린다.]*
W Hey, Kyle. Did you get home okay? We're ¹⁾still at the restaurant.	여 안녕, Kyle. 집에 잘 도착했어? 우리는 아직 식당에 있어.
M Hi, April. Yeah, **but I realized I left my wallet there.**	남 안녕, April. 응, 그런데 그곳에 지갑을 두고 온 걸 깨달았어.
W I can check for you. **Do you remember** ²⁾where you put it?	여 내가 확인해 줄게. 어디에 뒀는지 기억나?
M Thank you. I think I put it on the table.	남 고마워. 테이블 위에 올려놓은 것 같아.

선택지 ① 잠깐만. 내 지갑을 가져올게.
② 걱정하지 마. 그냥 집에 가는 버스를 타면 돼.
③ 늦어서 미안해. 최대한 빨리 갈게.
④ 동감이야. 그 식당의 음식은 훌륭했어.
⑤ 고마워. 테이블 위에 올려놓은 것 같아.

남자가 지갑을 식당에 두고 온 것을 깨달았다고 하자 여자가 확인해 주겠다면서 지갑을 어디에 뒀는지 물었으므로, 이에 대한 응답으로는 지갑을 둔 위치를 언급하는 ⑤ 'Thank you. I think I put it on the table.'이 가장 적절하다.

어휘 get home 집에 도착하다 realize 통 깨닫다 wallet 명 지갑

13 긴 대화의 응답 파악

정답 ①

W Did we take all of the camping gear out of the car, honey?	여 우리 캠핑 장비를 차에서 다 꺼냈어, 여보?
M Yes, I moved it all into the campsite.	남 응, 캠핑장 안으로 다 옮겼어.
W Great. I've set up the camping chairs, too.	여 좋아. 내가 캠핑 의자도 설치해 놓았어.
M Now, we can finally relax. It has been a long day.	남 이제 겨우 쉴 수 있겠네. 긴 하루였어.
W Yes, that ¹⁾traffic getting here was terrible.	여 응, 여기 오는 길에 차가 너무 막혔어.
M It was. **So let's just rest at the campground today.** We can start exploring tomorrow.	남 맞아. 그러니까 오늘은 그냥 캠핑장에서 쉬자. 내일부터 탐방을 시작해도 돼.
W That sounds good to me. **What should we make for dinner?**	여 그거 좋은 생각이야. 우리 저녁으로 무엇을 만들까?
M Well, we ²⁾have all the ingredients to make sandwiches.	남 음, 샌드위치를 만들 재료는 다 있어.
W **Let's cook the meat.** We can make sandwiches for lunch tomorrow.	여 고기를 굽자. 내일 점심으로 샌드위치를 만들어도 되니까.
M Okay. Then, we should start a fire.	남 좋아. 그럼, 불을 피워야겠네.
W I'll go ³⁾get some firewood. **Can you begin preparing the food in the meantime?**	여 장작을 좀 가져올게. 그사이에 음식 준비를 시작해줄 수 있어?
M Sure. I'll cut up the vegetables now.	남 물론이지. 지금부터 채소를 썰어 놓을게.

선택지 ① 물론이지. 지금부터 채소를 썰어 놓을게.
② 당연하지. 불 옆에 와서 앉아.
③ 좋은 생각이야. 내일 수영하러 가자.
④ 아직. 나는 여전히 캠핑장에서 멀리 떨어져 있어.
⑤ 됐어. 내 것에는 햄과 토마토를 올려 줘.

캠핑장에서 저녁을 준비하는 상황이다. 여자가 장작을 가져오는 사이에 음식 준비를 시작해줄 수 있는지 물었으므로, 이에 대한 응답으로는 물론이라고 대답하는 ① 'Sure. I'll cut up the vegetables now.'가 가장 적절하다.

어휘 gear 명 장비 set up ~을 설치하다 campground 명 캠핑장 explore 통 탐방하다, 탐험하다 ingredient 명 재료 start a fire 불을 피우다 firewood 명 장작
in the meantime 그사이에, 그동안

14 긴 대화의 응답 파악

정답 ③

[Cell phone rings.]	*[휴대폰이 울린다.]*
W Hello. This is Linda Allen.	여 여보세요. Linda Allen입니다.
M Hi. I'm calling from Belmont Auto Repair.	남 안녕하세요. Belmont Auto Repair에서 전화드렸습니다.
W Oh, yes. Did you find out what's ¹⁾wrong with my car?	여 오, 네. 제 차에 무슨 문제가 있는지 찾아내셨나요?
M We did. There's a problem with the engine.	남 알아냈어요. 엔진에 문제가 있어요.
W Okay. **How long will it take to fix?**	여 알겠습니다. 수리하는 데 얼마나 걸리나요?
M **It could take up to two weeks.** We have to ²⁾order some special parts.	남 최대 2주까지 걸릴 수 있어요. 특수 부품을 주문해야 해서요.
W Two weeks? I can't go without my car for that long.	여 2주라고요? 전 그렇게 오래 차 없이 못 지내요.
M **We can give you a rental car in the meantime.** You'll get a large discount on it because of your situation.	남 저희가 그동안 렌터카를 드릴 수 있어요. 고객님 상황 때문에 크게 할인받으실 거예요.
W That's fine, then. Is there anything that ³⁾I need for the rental?	여 그럼 괜찮아요. 제가 대여할 때 필요한 것이 있나요?
M You just need to bring your license to the shop when you come. You'll have to sign some paperwork, too.	남 오실 때 가게에 면허증만 가져오시면 됩니다. 서류에도 서명하셔야 해요.
W Great. **When can I pick up the car?**	여 좋아요. 언제 차를 가지러 가면 되나요?
M **We are open until 7 p.m. today, so** ⁴⁾any time before then.	남 오늘 오후 7시까지 영업하니, 그 전에 아무 때나 됩니다.
W Got it. I'll come by around 5 p.m.	여 알겠습니다. 오후 5시쯤에 들를게요.

자동차 수리가 늦어져서 대신 렌터카를 빌려야 하는 상황이다. 여자가 언제 차를 가지러 가면 되는지 묻자 남자가 오늘 오후 7시까지 영업하니 그 전에 아무 때나 된다고 답했으므로, 이에 대한 응답으로는 방문 시각을 말해주는 ③ 'Got it. I'll come by around 5 p.m.'이 가장 적절하다.

어휘 find out ~을 찾아내다 wrong 혱 문제가 있는, 잘못된 fix 동 수리하다 up tp 최대 ~까지 go without ~ 없이 지내다 situation 몡 상황 license 몡 면허증
paperwork 몡 서류; 서류 작업

15 상황에 적절한 말 파악
정답 ⑤

M Rose is a high school student. Recently, she took ¹⁾an important test in her math class. Today, she found out that she received a poor grade, so she feels very disappointed. Rose knows that her friend Daniel got an A on the test. So she asks him what she should do ²⁾to get better grades. He thinks that concentrating is the most important factor when studying. He knows that when Rose studies, she cannot concentrate for more than 10 minutes at a time. In his opinion, this ³⁾isn't long enough. **So Daniel wants to tell Rose that she should try to ⁴⁾train herself to focus for more than an hour.** In this situation, what would Daniel most likely say to Rose?

남 Rose는 고등학생입니다. 최근 그녀는 수학 시간에 중요한 시험을 치렀습니다. 오늘, 그녀는 형편없는 점수를 받았다는 것을 알게 되어서, 매우 실망했습니다. Rose는 그녀의 친구 Daniel이 시험에서 A를 받았다는 것을 알고 있습니다. 그래서, 그에게 더 나은 성적을 얻기 위해 무엇을 해야 하는지 물어봅니다. 그는 공부할 때 집중력이 가장 중요한 요소라고 생각합.니다. 그는 Rose가 공부할 때, 한 번에 10분 이상 집중할 수 없다는 것을 알고 있습니다. 그의 생각으로는, 이것은 충분히 길지 않습니다. 그래서, Daniel은 Rose에게 한 시간 이상 집중할 수 있도록 훈련해야 한다고 말하고 싶습니다. 이러한 상황에서, Daniel이 Rose에게 가장 할 것 같은 말은 무엇입니까?

선택지 ① 수학 선생님 말에 더 주의를 기울여야 해.

② 너 자신을 위한 학습 일정을 짜는 것은 중요해.

③ 성적에 대해 그렇게 많이 걱정하는 것은 도움이 되지 않는 것 같아.

④ 10분 안에 수학 문제를 다시 검토할 수 있어.

⑤ 한 시간 이상 집중하는 법을 배워야 해.

Rose가 공부할 때 10분 이상 집중할 수 없다는 것을 알고, Daniel은 한 시간 이상 집중할 수 있도록 훈련해야 한다고 말하려 한다. 따라서, Daniel이 할 말로 ⑤ 'You need to learn how to concentrate for more than an hour.'가 가장 적절하다.

어휘 receive 동 받다 poor 혱 형편없는; 가난한 concentrate 동 집중하다 factor 몡 요소 in one's opinion ~의 생각으로는 train 동 훈련하다 몡 기차
pay attention to ~에 주의를 기울이다

16-17 세트 문항
정답 16 ③ 17 ④

W Hello, students. In the last class, we learned about different ways that animals catch their prey. **Today, we'll go over some of the ways that animals ¹⁾protect themselves from danger.** First, let's talk about **bees**. These insects are usually harmless. But if they feel that their hive is threatened, they will use their stinger ²⁾to attack the threat. Second, I should mention **skunks**, which have a powerful weapon. This gentle creature has a bad-smelling spray that it will use if danger is close by. Third, **squid** ³⁾squirt dark ink into the water when predators are near. The ink creates a dark cloud that confuses the predator and allows the squid to quickly escape. Lastly, there are **turtles**. When a turtle ⁴⁾senses danger, it simply hides inside its shell until the threat is gone. Now, let's watch a video that shows these animals and others in action.

여 안녕하세요, 학생 여러분. 지난 수업에서, 우리는 동물들이 먹이를 잡는 다양한 방법에 대해 배웠습니다. 오늘은, 동물들이 위험으로부터 스스로를 보호하는 몇 가지 방법을 살펴보겠습니다. 먼저, 벌에 대해 이야기해 보겠습니다. 이 곤충들은 보통 해롭지 않습니다. 하지만 만약 벌집이 위협을 받는다고 느낀다면, 그들은 위협적인 존재를 공격하기 위해 침을 사용할 것입니다. 두 번째로, 강력한 무기를 가진 스컹크를 언급하겠습니다. 이 온화한 생명체는 위험이 가까이에 있을 때 사용할 악취가 나는 분무액이 있습니다. 세 번째로, 오징어는 포식자들이 가까이에 있을 때 물속으로 먹물을 내뿜습니다. 먹물은 먹구름을 만들어 포식자를 혼란스럽게 하고 오징어가 빠르게 탈출할 수 있게 합니다. 마지막으로 거북이들이 있습니다. 거북이가 위험을 감지하면, 그 위협적인 존재가 사라질 때까지 단순히 껍질 안에 숨습니다. 이제, 이 동물들과 다른 동물들이 행동하는 것을 보여주는 영상을 보겠습니다.

선택지 16 ① 어떤 동물들은 반려동물로 길들여지지 않는 이유

② 몇몇 동물들이 서로 돕는 방법

③ 동물들이 위험으로부터 스스로를 보호하는 방법

④ 동물들이 먹이를 잡는 다양한 방법

⑤ 야생에서 피해야 할 위험한 동물

17 ① 벌 ② 스컹크 ③ 오징어 ④ 뱀 ⑤ 거북이

16 동물들이 위험으로부터 스스로를 보호하는 몇 가지 방법을 살펴보고 있으므로 여자가 하는 말의 주제로 ③ 'how animals protect themselves from danger'가 가장 적절하다.

17 벌, 스컹크, 오징어, 거북이는 언급했지만 ④ 'snakes'는 언급하지 않았다.

어휘 prey 몡 먹이 go over ~을 살펴보다 protect 동 보호하다 danger 몡 위험 harmless 혱 해롭지 않은 hive 몡 벌집 stinger 몡 침 threat 몡 위협적인 존재, 위험
gentle 혱 온화한; 부드러운 creature 몡 생명체; 창조물 spray 몡 분무액 squirt 동 내뿜다 predator 몡 포식자 escape 동 탈출하다 sense 동 감지하다 몡 감각 shell 몡 껍질
tame 동 길들이다

1	④	2	③	3	②	4	⑤	5	②	6	②	7	⑤	8	①	9	④	10	③
11	④	12	①	13	⑤	14	①	15	①	16	③	17	③						

• 각 문제의 정답 근거는 굵은 글씨로, Dictation 정답은 밑줄로 표시되어 있습니다.

---

1 목적 파악

정답 ④

W Hello, WPR radio station listeners! Are you tired of planning meals every week? Are you too busy to 1)shop for groceries? **Then, sign up for Green Meal Kits. With this service, you'll get all the** 2)ingredients and recipes **to make delicious meals every day.** With Green Meal Kits, you don't need any special 3)cooking skills or kitchen tools. Our service offers a variety of dishes, and you can make them all in under 40 minutes. Get anywhere from two to seven kits delivered right to your door so you can avoid the 4)hassle of organizing meals. Just visit our website at www.greenmeals.com for more information today!

여 안녕하십니까, WPR 라디오 방송국 청취자 여러분! 매주 식단을 짜는 데 싫증이 나셨습니까? 너무 바빠서 식료품을 사러 갈 수 없으십니까? 그렇다면 Green Meal Kits를 신청하십시오. 이 서비스로 맛있는 음식을 만들기 위한 모든 재료와 요리법을 매일 얻으실 수 있습니다. Green Meal Kits가 있다면, 어떤 특별한 요리 기술이나 주방 도구도 필요하지 않습니다. 저희 서비스는 다양한 요리를 제공하고 있으며, 모두 40분 이내에 만들 수 있습니다. 식사 준비의 번거로움을 피하실 수 있도록 2개에서 7개의 키트를 어디서든 집 앞까지 배달해 드립니다. 더 많은 정보를 원하시면 그냥 오늘 바로 저희 웹사이트 www.greenmeals.com을 방문하십시오!

여자가 Green Meal Kits를 신청하라고 하면서, 해당 서비스로 음식 재료와 요리법을 매일 배달시킬 수 있다고 설명하고 있다. 따라서, 여자가 하는 말의 목적으로 ④ '밀키트 배달 서비스를 홍보하려고'가 가장 적절하다.

어휘 be tired of ~에 싫증이 나다 sign up for ~을 신청하다 ingredient 명 재료 a variety of 다양한 hassle 명 번거로움

---

2 의견 파악

정답 ③

M Hey, Christine. Are you going to Justin's wedding?
W Yes. But I don't have anything to wear. I need to go shopping for a dress.
M Oh, where will you go?
W I'm thinking about going to the mall. I'll definitely find something there.
M Yeah, **but I think it would be better to go to** 1)a secondhand shop **instead.**
W Why do you think so?
M I read that buying used clothes helps the environment. Making new clothes 2)uses up lots of water and creates pollution.
W I had no idea.
M People throw away clothes all the time. Wearing secondhand clothing helps reduce that waste.
W That makes sense. I guess it also saves money.
M Exactly. And you can find a 3)unique product.
W You're right. I'll visit a secondhand shop this week.

남 안녕, Christine. 너 Justin의 결혼식에 갈 거니?
여 응. 그런데 입을 옷이 없어. 원피스 사러 가야 해.
남 아, 어디로 갈 거야?
여 쇼핑몰에 갈까 생각 중이야. 거기서 뭔가 꼭 찾을 수 있을 거야.
남 그래, 하지만 대신 중고품 가게에 가는 게 좋을 것 같아.
여 왜 그렇게 생각해?
남 헌 옷을 사는 게 환경에 도움이 된대. 새 옷을 만드는 데는 많은 물이 쓰이고 오염을 일으켜.
여 전혀 몰랐어.
남 사람들은 항상 옷을 버리잖아. 중고 옷을 입는 건 그런 낭비를 줄이는 데도 도움이 돼.
여 일리 있는 말이야. 돈도 절약되는 것 같고.
남 정확해. 그리고 독특한 제품을 찾을 수도 있어.
여 네 말이 맞아. 이번 주에 중고품 가게를 방문할게.

원피스를 사러 쇼핑몰에 가려는 여자에게 남자가 중고품 가게에 가는 게 좋겠다고 했다. 따라서, 남자의 의견으로 ③ '중고품 가게에서 쇼핑하는 편이 좋다.'가 가장 적절하다.

어휘 secondhand 형 중고품의, 헌 pollution 명 오염 throw away ~을 버리다 reduce 통 줄이다

---

3 관계 파악

정답 ②

W Hi, Mr. Walker. How are you today?
M Not great. **I'm experiencing some** 1)pain in my jaw.
W All right. Let's see. [Pause] **Well, it looks like one of your back teeth is causing the pain.**
M What can you do to treat it?
W I'm afraid the tooth needs to be pulled.
M Oh, no... What's that process like?
W Well, I will perform surgery to remove it. And a few months later, I'll put a replacement in.
M I see. Does the surgery take a long time?
W No. The 2)procedure is quite fast, but you'll need a few days to recover afterward.

여 안녕하세요, Walker 씨. 오늘은 어떠세요?
남 좋진 않아요. 턱에 통증이 좀 있어요.
여 알겠습니다. 어디 볼게요. [잠시 멈춤] 음, 뒤쪽에 있는 치아 하나가 통증을 일으키고 있는 것 같군요.
남 어떻게 치료할 수 있죠?
여 유감스럽게도 그 치아를 뽑아야 할 것 같네요.
남 오, 이런... 그 과정은 어떤 건가요?
여 음, 그걸 제거하는 수술을 할 거예요. 그리고 몇 달 후에, 대체 치아를 삽입할 거예요.
남 그렇군요. 수술 시간이 오래 걸리나요?
여 아니요. 수술 과정은 꽤 빠른데, 그 후에 회복되려면 며칠이 걸릴 거예요.

M	**This is the busy season for my restaurant, so I can't take time off until next month.** Is that okay?	남	지금은 제 식당이 바쁜 철이라서, 다음 달은 되어야 휴가를 낼 수 있어요. 괜찮을까요?
W	That should be fine. Let's ³⁾schedule an appointment, then. I'll give you some pain medicine for now.	여	괜찮을 거예요. 그러면 예약 날짜를 잡죠. 일단은 진통제를 좀 드릴게요.
M	Okay. Thanks for your help.	남	알겠습니다. 도와주셔서 고맙습니다.

두 사람이 남자의 턱 통증 및 치료 과정에 관해 이야기하고 있다. 여자는 남자의 치아에 문제가 있다고 하면서 수술 과정을 설명하고 있고, 남자는 지금은 본인의 식당이 바쁜 철이라서 다음 달에나 수술받을 수 있다고 하는 것으로 보아 두 사람의 관계로 ② '치과 의사 — 식당 주인'이 가장 적절하다.

어휘 jaw 뎽 턱 pull 통 뽑다; 당기다 process 뎽 과정 perform surgery 수술을 하다 procedure 뎽 과정; 절차 not A until B B는 되어야 A하다 take time off 휴가를 내다
pain medicine 진통제 for now 일단은, 당분간은

---

4 그림 내용 불일치 파악   정답 ⑤

M	Hi, Jenny. Are you finished setting up your classroom?	남	안녕, Jenny. 너 교실 배치는 끝냈니?
W	Yes, I'm all done. Do you want to see a photo of it?	여	응, 다 했어. 교실 사진 볼래?
M	Of course.	남	물론이지.
W	Here it is. That's my desk at the front of the room.	여	여기 있어. 교실 앞에 저게 내 책상이야.
M	Oh, everything looks great. I love that ¹⁾globe beside your computer.	남	오, 모든 게 좋아 보여. 네 컴퓨터 옆에 있는 지구본이 너무 좋다.
W	Thanks. I thought it would be useful for when we learn about other countries.	여	고마워. 그건 다른 나라들에 대해 배울 때 유용할 것 같았어.
M	And what are those ²⁾two striped boxes on the table for?	남	탁자 위에 있는 줄무늬 상자 두 개는 뭘 위한 거야?
W	The students will put their homework there.	여	학생들이 숙제를 거기에 둘 거야.
M	Your chalkboard behind the table is also nice and big.	남	탁자 뒤에 있는 칠판도 크고 괜찮네.
W	Yes. I wanted a large one for teaching.	여	응. 가르치려면 큰 게 좋았어.
M	**And what is that ³⁾speaker standing by the board for?**	남	그리고 칠판 옆에 세워진 스피커는 뭐에 쓸 거야?
W	Sometimes we watch videos in class, so I thought it would be good to have a speaker for that.	여	가끔 수업 시간에 동영상을 보니까, 그러려면 스피커가 있으면 좋을 것 같았어.
M	Yeah, that makes sense.	남	그러게, 맞는 말이야.

대화에서 남자가 칠판 옆에 스피커가 세워져 있다고 말했는데, ⑤에는 스피커가 벽에 달린 형태로 그려져 있다.

어휘 globe 뎽 지구본; 지구 chalkboard 뎽 칠판

---

5 할 일 파악   정답 ②

M	Ashley, I can't believe the fall festival is this week.	남	Ashley, 가을 축제가 이번 주라니 믿을 수가 없어.
W	Me neither. I think our photo booth will be popular, but we should go over our preparations.	여	나도 그래. 우리 포토 부스가 인기 좋을 것 같긴 한데, 준비한 것들을 점검해봐야겠어.
M	All right. I'm buying some paper tomorrow so we can decorate it. You bought some paint yesterday, right?	남	좋아. 내가 내일 종이를 사면 우린 그걸 꾸미면 돼. 넌 어제 물감을 좀 샀지, 그렇지?
W	Yes. I also ¹⁾collected different hats and sunglasses to put in the booth.	여	응. 부스에 둘 여러 가지 모자와 선글라스도 모아뒀어.
M	And we already made the backgrounds for the booth.	남	그리고 부스 배경은 이미 만들었지.
W	Yeah, they look really good. What about cameras?	여	그래, 정말 좋아 보여. 카메라는?
M	I think I'll rent an extra one. I'm ²⁾worried about technical issues.	남	하나 더 빌릴까 싶어. 기술적인 문제가 걱정돼.
W	That's a good idea.	여	좋은 생각이야.
M	Now, we just need T-shirts for our uniform. Did you like the design I sent you?	남	이제 우리 유니폼으로 입을 티셔츠만 있으면 돼. 내가 보내줬던 디자인은 마음에 들었니?
W	Yeah. **Those T-shirts should be perfect.**	여	그래. 그 티셔츠면 완벽할 거야.
M	**Then, let's order them.**	남	그러면 주문하자.
W	**Let me ³⁾take care of it.** You're so busy these days.	여	그건 내가 처리할게. 넌 요즘 너무 바쁘잖아.

가을 축제에서 열 포토 부스에 관해 이야기하고 있다. 남자가 유니폼으로 입을 티셔츠를 주문하자고 제안하자, 여자가 본인이 처리하겠다고 했으므로 여자가 할 일로 ② '티셔츠 주문하기'가 가장 적절하다.

어휘 go over ~을 점검하다 background 뎽 배경 technical 휑 기술적인

6 금액 정보 파악

정답 ②

M	Good morning. What can I help you with?
W	**I need some new running shoes.**
M	Well, this is our most popular pair right now.
W	Oh, those look nice. How much are they?
M	They're usually $120, **but they're** ¹⁾<u>on sale right now</u> for $100.
W	**Great.** Do you have a size 8?
M	We do have your size. **And would you like some new socks as well?**
W	Yeah. I do need some new ones.
M	I recommend these. **They're $5, but they are high quality.**
W	Okay. I'll ²⁾<u>take two pairs</u> of those, then.
M	So you would like the shoes and two pairs of socks. Is that right?
W	It is. **I also** ³⁾<u>have this coupon</u> for a 10% discount. Can I use it?
M	**Yes, you can.** And do you need a shopping bag?
W	No, thank you. Here's my card.

남	좋은 아침입니다. 무엇을 도와 드릴까요?
여	새 운동화가 필요해요.
남	음, 이게 지금 가장 인기 있는 거예요.
여	오, 그거 멋져 보여요. 얼마예요?
남	보통 120달러인데, 지금은 할인해서 100달러에 팔고 있어요.
여	좋아요. 8사이즈 있나요?
남	물론 있죠. 그리고 새 양말도 좀 사시겠어요?
여	네. 정말로 새것이 필요하긴 해요.
남	이것들을 추천합니다. 5달러이지만 질이 좋아요.
여	알겠어요. 그러면 두 켤레 살게요.
남	그러니까, 그 신발이랑 양말 두 켤레를 원하시는 거군요. 맞나요?
여	맞아요. 그리고 제게 10% 할인 쿠폰이 있는데요. 써도 돼요?
남	네, 쓰실 수 있어요. 그리고 쇼핑백은 필요하세요?
여	아뇨, 괜찮습니다. 여기 제 카드요.

여자가 할인 중인 운동화 한 켤레($100)와 양말 두 켤레($5×2=$10)를 구매했고, 10% 할인($110×0.9=$99)을 받았으므로 정답은 ② '$99'이다.

어휘 on sale 할인하여 as well ~도, 또한 recommend 통 추천하다 quality 명 질, 품질

7 이유 파악

정답 ⑤

W	Hey, Ron. How are you?
M	I just booked a trip for the summer, so I'm happy. It ¹⁾<u>took me a long time</u> to decide where to go.
W	Where are you going?
M	I'm going to Vietnam.
W	I've always wanted to go there.
M	Are you traveling anywhere this summer?
W	No. I can't. I'll stay here.
M	Is it because you want to ²⁾<u>save money</u>? I know you want to buy a new cell phone.
W	I actually bought one already.
M	Oh, then is it because you want to spend time with your family at home?
W	That's not it, either. **I'm** ³⁾<u>volunteering at the national park</u>.
M	Oh, that's really cool. I bet that will be fun.
W	I think I'll be busy most of the time, but I'm looking forward to being in the forest.

여	안녕, Ron. 잘 지내지?
남	방금 여름에 갈 여행을 예약해서, 행복해. 어디로 갈지 결정하는 데 오랜 시간이 걸렸어.
여	어디로 가니?
남	베트남에 갈 거야.
여	난 항상 거기 가고 싶었는데.
남	넌 이번 여름에 어디 여행 갈 거니?
여	아니. 못 가. 나는 여기 남아 있을 거야.
남	돈을 아끼고 싶어서 그런 거야? 내가 알기로 너 새 휴대폰을 사고 싶어 하잖아.
여	사실 이미 하나 샀어.
남	아, 그러면 집에서 가족과 시간을 보내고 싶어서 그런 거니?
여	그것도 아니야. 나는 국립공원에서 자원봉사를 할 거야.
남	오, 정말 멋진걸. 분명 재미있을 거야.
여	대부분의 시간은 바쁠 것 같긴 한데, 숲속에 있을 게 기대돼.

여자가 이번 여름에 여행을 못 간다고 하면서 국립공원에서 자원봉사를 하느라 바쁠 것 같다고 말했으므로, 여자가 여행을 갈 수 없는 이유는 ⑤ '국립공원에서 봉사활동을 해서'이다.

어휘 stay 통 남아 있다, 머물다 volunteer 통 자원봉사 하다 forest 명 숲

8 언급 유무 파악

정답 ①

M	Honey, are you busy next weekend?
W	No. Why do you ask?
M	I'd really like to go to the Jamestown Whale Festival.
W	What is that?
M	It's an event that ¹⁾<u>celebrates the return</u> of gray whales. It will include **whale watching, a parade, and musical performances**.
W	That sounds fun. Does the festival take place all weekend?
M	This advertisement says that it will ²⁾<u>go from 11 a.m. to 5 p.m.</u> on both Saturday and Sunday.
W	Do we have to buy tickets for it?
M	Yes, but they're only **$10**.
W	All right. Let's buy tickets now in that case.
M	Sure. It says to purchase them online. And I guess we'll have to rent a car for the festival. The advertisement recommends **driving**, since there's ³⁾<u>no nearby public transportation</u>.
W	That's fine. I can't wait to go!

남	여보, 다음 주말에 바빠?
여	아니. 왜 물어보는데?
남	난 Jamestown Whale Festival에 정말 가고 싶어.
여	그게 뭐야?
남	회색 고래의 귀환을 축하하는 행사야. 고래 관찰, 퍼레이드, 그리고 음악 공연이 포함돼 있어.
여	재미있을 것 같아. 축제가 주말 내내 열려?
남	광고에 토요일과 일요일 둘 다 오전 11시부터 오후 5시까지 진행될 거라고 쓰여 있어.
여	티켓을 사야 해?
남	응, 하지만 겨우 10달러야.
여	알겠어. 그렇다면 지금 티켓을 사자.
남	좋아. 온라인으로 구매하래. 그리고 축제에 가려면 차를 빌려야 할 것 같아. 광고에서 근처에 대중교통이 없으니까 운전하는 걸 추천하고 있어.
여	괜찮아. 빨리 가고 싶다!

프로그램(고래 관찰, 퍼레이드, 음악 공연), 운영 시간(오전 11시부터 오후 5시까지), 티켓 가격(10달러), 추천 교통편(개인 차량 운전)에 대해 언급했고, ① '장소'는 언급하지 않았다.

어휘 advertisement 몡 광고 rent 통 빌리다 public transportation 대중교통 can't wait to 빨리 ~하고 싶다

---

9 내용 불일치 파악

정답 ④

W Hello, viewers! Have you ever wanted to be a guest on *The Geography Quiz*? Well, this is your ¹⁾chance to appear on the hit TV show where players answer questions about places around the world. From now until January 15th, we ²⁾are accepting applications on our website for the new season. We will contact everyone who is selected to participate by the 31st. Your application should include your current contact information and a video introducing yourself. ³⁾To apply, you must not have appeared on the show before. Filming will begin in February. It will ⁴⁾take place at our studio downtown every Tuesday night at 7 p.m. We hope to see you there!

여 안녕하십니까, 시청자 여러분! <The Geography Quiz>에 게스트로 나오고 싶으신 적 있으십니까? 자, 이것은 참가자들이 전 세계의 장소에 관한 질문에 대답하는 인기 있는 TV쇼에 출연할 기회입니다. 지금부터 1월 15일까지, 저희 웹사이트에서 새 시즌 지원서를 받을 예정입니다. 31일까지 참가자로 선정된 모든 분께 연락드리겠습니다. 지원서에는 현재 연락처 정보와 자신을 소개하는 동영상이 포함되어야 합니다. 지원하시려면, 이전에 저희 쇼에 출연하신 적이 없어야 합니다. 촬영은 2월에 시작됩니다. 매주 화요일 저녁 7시에 시내 스튜디오에서 진행될 것입니다. 그곳에서 뵙기를 바랍니다!

퀴즈쇼에 출연할 참가자 모집 안내 방송이다. 여자가 지원하려면 이전에 쇼에 출연한 적이 없어야 한다고 했으므로 ④ '지원자들은 쇼에 참가한 적이 있어도 된다.'는 내용과 일치하지 않는다.

어휘 appear 통 출연하다; ~인 것 같다 application 몡 지원서; 지원 select 통 선정하다 current 혱 현재의

---

10 도표 정보 파악

정답 ③

M Tory, what are you shopping for online?

W I'm looking at options for a new grocery cart. Do you want to help me choose one?

M Okay. Let's see. *[Pause]* They all seem nice. But ¹⁾what kind of material do you want it to be made of?

W I need something durable. **I don't think fabric is strong enough.** The other materials are okay, though.

M So you have four options left. What about price?

W **My budget is $100. I ²⁾can't afford anything over that.**

M All right. Then, you need to consider how many wheels it has. **I think you should get one ³⁾with four wheels.** It'll be much easier to move around.

W You're right. That'll be better.

M So the only thing now is color.

W **The black one looks really nice.**

M I agree.

W Okay. I'll go with this one, then. Thanks!

남 Tory, 온라인으로 뭘 사려고 하는 거야?

여 새 쇼핑 카트를 사려고 선택 사항들을 보는 중이야. 내가 고르는 것 좀 도와줄래?

남 알았어. 어디 봐. [잠시 멈춤] 다 좋아 보이네. 그런데 넌 어떤 소재로 그게 만들어진 거면 좋겠어?

여 내구성 있는 게 필요해. 천은 충분히 튼튼하지 않은 것 같아. 그래도 다른 소재들은 괜찮아.

남 이제 네 가지 선택지가 남았어. 가격은 어때?

여 내 예산은 100달러야. 그걸 넘는 건 어떤 것도 살 여유가 없어.

남 좋아. 그러면 바퀴가 몇 개 있는지 고려해야 해. 내 생각엔 바퀴가 네 개 달린 걸 사야 해. 돌아다니기 훨씬 편할 거야.

여 네 말이 맞아. 그게 더 낫겠어.

남 자, 이제 색깔뿐이야.

여 검은색이 정말 멋져 보여.

남 동의해.

여 좋아. 그러면 이걸로 할게. 고마워!

여자는 천 소재가 아니면서, 100달러를 넘지 않고, 바퀴가 4개 달린 것 중에서, 검은색인 쇼핑 카트를 골랐다.

어휘 durable 혱 내구성 있는 afford 통 살 여유가 있다 wheel 몡 바퀴

---

11 짧은 대화의 응답 파악

정답 ④

W Honey, do you want to see a movie this afternoon? **The new action film you've been ¹⁾waiting for is out.**

M Sure, but I have to ²⁾go mail this package first. **How about coming along with me to the post office?**

W Okay. **How are we going to get to the theater?**

M We can catch a bus in front of the post office.

여 여보, 오늘 오후에 영화 볼래? 당신이 기다려왔던 신작 액션 영화가 나왔어.

남 물론이지, 하지만 우선 이 소포를 부치러 가야 해. 나랑 같이 우체국 가는 게 어때?

여 알았어. 극장에는 어떻게 갈 거야?

남 우체국 앞에서 버스를 타면 돼.

선택지 ① 겨우 10분 정도 걸릴 거야.

② 오후 6시나 7시 중에 하나로 보면 돼.

③ 극장보다는 공원에 가는 게 낫겠어.

④ 우체국 앞에서 버스를 타면 돼.

⑤ 캐나다에 있는 친구에게 간식을 좀 보낼 거야.

남자가 영화를 보러 가기 전에 우선 우체국에 같이 가자고 제안하자 여자가 극장에는 어떻게 갈 것인지 물었으므로, 이에 대한 응답으로는 극장까지의 교통편을 말하는 ④ 'We can catch a bus in front of the post office.'가 가장 적절하다.

어휘 package 몡 소포 come along with ~와 같이 가다 either A or B A나 B 중에 하나 would rather A than B B보다 A가 낫다

12 짧은 대화의 응답 파악

정답 ①

M What can I do for you today, Daisy? Your hair has ¹⁾grown a lot.	남 오늘은 어떻게 해줄까요, Daisy? 머리가 많이 자랐네요.
W I'd like to get it cut, **but my hair also feels a little dry lately.** Is there anything you can do to make it softer?	여 머리를 자르고 싶은데, 요즘 모발이 약간 건조한 것 같기도 해요. 더 부드럽게 할 수 있는 방법이 있을까요?
M Of course. **There is a good treatment for that, though** ²⁾it's quite expensive.	남 물론이죠. 꽤 비싸긴 하지만, 좋은 치료법이 있어요.
W It'll be worth it if it helps.	여 도움이 된다면 그만한 가치가 있겠죠.

선택지 ① 도움이 된다면 그만한 가치가 있겠죠.
② 새로 자른 머리 모양이 정말 멋져 보여요.
③ 모발이 왜 건조해지는지 모르겠어요.
④ 치료받으려면 병원에 가야겠어요.
⑤ 여기서 머리를 좀 더 짧게 잘라 줄래요?

미용실에서 여자가 머리가 건조하다면서 해결 방법을 묻자 남자가 비싸지만 좋은 치료법이 있다고 했으므로, 이에 대한 응답으로는 도움이 된다면 치료받을 만하겠다는 ① 'It'll be worth it if it helps.'가 가장 적절하다.

어휘 treatment 圀 치료법   haircut 圀 자른 머리 모양; 이발   worth 圀 ~할 가치가 있는

13 긴 대화의 응답 파악

정답 ⑤

[Cell phone rings.]	[휴대폰이 울린다.]
M Hello. This is Trevor Stanton.	남 여보세요. Trevor Stanton입니다.
W Hi. This is Cecilia Johnson from Seaside Gallery.	여 안녕하세요. 씨사이드 미술관의 Cecilia Johnson입니다.
M Oh, is this about the art competition?	남 아, 미술 대회에 관한 용건이신가요?
W Yes. **Our judges have** ¹⁾selected your painting as one of the winners.	여 네. 심사위원들이 당신의 그림을 수상작 중 하나로 선정했어요.
M Wow, that's amazing! I can't believe it.	남 와, 정말 놀랍군요! 믿을 수가 없어요.
W We'd like to invite you to the award ceremony for the competition so we can ²⁾honor your work. Would you be able to attend next Friday?	여 당신의 작품을 기릴 수 있도록 대회 시상식에 초대하고 싶은데요. 다음 주 금요일에 참석하실 수 있나요?
M I think so. What time will it start?	남 그럴 것 같아요. 몇 시에 시작하나요?
W It will go from 6 p.m. to 9 p.m.	여 오후 6시부터 9시까지 진행될 거예요.
M That's perfect. I'll definitely be there.	남 완벽해요. 꼭 갈게요.
W Excellent. Food will be served at the event, and we will display your art, too.	여 좋아요. 음식은 행사장에서 제공될 예정이고, 저희가 당신 작품을 전시하기도 할 거예요.
M Great. Is it okay if I bring my family?	남 좋아요. 제가 가족들을 데려가도 괜찮을까요?
W You can bring as many guests as you'd like. **And we'd also like you to** ³⁾make an acceptance speech, **if you're willing.**	여 원하는 만큼 데려오셔도 돼요. 그리고 당신이 할 의향이 있으시다면, 수상 소감 연설 또한 해주시면 좋겠어요.
M It would be my honor to do that.	남 그렇게 한다면 제겐 영광스러운 일이죠.

선택지 ① 당신의 제출작에 대한 더 많은 정보가 필요해요.
② 제 일정을 확인하고 나중에 다시 연락드릴게요.
③ 아내와 아이들을 데리고 갈게요.
④ 업적을 이루신 걸 축하드려요!
⑤ 그렇게 한다면 제겐 영광스러운 일이죠.

미술관에서 대회 수상자에게 수상 소식을 알리는 상황이다. 여자가 남자에게 수상 소감 연설을 해주면 좋겠다고 부탁했으므로, 이에 대한 응답으로는 그러면 영광이라고 대답하는 ⑤ 'It would be my honor to do that.'이 가장 적절하다.

어휘 award ceremony 시상식   honor 圐 기리다 圀 영광   display 圐 전시하다   acceptance speech 수상 소감 연설   willing 圀 할 의향이 있는, 기꺼이 하는   submission 圀 제출작; 제출   get back to ~에게 나중에 다시 연락하다   achievement 圀 업적, 성취

14 긴 대화의 응답 파악

정답 ①

M Wow, the weather is beautiful today, honey.	남 와, 오늘 날씨가 정말 좋아, 여보.
W Yes, it is. **I'm so glad we came to the river.**	여 응, 그렇네. 강에 오길 정말 잘했어.
M It was a good idea to ¹⁾bring a blanket, too.	남 담요를 가져온 것도 좋은 생각이었어.
W Thanks. I thought we would enjoy sitting and reading for a while.	여 고마워. 난 우리가 한동안 앉아서 독서를 즐길 거라고 생각했거든.
M For sure. **I'm starting to get a little hungry, though.**	남 물론이지. 그래도 조금 배가 고파지기 시작하네.
W Yeah, me too. Do you want to go eat somewhere?	여 맞아, 나도 그래. 어디 가서 밥 먹을래?
M I don't know. I don't really want to ²⁾leave this spot.	남 모르겠어. 진짜로 이 자리를 떠나고 싶지 않아.
W I could go pick something up. There's a pizza place close by.	여 내가 뭔가 사 올 수도 있어. 근처에 피자집이 있어.
M That's a good idea. But I don't really want pizza.	남 좋은 생각이야. 하지만 피자는 별로 먹고 싶지 않아.
W **What about that café over there?**	여 저기 있는 카페는 어때?
M That would be perfect. I'd love a latte ³⁾and a sandwich.	남 그러면 정말 좋겠어. 라테 한 잔과 샌드위치 하나를 먹고 싶어.
W All right. I'll be back soon.	여 좋아. 곧 돌아올게.

선택지 ① 좋아. 곧 돌아올게.
② 물론이지. 담요는 차 안에 있어.
③ 알았어. 피자가 곧 도착할 거야.
④ 동감이야. 여기 해가 드는 곳에 앉자.
⑤ 좋아. 난 오늘 책을 다 읽고 싶어.

강으로 놀러 와서 먹을거리를 정하는 상황이다. 여자가 뭔가 사 오겠다고 한 후 카페가 어떤지 묻자 남자가 라테와 샌드위치를 먹고 싶다고 했으므로, 이에 대한 응답으로는 곧 사 오겠다고 대답하는 ① 'All right. I'll be back soon.'이 가장 적절하다.

어휘 blanket 명 담요 For sure. 물론이지. spot 명 자리, 장소

15 상황에 적절한 말 파악   정답 ①

M Emily and David work in the marketing department of a company. At the moment, their department is working on a campaign to advertise the company's new electric car. Their task is to [1)]research the reasons that consumers like electric cars. Although they have found a large amount of useful data, David is worried that the report they're writing will be too hard for people to understand. [2)]No matter how many statistics it includes, the report won't be useful unless readers have a clear idea of what the numbers mean. **So David wants to tell Emily that they should [3)]add some charts to the report.** In this situation, what would David most likely say to Emily?

남 Emily와 David는 회사의 마케팅 부서에서 일합니다. 현재, 그들의 부서는 그 회사의 새로운 전기차를 광고하기 위한 캠페인을 진행하고 있습니다. 그들의 업무는 소비자들이 전기차를 좋아하는 이유를 연구하는 것입니다. 비록 그들이 많은 양의 유용한 데이터를 발견하긴 했지만, David는 그들이 작성 중인 보고서가 사람들이 이해하기에 너무 어려울까 봐 걱정하고 있습니다. 아무리 많은 통계 수치를 포함하고 있더라도, 읽는 사람이 숫자가 의미하는 바를 명확하게 이해하지 못하는 한 보고서는 유용하지 않을 것입니다. 그래서 David는 Emily에게 그들이 보고서에 도표를 추가해야 한다고 말하고 싶습니다. 이러한 상황에서, David가 Emily에게 가장 할 것 같은 말은 무엇입니까?

선택지 ① 보고서에 도표가 포함되어야 할 것 같아요.
② 이 부분을 더 쉽게 읽히도록 다시 써 줄래요?
③ 보고서를 작성하기 전에 조사를 좀 해야 해요.
④ TV 광고에 이런 세부 사항들을 추가해야 해요.
⑤ 대부분의 고객이 전기차를 선호하는 것 같아요.

Emily와 함께 전기차 관련 연구 업무를 하는 David가 보고서에 도표를 추가하자고 제안하려 한다. 따라서, David가 할 말로 ① 'I think the report needs to include charts.'가 가장 적절하다.

어휘 department 명 부서 at the moment 현재 statistics 명 통계 수치; 통계학 have a clear idea of ~을 명확하게 이해하다 chart 명 도표

16-17 세트 문항   정답 16 ③ 17 ③

W Hello, teachers. Technology has changed many areas of our lives, including education. **Today, let's look at how technology can be used in the classroom to improve learning.** First, **computers** can be used to change the way you [1)]teach your lessons. You can make presentations or show video clips to the students to engage them. Next, **tablets** can replace textbooks in the classroom. Tablets are lighter and more convenient to carry around. Plus, tablets make it [2)]possible to access different books and information online. We can also use **VR technology** in the classroom. It enables students to take [3)]virtual field trips and explore places they might not be able to visit in person. Finally, **3D printing** has a lot of potential. For instance, with 3D printing, biology students can easily make models of body parts and cells. This will improve their ability to [4)]visualize and understand complex ideas. I hope you've enjoyed hearing about ways to incorporate technology into your teaching. Now, let's look at specific examples of lessons that use these technologies.

여 안녕하십니까, 선생님 여러분. 기술은 교육을 포함하여 우리 삶의 많은 영역을 변화시켜 왔습니다. 오늘은, 학습을 향상시키기 위해 교실에서 기술이 어떻게 사용될 수 있는지 살펴보겠습니다. 첫째로, 컴퓨터는 여러분이 수업하는 방식을 바꾸는 데 사용될 수 있습니다. 여러분은 학생들을 참여시키기 위해 그들에게 프레젠테이션을 하거나 동영상을 보여줄 수 있습니다. 다음으로, 태블릿은 교실의 교과서를 대체할 수 있습니다. 태블릿은 더 가볍고 휴대하기 더 편리합니다. 또한, 태블릿은 온라인으로 다양한 책과 정보에 접근하는 것을 가능하게 해줍니다. 우리는 또한 교실에서 VR 기술을 사용할 수 있습니다. 그것은 학생들이 가상 현장 학습을 하고 그들이 직접 방문할 수 없을 수도 있는 장소들을 탐험할 수 있게 해줍니다. 마지막으로, 3D 프린팅은 많은 잠재력을 가지고 있습니다. 예를 들어, 생물학과 학생들은 3D 프린팅으로 신체 부위와 세포의 모형들을 쉽게 만들 수 있습니다. 이것은 복잡한 아이디어를 시각화하여 이해하는 능력을 향상시킬 것입니다. 저는 여러분들이 수업에 기술을 접목하는 방법에 대해 재미있게 들으셨기를 바랍니다. 이제, 이러한 기술을 사용하는 수업의 구체적인 사례를 살펴보겠습니다.

선택지 16 ① 기술이 학생들의 집중력에 끼치는 영향
② 교실에서 학생들을 참여시키는 문제
③ 교육을 개선하기 위한 다양한 기술의 활용
④ 교실에서 기술을 사용하는 것이 왜 그렇게 중요한지
⑤ 학교에서 기술에 대한 학생들의 접근을 제한하는 것의 장점
17 ① 컴퓨터 ② 태블릿 ③ 스마트폰 ④ VR 기술 ⑤ 3D 프린팅

16 학습을 향상시키기 위해 교실에서 기술이 어떻게 사용될 수 있는지 살펴보고 있으므로 여자가 하는 말의 주제로 ③ 'utilization of different technologies to improve education'이 가장 적절하다.
17 컴퓨터, 태블릿, VR 기술, 3D 프린팅은 언급했지만 ③ 'smartphones'는 언급하지 않았다.

어휘 education 명 교육 engage 통 참여시키다 replace 통 대체하다 access 통 접근하다 enable 통 가능하게 하다 virtual 형 가상의 explore 통 탐험하다 in person 직접
biology 명 생물학 cell 명 세포 visualize 통 시각화하다 complex 형 복잡한 incorporate A into B A를 B에 접목시키다 specific 형 구체적인 utilization 명 활용

1	①	2	②	3	③	4	⑤	5	④	6	②	7	②	8	③	9	②	10	②
11	③	12	①	13	⑤	14	③	15	④	16	⑤	17	④						

• 각 문제의 정답 근거는 굵은 글씨로, Dictation 정답은 밑줄로 표시되어 있습니다.

---

1   목적 파악

정답 ①

M Hello, listeners. Do you want to become stronger and healthier? Would you like to have fun while doing this? **Then, 1)you should check out Blue Hawaii Sports Center.** At Blue Hawaii, we offer a wide range of 2)sports activities for you to choose from. Our facilities include tennis and basketball courts, a swimming pool, and a yoga studio with beautiful views of the ocean. At our gym, you can work out on the latest exercise machines. We have 3)professional trainers to help you achieve your fitness goals. You can even sign up for a group fitness class. So what are you waiting for? Visit our website for more details.

남 안녕하세요, 청취자 여러분. 더 강하고 건강해지고 싶으신가요? 이렇게 하면서도 즐기고 싶으신가요? 그렇다면, Blue Hawaii Sports Center를 살펴보시죠. Blue Hawaii에서는, 여러분께서 선택하실 수 있는 다양한 스포츠 활동을 제공합니다. 저희 시설에는 테니스와 농구 코트, 수영장, 아름다운 바다의 경치를 볼 수 있는 요가 스튜디오가 있습니다. 헬스장에서는 최신 운동기구로 운동을 하실 수 있습니다. 여러분의 체력 단련 목표를 달성할 수 있도록 도와줄 전문 트레이너가 있습니다. 심지어 그룹 피트니스 수업에 등록하실 수도 있습니다. 그러니 뭘 더 기다리십니까? 더 자세한 내용을 원하시면 저희 웹 사이트에 방문해주세요.

남자가 Blue Hawaii Sports Center의 시설을 소개하면서 센터에 대한 관심을 유도하고 있다. 따라서, 남자가 하는 말의 목적으로 ① '스포츠 센터를 홍보하려고'가 가장 적절하다.

[어휘] **check out** ~을 살펴보다 **a wide range of** 다양한 **facility** 몡 시설 **work out** 운동하다 **latest** 혱 최신의 **achieve** 통 달성하다 **fitness** 몡 체력 단련, 피트니스 **goal** 몡 목표
sign up for ~에 등록하다

---

2   의견 파악

정답 ②

W Hey, David. Are you feeling better today?
M Not really. But I'll just eat soup and drink lots of water for a few days. The illness 1)should go away.
W You've been sick for a while. Maybe that's not enough.
M Well, it's just the flu. I'll be fine.
W I understand, **but I believe you should go to the doctor even if your symptoms 2)are not serious.**
M I don't really want to spend a lot of time at the doctor's office, though.
W But the doctor will 3)run some tests to find out exactly what's wrong with you.
M That's true. I could also get the right medicine, then.
W Definitely. That will help you get better more quickly. **It's always a good idea to see a doctor if you're sick.**
M You're right. I'll go today.

여 안녕, David. 오늘은 좀 나아졌니?
남 그렇지 않아. 하지만 며칠 동안은 그냥 수프를 먹고 물을 많이 마실 거야. 병이 사라지겠지.
여 너 한동안 아팠잖아. 아마 그걸로는 충분하지 않을 거야.
남 음, 그냥 독감인걸. 괜찮을 거야.
여 이해는 하지만, 증상이 심각하지 않더라도 병원에 가봐야 한다고 생각해.
남 그렇지만 진료실에서 많은 시간을 보내고 싶지는 않아.
여 하지만 의사 선생님이 정확히 무슨 문제가 있는지 알아내기 위해 몇 가지 검사를 하실 거야.
남 맞아. 그러면 적합한 약도 받을 수 있겠지.
여 물론이지. 그렇게 하는 게 더 빨리 회복하는 데 도움이 될 거야. 아프면 진찰을 받는 건 항상 좋은 방법이야.
남 네 말이 맞아. 오늘 갈게.

독감에 걸렸지만 증상이 경미하다는 이유로 병원에 가지 않으려는 남자에게 여자가 증상이 심각하지 않더라도 병원에 가봐야 한다면서 진찰을 받는 것이 좋다고 했다. 따라서, 여자의 의견으로 ② '증상이 경미하더라도 진료를 받는 것이 좋다.'가 가장 적절하다.

[어휘] **illness** 몡 병 **go away** 사라지다 **for a while** 한동안 **go to the doctor** 병원에 가다 **symptom** 몡 증상 **the doctor's office** 진료실 **run** 통 (테스트, 검사 등을) 하다; 달리다
find out ~을 알아내다 **Definitely.** 물론이지. **get better** 회복하다 **see a doctor** 진찰을 받다

3 관계 파악

정답 ③

W	What's wrong? I think the actors look great.	여	무슨 문제 있나요? 배우들 모습이 멋진 것 같은데요.
M	I don't know. I'm not happy with the clothes they have on. Their costumes ¹⁾seem all wrong.	남	모르겠어요. 그들이 입고 있는 옷이 마음에 들지 않아요. 그들의 의상이 모두 잘못된 것 같아요.
W	That was the clothing style back in the 1940s. I'm sure my research is correct.	여	1940년대의 옷 스타일인걸요. 제가 조사한 내용이 옳다고 확신해요.
M	You're right, **but they don't have the feel I want for this scene.**	남	당신 말이 맞긴 하지만, 제가 이 장면에서 원하는 느낌이 안 나요.
W	Well, ²⁾what kind of feel are you looking for?	여	음, 어떤 느낌을 원하세요?
M	This is supposed to be a sad scene. But the colors are too bright and cheerful.	남	이건 슬픈 장면이 되어야 해요. 하지만 색깔이 너무 밝고 경쾌하군요.
W	**So you want darker costumes to fit the mood. Are the designs okay?**	여	그럼 분위기에 맞는 어두운 의상을 원하시는군요. 디자인은 괜찮은가요?
M	The designs are good. It's only the colors that need to be changed.	남	디자인은 좋아요. 색상만 변경하면 됩니다.
W	**Okay, I'll ³⁾bring some different costumes for you to choose from.** I need at least a couple of hours.	여	네, 고르실 수 있도록 다른 의상들을 가져올게요. 적어도 두어 시간은 필요해요.
M	Take your time. **I want my movie to be perfect.**	남	천천히 하세요. 저는 제 영화가 완벽했으면 좋겠어요.

두 사람이 영화 촬영 중 의상에 대해 이야기하고 있다. 여자는 디자인 등에 대한 의견을 물어본 후 남자에게 다른 의상을 가져오겠다고 했고, 남자는 옷의 색상이 장면의 분위기와 맞지 않는다고 의견을 주면서 자신의 영화가 완벽했으면 좋겠다고 하는 것으로 보아 두 사람의 관계로 ③ '의상 담당자 — 영화감독'이 가장 적절하다.

어휘 I'm not happy with ~. ~가 마음에 들지 않아요. costume 뗑 의상 scene 뗑 장면 cheerful 톙 경쾌한 fit 동 맞다, 어울리다 mood 뗑 분위기 a couple of 둘의, 두 개의 Take your time. 천천히 하세요.

4 그림 내용 불일치 파악

정답 ⑤

W	I can't believe how quickly you've set up the new children's library, Brian.	여	당신이 얼마나 빨리 새 어린이 도서관을 준비했는지 믿을 수가 없어요, Brian.
M	I know. Does it look okay?	남	그러게요. 괜찮아 보이나요?
W	It looks amazing. But what's inside that big wooden box ¹⁾beside the bookshelf on the wall?	여	정말 멋져 보여요. 그런데 벽에 붙은 책장 옆 저 큰 나무 상자 안에는 무엇이 들어 있나요?
M	Oh, that's filled with some cushions and blankets for the kids when they're reading.	남	오, 아이들이 책을 읽을 때 쓸 쿠션과 담요로 가득 차 있어요.
W	Good idea. I also love ²⁾the striped carpet. It looks soft.	여	좋은 생각이네요. 저는 줄무늬 카펫도 너무 맘에 들어요. 부드러워 보여요.
M	Yes, I wanted this area to be as comfortable as possible for everyone.	남	네, 저는 이 공간이 모든 사람들에게 최대한 편안한 곳이 되기를 원했어요.
W	What's on that poster?	여	저 포스터에 그려진 건 뭔가요?
M	It's a large tree. Do you like it?	남	큰 나무예요. 마음에 드세요?
W	I do. I think it goes well with the other decorations.	여	그래요. 다른 장식들과 잘 어울리는 것 같아요.
M	We also set up a round table in that corner of the room. **And we put ³⁾five chairs around it.**	남	방의 저쪽 구석에 원형 테이블도 설치했어요. 그리고 그 주위에 의자 5개를 배치했죠.
W	It fits the space nicely. Then, the children can also write or do their homework.	여	공간에 딱 맞네요. 그러면 아이들은 뭔가를 쓰거나 숙제를 할 수도 있겠어요.
M	That's what I was thinking.	남	제가 생각했던 게 바로 그거예요.

대화에서 남자가 원형 테이블 주위에 의자 5개를 배치했다고 말했는데, ⑤에는 의자가 2개만 그려져 있다.

어휘 set up ~을 준비하다, 설치하다 wooden 톙 나무로 된, 목재의 bookshelf 뗑 책장 be filled with ~으로 가득 차 있다 blanket 뗑 담요 go well with ~과 잘 어울리다 decoration 뗑 장식

5 할 일 파악

정답 ④

M	Hi, Marisa. How's your project for art class going?	남	안녕, Marisa. 미술 수업 수행평가는 잘 되고 있니?
W	I haven't started yet, Ben. Actually, I wanted to ask you something related to that.	여	아직 시작 안 했어, Ben. 사실, 네게 그것과 관련된 걸 부탁하고 싶었어.
M	Really? What is it?	남	정말? 뭔데?
W	This semester I'm taking a sculpture class, **so I need to ¹⁾make a sculpture.**	여	이번 학기에 조각 수업을 들어서, 조각을 만들어야 해.
M	I don't know much about art. I'm not sure how I could help you out.	남	난 예술에 대해 잘 몰라. 내가 어떻게 도와줄 수 있을지 잘 모르겠어.
W	Well, you are in the archery club, right?	여	음, 너 양궁부에 있지, 그렇지?
M	Yeah, I've been a member for a long time.	남	응, 난 오래된 부원이야.
W	**I'd like you ²⁾to pose for me with a bow and arrow.**	여	네가 활과 화살을 가지고 포즈를 취해주면 좋겠어.
M	**Sure.** That sounds fun. I can bring my own equipment, too.	남	물론이지. 재미있겠는데. 내 장비도 가져올 수 있어.
W	Perfect. I'll ³⁾take some photos of you and do a few sketches.	여	완벽해. 네 사진을 몇 장 찍고 스케치를 좀 할게.
M	What a relief! I thought I'd have to stay in the same position for hours!	남	정말 다행이다! 몇 시간 동안 같은 자세로 있어야 할 줄 알았어!

여자의 미술 수행평가에 대해 이야기하고 있다. 여자가 조각을 만들어야 한다면서 남자에게 포즈를 취해주면 좋겠다고 부탁하자, 남자가 승낙했으므로 남자가 여자를 위해 할 일로 ④ '조각 작품 모델 되기'가 가장 적절하다.

어휘 related to ~과 관련된 sculpture 뗑 조각 archery 뗑 양궁 bow 뗑 활 arrow 뗑 화살 equipment 뗑 장비 What a relief! 정말 다행이다!

6 금액 정보 파악

정답 ②

[Phone rings.]	[전화기가 울린다.]
M Green Springs Gourmet Food. How may I help you?	남 Green Springs Gourmet Food입니다. 무엇을 도와드릴까요?
W Hi. This is Rose Whitfield. I'd like to make ¹⁾an order for delivery, please.	여 안녕하세요. Rose Whitfield입니다. 배달 주문을 하고 싶은데요.
M Yes, Ms. Whitfield. What would you like?	남 네, Whitfield 씨. 어떤 것으로 하시겠어요?
W **I'd like five orders of seafood pasta. Each order is $20, right?**	여 해물 파스타 다섯 접시 주문할게요. 한 접시에 20달러 맞죠?
M **Yes, that's correct.** Would you like anything else?	남 네, 맞아요. 더 필요한 것 있으세요?
W I'd also like a small cheesecake.	여 작은 치즈 케이크도 주세요.
M That would be $20. **But if you order ²⁾the large one for $30, you can get a 10% discount on your order.**	남 20달러 되겠습니다. 하지만 30달러짜리 큰 것을 주문하시면, 주문 금액에서 10% 할인을 받을 수 있으세요.
W Oh, why is that?	여 오, 왜 그런가요?
M It's our special weekly promotion.	남 주간 특별 행사예요.
W All right. **I'll take the large cheesecake, then.**	여 좋아요. 큰 치즈 케이크로 할게요, 그럼.
M Okay. So that's ³⁾five seafood pastas and one large cheesecake. How would you like to pay?	남 네. 그럼, 해물 파스타 다섯 접시랑 치즈 케이크 큰 것 하나네요. 계산은 어떻게 하시겠어요?
W I'll pay by card.	여 카드로 계산할게요.
M Okay. The delivery person will process your payment. It will take about 45 minutes for your order to arrive.	남 네. 배달원이 결제를 처리해드릴 거예요. 도착까지 45분 정도 소요될 겁니다.
W Thank you.	여 감사합니다.

여자가 해물 파스타 다섯 접시($20×5=$100)와 큰 치즈 케이크 하나($30)를 구매했고, 주문 금액에서 10% 할인($130×0.9=$117)을 받았으므로 정답은 ② '$117'이다.

[어휘] weekly 휑 주간의, 매주의 promotion 똉 (판촉) 행사; 승진 delivery person 배달원 process 동 처리하다

7 이유 파악

정답 ②

M Have you picked a destination for your summer trip, Penny?	남 여름 여행을 갈 목적지는 정했어, Penny?
W Not yet. But I've decided I'll choose a city in Europe. Do you have any recommendations?	여 아직. 그렇지만 유럽에 있는 도시를 선택하기로 했어. 추천해 줄 곳이 있니?
M I think you should go to Barcelona in Spain.	남 스페인의 바르셀로나에 가보는 게 좋을 것 같아.
W Why? Is it because of the beaches there?	여 왜? 그곳의 해변 때문이니?
M No. They're pretty, but they get too crowded ¹⁾in the summer.	남 아니. 해변이 예쁘긴 한데, 여름에는 너무 붐벼.
W Oh, then I guess it's because of the famous Spanish food. The dishes all look amazing.	여 오, 그럼 유명한 스페인 음식 때문인가 보구나. 요리들이 다 맛있어 보이더라.
M It's very good, but that's not what I meant to say. **Actually, I think the top reason to visit Barcelona is ²⁾the architecture.**	남 음식도 아주 좋지만, 내가 하려던 말은 그게 아니야. 사실, 바르셀로나를 방문해야 하는 가장 큰 이유는 건축물이라고 생각해.
W Really? I didn't know that Barcelona was famous for its architecture.	여 정말? 난 바르셀로나가 건축물로 유명한지 몰랐어.
M It is. **There are ³⁾many interesting buildings like palaces and churches.**	남 정말이야. 왕궁과 교회 같은 흥미로운 건물들이 많이 있거든.
W That sounds cool. Maybe I'll look into going there after all.	여 그거 멋지겠는데. 무엇보다도 그곳에 가는 것을 자세히 살펴봐야겠어.
M You should. I think you'd love it.	남 그래야 해. 네가 좋아할 것 같아.

남자는 여자에게 바르셀로나를 여행지로 추천하면서 바르셀로나를 방문해야 하는 가장 큰 이유는 건축물이며 흥미로운 건물들이 많이 있다고 했으므로, 남자가 바르셀로나를 여행지로 추천한 이유는 ② '흥미로운 건축물들이 많아서'이다.

[어휘] destination 똉 목적지 recommendation 똉 추천 get crowded 붐비다, 혼잡하다 architecture 똉 건축물; 건축 양식 be famous for ~으로 유명하다 look into ~을 자세히 살펴보다 after all 무엇보다도

8 언급 유무 파악

정답 ③

W Are you doing anything special for New Year's Eve, Daniel?	여 새해 전야에 특별한 일 있니, Daniel?
M I am! I'm going to the city's New Year's Eve Concert.	남 응! 나는 시에서 여는 New Year's Eve Concert에 갈 거야.
W I ¹⁾hadn't heard about that. Where is it going to be?	여 그건 못 들어봤네. 어디서 열리니?
M It will be held at **the river park by Williams Bridge**. I have the event information here on my phone.	남 윌리엄스 다리 옆에 있는 강변 공원에서 열릴 거야. 여기 내 휴대폰에 행사에 대한 정보가 있어.
W Okay. So it's **from 8 p.m. to 12:30 a.m.**	여 그래. 그러니까, 저녁 8시부터 새벽 12시 30분까지 하는구나.
M Yes. **They'll have a few ²⁾bands play earlier in the evening. Then, there's a fireworks show at midnight.**	남 응. 이른 저녁에는 몇몇 밴드가 연주할 거야. 그리고, 자정에는 불꽃놀이 쇼가 있어.
W I really want to go. But parking will probably be a nightmare.	여 정말 가고 싶다. 하지만 주차하는 게 아마 아주 끔찍할 거야.
M You're right. I'm going to ³⁾take the subway since there's a Line 2 stop nearby.	남 맞아. 근처에 2호선 역이 있어서 난 지하철을 타려고 해.

W Then, why don't I meet you in the subway station?	여 그럼, 지하철역에서 만나는 게 어때?
M That would be great.	남 그게 좋겠다.

장소(윌리엄스 다리 옆 강변 공원), 시간(저녁 8시부터 새벽 12시 30분까지), 행사 순서(밴드 연주 후 불꽃놀이 쇼), 교통수단(지하철)에 대해 언급했고, ③ '티켓 가격'은 언급하지 않았다.

어휘 New Year's Eve 새해 전야(12월 31일) firework 명 불꽃놀이 midnight 명 자정 be a nightmare 아주 끔찍하다, 악몽 같다 nearby 부 근처에 형 인근의

---

9 내용 불일치 파악   정답 ②

W Hello, students! The Clarkson High School Physics Club is inviting all students to enter our Bridge Design Contest, which takes place ¹⁾every year. Students came up with some very creative designs last year, and we can't wait to see what they do this year. **However, we are introducing some ²⁾new contest rules this year.** The bridge must be made of regular wooden toothpicks and have a length of 33 centimeters. Students will be given four hours to build the bridge. The judge will be our physics teacher, Mr. Weston. He will test how much weight each bridge can hold. Prizes will be awarded to ³⁾the three strongest bridges. For more details, go to the Physics Club website or check out the notice posted on all bulletin boards.	여 안녕하세요, 학생 여러분! 클락슨 고등학교 물리학 동아리에서 매년 여는 다리 설계 대회에 모든 학생들을 초대합니다. 작년에 학생들은 매우 창의적인 설계안을 생각해 냈는데, 올해에는 어떤 것을 해낼지 빨리 보고 싶습니다. 그렇지만, 올해에는 몇 가지 새로운 대회 규칙을 도입할 예정입니다. 다리는 일반적인 나무 이쑤시개로 만들어져야 하며 길이는 33cm여야 합니다. 학생들에게 다리를 만드는 데 4시간이 주어질 것입니다. 심사위원은 물리 선생님이신 Weston 선생님께서 맡으십니다. 선생님께서 각 다리가 얼마나 많은 무게를 지탱할 수 있는지 시험하실 것입니다. 가장 튼튼한 3개의 다리에 상이 수여될 것입니다. 더 자세한 내용을 원하시면 물리학 동아리 웹 사이트를 방문하거나 모든 게시판에 게시된 공지를 확인하세요.

학교에서 열리는 다리 설계 대회에 대한 안내 방송이다. 여자가 올해 몇 가지 새로운 대회 규칙을 도입할 예정이라고 했으므로 ② '대회의 규칙은 작년과 동일하다.'는 내용과 일치하지 않는다.

어휘 physics 명 물리학 take place 열리다, 개최되다 come up with ~을 생각해 내다 be made of ~으로 만들어지다 toothpick 명 이쑤시개 judge 명 심사위원 통 심사하다 bulletin board 게시판

---

10 도표 정보 파악   정답 ②

W What are you looking at, Joe?	여 뭘 보고 있어, Joe?
M I'm reviewing different cars we can buy. These are our top options.	남 우리가 살 수 있는 각종 차량을 검토하고 있어. 이것들이 우리가 가진 최선의 선택지야.
W Oh, let's see. *[Pause]* Well, I think that this one is too big for us.	여 오, 어디 보자. *[잠시 멈춤]* 음, 이건 우리에게 너무 큰 것 같아.
M I agree. **We don't need ¹⁾space for six people since it's just us two.**	남 동의해. 우리 둘만 타는 거라서 6명이 탈 수 있는 공간은 필요 없어.
W That kind of car is also harder to park.	여 그런 종류의 차는 주차하기도 더 어렵지.
M What about the year it was made? Does that matter?	남 생산 연도는 어때? 중요하니?
W I don't want one that is too old. **Let's not buy anything ²⁾made before 2020.**	여 너무 오래된 것은 원하지 않아. 2020년 이전에 만들어진 것은 사지 말자.
M Okay. And what about the price?	남 알았어. 그리고 가격은 어때?
W **I'd like to keep it under $400 a month.** We're on a limited budget.	여 한 달에 400달러 미만으로 하고 싶어. 예산이 한정되어 있잖아.
M You're right. Now, we should decide if we want an electric car or not.	남 맞아. 이제, 우리가 전기차를 원하는지 아닌지 결정해야 해.
W I think we should ³⁾get an electric car. It's better for the environment.	여 전기차를 사야 할 것 같아. 그게 환경에 더 좋거든.
M Okay. Then, let's go with this one.	남 좋아. 그럼 이걸로 하자.

두 사람은 탑승 인원이 6명보다 적으면서, 2020년 이전에 생산되지 않았고, 한 달에 400달러 미만인 것 중에서, 전기차인 승용차를 골랐다.

어휘 review 통 검토하다 park 통 주차하다 명 공원 on a limited budget 예산이 한정된 electric car 전기차

---

11 짧은 대화의 응답 파악   정답 ③

W Honey, I want to ¹⁾hang these paintings on the wall. I think they'll look nice in the living room.	여 여보, 이 그림들을 벽에 걸고 싶어. 거실에 있으면 멋있어 보일 것 같아.
M Sure, I can do it right now. **I just need the hammer and some nails.**	남 물론이지, 내가 당장 할 수 있어. 망치랑 못 몇 개만 있으면 돼.
W Okay, I'll get them. ²⁾Where did you put them last?	여 알았어, 내가 가져올게. 그것들을 마지막으로 어디에 두었어?
M They're in a box below the sink.	남 싱크대 아래 상자 안에 있어.

	선택지 ① 난 파란 그림이 더 좋아.
	② 30분 정도 걸릴 거야.
	③ 싱크대 아래 상자 안에 있어.
	④ 슈퍼마켓에서 샀어.
	⑤ 오른쪽에 거는 게 좋을 것 같아.

남자가 그림을 벽에 걸 망치와 못이 필요하다고 하자 여자가 가져오겠다고 하면서 그것들을 마지막으로 어디에 두었는지 물었으므로, 이에 대한 응답으로는 위치를 알려주는 ③ 'They're in a box below the sink.'가 가장 적절하다.

어휘 hammer 명 망치 nail 명 못; 손톱 last 부 마지막으로

12 짧은 대화의 응답 파악

정답 ①

M Let's try this café, Mia. It's crowded, but I heard the coffee is really ¹⁾<u>good here</u>.	남 이 카페에 가보자, Mia. 붐비긴 하지만, 여기 커피가 정말 맛있다고 들었어.
W Okay. **But all of the tables outside and inside are** ²⁾<u>full right now.</u> What should we do?	여 알았어. 하지만 지금은 안팎의 테이블이 모두 꽉 찼네. 우리 어떻게 하지?
M **We should get our coffees to go.**	남 커피를 테이크아웃하자.
W Okay. Then, we can walk around with them.	여 <u>좋아. 그럼 들고 다닐 수 있겠어.</u>

선택지 ① 좋아. 그럼 들고 다닐 수 있겠어.
② 알겠어. 그들에게 전화해서 예약할게.
③ 물론이지. 입구 쪽 테이블을 잡을게.
④ 좋은 생각이야. 오늘 바깥 날씨가 너무 추워.
⑤ 됐어. 난 아직도 배가 불러.

카페에 자리가 없는 상황에서 남자가 커피를 테이크아웃해가자고 제안했으므로, 이에 대한 응답으로는 제안을 승낙하는 ① 'Okay. Then, we can walk around with them.'이 가장 적절하다.

어휘 full 휑 꽉 찬; 배부른 to go 테이크아웃하는, 포장해가는 grab 통 잡다, 쥐다 entrance 몡 입구

13 긴 대화의 응답 파악

정답 ⑤

W Is there any interesting news today?	여 오늘 무슨 재미있는 뉴스라도 있어?
M Yes. A company called Star Enterprises has announced its first space mission.	남 응. Star Enterprises라는 회사가 첫 번째 우주 탐사 임무를 발표했거든.
W Wow. Tell me more about it.	여 우와. 더 자세히 말해줘.
M **Well, the article I read said the research mission will cost about $4 billion.**	남 음, 내가 읽은 기사에 따르면 연구 임무에 약 40억 달러가 들 거래.
W $4 billion? That's ¹⁾<u>so much money</u>.	여 40억 달러? 정말 큰돈이네.
M Space exploration is never cheap.	남 우주 탐사는 절대 저렴하지 않지.
W But what are they going to spend all that money on?	여 그런데 그 돈을 다 어디에 쓰는 거야?
M Well, rockets are expensive, and very few of their parts can be reused after they launch into space.	남 글쎄, 로켓은 비싼데 우주로 발사된 후에 재사용할 수 있는 부품은 거의 없어.
W That sounds wasteful to me. The money could be used ²⁾<u>for more meaningful things</u>, like supporting hungry people.	여 낭비적인 것 같아. 그 돈은 배고픈 사람들을 지원하는 것과 같이, 더 의미 있는 일에 사용될 수 있잖아.
M That's true. But space research leads to the development of new technologies that help everyone. GPS is a good example of this.	남 맞아. 하지만 우주 연구는 모두에게 도움이 되는 신기술 개발로 이어져. GPS가 좋은 예야.
W **But I still believe it's better to spend money to assist** ³⁾<u>those in need.</u> **Don't you think so?**	여 하지만 난 여전히 도움이 필요한 사람들을 돕는 데 그 돈을 사용하는 게 더 낫다고 생각해. 그렇게 생각하지 않니?
M <u>Sure. But it's also important to make scientific progress.</u>	남 <u>물론이지. 하지만 과학적인 발전을 이루는 것도 중요해.</u>

선택지 ① 맞아. 우리는 사람들을 달에 보내야 해.
② 동의해. 세계 기아를 해결할 쉬운 방법은 없어.
③ 그렇고말고. 그 회사는 프로젝트를 완수했어.
④ 응. 우리가 쓰는 돈의 양을 줄여야 해.
⑤ 물론이지. 하지만 과학적인 발전을 이루는 것도 중요해.

우주 탐사 비용에 대해 토론하는 상황이다. 여자가 우주 탐사에 쓰이는 돈을 도움이 필요한 사람들에게 쓰는 것이 낫다면서 한번 더 의견을 피력했으므로, 이에 대한 응답으로는 동의하되 우주 탐사의 중요성도 말하는 ⑤ 'Sure. But it's also important to make scientific progress.'가 가장 적절하다.

어휘 space mission 우주 탐사 임무 cost 통 (비용이) 들다 billion 몡 10억 exploration 몡 탐사 launch 통 발사하다; 시작하다 wasteful 휑 낭비적인, 낭비하는 hunger 몡 기아, 배고픔 progress 몡 발전

14 긴 대화의 응답 파악

정답 ③

M Welcome to the passport office. May I help you?	남 여권 사무소에 오신 것을 환영합니다. 도와드릴까요?
W I'm afraid I've ¹⁾<u>lost my passport</u>.	여 여권을 잃어버렸어요.
M Are you certain you didn't just misplace it?	남 그냥 둔 곳을 잊어버리신 건 아니시죠?
W Yes. My backpack was stolen, and my passport was inside it.	여 네. 제 배낭을 도난당했고, 여권이 그 안에 있었어요.
M When did this happen?	남 언제 그런 일이 있었나요?
W It happened earlier today. I hope you can help me. I'm going on vacation, and I ²⁾<u>need it to fly</u>.	여 오늘 아침에 일어났어요. 선생님께서 도와주실 수 있었으면 좋겠어요. 휴가를 갈 거라서, 비행기를 타려면 필요해요.
M Okay. Did you already report your passport stolen to the police?	남 알겠습니다. 여권을 도난당했다고 경찰에 이미 신고하셨나요?
W Yes. Here's a copy of the police report.	여 네. 여기 경찰 보고서 사본이에요.
M I'll get the passport replaced for you. Do you have any other identification?	남 여권을 교체해 드릴게요. 다른 신분증 있으신가요?
W I only have this driver's license.	여 이 운전면허증밖에 없어요.
M I see. When is your flight?	남 그렇군요. 비행시간은 언제인가요?
W **I'm supposed to leave tomorrow morning. Will it be ready by then?**	여 내일 아침에 출발하기로 되어 있어요. 그때까지 준비될까요?

M No. It won't be possible. Can you ³⁾change your flight?

W I'll check with the airline right away.

남 아뇨. 불가능할 거예요. 비행편을 바꾸실 수 있으세요?

여 바로 항공사에 확인해 볼게요.

선택지 ① 다른 신분증이 있을지도 몰라요.

② 지금 사본 한 부 더 드릴게요.

③ 바로 항공사에 확인해 볼게요.

④ 티켓을 미리 인쇄해야 해요.

⑤ 경찰이 도와줄 수 있을 거예요.

여권을 도난당한 여자가 여권 사무소에 가서 재발급을 신청하는 상황이다. 여자가 내일까지 여권을 준비해달라고 요청하자 남자가 불가능하다면서 비행편을 바꿀 수 있는지 물었으므로, 이에 대한 응답으로는 항공사에 확인해보겠다는 ③ 'I'll check with the airline right away.'가 가장 적절하다.

어휘 misplace 통 둔 곳을 잊다, 잘못 두다   report 통 신고하다; 알리다   a copy of 사본 (한 부)   replace 통 교체하다   identification 명 신분증   be ready by ~까지 준비되다
beforehand 분 미리, 사전에

15 상황에 적절한 말 파악

정답 ④

W Victoria and James are in the same biology class. Their teacher has asked the students to prepare a presentation about marine life. Victoria and James decided to do a presentation ¹⁾on seashells. They are interested in this topic, and they have prepared a lot of material for their project. However, James is worried that the students will think ²⁾the topic is boring compared to the other presentations, so he speaks to Victoria about his concern. Victoria disagrees with him. She thinks that they ³⁾don't need to change their topic. **So Victoria wants to tell James that their topic will be ⁴⁾popular with the other students.** In this situation, what would Victoria most likely say to James?

여 Victoria와 James는 같은 생물학 수업을 듣습니다. 그들의 선생님은 학생들에게 해양 생물에 대한 발표를 준비할 것을 요청했습니다. Victoria와 James는 조개에 대해 발표를 하기로 결정했습니다. 그들은 이 주제에 관심이 있고, 과제를 위해 많은 자료를 준비했습니다. 하지만 James는 학생들이 다른 발표에 비해 주제가 지루하다고 생각할까 봐 걱정되어, Victoria에게 자신의 고민을 털어놓았습니다. Victoria는 그의 의견에 동의하지 않습니다. 그녀는 주제를 바꿀 필요가 없다고 생각합니다. 그래서, Victoria는 James에게 그들의 주제가 다른 학생들에게 인기가 있을 것이라고 말하고 싶습니다. 이런 상황에서, Victoria가 James에게 가장 할 것 같은 말은 무엇입니까?

선택지 ① 선생님께 의견을 여쭤보자.

② 우리 해변에서 조개를 수집해야 할 것 같아.

③ 우리 주제를 더 인기 있는 걸로 바꾸는 게 어때?

④ 반 친구들이 이 주제를 좋아할 거야.

⑤ 조개가 정말 알록달록해, 그렇지 않니?

James가 함께 준비하는 발표 주제가 지루할까 봐 걱정하는 것을 보고, Victoria는 그들의 주제가 다른 학생들에게 인기 있을 것이라고 말하려 한다. 따라서, Victoria가 할 말로 ④ 'Our classmates are going to love this topic.'이 가장 적절하다.

어휘 biology 명 생물학   ask A to B A에게 B할 것을 요청하다   marine 형 해양의, 바다의   seashell 명 조개, 조개껍데기   compared to ~에 비해   disagree with ~의 의견에 동의하지 않다

16-17 세트 문항

정답 16 ⑤ 17 ④

M Good afternoon. In yesterday's class, we talked about the causes of stress in our life. **Today, I want to introduce some foods that can help you ¹⁾manage your stress.** First, **chocolate** is not just a sweet snack. It can also improve your mood. This is because it contains chemicals that cause your body to produce happiness hormones. Second, eating **almonds** will enable you to respond to stress better. Several studies have shown that people who eat almonds regularly do ²⁾not react as strongly to stressful situations. Next, eating **strawberries** is another effective way to cope with stress. They are high in vitamin C, which helps to lower the amount of stress-causing chemicals in your body. Finally, warm **milk** is a great nighttime drink if you are ³⁾feeling stressed out. It has a calming effect on the mind and can help you get a good night's sleep. I hope today's class has given you some useful tips for managing your stress.

남 안녕하세요. 어제 수업에서, 우리는 생활 속 스트레스의 원인에 대해 이야기했습니다. 오늘은, 여러분의 스트레스를 관리하는 데 도움이 되는 음식들을 소개하려고 합니다. 첫째, 초콜릿은 그저 달콤한 간식만이 아닙니다. 그것은 여러분의 기분을 더 좋게 할 수 있습니다. 이는 초콜릿이 몸에서 행복 호르몬을 분비하게 하는 화학물질을 함유하고 있기 때문입니다. 둘째, 아몬드를 먹는 것은 스트레스에 더 좋게 반응할 수 있게 합니다. 여러 연구들은 아몬드를 규칙적으로 먹는 사람들이 스트레스를 받는 상황에 그다지 강하게 반응하지 않는다는 것을 보여줬습니다. 다음으로, 딸기를 먹는 것은 스트레스에 대처하는 또 다른 효과적인 방법입니다. 딸기에는 비타민 C가 풍부한데, 이것은 몸속 스트레스를 유발하는 화학물질의 양을 줄이는 데 도움을 줍니다. 마지막으로, 만약 여러분이 스트레스를 많이 받고 있다면 따뜻한 우유는 훌륭한 저녁 음료가 될 것입니다. 그것에는 마음을 진정시키는 효과가 있고 여러분이 숙면을 취하도록 도울 수 있습니다. 저는 오늘 수업이 스트레스를 관리하는 데 유용한 조언을 여러분에게 주었기를 바랍니다.

선택지 16 ① 개인적인 스트레스의 다양한 원인

② 비타민이 사람의 건강에 미치는 영향

③ 건강에 좋은 간식을 먹는 것의 중요성

④ 스트레스를 받는 상황에 대처하는 방법

⑤ 스트레스를 조절하는 데 도움을 줄 수 있는 음식

17 ① 초콜릿   ② 아몬드   ③ 딸기   ④ 바나나   ⑤ 우유

16 스트레스를 관리하는 데 도움이 되는 음식들을 소개하고 있으므로 남자가 하는 말의 주제로 ⑤ 'foods that can help to control stress'가 가장 적절하다.

17 초콜릿, 아몬드, 딸기, 우유는 언급했지만 ④ 'bananas'는 언급하지 않았다.

어휘 manage 통 관리하다   improve 통 더 좋게 하다, 개선하다   enable A to B A가 B하도록 하다   respond to ~에 반응하다   react 통 반응하다   cope with ~에 대처하다
stress-causing 형 스트레스를 유발하는   calm 통 진정시키다 형 침착한

| 1 | ① | 2 | ⑤ | 3 | ③ | 4 | ⑤ | 5 | ④ | 6 | ② | 7 | ⑤ | 8 | ③ | 9 | ② | 10 | ③ |
| 11 | ⑤ | 12 | ① | 13 | ① | 14 | ② | 15 | ① | 16 | ④ | 17 | ③ | • 각 문제의 정답 근거는 굵은 글씨로, Dictation 정답은 밑줄로 표시되어 있습니다. | | | | | |

---

1 목적 파악

정답 ①

M Good morning, shoppers. Autumn is coming to an end, which means that it's almost ¹⁾time for winter sports. **Whether you are into skating, skiing, sledding, or just playing in the snow, Dolson Sports Equipment has got you covered.** We've been providing residents of the Hartford area with high-quality ²⁾gear for a decade now. **And to celebrate our first 10 years in operation, we'll be holding a ³⁾massive storewide sale from November 10th to 25th.** Every item will be marked down, and you can expect savings ranging from 20% to 35%. If you are planning to have fun in ⁴⁾the great outdoors this winter, make sure to come visit us. We look forward to seeing you!

남 안녕하십니까, 쇼핑객 여러분. 가을이 끝나가고 있는데, 이는 겨울 스포츠를 할 때가 되었다는 의미죠. 스케이트, 스키, 썰매 타기에 관심이 있든 또는 그냥 눈 위에서 노는 것에 관심이 있든 간에, Dolson Sports Equipment가 여러분을 책임지겠습니다. 저희는 하트포드 지역 주민들에게 고품질의 장비를 현재 10년째 제공해 왔습니다. 그리고 운영 10주년을 기념하여 11월 10일부터 25일까지 대대적인 전 매장 세일을 진행할 예정입니다. 모든 품목이 할인될 것이며, 20%에서 35%에 이르는 절약을 기대할 수 있습니다. 만약 이번 겨울에 멋진 야외에서 즐거운 시간을 보낼 계획이라면, 꼭 저희를 방문해주세요. 여러분을 만나 뵙기를 기대합니다!

남자가 겨울 스포츠를 할 때가 되었다면서, Dolson Sports Equipment에서 진행할 대대적인 할인 행사에 대한 정보를 주고 있다. 따라서, 남자가 하는 말의 목적으로 ① '스포츠용품점의 할인 행사를 홍보하려고'가 가장 적절하다.

어휘 be into ~에 관심이 있다 sled 图 썰매 타다 have got ~ covered ~를 책임지다 resident 图 주민 gear 图 장비 decade 图 10년 operation 图 운영 massive 图 대대적인 mark down ~을 할인하다 range from A to B A에서 B에 이르다

---

2 의견 파악

정답 ⑤

M Hello, Anne. What ¹⁾are you up to this afternoon?
W I'm going to my Italian class at the community center.
M I didn't know you were studying Italian.
W I've been taking the class for over a month now.
M Do you find the class interesting?
W Yes. The teacher is amazing. **And taking a language class is a great way to ²⁾study a country's culture.**
M Can you give me an example?
W Today, we learned a famous Italian expression. It can be translated as, "No matter where you go, you end up at home."
M What does it mean?
W It shows ³⁾how important the family is for Italians. Throughout their life, they stay in close contact with their parents and ⁴⁾other relatives.
M Fascinating. You will be an expert on Italy soon.

남 안녕, Anne. 오늘 오후에 뭐 해?
여 주민센터에서 하는 이탈리아어 수업에 갈 거야.
남 네가 이탈리아어를 공부하는 줄 몰랐어.
여 지금 한 달 넘게 수업을 듣고 있는 중이야.
남 그 수업 재미있어?
여 응. 선생님이 정말 멋지셔. 그리고 어학 수업을 듣는 것은 그 나라의 문화를 공부하기에 좋은 방법이야.
남 예를 들어줄래?
여 오늘은 유명한 이탈리아어 표현을 배웠어. 그건 '어디를 가든 결국 집에 있게 된다'는 뜻으로 번역돼.
남 그게 무슨 뜻이야?
여 이탈리아인들에게 가족이 얼마나 중요한지 보여주는 표현이야. 일생 동안, 그들은 부모님 그리고 다른 친척들과 긴밀한 관계를 유지해.
남 흥미진진하네. 너는 곧 이탈리아 전문가가 되겠어.

주민센터에서 이탈리아어 수업을 수강 중인 여자가 어학 수업을 듣는 것은 그 나라의 문화를 공부하기에 좋은 방법이라고 했다. 따라서, 여자의 의견으로 ⑤ '어학 수업은 그 나라의 문화를 공부하기에 좋은 방법이다.'가 가장 적절하다.

어휘 translate 图 번역하다 end up 결국 ~하게 되다 stay in close contact 긴밀한 관계를 유지하다 relative 图 친척 fascinating 图 흥미진진한; 매혹적인 expert 图 전문가

---

3 관계 파악

정답 ③

M Hello. Are you the person who called me?
W Yes. **I need some ¹⁾assistance with a lock.**
M Can you describe the problem for me?
W **My key broke off in the lock, so I can't get the shutter open.**
M **I can help. But I need to make sure that you ²⁾manage this pharmacy.** Do you have any documents you can show me?
W Yes, I have one with me. *[Pause]* Here it is.
M Okay, and would you like me to replace your current system? Maybe you would ³⁾prefer a security system with a keypad.

남 안녕하세요. 제게 전화하셨던 분이신가요?
여 네. 자물쇠에 관해 도움이 필요해요.
남 문제를 설명해 주시겠어요?
여 열쇠가 자물쇠 속에서 부러져서 셔터를 열 수가 없어요.
남 제가 도와드릴 수 있어요. 하지만 당신이 이 약국을 운영하는지 확실히 해야 해요. 저에게 보여줄 수 있는 서류가 있나요?
여 네, 하나 가지고 있어요. *[잠시 멈춤]* 여기요.
남 알겠습니다, 그리고 지금의 장치를 교체해 드릴까요? 아마 키패드가 있는 보안 장치를 선호하실 것 같군요.

W	Yes, I think it's time for an upgrade. But please hurry. We're supposed to open in an hour.	여	네, 업그레이드할 때가 된 것 같아요. 하지만 서둘러 주세요. 한 시간 후에 문을 열기로 되어 있어서요.
M	Don't worry. I won't keep your customers waiting.	남	걱정하지 마세요. 당신의 고객분들을 기다리게 하지 않을게요.
W	And there's 4)a delivery of medicine arriving soon.	여	그리고 곧 약 배송도 올 거예요.
M	I understand. I'll work as fast as I can.	남	이해해요. 가능한 한 빨리 작업할게요.
W	Thank you so much!	여	정말 감사합니다!

두 사람이 약국의 고장 난 자물쇠에 관해 이야기하고 있다. 남자는 자물쇠를 고칠 수 있다면서 키패드가 있는 보안 장치로 교체할 것을 권했고, 여자는 열쇠가 자물쇠 속에서 부러져 운영 중인 약국 셔터를 열 수 없다고 하는 것으로 보아 두 사람의 관계로 ③ '열쇠 수리공 — 약사'가 가장 적절하다.

어휘 assistance 명 도움 describe 통 설명하다 break off 부러지다, 분리되다 pharmacy 명 약국 document 명 서류 security 명 보안 delivery 명 배송, 배달

4 그림 내용 불일치 파악 정답 ⑤

M	Honey, did you see the picture our daughter sent us?	남	여보, 우리 딸이 보낸 사진 봤어?
W	Not yet. Can you show me?	여	아니 아직. 내게 보여줄래?
M	Sure. She wants to know what we think about the living room in her new apartment.	남	물론이지. 우리 딸은 그녀의 새 아파트 거실에 대해 우리가 어떻게 생각하는지 알고 싶어 해.
W	Oh, I like the rug on the floor. 1)Its dot pattern makes it really stand out.	여	오, 바닥에 깔린 러그가 마음에 들어. 물방울무늬가 러그를 정말 돋보이게 하네.
M	That's for sure. And the round coffee table on it is beautiful. It 2)looks like an antique.	남	확실히 그래. 그리고 그 위에 있는 둥근 커피 테이블이 아름다워. 골동품 같아.
W	But I wonder why she decided to put two sofas in her living room.	여	그런데 왜 거실에 소파를 두 개 두었는지 의문이야.
M	Her friends visit her often. She probably wants to make sure there are 3)enough seats for everyone.	남	친구들이 자주 방문하거든. 아마 모두 앉을 자리가 충분하도록 하고 싶었을 거야.
W	Maybe her friends are the people in that picture on the wall.	여	벽에 걸린 저 사진 속의 사람들이 그녀의 친구들일지도 몰라.
M	That makes sense. What do you think of the curtains?	남	일리 있는 말이야. 커튼은 어떻게 생각해?
W	The 4)floral pattern doesn't really match the rest of the room, in my opinion.	여	내 생각에는 꽃무늬가 방의 나머지 부분과 별로 어울리지 않는 것 같아.
M	I agree. She should have chosen something simpler.	남	동의해. 더 단순한 걸 선택했어야 했어.

대화에서 여자가 커튼의 꽃무늬가 방의 나머지 부분과 별로 어울리지 않는 것 같다고 말했는데, ⑤에는 줄무늬 커튼이 그려져 있다.

어휘 dot pattern 물방울무늬 stand out 돋보이다 antique 명 골동품 floral 형 꽃무늬의 match 통 어울리다 rest 명 나머지

5 할 일 파악 정답 ④

M	I'm glad we decided to throw a surprise birthday party for Mom tonight. Aren't you?	남	오늘 밤에 엄마를 위해 깜짝 생일 파티를 열기로 해서 좋아. 넌 안 그래?
W	To be honest, I'm getting a bit stressed, Matthew. We only have two hours before she 1)comes home from work.	여	솔직히 말해서, 난 스트레스를 좀 받고 있어, Matthew. 엄마가 퇴근해서 집에 오기까지 두 시간밖에 안 남았어.
M	Well, what else do we still need to do?	남	음, 또 뭘 더 해야 하는데?
W	Hmm... Let me think.	여	흠... 생각해 볼게.
M	Do you want me to buy some snacks from the store?	남	가게에서 간식을 좀 사 올까?
W	No. It's okay. Dad is doing that now. He'll also get some flowers on his way home.	여	아니. 괜찮아. 아빠가 지금 그걸 하고 있어. 집에 오는 길에 꽃도 좀 사 올 거야.
M	Have you called everyone who's invited?	남	초대받은 사람들 모두에게 전화했어?
W	Of course. I 2)contacted all the guests earlier this week.	여	물론이지. 이번 주 초에 모든 손님들에게 연락했어.
M	Then, what should I do?	남	그럼 난 뭘 해야 해?
W	Well, I haven't 3)picked up the cake from the bakery on 5th Street yet.	여	음, 5번가에 있는 제과점에서 케이크를 아직 못 찾아왔어.
M	I'll head over there and do that now.	남	내가 지금 그곳으로 가서 그렇게 할게.
W	Great! While you're doing that, I'll 4)start decorating the house. I've got a lot of balloons to blow up.	여	좋아! 네가 그걸 하는 동안, 나는 집을 꾸미기 시작할게. 불어야 할 풍선이 많거든.

엄마를 위한 깜짝 생일 파티에 대해 이야기하고 있다. 여자가 5번가에 있는 제과점에서 케이크를 아직 못 찾아왔다고 하자, 남자가 지금 그곳으로 가서 그렇게 하겠다고 했으므로 남자가 할 일로 ④ '케이크 찾아오기'가 가장 적절하다.

어휘 throw a party 파티를 열다 to be honest 솔직히 말해서 contact 통 연락하다 head over ~로 가다 decorate 통 꾸미다, 장식하다 blow up (풍선 등을) 불다

6 금액 정보 파악 정답 ②

W	Welcome to West Shore Auto. How can I help you?	여	West Shore Auto에 오신 것을 환영합니다. 무엇을 도와드릴까요?
M	Hi. I flew here ¹⁾for a conference, and I would like to rent a car.	남	안녕하세요. 회의 때문에 이곳으로 비행기를 타고 왔는데, 차를 빌리고 싶어요.
W	Of course. **We have a sedan available at $30 per day and an SUV at $45 per day.**	여	물론이죠. 하루에 30달러인 세단과 45달러인 SUV가 이용 가능합니다.
M	**The sedan is fine. I'll need it for two days.**	남	세단이 괜찮아요. 이틀 동안 필요할 거예요.
W	Okay. Do you have ²⁾any special requests for the vehicle?	여	알겠습니다. 차량에 대한 특별한 요청 사항이 있으신가요?
M	**Actually, is it possible to have it delivered to my hotel at 4 p.m. today?**	남	실은, 오늘 오후 4시에 제 호텔로 배달해 주실 수 있나요?
W	Which hotel are you staying at?	여	어느 호텔에 묵고 계세요?
M	The Grand Pavilion.	남	Grand Pavilion입니다.
W	No problem. **But there will be an ³⁾additional $20 charge for that service.**	여	문제없습니다. 하지만 그런 서비스에는 20달러의 추가 요금이 부과될 거예요.
M	**That's fine. I'll pay the fee.**	남	괜찮아요. 요금을 낼게요.
W	Okay. **And if you download our app, you can get a 10% discount on your total.**	여	알겠습니다. 그리고 저희 앱을 다운받으시면 총액의 10%를 할인받으실 수 있어요.
M	Really? I'll do that right now.	남	정말요? 지금 바로 그렇게 할게요.
W	Sure. [Pause] **The coupon ⁴⁾is confirmed.** I'll ring you up.	여	그럼요. [잠시 멈춤] 쿠폰이 확인되었습니다. 계산해 드릴게요.

남자가 이틀 동안 세단($30×2=$60)을 빌리고, 배달 서비스($20)를 요청했고, 총액에서 10% 할인($80×0.9=$72)을 받았으므로 정답은 ② '$72'이다.

어휘 conference 명 회의 rent 통 빌리다 request 명 요청 사항 통 요청하다 vehicle 명 차량 confirm 통 확인하다 ring up 계산하다

---

7 이유 파악 정답 ⑤

M	Sarah, you're a big fan of the Golden Stripes, right?	남	Sarah, 너 Golden Stripes의 열렬한 팬이지, 그렇지?
W	Yeah. That's one of my favorite bands.	여	응. 내가 가장 좋아하는 밴드 중 하나야.
M	Well, my cousin gave me ¹⁾two tickets to their concert on Saturday evening at Domingo Hall. Do you want to go with me?	남	음, 내 사촌이 토요일 저녁에 도밍고 홀에서 열리는 그들의 콘서트 티켓 두 장을 줬어. 나랑 같이 갈래?
W	Saturday? I'd love to, but I'm afraid I can't.	여	토요일? 그러고 싶지만, 유감스럽게도 못 갈 것 같아.
M	Oh, are you meeting your friends?	남	오, 친구들 만날 거니?
W	Nope. I won't be able to see them at all this weekend.	여	아니. 이번 주말에는 친구들을 전혀 볼 수 없을 거야.
M	You must have a lot of homework, then.	남	그럼 숙제가 많은가 보구나.
W	That's not it. **I'm going to be ²⁾out of town visiting my grandparents.**	여	그게 아니야. 우리 조부모님을 뵈러 마을 밖으로 나가 있을 거야.
M	Too bad. If you'd like, I can ³⁾make a video of the show. Then, you can watch it when you get back.	남	안타깝네. 네가 원한다면, 그 공연의 영상을 찍어줄 수 있어. 그러면, 네가 돌아와서 그걸 볼 수 있잖아.
W	Thanks. I really appreciate that.	여	고마워. 정말 고마워.

여자는 토요일에 열리는 콘서트를 못 간다고 하면서 조부모님을 뵈러 마을 밖으로 나가 있을 것이라고 했으므로, 여자가 콘서트를 보러 갈 수 없는 이유는 ⑤ '조부모님을 뵈러 갈 예정이어서'이다.

어휘 cousin 명 사촌 not ~ at all 전혀 ~ 아닌

---

8 언급 유무 파악 정답 ③

W	Hi, Raymond. I haven't seen you in ages. What ¹⁾have you been up to?	여	안녕, Raymond. 오랜만에 보네. 요즘 뭐 하고 지내?
M	Well, I joined the Westgate Rock-Climbing Club.	남	음, 나는 Westgate Rock-Climbing Club에 가입했어.
W	Really? What types of activities do you do?	여	정말? 어떤 종류의 활동을 하니?
M	We mostly **go to local climbing gyms to climb indoor walls.** But once in a while, we go to the mountains ²⁾in nearby national parks.	남	우리는 주로 지역에 있는 클라이밍 체육관에 가서 실내 벽을 등반해. 하지만 가끔은 근처 국립공원에 있는 산에 가기도 해.
W	Interesting. Are there many people in your group?	여	흥미롭네. 모임에 많은 사람들이 있어?
M	Not really. There are **12 members** in total. We hope more people will join, though.	남	그렇지 않아. 총 12명의 회원이 있어. 그런데 우리는 더 많은 사람들이 가입하기를 바라고 있어.
W	Is there a fee for members?	여	회원들에게 회비가 있어?
M	Yeah. We each pay **$50 per month** to ³⁾cover the various group expenses.	남	응. 여러 가지 단체 비용을 부담하기 위해 각자 한 달에 50달러를 내고 있어.
W	It sounds like something I would really enjoy. How can I sign up?	여	내가 정말 좋아할 만한 것 같아. 어떻게 가입할 수 있어?
M	Just **stop by our next meeting, and fill out** ⁴⁾a registration form. You can come with me, if you want.	남	그냥 다음 우리 모임에 들러서 가입 신청서를 작성하면 돼. 원한다면 나랑 같이 가도 돼.
W	Perfect. Thanks!	여	완벽해. 고마워!

주요 활동(지역 클라이밍 체육관에 가서 실내 벽 등반), 회원 수(12명), 월별 회비(50달러), 가입 방법(모임 방문 후 가입 신청서 작성)에 대해 언급했고, ③ '모임 횟수'는 언급하지 않았다.

어휘 in ages 오랫동안 indoor 형 실내의 once in a while 가끔 nearby 형 근처의 cover 통 (비용 등을) 부담하다; 덮다 expense 명 비용 stop by ~에 들르다 fill out ~을 작성하다

9 내용 불일치 파악

정답 ②

M Welcome back to *Community Update* on LHF Radio. The third annual Greenville Marathon will take place on Saturday, May 17th. **There is** ¹⁾**no fee to** <u>participate</u> in this event, and both amateur and professional athletes are welcome. The starting line will be directly in front of city hall, and the race will begin at 10 a.m. The course is 10 kilometers long, and ²⁾<u>most of it follows</u> the scenic Elk River. The race will end at Meadow Park, where Mayor Adams will hold a short ceremony to announce the winner. The person ³⁾<u>who comes in first</u> this year will receive a trophy and $500. For more information about the event, visit www.greenvillemarathon.com.	남 LHF 라디오의 <Community Update>를 다시 듣게되신 것을 환영합니다. 제3회 연례 Greenville Marathon이 5월 17일 토요일에 열립니다. 이 행사에 참가하는 것은 무료이며, 아마추어와 프로 선수 모두 환영입니다. 출발선은 시청 바로 앞에 놓일 예정으로, 경기는 오전 10시에 시작됩니다. 코스는 10km 길이이고, 대부분은 경치가 아름다운 엘크강을 따라 이어집니다. 경기는 메도우 공원에서 끝날 예정인데, 그곳에서 Adams 시장이 수상자를 발표하는 짧은 시상식을 개최하겠습니다. 올해 1위로 들어온 사람은 트로피와 500달러를 받을 예정입니다. 행사에 대한 더 많은 정보를 얻으시려면 www.greenvillemarathon.com을 방문하십시오.

마라톤 대회에 대한 안내 방송이다. 남자가 이 행사에 참가하는 것은 무료라고 했으므로 ② '프로 마라토너는 참가비를 내야 한다.'는 내용과 일치하지 않는다.

어휘 directly 분 바로 scenic 형 경치가 아름다운 receive 동 받다

10 도표 정보 파악

정답 ③

W Honey, have you booked your flight for your business trip to Boston?	여 여보, 보스턴 출장 항공편 예약했어?
M Actually, I'm looking on a travel website to see what's available. ¹⁾<u>The earliest flight</u> is at 8 a.m.	남 사실, 뭐가 예약 가능한지 알아보려고 여행 웹사이트를 보고 있어. 가장 빠른 항공편은 오전 8시야.
W But I won't be able to drive you to the airport before 9 a.m.	여 하지만 오전 9시 전에는 내가 당신을 공항까지 태워다 줄 수 없을 거야.
M In that case, I should look for flights that depart at 11 a.m. or later.	남 그렇다면 오전 11시나 그 이후에 출발하는 항공편을 찾아봐야겠네.
W How much will your company ²⁾<u>allow you to spend on</u> the plane ticket?	여 회사에서 항공편에 얼마나 쓰도록 해줄 예정인데?
M My boss wants me to keep the price under $250.	남 내 상사는 가격을 250달러 미만으로 해주길 원하고 있어.
W Well, that leaves you with these three flights to choose from.	여 음, 그러면 이 세 가지 항공편 중에서 선택할 수 있어.
M Now that I think about it, I'd ³⁾<u>prefer a direct flight</u>.	남 지금 생각해 보니까 직항편이 좋겠어.
W Okay. Do you want a window seat or an aisle seat?	여 알겠어. 창가 쪽 자리를 원해, 아니면 통로 쪽 자리를 원해?
M I'd like an aisle seat. That way, it's easier to go to the bathroom.	남 통로 쪽 자리가 좋아. 그래야 화장실에 가는 게 더 수월할 거야.
W Then, you should book this one.	여 그럼 이걸 예약해야겠네.

남자는 오전 11시 이후에 출발하고, 250달러 미만인 것 중에서, 직항이며, 통로 쪽 자리인 항공편을 골랐다.

어휘 business trip 출장 in that case 그렇다면 depart 동 출발하다 (departure 명 출발) now that ~하니까 direct flight 직항 aisle 명 통로, 복도

11 짧은 대화의 응답 파악

정답 ⑤

W Nate, did you take the garbage out? Tomorrow is the pickup day ¹⁾<u>for our neighborhood</u>.	여 Nate, 쓰레기 내놓았니? 내일은 우리 동네 수거 날이야.
M I completely forgot, Mom. I'm sorry. I'll take care of that now.	남 완전히 잊어버렸어요, 엄마. 죄송해요. 제가 지금 처리할게요.
W We ²⁾<u>can do it together</u> if you like. Then, we could go for a walk with the dog afterward.	여 원한다면 같이 할 수 있어. 그러면 그 후에 개랑 산책하러 갈 수도 있지.
M Okay. I'll go with you in that case.	남 좋아요. 그렇다면 같이 갈게요.
	선택지 ① 아니요. 수요일마다 쓰레기를 수거하는걸요.
	② 죄송해요. 다음에는 잊지 않고 할게요.
	③ 네. 그건 쓰레기통에 넣어주세요.
	④ 그럴 필요 없어요. 제가 한 시간 전에 개에게 먹이를 줬거든요.
	⑤ 좋아요. 그렇다면 같이 갈게요.

남자가 쓰레기 내놓는 것을 잊었다고 하자 여자가 원한다면 같이 할 수 있고 그 후에 개와 산책할 수도 있다고 제안했으므로, 이에 대한 응답으로는 제안을 승낙하는 ⑤ 'Okay. I'll go with you in that case.'가 가장 적절하다.

어휘 garbage 명 쓰레기 neighborhood 명 동네; 이웃 completely 분 완전히 take care of ~을 처리하다 go for a walk 산책하러 가다 afterward 분 그 후에 feed 동 먹이를 먹이다

12 짧은 대화의 응답 파악   정답 ①

M	Honey, I ¹⁾feel too lazy to cook dinner tonight. **Why don't we order in?**
W	That's a good idea. **There's a new Mexican place that I've wanted to** ²⁾**try** for a while now.
M	Mexican food? I'm not really in the mood for spicy food tonight. **How about getting something else?**
W	Sure. What do you suggest?

남	여보, 오늘 저녁 요리하기 너무 귀찮아. 음식을 배달시키는 게 어때?
여	좋은 생각이야. 예전부터 시도해 보고 싶었던 새로운 멕시코 음식점이 있어.
남	멕시코 음식? 오늘 밤은 별로 매운 음식을 먹고 싶은 기분이 나지 않아. 다른 걸 먹는 게 어때?
여	물론이지. 뭐가 좋겠어?

선택지 ① 물론이지. 뭐가 좋겠어?
② 괜찮아. 당신 순한 맛으로 음식 주문한 거야?
③ 미안해. 내가 게으름을 피우지 말아야 했는데.
④ 걱정하지 마. 내가 이미 저녁을 준비했어.
⑤ 좋아. 20분 후에 음식을 가지러 가면 돼.

배달 음식을 정하는 상황에서 여자가 멕시코 음식점을 제안하자 남자가 매운 음식을 먹고 싶은 기분이 아니라면서 다른 것을 먹자고 제안했으므로, 이에 대한 응답으로는 제안을 수락하면서 무엇을 먹고 싶은지 되묻는 ① 'Sure. What do you suggest?'가 가장 적절하다.

어휘 order in 음식을 배달시키다   be in the mood for ~할 기분이 나다   spicy 휑 매운   mild 휑 (음식 등이) 순한

13 긴 대화의 응답 파악   정답 ①

W	Why the long face, Greg? Did something happen at school today?
M	Yeah, Mom. **Do you remember how I wanted to join the school's baseball team?**
W	Oh, right. **The tryouts were today.** I guess things ¹⁾didn't go well for you.
M	You can say that again. **I made a lot of mistakes, so the coach didn't pick me for the team.** It was really embarrassing.
W	But your skills improved a lot over the summer. What went wrong?
M	I got really nervous ²⁾with everyone watching me, and then I couldn't do anything right.
W	So there is no chance of you joining the team?
M	**Not until next year. Maybe I should just give up.**
W	You shouldn't! You really want to be a baseball player.
M	But I will have to ³⁾wait so long before I can try out again.
W	**Yes, but that will give you more** ⁴⁾**time to prepare.**
M	You're right. I'll just keep practicing.

여	왜 시무룩한 얼굴이니, Greg? 오늘 학교에서 무슨 일 있었어?
남	네, 엄마. 제가 학교 야구팀에 들어가고 싶어 했던 거 기억하세요?
여	오, 그래. 오늘 선발 시험이 있었지. 일이 잘 안 풀렸나 보네.
남	정말 그래요. 제가 실수를 많이 해서 코치님이 저를 팀에 뽑지 않으셨어요. 전 정말 창피했어요.
여	하지만 넌 여름 동안 실력이 많이 늘었는데. 뭐가 잘못됐어?
남	모든 사람들이 저를 쳐다보고 있어서 정말 긴장했고, 그러고 나니 저는 아무것도 제대로 할 수 없었어요.
여	그러니까 팀에 합류할 가능성은 없는 거니?
남	내년까지는 안 돼요. 어쩌면 그냥 포기해야 할 것 같아요.
여	그러면 안 돼! 너는 정말 야구 선수가 되고 싶어 하잖니.
남	하지만 다시 도전하기까지 정말 오래 기다려야 하잖아요.
여	그래, 그렇지만 그건 네게 준비할 시간을 더 많이 주는 셈이란다.
남	맞아요. 그냥 계속 연습할게요.

선택지 ① 맞아요. 그냥 계속 연습할게요.
② 동의해요. 훌륭한 야구 선수가 되실 거예요.
③ 몰라요. 스포츠를 별로 좋아하지 않거든요.
④ 말도 안 돼요. 선발 시험이 일주일도 남지 않았어요.
⑤ 그럼요. 다음 경기는 코치님을 실망시키지 않을게요!

남자가 야구팀 선발 시험에 떨어진 상황이다. 남자가 내년에야 다시 도전할 수 있다면서 포기하려 하자 여자가 오히려 준비 시간이 더 생긴 것이라고 설득했으므로, 이에 대한 응답으로는 설득에 수긍하는 ① 'You're right. I'll just keep practicing.'이 가장 적절하다.

어휘 long face 시무룩한 얼굴   tryout 휑 선발 시험   You can say that again. 정말 그래요.   chance 휑 가능성   give up 포기하다   try out 도전하다   let ~ down ~를 실망시키다

14 긴 대화의 응답 파악   정답 ②

	[Telephone rings.]
M	Thank you for calling Brighton Dental Clinic. How can I help you?
W	Good morning. I'm calling about my appointment with Dr. Nicks this afternoon.
M	Could I get your name, please?
W	It's Jane Scott.
M	You're scheduled for a ¹⁾routine teeth cleaning at 1 p.m., right?
W	That's correct. But there's a problem at work, and I have to go to the office to sort it out.
M	**So you need to** ²⁾**reschedule your appointment?**
W	That's right. I apologize for the short notice.
M	That's fine. Are you available later this afternoon?
W	I don't think ³⁾I can come at all today. And I will be out of town tomorrow. **Is there an appointment time available on Monday?**
M	Let me check. *[Typing sound]* **How about 10:30 a.m. or 2 p.m.?**
W	I think the morning would work best for me.

	[전화기가 울린다.]
남	Brighton Dental Clinic에 전화해 주셔서 감사합니다. 무엇을 도와드릴까요?
여	안녕하세요. 오늘 오후에 Nicks 의사 선생님과 진료 예약이 잡혀 있어서 전화 드렸어요.
남	성함이 어떻게 되시죠?
여	Jane Scott이에요.
남	오후 1시에 정기 스케일링을 받으실 예정이네요, 맞죠?
여	맞아요. 그런데 회사에 문제가 있어서, 그걸 해결하러 사무실에 가야 해요.
남	그럼, 예약 일정을 변경하셔야 하나요?
여	맞아요. 촉박하게 알려드려서 죄송해요.
남	괜찮아요. 오늘 오후 늦게는 가능하세요?
여	오늘은 아예 못 갈 것 같아요. 그리고 제가 내일 마을에 없을 거라서요. 월요일에 예약 가능한 시간이 있나요?
남	확인해 볼게요. *[타자 치는 소리]* 오전 10시 30분이나 오후 2시는 어떠세요?
여	오전이 가장 좋을 것 같아요.

<선택지> ① 출장 때문에 마을에 없을 거예요.

② 오전이 가장 좋을 것 같아요.

③ 편하실 때 언제든지 오세요.

④ 예약 시간을 확인해 주셔서 감사합니다.

⑤ 마지막으로 스케일링을 받으신 게 언제죠?

치과 예약 일정을 변경하는 상황이다. 여자가 월요일에 예약 가능한 시간이 있는지 묻자 남자가 오전 10시 30분이나 오후 2시는 어떤지 제안했으므로, 이에 대한 응답으로는 오전이 좋다고 언급하는 ② 'I think the morning would work best for me.'가 가장 적절하다.

[어휘] routine 혱 정기적인 teeth cleaning 스케일링 sort out ~을 해결하다 reschedule 통 일정을 변경하다

15 상황에 적절한 말 파악   정답 ①

M Dan is the owner of a catering company, and Zoe is the manager of an art gallery. Zoe recently hired Dan's company to provide the food for [1)]an exhibit opening at her gallery. Yesterday, Dan sent her the menu for the event to review. She is happy with the dishes he intends to serve. She also likes that he is planning to use [2)]organic ingredients because she wants to provide her guests with healthy food. However, she is concerned because there are no vegetarian dishes on the menu. **Therefore, Zoe wants to ask Dan to [3)]prepare some vegetarian dishes for her guests as well.** In this situation, what would Zoe most likely say to Dan?

남 Dan은 케이터링 회사의 사장이고, Zoe는 미술관 매니저입니다. Zoe는 최근 미술관의 전시회 개막식에 음식을 제공하기 위해 Dan의 회사를 고용했습니다. 어제 Dan은 그녀에게 검토할 행사 메뉴를 보냈습니다. 그녀는 그가 제공하려고 생각하는 요리에 만족합니다. 그녀는 또한 손님들에게 건강한 음식을 제공하기를 원하기 때문에, 그가 유기농 재료를 사용할 계획이라는 것이 마음에 듭니다. 하지만 그녀는 메뉴에 채식 요리가 없어서 걱정입니다. 따라서, Zoe는 Dan에게 손님들을 위해 채식 요리도 준비해달라고 부탁하고 싶습니다. 이러한 상황에서, Zoe가 Dan에게 가장 할 것 같은 말은 무엇입니까?

<선택지> ① 손님들을 위해 고기가 없는 옵션을 포함해 주실 수 있나요?

② 유기농 재료를 어디서 살 건지 말해주세요.

③ 건강에 좋은 음식을 준비하려는 귀하의 노력에 정말 감사드려요.

④ 메뉴를 개선하는 방법에 대해 제안해 주실 게 있나요?

⑤ 행사에서 채식 요리만 제공할 수 있을까요?

Dan이 보낸 행사 메뉴에 채식 요리가 없는 것을 보고, Zoe는 채식 요리도 준비해달라고 부탁하려 한다. 따라서, Zoe가 할 말로 ① 'Could you include some meatless options for my guests?'가 가장 적절하다.

[어휘] hire 통 고용하다 exhibit 몡 전시회; 전시 review 통 검토하다 intend to ~하려고 생각하다 serve 통 제공하다 organic 혱 유기농의 ingredient 몡 재료
vegetarian 혱 채식의 몡 채식주의자 meatless 혱 고기가 없는

16-17 세트 문항   정답 16 ④ 17 ③

W Good morning, students. Yesterday, we began talking about the harsh desert environment. **In today's class, we will look at the traits that animals have developed to survive there.** Finding and storing water is an issue all animals in the desert must overcome. The **kangaroo rat** has an advantage in this respect. It can survive [1)]without drinking water. Instead, it gets all its moisture from the seeds it eats. The **camel** is also well-suited to desert life. It can drink more than 75 liters of water at once. This [2)]ability lets it store several days' worth of water, allowing it to walk long distances in the desert. Another challenge facing desert animals is the extreme heat. The **fennec fox** avoids overheating by [3)]releasing its body heat through its extremely large ears. And the **banded gecko** avoids the sun entirely. It spends the day hiding under rocks, and then it [4)]comes out at night to hunt. I hope this lesson has helped you develop a better understanding of desert life. Now, let's have a look at a brief video.

여 좋은 아침입니다, 학생 여러분. 어제, 우리는 혹독한 사막의 환경에 대해 이야기하기 시작했습니다. 오늘 수업에서는, 동물들이 그곳에서 살아남기 위해 발달시킨 특성들을 살펴볼 것입니다. 물을 찾고 저장하는 것은 사막의 모든 동물들이 극복해야 하는 문제입니다. 캥거루쥐는 이러한 점에 있어서 이점이 있습니다. 그것은 물을 마시지 않고도 살아남을 수 있습니다. 대신, 그것은 그것이 먹는 씨앗으로부터 모든 수분을 얻습니다. 낙타도 사막 생활에 적절합니다. 그것은 한 번에 75L 이상의 물을 마실 수 있습니다. 이 능력은 며칠 분량의 물을 저장할 수 있게 해주고, 사막에서 먼 거리를 걸을 수 있게 합니다. 사막 동물들이 직면하는 또 다른 문제는 극심한 더위입니다. 사막여우는 극도로 큰 귀를 통해 체온을 방출함으로써 과열을 피합니다. 그리고 줄무늬 도마뱀은 태양을 완전히 피합니다. 그것은 바위 밑에 숨어서 낮을 보내고, 밤에는 나와서 사냥을 합니다. 이 수업이 사막의 생물에 대한 여러분의 이해를 높이는 데 도움이 되었기를 바랍니다. 이제 간단한 영상을 시청하겠습니다.

<선택지> **16** ① 사막의 물리적 특징

② 건조한 생태계의 수자원

③ 야생 생물의 사냥 기술

④ 혹독한 사막 환경에 대한 동물의 적응

⑤ 동물들이 체온을 방출하기 위해 사용하는 여러 가지 방법

17 ① 캥거루쥐 ② 낙타 ③ 뱀 ④ 사막여우 ⑤ 줄무늬 도마뱀

16 동물들이 사막에서 살아남기 위해 발달시킨 특성들에 대해 살펴보고 있으므로 여자가 하는 말의 주제로 ④ 'animal adaptations to harsh desert environments'가 가장 적절하다.
17 캥거루쥐, 낙타, 사막여우, 줄무늬 도마뱀은 언급했지만 ③ 'snake'는 언급하지 않았다.

[어휘] harsh 혱 혹독한 environment 몡 환경 trait 몡 특성 survive 통 살아남다, 생존하다 overcome 통 극복하다 advantage 몡 이점 in this respect 이러한 점에 있어서
well-suited 혱 적절한 face 통 직면하다 몡 얼굴 release 통 방출하다 entirely 튄 완전히 ecosystem 몡 생태계 adaptation 몡 적응

1	①	2	⑤	3	②	4	⑤	5	③	6	④	7	①	8	②	9	⑤	10	④
11	①	12	④	13	②	14	③	15	⑤	16	②	17	④						

• 각 문제의 정답 근거는 굵은 글씨로, Dictation 정답은 밑줄로 표시되어 있습니다.

---

1 목적 파악

정답 ①

M Good morning, residents. I'm John Miller, the president of the Lexton Apartment Committee. **As you know, we'll hold our annual food donation event soon. However, we are going to** ¹⁾change the method **of participation from this year.** To make sure the donations include a good variety of items, we've set up a new online sign-up sheet this year. You can ²⁾select specific items for donation, such as canned meat, frozen vegetables, and dried fish. The link is in the text message we sent you this morning. We are ³⁾looking forward to the event, and we hope everyone joins us in helping out our community.

남 주민 여러분, 좋은 아침입니다. 저는 렉스턴 아파트 운영위원장인 John Miller입니다. 아시다시피, 저희는 곧 연례 식품 기부 행사를 열 예정입니다. 하지만, 저희는 올해부터 참여 방식을 바꾸고자 합니다. 기부에 다양한 물품이 포함될 수 있도록, 저희는 올해 새로운 온라인 참가 신청서를 마련했습니다. 통조림 고기, 냉동 야채, 건어물 등 특정 기부 품목을 선택할 수 있습니다. 링크는 저희가 오늘 아침에 보내드린 문자 메시지에 있습니다. 저희는 이 행사를 기대하고 있고, 모두가 저희 지역사회를 돕는 데 동참하기를 바랍니다.

아파트 운영위원장인 남자가 연례 식품 기부 행사에 대해 말하면서, 올해부터 바뀌는 참여 방식을 안내하고 있다. 따라서, 남자가 하는 말의 목적으로 ① '기부 행사 참여 방법 변경을 안내하려고' 가 가장 적절하다.

어휘 committee 몡 운영위원회 donation 몡 기부 participation 몡 참여, 참가 sign-up sheet 참가 신청서 canned 혱 통조림의 frozen 혱 냉동의, 언 dried fish 건어물 community 몡 지역사회, 공동체

---

2 의견 파악

정답 ⑤

W Are you going somewhere, Liam?
M I'm meeting some classmates at the library, Mom.
W Oh, are you ¹⁾working on a group project together?
M Yeah. We're supposed to write a report about a famous person in history.
W That sounds interesting. **Group projects are a great way to learn** ²⁾how to cooperate **with others.**
M To be honest, it's not going well. Everyone keeps arguing about the topic.
W That must be hard, but you'll end up resolving the arguments.
M Hmm... Why are you so sure about that?
W Well, you have ³⁾a common goal of writing a good report. So as you try to accomplish that goal, you'll learn how to work together.
M That sounds like a good lesson, but it's a difficult one.
W I know, but ⁴⁾keep trying!
M Okay. I will, Mom.

여 어디 가니, Liam?
남 도서관에서 반 친구들을 만나기로 했어요, 엄마.
여 아, 조별 과제를 같이 하는 거니?
남 네. 역사상 유명한 사람에 대한 보고서를 쓰기로 되어 있어요.
여 그거 재미있겠네. 조별 과제는 다른 사람들과 협력하는 방법을 배울 수 있는 좋은 방법이란다.
남 솔직히 말해서, 잘 되어 가고 있지 않아요. 모두가 주제에 대해 계속 언쟁하고 있어요.
여 힘들겠지만, 결국 언쟁을 해결하게 될 거야.
남 흠... 왜 그렇게 확신을 하세요?
여 글쎄, 너희들은 좋은 보고서를 쓰겠다는 공통된 목표를 가지고 있잖니. 그래서, 너희가 그 목표를 성취하기 위해 노력하면서, 함께 일하는 방법을 배우게 될 거란다.
남 좋은 교훈처럼 들리지만, 어렵네요.
여 그래, 하지만 계속 노력해 보렴!
남 알았어요. 그렇게 할게요, 엄마.

조별 과제를 하면서 어려움을 겪고 있는 남자에게 여자가 조별 과제는 다른 사람들과 협력하는 방법을 배울 수 있는 좋은 방법이라고 했다. 따라서, 여자의 의견으로 ⑤ '조별 과제를 통해 사람들과 협력하는 법을 배울 수 있다.'가 가장 적절하다.

어휘 cooperate 동 협력하다 to be honest 솔직히 말해서 go well 잘 되어 가다 argue 동 언쟁하다 (argument 몡 언쟁, 논쟁) end up 결국 ~하게 되다 resolve 동 해결하다 common 혱 공통된; 흔한 goal 몡 목표 accomplish 동 성취하다 lesson 몡 교훈; 수업

---

3 관계 파악

정답 ②

M Welcome to *Weekend Sports*, Ms. Davis.
W Thanks. I am a long-time fan of your show.
M I appreciate that. **I'm sure many of my listeners are excited to cheer for your team in the international soccer tournament that starts tomorrow. How** ¹⁾have you prepared **for it?**
W Well, I've organized practices for the players on my team every day for the last two months.
M Isn't that schedule tiring?
W Sure. But the players know they ²⁾need to work hard to win difficult matches.

남 <Weekend Sports>에 오신 것을 환영합니다, Davis 씨.
여 고맙습니다. 전 당신 쇼의 오랜 팬이에요.
남 감사합니다. 내일부터 시작되는 국제 축구 토너먼트 경기에서 저희의 많은 청취자분들이 당신의 팀을 응원할 생각에 신이 나 계시는데요. 경기를 어떻게 준비하셨나요?
여 음, 지난 두 달 동안 우리 팀 선수들을 위한 훈련을 매일 준비했어요.
남 그 일정이 피곤하지는 않았나요?
여 물론이죠. 하지만 선수들은 어려운 경기에서 이기려면 열심히 노력해야 한다는 것을 알고 있습니다.

M Your star player Nancy Aston injured her leg recently. Is it serious?	남 당신의 스타 선수 Nancy Aston이 최근에 다리를 다쳤어요. 심각한 건가요?
W No. The team doctor expects it to heal in about a week.	여 아니요. 팀 의사 선생님은 일주일 정도면 나을 거라고 예상하고 있어요.
M Will she be able to play well in the tournament?	남 그녀가 토너먼트 경기에서 잘 뛸 수 있을까요?
W Yes, I believe so. Everyone is feeling confident that we can ³⁾lift the championship trophy at the end of the tournament.	여 네, 그럴 거라고 봅니다. 모두가 대회가 끝날 때 우승 트로피를 들어 올릴 수 있겠다는 자신감을 느끼고 있습니다.
M Great. Best of luck to you.	남 멋집니다. 행운을 빌어요.

두 사람이 내일부터 시작되는 국제 축구 토너먼트 경기에 대해 이야기하고 있다. 남자는 자신의 청취자들을 대변하여 인터뷰를 하고 있고, 여자는 자신의 팀이 경기를 준비한 과정을 답변해주고 있는 것으로 보아 두 사람의 관계로 ② '라디오 진행자 — 축구 감독'이 가장 적절하다.

어휘 cheer for ~를 응원하다 tournament 명 토너먼트 경기 organize 통 준비하다; 조직하다 confident 형 자신감 있는 lift 통 들어올리다 Best of luck to you. 행운을 빌어요.

4 그림 내용 불일치 파악
정답 ⑤

M Honey, we finally finished redecorating the guestroom.	남 여보, 우리 드디어 손님 방을 다시 꾸미는 것을 마쳤네.
W I think it looks amazing. What do you think?	여 정말 멋진 것 같아. 당신 생각은 어때?
M I agree. ¹⁾I particularly like the checked rug on the floor.	남 동의해. 특히 바닥에 있는 체크무늬 러그가 좋아.
W Me too. I'm not sure if the wardrobe next to the window is big enough, though.	여 나도. 하지만 창문 옆에 있는 옷장이 충분히 큰지는 잘 모르겠어.
M It's fine. Hmm, do you think we need to put in another lamp?	남 괜찮아. 흠, 램프를 하나 더 놓아야 할까?
W No. The floor lamp ²⁾next to the bed is actually quite bright.	여 아니. 침대 옆에 있는 플로어 스탠드 조명이 사실 꽤 밝거든.
M Good. I want to make sure the painting you hung above the bed is easy to see.	남 좋아. 당신이 침대 위에 걸어놓은 그림이 확실히 보기 쉽게 하고 싶거든.
W The flowers in that painting are beautiful. I hope our guests like it.	여 저 그림 속의 꽃들은 아름다워. 손님들이 좋아했으면 좋겠어.
M I'm sure they will. **Oh, maybe we should move the round table ³⁾closer to the wall.**	남 분명 그럴 거야. 아, 어쩌면 원형 탁자를 벽 쪽으로 더 가까이 옮기는 게 좋겠어.
W I don't think that's necessary. **I like the table on the rug where it is now.**	여 그럴 필요는 없을 것 같아. 지금처럼 러그 위에 있는 게 좋아.
M Great. Then, I guess we don't need to change anything.	남 훌륭해. 그럼, 우리는 아무것도 바꿀 필요가 없겠네.

대화에서 남자가 러그 위에 있는 원형 탁자를 벽 쪽으로 더 가까이 옮기는 것이 좋겠다고 말했는데, ⑤에는 사각 탁자가 그려져 있다.

어휘 redecorate 통 다시 꾸미다 particularly 부 특히 checked 형 체크무늬의 wardrobe 명 옷장 quite 부 꽤 bright 형 밝은 make sure ~을 확실히 하다

5 할 일 파악
정답 ③

W Hey, Eric. Do you want to head over to the studio to record our video about woodworking?	여 안녕, Eric. 스튜디오로 가서 목공에 관한 영상을 녹화할래?
M Just a moment. Let's make sure everything is ready.	남 잠깐만. 모든 것이 준비되었는지 확실히 하자.
W Right. I don't want to find out that we forgot something after we start filming.	여 그래. 촬영을 시작한 후에 뭔가를 잊어버렸다는 것을 알고 싶지는 않네.
M Exactly. ¹⁾made a checklist on my phone.	남 맞아. 내가 휴대폰에 체크리스트를 만들어두었어.
W Thanks. What is the first thing we should confirm?	여 고마워. 우리가 가장 먼저 확인해야 할 것은 뭐야?
M Do we have the wood and the power tools for ²⁾building the shoe rack?	남 신발장을 만들 목재와 전동 공구는 있어?
W All of the equipment is packed into the van.	여 모든 장비는 밴 안에 들어 있어.
M What about the camera and the microphones?	남 카메라랑 마이크는?
W I brought those over to the studio earlier. They're all set up.	여 전에 스튜디오에 가지고 갔었어. 다 설치가 되어있어.
M Great. **We still need to ³⁾select some background music to play in the video, right?**	남 좋아. 우린 아직 영상에서 재생할 배경 음악을 선택해야 해, 그렇지?
W **Yeah. I can pick a song now.**	여 응. 내가 지금 음악을 고를 수 있어.
M Perfect. I'll put the song in the video when editing it.	남 완벽해. 편집할 때 영상에 그 음악을 넣을게.

영상 녹화에 필요한 준비물에 대해 이야기하고 있다. 남자가 영상에서 재생할 배경음악을 선택해야 하는지 묻자 여자가 본인이 지금 음악을 고를 수 있다고 했으므로 여자가 할 일로 ③ '배경 음악 고르기'가 가장 적절하다

어휘 head over to ~로 가다, 향하다 record 통 녹화하다 woodworking 명 목공 power tool 전동 공구 shoe rack 신발장 equipment 명 장비 edit 통 편집하다

6 금액 정보 파악

정답 ④

M Welcome to the Grand Canyon Souvenir Shop. How can I help you?	남 그랜드 캐니언 기념품 가게에 오신 것을 환영합니다. 무엇을 도와드릴까요?
W Hi. I want to get some T-shirts for ¹⁾my friends back home.	여 안녕하세요. 고향에 있는 친구들에게 줄 티셔츠를 좀 사고 싶어요.
M What about these? **The one with the cactus on it is $15, and the one with the picture of the Grand Canyon is $20.**	남 이건 어떠세요? 선인장이 그려진 것은 15달러이고, 그랜드 캐니언의 사진이 있는 것은 20달러예요.
W **I'll take two with the cactus and one with the picture of the Grand Canyon.**	여 선인장이 그려진 것 두 개, 그랜드 캐니언 사진이 있는 것 하나 주세요.
M Here you go. Is there anything else you need?	남 여기 있습니다. 그 밖에 더 필요한 건 없으시나요?
W **I was also thinking of buying some magnets.**	여 자석도 좀 살까 생각 중이었어요.
M Well, this one is very popular, **and it's only $10.**	남 음, 이것은 아주 인기가 있는데, 10달러밖에 안 해요.
W Perfect. I'll ²⁾take four, please.	여 완벽해요. 네 개 주세요.
M So you want two T-shirts with the cactus, one with the picture of the canyon, and four of these magnets, right?	남 그럼 선인장이 그려진 티셔츠 두 장, 협곡 사진이 있는 티셔츠 한 장, 자석 네 개를 원하시는 거죠?
W Yes. That's everything.	여 네. 그게 다예요.
M Okay. Oh, I ³⁾forgot to mention that we are having a sale today. **Every item is 10% off.**	남 알겠습니다. 아, 오늘 세일 중이라고 말하는 걸 깜빡했네요. 모든 품목이 10% 할인돼요.
W Wonderful. Here's my credit card.	여 훌륭해요. 여기 제 신용 카드요.

여자가 선인장이 그려진 티셔츠 두 장($15×2=$30)과 협곡 사진이 있는 티셔츠 한 장($20), 자석 네 개($10×4=$40)를 구매했고, 모든 품목에 10% 할인($90×0.9=$81)을 받았으므로 정답은 ④ '$81'이다.

어휘 home 몡 고향; 집 cactus 몡 선인장 magnet 몡 자석 canyon 몡 협곡 mention 통 말하다; 언급하다 have a sale 세일하다

7 이유 파악

정답 ①

W Brandon, are you excited about our class field trip on Friday?	여 Brandon, 금요일에 있을 우리 반 현장학습이 기대되니?
M Yes. I'm really looking forward to hiking in the national park. But I think I need a new backpack. Mine is pretty old.	남 응. 국립공원에서 하이킹하는 것을 정말 기대하고 있어. 그런데 새 배낭이 필요할 것 같아. 내 것은 꽤 낡았거든.
W I want to ¹⁾buy a new one, too. Do you want to go shopping with me this afternoon?	여 나도 새 걸 사고 싶어. 오늘 오후에 나랑 함께 쇼핑하러 갈래?
M I'd love to, but I have plans.	남 그러고 싶지만, 계획이 있어.
W Oh, you have a piano lesson today, right?	여 아, 오늘 피아노 수업이 있지?
M No. My lesson is tomorrow, actually.	남 아니. 사실 수업은 내일 있어.
W Really? Then, are you supposed to ²⁾spend time with your family?	여 정말? 그럼, 가족과 함께 시간을 보내기로 되어 있니?
M No. **I have to visit the dentist at 2 p.m. this afternoon. It's time for ³⁾my annual checkup.**	남 아니. 오늘 오후 2시에 치과에 가야 해. 연례 검진을 받을 때거든.
W I see. I'll ask Jenna to go to the mall with me instead. Will you have time to study for history class with me tomorrow?	여 그렇구나. 대신 Jenna에게 쇼핑몰에 같이 가자고 할게. 내일 나랑 역사 수업 공부할 시간은 있니?
M Of course. See you then.	남 물론이지. 그때 봐.

남자는 쇼핑하러 가자는 여자의 제안에 계획이 있다고 하면서 치과에 연례 검진을 받으러 간다고 말했으므로, 남자가 쇼핑하러 갈 수 없는 이유는 ① '치과 검진을 받아야 해서'이다.

어휘 field trip 현장학습 look forward to ~을 기대하다 national park 국립공원 be supposed to ~하기로 되어 있다 annual 혱 연례의, 연간의 checkup 몡 검진, 검사

8 언급 유무 파악

정답 ②

M Gina, are you busy on Saturday? I'd like to visit the art museum with you.	남 Gina, 토요일에 바빠? 너와 함께 미술 박물관을 방문하고 싶어.
W I appreciate the invitation, but I can't go. I'm taking the Emergency First Aid Course. It starts ¹⁾at 10 a.m. on Saturday.	여 초대는 고맙지만, 갈 수 없어. 비상시 응급 처치 과정 수업을 들을 예정이거든. 토요일 오전 10시에 시작해.
M What about ²⁾visiting the museum in the afternoon?	남 오후에 박물관을 방문하는 건 어때?
W It's **a four-hour class.** I'll be too tired to do anything afterward.	여 4시간짜리 수업이야. 나는 너무 피곤해서 그 후에는 아무것도 할 수 없을 거야.
M I understand. That sounds exhausting. Where are you taking the course?	남 이해해. 피로할 것 같네. 어디서 수업을 들어?
W At **the Robertson Community Center.** It's just ³⁾a couple of blocks from my home.	여 로버트슨 주민 센터에서. 우리 집에서 두어 블록만 가면 돼.
M That's convenient. It won't take you long to walk there. By the way, who is the instructor?	남 편리하네. 거기까지 걸어가는 데 오래 걸리지 않겠어. 그런데, 강사는 누구야?
W The course is being taught by **Evan Williams.** He's ⁴⁾a retired doctor who teaches classes at the center.	여 이 수업은 Evan Williams님이 가르치고 있어. 센터에서 수업을 가르치는 은퇴한 의사셔.
M That sounds great. I'm sure you'll learn a lot.	남 좋네. 많은 것을 배울 수 있을 거야.
W Thanks! And I hope you have fun at the museum.	여 고마워! 그리고 네가 박물관에서 즐거운 시간 보내면 좋겠어.

시작 시각(오전 10시), 소요 시간(4시간), 수업 장소(로버트슨 주민 센터), 강사 이름(Evan Williams)에 대해 언급했고, ② '참가 인원'은 언급하지 않았다.

어휘 take a course 수업을 듣다 emergency 몡 비상시, 비상사태 first aid 응급 처치 afterward 뷔 그 후 exhausting 혱 피로하게 하는 convenient 혱 편리한 by the way 그런데
instructor 몡 강사 retired 혱 은퇴한

---

9 내용 불일치 파악   정답 ⑤

M Good morning. You are listening to *Around Town*. If you enjoy watching fireworks, don't miss the sixth annual Summer Fireworks Festival on Sunday. The event will begin at 9 p.m. and end at 11 p.m. It ¹⁾will be held in Harbor Park. Teams from four countries will compete to put on the best fireworks display. You are sure to have a great time. And if you get hungry during the festival, don't worry. There will be many vendors selling snacks and drinks. **Parking ²⁾will be available in the lot on the east side of the park and will cost $15 for three hours.** However, space is limited, so attendees are advised to ³⁾use public transportation. For more information, visit www.summerfireworks.com.	남 좋은 아침입니다. 여러분은 <Around Town>을 듣고 계십니다. 만약 여러분이 불꽃놀이 보는 것을 즐긴다면, 일요일에 열리는 여섯 번째 연례 Summer Fireworks Festival을 놓치지 마세요. 행사는 저녁 9시에 시작해서 11시에 끝날 것입니다. 하버 공원에서 열릴 예정이지요. 4개국에서 온 팀들이 참가하여 최고의 불꽃놀이 공연을 할 것입니다. 여러분은 분명 즐거운 시간을 보낼 거예요. 그리고 축제 동안 배가 고파져도 걱정하지 마세요. 간식과 음료를 파는 많은 노점상들이 있을 것입니다. 주차는 공원 동쪽에 있는 주차장에 하시면 되고 3시간에 15달러 되겠습니다. 하지만, 공간이 한정되어 있어서, 참석자분들에게 대중교통을 이용하시기를 권고합니다. 더 많은 정보를 원하시면, www.summerfireworks.com을 방문하세요.

불꽃놀이 축제에 대한 안내 방송이다. 남자가 주차는 3시간에 15달러가 되겠다고 했으므로 ⑤ '무료 주차 공간이 제공될 예정이다.'는 내용과 일치하지 않는다.

어휘 firework 몡 불꽃놀이 annual 혱 연례의 compete 통 참가하다; 경쟁하다 put on ~을 공연하다 vendor 몡 노점상 limit 통 제한하다 몡 한계 attendee 몡 참석자
advise 통 권고하다, 조언하다 public transportation 대중교통

---

10 도표 정보 파악   정답 ④

W Honey, have you ¹⁾reserved the rental car for our ski trip to Denver?	여 여보, 덴버로 스키 여행 갈 때 쓸 렌터카 예약했어?
M I'm just looking at the agency's website. What about this one?	남 지금 막 대리점 웹사이트를 보는 중이야. 이거 어때?
W It only has seats for two people.	여 이 차엔 두 사람만 앉을 수 있어.
M I didn't notice that. That will be too small. **There will be four of us traveling together.**	남 그건 몰랐네. 너무 작을 거야. 우리는 4명이 함께 여행할 거니까.
W And it is going to ²⁾be a long trip, so we will need a vehicle that's fuel efficient.	여 그리고 긴 여행이 될 테니, 연료 효율이 좋은 차량이 필요할 거야.
M Yeah. **It should get at least 12 kilometers to the liter.**	남 응. 1L당 적어도 12km는 가야지.
W Right. **And I don't want to spend more than $50 per day on the rental.**	여 맞아. 그리고 렌트하는 데 하루에 50달러 이상을 쓰고 싶지는 않아.
M Me neither. **Oh, look!** One of ³⁾the remaining cars has a ski rack.	남 나도 그래. 오, 봐! 남아있는 차들 중 하나는 스키 거치대가 있어.
W **We definitely need one to hold the skis.**	여 스키판을 둘 수 있는 게 꼭 필요해.
M I agree. I guess we should reserve this car, then.	남 동의해. 그럼 이 차를 예약해야겠네.

두 사람은 4명 이상이 탈 수 있고, 1L당 12km 이상 가며, 렌트비가 하루에 50달러 미만인 것 중에서, 스키 거치대가 있는 렌터카를 골랐다.

어휘 reserve 통 예약하다 agency 몡 대리점 vehicle 몡 차량 fuel efficient 연료 효율이 좋은 remaining 혱 남아있는 ski rack 스키 거치대 capacity 몡 수용력, 용량
rental fee 렌트비, 대여료

---

11 짧은 대화의 응답 파악   정답 ①

M Mom, have you called a taxi yet? We need to leave for the airport soon.	남 엄마, 택시 부르셨어요? 우리 곧 공항으로 떠나야 해요.
W Oh, I ¹⁾completely forgot. Can you do that?	여 아, 완전히 잊어버렸네. 네가 해줄 수 있니?
M Sure. *[Pause]* **I just ²⁾got a taxi with an app!** Hopefully, it won't take too long to get here.	남 물론이죠. *[잠시 멈춤]* 방금 앱으로 택시를 잡았어요! 바라건대 여기 오는 데 너무 오래 걸리지 않으면 좋겠네요.
W It should arrive in about 10 minutes.	여 10분 정도면 도착할 거야.

선택지 ① 10분 정도면 도착할 거야.
② 택시 요금을 신용 카드로 결제했어.
③ 공항에 도착하자마자 문자 주렴.
④ 운전이 예상보다 오래 걸렸어.
⑤ 우리 비행기가 연착되지 않으면 좋겠네.

여자가 택시를 불러달라고 하자 남자가 앱으로 택시를 잡았다면서 이곳으로 오는 데 너무 오래 걸리지 않으면 좋겠다고 했으므로, 이에 대한 응답으로는 택시의 도착 시간을 예상하는 ① 'It should arrive in about 10 minutes.'가 가장 적절하다.

어휘 leave for ~으로 떠나다 completely 뷔 완전히 hopefully 뷔 바라건대 as soon as ~하자마자

12 짧은 대화의 응답 파악   정답 ④

W Honey, ¹⁾would you mind stopping at the supermarket on your way home from work tonight? M Of course not. What do you need me to pick up from the store? W I'm planning on baking a cake tomorrow. **Could you ²⁾buy me some flour?** M Sure. Is there a particular brand you like?	여 여보, 오늘 밤 퇴근하는 길에 슈퍼마켓에 들러 줄래? 남 물론이지. 가게에서 뭘 사 오길 원해? 여 내일 케이크를 구울 계획이야. 밀가루 좀 사다 줄 수 있어? 남 물론이지. 특별히 좋아하는 브랜드가 있어? 선택지 ① 괜찮아. 이 케이크가 너무 달아. ② 응. 그 가게는 그린우드가에 있어. ③ 미안해. 꽃 배달이 늦을 예정이야. ④ 물론이지. 특별히 좋아하는 브랜드가 있어? ⑤ 걱정 마. 퇴근하고 당신을 데리러 갈게.

여자가 내일 케이크를 구울 계획이라면서 남자에게 슈퍼마켓에서 밀가루를 사달라고 했으므로, 이에 대한 응답으로는 특별히 좋아하는 밀가루 브랜드가 있는지 되묻는 ④ 'Sure. Is there a particular brand you like?'가 가장 적절하다.

어휘 stop 통 들르다, 멈추다   bake 통 굽다   flour 명 밀가루

---

13 긴 대화의 응답 파악   정답 ②

[Phone rings.] W You've reached the front desk at the Sunset Hotel. M Hi. This is Steve Harris in Room 303. W Good evening, Mr. Harris. How can I help you? M **The people in ¹⁾the room next to mine are very noisy.** W Oh, I see. Is the noise disturbing you? M Yes. Would it be possible to get a different room? W I'll check if there are any rooms available now, Mr. Harris. *[Typing sound]* I'm very sorry, but we are ²⁾fully booked tonight. I can have you moved to another one tomorrow. M But that doesn't help me now. I'm trying to prepare for an important meeting tomorrow, but I can't focus on my work. W I'll ask the guests in that room to be quiet. M Thanks. I really ³⁾appreciate your assistance. W No problem. **Could you tell me which room the noise is coming from?** M I am pretty sure it is the people in Room 302.	*[전화기가 울린다.]* 여 선셋 호텔 안내 데스크입니다. 남 안녕하세요. 303호의 Steve Harris입니다. 여 안녕하세요, Harris 씨. 무엇을 도와드릴까요? 남 제 옆 방 사람들이 너무 시끄러워요. 여 아, 그렇군요. 소음이 방해되나요? 남 네. 다른 방으로 배정받을 수 있을까요? 여 지금 이용하실 수 있는 방이 있는지 알아볼게요, Harris 씨. *[타자 치는 소리]* 정말 죄송합니다만, 오늘 밤은 예약이 꽉 찼네요. 내일 다른 곳으로 옮겨 드릴 수 있어요. 남 하지만 지금은 그게 도움이 안 돼요. 내일 있는 중요한 회의를 준비하려고 하는데, 일에 집중할 수가 없어요. 여 그 방에 있는 손님들에게 조용히 해달라고 요청하겠습니다. 남 고마워요. 도와주셔서 정말 감사해요. 여 천만에요. 어느 방에서 소음이 나는지 말씀해 주시겠어요? 남 302호에 있는 사람들이라고 꽤 확신해요. 선택지 ① 회의는 오전 9시에 시작하기로 되어 있어요. ② 302호에 있는 사람들이라고 꽤 확신해요. ③ 바다가 보이는 방으로 주세요. ④ 내일 몇 시에 체크인이 가능할까요? ⑤ 저의 새로운 방이 준비되었는지 확인해 주세요.

호텔 투숙객인 남자가 옆 방이 너무 시끄러워서 안내 데스크에 전화를 건 상황이다. 호텔 직원인 여자가 어느 방에서 소음이 나는지 물었으므로, 이에 대한 응답으로는 방 호수를 언급하는 ② 'I am pretty sure it is the people in Room 302.'가 가장 적절하다.

어휘 noise 명 소음   disturb 통 방해하다   available 형 이용할 수 있는   focus on ~에 집중하다   assistance 명 도움

---

14 긴 대화의 응답 파악   정답 ③

W I can't believe how tired I am today, David. M Did you stay up late last night? W Yeah. **I've been having trouble sleeping lately.** M That's unfortunate. I used to have the same problem as well. W Really? Did you figure out a way to deal with it? M Well, one thing that is very important is to avoid using your computer or phone ¹⁾right before bed. W I've heard people say that. But I don't understand why it's so important. M ²⁾Exposure to the light from these devices can make you feel more alert. W I see what you mean. Did you change anything else? M **I'd also suggest exercising every day. I read that it ³⁾helped with sleep.** W Did that work for you? M Yes. **I joined a gym, and I've been sleeping better ever since.** W Interesting. I may have to give your suggestions a try.	여 David, 오늘 얼마나 피곤한지 믿을 수가 없네. 남 어젯밤 늦은 시간까지 깨어있었어? 여 응. 요즘 잠을 잘 못 자고 있어. 남 유감이네. 나도 예전에 같은 문제가 있었어. 여 정말? 그걸 해결할 방법을 알아냈어? 남 음, 아주 중요한 한 가지는 자기 직전에 컴퓨터나 휴대폰 사용을 피하는 거야. 여 사람들이 그렇게 말하는 걸 들어본 적 있어. 하지만 그게 왜 그렇게 중요한지 이해가 안 돼. 남 그 기기들에서 나오는 빛에 노출되면 정신이 더 깰 수 있거든. 여 무슨 말인지 알겠어. 다른 건 바꾼 거 없어? 남 매일 운동하는 것도 제안할게. 그게 수면에 도움이 된다는 내용을 읽어봤거든. 여 그게 효과가 있었니? 남 응. 체육관에 등록했는데, 그 이후로 계속 잠을 더 잘 잤어. 여 흥미롭네. 너의 제안을 시도해 봐야 할 것 같아.

선택지 ① 아직. 나는 주말마다 늦게까지 늦잠 자는 것을 좋아하거든.

② 모르겠어. 나는 아침에 운동하는 것을 선호해.

③ 흥미롭네. 너의 제안을 시도해 봐야 할 것 같아.

④ 잘됐네. 너희 체육관에 나를 등록해 줘서 기뻐.

⑤ 좋은 생각이야. 자기 전에 휴대폰을 무음으로 해둘게.

여자가 요즘 잠을 잘 못 잔다고 말하자 남자가 조언해주는 상황이다. 남자가 자기 직전 컴퓨터나 휴대폰 사용을 피하고 매일 운동을 하는 등의 방법을 조언하면서 그 효과를 설명했으므로, 이에 대한 응답으로는 남자의 제안을 시도해보겠다고 말하는 ③ 'Interesting. I may have to give your suggestions a try.'가 가장 적절하다.

어휘 **stay up late** 늦은 시간까지 깨어있다 **unfortunate** 형 유감스러운; 불행한 **figure out** ~을 알아내다 **deal with** ~을 해결하다 **avoid** 동 피하다 **exposure** 명 노출 **device** 명 기기, 장치 **feel alert** 정신이 깨다 **ever since** 그 이후로 계속 **sleep in** 늦잠을 자다 **give ~ a try** ~을 시도해 보다

---

15 상황에 적절한 말 파악

정답 ⑤

W Carl and Brenda live in the same apartment building. Their building provides each resident with an individual parking space. Carl's parking space is [1)]near the main entrance of the building, but Brenda's is about 30 meters away from the door. Last week, Brenda slipped on the icy pavement and sprained her ankle. When Carl came home from work today, he noticed that she was [2)]having problems walking from her car to the building's entrance. **Therefore, Carl wants to tell Brenda that she can use his parking space and he will use hers while [3)]her injury heals.** In this situation, what would Carl most likely say to Brenda?

여 Carl과 Brenda는 같은 아파트에 살고 있습니다. 그들의 건물은 각 거주민에게 개별 주차 공간을 제공합니다. Carl의 주차 공간은 건물 정문 근처에 있지만, Brenda의 것은 현관에서 약 30m 떨어져 있습니다. 지난주, Brenda는 빙판길에서 미끄러져 발목을 삐었습니다. Carl이 오늘 퇴근하고 집에 왔을 때, 그는 그녀가 차에서 건물 입구까지 걸어가는 데 문제가 있다는 것을 알아챘습니다. 따라서, Carl은 Brenda에게 그녀가 자신의 주차 공간을 사용할 수 있고, 그가 Brenda의 부상이 낫는 동안 그녀의 주차 공간을 사용하겠다고 말하고 싶습니다. 이러한 상황에서, Carl이 Brenda에게 가장 할 것 같은 말은 무엇입니까?

선택지 ① 당신 주차 공간이 어디에 있는지 알려줘요.

② 어째서 저번에 제 공간에 주차했나요?

③ 건물 관리자에게 새로운 주차 공간을 요청해야 해요.

④ 발을 다친 상태에서 운전하는 건 안전하지 않다고 생각해요.

⑤ 당신이 나을 때까지 우리 주차 공간을 바꾸는 게 어때요?

Brenda가 발목을 삐어 걷는 데 어려움을 겪는 것을 보고, Carl은 그녀의 부상이 낫는 동안 자신의 주차 공간과 바꾸어 사용하자고 제안하려 한다. 따라서, Carl이 할 말로 ⑤ 'Why don't we trade parking spaces until you are feeling better?'가 가장 적절하다.

어휘 **provide** 동 제공하다 **resident** 명 거주민, 거주자 **individual** 형 개별의; 개인의 **slip** 동 미끄러지다 **pavement** 명 길, 인도 **sprain one's ankle** 발목을 삐다 **injury** 명 부상 **heal** 동 낫다, 치유되다 **How come ~?** 어째서 ~예요? **trade** 동 바꾸다, 교환하다

16-17 세트 문항

정답 16 ② 17 ④

M Good afternoon. Last class, we started talking about how people in early societies lived. **Today, I want to focus on the various types of shelters that they used.** First, **caves** were one of the [1)]earliest homes for humans. In fact, one cave in Eastern Europe was inhabited about 54,000 years ago. Second, **tents** were best for people who moved from place to place in search of food. These [2)]temporary shelters were usually made with animal skins and wooden poles. Some of them were large enough for 10 to 15 people to live in comfortably. Third, **igloos** have been made for thousands of years by people living in the Arctic. These are built using blocks of snow, and they provide excellent [3)]protection from the cold weather of this region. Lastly, prehistoric people also constructed **stone buildings**. The oldest known example is on an island in the Middle East. It is believed to be over 8,500 years old. Now, let's look at some photos of these shelters.

남 안녕하십니까. 지난 수업에서, 우리는 초기 인류 사회의 사람들이 어떻게 살았는지에 대해 이야기하기 시작했습니다. 오늘은, 그들이 사용한 다양한 유형의 주거지에 초점을 맞추고 싶습니다. 첫째로, 동굴은 인류의 가장 초기 집 중 하나였습니다. 사실, 동유럽의 한 동굴에는 약 54,000년 전에 사람이 살고 있었습니다. 둘째, 텐트는 음식을 찾아서 여기저기로 이동하는 사람들에게 최고였습니다. 이 임시 주거지는 보통 동물의 가죽과 나무 막대기로 만들어졌습니다. 그것들 중 일부는 10명에서 15명의 사람들이 편안하게 살 수 있을 정도로 충분히 컸습니다. 셋째, 이글루는 북극에 사는 사람들에 의해 수천 년 동안 만들어져왔습니다. 이것들은 눈으로 된 벽돌을 사용하여 지어지고, 이 지역의 추운 날씨로부터 탁월한 보호를 제공합니다. 마지막으로, 선사시대 사람들도 석조 건물을 세웠습니다. 가장 오래된 것으로 알려진 예는 중동의 한 섬에 있습니다. 그것은 8,500년 이상 되었다고 여겨집니다. 이제, 이 주거지들의 사진을 몇 장 보겠습니다.

선택지 16 ① 최초의 인류 사회의 특징

② 초기 인류가 사용한 거주지의 종류

③ 사람들이 동굴을 쉼터로 사용한 이유

④ 건축 자재로서의 석재의 이점

⑤ 전 세계에 선사시대 사람들의 확산

17 ① 동굴 ② 텐트 ③ 이글루 ④ 통나무집 ⑤ 석조 건물

16 초기 인류 사회의 사람들이 사용한 다양한 유형의 주거지에 초점을 맞추고 있으므로 남자가 하는 말의 주제로 ② 'types of residences used by early humans'가 가장 적절하다.

17 동굴, 텐트, 이글루, 석조 건물은 언급했지만 ④ 'log houses'는 언급하지 않았다.

어휘 **early** 부 초기의; 이른 **shelter** 명 주거지; 쉼터 **cave** 명 동굴 **inhabit** 동 살다, 거주하다 **from place to place** 여기저기로 **in search of** ~을 찾아서 **temporary** 형 임시의, 일시적인 **skin** 명 가죽; 피부 **pole** 명 막대기 **region** 명 지역 **prehistoric** 형 선사시대의 **construct** 동 세우다, 건설하다

23회 고난도 영어듣기 모의고사

1	①	2	⑤	3	②	4	⑤	5	①	6	②	7	①	8	③	9	③	10	④
11	⑤	12	②	13	④	14	①	15	②	16	⑤	17	③						

• 각 문제의 정답 근거는 굵은 글씨로, Dictation 정답은 밑줄로 표시되어 있습니다.

1 목적 파악

정답 ①

W Are you trying to exercise more often? Do you find it hard ¹⁾to stay motivated while working out alone? If so, we have some great news for you. **The Center Street Gym will have its** ²⁾grand opening **on May 15th. We encourage everyone to come check it out!** Conveniently located near the Bayside Subway Station, our facility will include state-of-the-art equipment. Best of all, each member ³⁾will receive access to personal trainers and a wide variety of group classes including yoga and aerobics. There will always be someone to ⁴⁾give you encouragement to meet your fitness goals. Visit www.centergym.com for more information about our gym.

여 운동을 더 자주 하려고 노력하고 있나요? 혼자 운동하는 동안 의욕을 갖도록 유지하는 것이 어렵나요? 만약 그렇다면, 저희에게 좋은 소식이 있습니다. Center Street Gym이 5월 15일에 개장합니다. 모두 많이 구경 와주십시오! 베이사이드 지하철역 근처의 교통이 편리한 곳에 자리 잡은 저희 시설에는 최신 장비가 포함될 것입니다. 무엇보다도, 각 회원들은 개인 트레이너 그리고 요가와 에어로빅을 포함한 다양한 그룹 수업을 받을 것입니다. 여러분의 운동 목표를 달성하도록 격려해 줄 누군가가 항상 있을 겁니다. 저희 체육관에 대한 더 많은 정보를 원하시면 www.centergym.com을 방문하십시오.

여자가 Center Street Gym이 개장할 것이라고 하면서, 개관일과 위치 및 수업 등에 대한 정보를 주고 있다. 따라서, 여자가 하는 말의 목적으로 ① '체육관 개관을 홍보하려고'가 가장 적절하다.

[어휘] motivate ⑧ 의욕을 갖게 하다 work out 운동하다 grand opening 개장 conveniently located 교통이 편리한 곳에 자리 잡은 facility ⑲ 시설 state-of-the-art ⑲ 최신의 best of all 무엇보다도 receive ⑧ 받다 meet a goal 목표를 달성하다 fitness ⑲ 운동, 체력 단련

2 의견 파악

정답 ⑤

M What are you doing, Emma?
W I'm writing an essay about Shakespeare.
M You seem frustrated. Are you ¹⁾having trouble with the topic?
W Well, it's not the topic but the writing. I think my writing is too simple, and I keep using the same words.
M There's an easy way to fix that.
W Really? What's that?
M **You should read a lot of different books,** ²⁾like novels, biographies, **and even comics, whenever you can.**
W I don't see how that can help.
M The books are all written in different styles and ³⁾use a variety of words and phrases. You would become familiar with many types of writing.
W But ⁴⁾reading is different from writing.
M That doesn't matter. **Just by reading a lot, your vocabulary naturally increases and your writing improves.**
W I get it. I'll give it a try!

남 Emma, 뭐 하고 있니?
여 셰익스피어에 대한 에세이를 쓰고 있어.
남 불만이 있어 보여. 주제와 관련된 곤란을 겪고 있니?
여 음, 주제가 아니라 글쓰기가 문제야. 나는 내 글이 너무 단순하고, 계속 같은 단어를 반복해서 사용한다고 생각해.
남 그걸 고칠 수 있는 쉬운 방법이 있어.
여 정말? 그게 뭐야?
남 소설, 전기, 심지어 만화와 같은 다양한 책들을 가능할 때마다 많이 읽어야 해.
여 그게 어떻게 도움이 되는지 모르겠어.
남 그 책들은 모두 다른 스타일로 쓰였고 다양한 단어와 어구를 사용해. 너는 많은 종류의 글에 익숙해질 거야.
여 하지만 읽는 것과 쓰는 것은 달라.
남 그건 중요하지 않아. 책을 많이 읽는 것만으로도 자연스럽게 어휘가 늘어나고 글쓰기도 좋아져.
여 알겠어. 한번 시도해 볼게!

여자는 자신의 글쓰기 문제에 대한 불만 사항을 남자에게 이야기하고 있다. 남자는 여자의 문제를 고치려면 다양한 책들을 가능할 때마다 많이 읽어야 하고, 그것만으로도 자연스럽게 어휘가 늘어나고 글쓰기도 좋아진다고 했다. 따라서 남자의 의견으로 ⑤ '다양한 책을 많이 읽는 것만으로 작문 실력이 향상될 수 있다.'가 가장 적절하다.

[어휘] frustrated ⑲ 불만이 있는, 혼란스러운 have trouble with ~과 관련된 곤란을 겪다 novel ⑲ 소설 biography ⑲ 전기, 위인전 a variety of 다양한 phrase ⑲ 어구, 구절

3 관계 파악

정답 ②

[Cell phone rings.]
W Hello? You've reached Audrey Jones.
M Hi. This is Ronald Stein from the Kenwood History Museum. **I'm calling to invite you to our museum's event.**
W Oh? What's the event?
M It's a 150th celebration of the founding of our city. **We're** ¹⁾having different speakers talk **about its history.**
W That sounds wonderful. Is there anything specific you'd like me to talk about?

[휴대폰이 울린다.]
여 여보세요? Audrey Jones입니다.
남 안녕하세요. 저는 켄우드 역사박물관의 Ronald Stein입니다. 저는 귀하를 저희 박물관 행사에 초대하고자 전화했습니다.
여 오? 무슨 행사인가요?
남 저희 도시의 건설 150주년 기념행사입니다. 저희는 다양한 발표자들이 도시의 역사에 대해 이야기하도록 하려고 합니다.
여 그거 멋진데요. 제가 이야기했으면 하는 구체적인 사항이 있나요?

M	Your research on what happened in our city during the 1980s is renowned. We would be honored if you could speak about that time period.	남	1980년대에 저희 도시에서 어떤 일이 일어났는지에 관한 귀하의 연구는 유명하잖아요. 그 시기에 대해 말씀해 주시면 감사하겠습니다.
W	I'd love to. ²⁾<u>When is the event</u>?	여	얼마든지요. 행사는 언제입니까?
M	It's on May 7th at 4 p.m. It'll be held in the museum's lecture hall.	남	5월 7일 오후 4시예요. 박물관 내에 있는 강의실에서 열릴 것입니다.
W	I'll be there. And is it possible for me to bring my assistant?	여	참석하겠습니다. 그리고 제 조수를 데려와도 될까요?
M	Of course. That's absolutely fine.	남	물론이죠. 그건 당연히 괜찮습니다.
W	Thank you. She usually ³⁾<u>helps me prepare for</u> public speeches.	여	감사합니다. 그녀는 보통 제가 대중을 대상으로 하는 연설을 준비하는 것을 도와주거든요.
M	That won't be a problem. I look forward to seeing you!	남	안 될 것 없습니다. 귀하를 뵙기를 기대하겠습니다!

여자가 남자의 박물관에서 주최하는 도시 건설 150주년 기념행사에 초청받고 있다. 그 도시의 1980년대에 관한 여자의 연구가 유명하므로 행사에서 이에 대해 강연해달라고 부탁받는 것으로 보아 두 사람의 관계로 ② '역사학자 — 박물관 직원'이 가장 적절하다.

어휘 celebration 몡 기념행사 specific 혱 구체적인 renowned 혱 유명한 period 몡 시기, 기간 hall 몡 ~실, 방 assistant 몡 조수 absolutely 뷔 당연히 look forward to ~을 기대하다

4 그림 내용 불일치 파악   정답 ⑤

M	Katie, there you are! Are you doing your painting for the art contest here?	남	Katie, 여기 있었구나! 미술 대회에 제출할 그림을 여기서 그리는 거니?
W	Yeah. Isn't this spot perfect?	여	응. 이 자리 정말 완벽하지 않아?
M	This maple tree you're sitting under is so beautiful!	남	네가 앉아있는 곳의 이 단풍나무 정말 예쁘다!
W	I know! It inspired me to paint here.	여	맞아! 그래서 여기서 그림을 그리게 됐어.
M	I thought you would bring the checkered mat, but the one you ¹⁾<u>brought is plain</u>.	남	난 네가 체크무늬 돗자리를 가져올 줄 알았는데, 가져온 건 무늬가 없는 것이구나.
W	Yeah. I prefer to sit on this because it's more comfortable, and it's also big enough. I put all of my paints and sketchbook here, too.	여	응. 더 편해서 이것 위에 앉는 걸 더 좋아해. 그리고 크기도 충분히 크거든. 내 물감이랑 스케치북도 다 여기에 올려뒀어.
M	Did you see those ²⁾<u>three lovely flowers</u> by the corner of the mat?	남	돗자리 모서리 쪽에 있는 예쁜 꽃 세 송이 봤어?
W	Actually, I already put those flowers in my painting.	여	사실, 이미 난 내 그림에 저 꽃들을 담았어.
M	Oh, look at that! There's ³⁾<u>a rabbit over there</u>.	남	오, 이것 좀 봐! 저기에 토끼 한 마리가 있네.
W	How cute! It's eating some grass. Maybe I should add that to my painting.	여	귀엽다! 풀을 먹고 있어. 내 그림에 저걸 추가하는 게 좋을지도 모르겠어.
M	That's a good idea. Anyway, do you mind if I work on my painting here?	남	그건 좋은 생각이야. 아무튼, 나도 여기서 그림 그려도 될까?
W	No problem. Have a seat.	여	문제없지. 자리에 앉아.

대화에서 남자가 저쪽에 토끼 한 마리가 있다고 말했는데, ⑤에는 토끼가 두 마리 그려져 있다.

어휘 spot 몡 자리; 점 maple tree 단풍나무 mat 몡 돗자리, 매트 plain 혱 무늬가 없는; 보통의 paint 몡 물감 통 (물감을) 칠하다 grass 몡 풀, 잔디 Do you mind if ~? ~해도 될까? Have a seat. 자리에 앉아.

5 할 일 파악   정답 ①

W	Good morning, honey. How did you sleep?	여	좋은 아침이야, 여보. 잘 잤어?
M	Great. You must be tired from our dinner party last night.	남	잘 잤어. 당신은 어젯밤 우리 저녁 파티 때문에 피곤하겠다.
W	I'm fine. Thanks again for ¹⁾<u>cooking that fish</u> for our guests. They really enjoyed it.	여	괜찮아. 손님들을 위해 생선 요리를 해 줘서 다시 한번 고마워. 그분들이 그걸 정말 좋아하더라.
M	I'm glad. I also loved the dessert you prepared.	남	기쁘네. 나도 당신이 준비한 디저트 너무 좋았어.
W	Thank you. I ²⁾<u>found the recipe online</u>.	여	고마워. 인터넷에서 레시피를 찾았어.
M	Well, it's time for us to do some housework. I'll get started on the laundry.	남	자, 이제 집안일을 할 시간이네. 나는 빨래를 시작할게.
W	That's okay. I did that earlier this morning.	여	놔둬. 오늘 아침 일찍 내가 이미 했어.
M	That's so sweet of you. Then, what's left? Let me know ³⁾<u>what I can do</u>.	남	당신 정말 다정하다. 그럼, 뭐가 남았지? 내가 할 수 있는 일을 알려 줘.
W	You could take the dog for a walk or clean the bathroom. It's up to you.	여	개를 데리고 산책하러 가거나 화장실을 청소하면 돼. 당신 선택에 달렸어.
M	I'll ⁴⁾<u>clean the bathroom</u>. Why don't you get some fresh air with the dog?	남	내가 화장실을 청소할게. 당신은 개와 함께 바람을 쐬는 게 어때?
W	Great. Then, we can get coffee together afterwards.	여	좋아. 그럼 그 뒤에는 같이 커피 마실 수 있겠다.

두 사람이 지난밤 파티 이후 해야 할 집안일에 관하여 이야기하고 있다. 여자가 남자에게 개를 데리고 산책하러 가거나 화장실을 청소하면 된다고 하자, 남자가 자신이 화장실을 청소하겠다고 했으므로 남자가 할 일로 ① '욕실 청소하기'가 가장 적절하다.

어휘 recipe 몡 레시피, 조리법 do housework 집안일을 하다 It's up to you. 당신 선택에 달렸어. get some fresh air 바람을 쐬다 afterwards 뷔 그 뒤에, 그 후에

6 금액 정보 파악

정답 ②

M	Hello. Can I take your order?	남	안녕하세요. 주문하시겠습니까?
W	Hi. We're thinking of ordering the Set Menu Special.	여	안녕하세요. 세트 메뉴 스페셜을 주문하려고 하는데요.
M	Okay. We have two options. Would you like me ¹⁾to explain them to you?	남	네. 두 가지 옵션이 있습니다. 제가 설명해 드릴까요?
W	That would be great.	여	그렇게 해 주시면 정말 좋겠네요.
M	Set A includes a salad, chicken dish, and dessert. Set B includes a salad, pasta, steak, and dessert.	남	A세트에는 샐러드, 치킨 요리, 디저트가 포함되어 있습니다. B세트에는 샐러드, 파스타, 스테이크, 디저트가 포함되어 있고요.
W	What's the price difference?	여	가격 차이가 얼마나 나요?
M	**Set A is $30, and Set B is $50.**	남	A세트는 30달러이고, B세트는 50달러입니다.
W	**Well, we are pretty hungry, so we'll ²⁾go with two orders of Set B.**	여	음, 저희는 배가 꽤나 고파서 B세트로 두 개 주문할게요.
M	Oh, that might be too much for two of you.	남	오, 두 분께는 너무 많을지도 몰라요.
W	Actually, our friends will be joining us soon, so there will be ³⁾four of us in total.	여	사실, 저희 친구들이 곧 합류할 거라서, 저희는 모두 4명이 될 거예요.
M	That should be perfect, then. **Also, we're offering 10% off your total if you post a picture and mention us on social media.**	남	그럼 딱 좋으실 거예요. 또한 SNS에 사진을 올려주시고 저희 가게를 언급해 주시면 총액에서 10% 할인해 드려요.
W	**Oh, great. I'll ⁴⁾do that right now.**	여	오, 좋아요. 지금 바로 그렇게 할게요.

여자가 B세트를 2개($50×2=$100) 주문했고, 총액에서 10% 할인($100×0.9=$90)을 받았으므로 정답은 ② '$90'이다.

어휘 option 몡 옵션, 선택지 mention 통 언급하다 social media SNS, 소셜 미디어

7 이유 파악

정답 ①

M	Christine, I have a favor to ask.	남	Christine, 나 부탁이 있어.
W	Sure. How can I help?	여	뭐든지 말해. 뭘 도와줄까?
M	My school choir has a performance this weekend, but ¹⁾our piano player hurt her finger and can't play for us.	남	우리 학교 합창단이 이번 주말에 공연이 있는데, 피아노 연주자가 손가락을 다치는 바람에 연주할 수가 없게 됐어.
W	I'm sorry to hear that. ²⁾Do you need me to fill in?	여	안타깝다. 내가 대신해 줄까?
M	Could you do it? There isn't much time to practice, but you're such a great pianist. I'm sure you'll be able to learn the songs.	남	해줄 수 있겠어? 연습할 시간이 별로 없지만, 넌 정말 훌륭한 피아니스트잖아. 난 네가 곡들을 익힐 수 있을 거라고 확신해.
W	Well... When is it?	여	음... 공연이 언젠데?
M	It's this Saturday afternoon at 3.	남	이번 주 토요일 오후 3시야.
W	I'm sorry. ³⁾I can't make it.	여	미안해. 난 못 할 것 같아.
M	Oh, I forgot. You're going on a family trip.	남	오, 깜빡했네. 넌 가족 여행을 갈 예정이지.
W	That's not the problem. We canceled our trip.	여	그게 문제가 아니야. 우린 여행을 취소했어.
M	Then, why not?	남	그럼, 왜 안 돼?
W	My ⁴⁾mom's retirement party is that day. Her coworkers have been preparing it as a surprise for her.	여	우리 엄마의 은퇴 기념 파티가 그날이야. 엄마 동료분들이 엄마를 위해 깜짝 선물로 준비해오고 있어.
M	I see. Then, I'll find someone else.	남	그렇구나. 그럼, 다른 사람을 찾아볼게.

여자는 남자가 부탁한 피아노 반주를 대신해 줄 수 없다고 하면서 그날 어머니의 은퇴 기념 파티가 있다고 말했으므로, 여자가 피아노 반주를 대신해 줄 수 없는 이유는 ① '은퇴 기념 파티에 참석해야 해서'이다.

어휘 favor 몡 부탁 choir 몡 합창단 fill in 대신하다, 채우다 cancel 통 취소하다 retirement 몡 은퇴 coworker 몡 동료

8 언급 유무 파악

정답 ③

W	What's that, Tyler?	여	그게 뭐야, Tyler?
M	I'm looking at a post online about the International Sand Sculpture Competition. It sounds like a lot of fun.	남	국제 모래 조각 대회에 관한 게시물을 온라인으로 보고 있어. 아주 재미있을 것 같아.
W	Why don't we ¹⁾go watch it together? When is it?	여	같이 보러 가지 않을래? 그게 언제야?
M	It begins on **September 29th,** and the competitors' pieces will be available for public viewing for one week.	남	9월 29일에 시작하고, 출전자들의 작품을 일주일 동안 대중이 볼 수 있도록 할 거래.
W	Great. Isn't it being held at **Logan Beach**?	여	좋은걸. 그거 로건 해변에서 열리지 않니?
M	That's right. Apparently ²⁾32 sand sculptors from all over the world are competing.	남	맞아. 보아하니 전 세계에서 온 32명의 모래 조각가들이 경쟁할 거야.
W	Wow. I wonder what kind of sculptures they will make.	여	우와. 그들이 어떤 종류의 조각을 만들지 궁금해지네.
M	It says the competition is about ³⁾legendary sea animals. So I'm guessing there will be things like mermaids and sea dragons!	남	여기에 이 대회가 전설적인 바다 동물들에 관한 대회라고 쓰여 있어. 그러니 내 추측으로는 인어와 해룡 같은 것들이 있을 것 같아.
W	That sounds amazing. How much does it cost?	여	그거 굉장한데. 비용은 얼마야?
M	**Tickets are only $8 for adults, and kids are free.**	남	성인은 8달러밖에 안 하고, 아이들은 무료야.

| W Great. Then, let's buy them now. I'm sure it'll be a unique experience. | 여 좋아. 그럼, 지금 구매하자. 장담컨대 독특한 경험이 될 거야. |

날짜(9월 29일), 장소(로건 해변), 조각 주제(전설적인 바다 동물), 티켓 가격(성인은 8달러, 아이는 무료)에 대해 언급했고, ③ '예상 관중 수'는 언급하지 않았다.

[어휘] apparently 튀 보아하니 sculptor 명 조각가 legendary 형 전설적인 mermaid 명 인어 unique 형 독특한

9 내용 불일치 파악
정답 ③

| W Okay, class. Before you leave, I'd like to remind you about the Westbrook Cultural Exchange Program that the city ¹⁾is running this summer. As you know, all selected participants will travel to Spain. The program will take place over nine days. **However, participants who would like to explore the country on their own ²⁾may arrive earlier or stay longer.** There are still three spaces left in the program. If you're interested in going, please visit the program's website, whose address I've written ³⁾on the board for you. Please note that you'll have to submit an essay about why you want to participate. The deadline for applications is next Monday. I encourage you all ⁴⁾to apply for this wonderful opportunity. | 여 좋아요, 여러분. 떠나시기 전에, 시에서 올여름에 운영할 웨스트브룩 문화교류 프로그램에 대해 상기시켜드리고 싶습니다. 아시다시피, 선정된 모든 참가자들은 스페인으로 여행을 갈 것입니다. 이 프로그램은 9일에 걸쳐 진행될 것입니다. 하지만, 그 나라를 스스로 여행하고 싶은 참가자들은 더 일찍 도착하거나 더 오래 머물러도 됩니다. 이 프로그램에는 아직 3개의 자리가 남아 있습니다. 갈 의향이 있으시다면, 제가 칠판에 적어 둔 프로그램 웹사이트 주소를 통해 방문해 주시기 바랍니다. 참여하고자 하는 이유에 대한 에세이를 제출해야 한다는 점 참고해 주세요. 지원 마감일은 다음 주 월요일입니다. 저는 여러분 모두가 이 멋진 기회에 지원해 보시기를 권장 드립니다. |

문화 교류 프로그램에 대한 안내이다. 여자가 프로그램 참가자들 중 그 나라를 스스로 여행하고 싶은 사람들은 더 일찍 도착하거나 더 오래 머물러도 된다고 했으므로 ③ '참가자들은 프로그램 기간에 맞춰 출국해야 한다.'는 내용과 일치하지 않는다.

[어휘] remind 통 상기시키다 run 통 운영하다; 달리다 on one's own 스스로, 개별적으로 be interested in ~할 의향이 있다 submit 통 제출하다 application 명 지원, 신청 encourage 통 권장하다 apply for ~에 지원하다 opportunity 명 기회

10 도표 정보 파악
정답 ④

M Hey, Rose. What are you doing?	남 안녕, Rose. 뭐 하고 있어?
W I'm trying to buy a set of coffee mugs online. ¹⁾Do you want to see?	여 인터넷에서 커피 머그잔 세트 하나를 사려고 해. 너도 볼래?
M Okay. [Pause] They all look nice. But this set is pretty expensive.	남 좋아. [잠시 멈춤] 다 멋있어 보이네. 하지만 이 세트는 꽤 비싼걸.
W Yeah. **I want to stick to a price under $60.**	여 맞아. 나는 60달러 미만의 가격을 고수하고 싶어.
M What about size? How big do you want the mugs to be?	남 사이즈는? 머그잔의 크기는 얼마나 컸으면 좋겠어?
W **I prefer ²⁾medium or large ones.** I drink a lot of coffee, so those small cups aren't big enough.	여 중간이나 큰 게 좋아. 난 커피를 많이 마셔서, 저 작은 컵들은 충분히 크지 않아.
M Now, you have to consider the colors. Do any of them stand out to you?	남 이제 색깔을 고려해야 해. 저것들 중 눈에 띄는 것이 있니?
W **I don't really like ³⁾the white ones.** They will get stained easily.	여 흰색은 별로 마음에 안 들어. 쉽게 얼룩질 거야.
M Then, these two are your last options. They both come with a free gift, too.	남 그럼 이 두 가지가 마지막 남은 선택지야. 둘 다 사은품이 딸려 나오네.
W Oh, that's great. I love coffee of course, **but I think ⁴⁾tea spoons would be pretty useful. I'll go with that one.**	여 오, 잘 됐네. 나는 물론 커피를 좋아하지만, 티스푼이 꽤 유용할 것 같아. 저걸로 해야겠어.
M Great. Looks like you've made your choice.	남 좋아. 결정을 내린 것 같네.

여자는 60달러 미만의 가격을 고수하면서, 중간이나 큰 사이즈이고, 흰색을 제외한 색 중에서, 티스푼이 사은품으로 딸려 나오는 커피 머그잔 세트를 골랐다.

[어휘] pretty 튀 꽤 stick to 고수하다, 지키다 stand out 눈에 띄다 stain 통 얼룩지게 하다, 더러워지다 come with ~이 딸려 나오다 free gift 사은품, 경품 make one's choice 결정을 내리다, 선택하다

11 짧은 대화의 응답 파악
정답 ⑤

W Are you okay, Marcus? You've barely touched your dinner.	여 괜찮니, Marcus? 저녁밥을 거의 손도 안 댔구나.
M Sorry, Mom. I ¹⁾was thinking about my classmate. He just transferred from another school, and he always ²⁾looks so lonely.	남 죄송해요, 엄마. 우리 반 친구를 생각하고 있었어요. 그는 다른 학교에서 전학 온 지 얼마 안 됐는데, 항상 너무 외로워 보여요.
W That's tough. **I know you're shy, but why don't you try talking to him?**	여 어려운 상황이구나. 네가 부끄러움을 많이 타는 것은 알지만, 그 친구에게 한번 말을 걸어 보는 것이 어떠니?
M Okay. I'll start a conversation when I see him.	남 알았어요. 그를 만나면 말을 걸어 볼게요.
	[선택지] ① 그렇군요. 근데 그는 말이 너무 많아요.
	② 괜찮아요. 오늘 점심을 많이 먹었어요.
	③ 그래요? 저는 그가 꽤 인기가 있다고 생각했어요.
	④ 걱정하지 마세요. 새로운 반 친구를 좋아하게 되실 거예요.
	⑤ 알았어요. 그를 만나면 말을 걸어 볼게요.

남자가 전학 온 친구가 외로워 보인다고 걱정하자 여자가 그 친구에게 한번 말을 걸어 보라고 제안했으므로, 이에 대한 응답으로는 그렇게 하겠다는 ⑤ 'Okay. I'll start a conversation when I see him.'이 가장 적절하다.

[어휘] barely 튀 거의 ~ 않다 classmate 명 반 친구 transfer 통 전학 오다; 옮기다 tough 형 어려운, 힘든 shy 형 부끄러움을 잘 타는, 수줍은 start a conversation 말을 걸다, 대화를 시작하다

12 짧은 대화의 응답 파악
정답 ②

M Hello. **I'm the restaurant manager.** Did you ¹⁾<u>make a reservation</u> for dinner tonight?	남 안녕하세요. 저는 식당의 매니저입니다. 오늘 저녁 식사를 예약하셨나요?
W No, I didn't. Hmm... I didn't know I could make reservations here.	여 아뇨, 안 했어요. 흠... 저는 이곳을 예약할 수 있는지 몰랐네요.
M Oh, you can find the booking system on our website. **Unfortunately, we are ²⁾<u>all booked for</u> tonight.**	남 아, 저희 웹사이트에서 예약 시스템을 찾으실 수 있습니다. 안타깝게도, 오늘 밤은 예약이 다 찼습니다.
W <u>It's all right. We'll just come back another day.</u>	여 <u>알겠어요. 그냥 다른 날에 다시 올게요.</u>

선택지 ① 그렇군요. 저녁 7시로 자리를 예약하고 싶어요.
② 알겠어요. 그냥 다른 날에 다시 올게요.
③ 괜찮아요. 저희는 저쪽 테이블에 앉으면 돼요.
④ 신경 쓰지 마세요. 시스템이 다시 작동하는 것 같습니다.
⑤ 당연하죠. 지금 예약을 위해 식당에 전화할게요.

남자가 식당을 찾은 여자에게 오늘 밤 예약이 다 찼다고 말했으므로, 이에 대한 응답으로는 다른 날에 다시 오겠다는 의사를 표하는 ② 'It's all right. We'll just come back another day.' 가 가장 적절하다.

어휘 reservation 몡 예약 booking 몡 예약 unfortunately 뷔 안타깝게도, 애석하게도

13 긴 대화의 응답 파악
정답 ④

W Excuse me. Do you mind helping me?	여 실례합니다. 저 좀 도와주시겠어요?
M I'd be happy to. What do you need?	남 얼마든지요. 무엇이 필요하세요?
W I'm ¹⁾<u>trying to buy</u> a new television, but I can't decide which one to get. How about this one?	여 새 텔레비전을 사려고 하는데, 어떤 걸 살지 결정을 못 내리겠어요. 이건 어떤가요?
M Well, it is our best-selling model. But it's ²⁾<u>a little expensive</u>.	남 음, 그건 가장 잘 팔리는 모델이에요. 하지만 조금 비쌉니다.
W Then, could you recommend a more affordable model?	여 그럼, 더 저렴한 제품을 추천해주실래요?
M There's this one. You ³⁾<u>might have to wait</u> a few weeks for it to be delivered, though. It's currently sold out everywhere.	남 여기 이게 있어요. 하지만 이건 배달되기까지 몇 주를 기다리셔야 할 수도 있어요. 현재 모든 곳에서 품절이거든요.
W Oh, really? That's too bad.	여 아, 그래요? 안됐군요.
M **Or if you don't want to wait, we do have one in the back. But the box is open.** A customer returned it for a refund.	남 아니면 혹시 기다리고 싶지 않으시다면, 뒤편에 하나가 있어요. 하지만 개봉된 적이 있는 상태예요. 고객 한 분이 환불받으려고 반품하셨거든요.
W Are there any problems with it?	여 무슨 문제라도 있나요?
M No. It's perfectly fine. He decided to buy a bigger one.	남 아뇨. 아주 완벽해요. 그분은 더 큰 것을 사기로 결정하셨거든요.
W I see. **Can you ⁴⁾<u>give me a discount</u> on it?**	여 그렇군요. 할인을 해주실 수 있나요?
M **We can offer you 20% off the regular price.**	남 정가에서 20% 할인해 드릴 수 있어요.
W <u>That's great. This deal is too good to pass up.</u>	여 <u>잘됐네요. 이 제안은 거절하기에는 너무 좋네요.</u>

선택지 ① 안 돼요. 더 이상 켜지지 않아요.
② 잘 모르겠어요. 더 작은 사이즈가 필요하실지도 몰라요.
③ 괜찮아요. 수리 기사가 내일 올 거예요.
④ 잘됐네요. 이 제안은 거절하기에는 너무 좋네요.
⑤ 물론이죠! 오늘 배송이 될 겁니다.

여자가 텔레비전을 사러 온 상황이다. 여자는 비록 개봉된 적 있는 제품이지만 기다리지 않아도 되는 것을 구매하기에 앞서 할인 여부를 물었고 남자가 20%를 할인해 줄 수 있다고 말했으므로, 이에 대한 응답으로는 할인 조건에 만족을 표하는 ④ 'That's great. This deal is too good to pass up.'이 가장 적절하다.

어휘 bestselling 휑 가장 잘 팔리는, 베스트셀러의 affordable 휑 저렴한, 감당할 수 있는 currently 뷔 현재, 지금 regular price 정가 pass up ~을 거절하다

14 긴 대화의 응답 파악
정답 ①

W Honey, what did the doctor say at the hospital?	여 여보, 병원에서 의사가 뭐라고 했어?
M **He recommended knee surgery.**	남 무릎 수술을 권하더라.
W I'm not surprised... Is it a serious procedure?	여 놀랄 일도 아니지... 심각한 수술이야?
M No. It's a pretty minor one. I'll be in and out of the hospital ¹⁾<u>on the same day</u>.	남 아니. 꽤 작은 수술이야. 병원에 입원했다가 같은 날 퇴원할 거야.
W Good. When is it scheduled?	여 좋아. 언제로 예정되어 있어?
M It'll be next Thursday.	남 다음 주 목요일이야.
W Okay. I'll ²⁾<u>drive you there</u>. What is the recovery time?	여 알았어. 내가 태워다 줄게. 회복 기간은 어떻게 돼?
M It'll take a few weeks. The doctor also advised me not to walk for at least a week after leaving the hospital.	남 몇 주 걸릴 거야. 의사도 퇴원 후에 적어도 일주일 동안은 걷지 말라고 조언했어.
W **Oh, will we need to get you a wheelchair?**	여 아, 우리가 휠체어를 구하는 게 좋을까?
M **Just for that first week.** I think the hospital can lend us one.	남 그 첫 주 동안만. 내 생각엔 병원에서 하나 빌려줄 수 있을 것 같아.
W **Then, maybe I should ³⁾<u>reorganize the furniture</u> so that it's easier for you to move around in the wheelchair.**	여 그럼, 당신이 휠체어를 타고 돌아다니기 편하도록 가구들을 다시 배치하는 게 좋을지도 모르겠어.
M That would be great. Thank you.	남 그거 정말 좋겠다. 고마워.

W	No problem. **Should I start preparing the house today?**
M	Sure. I might be able to help carry some light items.

여 천만에. 오늘부터 집을 준비해두기 시작할까?
남 물론이지. 내가 가벼운 물건들은 옮기는 걸 도와줄 수 있을지도 몰라.

선택지 ① 물론이지. 내가 가벼운 물건들은 옮기는 걸 도와줄 수 있을지도 몰라.
② 응. 수술 후에 많이 좋아지기 시작했어.
③ 그건 불가능해. 나는 앞으로 몇 주 동안 병원에 입원해 있을 거야.
④ 걱정하지 마. 이 휠체어는 타고 돌아다니기 편해.
⑤ 아니. 의사가 내 무릎 부상 때문에 가면 안 된대.

무릎 수술을 앞둔 남자와 여자가 대화를 하는 상황에서, 여자가 수술 후 휠체어를 타야 하는 남자를 위해 집안 가구들을 오늘부터 미리 재배치해야 하는지 물었으므로, 이에 대한 응답으로는 그 계획에 동의하며 자신도 돕겠다는 ① 'Sure. I might be able to help carry some light items.'가 가장 적절하다.

어휘 surgery 몡 수술 procedure 몡 수술; 절차 minor 혱 작은, 미미한 recovery 몡 회복 advise A to B A에게 B할 것을 조언하다 reorganize 통 재배치하다, 재조직하다
light 혱 가벼운 몡 빛 hospitalize 통 입원시키다

---

15 상황에 적절한 말 파악

정답 ②

M	Carl is a photographer and will have his photos exhibited at a gallery soon. His work mainly focuses on rare plants and animals. Carl is excited because it's [1]the first time his photographs will be hung up in a gallery. However, he's having a difficult time selecting the photographs for his exhibition. He knows that his friend Emily [2]has much more experience with photography exhibits than he does. Carl asks her for advice about which pictures to select. Because the gallery already features a lot of plant photographs, Emily believes Carl should show pictures of animals to stand out. **So Emily wants to suggest that Carl select photographs [3]of uncommon animals.** In this situation, what would Emily most likely say to Carl?

남 Carl은 사진작가이고 곧 그의 사진을 갤러리에 전시할 예정입니다. 그의 작품은 주로 희귀한 식물과 동물에 초점을 두고 있습니다. Carl은 그의 사진이 갤러리에 걸리는 것은 이번이 처음이기 때문에 신이 났습니다. 하지만, 그는 그의 전시회를 위한 사진을 고르는 데 어려움을 겪고 있습니다. 그는 그의 친구 Emily가 그보다 사진 전시에 있어 훨씬 더 경험이 많다는 것을 알고 있습니다. Carl은 그녀에게 어떤 그림을 고를지 조언을 구합니다. 갤러리에는 이미 많은 식물 사진을 특히 포함하고 있기 때문에, 눈에 띄기 위해서는 Carl이 동물 사진을 보여주어야 한다고 Emily는 생각합니다. 그래서 Emily는 Carl에게 희귀한 동물 사진을 골라보라고 제안하고 싶습니다. 이러한 상황에서, Emily가 Carl에게 가장 할 것 같은 말은 무엇입니까?

선택지 ① 넌 이 사진들의 가격을 확인해야 해.
② 독특한 동물 사진들을 골라보는 게 어때?
③ 내가 이미 그 지역의 다른 갤러리들을 알아봤어.
④ 네 사진들을 어디에 걸지 다시 생각해보는 게 좋을걸.
⑤ 우리 오늘 오후에 전시회에 방문하는 게 어때?

Carl의 사진이 전시될 갤러리에는 이미 식물 사진이 많이 포함되어 있기 때문에, Emily는 희귀한 동물 사진을 골라 전시하라고 조언하려 한다. 따라서, Emily가 할 말로 ② 'How about choosing pictures of unique animals?'가 가장 적절하다.

어휘 mainly 뷔 주로 focus on ~에 초점을 두다 hang up ~을 걸다 have a difficult time 어려움을 겪다 feature 통 특히 포함하다 몡 특징, 특색 uncommon 혱 희귀한, 흔치 않은

16-17 세트 문항

정답 16 ⑤ 17 ③

W	Hi, everyone. Last time, we talked about why it is so important to keep public spaces clean. **Today, I want to talk about objects in your home where [1]a large number of germs live. Door knobs** are the first example I should mention. Bacteria on our hands transfer to these every time we open or close a door. And what's more, [2]people rarely clean them because they don't appear to be dirty. Second up are **smartphones.** Disease-causing germs are able to grow quickly on their glass surfaces because we're constantly touching them throughout the day. Third, we have **light switches.** We use them often, and hardly wash our hands before touching them. And because they [3]are made of plastic, viruses can survive on them for a long time. Finally, **kitchen sponges** are one of the dirtiest objects in our houses. Sponges provide a favorable humid environment for bacteria, and [4]they often touch food waste that feeds the germs. Okay. Now, I'll show you a video about properly cleaning these things.

여 안녕하십니까, 여러분. 지난 시간에, 우리는 공공장소를 깨끗하게 유지하는 것이 왜 그리 중요한지에 대해 이야기했습니다. 오늘은, 여러분의 가정에 있는 물건 중 정말 많은 세균이 살고 있는 것들에 관해 이야기하고자 합니다. 문손잡이는 제가 이야기해야 할 첫 번째 사례입니다. 우리 손에 있는 박테리아는 문을 열거나 닫을 때마다 이 손잡이로 옮겨갑니다. 게다가, 사람들은 손잡이가 더러워 보이지 않기 때문에 그것들을 거의 닦지 않습니다. 두 번째는 스마트폰입니다. 우리가 온종일 스마트폰을 계속 만지기 때문에 병을 일으키는 세균이 액정 표면에서 빠르게 자라날 수 있습니다. 셋째, 전등 스위치입니다. 우리는 그것들을 자주 사용하고, 그것들을 만지기 전에 거의 손을 씻지 않습니다. 그리고 스위치가 플라스틱으로 만들어졌기 때문에, 바이러스가 그 위에서 오랫동안 생존할 수 있습니다. 마지막으로, 부엌 스펀지는 가정에서 가장 더러운 물건 중 하나입니다. 스펀지는 박테리아에 유리한 습한 환경을 제공하고, 세균의 먹잇감이 되는 음식물 쓰레기에 자주 닿습니다. 좋습니다. 이제 이 물건들을 제대로 닦는 것에 관한 동영상을 보여드리겠습니다.

선택지 16 ① 세균이 질병을 초래하는 방식
② 공공장소가 몹시 더러운 이유
③ 집을 자주 청소하는 것의 장점
④ 박테리아가 새로운 곳으로 옮겨가는 방법
⑤ 많은 세균이 들어 있는 가정용품
17 ① 문손잡이 ② 스마트폰 ③ 리모컨 ④ 전등 스위치
⑤ 부엌 스펀지

16 가정에 있는 물건 중 정말 많은 세균이 살고 있는 것들에 대해 이야기하고 있으므로 여자가 하는 말의 주제로 ⑤ 'household objects that contain many germs'가 가장 적절하다.
17 문손잡이, 스마트폰, 전등 스위치, 부엌 스펀지는 언급했지만 ③ 'remote controls'는 언급하지 않았다.

어휘 object 몡 물건 germ 몡 세균 knob 몡 손잡이 transfer 통 옮겨가다, 옮기다 what's more 게다가 throughout 젠 종일, 내내 hardly 뷔 거의 ~않다 favorable 혱 유리한; 호의적인
humid 혱 습한, 축축한 lead to ~을 초래하다 household 혱 가정용의 몡 가정

1	③	2	④	3	②	4	⑤	5	①	6	④	7	②	8	⑤	9	⑤	10	③
11	③	12	①	13	⑤	14	②	15	①	16	③	17	②						

• 각 문제의 정답 근거는 굵은 글씨로, Dictation 정답은 밑줄로 표시되어 있습니다.

1 목적 파악

정답 ③

W Dear shoppers. I'm Chelsea Anderson from the Galleria Mall. **I'd like to let you know about our** ¹⁾<u>ongoing customer satisfaction survey.</u> The deadline for this feedback is December 8th. However, with just a week left, we have only received a small number of replies. **So I'd like to encourage everyone** ²⁾<u>to fill out</u> this survey. It's a great opportunity for you to help us improve. Please let us know what we're doing right and what we can do better. In particular, we'd like to hear your opinions on the recent changes to ³⁾<u>our refund policy.</u> We hope you take the time to help us make our mall a better place for our valued customers. Thank you.

여 친애하는 쇼핑객 여러분. 저는 Galleria Mall의 Chelsea Anderson입니다. 현재 진행 중인 고객 만족도 조사에 대해 알려드리고자 합니다. 피드백을 주실 수 있는 마감일은 12월 8일입니다. 하지만, 단 일주일밖에 남지 않은 상황에서, 저희는 적은 수의 회신만을 받았습니다. 그래서 저는 여러분들께 이 설문조사를 작성해 주시기를 권하고 싶습니다. 이것은 여러분이 저희의 발전을 도울 수 있는 좋은 기회입니다. 저희가 무엇을 잘하고 있는지, 무엇을 더 잘할 수 있는지 알려 주십시오. 특히, 최근 환불 정책 변경에 대한 여러분들의 의견을 듣고 싶습니다. 저희는 소중한 고객들을 위해 저희의 매장을 더 좋은 곳으로 만들도록 여러분들께서 시간을 내 도와주시기를 바랍니다. 감사합니다.

여자가 Galleria Mall에서 진행하는 서비스 만족도 조사에 대해 알려주면서, 고객들의 설문조사 참여를 권하고 있다. 따라서, 여자가 하는 말의 목적으로 ③ '고객 만족도 조사 참여를 요청하려고'가 가장 적절하다.

어휘 ongoing 휑 현재 진행 중인 satisfaction 뗑 만족도, 충족 survey 뗑 (설문) 조사 deadline 뗑 마감일 reply 뗑 회신, 답장 encourage 통 권하다 opportunity 뗑 기회 in particular 특히 policy 뗑 정책 valued 휑 소중한

2 의견 파악

정답 ④

W Hey, Adam. Did you watch that TV documentary on robots I mentioned?
M Yeah, I saw it last night.
W Didn't you think the technology was scary?
M **Actually, I think robots are going to have an** ¹⁾<u>overall positive effect</u> **on human lives.**
W I'm surprised you feel that way.
M Robots are already useful. They are used to ²⁾<u>manufacture things in factories.</u>
W But aren't you worried that people will lose their jobs to robots in the future?
M Not really. Robots will mostly be used for tasks that people don't want to do.
W What do you mean?
M For instance, robots can be used to stop wildfires or ³⁾<u>clean up toxic waste.</u>
W Ah, I see. So they will let humans avoid dangerous situations.
M Exactly. **That's why I think robots will be a good thing for people.**

여 안녕, Adam. 내가 말한 로봇에 관한 TV 다큐멘터리 봤어?
남 응, 어젯밤에 봤어.
여 그 기술이 소름 끼친다고 생각하지 않았어?
남 사실, 나는 로봇이 인간의 삶에 전반적으로 긍정적인 영향을 끼칠 거라고 생각해.
여 네가 그렇게 생각한다니 놀랍네.
남 로봇은 이미 유용해. 그것들은 공장에서 물건을 제조하는 데 사용되고 있어.
여 하지만 미래에 사람들이 로봇 때문에 일자리를 잃는 게 걱정되지는 않아?
남 딱히. 로봇은 대부분 사람들이 원치 않는 일에 사용될 거야.
여 무슨 말이야?
남 예를 들자면, 로봇은 산불을 멈추거나 유독성 폐기물을 청소하는 데 사용될 수 있어.
여 아, 그렇구나. 그래서 그것들은 사람들이 위험한 상황을 피하도록 해주겠구나.
남 정확해. 그래서 난 로봇이 사람들에게 좋은 것이 될 거라고 생각해.

로봇의 영향력을 걱정하는 여자에게 남자가 로봇은 인간의 삶에 전반적으로 긍정적인 영향을 끼치는 좋은 것이 되리라고 했다. 따라서, 남자의 의견으로 ④ '로봇은 사람들의 삶에 긍정적인 영향을 줄 것이다.'가 가장 적절하다.

어휘 overall 闬 전반적으로 manufacture 통 제조하다 lose A to B B 때문에 A를 잃다 task 뗑 일, 작업 wildfire 뗑 산불 toxic 휑 유독성의, 중독의 waste 뗑 폐기물, 노폐물

3 관계 파악

정답 ②

W I feel like I let everyone down tonight, Mr. Campbell.
M We all have good days and bad days. Don't be so hard on yourself, Rebecca.
W **I missed** ¹⁾<u>so many shots,</u> **even when the basket was wide open.**
M I'll tell you a story. During my first game in college, I was so nervous that I could ²⁾<u>barely dribble the ball.</u>
W Really? But you were voted MVP for three years, and then you became a professional player.
M Exactly. If I had ³⁾<u>decided to give up</u> after that first game, I wouldn't be where I am today.
W I see. Do you miss playing?

여 오늘 밤 제가 모두를 실망시킨 것 같아요, Campbell 선생님.
남 우리 모두 잘 풀리는 날도 있고 안 풀리는 날도 있어. 스스로를 너무 심하게 대하지 마렴, Rebecca.
여 저는 너무 많은 슛을 놓쳤어요, 심지어 농구 골대가 활짝 비었을 때도요.
남 내가 뭐 하나만 이야기해 줄게. 대학 시절 첫 경기 중에, 나는 너무 긴장한 나머지 드리블도 간신히 할 정도였어.
여 진짜요? 그렇지만 선생님은 3년간 MVP로 뽑혔었고, 그 이후 프로 선수가 되셨잖아요.
남 맞아. 만약 내가 그 첫 경기 이후 포기하기로 결정했다면, 나는 지금의 내가 있는 곳에 없었을 거야.
여 그렇군요. 운동하던 때가 그리우세요?

M	Sometimes. **But** **4)teaching young people** like you is my greatest joy these days.	남	가끔 그렇지. 하지만 너 같은 젊은 사람들을 가르치는 게 요즘 나의 가장 큰 기쁨이야.
W	That's good. But I don't know how I can recover from this.	여	잘 됐네요. 하지만 전 어떻게 회복할 수 있을지 모르겠어요.
M	Trust me. Just pick yourself up and get back out there.	남	날 믿으렴. 그냥 스스로 마음을 다잡고 벗어나면 돼.
W	Okay, thank you. I won't give up.	여	알겠어요, 감사합니다. 포기하지 않을게요.

두 사람이 여자의 불만족스러운 경기 내용에 관해 이야기하고 있다. 여자는 농구 골대가 비었어도 슛을 놓치는 등 경기 중에 저지른 구체적인 실수를 언급하고 있고, 남자는 여자를 격려하며 현재 젊은 사람들을 가르치는 것이 가장 기쁘다고 하는 것으로 보아 두 사람의 관계로 ② '농구 선수 — 코치'가 가장 적절하다.

어휘 let ~ down ~를 실망시키다 be hard on ~를 심하게 대하다 shot 명 슛; 발사 basket 명 (농구) 골대; 바구니 barely 부 간신히, 겨우 recover 통 회복하다
pick oneself up (마음 등을) 다잡다

4 그림 내용 불일치 파악

정답 ⑤

M	Hey, Collette. What are you looking at?	남	안녕, Collette. 뭘 보고 있어?
W	It's a photo of a hotel room in Paris. I might book this one for my vacation.	여	파리에 있는 호텔 방 사진이야. 내 휴가를 위해 여길 예약할까 봐.
M	Oh, the bed looks so **1)cozy** and **comfortable**.	남	오, 침대가 정말 아늑하고 편안해 보여.
W	I know. And the painting of the lily on the wall is beautiful.	여	그러게. 그리고 벽에 있는 백합 그림이 아름다워.
M	Look at that crystal chandelier **2)hanging** **from** **the** **ceiling**. That's so luxurious!	남	천장에 달려 있는 수정 샹들리에 좀 봐. 정말 고급스러워!
W	Yes. But the best part is the nice view through the window.	여	맞아. 하지만 제일 멋진 건 창문으로 보이는 근사한 풍경이야.
M	Wow, you can see the Eiffel Tower from the room.	남	우와, 방에서 에펠탑도 볼 수 있네.
W	Yeah, that's amazing.	여	맞아, 정말 멋져.
M	Oh, there's a round table with **3)two** **chairs** **by** **the** **window**. Do you think you'll use it?	남	아, 창가에는 의자 두 개와 원형 탁자가 있어. 그걸 사용할 것 같아?
W	Yes. I can't wait to have my coffee and baguette there every morning.	여	응. 매일 아침 거기서 커피와 바게트를 먹는 일이 너무 기대돼.
M	I think you should go ahead and book it.	남	내 생각엔 실행에 옮겨서 예약하는 게 좋을 것 같아.
W	Yes, I agree.	여	응, 동감이야.

대화에서 남자가 창가에 의자 두 개와 원형 탁자가 있다고 말했는데, ⑤에는 의자가 한 개만 그려져 있다.

어휘 cozy 형 아늑한 luxurious 형 고급스러운 go ahead 실행에 옮기다

5 할 일 파악

정답 ①

M	Hi, Grace. Are you walking over to the library?	남	안녕, Grace. 도서관으로 걸어가는 중이니?
W	No. Why do you ask? Is something going on?	여	아니. 왜? 무슨 일 있니?
M	Some of our classmates are going there now **1)to** **study** **together** for the math exam.	남	우리 반 친구들 몇 명이 수학 시험공부를 같이 하려고 거기에 가고 있거든.
W	Oh, I didn't know. Are you going?	여	아, 나는 몰랐어. 너도 가는 거야?
M	Yes. I **2)need** **all** **the** **help** I can get.	남	응. 나는 내가 받을 수 있는 모든 도움이 필요해.
W	Well, I won't be able to join you. I have a drum lesson this afternoon.	여	음, 나는 너와 함께 하지는 못할 것 같아. 오늘 오후에 드럼 수업이 있거든.
M	Oh, do you play the drums? When did you start to learn?	남	오, 너 드럼 치니? 언제부터 배우기 시작했어?
W	I just started six months ago. I'm planning to sign up for an amateur drummer contest next year.	여	6개월 전에 막 시작했어. 내년에 아마추어 드러머 대회에 참가할 계획이야.
M	Sounds great! Then, are you **3)heading** **to** **the** **academy** now for your lesson?	남	멋진걸! 그럼, 너는 지금 수업받으러 학원으로 가는 거야?
W	No. **My mom asked me to walk my sister home. I have to** **4)pick** **her** **up** **from** **her kindergarten first.**	여	아니. 엄마가 여동생을 집까지 데려다주라고 했어. 나는 먼저 유치원에 동생을 데리러 가야 해.
M	All right. See you tomorrow.	남	알겠어. 내일 보자.

우연히 마주친 두 사람이 이후의 일정에 대해 이야기하고 있다. 남자가 여자에게 드럼 수업을 받으러 가는지 묻자, 여자가 여동생을 유치원에서 집으로 데려다줘야 한다고 했으므로 여자가 할 일로 ① '여동생 데리러 가기'가 가장 적절하다.

어휘 classmate 명 반 친구 sign up for ~에 참가하다 contest 명 대회 academy 명 학원; 학술원 kindergarten 명 유치원

6   금액 정보 파악

정답 ④

M Welcome to the Orlando Pottery Museum. Can I help you?	남 올랜도 도자기 박물관에 오신 것을 환영합니다. 도와드릴까요?
W Hello. I want to buy some tickets.	여 안녕하세요. 티켓을 좀 사고 싶은데요.
M All right. **They're** ¹⁾$20 for adults and $10 for children.	남 네. 성인은 20달러, 어린이는 10달러입니다.
W Great. **I'll take two adult tickets for me and my friend.** Also, we are students. Is there a discount?	여 좋아요. 저와 제 친구를 위해 성인용 티켓 2장을 살게요. 그리고, 저희는 학생인데요. 할인이 있나요?
M Yes. You can get 10% off of the tickets. May I see your student IDs?	남 네. 티켓 값을 10% 할인받을 수 있어요. 학생증 좀 보여 주시겠어요?
W Sure. *[Pause]* Here you go.	여 그럼요. *[잠시 멈춤]* 여기요.
M Thanks. **And I should** ²⁾let you know that we are offering a pottery-making experience for visitors today.	남 감사합니다. 그리고 오늘 방문객들에게 도자기 만들기 체험을 제공하고 있다는 것을 알려드려야겠군요.
W That sounds fun. How much is it?	여 재미있겠네요. 얼마인가요?
M **It's $15 per person. But there isn't a student discount for it.**	남 1인당 15달러입니다. 하지만 여기엔 학생 할인이 없어요.
W That's okay. **We'll** ³⁾take two of those as well.	여 괜찮아요. 그것도 두 장 주세요.
M So you want two admission tickets with a student discount and two pottery session passes, right?	남 그럼, 학생 할인을 받은 입장권 두 장과 도자기 수업 이용권 두 장을 원하시는 거군요, 그렇죠?
W That's correct. Here's my card.	여 맞아요. 여기 제 카드요.

여자는 10% 할인을 받아 성인용 티켓 2장($20×2×0.9=$36)을 구매했고, 도자기 만들기 수업 이용권을 할인 없이 2장($15×2=$30) 구매했으므로 정답은 ④ '$66'이다.

[어휘] pottery 몡 도자기   admission 몡 입장; 승인   session 몡 수업; 시간   pass 몡 이용권, 입장권 통 통과하다

7   이유 파악

정답 ②

W Noah, is that you? You've ¹⁾grown up so much since I last saw you.	여 Noah, 너 맞지? 내가 널 마지막으로 본 이후로 정말 많이 자랐구나.
M Hi, Ms. Murphy! I haven't seen you since I graduated from middle school. But I've really missed you.	남 안녕하세요, Murphy 선생님! 제가 중학교를 졸업한 이후로 뵌 적이 없었네요. 하지만 정말 보고 싶었어요.
W I'm so glad to run into you. How are you?	여 우연히 널 만나서 정말 기쁘구나. 잘 지내지?
M Great. I'm going to be a sophomore in college next year.	남 좋죠. 저는 내년에 대학교 2학년이 돼요.
W Wow, ²⁾time sure flies. It seems like yesterday that you were in my class.	여 와, 시간 참 빠르네. 네가 내 반에 있었던 게 엊그제 같은데.
M I just got my driver's license, too.	남 전 최근에 운전면허증도 땄어요.
W That's wonderful. Are you coming to the ³⁾middle school reunion on Saturday? We're planning a barbecue.	여 굉장하구나. 토요일에 중학교 동창회에 올 거니? 우리는 바비큐 파티를 계획하고 있어.
M No. I can't make it.	남 아뇨. 저는 못 가요.
W That's too bad. There will be lots of fun games with small prizes.	여 유감이구나. 작은 상품들과 함께 재미있는 게임들이 많이 있을 건데 말이야.
M I know. **But my grandmother is** ⁴⁾coming to visit that day.	남 그러게요. 하지만 그날 할머니가 방문하러 오신대요.
W Oh, that's so nice. Have a great time with her.	여 오, 참 잘됐구나. 할머니와 즐거운 시간 보내렴.
M Thanks, Ms. Murphy.	남 고마워요, Murphy 선생님.

남자는 중학교 동창회에 못 간다고 하면서 그날 할머니가 자신을 보러 온다고 말했으므로, 남자가 동창회에 참석할 수 없는 이유는 ② '할머니가 오시기로 해서'이다.

[어휘] graduate from ~을 졸업하다   run into ~를 우연히 만나다   sophomore 몡 대학교 2학년   driver's license 운전면허증   reunion 몡 동창회

8   언급 유무 파악

정답 ⑤

M Katie, have you seen that letter I was reading earlier?	남 Katie, 아까 내가 읽고 있던 편지 봤니?
W Is this it, Dad? It's from **the Canadian Cancer Foundation**.	여 이건가요, 아빠? 캐나다 암 재단에서 온 거요.
M Yeah! That's the one. It has some details about that organization's ¹⁾charity event.	남 맞아! 그거야. 그 편지에는 그 단체의 자선 행사에 대한 세부 사항이 담겨 있단다.
W What kind of event is it?	여 어떤 종류의 행사인가요?
M It's a sale. The foundation sells new and used items that people donate to them. The purpose is **to** ²⁾raise money for cancer research.	남 판매 행사야. 그 재단은 사람들이 그들에게 기부하는 새 물건과 중고품을 판매한단다. 암 연구를 위한 기금을 모으려는 목적이지.
W Oh, that sounds like a good cause. When is it?	여 오, 좋은 취지인 것 같아요. 언제예요?
M Let me check. *[Pause]* It's on **June 17th**.	남 확인해 볼게. *[잠시 멈춤]* 6월 17일이구나.
W How can we donate items?	여 어떻게 물건을 기부할 수 있나요?
M **They will** ³⁾pick up our donations whenever it's convenient for us. I just have to call them the day before.	남 그들은 우리가 편할 때면 언제든 기부 물건을 찾으러 올 거야. 내가 그냥 전날 전화를 하기만 하면 된다.
W I have some toys that I don't play with anymore.	여 제겐 더 이상 가지고 놀지 않는 장난감이 몇 개 있어요.
M Great. Should I have them stop by tomorrow afternoon, then?	남 좋아. 그럼 내일 오후에 들르라고 할까?
W Sure. I'll get everything ready tonight.	여 그럼요. 오늘 밤 안에 모든 걸 준비해둘게요.

주최 기관(캐나다 암 재단), 행사 목적(암 연구를 위한 기금 모금), 행사 날짜(6월 17일), 기부 방법(전날 전화하면 기부 물건을 찾으러 옴)에 대해 언급했고, ⑤ '기부 제한 품목'은 언급하지 않았다.

어휘 cancer 명 암 foundation 명 재단; 창립 organization 명 단체 cause 명 취지, 대의명분; 원인 whenever 접 언제든지 convenient 형 편한, 편리한 stop by 들르다

---

9 내용 불일치 파악

정답 ⑤

W Good morning, students of Applewood High School. I'm Ms. Barnes, the advisor for the school drama club. Our club will have an event called Applewood Play Night next Friday evening. We'll perform brief plays 1)in the school auditorium. All students are encouraged to attend. Each student is permitted to invite 2)a maximum of three guests. The performance will begin at 7 p.m., but the doors to the auditorium will be closed at 6:55 p.m. Those who arrive after that time will not be allowed to enter. So make sure that your guests arrive no later than that. 3)**Following the performance**, **free refreshments will be served in the hall outside of the auditorium.** I hope all of you enjoy our event. Thank you.	여 좋은 아침입니다, 애플우드 고등학교 학생 여러분. 저는 학교 연극 동아리의 고문인 Barnes 선생님입니다. 저희 동아리는 다음 주 금요일 저녁에 Applewood Play Night라는 행사를 할 예정입니다. 저희는 학교 강당에서 짧은 연극들을 공연할 것입니다. 모든 학생들에게 참석할 것이 권장됩니다. 각 학생은 최대 3명의 손님을 초대하는 것이 허용됩니다. 공연은 저녁 7시에 시작되지만, 강당 문은 6시 55분에 닫힐 것입니다. 그 시간 이후에 도착한 사람들은 입장할 수 없습니다. 따라서 여러분의 초대객이 꼭 그 전에 도착하도록 해주십시오. 공연 후에는 강당 밖 홀에서 무료 다과가 제공될 예정입니다. 여러분 모두가 행사를 즐기시기를 바랍니다. 감사합니다.

학교 연극 동아리에서 주최하는 연극 공연 행사에 대한 안내 방송이다. 여자가 공연 후에 강당 밖 홀에서 무료 다과가 제공될 예정이라고 했으므로 ⑤ '공연 전에 무료 다과가 제공될 것이다.'는 내용과 일치하지 않는다.

어휘 advisor 명 고문 brief 형 짧은, 간단한 auditorium 명 강당 permit 통 허용하다, 허락하다 maximum 명 최대 following 전 ~ 후에 refreshment 명 다과

---

10 도표 정보 파악

정답 ③

W Hi, Derek. Can I get your opinion on something? **M** Of course. What is it? **W** I want to buy a standing desk, but I can't decide which model to choose. **M** How much can you spend? **W** I 1)**can't afford** a standing desk over $300. **M** We can cross one off the list, then. What type of adjustment method do you want? **W** I want 2)**an electric desk**, not a manual one. **M** Good idea. Then, you just have to push a button to make it go up and down. **W** Also, my computer screen is really wide. **So the desk should be** 3)**wider than 90 centimeters.** **M** In that case, you're down to these two models. What about the color? **W** I'm looking for something to 4)match my light office interior. **So I shouldn't pick the black one.** **M** You should get this one, then.	여 안녕, Derek. 네 의견을 좀 들을 수 있을까? 남 물론이지. 뭔데? 여 스탠딩 책상을 하나 사고 싶은데, 어떤 모델을 선택해야 할지 모르겠어. 남 돈은 얼마나 쓸 수 있어? 여 300달러가 넘는 스탠딩 책상은 살 여유가 없어. 남 그럼 목록에서 하나 지울 수 있겠어. 어떤 종류의 조정 방법을 원해? 여 수동이 아닌 전동 책상을 원해. 남 좋은 생각이야. 그럼 위아래로 움직이게 하려면 버튼을 누르기만 하면 되잖아. 여 그리고, 내 컴퓨터 화면은 정말 넓어. 그래서, 책상이 90cm보다 더 넓어야 해. 남 그런 상황이라면, 이 두 모델밖에 남지 않았어. 색깔은 어때? 여 내 밝은 사무실 인테리어에 어울리는 걸로 찾고 있어. 그래서 검은색은 고르면 안 돼. 남 그럼 이걸 사야겠어.

여자는 300달러를 넘지 않는 것 중에서, 전동으로 조정이 가능하고, 90cm보다 넓은 크기이면서, 검은색이 아닌 스탠딩 책상을 골랐다.

어휘 afford 통 살 여유가 있다 cross A off B B에서 A를 지우다 adjustment 명 조정, 적응 manual 형 수동의 be down to ~밖에 남지 않다 width 명 너비, 폭

---

11 짧은 대화의 응답 파악

정답 ③

M Where are you going, Taylor? **W** I'm 1)on my way to a pop-up event. **My favorite singer, Serena Tillman, has launched her own beauty brand.** **M** Oh, I heard her perfume 2)**has a nice scent.** **W** Me too. I was thinking of buying a bottle of it.	남 어디 가, Taylor? 여 팝업 행사에 가는 길이야. 내가 가장 좋아하는 가수인 Serena Tillman이 그녀만의 화장품 브랜드를 출시했거든. 남 오, 그녀의 향수에서 좋은 향기가 난다고 들었어. 여 나도 들었어. 그걸 한 병 살까 생각 중이었어. 선택지 ① 안 돼. 출시 행사는 금요일에 있어. ② 왜 아니겠어? 화장품은 누구나 좋아한다고. ③ 나도 들었어. 그걸 한 병 살까 생각 중이었어. ④ 맞아. 우리는 그녀의 노래를 다시 들어야 해. ⑤ 물론이지. 나는 방금 그녀의 새 앨범을 샀어.

가수가 출시한 화장품 브랜드에 대해 이야기하는 상황에서 남자가 그 브랜드의 향수에서 좋은 향기가 난다는 말을 들었다고 했으므로, 이에 대한 응답으로는 남자의 말에 동의하면서 향수를 사려했다고 말하는 ③ 'Me too. I was thinking of buying a bottle of it.'이 가장 적절하다.

어휘 launch 통 출시하다; 발사하다 perfume 명 향수 scent 명 향기, 향

12 짧은 대화의 응답 파악

정답 ①

W Max, are you okay? Did something happen at the park today?	여 Max, 괜찮니? 오늘 공원에서 무슨 일 있었어?
M Well, I was skateboarding with my friends. But I ¹⁾fell and injured myself, Mom.	남 음, 친구들과 스케이트보드를 탔어요. 그런데 넘어져서 다쳤어요, 엄마.
W Oh, no! Let me have a look. ²⁾Where does it hurt?	여 오, 이런! 엄마가 한번 보자. 어디를 다쳤니?
M I have some cuts on my arm.	남 팔에 베인 상처가 있어요.

선택지
① 팔에 베인 상처가 있어요.
② 어젯밤에 약을 조금 먹었어요.
③ 오늘 공원은 정말 붐볐어요.
④ 왜 헬멧을 쓰지 않았나요?
⑤ 공원에서 스케이트보드를 빌릴 수 있어요.

남자가 스케이트보드를 타다가 다친 상황에서 여자가 어디를 다쳤는지 물었으므로, 이에 대한 응답으로는 다친 부위를 언급하는 ① 'I have some cuts on my arm.'이 가장 적절하다.

어휘 injure 통 다치게 하다, 부상을 입히다 cut 명 베인 상처, 자상 통 베다 crowded 형 붐비는

13 긴 대화의 응답 파악

정답 ⑤

W Joshua! There you are.	여 Joshua! 거기 있었구나.
M Hey, Rachel. **Are you ready for the ¹⁾camping trip tomorrow?**	남 안녕, Rachel. 내일 캠핑 여행 준비는 다 됐니?
W Not even close. We have so much to prepare!	여 전혀 아니야. 준비해야 할 게 너무 많아!
M Let's ²⁾make a list of what we all need. Then, I can go to the store and pick up some things.	남 우리한테 필요한 모든 걸 목록으로 작성해 보자. 그러면, 내가 가게에 가서 물건을 좀 사 올 수 있을 거야.
W Yes, please! Could we add marshmallows to the list? It was so nice to roast them on our last camping trip.	여 응, 그렇게 해줘! 마시멜로를 목록에 추가해도 돼? 우리 지난번 캠핑 여행에서 그걸 구웠던 게 너무 좋았어.
M Definitely. I also might buy handheld electric fans ³⁾because of the weather.	남 물론이지. 나도 날씨 때문에 휴대용 선풍기를 사야겠어.
W Is it going to be really hot?	여 엄청나게 더울까?
M Yes, so we better pack lots of shorts and T-shirts.	남 응, 그래서 반바지와 티셔츠를 많이 챙기는 게 좋겠어.
W I'm a little worried about bugs, then.	여 그렇다면 벌레가 좀 걱정되네.
M Me too. **I think there will be lots of mosquitoes.**	남 나도. 모기가 엄청 많을 거야.
W Well, how can we ⁴⁾prevent bites?	여 음, 물리는 걸 어떻게 막을 수 있을까?
M Why don't we buy some bug spray?	남 벌레 스프레이를 사는 게 어때?

선택지
① 나는 밤에 모닥불 피우는 걸 좋아해.
② 어쩌면 다른 주말에 가는 게 좋겠어.
③ 일기예보에서 대체로 맑을 거라고 했어.
④ 길 아래에 있는 가게로 가자.
⑤ 벌레 스프레이를 사는 게 어때?

두 사람이 캠핑 여행을 준비하는 상황이다. 남자가 모기가 많을 것이라고 하자 여자가 벌레에 물리는 것을 어떻게 막을 수 있을지 물었으므로, 이에 대한 응답으로는 해결책을 제시하는 ⑤ 'Why don't we buy some bug spray?'가 가장 적절하다.

어휘 Not even close. 전혀 아니야. roast 통 굽다 handheld 형 휴대용의, 손에 쥘 수 있는 electric fan 선풍기 shorts 명 반바지 mosquito 명 모기 bite 명 물리는 것; 물린 자국

14 긴 대화의 응답 파악

정답 ②

M What are you making, Crystal?	남 Crystal, 뭘 만들고 있니?
W Hi, Pete. **It's a poster for the beach clean-up event I'm organizing.**	여 안녕, Pete. 이건 내가 기획하고 있는 해변 청소 행사의 포스터야.
M That's a great idea. What is involved in this event?	남 좋은 생각인걸. 행사에 어떤 게 포함돼 있어?
W We'll ¹⁾pick up trash at Turtle Beach.	여 터틀 해변에서 쓰레기를 주울 거야.
M Great. I saw so much garbage the last time I went there. I didn't want to swim.	남 훌륭하네. 저번에 내가 거기에 갔을 때 정말 많은 쓰레기를 봤어. 수영하고 싶지 않더라.
W Yeah. And when trash gets into the ocean, it ²⁾harms the animals.	여 맞아. 그리고 쓰레기가 바다에 들어가면 동물들에게 피해를 줘.
M I've read that many sea turtles have died from eating plastic bags. It's really sad.	남 많은 바다거북이들이 비닐봉지를 먹고 죽었다는 걸 읽어본 적 있어. 너무 슬퍼.
W But we can do something about the problem.	여 그래도 그 문제에 대해 뭔가 할 수 있을 거야.
M You're right. **I'd love to volunteer for your event. How can I help?**	남 네 말이 맞아. 나는 너의 행사에 지원하고 싶어. 내가 어떻게 도울 수 있을까?
W Well... I need someone ³⁾to put up posters, and I still need to figure out how to take care of the collected trash.	여 음... 포스터를 붙여줄 사람이 필요하고, 모은 쓰레기를 어떻게 처리해야 할지 여전히 방법을 생각해 내야 해.
M I have a suggestion. Let's ⁴⁾borrow my dad's truck for that.	남 한 가지 제안이 있어. 우리 아빠 트럭을 빌리자.
W Really? Are you sure he would let us use it?	여 정말? 우리가 그걸 사용하도록 허락하실 거라고 확신해?

선택지
① 그러게. 사람들은 재활용을 더 많이 해야 해.
② 정말? 우리가 그걸 사용하도록 허락하실 거라고 확신해?
③ 물론이지. 플라스틱 쓰레기는 많은 동물들에게 해를 끼쳐.

④ 맞아. 청소 행사는 대성공이었어.

⑤ 좋아. 널 위해 곧 포스터를 준비해 둘게.

여자가 기획한 해변 청소 행사를 남자가 도와주려는 상황이다. 여자가 모은 쓰레기를 어떻게 처리할지 고민하자 남자가 그의 아버지 트럭을 빌리자고 제안했으므로, 이에 대한 응답으로는 빌리는 것이 정말 가능한지 확인하는 ② 'Really? Are you sure he would let us use it?'이 가장 적절하다.

어휘 organize 통 기획하다; 조직하다 involve 통 포함하다 harm 통 피해를 주다 plastic bag 비닐봉지 figure out ~을 생각해 내다 collected 형 모은, 수집한 recycle 통 재활용하다

15 상황에 적절한 말 파악
정답 ①

W Vanessa and Matt are high school freshmen who have never met before. Today is their first day at their new school. Both of them are assigned to the same homeroom class, and they happen to sit down 1)next to one another. When class begins, their teacher asks everyone to introduce themselves to their new classmates. When Matt greets Vanessa, she immediately notices that he has a big piece of 2)spinach on his front tooth. Vanessa knows that Matt is about to meet everyone else in the class for the first time, and she doesn't want him to embarrass himself. **So Vanessa wants to tell him that he should go look at 3)himself in the mirror.** In this situation, what would Vanessa most likely say to Matt?

여 Vanessa와 Matt는 전에 만난 적이 없는 고등학교 신입생입니다. 오늘은 그들의 새 학교에서의 첫날입니다. 두 사람 모두 같은 반에 배정되었고, 우연히 서로 나란히 앉게 되었습니다. 수업이 시작되자, 그들의 선생님은 새로운 반 친구들에게 스스로를 소개해달라고 모두에게 요청합니다. Matt가 Vanessa에게 인사를 할 때, 그녀는 그의 앞니에 커다란 시금치 조각이 붙어 있다는 것을 곧바로 알아차립니다. Vanessa는 Matt가 곧 학급의 다른 모든 사람들을 처음으로 만나게 될 참이라는 것을 알고 있고, 그가 스스로를 난처하게 만들지 않았으면 합니다. 그래서, Vanessa는 그에게 거울로 자신의 모습을 보러 가야 한다고 말하고 싶습니다. 이러한 상황에서, Vanessa가 Matt에게 가장 할 것 같은 말은 무엇입니까?

선택지 ① 거울을 확인해 보는 게 좋을 것 같아.

② 좋은 인상을 주는 건 중요해.

③ 너 수업 전에 시금치를 먹었나 보구나.

④ 아마도 너는 아침 먹을 시간이 없었나 보네.

⑤ 우리가 자기소개를 할 기회가 생겨서 기뻐.

Matt의 앞니에 시금치 조각이 붙어 있는 것을 보고, Vanessa는 거울로 모습을 확인해 보라고 조언하려 한다. 따라서, Vanessa가 할 말로 ① 'I think you may want to check the mirror.'가 가장 적절하다.

어휘 freshmen 명 신입생 assign 통 배정하다 happen to 우연히 ~ 하다 greet 통 인사하다 spinach 명 시금치 be about to 곧 ~할 참이다 embarrass 통 난처하게 만들다 impression 명 인상

16-17 세트 문항
정답 16 ③ 17 ②

M Hello, students. Last time, we talked about the development of artificial intelligence. As we make new progress in technology, AI is 1)becoming more popular all over the world. **So today, we'll discuss how AI is applied in various fields.** First, AI has become essential to **agriculture**. Not only do farmers use AI to monitor drones and drive tractors, but this technology can also 2)track the condition of plants. Next, AI is being heavily incorporated into **transportation**. AI is needed for the smooth operation of self-driving buses and cars. With the help of this technology, these vehicles can actually understand their surroundings in order to navigate. Another developing AI industry is **healthcare**. AI is revolutionizing how patients are diagnosed, analyzed, and monitored. In addition, it's enabling scientists to discover new treatments. Finally, AI has led to changes in **finance**. 3)Instead of consulting with financial experts, people can use AI investors. These virtual assistants analyze market trends and provide advice on which stocks to buy or sell. Now, let's watch a video about how AI accomplishes these feats.

남 안녕하세요, 학생 여러분. 지난 시간에는 인공 지능의 발전에 대해 이야기했습니다. 우리가 기술에서의 새로운 진보를 만들어냄에 따라, 인공 지능은 전 세계적으로 더 인기를 얻고 있습니다. 따라서 오늘은 인공 지능이 어떻게 다양한 분야에 적용되는지 알아보겠습니다. 첫째, 인공 지능은 농업에 필수적인 요소가 되었습니다. 농부들은 드론을 추적하고 트랙터를 운전하기 위해 인공 지능을 사용할 뿐만 아니라, 이 기술은 식물의 상태도 추적할 수 있습니다. 다음으로, 인공 지능은 교통에 몹시 결합되고 있습니다. 자율 주행 버스와 자동차의 원활한 운행을 위해 인공 지능이 필요합니다. 이 기술의 도움으로, 이러한 차량들은 주행하기 위해 실제로 주변 환경을 이해할 수 있습니다. 성장하고 있는 또 다른 인공 지능 산업은 의료입니다. 인공 지능은 환자를 진단, 분석, 그리고 추적 관찰하는 방법에 혁신을 일으키고 있습니다. 게다가, 그것은 과학자들이 새로운 치료법을 발견할 수 있게 해주고 있습니다. 마지막으로, 인공 지능은 금융의 변화를 이끌어 왔습니다. 금융 전문가와 상담하는 대신, 사람들은 인공 지능 투자자를 이용할 수 있습니다. 이 가상의 보조자는 시장 동향을 분석하고 매수 또는 매도할 주식에 대한 조언을 제공합니다. 이제 인공 지능이 어떻게 이러한 업적을 달성하는지에 대한 영상을 시청해 보겠습니다.

선택지 16 ① 인공 지능으로 인한 인간 노동력의 감소

② 인공 지능 사용과 관련된 위험 요인

③ 다른 산업에서 인공 지능을 활용하는 방법

④ 경제를 변화시킬 수 있는 인공 지능의 잠재력

⑤ 인공 지능 시스템을 개발하는 과정

17 ① 농업 ② 교육 ③ 교통 ④ 의료 ⑤ 금융

16 인공 지능이 어떻게 다양한 분야에 적용되는지에 대해 알아보고 있으므로 남자가 하는 말의 주제로 ③ 'ways different industries utilize AI'가 가장 적절하다.

17 농업, 교통, 의료, 금융은 언급했지만, ② 'education'은 언급하지 않았다.

어휘 AI(Artificial Intelligence) 명 인공 지능 progress 명 진보 agriculture 명 농업 monitor 통 추적하다, 감시하다 track 통 추적하다 incorporate 통 결합하다, 포함하다 operation 명 운행 surroundings 명 주변 환경 navigate 통 주행하다; 항해하다 industry 명 산업 revolutionize 통 혁신을 일으키다 diagnose 통 진단하다 enable A to B A가 B할 수 있게 하다 treatment 명 치료법 finance 명 금융, 재정 consult with ~와 상담하다 expert 명 전문가 investor 명 투자자 virtual 형 가상의 stock 주식; 재고 accomplish 통 달성하다, 성취하다 feat 명 업적, 위업 potential 명 잠재력 labor 명 노동력

24회 고난도 영어듣기 모의고사 해커스 수능영어듣기 모의고사 20+4회 기본

MEMO

수능 1등급을 위한 **완벽한 실전 대비서**

해커스
수능영어듣기
모의고사 20+4회
기본